(continued from front flap)

interpret, and evaluate these inequalities. Part IV discusses differential life chances, and ways of life, while Part V examines social mobility.

Part VI concentrates on ethnicity, race, and class, and Part VII on change in stratification systems. The last part of the book consists of articles concerning two major issues of contemporary theory: the question of the nature of stratification in general, and the question of the nature of the newly emerging stratification system in an advanced industrial society. Since contemporary theory is dominated by controversy, the reader will be better equipped to evaluate the significance of each position using the empirical studies found in preceding sections of the book.

Change and the new system of structured social inequality that is now evolving are uniquely featured in this text. Explanatory footnotes and a fully articulated index will be helpful to the student.

APC

STRUCTURED SOCIAL INEQUALITY

Structured Social Inequality

A Reader in Comparative Social Stratification

EDITED AND WITH INTRODUCTIONS BY

Celia S. Heller

HUNTER COLLEGE OF THE CITY UNIVERSITY OF NEW YORK

The Macmillan Company
NEW YORK
Collier-Macmillan Limited
LONDON

Library of Congress catalog card number: 69–10021

THE MACMILLAN COMPANY, NEW YORK
COLLIER-MACMILLAN CANADA, LTD., TORONTO, ONTARIO

Printed in the United States of America

To my sister Ann

PREFACE

This volume is intended to serve as a textbook for both undergraduate and graduate levels. The introductions to the eight parts of the book together aim to cover the major areas of stratification. Each introduction places the articles of that section into the larger context of the particular area to which they pertain. Thus an instructor can rely entirely on this book as the textbook for his course. Or, if he prefers, he can use it as a supplement to a standard textbook, selecting from among the readings those that correspond to the topics in that textbook. To conserve space and to make possible the inclusion of more readings, I have abridged slightly the selections from scholarly journals. In those selections from books the abridgment of material has also facilitated a wider coverage of ideas from each author. (Where passages have been omitted, the conventional ellipsis sign appears.) In a number of readings I have added editorial footnotes, and these carry my initials to distinguish them from the author's original footnotes.

Before I close, I would like to acknowledge my debts to those who have directly or indirectly influenced this work. I am most grateful to my grandfather, Saul Rosenman, for opening the door to the magic world of ideas for me when I was still a child and for directing my eyes to the injustices of inequality. As a sociologist, I am deeply indebted intellectually to my teachers: Conrad Arensberg, Robert K. Merton, Paul Lazarsfeld, Herbert Hyman, and Hans Zetterberg. In preparing this book, I benefited from the discussions with and advice from my friends and colleagues: Alfonso Pinkney, Suzanne Keller, Richard A. Schermerhorn, George Fischer, Judith Kramer, Wanda Wendt, Philip Weintraub, Barbara Bauman, Gerda Lorenz, and Sarah Karant. The comments by Dennis Wrong on the introductions to and choices of selections—a number of which led to revisions—are much appreciated. And I am very grateful to John Moore, an ally in this venture, for his patience, encouragement, generosity, and editorial help.

C. S. H.

CONTENTS

GENERAL
INTRODUCTION

The study of social stratification is one of the most flourishing areas of American sociology today. Hardly an issue of the leading sociological journals appears that does not contain one or more articles on this topic. However, this field, now well developed and thriving as a basic branch of sociology, was long neglected as a subject of systematic investigation in the United States. The systematic study of social stratification is a phenomenon of only the last three decades. It is reflected in the fact that in 1929 the authors of the book *Trends in American Sociology,* much acclaimed in its day, found no materials on social stratification worthy of a chapter.[1] Another indicator of the neglect is the late appearance of textbooks on this subject. The first general work suitable for university students was the collection of readings by Bendix and Lipset that was issued in 1953.[2] Then, in 1955, came the short but succinct paperback *Class and Society* by Kurt B. Mayer.[3] But the first textbooks in the traditional sense of the word did not appear until 1957.[4]

The growth of empirical studies of social stratification can be traced to the Great Depression and to the influence of Marxist thought on the intellectuals of that epoch. But even if the systematic study of stratification in the United States goes back only that far, the interest in this phenomenon is as old as sociology itself. Auguste Comte touched on it in his discussion of division of labor and social solidarity. It was at the heart of Saint-Simon's preoccupation with how industrial society is to be organized to bring about a moral regeneration. Herbert Spencer gave it some attention, particularly in his *Study of Sociology* when he wrote about *class bias* as a serious obstacle to sociological thought. He made the "modern" sounding observation that the ideas and sentiments of the class to which the sociologist himself belongs "affect alike his conceptions of the past, his interpretations of present, his anticipations of the future."[5] The same could be said about early American sociologists—Lester F. Ward, William Graham Sumner, Charles H. Cooley—for, as has been convincingly demonstrated by Charles Page, they too were concerned with the subject of social stratification.[6] And it was at the very center of the thought of those theorists from whose writings constitute the first readings of this book: Marx, Weber, Pareto, and Schumpeter.

[1] G. A. Lundberg, *et al., Trends in American Sociology,* New York: Harpers, 1929, as reported by Charles H. Page, *Class in Amercian Sociology,* New York: Dial Press, 1940.
[2] Reinhard Bendix and Seymour Martin Lipset, eds., *Class, Status and Power,* Glencoe, Illinois: Free Press, 1953.
[3] Kurt B. Mayer, *Class and Society,* New York: Random House, 1955.
[4] Bernard Barber, *Social Stratification,* New York: Harcourt, Brace and Company, 1957; Joseph A. Kahl, *The American Class Structure,* New York: Holt, Rinehart and Winston, 1957.
[5] Herbert Spencer, "The Class Bias," in C. Wright Mills, ed., *Images of Man,* New York: George Braziller, 1960, p. 64.
[6] Page, *op. cit.*

It is not enough to indicate that interest in social stratification is as old as sociology itself, for, as a matter of fact, it preceded the nineteenth-century beginnings of sociology.

Among the earliest written thoughts and judgments about social inequality were those of the Hebrew prophets who denounced the excesses of the rich and mighty. And as could easily be guessed—because there is hardly a subject that cannot be traced to them—Plato and Aristotle paid attention to this phenomenon. Plato was preoccupied with the conception of a society in which social inequality would correspond perfectly to the inherent inequality of men. Thus, his Republic is a utopian society where each man assumes the occupation for which he is best fitted. Aristotle, the great classifier, gave us the scheme of three classes present in all states: "One class is very rich, another very poor, and a third is a mean." [7] Knowing his preference for the *mean* in all things, it is not surprising that he thought the middle class the best of the three and those states possessing a large middle class the best administered. In his *Politics* we also find differing dichotomous schemes: One is the basic division of people everywhere into free and slave; and the other is the division of every population into those who work and those who do not.

From his selection of written materials on social inequality spanning several thousand years, the Polish sociologist Stanislaw Ossowski isolated two major perspectives:

1. Those who approve of the existing social order: They see social inequality as basically just, for it consists of everyone getting his due. In this view, social inequality is a natural scheme of things in which one gets what he deserves. Approval of the existing order, says Ossowski, has somehow always developed into apologetics for it.

2. Those who question the existing social order: They see inequality as unjust, measuring it against the ideal of equality: ". . . an ideal which over the centuries has been extinguished and reborn, aroused people to action, taken the form of unrealizable dreams or glimmered in the mists of an afterworld, but which has always managed to emerge from the recesses of the social consciousness to disturb the existing state of affairs." [8]

In both instances, Ossowski shows, it is not merely a question of perspective: each suggests "different practical policies." If so, then the increasingly frequent argument that the above two contrasting perspectives also run through the contemporary sociological theories of stratification assume special significance. According to them, the *functionalist* theory stems from the first, the *conservative tradition* and its competitor, conflict theory, grows out of the latter, the *radical tradition.* [9] To oversimplify for the sake of brevity, functional theory holds that stratification is a necessary requirement for the existence of society. According to conflict theory, *power* not functional necessity is the key to stratification. The differential distribution of power accounts for the inequality in valued goods and services. (Expositions of these competing theories appear in the final part of this book). What makes these theories different from all the conservative and radical

---

[7] Aristotle, *Politics,* trans. by Benjamin Jowett, New York: Modern Library, 1943, p. 190.

[8] Stanislaw Ossowski, *Class Structure in the Social Consciousness,* New York: Free Press, 1963, p. 179.

[9] See Gerhard E. Lenski, *Power and Privilege,* New York: McGraw-Hill Book Company, 1966, pp. 14–17; Also Ralf Dahrendorf, *Class and Class Conflict in Industrial Society,* Stanford: Stanford University Press, 1959, p. 158. For an earlier statement to the same effect, see S. M. Lipset and Reinhard Bendix, "Social Status and Social Structure," *British Journal of Sociology,* Vol. II, 1952, p. 150.

formulations that preceded them—say some sociologists in the role of critics—is that they are phrased in morally neutral terms. But beyond that façade, as it were, are premises no different from those inherent in the other formulations.

In light of such assertions, it would seem only proper for the editor of a volume such as this to make explicit to which "camp" she belongs. But a third alternative is emerging: Voices are beginning to be raised about the need for a synthesis of functionalist and conflict theories and some even claim that much has already been achieved toward developing such a synthesis. These voices reflect an explicit or implicit adherence to the Hegelian dialectic, to the concept that the historical process is characterized by the principle of the struggle of opposites (*thesis* and *antithesis*) and their continual resolution (*synthesis*). Convinced of the dialectical principle in intellectual development—that ideas give rise to opposite ideas and that the struggle between them results in an eventual synthesis, a new and different entity containing elements of both within it—I am confident that ultimately such a synthesis will emerge in stratification theory. Clearly, however, it would be foolish at this point to attempt a premature collection of readings in stratification to represent such a synthesis. This book after all is intended primarily as a textbook for courses on social stratification. That is why it is eclectic (hopefully in the better sense of the word) in its selections: It espouses no one sociological position to the exclusion of others. The reader will find both major theoretical viewpoints and the attempts at synthesis represented here.

What consciously guided me in the selection of articles was first of all a concern for excellence. A second concern was to cover the major aspects of the field of stratification as it has so far developed. And a third consideration was to represent the comparative orientation in its coverage. To accomplish these aims, I have not confined myself to the work of sociologists, but occasionally have drawn on that of anthropologists, economists, historians, and political scientists. I have also included a few readings that appear in print for the first time here. To these, insofar as this is its first appearance in English, belongs the portion from Theodor Geiger's *Die Klassengesellschaft im Schmelztiegel,* which has exercised a profound influence on European sociological thought, but is little known in the United States.

The book consists of eight parts. It begins with classical theory and finishes with contemporary theory. The logic behind it is, first, that classical theory—represented in this book by Weber, Marx, and Pareto—has exercised a profound influence on the empirical studies in stratification. And such studies heavily dominate the next six parts of the book. Secondly, the reason contemporary theory is placed at the end of the book rather than together with classical theory is, as has already been indicated, that it is dominated by controversy. The reader should be able to judge the merits of each position better, armed with the knowledge of the empirical studies.

Social stratification is too often treated as if it were synonymous with social differentiation, which it is not. Social differentiation is a universal phenomenon: In all societies we have a separation of positions and roles, some division of functions and labor. But social differentiation alone does not constitute stratification. First of all, social differentiation does not always involve differential evaluation or ranking of positions, whereas stratification does. Positions may be differentiated from one another and yet not *ranked* relative to each other. For example, in our society the position of the adolescent is generally not considered superior to that of infant, merely different.

Social stratification, however, can be considered a certain type of social differentiation. To put it differently, whenever you have stratification you have social differentiation, but not the other way around. Although the universality of social differentiation is undisputed, there is some controversy about whether stratification is universal. Scattered throughout this book, the reader will find statements declaring that it is. Those making the statements generally also consider stratification *necessary* in all social systems. But others point to some primitive societies without stratification. There is, however, general agreement among sociologists that stratification has been present in all complex societies to date. Although many deduce from this and argue that stratification is a necessary *condition* for complex society, the proposition is a bit shaky. It could just as well be that stratification is a *consequence* of complexity and that therefore mechanisms might evolve or consciously be introduced that could counteract this consequence. What I am suggesting is that it is a logical fallacy to deduce, as many do, inevitability from universality.

To this writer the crucial question in examining a society at a given time is not whether it is stratified or not but the degree to and way in which it is stratified. Minimally stratified systems must be distinguished from highly stratified ones, because they involve social relations that are qualitatively different and because they have qualitatively different consequences for their members. Despite the manifold variations in the phenomenon of stratification, through time and space, the following ideal types can be distinguished: slave, caste, estate, and class and stratification in advanced industrial society. The readings in Part II of this book deal with principal types of stratification systems.

Although we have specified that stratification is not synonymous with social differentiation and that it involves differential ranking, we have not yet made clear what stratification means. To say that this is the subject of this book is not to beg the question but rather to point to the great complexity of the phenomenon known as stratification. As the reader will gather from the following selections, and especially those in the first part, there is no uniform definition of social stratification. Perhaps the most common meaning that runs through the numerous contemporary definitions is that it refers to an arrangement of positions in a graded hierarchy of socially superior and inferior ranks.[10] As suggested by the title of this book I find it convenient to think of stratification as a system of structured inequality in the things that count in a given society, that is, both tangible and symbolic goods of that society. The term *structured* indicates an arrangement of elements: the inequality is not random but follows a pattern, displays relative constancy and stability, and is backed by ideas that legitimize and justify it. The various forms of patterning, the degree of stability, and the extent of institutionalization vary from one system to another. But several principal types, as has already been said, can be distinguished. They are the subject of the readings in the Part II of this book. The nature of the things that count and how unequal is their distribution in modern society, is treated in Part III, "Major Dimensions of Stratification." The readings deal with the actual inequalities—in income, wealth, power, and prestige—as well as how the members of society perceive, interpret, and evaluate these inequalities.

When we say that the preceding—wealth, power, prestige—are things that count,

---

[10] Mayer, *op. cit.,* p. 4.

we have in mind the consequences for the people who have or lack them, who possess more or less of these goods. The consequences manifest themselves in almost every aspect of life. The readings in Part IV, "Differential Life Chances and Ways of Life," cover some of them: how strata differ in the basic chance to stay alive, in value orientations, family organization, type of home socialization, the quality of formal education, and so on.

Although we conceptualize these differential patterns of social behavior as consequences of stratification, we are nevertheless fully aware that they in turn affect the stratification system. The pattern of mutual dependence is operating here as in social phenomena in general.[11] Effects of conditions react on the conditions themselves or, as Homans expressed it, "they wax and wane together."[12] Where this manifests itself dramatically is in the realm of social mobility. The same pattern of behavior that may represent a positive adjustment to one's situation in the stratification system may be dysfunctional for social mobility. For example, the low aspiration levels of youths in the lower strata helps to avoid inevitable frustrations, because there is not enough room "on top" for many of them. At the same time, however, such low aspirations eliminate from the race, individuals who might be able to achieve the positions that are open.

Social mobility—the transition from one social position to another in the stratification system—is the subject of Part VI of this book. The readings deal with extent of social mobility, its types, factors that affect it, and modes of mobility. They lead rather easily to the selections in Part VI on ethnicity (including race) and social stratification. Ethnicity and social stratification are two major and related features of a number of contemporary societies and it is therefore important to explore the connection between them. Mindful that such exploration is especially crucial in understanding the Negro revolts in contemporary American cities, we have purposefully included in this part, in contrast to the rest of the book, selections primarily concerning stratification and ethnicity in the United States.

To reiterate then, this book aims to be comparative in its approach, a perspective that is gaining ground in contemporary American sociology. Perhaps in no other area of sociology have we moved as far away from parochialism as in the study of stratification. Hopefully these selections will reflect it. In so far as it was possible, an attempt was made to include, in all those parts of the book that deal with modern stratification, readings about the various aspects of the Soviet type of stratification as well as the Western type.

The comparative approach manifests itself perhaps most fully in Part VII, "Change in Stratification Systems." It begins with a general article about change in preindustrial stratification systems and concludes with one dealing with change in the stratification systems of advanced industrial societies.

The last part of this book, "Unresolved Issues in Stratification Theory," consists of articles concerning the two major issues: (1) the old, and as yet unresolved, question of the nature of stratification in general and (2) the new question of the nature of the now emerging stratification system in advanced industrial society. We already referred to the readings dealing with the first in explaining why this book begins and ends with theoretical statements. As for the selections

---

[11] For the classic criticism of the concept of one-sided causation in the study of social phenomena, see Vilfredo Pareto: *The Mind and Society*, New York: Harcourt, Brace and Co., 1935, pp. 68–74; 254–256.

[12] George C. Homans, *The Human Group*, New York: Harcourt, Brace and Co., 1950, p. 7.

regarding the latter issue, they struggle to grasp the outline of the new system of structured inequality that is now shaping. Perhaps it is only fitting that the readings on both of these issues constitute our final readings, for they help us to pinpoint what we know and what we do not yet know about structured social inequality.

PART I
Theories of Stratification— The Classic Tradition

The readings in the first part of this book are not the only theoretical ones included. Such statements are to some extent dispersed throughout and are concentrated again in Part VIII. What distinguishes the first readings in theory from the rest is that they are, to borrow C. Wright Mills' designation, in the "classic tradition"[1] and as such are indispensable to the student of stratification. They have served in the past and continue to serve even today as points of orientation for the work of others. The extent to which the theorists represented here have influenced research and thought will become clear when one encounters the numerous references to them in the rest of the readings on the many aspects of stratification.

The two giants of stratification theory are Karl Marx (1818–1883) and Max Weber (1864–1920). We begin with Marx not only because his work chronologically preceded Weber's but also because it was part of Weber's intellectual tradition. To Weber, Marxism in general seemed an "untenable monocausal theory": It reduced the multiplicity of causal factors to a single-factor theorem.[2] Yet Weber's theory of stratification could not be well understood by one ignorant of Marx's ideas on class. In a sense all Weber's work (and particularly that on stratification) was shaped by his *intellectual dialogue* with Marx.

In contrast to Weber's concise statement on stratification—the second selection here—Marx's extensive writings do not contain an explicit exposition of his class theory.[3] (He undertook this task for the last chapter of *Capital,* entitled "The

---

[1] C. Wright Mills, *Images of Man,* New York: George Braziller, 1960, p. 2.

[2] H. H. Gerth and C. Wright Mills, "Intellectual Orientation," in *From Max Weber: Essays in Sociology,* New York: Oxford University Press, 1958, pp. 46–47.

[3] Among the best known essays written by sociologists on Marx's theory of class are Reinhard Bendix and Seymour Martin Lipset, "Karl Marx's Theory of Social Classes," in *Class, Status and Power,* Glencoe:, Illinois: Free Press, 1953, pp. 26–35; Ralf Dahrendorf, "Karl Marx's Model of the Class Society," in *Class and Class Conflict in Industrial Society,* Stanford: Stanford University Press, 1959, pp. 3–36 and Stanislaw Ossowski, "The Marxian Synthesis," in *Class Structure in the Social Consciousness,* New York: Free Press, 1963, pp. 69–88.

Classes," but he had written only a little more than a page when death interrupted him).

However, there is hardly a work by Marx in which he did not make generaliza-itons about class or analyze concrete social structures or historical events in terms of his class theory. Included here are excerpts from four of them that convey the essential elements of his thought on class. The first is the beginning of the systematic and scholarly exposition that he never finished (p. 14). Right here we become aware that Marx did not always employ a two-class model (capitalists, alternately termed the "bourgeoisie," and the proletarians) for which he is often accused. He speaks of the "three big classes" in the modern society of his day. In this brief beginning he did pose the question "What constitutes a class?" but the manuscript broke off just when he was about to provide the answer. His collaborator Engels did not take up the unanswered question.[4]

It is hoped that the reader will find at least a partial answer in the portion of the *Communist Manifesto* reprinted here (pp. 14–21), although this is an early work by Marx. His thoughts on class gained in precision in later writings. Despite this and despite its propagandistic rather than scholarly tone the *Manifesto* possesses a historical importance on which there is no need to elaborate. Furthermore, it contains almost all the elements of Marx's concept of class developed in his later works—even if often in less precise form. Wresting the theory from the propaganda is not easy, for the text is full of ambiguous generalizations. Take, for example, the opening sentence: What does it really mean that the ". . . history of all hitherto existing society is the history of class struggle?" It is clearly fallacious if it signifies that there has not been cooperation among classes. If it means that the class struggle is the only factor in social change, it is again wrong.[5] We may set it aside as expressing in the categorical rhetoric of propaganda Marx's theory of class, which is to be discovered from the rest of the selection.

Marx uses the term *class* in a generic sense, in the modern sense of stratum in general rather than type of stratum characteristic of capitalism. Thus he speaks of "classes" under slavery and feudalism as well as capitalism. He sees these classes not as monolithic structures but as containing distinct subdivisions whose interests often diverge. For the latter he sometimes uses the term *gradations* and other times *fractions* so that, for example, "the *lower* middle class" is such a fraction of the middle class (p. 20). He also designates these subdivisions as *strata* and thus speaks of the "lower strata of the middle class" (p. 18).

In the excerpt here from the *Manifesto,* the dichotomous conception of class appears to contradict the fragment of *Capital* where Marx referred to three classes. Marx employs the term class in two different ways, depending on context: (1) as a designation of concrete entities—strata at a given time—for example, wage laborers, capitalists, and landowners as the three "big classes" of his day (p. 14) and (2) as an analytic concept. In the latter sense, class is presented as a dichotomous scheme used to explain change from one social system to another, as well as to project the direction in which capitalist society would develop. Throughout history two dominant classes are in conflict with each other and this generates change. Capitalist society, according to Marx, was moving in the direction of the

---

[4] Recently Dahrendorf, *op. cit.,* made an effort to reconstruct this answer by stringing together quotations from the various writings by Marx.

[5] Pitirim Sorokin, *Contemporary Sociological Theories,* New York: Harper Brothers, 1928, pp. 540–543.

elimination of all other classes but the bourgeoisie and the proletariat. The other classes would "decay and finally disappear in the face of modern industry" (p. 20). He predicted that capitalist society would achieve "this dichotomy in full in the penultimate act of the drama," in the period that precedes the collapse of capitalism.[6]

Because Marx's dichotomous conception of class has been subject to much criticism, it may be interesting to note that such formulations have long preceded him. As Ossowski demonstrates, throughout cultural history there has been a tendency to conceive of hierarchical divisions of society in dichotomous terms. Aristotle, for example, saw the basic division in the social structure as the distinction between free men and slaves. In the writings of the Fathers of the Church society was divided into two strata: the rich and the poor.[7] And as we think of the history of the United States, the words of Alexander Hamilton come to mind: "All communities divide themselves into the few and the many. The first are the rich and well-born and the other the mass of the people who seldom judge or determine right."[8] This last example could also serve to illustrate the proposition that dichotomous conceptions of stratification are not necessarily the products of radical thought. Hamilton was supporting his argument for an aristocratic Senate elected for life.

By reading the section from the *Manifesto* the discerning will also discover that, contrary to what some sociology textbooks assert,[9] Marx did not disregard other aspects of stratification by emphasizing the economic one. On the contrary, the essential feature of social inequality, according to him, is power. Society is divided into those who have it, *the oppressors* and those who do not have it *the oppressed*. Marx's "economic interpretation" is an explanation of what accounts for this inequality in power. He maintains that the relation to the means of production is the determining factor. Those who own the means of production have the power to rule and oppress those who do not own it. The idea of the *ruling class* encountered in the *Manifesto* is elaborated in the pages here reprinted from *The German Ideology,* especially the thesis on how this class controls the prevailing ideas in a given society.

In the *Manifesto* one also finds Marx's important concept of class consciousness. Although he does spell out in this pamphlet the conditions under which such consciousness arises, also included here are some pages from his *Poverty of Philosophy,* where additional subjective aspects of class are delineated. Here also the two separate concepts that the sociologist of today would designate as *objective class* and *subjective class* are found. Individuals in the same economic situation constitute a class (objective) even when no awareness of its distinctive interests exists among them. To this Marx elsewhere refers as "class in itself," *Klasse an sich.* When such a class develops consciousness of its distinct interests it becomes a "class for itself," *Klasse für sich* (subjective class).

We turn next to the Max Weber selection, "Class, Status, Party." Of all the theoretical writings about stratification, this essay is probably the one most often referred to in American articles and books on this subject. That Weber's theory

---

[6] Ossowski, *op. cit.,* p. 75.

[7] *Ibid.,* pp. 19–37.

[8] Quoted in Arthur Schlessinger, Jr., *Age of Jackson,* Boston: Little Brown, 1945, p. 10.

[9] For example, Chinoy says that Marx "overlooked" other factors of stratification and "seriously neglected the ubiquitous problem of political power." See Ely Chinoy, *Society—An Introduction to Sociology,* New York: Random House, 1962, p. 133.

has had a much larger influence on stratification studies in the United States than has the theory of Marx may be partly because of the fact that Weber, in sharp contrast to Marx, set forth his entire theory in a single essay. But the more important reason lies in the nature of the concepts: those of Weber are narrower and lend themselves more to the technique of modern research.

What Marx assumed—that those who had the economic means also had the power and prestige—Weber made problematical by creating three distinct concepts: class, status, and power. In studying a given stratification system, the sociologist—if he has learned his leason from Weber—will not assume that the distribution of the above three factors coincides. The burden will rest on him to investigate to what degree prestige and power correlate with class.

Weber's concept of class resembles Marx's only in so far as it refers to an economic stratum. But even here it must not be overlooked that for Weber the importance of the economic factor lies elsewhere than in the relation to the means of production. His concept of class is narrower than that of Marx because it denotes only one type of strata in such a system. The other important type, based on prestige rather than economic criteria, is the *status group*.

A substantial part of the reprinted essay deals with status stratification and especially its relation to economic stratification. However, reading Weber critically one may discover that he is quite ambiguous about the latter. On one hand he stresses that status groups and classes are *empirically* distinct from each other, asserting that "'status groups' hinder the strict carrying through of the sheer market principle" (p. 27) and that "Both propertied and propertyless people can belong to the same status group, and frequently they do" (p. 28). But on the other hand, he qualified statements of this kind in a way that makes one conclude that class and status are in fact very much connected. Take, for example, his generalization that "Property as such is not always recognized as a status qualification, but in the long run it is, and with extraordinary regularity" (p. 28). What Weber fails to make explicit in this essay is that one has to separate *analytically* the economic and status factors that *actually* are closely joined together, precisely in order to understand the nature of the connection in a given society at a given time. Perhaps the ambiguity could be traced to Weber's failure to differentiate the competing bases of honor in Europe during the transition from feudalism to capitalism. The rising bourgeoisie did claim honor based on sheer economic considerations, but the aristocracy refused at first to recognize it. The latter had a vested interest in honor based on feudal values such as chivalry and lineage. In America, with no background of feudalism, the "self-made man" was accorded honor from the outset.

Weber perhaps expressed the relation between class and status more succinctly in his *Religion of India* than in the reprinted essay when he stated that "Social honor [status] can adhere directly to a class situation and it is also, indeed most of the time, determined by the average class situation of the status group members. This, however, is not necessarily the case. Status membership, in turn, influences the class situation in that the style of life required by status groups makes them prefer special kinds of property or gainful pursuits and reject others."[10]

As for power, the reprinted essay begins with an explanation and definition of it, but Weber does not elaborate on the distribution of power. It should be noted,

[10] Max Weber, *Religion of India*, Glencoe, Illinois: Free Press, 1958, p. 39.

however, that his definition lends itself to the concept of a continuum in the distribution of power, contrasting with Marx's dichotomous conception.

Power is the main subject of our third selection from the lengthy work of Vilfredo Pareto (1848–1923), the *Tratado di Sociologia Generale,* which appeared in its English edition under the title *Mind and Society.* The pages reprinted here contain perhaps the best known part of this magnum opus and the thoughts contained in them are often referred to as his *theory of circulation of elites.*

It is particularly important to pay attention to Pareto's concept of *elite,* for this term is common in the current literature and yet is used in a variety of meanings. Although Pareto defines elite in terms of the distribution of certain attributes, he does not operate with this concept in his theory of elite circulation but with the narrower one of *governing elite.* The theory deals with the relation between those who have power, the governing elite, and those who do not, the nonelite.

In this it resembles closely the thoughts of Mosca, [11] another "Machiavellian," as James Burnham labeled him. First of all, the concepts of political or ruling class (Mosca) and governing elite (Pareto) are very similar. Then, too, we encounter in both of them, as in Marx, a dichotomous conception of power. They see power as the universal aspect of stratification: all societies are divided into two strata— the rulers and the ruled. (This similarity between the Machiavellians and Marx are especially noteworthy because they opposed and sharply criticized Marx's social theory).

From a historical perspective, it may be interesting to recall here that the similarities in the theories of Pareto and Mosca gave rise to heated polemics as to who borrowed from whom; they were begun by Mosca himself who first raised the question of indebtedness.[12] By now we know enough about the sociology of knowledge to recognize that similarities do not necessarily imply "borrowing," often a euphemism for stealing. The intellectual climate of a given time focuses the attention of thinkers on certain problems.

In the Marx selection are some comments on what would go today under the heading of social mobility: how individuals rise or sink from one class to another. Such mobility in Marx's theory is connected with social change: with the transformation from feudalism to capitalism or with the development of capitalism. Pareto's contribution is toward the understanding of social mobility as a universal phenomenon, present in all societies to a larger or smaller extent.

He begins the exposition of his theory with the empirical generalization—the truth of which has withstood the test of time—that no stratification system, even that of caste, is completely closed. Systems do, however, differ in amount of interstrata mobility. In addition, he makes the important distinction between the normative and factual state (p. 37), which could serve us well later when we come to the readings about various types of stratification systems (Part II of this book). To rephrase Pareto, the norms of a given society may preclude mobility and yet mobility will take place (caste society). Conversely, the norms may postulate unlimited mobility (capitalist society) while actually the amount is limited.

Here too we find a similarity to Mosca. Mosca's contention, translated into current sociological terms, is that society makes use of both ascribed and achieved status, but that societies differ in the degree in which they rely on one or the other.

[11] Gaetano Mosca, *The Ruling Class,* New York: McGraw-Hill Book Company, 1939.
[12] Arthur Livingston, "Introduction," *Ibid.,* pp. ix–xvi.

He declares that in every society there are two tendencies in conflict with each other. One he calls democratic, the tendency toward an open structure that allows able people to rise. The other is aristocratic, the tendency toward closure: those on top set up barriers for those who want to climb.[13]

In criticizing Pareto's theory of elite circulation, Bottomore asserts, and we could take issue with this, that its analytical quality is less impressive than the glamour of the style. He considers it a major difficulty of this theory that it does not differentiate clearly and precisely between the process in which *individuals* circulate between the elite and nonelite and the process in which *one governing elite* is replaced by another.[14]

Although Pareto does refer to both processes by the same designation—circulation of elites—the preceding criticism may not be entirely valid. Pareto makes clear that he is primarily interested in the first process. Furthermore, he shows that the second process is dependent on the first (p. 38). A governing elite "crashes to ruin" when upward movement into it and downward movement out of it are severely curtailed. The reason is that it retains those members who are not capable of exercising power (no downward movement out of the elite) and fails to absorb capable nonelite individuals who eventually bring about its downfall and replace it (no upward movement into the elite). Pareto also points to force as an important element in the change of governing elites. The replacement of such an elite, he maintains, may be the result of its failure to use force.

Again one might point to the resemblence between Pareto's and Mosca's thought. Mosca also speaks of the disastrous consequences for the ruling classes that result from their being too closed to individuals from below. For when they are open to such individuals they ". . . are continually replenished through the admission of new elements who have inborn talents for leadership and will to lead". And this ". . . prevents that exhaustion of aristocracies of birth which usually paves the way for great social cataclysms."[15]

Joseph Schumpeter (1883–1950) also sees the aforenamed processes as connected, but analytically he differentiates one from the other more sharply than does Pareto. Thus his essay "Social Classes in an Ethnically Homogenous Environment," contains two separate sections: one dealing with the "Movement Across Class Lines,"[16] and the other—Part 2 of the Schumpeter selection—with the "Rise and Fall of Whole Classes."

First we should note that Schumpeter uses the term *classes* in the broad sense of strata, rather than in the Weberian sense. Hence he speaks of classes in feudal as well as capitalist society. His theory of the rise and fall of strata, as well as their relative rank, is a functional one. He explains the connection between the rank of a stratum, which he calls class, and its function in society. Its rank depends on the significance that *is attributed* to that function and how successfully it performs that function. Every class that has once enjoyed an elevated position, Schumpeter tells us, is greatly aided in seizing new functions "because the sources and gains of its prior function survive for some time."

Although Schumpeter's theory is a functional one, it does not suffer in my estimation from the shortcoming of current functional theories which cannot be

[13] *Ibid.*, pp. 56–68; 116–119; 405–420.
[14] T. B. Bottomore, *Elites and Society*, New York: Basic Books, 1964, pp. 42–43.
[15] Mosca, *op. cit.*, p. 416.
[16] Joseph Schumpeter, *Imperialism and Social Classes*, New York: Meridian Books, 1955, pp. 124–134.

used to explain change adequately. The Schumpeter theory of rise and fall of classes is precisely a theory of how stratification systems change and become replaced.

The historical case Schumpeter uses in detail to illustrate his theory is that of the rise and fall of the feudal aristocracy in Europe and more specifically in Germany. It would serve us well to acquaint ourselves with this material because feudalism is included in the next part of our book, Major Types of Stratification Systems. And in proceeding to that part we will also benefit from Schumpeter's historical perspective. He demonstrates convincingly that a stratification system at a given time cannot be understood without taking into account the system that preceded it.

ON CLASS
Karl Marx

I.

The owners merely of labour-power, owners of capital, and landowners, whose respective sources of income are wages, profit, and ground-rent, in other words, wage-labourers, capitalists, and land-owners constitute the three big classes of modern society based upon the capitalist mode of production.

In England, modern society is indisputably most highly and classically developed in economic structure. Nevertheless, even here the stratification of classes does not appear in its pure form. Middle and intermediate strata even here obliterate lines of demarcation everywhere (although incomparably less in rural districts than in the cities). However, this is immaterial for our analysis. We have seen that the continual tendency and law of development of the capitalist mode of production is more and more to divorce the means of production from labour, and more and more to concentrate the scattered means of production into large groups, thereby transforming labour into wage-labour and the means of production into capital. And to this tendency, on the other hand, corresponds the independent separation of landed property from capital and labour,[1] or the transformation of all landed property into the form of landed property corresponding

Section I is the unfinished last chapter from *Capital: A Critique of Political Economy*. Section II consists of pages from Part I of the *Manifesto of the Communist Party* by Karl Marx and Friedrich Engels. Section III is from Karl Marx and Friedrich Engels, *The German Ideology*. Section IV is from *The Poverty of Philosophy*.

[1] F. List remarks correctly: "The prevalence of a self-sufficient economy on large estates demonstrates solely the lack of civilization, means of communication, domestic trades and wealthy cities. It is to be encountered, therefore, throughout Russia, Poland, Hungary and Mecklenburg. Formerly, it was also prevalent in England; with the advance of trades and commerce, however, this was replaced by the breaking up into middle estates and the leasing of land." (*Die Ackerverfassung, die Zwergwirtschaft und die Auswanderung*, 1842, p. 10.)

to the capitalist mode of production.

The first question to be answered is this: What constitutes a class?—and the reply to this follows naturally from the reply to another question, namely: What makes wage-labourers, capitalists, and landlords constitute the three great social classes?

At first glance—the identity of revenues and sources of revenue. There are three great social groups whose members, the individuals forming them, live on wages, profit, and ground-rent respectively, on the realization of their labour-power, their capital, and their landed property.

However, from this standpoint, physicians and officials, e.g., would also constitute two classes, for they belong to two distinct social groups, the members of each of these groups receiving their revenue from one and the same source. The same would also be true of the infinite fragmentation of interest and rank into which the division of social labour splits labourers as well as capitalists and landlords—the latter, e.g., into owners of vineyards, farm owners, owners of forests, mine owners, and owners of fisheries.

[Here the manuscript breaks off.]

II.

BOURGEOIS AND PROLETARIANS[2]

The history of all hitherto existing society[3] is the history of class struggles.

[2] By bourgeoisie is meant the class of modern capitalists, owners of the means of social production and employers of wage-labour; by proletariat, the class of modern wage-labourers who, having no means of production of their own, are reduced to selling their labour power in order to live.

[3] That is, all *written* history. In 1837, the pre-history of society, the social organisation existing previous to recorded history, was all but unknown. Since then Haxthausen [August von, 1792-1866] discovered common ownership of land in Russia, Maurer [Georg Ludwig von] proved it to be the social foundation from which all Teutonic races started in history, and, by and by, village communities were found to be, or to have been, the primitive form of society everywhere from India to Ireland. The inner organisation of this primitive communistic society was laid bare, in its typical form, by Morgan's [Lewis H., 1818-1881] crowning discovery of the true nature of the *gens* and its relation to the *tribe*. With the dissolution of these primæval communities, society begins to be differentiated into separate and finally antagonistic classes. I have attempted to retrace this process of dissolution in *The Origin of the Family, Private Property and the State*.

Freeman and slave, patrician and plebeian, lord and serf, guild-master[4] and journeyman, in a word, oppressor and oppressed, stood in constant opposition to one another, carried on an uninterrupted, now hidden, now open fight, a fight that each time ended, either in a revolutionary reconstitution of society at large, or in the common ruin of the contending classes.

In the earlier epochs of history, we find almost everywhere a complicated arrangement of society into various orders, a manifold gradation of social rank. In ancient Rome we have patricians, knights, plebeians, slaves; in the Middle Ages, feudal lords, vassals, guild-masters, journeymen, apprentices, serfs; in almost all of these classes, again, subordinate gradations.

The modern bourgeois society that has sprouted from the ruins of feudal society, has not done away with class antagonisms. It has but established new classes, new conditions of oppression, new forms of struggle in place of the old ones.

Our epoch, the epoch of the bourgeoisie, possesses, however, this distinctive feature: It has simplified the class antagonisms. Society as a whole is more and more splitting up into two great hostile camps, into two great classes directly facing each other— bourgeoisie and proletariat.

From the serfs of the Middle Ages sprang the chartered burghers of the earliest towns. From these burgesses the first elements of the bourgeoisie were developed.

The discovery of America, the rounding of the Cape, opened up fresh ground for the rising bourgeoisie. The East-Indian and Chinese markets, the colonisation of America, trade with the colonies, the increase in the means of exchange and in commodities generally, gave to commerce, to navigation, to industry, an impulse never before known, and thereby, to the revolutionary element in the tottering feudal society, a rapid development.

The feudal system of industry, in which industrial production was monopolised by closed guilds, now no longer sufficed for the growing wants of the new markets. The manufacturing system took its place. The

guild-masters were pushed aside by the manufacturing middle class; division of labour between the different corporate guilds vanished in the face of division of labour in each single workshop.

Meantime the markets kept ever growing, the demand ever rising. Even manufacture no longer sufficed. Thereupon, steam and machinery revolutionised industrial production. The place of manufacture was taken by the giant, modern industry, the place of the industrial middle class, by industrial millionaires—the leaders of whole industrial armies, the modern bourgeois.

Modern industry has established the world market, for which the discovery of America paved the way. This market has given an immense development to commerce, to navigation, to communication by land. This development has, in its turn, reacted on the extension of industry; and in proportion as industry, commerce, navigation, railways extended, in the same proportion the bourgeoisie developed, increased its capital, and pushed into the background every class handed down from the Middle Ages.

We see, therefore, how the modern bourgeoisie is itself the product of a long course of development, of a series of revolutions in the modes of production and of exchange.

Each step in the development of the bourgeoisie was accompanied by a corresponding political advance of that class. An oppressed class under the sway of the feudal nobility, it became an armed and self-governing association in the mediæval commune;[5] here independent urban republic (as in Italy and Germany), there taxable "third estate" of the monarchy (as in France); afterwards, in the period of manufacture proper, serving either the semi-feudal or the absolute monarchy as a counterpoise against the nobility, and, in fact, corner-stone of the great monarchies in

---

[4] Guild-master, that is a full member of a guild, a master within, not a head of a guild.

[5] "Commune" was the name taken in France by the nascent towns even before they had conquered from their feudal lords and masters local self-government and political rights as the "Third Estate." Generally speaking, for the economic development of the bourgeoisie, England is here taken as the typical country, for its political development, France.

general—the bourgeoisie has at last, since the establishment of modern industry and of the world market, conquered for itself, in the modern representative state, exclusive political sway. The executive of the modern state is but a committee for managing the common affairs of the whole bourgeoisie.

The bourgeoisie has played a most revolutionary rôle in history.

The bourgeoisie, wherever it has got the upper hand, has put an end to all feudal, patriarchal, idyllic relations. It has pitilessly torn asunder the motley feudal ties that bound man to his "natural superiors," and has left no other bond between man and man than naked self-interest, than callous "cash payment." It has drowned the most heavenly ecstasies of religious fervour, of chivalrous enthusiasm, of philistine sentimentalism, in the icy water of egotistical calculation. It has resolved personal worth into exchange value, and in place of the numberless indefeasible chartered freedoms, has set up that single, unconscionable freedom—Free Trade. In one word, for exploitation, veiled by religious and political illusions, it has substituted naked, shameless, direct, brutal exploitation.

The bourgeoisie has stripped of its halo every occupation hitherto honoured and looked up to with reverent awe. It has converted the physician, the lawyer, the priest, the poet, the man of science, into its paid wage-labourers.

The bourgeoisie has torn away from the family its sentimental veil, and has reduced the family relation to a mere money relation.

The bourgeoisie has disclosed how it came to pass that the brutal display of vigour in the Middle Ages, which reactionaries so much admire, found its fitting complement in the most slothful indolence. It has been the first to show what man's activity can bring about. It has accomplished wonders far surpassing Egyptian pyramids, Roman aqueducts, and Gothic cathedrals; it has conducted expeditions that put in the shade all former migrations of nations and crusades.

The bourgeoisie cannot exist without constantly revolutionising the instruments of production, and thereby the relations of production, and with them the whole relations of society. Conservation of the old modes of production in unaltered form, was, on the contrary, the first condition of existence for all earlier industrial classes. Constant revolutionising of production, uninterrupted disturbance of all social conditions, everlasting uncertainty and agitation distinguish the bourgeois epoch from all earlier ones. All fixed, fast-frozen relations, with their train of ancient and venerable prejudices and opinions, are swept away, all new-formed ones become antiquated before they can ossify. All that is solid melts into air, all that is holy is profaned, and man is at last compelled to face with sober senses his real conditions of life and his relations with his kind.

The need of a constantly expanding market for its products chases the bourgeoisie over the whole surface of the globe. It must nestle everywhere, settle everywhere, establish connections everywhere.

The bourgeoisie has through its exploitation of the world market given a cosmopolitan character to production and consumption in every country. To the great chagrin of reactionaries, it has drawn from under the feet of industry the national ground on which it stood. All old-established national industries have been destroyed or are daily being destroyed. They are dislodged by new industries, whose introduction becomes a life and death question for all civilised nations, by industries that no longer work up indigenous raw material, but raw material drawn from the remotest zones; industries whose products are consumed, not only at home, but in every quarter of the globe. In place of the old wants, satisfied by the production of the country, we find new wants, requiring for their satisfaction the products of distant lands and climes. In place of the old local and national seclusion and self-sufficiency, we have intercourse in every direction, universal inter-dependence of nations. And as in material, so also in intellectual production. The intellectual creations of individual nations become common property. National one-sidedness and narrow-mindedness become more and more impossible, and from the numerous national and local literatures there arises a world literature.

The bourgeoisie, by the rapid improvement of all instruments of production, by the immensely facilitated means of communication, draws all nations, even the most barbarian, into civilisation. The cheap prices of its commodities are the heavy artillery with which it batters down all Chinese walls, with which it forces the barbarians' intensely obstinate hatred of foreigners to capitulate. It compels all nations, on pain of extinction to adopt the bourgeois mode of production; it compels them to introduce what it calls civilisation into their midst, *i.e.,* to become bourgeois themselves. In a word, it creates a world after its own image.

The bourgeoisie has subjected the country to the rule of the towns. It has created enormous cities, has greatly increased the urban population as compared with the rural, and has thus rescued a considerable part of the population from the idiocy of rural life. Just as it has made the country dependent on the towns, so it has made barbarian and semi-barbarian countries dependent on the civilised ones, nations of peasants on nations of bourgeois, the East on the West.

More and more the bourgeoisie keeps doing away with the scattered state of the population, of the means of production, and of property. It has agglomerated population, centralised means of production, and has concentrated property in a few hands. The necessary consequence of this was political centralisation. Independent, or but loosely connected provinces, with separate interests, laws, governments and systems of taxation, became lumped together into one nation, with one government, one code of laws, one national class interest, one frontier and one customs tariff.

The bourgeoisie, during its rule of scarce one hundred years, has created more massive and more colossal productive forces than have all preceding generations together. Subjection of nature's forces to man, machinery, application of chemistry to industry and agriculture, steam-navigation, railways, electric telegraphs, clearing of whole continents for cultivation, canalisation of rivers, whole populations conjured out of the ground—what earlier century had even a presentiment that such productive forces slumbered in the lap of social labour?

We see then that the means of production and of exchange, which served as the foundation for the growth of the bourgeoisie were generated in feudal society. At a certain stage in the development of these means of production and of exchange, the conditions under which feudal society produced and exchanged, the feudal organisation of agriculture and manufacturing industry, in a word, the feudal relations of property became no longer compatible with the already developed productive forces; they became so many fetters. They had to be burst asunder; they were burst asunder.

Into their place stepped free competition, accompanied by a social and political constitution adapted to it, and by the economic and political sway of the bourgeois class.

A similar movement is going on before our own eyes. Modern bourgeois society with its relations of production, of exchange and of property, a society that has conjured up such gigantic means of production and of exchange, is like the sorcerer who is no longer able to control the powers of the nether world whom he has called up by his spells. For many a decade past the history of industry and commerce is but the history of the revolt of modern productive forces against modern conditions of production, against the property relations that are the conditions for the existence of the bourgeoisie and of its rule. It is enough to mention the commercial crises that by their periodical return put the existence of the entire bourgeois society on trial, each time more threateningly. In these crises a great part not only of the existing products, but also of the previously created productive forces, are periodically destroyed. In these crises there breaks out an epidemic that, in all earlier epochs, would have seemed an absurdity—the epidemic of overproduction. Society suddenly finds itself put back into a state of momentary barbarism; it appears as if a famine, a universal war of devastation had cut off the supply of every means of subsistence; industry and commerce seem to be destroyed. And why? Because there is too much civilisation, too much means of subsistence, too much industry, too much commerce. The productive forces at the disposal of society no longer tend to further the development of the conditions of bourgeois property; on the contrary, they have become too powerful for these conditions, by which they are fettered, and no sooner do they overcome these fetters than they bring disorder into the whole of bourgeois society, endanger the existence of bourgeois property. The conditions of bourgeois society are too narrow to comprise the wealth created by them. And how does the bourgeoisie get over these crises? On the one hand by enforced destruction of a mass of productive forces; on the other, by the conquest of new markets, and by the more thorough exploitation of the old ones. That is to say, by paving the way for more extensive and more destructive crises, and by diminishing the means whereby crises are prevented.

The weapons with which the bourgeoisie felled feudalism to the ground are now turned against the bourgeoisie itself.

But not only has the bourgeoisie forged the weapons that bring death to itself; it has also called into existence the men who are to wield those weapons—the modern working class—the proletarians.

In proportion as the bourgeoisie, *i.e.,* capital, is developed, in the same proportion is the probetariat, the modern working class, developed—a class of labourers, who live only so long as they find work, and who find work only so long as their labour increases capital. These labourers, who must sell themselves piecemeal, are a commodity, like every other article of commerce, and are consequently exposed to all the vicissitudes of competition, to all the fluctuations of the market.

Owing to the extensive use of machinery and to division of labour, the work of the proletarians has lost all individual character, and, consequently, all charm for the workman. He becomes an appendage of the machine, and it is only the most simple, most montonous, and most easily acquired knack, that is required of him. Hence, the cost of production of a workman is restricted, almost entirely, to the means of subsistence that he requires for his maintenance, and for the propagation of his race. But the price of a commodity, and therefore also of labour, is equal to its cost of production. In proportion, therefore, as the repulsiveness of the work increases, the wage decreases. Nay more, in proportion as the use of machinery and division of labour increases, in the same proportion the burden of toil also increases, whether by prolongation of the working hours, by increase of the work exacted in a given time, or by increased speed of the machinery, etc.

Modern industry has converted the little workshop of the patriarchal master into the great factory of the industrial capitalist. Masses of labourers, crowded into the factory, are organised like soldiers. As privates of the industrial army they are placed under the command of a perfect hierarchy of officers and sergeants. Not only are they slaves of the bourgeois class, and of the bourgeois state; they are daily and hourly enslaved by the machine, by the overlooker, and, above all, by the individual bourgeois manufacturer himself. The more openly this despotism proclaims gain to be its end and aim, the more petty, the more hateful and the more embittering it is.

The less the skill and exertion of strength implied in manual labour, in other words, the more modern industry develops, the more is the labour of men superseded by that of women. Differences of age and sex have no longer any distinctive social validity for the working class. All are instruments of labour, more or less expensive to use, according to their age and sex.

No sooner has the labourer received his wages in cash, for the moment escaping exploitation by the manufacturer, than he is set upon by the other portions of the bourgeoisie, the landlord, the shopkeeper, the pawnbroker, etc.

The lower strata of the middle class—the small tradespeople, shopkeepers, and retired tradesmen generally, the handicraftsmen and peasants—all these sink gradually into the proletariat, partly because their diminutive capital does not suffice for the scale on which modern industry is carried on, and is swamped in the competition with the large capitalists, partly because their specialised skill is rendered worthless by new methods of production. Thus the proletariat is recruited from all classes of the population.

The proletariat goes through various

stages of development. With its birth begins its struggle with the bourgeoisie. At first the contest is carried on by individual labourers, then by the work people of a factory, then by the operatives of one trade, in one locality against the individual bourgeois who directly exploits them. They direct their attacks not against the bourgeois conditions of production, but against the instruments of production themselves; they destroy imported wares that compete with their labour, they smash machinery to pieces, they set factories ablaze, they seek to restore by force this vanished status of the workman of the Middle Ages.

At this stage the labourers still form an incoherent mass scattered over the whole country, and broken up by their mutual competition. If anywhere they unite to form more compact bodies, this is not yet the consequence of their own active union, but of the union of the bourgeoisie, which class, in order to attain its own political ends, is compelled to set the whole proletariat in motion, and is moreover still able to do so for a time. At this stage, therefore, the proletarians do not fight their enemies, but the enemies of their enemies, the remnants of absolute monarchy, the landowners, the non-industrial bourgeois, the petty bourgeoisie. Thus the whole historical movement is concentrated in the hands of the bourgeoisie; every victory so obtained is a victory for the bourgeoisie.

But with the development of industry the proletariat not only increases in number; it becomes concentrated in greater masses, its strength grows, and it feels that strength more. The various interests and conditions of life within the ranks of the proletariat are more and more equalised, in proportion as machinery obliterates all distinctions of labour and nearly everywhere reduces wages to the same low level. The growing competition among the bourgeois, and the resulting commercial crises, make the wages of the workers ever more fluctuating. The unceasing improvement of machinery, ever more rapidly developing, makes their livelihood more and more precarious; the collisions between individual workmen and individual bourgeois take more and more the character of collisions between two classes. Thereupon the workers begin to form combinations (trade unions) against the bourgeoisie; they club together in order to keep up the rate of wages; they found permanent associations in order to make provision beforehand for these occasional revolts. Here and there the contest breaks out into riots.

Now and then the workers are victorious, but only for a time. The real fruit of their battles lies, not in the immediate result, but in the ever expanding union of the workers. This union is furthered by the improved means of communication which are created by modern industry, and which place the workers of different localities in contact with one another. It was just this contact that was needed to centralise the numerous local struggles, all of the same character, into one national struggle between classes. But every class struggle is a political struggle. And that union, to attain which the burghers of the Middle Ages, with their miserable highways, required centuries, the modern proletarians, thanks to railways, achieve in a few years.

This organisation of the proletarians into a class, and consequently into a political party, is continually being upset again by the competition between the workers themselves. But it ever rises up again, stronger, firmer, mightier. It compels legislative recognition of particular interests of the workers, by taking advantage of the divisions among the bourgeoisie itself. Thus the ten-hour bill in England was carried.

Altogether, collisions between the classes of the old society further the course of development of the proletariat in many ways. The bourgeoisie finds itself involved in a constant battle. At first with the aristocracy; later on, with those portions of the bourgeoisie itself whose interests have become antagonistic to the progress of industry at all times with the bourgeoisie of foreign countries. In all these battles it sees itself compelled to appeal to the proletariat, to ask for its help, and thus, to drag it into the political arena. The bourgeoisie itself, therefore, supplies the proletariat with its own elements of political and general education, in other words, it furnishes the proletariat with weapons for fighting the bourgeoisie.

Further, as we have already seen, entire

sections of the ruling classes are, by the advance of industry, precipitated into the proletariat, or are at least threatened in their conditions of existence. These also supply the proletariat with fresh elements of enlightenment and progress.

Finally, in times when the class struggle nears the decisive hour, the process of dissolution going on within the ruling class, in fact within the whole range of old society, assumes such a violent, glaring character, that a small section of the ruling class cuts itself adrift, and joins the revolutionary class, the class that holds the future in its hands. Just as, therefore, at an earlier period, a section of the nobility went over to the bourgeoisie, so now a portion of the bourgeoisie goes over to the proletariat, and in particular, a portion of the bourgeois ideologists, who have raised themselves to the level of comprehending theoretically the historical movement as a whole.

Of all the classes that stand face to face with the bourgeoisie today, the proletariat alone is a really revolutionary class. The other classes decay and finally disappear in the face of modern industry; the proletariat is its special and essential product.

The lower middle class, the small manufacturer, the shopkeeper, the artisan, the peasant, all these fight against the bourgeoisie, to save from extinction their existence as fractions of the middle class. They are therefore not revolutionary, but conservative. Nay more, they are reactionary, for they try to roll back the wheel of history. If by chance they are revolutionary, they are so only in view of their impending transfer into the proletariat; they thus defend not their present, but their future interests; they desert their own standpoint to adopt that of the proletariat.

The "dangerous class," the social scum (*Lumpenproletariat*), that passively rotting mass thrown off by the lowest layers of old society, may, here and there, be swept into the movement by a proletarian revolution; its conditions of life, however, prepare it far more for the part of a bribed tool of reactionary intrigue.

The social conditions of the old society no longer exist for the proletariat. The proletarian is without property; his relation to his wife and children has no longer anything in common with bourgeois family relations; modern industrial labour, modern subjection to capital, the same in England as in France, in America as in Germany, has stripped him of every trace of national character. Law, morality, religion, are to him so many bourgeois prejudices, behind which lurk in ambush just as many bourgeois interests.

All the preceding classes that got the upper hand, sought to fortify their already acquired status by subjecting society at large to their conditions of appropriation. The proletarians cannot become masters of the productive forces of society, except by abolishing their own previous mode of appropriation, and thereby also every other previous mode of appropriation. They have nothing of their own to secure and to fortify; their mission is to destroy all previous securities for, and insurance of, individual property.

All previous historical movements were movements of minorities, or in the interest of minorities. The proletarian movement is the self-conscious, independent movement of the immense majority, in the interest of the immense majority. The proletariat, the lowest stratum of our present society, cannot stir, cannot raise itself up, without the whole superincumbent strata of official society being sprung into the air.

Though not in substance, yet in form, the struggle of the proletariat with the bourgeoisie is at first a national struggle. The proletariat of each country must, of course, first of all settle matters with its own bourgeoisie.

In depicting the most general phases of the development of the proletariat, we traced the more or less veiled civil war, raging within existing society, up to the point where that war breaks out into open revolution, and where the violent overthrow of the bourgeoisie lays the foundation for the sway of the proletariat.

Hitherto, every form of society has been based, as we have already seen, on the antagonism of oppressing and oppressed classes. But in order to oppress a class, certain conditions must be assured to it under which it can, at least, continue its slavish existence. The serf, in the period of serfdom, raised himself to membership in the commune, just as the petty bourgeois under the yoke of feudal absolutism, managed to develop into a bourgeois. The modern labourer, on the contrary, instead of rising with the progress of industry, sinks deeper and deeper below the conditions of existence of his own class. He becomes a pauper, and pauperism develops more rapidly than population and wealth. And here it becomes evident, that the bourgeoisie is unfit any longer to be the ruling class in society, and to impose its conditions of existence upon society as an over-riding law. It is unfit to rule because it is incompetent to assure an existence to its slave within his slavery, because it cannot help letting him sink into such a state, that it has to feed him, instead of being fed by him. Society can no longer live under this bourgeoisie, in other words, its existence is no longer compatible with society.

The essential condition for the existence and sway of the bourgeois class, is the formation and augmentation of capital; the condition for capital is wage-labour. Wage-labour rests exclusively on competition between the labourers. The advance of industry, whose involuntary promoter is the bourgeoisie, replaces the isolation of the labourers, due to competition, by their revolutionary combination, due to association. The development of modern industry, therefore, cuts from under its feet the very foundation on which the bourgeoisie produces and appropriates products. What the bourgeoisie therefore produces, above all, are its own grave-diggers. Its fall and the victory of the proletariat are equally inevitable.

. . . .

III.

The ideas of the ruling class are in every epoch the ruling ideas: i.e. the class, which is the ruling material force of society, is at the same time its ruling intellectual force. The class which has the means of material production at its disposal, has control at the same time over the means of mental production, so that thereby, generally speaking, the ideas of those who lack the means of mental production are subject to it. The ruling ideas are nothing more than the ideal expression of the dominant material relationships, the dominant material relationships grasped as ideas; hence of the relationships which make the one class the ruling one, therefore the ideas of its dominance. The individuals composing the ruling class possess among other things consciousness, and therefore think. In so far, therefore, as they rule as a class and determine the extent and compass of an epoch, it is self-evident that they do this in their whole range, hence among other things rule also as thinkers, as producers of ideas, and regulate the production and distribution of the ideas of their age: thus their ideas are the ruling ideas of the epoch. For instance, in an age and in a country where royal power, aristocracy and bourgeoisie are contending for mastery and where, therefore, mastery is shared, the doctrine of the separation of powers proves to be the dominant idea and is expressed as an "eternal law." The division of labour, which we saw above as one of the chief forces of history up till now, manifests itself also in the ruling class as the division of mental and material labour, so that inside this class one part appears as the thinkers of the class (its active, conceptive ideologists, who make the perfecting of the illusion of the class about itself their chief source of livelihood), while the others' attitude to these ideas and illusions is more passive and receptive, because they are in reality the active members of this class and have less time to make up illusions and ideas about themselves. Within this class this cleavage can even develop into a certain opposition and hostility between the two parts, which, however, in the case of a practical collision, in which the class itself is endangered, automatically comes to nothing, in which case there also vanishes the semblance that the ruling ideas were not the ideas of the ruling class and had a power distinct from the power of this class. The existence of revolutionary ideas in a particular period presupposes the existence of a revolutionary class; about the premises for the latter sufficient has already been said above.

If now in considering the course of history we detach the ideas of the ruling class from the ruling class itself and attribute to them an independent existence, if we confine ourselves to saying that these or those ideas were dominant, without bothering ourselves about the conditions of production and the producers of these ideas, if we then ignore the individuals and world conditions which are the source of the ideas, we can say, for instance, that during the time that the aristocracy was dominant, the concepts honour, loyalty, etc., were dominant, during the dominance of the bourgeoisie the concepts freedom, equality, etc. The ruling class itself on the whole imagines this to be so. This conception of history, which is common to all historians, particularly since the eighteenth century, will necessarily come up against the phenomenon that increasingly abstract ideas hold sway, i.e. ideas which increasingly take on the form of universality. For each new class which puts itself in the place of one ruling before it, is compelled, merely in order to carry through its aim, to represent its interest as the common interest of all the members of society, put in an ideal form; it will give its ideas the form of universality, and represent them as the only rational, universally valid ones. The class making a revolution appears from the very start, merely because it is opposed to a *class*, not as a class but as the representative of the whole of society; it appears as the whole mass of society confronting the one ruling class. It can do this because, to start with, its interest really is more connected with the common interest of all other non-ruling classes, because under the pressure of conditions its interest has not yet been able to develop as the particular interest of a particular class. Its victory, therefore, benefits also many individuals of the other classes which are not winning a dominant position, but only in so far as it now puts these individuals in a position to raise themselves into the ruling class. When the French bourgeoisie overthrew the power of the aristocracy, it thereby made it possible for many proletarians to raise themselves above the proletariat, but only in so far as they became bourgeois. Every new class, therefore, achieves its hegemony only on a broader basis than that of the class ruling previously, in return for which the opposition of the non-ruling class against the new ruling class later develops all the more sharply and profoundly. Both these things determine the fact that the struggle to

be waged against this new ruling class, in its turn, aims at a more decided and radical negation of the previous conditions of society than could all previous classes which sought to rule.

This whole semblance, that the rule of a certain class is only the rule of certain ideas, comes to a natural end, of course, as soon as society ceases at last to be organized in the form of class-rule, that is to say as soon as it is no longer necessary to represent a particular interest as general or "the general interest" as ruling.

· ·

IV.

Feudalism also had its proletariat—serfdom, which contained all the germs of the bourgeoisie. Feudal production also had two antagonistic elements which are likewise designated by the name of the *good side* and the *bad side* of feudalism, irrespective of the fact that it is always the bad side that in the end triumphs over the good side. It is the bad side that produces the movement which makes history, by providing a struggle. If, during the epoch of the domination of feudalism, the economists, enthusiastic over the knightly virtues, the beautiful harmony between rights and duties, the patriarchal life of the towns, the prosperous condition of domestic industry in the countryside, the development of industry organized into corporations, guilds and fraternities, in short, everything that constitutes the good side of feudalism, had set themselves the problem of eliminating everything that cast a shadow on this picture—serfdom, privileges, anarchy—what would have happened? All the elements which called forth the struggle would have been destroyed, and the development of the bourgeoisie nipped in the bud. One would have set oneself the absurd problem of eliminating history.

After the triumph of the bourgeoisie there was no longer any question of the good or the bad side of feudalism. The bourgeoisie took possession of the productive forces it had developed under feudalism. All the old economic forms, the corresponding civil relations, the political state which was the official expression of the old civil society, were smashed.

Thus feudal production, to be judged properly, must be considered as a mode of production founded on antagonism. It must be shown how wealth was produced within this antagonism, how the productive forces were developed at the same time as class antagonisms, how one of the classes, the bad side, the drawback of society, went on growing until the material conditions for its emancipation had attained full maturity. Is not this as good as saying that the mode of production, the relations in which productive forces are developed, are anything but eternal laws, but that they correspond to a definite development of men and of their productive forces, and that a change in men's productive forces necessarily brings about a change in their relations of production? As the main thing is not to be deprived of the fruits of civilization, of the acquired productive forces, the traditional forms in which they were produced must be smashed. From this moment the revolutionary class becomes conservative.

The bourgeoisie begins with a proletariat which is itself a relic of the proletariat of feudal times. In the course of its historical development, the bourgeoisie necessarily develops its antagonistic character, which at first is more or less disguised, existing only in a latent state. As the bourgeoisie develops, there develops in its bosom a new proletariat, a modern proletariat; there develops a struggle between the proletarian class and the bourgeois class, a struggle which, before being felt, perceived, appreciated, understood, avowed and proclaimed aloud by both sides, expresses itself, to start with, merely in partial and momentary conflicts, in subversive acts. On the other hand, if all the members of the modern bourgeoisie have the same interests inasmuch as they form a class as against another class; they have opposite, antagonistic interests inasmuch as they stand face to face with one another. This opposition of interests results from the economic conditions of their bourgeois life. From day to day it thus becomes clearer

that the production relations in which the bourgeoisie moves have not a simple, uniform character, but a dual character; that in the selfsame relations in which wealth is produced, poverty is produced also; that in the selfsame relations in which there is a development of the productive forces, there is also a force producing repression; that these relations produce *bourgeois wealth*, i.e., the wealth of the bourgeois class, only by continually annihilating the wealth of the individual members of this class and by producing an evergrowing proletariat.

. . . .

Economic conditions had first transformed the mass of the people of the country into workers. The combination of capital has created for this mass a common situation, common interests. *This mass is thus already a class as against capital, but not yet for itself.* [Italics supplied.] In the struggle, of which we have noted only a few phases, this mass becomes united, and constitutes itself as a *class for itself*. [Italics supplied][6] The interests it defends become class interests. But the struggle of class against class is a political struggle.

In the bourgeoisie we have two phases to distinguish: that in which it constituted itself as a class under the regime of feudalism and absolute monarchy, and that in which, already constituted as a class, it overthrew feudalism and monarchy to make society into a bourgeois society. The first of these phases was the longer and necessitated the greater efforts. This too began by partial combinations against the feudal lords.

Much research has been carried out to trace the different historical phases that the bourgeoisie has passed through, from the commune up to its constitution as a class.

[6] The two last sentences are often cited and here they are in the German original: "So ist die Masse bereits eine Klasse gegenüber dem Kapital aber noch nicht für sich selbst. In dem Kampf . . . findet sich diese Masse zusammen, konstituiert sie sich als Klasse für sich selbst." *Das Elend der Philosophie* in *Karl Marx, Friedrich Engels Werke*, Berlin: Dietz Verlag, 1959, 4, p. 181. (C. S. H.)

But when it is a question of making a precise study of strikes, combinations[7] and other forms in which the proletarians carry out before our eyes their organization as a class, some are seized with real fear and others display a *transcendental* disdain.

An oppressed class is the vital condition for every society founded on the antagonism of classes. The emancipation of the oppressed class thus implies necessarily the creation of a new society. For the oppressed class to be able to emancipate itself it is necessary that the productive powers already acquired and the existing social relations should no longer be capable of existing side by side. Of all the instruments of production, the greatest productive power is the revolutionary class itself. The organization of revolutionary elements as a class supposes the existence of all the productive forces which could be engendered in the bosom of the old society.

Does this mean that after the fall of the old society there will be a new class domination culminating in a new political power? No.

The condition for the emancipation of the working class is the abolition of every class, just as the condition for the liberation of the third estate, of the bourgeois order, was the abolition of all estates[8] and all orders.

The working class, in the course of its development, will substitute for the old civil society an association which will exclude classes and their antagonism, and there will be no more political power properly so-called, since political power is precisely the official expression of antagonism in civil society.

. . . .

[7] Trade Unions. (C. S. H.)

[8] Estates here in the historical sense of the estates of feudalism, estates with definite and limited privileges. The revolution of the bourgeoisie abolished the estates and their privileges. Bourgeois society knows only *classes*. It was, therefore, absolutely in contradiction with history to describe the proletariat as the "fourth estate." [*Note by F. Engels to the German edition,* 1885].

CLASS, STATUS, PARTY
Max Weber

ECONOMICALLY DETERMINED POWER AND THE SOCIAL ORDER

Law exists when there is a probability that an order will be upheld by a specific staff of men who will use physical or psychical compulsion with the intention of obtaining conformity with the order, or of inflicting sanctions for infringement of it.[1] The structure of every legal order directly influences the distribution of power, economic or otherwise, within its respective community. This is true of all legal orders and not only that of the state. In general, we understand by "power" the chance of a man or of a number of men to realize their own will in a communal action even against the resistance of others who are not participating in the action.

"Economically conditioned" power is not, of course, identical with "power" as such. On the contrary, the emergence of economic power may be the consequence of power existing on other grounds. Man does not strive for power only in order to enrich himself economically. Power, including economic power, may be valued "for its own sake." Very frequently the striving for power is also conditioned by the social "honor" it entails. Not all power, however, entails social honor: The typical American Boss, as well as the typical big speculator, deliberately relinquishes social honor. Quite generally, "mere economic" power, and especially "naked" money power, is by no means a recognized basis of social honor. Nor is power the only basis of social honor. Indeed, social honor, or prestige, may even be the basis of political or economic power, and very frequently has been. Power, as well as honor, may be

From *From Max Weber: Essays in Sociology,* edited and translated by H. H. Gerth and C. Wright Mills. Copyright 1946 by Oxford University Press, Inc. Reprinted by permission.

[1] *Wirtschaft und Gesellschaft*, Part III, Chap. 4, pp. 631–640. The first sentence in paragraph one and the several definitions in this chapter in brackets do not appear in the original text. They have been taken from other contexts of *Wirtschaft und Gesellschaft*.

guaranteed by the legal order, but, at least normally, it is not their primary source. The legal order is rather an additional factor that enhances the chance to hold power or honor; but it cannot always secure them.

The way in which social honor is distributed in a community between typical groups participating in this distribution we may call the "social order." The social order and the economic order are, of course, similarly related to the "legal order." However, the social and the economic order are not identical. The economic order is for us merely the way in which economic goods and services are distributed and used. The social order is of course conditioned by the economic order to a high degree, and in its turn reacts upon it.

Now: "classes," "status groups," and "parties" are phenomena of the distribution of power within a community.

DETERMINATION OF CLASS-SITUATION BY MARKET-SITUATION

In our terminology, "classes" are not communities; they merely represent possible, and frequent bases for communal action. We may speak of a "class" when (1) a number of people have in common a specific causal component of their life chances, in so far as (2) this component is represented exclusively by economic interests in the possession of goods and opportunities for income, and (3) is represented under the conditions of the commodity or labor markets. [These points refer to "class situation," which we may express more briefly as the typical chance for a supply of goods, external living conditions, and personal life experiences, in so far as this chance is determined by the amount and kind of power, or lack of such, to dispose of goods or skills for the sake of income in a given economic order. The term "class" refers to any group of people that is found in the same class situation.]

It is the most elemental economic fact that the way in which the disposition over material property is distributed among a plurality of people meeting competitively in the market for the purpose of exchange, in itself creates specific life chances. According to the law of marginal utility this mode of distribution excludes the non-owners from competing for highly valued goods; it favors the owners and, in fact, gives to them a monopoly to acquire such goods. Other things being equal, this mode of distribution monopolizes the opportunities for profitable deals for all those who, provided with goods, do not necessarily have to exchange them. It increases, at least generally, their power in price wars with those who, being propertyless, have nothing to offer but their services in native form or goods in a form constituted through their own labor, and who above all are compelled to get rid of these products in order barely to subsist. This mode of distribution gives to the propertied a monopoly on the possibility of transferring property from the sphere of use as a "fortune," to the sphere of "capital goods"; that is, it gives them the entrepreneurial function and all chances to share directly or indirectly in returns on capital. All this holds true within the area in which pure market conditions prevail. "Property" and "lack of property" are, therefore, the basic categories of all class situations. It does not matter whether these two categories become effective in price wars or in competitive struggles.

Within these categories, however, class situations are further differentiated: on the one hand, according to the kind of property that is usable for returns; and, on the other hand, according to the kind of services that can be offered in the market. Ownership of domestic buildings; productive establishments; warehouses; stores; agriculturally usable land, large and small holdings—quantitative differences with possibly qualitative consequences—; ownership of mines; cattle; men (slaves); disposition over mobile instruments of production, or capital goods of all sorts, especially money or objects that can be exchanged for money easily and at any time; disposition over products of one's own labor or of others' labor differing according to their various distances from consumability; disposition over transferable monopolies of any kind—all these distinctions differentiate the class situations of the propertied just as does the "meaning" which they can and do give to the utilization of property, especially to property which has money equivalence.. Accordingly, the propertied, for instance, may belong to the class of rentiers or to the class of entrepreneurs.

Those who have no property but who offer services are differentiated just as much according to their kinds of services as according to the way in which they make use of these services, in a continuous or discontinuous relation to a recipient. But always this is the generic connotation of the concept of class: that the kind of chance in the *market* is the decisive moment which presents a common condition for the individual's fate. "Class situation" is, in this sense, ultimately "market situation." The effect of naked possession *per se*, which among cattle breeders gives the non-owning slave or serf into the power of the cattle owner, is only a forerunner of real "class" formation. However, in the cattle loan and in the naked severity of the law of debts in such communities, for the first time mere "possession" as such emerges as decisive for the fate of the individual. This is very much in contrast to the agricultural communities based on labor. The creditor-debtor relation becomes the basis of "class situations" only in those cities where a "credit market," however primitive, with rates of interest increasing according to the extent of dearth and a factual monopolization of credits, is developed by a plutocracy. Therewith "class struggles" begin.

Those men whose fate is not determined by the chance of using goods or services for themselves on the market, e.g. slaves, are not, however, a "class" in the technical sense of the term. They are, rather, a "status group."

COMMUNAL ACTION FLOWING FROM CLASS INTEREST

According to our terminology, the factor that creates "class" is unambiguously economic interest, and indeed, only those interests involved in the existence of the "market." Nevertheless, the concept of "class-interest" is an ambiguous one: even as an empirical concept it is ambiguous as soon as one understands by it something other than the factual direction of interests following with a certain prob-

ability from the class situation for a certain "average" of those people subjected to the class situation. The class situation and other circumstances remaining the same, the direction in which the individual worker, for instance, is likely to pursue his interests may vary widely, according to whether he is constitutionally qualified for the task at hand to a high, to an average, or to a low degree. In the same way, the direction of interests may vary according to whether or not a *communal* action of a larger or smaller portion of those commonly affected by the "class situation," or even an association among them, e.g. a "trade union," has grown out of the class situation from which the individual may or may not expect promising results. [Communal action refers to that action which is oriented to the feeling of the actors that they belong together. Societal action, on the other hand, is oriented to a rationally motivated adjustment of interests.] The rise of societal or even of communal action from a common class situation is by no means a universal phenomenon.

The class situation may be restricted in its effects to the generation of essentially *similar* reactions, that is to say, within our terminology, of "mass actions." However, it may not have even this result. Furthermore, often merely an amorphous communal action emerges. For example, the "murmuring" of the workers known in ancient oriental ethics: the moral disapproval of the work-master's conduct, which in its practical significance was probably equivalent to an increasingly typical phenomenon of precisely the latest industrial development, namely, the "slow down" (the deliberate limiting of work effort) of laborers by virtue of tacit agreement. The degree in which "communal action" and possibly "societal action," emerges from the "mass actions" of the members of a class is linked to general cultural conditions, especially to those of an intellectual sort. It is also linked to the extent of the contrasts that have already evolved, and is especially linked to the *transparency* of the connections between the causes and the consequences of the "class situation." For however different life chances may be, this fact in itself, according to all experience, by no means gives birth to "class action" (communal action by the members of a class). The fact of being conditioned and the results of the class situation must be distinctly recognizable. For only then the contrast of life chances can be felt not as an absolutely given fact to be accepted, but as a resultant from either (1) the given distribution of property, or (2) the structure of the concrete economic order. It is only then that people may react against the class structure not only through acts of an intermittent and irrational protest, but in the form of rational association. There have been "class situations" of the first category (1), of a specifically naked and transparent sort, in the urban centers of Antiquity and during the Middle Ages; especially then, when great fortunes were accumulated by factually monopolized trading in industrial products of these localities or in foodstuffs. Furthermore, under certain circumstances, in the rural economy of the most diverse periods, when agriculture was increasingly exploited in a profit-making manner. The most important historical example of the second category (2) is the class situation of the modern "proletariat."

TYPES OF "CLASS STRUGGLE"

Thus every class may be the carrier of any one of the possibly innumerable forms of "class action," but this is not necessarily so. In any case, a class does not in itself constitute a community. To treat "class" conceptually as having the same value as "community" leads to distortion. That men in the same class situation regularly react in mass actions to such tangible situations as economic ones in the direction of those interests that are most adequate to their average number is an important and after all simple fact for the understanding of historical events. Above all, this fact must not lead to that kind of pseudo-scientific operation with the concepts of "class" and "class interests" so frequently found these days and which has found its most classic expression in the statement of a talented author, that the individual may be in error concerning his interests but that the "class" is "infallible" about its interests. Yet, if classes as such are not communi-

ties, nevertheless class situation emerge only on the basis of communalization. The communal action that brings forth class situations, however, is not basically action between members of the identical class; it is an action between members of different classes. Communal actions that directly determine the class situation of the worker and the entrepreneur are: the labor market, the commodities market, and the capitalistic enterprise. But, in its turn, the existence of a capitalistic enterprise presupposes that a very specific communal action exists and that it is specifically structured to protect the possession of goods *per se,* and especially the power of individuals to dispose, in principle, freely over the means of production. The existence of a capitalistic enterprise is preconditioned by a specific kind of "legal order." Each kind of class situation, and above all when it rests upon the power of property *per se,* will become most clearly efficacious, when all other determinants of reciprocal relations are, as far as possible, eliminated in their significance. It is in this way that the utilization of the power of property in the market obtains its most sovereign importance.

Now "status groups" hinder the strict carrying through of the sheer market principle. In the present context they are of interest to us only from this one point of view. Before we briefly consider them, note that not much of a general nature can be said about the more specific kinds of antagonism between "classes" (in our meaning of the term). The great shift, which has been going on continuously in the past, and up to our times, may be summarized, although at the cost of some precision: the struggle in which class situations are effective has progressively shifted from consumption credit toward, first, competitive struggles in the commodity market, and, then, toward price wars on the labor market. The "class struggles" of antiquity—to the extent that they were genuine class struggles and not struggles between status groups—were initially carried on by indebted peasants, and perhaps also by artisans threatened by debt bondage and struggling against urban creditors. For debt bondage is the normal result of the differentiation of wealth in commercial cities, especially in seaport cities. A similar situation has existed among cattle breeders. Debt relationships as such produced class action up to the time of Cataline. Along with this, and with an increase in provision of grain for the city by transporting it from the outside, the struggle over the means of sustenance emerged. It centered in the first place around the provision of bread and the determination of the price of bread. It lasted throughout antiquity and the entire Middle Ages. The propertyless as such flocked together against those who actually and supposedly were interested in the dearth of bread. This fight spread until it involved all those commodities essential to the way of life and to handicraft production. There were only incipient discussions of wage disputes in antiquity and in the Middle Ages. But they have been slowly increasing up into modern times. In the earlier periods they were completely secondary to slave rebellions as well as to fights in the commodity market.

The propertyless of antiquity and of the Middle Ages protested against monopolies, pre-emption, forestalling, and the withholding of goods from the market in order to raise prices. Today the central issue is the determination of the price of labor.

This transition is represented by the fight for access to the market and for the determination of the price of products. Such fights went on between merchants and workers in the putting-out system of domestic handicraft during the transition to modern times. Since it is quite a general phenomenon we must mention here that the class antagonisms that are conditioned through the market situation are usually most bitter between those who actually and directly participate as opponents in price wars. It is not the rentier, the shareholder, and the banker who suffer the ill will of the worker, but almost exclusively the manufacturer and the business executives who are the direct opponents of workers in price wars. This is so in spite of the fact that it is precisely the cash boxes of the rentier, the share-holder, and the banker into which the more or less "unearned" gains flow, rather than into the pockets of the manufacturers or of the business executives. This simple state of

affairs has very frequently been decisive for the role the class situation has played in the formation of political parties. For example, it has made possible the varieties of patriarchal socialism and the frequent attempts—formerly, at least—of threatened status groups to form alliances with the proletariat against the "bourgeoisie."

STATUS HONOR

In contrast to classes, *status groups* are normally communities. They are, however, often of an amorphous kind. In contrast to the purely economically determined "class situation" we wish to designate as "status situation" every typical component of the life fate of men that is determined by a specific, positive or negative, social estimation of *honor*.[2] This honor may be connected with any quality shared by a plurality, and, of course, it can be knit to a class situation: class distinctions are linked in the most varied ways with status distinctions. Property as such is not always recognized as a status qualification, but in the long run it is, and with extraordinary regularity. In the subsistence economy of the organized neighborhood, very often the richest man is simply the chieftain. However, this often means only an honorific preference. For example, in the so-called pure modern "democracy," that is, one devoid of any expressly ordered status privileges for individuals, it may be that only the families coming under approximately the same tax class dance with one another. This example is reported of certain smaller Swiss cities. But status honor need not necessarily be linked with a "class situation." On the contrary, it normally stands in sharp opposition to the pretensions of sheer property.

Both propertied and propertyless people can belong to the same status group, and frequently they do with very tangible consequences. This "equality" of social esteem may, however, in the long run become quite precarious. The "equality"

[2] Because "status situation," *Ständische Lage*, is a distinctly Weberian concept, the definition is presented here in its German original: "eine typisch wirksam im Anspruch genommene positive oder negative Privilegierung in der socialen Schätzung." *Wirtschaft und Gesellschaft*, Tübingen: Mohr, 1925, p. 179. (C. S. H.)

of status among the American "gentlemen," for instance, is expressed by the fact that outside the subordination determined by the different functions of "business," it would be considered strictly repugnant—wherever the old tradition still prevails—if even the richest "chief," while playing billiards or cards in his club in the evening, would not treat his "clerk" as in every sense fully his equal in birthright. It would be repugnant if the American "chief" would bestow upon his "clerk" the condescending "benevolence" marking a distinction of "position," which the German chief can never dissever from his attitude. This is one of the most important reasons why in America the German "clubby-ness" has never been able to attain the attraction that the American clubs have.

GUARANTEES OF STATUS STRATIFICATION

In content, status honor is normally expressed by the fact that above all else a specific *style of life* can be expected from all those who wish to belong to the circle. Linked with this expectation are restrictions on "social" intercourse (that is, intercourse which is not subservient to economic or any other of business's "functional" purposes). These restrictions may confine normal marriages to within the status circle and may lead to complete endogamous closure. As soon as there is not a mere individual and socially irrelevant imitation of another style of life, but an agreed-upon communal action of this closing character, the "status" development is under way.

In its characteristic form, stratification by "status groups" on the basis of conventional styles of life evolves at the present time in the United States out of the traditional democracy. For example, only the resident of a certain street ("the street") is considered as belonging to "society," is qualified for social intercourse, and is visited and invited. Above all, this differentiation evolves in such a way as to make for strict submission to the fashion that is dominant at a given time in society. This submission to fashion also exists among men in America to a degree unknown in Germany. Such submission is considered to be an indication of the fact that a given man

pretends to qualify as a gentleman. This submission decides, at least *prima facie,* that he will be treated as such. And this recognition becomes just as important for his employment chances in "swank" establishments, and above all, for social intercourse and marriage with "esteemed" families, as the qualification for dueling among Germans in the Kaiser's day. As for the rest: certain families resident for a long time, and, of course, correspondingly wealthy, e.g. "F. F. V., i.e. First Families of Virginia," or the actual or alleged descendants of the "Indian Princess" Pocahontas, of the Pilgrim Fathers, or of the Knickerbockers, the members of almost inaccessible sects and all sorts of circles setting themselves apart by means of any other characteristics and badges ... all these elements usurp "status" honor. The development of status is essentially a question of stratification resting upon usurpation. Such usurpation is the normal origin of almost all status honor. But the road from this purely conventional situation to legal privilege, positive or negative, is easily traveled as soon as a certain stratification of the social order has in fact been "lived in" and has achieved stability by virtue of a stable distribution of economic power.

"ETHNIC" SEGREGATION AND "CASTE"

Where the consequences have been realized to their full extent, the status group evolves into a closed "caste." Status distinctions are then guaranteed not merely by conventions and laws, but also by *rituals.* This occurs in such a way that every physical contact with a member of any caste that is considered to be "lower" by the members of a "higher" caste is considered as making for a ritualistic impurity and to be a stigma which must be expiated by a religious act. Individual castes develop quite distinct cults and gods.

In general, however, the status structure reaches such extreme consequences only where there are underlying differences which are held to be "ethnic." The "caste" is, indeed, the normal form in which ethnic communities usually live side by side in a "societalized" manner. These ethnic communities believe in blood relationship and exclude exogamous marriage and social intercourse. Such a caste situation is part of the phenomenon of "pariah" peoples and is found all over the world. These people form communities, acquire specific occupational traditions of handicrafts or of other arts, and cultivate a belief in their ethnic community. They live in a "diaspora" strictly segregated from all personal intercourse, except that of an unavoidable sort, and their situation is legally precarious. Yet, by virtue of their economic indispensability, they are tolerated, indeed, frequently privileged, and they live in interspersed political communities. The Jews are the most impressive historical example.

A "status" segregation grown into a "caste" differs in its structure from a mere "ethnic" segregation: the caste structure transforms the horizontal and unconnected coexistences of ethnically segregated groups into a vertical social system of super- and subordination. Correctly formulated: a comprehensive societalization integrates the ethnically divided communities into specific political and communal action. In their consequences they differ precisely in this way: ethnic coexistences condition a mutual repulsion and disdain but allow each ethnic community to consider its own honor as the highest one; the caste structure brings about a social subordination and an acknowledgment of "more honor" in favor of the privileged caste and status groups. This is due to the fact that in the caste structure ethnic distinctions as such have become "functional" distinctions within the political societalization (warriors, priests, artisans that are politically important for war and for building, and so on). But even pariah people who are most despised are usually apt to continue cultivating in some manner that which is equally peculiar to ethnic and to status communities: the belief in their own specific "honor." This is the case with the Jews.

Only with the negatively privileged status does the "sense of dignity" take a specific deviation. A sense of dignity is the precipitation in individuals of social honor and of conventional demands which a positively privileged status group raises for the deportment of its members. The sense of dignity that characterizes positively privileged status groups is naturally related to their "being" which does not transcend itself, that is, it is to their "beauty and excellence" (καλο-κἀγαδια). Their kingdom is "of this world." They live for the present and by exploiting their great past. The sense of dignity of the negatively privileged strata naturally refers to a future lying beyond the present, whether it is of this life or of another. In other words, it must be nurtured by the belief in a providential "mission" and by a belief in a specific honor before God. The "chosen people's" dignity is nurtured by a belief either that in the beyond "the last will be the first," or that in this life a Messiah will appear to bring forth into the light of the world which has cast them out the hidden honor of the pariah people. This simple state of affairs, and not the "resentment" which is so strongly emphasized in Nietzsche's much admired construction in the *Genealogy of Morals,* is the source of the religiosity cultivated by pariah status groups. In passing, we may note that resentment may be accurately applied only to a limited extent; for one of Nietzsche's main examples, Buddhism, it is not at all applicable.

Incidentally, the development of status groups from ethnic segregations is by no means the normal phenomenon. On the contrary, since objective "racial differences" are by no means basic to every subjective sentiment of an ethnic community, the ultimately racial foundation of status structure is rightly and absolutely a question of the concrete individual case. Very frequently a status group is instrumental in the production of a thoroughbred anthropological type. Certainly a status group is to a high degree effective in producing extreme types, for they select personally qualified individuals (e.g. the Knighthood selects those who are fit for warfare, physically and psychically). But selection is far from being the only, or the predominant, way in which status groups are formed: Political membership or class situation has at all times been at least as frequently decisive. And today the class situation is by far the predominant factor, for of course the possibility of a style of life expected for members of a status group is usually conditioned economically.

STATUS PRIVILEGES

For all practical purposes, stratification goes hand in hand with a monopolization of ideal and material goods or opportunities, in a manner we have come to know as typical. Besides the specific status honor, which always rests upon distance and exclusiveness, we find all sorts of material monopolies. Such honorific preferences may consist of the privilege of wearing special costumes, of eating special dishes taboo to others, of carrying arms—which is most obvious in its consequences—the right to pursue certain non-professional dilettante artistic practices, e.g. to play certain musical instruments. Of course, material monopolies provide the most effective motives for the exclusiveness of a status group; although, in themselves, they are rarely sufficient, almost always they come into play to some extent. Within a status circle there is the question of inter-marriage: the interest of the families in the monopolization of potential bridegrooms is at least of equal importance and is parallel to the interest in the monopolization of daughters. The daughters of the circle must be provided for. With an increased inclosure of the status group, the conventional preferential opportunities for special employment grow into a legal monopoly of special offices for the members. Certain goods become objects for monopolization by status groups. In the typical fashion these include "entailed estates" and frequently also the possessions of serfs or bondsmen and, finally, special trades. This monopolization occurs positively when the status group is exclusively entitled to own and to manage them; and negatively when, in order to maintain its specific way of life, the status group must *not* own and manage them.

The decisive role of a "style of life" in status "honor" means that status groups are the specific bearers of all "conventions." In whatever way it may be manifest, all "stylization" of life either originates in status groups or is at least conserved by them. Even if the principles of status conventions differ greatly, they reveal certain typical traits, especially among those strata which are most privileged. Quite generally, among privileged status groups there is a status disqualification that operates against the performance of common physical labor. This disqualification is now "setting in" in America against the old tradition of esteem for labor. Very frequently every rational economic pursuit, and especially "entrepreneurial activity," is looked upon as a disqualification of status. Artistic and literary activity is also considered as degrading work as soon as it is exploited for income, or at least when it is connected with hard physical exertion. An example is the sculptor working like a mason in his dusty smock as over against the painter in his salon-like "studio" and those forms of musical practice that are acceptable to the status group.

ECONOMIC CONDITIONS AND EFFECTS OF STATUS STRATIFICATION

The frequent disqualification of the gainfully employed as such is a direct result of the principle of status stratification peculiar to the social order, and of course, of this principle's opposition to a distribution of power which is regulated exclusively through the market. These two factors operate along with various individual ones, which will be touched upon below.

We have seen above that the market and its processes "knows no personal distinctions": "functional" interests dominate it. It knows nothing of "honor." The status order means precisely the reverse, viz.: stratification in terms of "honor" and of styles of life peculiar to status groups as such. If mere economic acquisition and naked economic power still bearing the stigma of its extra-status origin could bestow upon anyone who has won it the same honor as those who are interested in status by virtue of style of life claim for themselves, the status order would be threatened at its very root. This is the more so as, given equality of status honor, property *per se* represents an addition even if it is not overtly acknowledged to be such. Yet if such economic acquisition and power gave the agent any honor at all, his wealth would result in his attaining more honor than those who successfully claim honor by virtue of style of life. Therefore all groups having interests in the status order react with special sharpness precisely against the pretensions of purely economic acquisition. In most cases they react the more vigorously the more they feel themselves threatened. Calderon's respectful treatment of the peasant, for instance, as opposed to Shakespeare's simultaneous and ostensible disdain of the *canaille* illustrates the different way in which a firmly structured status order reacts as compared with a status order that has become economically precarious. This is an example of a state of affairs that recurs everywhere. Precisely because of the rigorous reactions against the claims of property *per se*, the "parvenu" is never accepted, personally and without reservation, by the privileged status groups, no matter how completely his style of life has been adjusted to theirs. They will only accept his descendants who have been educated in the conventions of their status group and who have never besmirched its honor by their own economic labor.

As to the general *effect* of the status order, only one consequence can be stated, but it is a very important one: the hindrance of the free development of the market occurs first for those goods which status groups directly withheld from free exchange by monopolization. This monopolization may be effected either legally or conventionally. For example, in many Hellenic cities during the epoch of status groups, and also originally in Rome, the inherited estate (as is shown by the old formula for indiction against spendthrifts) was monopolized just as were the estates of knights, peasants, priests, and especially the clientele of the craft and merchant guilds. The market is restricted, and the power of naked property *per se,* which gives its stamp to "class formation," is pushed into the background. The results of this process can be most varied. Of course, they do not necessarily weaken the contrasts in the economic situation. Frequently they strengthen these contrasts, and in any case, where stratification by status permeates a community as strongly as was the case in all political communities of antiquity and of the Middle Ages, one can never speak of a genuinely

free market competition as we understand it today. There are wider effects than this direct exclusion of special goods from the market. From the contrariety between the status order and the purely economic order mentioned above, it follows that in most instances the notion of honor peculiar to status absolutely abhors that which is essential to the market: higgling. Honor abhors higgling among peers and occasionally it taboos higgling for the members of a status group in general. Therefore, everywhere some status groups, and usually the most influential, consider almost any kind of overt participation in economic acquisition as absolutely stigmatizing.

With some over-simplification, one might thus say that "classes" are stratified according to their relations to the production and acquisition of goods; whereas "status groups" are stratified according to the principles of their *consumption* of goods as represented by special "styles of life."

An "occupational group" is also a status group. For normally, it successfully claims social honor only by virtue of the special style of life which may be determined by it. The differences between classes and status groups frequently overlap. It is precisely those status communities most strictly segregated in terms of honor (viz. the Indian castes) who today show, although within very rigid limits, a relatively high degree of indifference to pecuniary income. However, the Brahmins seek such income in many different ways.

As to the general economic conditions making for the predominance of stratification by "status," only very little can be said. When the bases of the acquisition and distribution of goods are relatively stable, stratification by status is favored. Every technological repercussion and economic transformation threatens stratification by status and pushes the class situation into the foreground. Epochs and countries in which the naked class situation is of predominant significance are regularly the periods of technical and economic transformations. And every slowing down of the shifting of economic stratifications leads, in due course, to the growth of status structures and makes for a resuscitation of the important role of social honor.

PARTIES

Whereas the genuine place of "classes" is within the economic order, the place of "status groups" is within the social order, that is, within the sphere of the distribution of "honor." From within these spheres, classes and status groups influence one another and they influence the legal order and are in turn influenced by it. But "parties" live in a house of "power."

Their action is oriented toward the acquisition of social "power," that is to say, toward influencing a communal action no matter what its content may be. In principle, parties may exist in a social "club" as well as in a "state." As over against the actions of classes and status groups, for which this is not necessarily the case, the communal actions of "parties" always mean a societalization. For party actions are always directed toward a goal which is striven for in planned manner. This goal may be a "cause" (the party may aim at realizing a program for ideal or material purposes), or the goal may be "personal" (sinecures, power, and from these, honor for the leader and the followers of the party). Usually the party action aims at all these simultaneously. Parties are, therefore, only possible within communities that are societalized, that is, which have some rational order and a staff of persons available who are ready to enforce it. For parties aim precisely at influencing this staff, and if possible, to recruit it from party followers.

In any individual case, parties may represent interests determined through "class situation" or "status situation," and they may recruit their following respectively from one or the other. But they need be neither purely "class" nor purely "status" parties. In most cases they are partly class parties and partly status parties, but sometimes they are neither. They may represent ephemeral or enduring structures. Their means of attaining power may be quite varied, ranging from naked violence of any sort to canvassing for votes with coarse or subtle means: money, social influence, the force of speech, suggestion,

clumsy hoax, and so on to the rougher or more artful tactics of obstruction in parliamentary bodies.

The sociological structure of parties differs in a basic way according to the kind of communal action which they struggle to influence. Parties also differ according to whether or not the community is stratified by status or by classes. Above all else, they vary according to the structure of domination within the community. For their leaders normally deal with the conquest of a community. They are, in the general concept which is maintained here, not only products of specially modern forms of domination. We shall also designate as parties the ancient and medieval "parties," despite the fact that their structure differs basically from the structure of modern parties. By virtue of these structural differences of domination it is impossible to say anything about the structure of parties without discussing the structural forms of social domination *per se*. Parties, which are always structures struggling for domination, are very frequently organized in a very strict "authoritarian" fashion . . .

Concerning "classes," "status groups," and "parties," it must be said in general that they necessarily presuppose a comprehensive societalization, and especially a political framework of communal action, within which they operate. This does not mean that parties would be confined by the frontiers of any individual political community. On the contrary, at all times it has been the order of the day that the societalization (even when it aims at the use of military force in common) reaches beyond the frontiers of politics. This has been the case in the solidarity of interests among the Oligarchs and among the democrats in Hellas, among the Guelfs and among the Ghibellines in the Middle Ages, and within the Calvinist party during the period of religious struggles. It has been the case up to the solidarity of the landlords (international congress of agrarian landlords), and has continued among princes (holy alliance, Karlsbad decrees), socialist workers, conservatives (the longing of Prussian conservatives for Russian intervention in 1850). But their aim is not necessarily the establishment of new international political, i.e. *territorial* dominion. In the main they aim to influence the existing dominion.[3]

ELITES AND THEIR CIRCULATION

Vilfredo Pareto

· ·

Whether certain theorists like it or not, the fact is that human society is not a homogeneous thing, that individuals are physically, morally, and intellectually different. Here we are interested in things as they actually are. Of that fact, therefore, we have to take account. And we must also take account of another fact: that the social classes are not entirely distinct, even in countries where a caste system prevails; and that in modern civilized countries circulation among the various classes is exceedingly rapid. To consider at all exhaustively here this matter of the diversity of the vastly numerous social groups and the numberless ways in which they mix is out of the question. As usual, therefore, since we cannot have the more, we must rest content with the less and try to make the problem easier in order to have it the more manageable. That is a first step along a path that others may go on following. We shall consider the problem only in its bearing on the social equilibrium and try to reduce as far as possible the numbers of the groups and the modes of circulation, putting under one head phenomena that prove to be roughly and after a fashion similar.

Suppose we begin by giving a theoretical definition of the thing we are dealing with, making it as exact as possible, and then go

From *The Mind and Society* by Vilfredo Pareto, translated by A. Bongiorno and A. Livingston and edited by A. Livingston, Harcourt, Brace & Company, 1935. Reprinted by permission of the Pareto Fund.

[3] The posthumously published text breaks off here. We omit an incomplete sketch of types of "warrior estates."

on to see what practical considerations we can replace it with to get a first approximation. Let us for the moment completely disregard considerations as to the good or bad, useful or harmful, praiseworthy or reprehensible character of the various traits in individuals, and confine ourselves to degrees—to whether, in other words, the trait in a given case be slight, average, intense, or more exactly, to the index that may be assigned to each individual with reference to the degree, or intensity, in him of the trait in question.

Let us assume that in every branch of human activity each individual is given an index which stands as a sign of his capacity, very much the way grades are given in the various subjects in examinations in school. The highest type of lawyer, for instance, will be given 10. The man who does not get a client will be given 1—reserving zero for the man who is an out-and-out idiot. To the man who has made his millions—honestly or dishonestly as the case may be—we will give 10. To the man who has earned his thousands we will give 6; to such as just manage to keep out of the poor-house, 1, keeping zero for those who get in. To the woman "in politics," such as the Aspasia of Pericles, the Maintenon of Louis XIV, the Pompadour of Louis XV, who has managed to infatuate a man of power and play a part in the man's career, we shall give some higher number, such as 8 or 9; to the strumpet who merely satisfies the senses of such a man and exerts no influence on public affairs, we shall give zero. To a clever rascal who knows how to fool people and still keep clear of the penitentiary, we shall give 8, 9, or 10, according to the number of geese he has plucked and the amount of money he has been able to get out of them. To the sneak-thief who snatches a piece of silver from a restaurant table and runs away into the arms of a policeman, we shall give 1. To a poet like Carducci we shall give 8 or 9 according to our tastes; to a scribbler who puts people to rout with his sonnets we shall give zero. For chessplayers we can't get very precise indices, noting what matches, and how many, they have won. And so on for all the branches of human activity.

We are speaking, remember, of an actual,

not a potential, state. If at an English examination a pupil says: "I could know English very well if I chose to; I do not know any because I have never seen fit to learn," the examiner replies: "I am not interested in your alibi. The grade for what you know is zero." If, similarly, someone says: "So-and-so does not steal, not because he couldn't, but because he is a gentleman," we reply: "Very well, we admire him for his self-control, but his grade as a thief is zero."

There are people who worship Napoleon Bonaparte as a god. There are people who hate him as the lowest of criminals. Which are right? We do not choose to solve that question in connexion with a quite different matter. Whether Napoleon was a good man or a bad man, he was certainly not an idiot, nor a man of little account, as millions of others are. He had exceptional qualities, and that is enough for us to give him a high ranking, though without prejudice of any sort that might be raised as to the ethics of his qualities or their social utility.

In short, we are here as usual resorting to scientific analysis, which distinguishes one problem from another and studies each one separately. As usual, again, we are replacing imperceptable variations in absolutely exact numbers with the sharp variations corresponding to groupings by class, just as in examinations those who are passed are sharply and arbitrarily distinguished from those who are "failed," and just as in the matter of physical age we distinguish children from young people, the young from the aged.

So let us make a class of the people who have the highest indices in their branch of activity, and to that class give the name of *élite*.[1]

[1] Kolabinska, *La circulation des élites en France*, p. 5: "The outstanding idea in the term '*élite*' is 'superiority'. That is the only one I keep. I disregard secondary connotations of appreciation or as to the utility of such superiority. I am not interested here in what is desirable. I am making a simple study of what is. In a broad sense I mean by the *élite* in a society people who possess in marked degree qualities of intelligence, character, skill, capacity, of whatever kind. . . . On the other hand I entirely avoid any sort of judgment on the merits and utility of such classes." [The phrase "circulation of *élites*" is well established in

For the particular investigation with which we are engaged, a study of the social equilibrium, it will help if we further divide that class into two classes: a *governing élite*, comprising individuals who directly or indirectly play some considerable part in government, and a *non-governing élite*, comprising the rest.

A chess champion is certainly a member of the *élite*, but it is no less certain that his merits as a chess-player do not open the doors to political influence for him; and hence unless he has other qualities to win him that distinction, he is not a member of the governing *élite*. Mistresses of absolute monarchs have oftentimes been members of the *élite*, either because of their beauty or because of their intellectual endowments; but only a few of them, who have had, in addition, the particular talents required by politics, have played any part in government.

So we get two strata in a population: (1) A lower stratum, the *non-élite*, with whose possible influence on government we are not just here concerned; then (2) a higher stratum, *the élite*, which is divided into two: (*a*) a governing *élite*; (*b*) a non-governing *élite*.

In the concrete, there are no examinations whereby each person is assigned to his proper place in these various classes. That deficiency is made up for by other means, by various sorts of labels that serve the purpose after a fashion. Such labels are the rule even where there are examinations. The label "lawyer" is affixed to a man who is supposed to know something about the law and often does, though sometimes again he is an ignoramus. So, the governing *élite* contains individuals who wear labels appropriate to political offices of a certain altitude—ministers, Senators, Deputies, chief justices, generals, colonels, and so on—making the apposite exceptions for those who have found their way into that

Continental literature. Pareto himself renders it in Italian as "circulation of the élite (selected, chosen, ruling, 'better') classes." It is a cumbersome phrase and not very exact, and I see no reason for preferring it to the more natural and, in most connexions, the more exact English phrase, class-circulation.—A.L.]

exalted company without possessing qualities corresponding to the labels they wear.

Such exceptions are much more numerous than the exceptions among lawyers, physicians, engineers, millionaires (who have made their own money), artists of distinction, and so on; for the reason, among others, that in these latter departments of human activity the labels are won directly by each individual, whereas in the *élite* some of the labels—the label of wealth, for instance—are hereditary. In former times there were hereditary labels in the governing *élite* also—in our day hardly more than the label of king remains in that status; but if direct inheritance has disappeared, inheritance is still powerful indirectly; and an individual who has inherited a sizeable patrimony can easily be named Senator in certain countries, or can get himself elected to the parliament by buying votes or, on occasion, by wheedling voters with assurances that he is a democrat of democrats, a Socialist, an Anarchist. Wealth, family, or social connexions also help in many other cases to win the label of the *élite* in general, or of the governing *élite* in particular, for persons who otherwise hold no claim upon it.

In societies where the social unit is the family the label worn by the head of the family also benefits all other members. In Rome, the man who became emperor generally raised his freedmen to the higher class, and oftentimes, in fact, to the governing *élite*. For that matter, now more, now fewer, of the freedmen taking part in the Roman government possessed qualities good or bad that justified their wearing the labels which they had won through imperial bounty. In our societies, the social unit is the individual; but the place that the individual occupies in society also benefits his wife, his children, his connexions, his friends.

If all these deviations from type were of little importance, they might be disregarded, as they are virtually disregarded in cases where a diploma is required for the practice of a profession. Everyone knows that there are persons who do not deserve their diplomas, but experience shows that on the whole such exceptions may be overlooked. One might, further, from certain points

of view at least, disregard deviations if they remained more or less constant quantitatively—if there were only a negligible variation in proportions between the total of a class and the people who wear its label without possessing the qualities corresponding.

As a matter of fact, the real cases that we have to consider in our societies differ from those two. The deviations are not so few that they can be disregarded. Then again, their number is variable, and the variations give rise to situations having an important bearing on the social equilibrium. We are therefore required to make a special study of them.

Furthermore, the manner in which the various groups in a population intermix has to be considered. In moving from one group to another an individual generally brings with him certain inclinations, sentiments, attitudes, that he has acquired in the group from which he comes, and that circumstance cannot be ignored.

To this mixing, in the particular case in which only two groups, the *élite* and the non-*élite*, are envisaged, the term "circulation of élites" has been applied[2]—in French, *circulation des élites* [or in more general terms "class-circulation"].

In conclusion we must pay special attention (1), in the case of one single group, to the proportions between the total of the group and the number of individuals who are nominally members of it but do not possess the qualities requisite for effective membership; and then (2), in the case of various groups, to the ways in which transitions from one group to the other occur, and to the intensity of that movement—that is to say, to the velocity of the circulation.

Velocity in circulation has to be considered not only absolutely but also in relation to the supply of and the demand for certain social elements. A country that is

[2] [And most inappropriately, for, in this sense, the phrase never meant more than circulation within the *élite*. Furthermore, the *élite* is not the only class to be considered, and the principles that apply to circulation within the *élite* apply to circulation within such lower classes as one may choose for one purpose or another to consider.—

always at peace does not require many soldiers in its governing class, and the production of generals may be overexuberant as compared with the demand. But when a country is in a state of continuous warfare many soldiers are necessary, and though production remains at the same level it may not meet the demand. That, we might note in passing, has been one of the causes for the collapse of many aristocracies.[3]

Another example. In a country where there is little industry and little commerce, the supply of individuals possessing in high degree the qualities requisite for those types of activity exceeds the demand. Then industry and commerce develop and the supply, though remaining the same, no longer meets the demand.

We must not confuse the state of law with the state of fact. The latter alone, or almost alone, has a bearing on the social equilibrium. There are many examples of castes that are legally closed, but into which, in point of fact, new-comers make their way, and often in large numbers. On the other hand, what difference does it make if a caste is legally open, but conditions *de facto* prevent new accessions to it? If a person who acquires wealth thereby becomes a member of the governing class, but no one gets rich, it is as if the class were closed; and if only a few get rich, it is as if the law erected serious barriers against access to the caste. Something of that sort was observable towards the end of the Roman Empire. People who acquired wealth entered the order of the curials. But only a few individuals made any money. Theoretically we might examine any number of groups. Practically we have to confine ourselves to the more important.

[3] Kolabinska, *Op. cit.,* p. 10: "Inadequate recruiting in the *élite* does not result from a mere numerical proportion between new members and old. Account has to be taken of the number of persons who possess the qualities required for membership in the governing *élite* but are refused admittance; or else, in an opposite direction, the number of new members the *élite* might require but does not get. In the first case, the production of persons possessing unusual qualities as regards education may far surpass the number of such persons that the *élite* can accommodate, and then we get what has been called an 'intellectual proletariat.'"

We shall proceed by successive approximations, starting with the simple and going on to the complex.

Higher Class and Lower Class in General. The least we can do is to divide society into two strata: a higher stratum, which usually contains the rulers, and a lower stratum, which usually contains the ruled. That fact is so obvious that it has always forced itself even upon the most casual observation, and so for the circulation of individuals between the two strata. Even Plato had an inkling of class-circulation and tried to regulate it artificially. The "new man," the upstart, the *parvenu*, has always been a subject of interest, and literature has analyzed him unendingly. Here, then, we are merely giving a more exact form to things that have long been perceived more or less vaguely. Above ... we noted a varying distribution of residues in the various social groupings, and chiefly in the higher and the lower class. Such heterogeneousness is a fact perceived by the most superficial glance. ...

The upper stratum of society, the *élite*, nominally contains certain groups of peoples, not always very sharply defined, that are called aristocracies. There are cases in which the majority of individuals belonging to such aristocracies actually possess the qualities requisite for remaining there; and then again there are cases where considerable numbers of the individuals making up the class do not possess those requisites. Such people may occupy more or less important places in the governing *élite* or they may be barred from it.

In the beginning, military, religious, and commercial aristocracies and plutocracies —with a few exceptions not worth considering—must have constituted parts of the governing *élite* and sometimes have made up the whole of it. The victorious warrior, the prosperous merchant, the opulent plutocrat, were men of such parts, each in his own field, as to be superior to the average individual. Under those circumstances the label corresponded to an actual capacity. But as time goes by, considerable, sometimes very considerable, differences arise between the capacity and the label; while on the other hand, certain aristocracies originally figuring prominently in the rising *élite* end by constituting an insignificant element in it. That has happened especially to military aristocracies.

Aristocracies do not last. Whatever the causes, it is an incontestable fact that after a certain length of time they pass away. History is a graveyard of aristocracies. The Athenian "People" was an aristocracy as compared with the remainder of a population of resident aliens and slaves. It vanished without leaving any descent. The various aristocracies of Rome vanished in their time. So did the aristocracies of the Barbarians. Where, in France, are the descendants of the Frankish conquerors? The genealogies of the English nobility have been very exactly kept; and they show that very few families still remain to claim descent from the comrades of William the Conqueror. The rest have vanished. In Germany the aristocracy of the present day is very largely made up of descendants of vassals of the lords of old. The populations of European countries have increased enormously during the past few centuries. It is as certain as certain can be that the aristocracies have not increased in proportion.

They decay not in numbers only. They decay also in quality, in the sense that they lose their vigour, that there is a decline in the proportions of the residues which enabled them to win their power and hold it. The governing class is restored not only in numbers, but—and that is the more important thing—in quality, by families rising from the lower classes and bringing with them the vigour and the proportions of residues necessary for keeping themselves in power. It is also restored by the loss of its more degenerate members.

If one of those movements comes to an end, or worse still, if they both come to an end, the governing class crashes to ruin and often sweeps the whole of a nation along with it. Potent cause of disturbance in the equilibrium is the accumulation of superior elements in the lower classes and, conversely, of inferior elements in the higher classes. If human aristocracies were like thorough-breds among animals, which reproduce themselves over long periods of time with approximately the same traits, the history of the human race would be something altogether different from the history we know.

In virtue of class-circulation, the governing *élite* is always in a state of slow and continuous transformation. It flows on like a river, never being today what it was yesterday. From time to time sudden and violent disturbances occur. There is a flood —the river overflows its banks. Afterwards, the new governing *élite* again resumes its slow transformation. The flood has subsided, the river is again flowing normally in its wonted bed.

Revolutions come about through accumulations in the higher strata of society —either because of a slowing-down in class-circulation, or from other causes—of decadent elements no longer possessing the residues suitable for keeping them in power, and shrinking from the use of force; while meantime in the lower strata of society elements of superior quality are coming to the fore, possessing residues suitable for exercising the functions of government and willing enough to use force.

In general, in revolutions the members of the lower strata are captained by leaders from the higher strata, because the latter possess the intellectual qualities required for outlining a tactic, while lacking the combative residues supplied by the individuals from the lower strata.

Violent movements take place by fits and starts, and effects therefore do not follow immediately on their causes. After a governing class, or a nation, has maintained itself for long periods of time on force and acquired great wealth, it may subsist for some time still without using force, buying off its adversaries and paying not only in gold, but also in terms of the dignity and respect that it had formerly enjoyed and which constitute, as it were, a capital. In the first stages of decline, power is maintained by bargainings and concessions, and people are so deceived into thinking that the policy can be carried on indefinitely. So the decadent Roman Empire bought peace of the Barbarians with money and honours. So Louis XVI, in France, squandering in a very short time an ancestral inheritance of love, respect, and almost religious reverence for the monarchy, managed, by making repeated concessions, to be the King of the Revolution. So the English aristocracy managed to prolong its term of power in the second half of the nineteenth century down to the dawn of its decadence, which was heralded by the "Parliament Bill" in the first years of the twentieth.

. . . .

THE RISE AND FALL OF WHOLE CLASSES

Joseph Schumpeter

I.

. . . Every social situation is the heritage of preceding situations and takes over from them not only their cultures, their dispositions, and their "spirit," but also elements of their social structure and concentrations of power. This fact is of itself interesting. The social pyramid is never made of a single substance, is never seamless. There is no single *Zeitgeist*, except in the sense of a construct. This means that in explaining any historical course or situation, account must be taken of the fact that much in it can be explained only by the survival of elements that are actually alien to its own trends. . . . When applied to our problem, this means, first, that any theory of class structure, in dealing with a given historical period, must include prior class structures among its data; and then, that any general theory of classes and class formation must explain the fact that classes coexisting at any given time bear the marks of different centuries on their brow, so to speak—that they stem from varying conditions. This is in the essential nature of the matter, an aspect of the nature of the class phenomenon. Classes, once they have come into being, harden in their mold and perpetuate themselves, even when the social conditions

From *Imperialism and Social Classes*, by Joseph Schumpeter, Meridian Books, 1960. Copyright 1951. Reprinted by permission.

that created them have disappeared. . . .

Any study of classes and class situations therefore leads, in unending regression, to other classes and class situations, . . . Similarly—though less closely so—analysis of the economic value of goods always leads back from a use value to a cost value and back again to a use value, so that it seems to turn in a circle. Yet this very analogy points to the logical way out. The general and mutual interdependence of values and prices in an economic situation does not prevent us from finding an all-encompassing explanatory principle; and the fact of regression in our own case does not mean the non-existence of a principle that will explain the formation, nature, and basic laws of classes—though this fact naturally does not necessarily furnish us with such a principle. If we cannot derive the sought-for principle from the genesis of classes in a classless state, it may yet emerge from a study of how classes function and what happens to them especially from actual observation of the changes in the relationship of existing classes to one another and of individuals within the class structure— *provided* it can be shown that the elements explaining such changes also include the reason why classes exist at all. . . .

II.

We observe . . . that the class structure of a people . . . changes by virtue of the fact that the relative social position of the classes as such undergoes shifts. A question now poses itself that is analogous to the question concerning the reasons for shifts of individual families within the class. Why and how do classes change their relative position?

We see such a shift most plainly, not in cases where it is the result of a slow, organic process, but in those where it occurs by a single historical event. The most important instance of the latter process is the forcible subjugation of one social entity by another that is politically alien—usually nationally as well, though that is not essential to us now. What interests us in such an upheaval is the fact that classes that appear as "upper" or "ruling" even to superficial observation—especially *the* "ruling class" —are much more deeply affected than the "lower" classes, and in an altogether different way. True, even the lower classes may often—though not always or necessarily—be put in a worse economic plight, but their position as a class, their relative social rating, is affected only slightly or not at all, usually remaining essentially unchanged under the new overlord. The upper classes, on the other hand, are likely to lose the very core of their position—the more so the nearer they are to the top of the social pyramid. Let us, for example, take the conquest of certain Romanized regions by the Germans during the Great Migration. . . . There is only one way in which the upper class can maintain its full social position under such circumstances; that is when it is received into the corresponding class of the conqueror. . . . Thus it was a common policy of the East Roman Empire to accept the nobility of subjugated peoples (of Bulgaria, for example, in the time of the Macedonian emperors) into the imperial Byzantine nobility. But it will be seen at once that this constitutes no exception to our assertion; for it was not the old class itself that retained its social validity, but merely the sum of its members in their function as members of what now came to be the upper class.

Yet even this shift in the relative position of the classes toward each other does not quite tell us what we need to know. After all, it was the result of outside influence, which was accidental from the viewpoint of the class system in existence before. Let us, nevertheless, take note of the following two elements: to be conquered always means failure, and the failure applies particularly to the ruling classes. Apparently it is this inherent character of subjugation, so destructive to prestige, that has, in turn, much to do with the forfeiture of social position. A calamity lacking this special character—a great earthquake, for example —would not have such an effect, unless it were linked in the public mind with a failure, on the part of the upper classes, to entertain, let us say, good relations with the gods. This offers an obvious analogy with the effect of personal failure of a leader—a leader of mounted nomads, for example. The position of a monarchial family is typically rooted in class. Yet

nothing shakes its position so much as an unsuccessful war. It would be difficult to find any case of loss of monarchial position that did not have, at least indirectly, some connection with this element. Again, this matter of having been subjugated or of meeting with failure is not just a question of failure in general, failure in any field; the failure becomes relevant only when it occurs with respect to certain definite fields—not merely those fields which the observer, from the necessities he has grasped, deems important, but those for which the class in question is responsible in a way that other classes are not. Only when a class has thus been weighed and found wanting, in the light of the circumstances of the times, does its position toward other classes of citizens decline—all down the line, not merely in this point alone—although, of course, a position once gained may prove equal to quite a number of such tests.

Here, then, in a flash, we begin to see the underlying relationship that leads directly to an answer to our question. This is the connection between the social rank of a class and its function. Each class is always linked to such a special function. That is the real core of all theories of the division of labor and occupation in the field of class phenomena—except that these theories, in our opinion, evaluate this element incorrectly. . . . Every class, . . . has a definite function which it must fulfill according to its whole concept and orientation, and which it actually does discharge as a class and through the class conduct of its members. Moreover, the position of each class in the total national structure, depends, on the one hand, on the significance that is attributed to that function, and, on the other hand, on the degree to which the class successfully performs the function. Changes in relative class position are always explained by changes along these two lines, and in no other way. For the time being, the propositions just put forth are liable to obvious objections. Just what their meaning is will be shown by an example which at the same time may serve to demonstrate our line of reasoning for cases that are not dependent on the effect of outside forces. The proof cannot be absolute, for that would require an analysis of universal history.

. . . .

Now let us examine our example. At the time the Germans entered the limelight of history, their aristocracy was no more than the leading circle of a mounted nomad people. It was simply a circle of families of enhanced prestige—more precisely, a plurality of distinct circles, differing from one another by the degree of prestige they enjoyed. Their members had more to do with making the policies of the totality than the rest. . . . There were real or potential chieftains of larger or smaller groups and subgroups. Yet there was one distinction as against the case of the mounted nomads, a distinction which explains the sharply marked character of the picture. Even when we first catch sight of them, the Germans were in a very high stage of agriculture, normally and preeminently living by tilling the soil. . . . Agriculture, to a much higher degree than nomadic animal husbandry, destroys uniformity of behavior among the members of a community,[1] and *adds a new distinction to that between leaders and led.* Hence we encounter the Germanic aristocracy from the very outset in a more sharply circumscribed special function. We need scarcely fear contradiction when we characterize this function as that of military leadership—a leadership, however, that meant not merely the command of forces but, to an increasing degree during the ensuing centuries, the actual execution of combat actions. Nor need we fear contradiction when we assert that this is the primary explanation for the generally enhanced position of the aristocracy, for its association with further functions— presiding at group meetings, leadership in other group concerns. It is plausible that the predominance of the military function, in uncomplicated circumstances and where the group is small in numbers, inhibits the emergence of positions of a different character. In the course of the Great Migrations and the concluding Merovingian and

[1] More precisely, it is independent of positional elements that are recognizable before the event occurs. For the event may be—and generally is— tied to one of these elements.

Carolingian successes, this social class steadily rose in power and position—it is of small moment, in this connection, that actual family content may have turned over rather rapidly. There can be no doubt, after all, that we are still entitled to speak of the same class. The question now at issue is no sooner put than answered. How can we explain this rise, this shift in relative class position? Evidently from the fact that, in the circumstances of the time, the basic class function gained in actual importance—as understood by us, the observers —and that this importance was sensed, not necessarily consciously, by the rest of the people. Both aspects are essential. Without the former there would not, in the long run, be an adequate explanation, a link with the objective facts of life of the social group; without the latter the vital connections between those vital facts and the phenomenon they created would be lacking.

This enhanced importance is *reflected and objectified* in the rise of a definite institution among the Germans in their new territories—the creation of great manorial estates. This is their social meaning and they become incomprehensible when this element is left out of consideration. It is for this very reason that the problem of the rise of such estates is such a complex and controversial one in the literature of legal and social history. All of a sudden, as it were, the great estates are in existence in the Carolingian period. One can only conclude from this fact that far-reaching social transformations had taken place; and, as is often the case with problems that are more apparent than real, this one has given rise to labored theories that are not always free of unconscious humor. Actually it is no more than the expression and gradual realization of an administrative system that arose independently, under the impact of our factor of a previously shifted class structure. Like the feudal system itself, the manorial estates, in one of their aspects, are only the expression of an administrative system adapted to special outward circumstances and the special class structure of the times—to the legal system in general, to passive methods of disposing of natural resources. (The methods are not necessarily passive in every case.) With the establishment of the great estates and the development of a mode of life in keeping with their conception at the time, as well as of a body of law affecting all classes—vassalage, immunity, court privilege, village law, and so on—there commenced a great social process that was subject to many fluctuations and setbacks and that ended only in the nineteenth century with the complete abolition of manorial privileges, even then leaving a heritage of established position to later times. We shall call this process *patrimonialization.*

There are four factors that justify the proposition that, down to the threshold of the "modern age," the relative position of our class was rising rather than sinking. I think this is apparent from the fact that, for the most part, its actual and legal privileges were on the increase, while similarly those of the remaining classes were on the decline. The only exception in this respect is the urban bourgeoisie, even though its rise did not take place in a straight line. It did, however, demonstrate the ultimate impotence of legal and political restrictions, even when the outward resources of power are at the disposal of those that impose them. It burst out of the social pyramid of feudal society, slipped from the grasp of the nobility, and enhanced its own weight and function despite all class legislation.

True, in the course of the centuries there were radical upheavals within that other class. (Technically, we should really speak in the plural, or at least distinguish between high and low aristocracy, but for the sake of simplicity in presentation we shall here speak only of a single class of feudal lords). There were numerous shifts in the position of groups within the class—above all, a constant turnover of its constituents. There were losses as well as gains in all these respects, though in the long run the gains outweighed the losses, as far as concerns class position as such. This outcome is attributable to the following four reasons: In the first place, during this entire time war essentially retained its character as a mode of life—a character it has since increasingly lost. It was a normal thing, not a last resort, as it came to be later. War and instant readiness for war remained an

indispensable element of survival in every walk of life, in all socially characteristic situations. Those who could not themselves function along these lines were dependent on the protection of some individual warlord. Because this class function was so vital, it served to enhance the significance of another factor we should like to adduce in explaining shifts in class position. The class in question exercised its function with signal success. For, in the second place, the warrior of that period grew into an expert mounted fighter. Success in the profession of arms required not merely an aptitude for fighting, but constant application to technical mastery. Those who had other concerns were by that fact alone disqualified from the full exercise of this function. Today, special technical skill can be confined to the few who, in case of need, can in a short time train men drawn from their regular occupations. But that was not true then. Nor could the military rest content with working out measures for mobilization. The warlord himself constituted the machine on which everything rested. These circumstances lie at the very heart of the matter. . . . This also disposes of the seemingly plausible notion that possession of certain "means of production"—horse and armor—was the factor that led to the formation of the class. It is only necessary to realize that one of the objectives of the system of benefices must have been to furnish not only these immediate means but also those required for the life and profession of a knight in general to those who had already been chosen for other reasons. Yet these material elements and and the way in which they were provided did have the effect of elevating and securing class position. There were other mere consequences that worked in the same direction. On the one hand, the class base was broadened. Even relatively, the number of professional warriors was greater than that of the members of the nobility in the time of universal liability to military service. Then again, the qualities required and developed by the chivalric life were eminently suited to the defense of class position against other segments of the population, which in turn were in the process of losing these very qualities. A third reason for rising class position lay in the elaboration of functions that were originally subsidiary to the main function but that now, by virtue of the situation, were carefully preserved and even more closely associated with it. National horizons, interests, and tasks were expanding, and the upper class found ever new sources of activity and thus of power in the great problems of empire, which assumed reality for it alone. It should be pointed out, however, that the situation is by no means exhaustively characterized by mere reference to the interrelationship of these functions with the basic function that genetically explains class position. Two other relationships must be considered and conceptually differentiated from the one described. Quite apart from the fact that aptitude for war was necessary even for the exercise of these further functions—a qualification that gradually disappeared—it is manifestly significant that the exercise of these other functions was objectively related to the military preoccupations of a person of high rank. Here too it was a matter of deciding, commanding, leading, winning. This the knights—or at least a sufficient number of them—were able and willing to do. It was from their ranks that the emerging high nobility was recruited, and by no means exclusively nor even normally from the families of the earlier high nobility; and it was this section of the knighthood that maintained and enhanced the position of the entire knightly class. No such interrelationship was apparent in the economic sphere. The knight had neither the desire nor the ability to become a trader. Later on, as we shall presently see, this was reversed, though only in a special sense—a fact which again justifies our conception and explains the emergence of the bourgeois from the feudal class structure, as well as the already mentioned relative decline of the nobility as against this new group whose ancestors had once stood far beneath the nobility, whether they had been legally subordinate or not. The fundamental significance of this relationship to class development is evident, and it will later be formulated in general terms. Another relationship exists by virtue of the fact that, quite apart, for the moment, from the

two correlations described, members of an elevated class, especially when their position has materialized even outwardly into privileges, property, and organic functions, find easier access to new functions (which they may even monopolize) than members of other classes. A fourth reason for the rise in the position of our class lies in the opportunities it had to colonize frontier regions, either for its own benefit or at any rate for the benefit of small subgroups, in its capacity to exploit these opportunities, and in the fact that they *were* exploited with success. This led to rising wealth, to a position of dominance over aliens, which in turn enhanced class position at home.

Yet from the end of the fourteenth century down to the present day our class has been almost without interruption on the downgrade. This is seen not so much in its legal status which even gained rather than lost in the fifteenth, sixteenth, and seventeenth centuries and did not begin to be systematically undermined until the eighteenth century—which agrees with the general observation that of all the clearly marked elements of social life the "superstructure"[2] of law, custom, and so forth is always the last to change, always lags behind changes in the actual life situation. Nor is it expressed in a decline in "social" position which, on the contrary, has been surprisingly well maintained to the present day. Rather does this decline emerge in the invariable subjection of the class to a new social factor—new, at least, in this particular form—the state power. At first glance it may seem as though this holds nothing new from the viewpoint of our subject, as though this need not impinge on class position as such. For primarily the "state power" meant no more than the sum total of the powers of the sovereign; and subjection of this nature meant no more than subjection to a superior within the class. . . . But the fact is that the sovereign did not subjugate the nobility in his capacity as feudal overlord; he did so in his capacity as master over an entirely different power—and it was to this power that he

---

[2] I employ this term, suggestive of the economic interpretation of history, in order to give expression to my belief that our line of reasoning is entirely reconcilable with that approach.

bent the nobility. There arose an administrative machine, at first predominantly manned by the nobility—more of this presently—but one with which it was by no means identical. This machinery, being capable of functioning equally well and even better in other hands, could be—and was in fact wrested from the grasp of the nobility and even of the sovereign. Objectively and theoretically, this was a new kind of subordination—submission to something that *ultimately turned out to be alien and even hostile.*

What we mean by patrimonialization is the process that explains this unfavorable change in class position—a process that must itself be explained. The term, in other words, is used in a broader sense than its technical application in legal and social history. We mean, first of all, the familiar process by which, from the Carolingian period on, vital functions became hereditary. Briefly, imperfectly, and indeed incorrectly put, they tended to become objects of the law of property. This is the *patrimonialization of office.* Secondly, we mean the process by which landownership by the nobles became—at first in fact and then in law (in its extreme form this is the alodification of fiefs)—a thing apart from the unified feudal system, in time simply a source of income, a means of production, an object of traffic. This is the *patrimonialization of landed property.* Thirdly, we mean the process by which the individual emerged from the obligations and attitudes of the feudal relationship, becoming in theory a citizen left to his own devices, shaping his private sphere more or less at will, even though for the time being he was still invested with special privileges and tied to fixed social forms. This is the *patrimonialization of the individual.* The rococo period shows us an intermediate state that is highly illuminating. In many outward respects the position of the nobility was never more splendid. Socially, legally, and materially, it rested on the very extensive heritage of the feudal age, in part well preserved, for the rest showing itself highly resistant even in a state of impairment. In all three directions this position was strengthened by the fact that the new state machine, whatever it may have taken away

from the old position of overlordship, still needed to be staffed by the nobility, while in financial respects it proved at first to be an almost inexhaustible object of exploitation. What the historian, often quite superficially, describes as courtly extravagance at the whim of the sovereign, was actually the very essence of a social and political system which sought to transform the nobility from an independent gentry into a pliant court aristocracy, not merely by force, but also by economic temptation. Actually the time of that independence, when the nobles stood on their own two feet, was at an end. The essence and guarantee of independence had lain in the fact that in case of need the lord would mount his horse and defend himself, sword in hand, against dangers from above or below—the last example, already adulterated by other factors, is furnished by the sixteenth-century peasant wars. The time was past when the coronation formula of Aragon was a striking expression of an actual situation, when the concept of the "peer" had real meaning. Now the servility of the estates just as strikingly expressed a new situation of dependence on the favor and protection of the state machine. More and more the position of overlordship became a derivate, even where it antedated the state and had its foundations outside the state, even though it continued to enjoy the glory of ancient—and otherwise to an increasing degree borrowed—associations. In telling confirmation of our view, the complement to this situation was that the lower nobility was primarily preoccupied with its private concerns, while the higher nobility as such had nothing whatever to do. The facts are in part obscured by the circumstance that *members* of both groups were active in the service of the state, while there was an understandable tendency to continue the old functions in form rather than in substance. The rugged pugnacity of the knight remained as an ideal, to be refined into the fine arts of wielding the foil and riding according to the tenets of the classcial school, utterly devoid of any further significance in the social struggle for survival. Intervention in the affairs of state became a skillful ritual, an end in itself without relevance to the task in hand. If the action had any meaning at all, this was determined, not by the great lords who actually figured in the proceedings, but by other persons and interests. It is this survival of social and material position on the one hand, and the extensive decay of underlying functions on the other, that explain the characteristic charm and high culture of that period. True, even then this group had not completely closed ranks, but it had far fewer motives for accepting newcomers than any class immediately embroiled in the struggle for survival where it must stand up and show its mettle. Yet for a while, during the time in question, the nobility could utterly ignore the nature of the relationship between ruling and serving, could temporarily surrender to the illusion that the world was its oyster, that fun was the only purpose of life, that any act that was not pure entertainment represented a graciously conferred boon. All classes, including the ruling class, exercise rights just for the sake of maintaining them. But the rococo period was characterized by the exercise of rights (which were more and more losing their function) for purely selfish reasons—and this meant that the overlord really ceased to be one, in the essential meaning of his class position. Obviously the course of events in the eighteenth century supports our contention that such a situation could continue only because it was the heritage of an altogether different situation, and also because it never existed in the pure state and was always subject to numerous corrective and weakening factors. The only alternatives would have been a timely, voluntary surrender or adaptation to a process marked by legal continuity, or loss of position by events that break such continuity—in other words, retreat or defeat; and both contingencies lead to the same final result.

To the degree required for our purposes, we may enumerate the essential elements and causes of the process of patrimonialization under the four headings we have set forth. The scope of our study requires, however, that in each case we rest content with only the first links in causal chains that ultimately reach very deep. Thus we cannot immediately discuss why physical, armed combat ceased to be a mode of life

inside the national community, and gradually outside it as well. But the fact that this happened did pull the foundation from under the main function of our class. One has to ask oneself whether the competitive economy of the nineteenth century could have existed if industrial families had not had to be continually concerned over their survival and to give constant attention to current business decisions. Reflection will show why we assert that the occasional exercise of a function—no matter how frequent the occasion, how vital the preoccupation, how suitable the function to become the basis of a full-time vocation—is insufficient to intrench a special discipline and orientation in such a way that they become the very life of a class. Even when he serves in the army, the modern conscript remains at heart a civilian. The modern professional soldier is a soldier in the sense that a lawyer is a lawyer. He is *not* a warrior, even though the traditional officer corps, in order to engender or preserve such an orientation, cultivates a warrior ideology, even going so far as to keep alive the fiction of individual readiness for combat by tolerating or promoting the duel. But when combat is no longer a mode of life, when it is no longer imminent at any moment in defense of immediate, personal interests—then it is no longer *the* great task, foreordained and self-evident. Battle, even though it may still be frequent, soon becomes an emergency situation, foreign and disturbing to other spheres of life, and there is no longer occasion for every member of the class to be constantly trained in it with every fiber of his being. This carries two consequences. The basic cause for the slow demilitarization of the nobility must be sought in the whole trend of society, which more and more circumscribed the occasion and opportunity for defending individual and class position by force of arms. Ultimately, this demilitarization made the armed class struggle—if one wishes to use that term—altogether impossible, and thus one of the conspicuous guarantees of class position fell by the wayside. Of far greater importance was the fact that this demilitarization, and the resulting orientation toward other interests, more and more had the effect of turning the nobility against its own basic function, causing it to undermine the very foundations of its own social importance. To an ever-increasing degree military service was rejected. It was not that the obligation to render such service was denied, but it was regarded as onerous and the call to it was complied with only grudgingly, if at all. Proof is furnished by the fact that in the fifteenth and early sixteenth centuries the feudal lords used the call to military service as one of the ways of making the estates comply with their financial requirements— something that can be understood only when it is realized that such duty, while acknowledged, was also resented. In this way, a replacement was found for the nobility in that sphere where combat still remained vital to survival—a sphere in which the nobility might well have continued to play a role, preserving part of its social importance. We should not overrate the significance of technical innovations in this process. On the technical side there was nothing to keep the nobility from taking to small arms and ordnance, just as it had once, with similar social results, mastered the technique of mounted and armored combat. It is no valid objection to say that the new techniques led to an increase in the number of effectives. For apart from the fact that this was to a certain extent a consequence of the circumstance that the people replacing the nobility were available in greater numbers, the earlier introduction of the host of mounted knights had itself led to a numerical increase in the nobility, a process to which any class vigorously oriented toward its function readily submits. *It is only because this did not happen now* that we think of the nobility as clinging stubbornly to the fighting methods of the Middle Ages and that the very idea of the nobility's adapting itself to the new methods seems far-fetched and unreal. Yet the army of knighthood did not fail because the mercenary army came into being. Rather the system of mercenaries arose because the knightly host failed from inner causes. But once the new situation existed, once the mercenary system functioned—with the nobility in part furnishing the financial resources (though mostly from the pockets of its own copyholders) for the very purpose

of evading military service—*then* the army of knighthood had really grown obsolete and inferior. There was a stronger power in existence now, and this meant a fundamental change in the total social-class structure. As we shall presently have occasion to discuss again, the individual knight was still the most likely candidate for positions of leadership in the mercenary army; and significantly enough, he endeavored for a long time, by his bearing and appearance, to convey the impression that he was prepared at any moment to ride out full tilt with lowered lance to meet his enemy in indvidual combat—though in the end he was likely to don armor only when his portrait was to be painted. Even though this shed glamor on the class as a whole, it was something rather different from bearing the whole burden of combat. Yet the survival of such conspicuous externals served to slow down the full effect of the internal change. And with this, we have disposed not only of the first two of the four factors we enumerated as effecting changes in position, but also of the fourth, since the possibility of private colonization is obviously associated with the warrior function as a whole.

The process by which our class relinquished its basic class function implies not merely voluntary surrender and failure of will power, but also the pressure of the objective social situation which resulted in inactivity and flagging will. It implies not only *giving up*, but also, once that had begun, *taking away*. For the nobles this process was at the same time a process of individual emancipation, and it enabled the nobility as a class to loosen all the other feudal bonds—bonds which had already begun to lose meaning and to enter into a state of atrophy. This is just what we mean, in the case of the nobility, by "patrimonialization of the individual." But it is precisely because a decline in the social importance of a class function—the inadequate exercise and ultimate surrender of that function— *sets the members of the class free* that the decline in class position which might be expected occurs only if the class is unable to adapt itself to some other function that rates the same social importance as the old one. This fact, let us remark in passing, constitutes a severe limitation on the

explanatory value of the relationship between class and function. There can never be any lack of new functions, unless a people chances into a stagnant social situation, free of problems. And every class that has once enjoyed an elevated position is greatly aided in seizing on new functions, because the sources and gains of its prior function survive for some time. In our own case we see at once that two such functions automatically obtruded themselves on the nobility by virtue of their relation to its former positions as the warrior and master class, and to which it did, in fact, turn. These functions were the staffing of the state machine and the administration of its own landed estates. It is at once evident why these two functions were, on the one hand, able to slow down and soften the descent of the class, while, on the other hand, they were insufficient to preserve its old position. Orientation toward individually owned landed property did not occur everywhere at the same rate and in the same manner. The differences in this respect are highly instructive. Where the state machine arose on the basis of the princely domain [*Fürstenterritorium*]—which was the case precisely where the mercenary system was most strongly developed—this orientation took place much more rapidly and sharply than in cases where the state had other antecedents, the single important example of the latter being England. Longer than anywhere else, and to a certain extent down to the present day, the English nobility continued in a position of national leadership, though in the course of time it became an agent rather than a ruler. It was able to do so because it did not turn to agriculture as an occupation and thus, on the one hand, remained free of all economic activity, while, on the other, it never degenerated into a group of economic and political partisans, as the nobility of other countries did. Nevertheless, the causes, the broad outlines, and the ultimate results of the process were everywhere the same, except that they emerge with particular clarity where the nobleman turns husbandman, where landlordism develops in its pure form. *Just as the manorial system corresponds to the type of the knightly warrior-politician and warrior-administrator,*
so the system of large landed estates corresponds to the type of the aristocratic businessman. Naturally our process was determined by economic developments. Landlordism is possible only when population density has risen and when centers of consumption exist. The declining purchasing power of feudal money rents was a sharp incentive to the exploitation of inherited feudal resources for private economic gain, even though such exploitation was destructive of prestige. But the heart of the matter lies in the conquests of the period between the Merovingians and Hohenstaufens, which led to a situation in which the administration and enjoyment of what had been gained, individually and as a class, made for a full life, weakening the incentive for further headlong action—quite apart from the fact that outward opportunities for such action began to dwindle. These developments gave a calculating, private-economic direction to the nobility's attitude toward such matters as its own property, its relation to the peasantry, and the maintenance of feudal rights and duties. And all this, in turn, led to corresponding legal forms and constitutes the social content of the "patrimonialization of landed property."

The situation is basically similar in the case of the "patrimonialization of office." It too becomes the comprehensible from the same causal nexus. Here too, in the course of time, the successful families established themselves in the positions they had temporarily acquired, as though such a situation must automatically endure—just as the bourgeoisie in the early nineteenth century established itself in the positions it had created, invested those positions with appropriate legal standing, regarded individual control of the means and fruits of production as self-evident and, indeed, the whole order as permanent, because it was "natural." Yet this analogy does not extend all the way. It deserts us because of the circumstance that the old overlords, in order to administer and maintain their position, did not always have to repeat those actions that had led to the conquest of that position, while the position of the industrialists is rapidly dissipated unless it is constantly marked by the same kind of success that created it. That is the main reason why the analogy between feudal and industrial rule breaks down when applied seriously and in detail. There are, to be sure, other reasons as well, of which we shall mention the two most important. The feudal master class was once—and the bourgeoisie was never—the supreme pinnacle of a uniformly constructed social pyramid. The feudal nobility was once lord and master in every sphere of life—which constitutes a difference in prestige that can never be made up. Moreover, the feudal nobility was once—and the bourgeoisie was never—not only the sole possessor of physical power; it *was* physical power incarnate. The aforementioned main difference, however, means, on the one hand, that in the case of the nobility, class and individual family position endured far better and longer than in the case of the bourgeoisie. It means, on the other hand, that the objective social importance of the function of the bourgeoisie as a class is not as readily destroyed by its own failure as was true in the case of the nobility. The failing bourgeois family drops out of the class so swiftly that the class itself always consists of families which are normally equal to their function. Stated in a somewhat different way, with the emphasis on another factor: the nobility *conquered* the material complement to its position, while the bourgeoisie *created* this complement for itself.

. . . .

Not always, but predominantly—though to a declining degree—the functions involved in the attainment of outstanding success were exercised by members of the nobility.[3] There are many reasons for this. The existing class relationship facilitated mutual understanding and concerted action. By tradition the nobility was fitted for the tasks immediately in hand—quite apart from the traditions of war, there was. the lordly mode of life, the habit of command and of handling people, of much greater importance in practical action than mere technical competence; even in our own times

[3] To the extent that other persons were involved, they were "elevated" and assimilated to the nobility—not always voluntarily.

many outstanding presidents of English railway companies have been members of the court nobility. To complete the list of the most important considerations, there was finally the need to keep the nobility occupied, to tie it to the dynasty, to maintain its prestige among the people. This led to powerful customs and taboos which strengthened the position of the nobility all the more, since they perpetuated certain feudal and patrimonial elements which created the illusion of the continued existence of the old system. These customs included the long-maintained practice of reserving high government office to the nobility, the requirement that even ordinary army officers must show descent from a certain number of aristocratic ancestors, and so on. The practices of simony and patronage were specifically patrimonial and in most countries endured deep into the eighteenth century; in the English army, for example, they were abolished only during Gladstone's second ministry. Semi-dynastic succession in office likewise disappeared but slowly. As late as Louis XIV, Colbert and Louvois were succeeded by their sons in the same or similar offices, and the fact attracted not the slightest notice. It is nevertheless important to realize that this function of the nobility, though tending to preserve its position, merely shuffling the position of families, and serving to admit an infusion of new blood (the present-day high aristocracy was largely formed in this fashion), was something altogether different from the former warrior function of the nobility—this, of course, is self-evident —and also different from its position of leadership in public affairs during the Middle Ages. That position was then filled by warlords and by the military class generally, in their own right and with their own resources, regardless of feudal subordination. Now it was exercised at the behest, not of the feudal lord, but of the sovereign, in his borrowed right and power. The core of the system had vanished, its meaning and social content had changed. What did continue, maintaining the position of the nobility, though at a steadily declining rate, were merely accessory elements—ancient prestige, access to and fitness for certain key government jobs and political functions (now superseded by the modern trained expert), intimate contact between class members which facilitated survival, a material basis in agriculture and sometimes industry, stemming from land ownership, incidental opportunities of all kinds which were open to the individual in an "elevated" position. All this, however, tended to be swept away in time. And, confirming our basic view, the process did not take place uniformly and mechanically, but with characteristic differences, according to whether one or the other element of position could be made the basis for social function and success.

What we have been discussing is only an example, though one that demonstrates all the important elements essential in answering our question. It shows not only how our thesis may be proved, but also how it is meant to be understood. In particular there now emerges, much more clearly than would be possible from a general discussion, the sense in which we speak of a socially necessary function, of class activity and orientation to activity which we, the observers, understand to be necessary for the survival of the social group, under a given set of circumstances and with a given disposition on the part of the people, and which the group itself senses to be vital for survival. We have only to add the following:

All functions that can be distinguished in the case of a given people and in a given historical situation are "socially necessary." This criterion alone, therefore, cannot decide their relative evaluation. Evidently it is a question of how important the individual class member is in a given situation more particularly, to what degree he can be replaced. The individual warrior in the Middle Ages was less replaceable and individually more "important" than the peasant. The individual industrialist is less replaceable and individually more "important" than the individual worker.

The social importance of class members varies with our two basic elements—the importance of the class function and the degree of success in carrying out that function. But the relation is not always a direct one. Other causes often appear to be far more conspicuous and immediate. Yet such causes, on their part, can always be

reduced to those basic elements, just as, according to the economic interpretation of history, the flow of social events is always ultimately shaped by the inner logic of the economic machine, though very often this influence is anything but direct. It is especially the inertia of once solidly established positions that creates a discrepancy between theory and practice, opening up a long chapter of intermediate processes. But these positions themselves can be made comprehensible in accordance with our principle.

Only this latter element explains why the evaluation of a function and the evaluation (that is, the social value) of a class do not always run parallel; why, instead, changes in class evaluation tend to lag behind changes in the evaluation of functions. This also explains the fact that, on first impression, it is more correct to describe the evaluation of a function as dependent on the social rank of those who exercise it. We say, for example, that the social rank of a class depends on the evaluation of its function by the social group, or on its importance for survival. and that "function" often appears at first, not as the prime mover, but as an accessory factor, something quite separate.[4] And this impression is strengthened—but also fully explained— by still another factor: socially necessary functions are not simply coordinate specialties. They do not all have the same relation to the leadership of social groups. Quite apart from the question of the degree to which *individual* members of the class are replaceable, the *intensity* of this relation to leadership provides a criterion for ranking socially necessary functions above and below one another and not simply for placing them beside each other as mere social necessities. But social leadership can express itself in many different concrete activities, and those which are chosen by a once-dominant group will thereby achieve higher social evaluation.

When we survey the ideas set forth in this section, we see that the causes that account for shifts in the relative positions of classes also, *ipso facto,* account for the original

[4] It is more accurate, by the way, to say that class determines "occupation" than the other way round.

order of rank—the order in which we find them at the outset of any given period. We also see why it is not always easy to establish an unequivocal class hierarchy, why there cannot always be "ruling" classes. More than that, it follows immediately that the same factors which ultimately account for shifts in class position in historical time and for the existing class structure at any given point in time, also answer the question of why there is such a phenomenon as class structure at all. For a class *gains and loses position in the same way that it emerges and passes as a class;* and only because an individual class *does* emerge and pass is there the general problem of class structure.

PART II
Principal Types
of Stratification
Systems

The social strata of our day bear, to use Schumpeter's picturesque description, the marks of different centuries on their brow. One could say, more generally, that the stratification system of any given time bears marks of the systems that preceded it. Thus it is important to study the major types of stratification systems not only in order to gain knowledge about the range of variation in the phenomenon of social inequality but also to understand the patterns of inequality today. For example, the contemporary system of stratification in the United States, and particularly in the South, still shows evidence of eighteenth- and nineteenth-century slavery and cannot be fully comprehended without taking that into account.

This is one of the main reasons why the first reading in this section deals with slavery. It is surprising yet true that sociologists have almost completely neglected slavery as a system of stratification. They generally distinguish caste, estate, and class as the principal types of stratification systems and do not name slavery as one of them.[1] And yet the literate public has become aware that slavery still exists in some parts of the world. A report compiled for the United Nations Human Rights Commission by Dr. Mohamed Awad of the United Arab Republic estimates that there are more than two million slaves today in various parts of Asia, Africa, and South America.[2]

What we mean by *types* of stratification? Despite the manifold variations in social inequality, through time and space, the following ideal types can be distinguished: slave, caste, estate, class, and "modern" stratification in advanced industrial society. By designating them as ideal types we serve notice that concrete systems are never exact replicas of these; as a matter of fact they are often "mixed

[1] See, for example, Kurt B. Mayer, *Class and Society,* New York: Random House, 1955, p. 7; Kare Svalastoga, *Social Differentiation,* New York: David McKay, 1965, p. 40; T. B. Bottomore, *Classes in Modern Society*, New York: Pantheon Books, 1966, p. 9. A noteworthy exception is Egon E. Bergel's, *Social Stratification*, New York: McGraw-Hill Book Company, 1962. It includes a chapter entitled "The Basic Division: Freedom and Bondage."

[2] C. L. Sulzberger, "Foreign Affairs: Slaves and Science," *The New York Times,* March 1, 1967, p. 42. Also see "Group Urging U.N. to Halt Slavery," *The New York Times*, December 4, 1966, p. 166.

types," containing elements of different ideal types.[3] However, it is precisely in order to gain some understanding of these concrete historical structures that we focus on ideal tpyes. Admittedly, each of these types is complex and there are many unsettled questions about their distinguishing characteristics. Nevertheless, armed with the theoretical formulations in the preceding section, we can attempt to specify the criteria of relevance that are implicit in this array of principal types of stratification. The following criteria seem of paramount importance. It should be noted at the outset that some pertain to the normative side and others to the actual side of stratification.

1. *Normatively* open-closed. Do the norms call for open or closed strata? What is the degree of openness or closure that they prescribe, prefer, or permit?
2. (Related to the preceding but pertaining to recruitment or filling of positions). *Normative* ascription-achievement. How much reliance is supposed to be placed on ascription, as compared with achievement, in filling of positions. (Ascription refers to the investment of persons with distinct statuses and roles by virtue of some quality or qualities over which they have no control; achievement— statuses obtained by virtue of their own achievement.)
3. Degree and type of institutionalization of inequality. How is unequal access to positions of advantage institutionalized? On what basis? Is it buttressed, and to what extent, by custom, law, ideology, and so on?
4. The *actual* predominant factor of social inequality from which all other inequality tends to flow—is it the power factor, the economic one, or status?

In introducing the selections, which deal mostly with concrete cases, we shall pay attention to how each of them meets these criteria. We shall also try to indicate the relative weight of a discussed criterion in a given system, for even though the four criteria are relevant in all types of stratification systems, they are not of equal importance in all systems. Take, for example, slavery. The two criteria of utmost significance are three and four: a high degree of institutionalization and the type of economic inequality are its distinguishing characteristics. To use the words of the outstanding historian of Greek slavery M. J. Finley, slavery is a system of stratification in which ". . . a man is in the eyes of the *law* and of public opinion and with respect to all other parties a *possession* of another man." [Italics supplied].[4] It was the economic fact of being owned, of being a possession, not the nature of the work, that made one a slave. Finley demonstrates convincingly that in ancient Greece there was no type of work solely performed by slaves in which free men would not engage. "In the Greek scale of values," he tells us, "the crucial test was not so much the nature of the work as the condition [freedom or slavery] . . . under which it was carried on."

Regrettably, this fact about slavery has not been brought into the contemporary discussion of the functional explanation of stratification, as we shall have the opportunity to note later when we read some of its well-known statements. According

---

[3] It might be fitting to recall here Max Weber's explanation of what an ideal type is. "An ideal type is formed by the one-sided *accentuation* of one or more points of view and by the synthesis of a great many diffuse, discrete, more or less present and occasionally absent concrete individual phenomena, which are arranged to those one-sidedly emphasized view points into a unified *analytical* construct. In its conceptual purity this mental construct cannot be found anywhere in reality." Max Weber, *The Methodology of the Social Sciences*, Glencoe: Free Press, 1949, p. 90.

[4] M. J. Finley, *Slavery in Classical Antiquity*, Cambridge, England: W. Heffer & Sons, 1960, p. 145.

to the functional theory, those positions rank higher in any society that (1) have the greater importance for society, (2) require greater training. [5] It can be easily seen that this explanation does not fit the slave system. The position of a slave ranked low because he was legally a possession, whereas the free man ranked higher because he was not owned by another. With ownership of the person came complete power over him. Thus the low rank of the *slave position* was tied to both the economic and power relation inherent in it.

The prestige factor in slavery is inseparable from the economic and power factors—but only in regard to the position, not in regard to the individuals who occupied it. It was the worst position to be in, but it was not considered to reflect on the *intrinsic* worth of the person. This is tied to the ways in which slave positions were filled. The slave system relied partially on birth (slave status was inherited from the mother), but its main sources of supply were captives and victims of war and piracy.

As Finley expresses it succinctly, ". . . the condition of servitude was one which no man, woman, or child, regardless of status or wealth, could be sure to escape in case of war or some other unpredictable and uncontrollable emergency." It is understandable why under such circumstances the idea of natural slavery could not gain ground, for everyone, so to speak, was a potential slave. There were attempts to justify slavery as "part of the natural arrangement" of things but this formulation did not become prominent either in Greece or Rome. The predominating view was that slavery was a man-made arrangement, a conventional institution, universally practiced. [6] As Florentius, the Roman jurist, phrased it, "Slavery is an institution of the *ius gentium* whereby someone is subject to the *dominium* of another, contrary to nature." [7] This did not, however, make the Greeks or Romans accept slavery less or question it more than it was later in the American South. Slavery remained unchallenged for they saw it as a necessity. To the Greeks, Nietzsche said, slavery was ". . . a necessary disgrace, of which one feels *ashamed,* as a disgrace and necessity at the same time." [8] They, including their philosophers, could not imagine civilized society without slaves just as most people today, including many sociologists, cannot imagine industrial society without differential ranking of occupations.

Since the publication in 1947 of Frank Tannenbaum's *Slave and Citizen,* the most original and thoughtful studies have expounded the view that slavery in the United States had little in common with previous forms of servitude. [9] But Arnold A. Sio, in the reprinted essay, "Interpretations of Slavery: Slave Status," basing himself on recent scholarship, challenges this view. He draws a thorough comparison of slavery in the United States with slavery in Rome and more briefly compares it in the United States and in Latin America. He demonstrates convincingly that the *legal* status of the slave as property was essentially the same in Rome and in the United States. Neither did American slavery differ from ancient slavery in its pervasiveness. For there was hardly a branch of Greek life not

---

[5] Kingsley Davis and Wilbert E. Moore, "Some Principles of Stratification," see pp. 496–503 in this volume.

[6] Finley, *op. cit.,* pp. 145–164.

[7] *Ibid.,* p. 153.

[8] As quoted by Finley, *ibid.,* p. 70.

[9] David Brion Davis, *The Problem of Slavery in Western Culture,* Ithaca: Cornell University Press, 1966, p. 29.

affected in some way by the fact that many people in Greece were slaves or former slaves.

Sio's position is in accord with the subsequent monumental work by David Brion Davis, who minimizes the difference between ancient slave systems and the American one and maintains that "... a comparable analysis of historical forms of servitude reveals precedents for *most* of the striking traits of American slavery" (italics supplied).[10] Davis, however, makes clear that he is not implying that slavery in America lacked distinctive characteristics, such as its racial basis and its legal barriers against manumission. And he does assert that "In no ancient society was the distinction between slave and freedom so sharply drawn as in America."[11]

This distinction is tied to the manner of filling positions. As is shown in Sio's essay, the major difference between Southern slavery and that in Greece and Rome was that race was made the basis for filling slave positions in the United States. Greek and Roman slavery had no color line. But we gather from David Brion Davis' work that the color line in America was not entirely unique. Racial distinctions were of some importance in the Arab world and in Mameluke Egypt, where Negro slaves were far more prevalent than in the Roman Empire. According to Davis, "Moslems not only accepted the legitimacy of Negro enslavement, but were inclined to think of black Africans as a docile race who were born to be slaves." And he shows that in China during the T'ang Dynasty "... there was a definite connection between slavery and racial prejudice."[12]

Sio questions the widely accepted thesis of the profound differences between slavery in the United States and Latin America. However, in surveying the work done in this field, he finds it insufficient and calls for more comparative studies. Since then a number of the kind of studies he called for have appeared, such as those by Eugene Genovese, Herbert S. Klein, and David Brion Davis.[13] In a review article of these studies, Sio says that "... they provide us with the beginning of a significant body of scholarship on slavery in the Americas."[14] According to Genovese the slave system of the South was not unique; what was unique was the civilization of the South. As far as its slavery is concerned, it represents a case of a "mature, commercially oriented slave system."[15] David Brion Davis, too, stresses the similarities between slavery in the United States and Latin America. He challenges the assumption of modern historians that Latin Americans were more sensitive to the essential humanity of their slaves. It is true, says he, that slavery in Latin America was less affected by competitive capitalism and closer to a patriarchal system than that in North America. But evidence shows that at times an exploitative, capitalistic form of servitude existed in Brazil and Spanish America and that, on the other hand, at certain times and places the paternalistic pattern existed in North America and the humanity of slaves was openly acknowledged. He concludes therefore that "... it may be that the differences between Latin America and the United States were no greater than regional or temporal differences

---

[10] *As quoted by Finley, ibid.,* p. 31.

[11] *Ibid.,* pp. 30, 47.

[12] *Ibid.,* pp. 50–51.

[13] Eugene D. Genovese, *The Political Economy of Slavery: Studies in the Economy and Society of the Slave South,* New York: Pantheon Books, 1965; Herbert S. Klein, *Slavery in the Americas—A Comparative Study of Cuba and Virginia,* Chicago: University of Chicago Press, 1967.

[14] Arnold A. Sio, "Society, Slavery, and the Slave," *Social and Economic Studies,* Vol. 16, September, 1967, pp. 330–344.

[15] Genovese, *op. cit.,* p. 8.

within the countries themselves." And this conclusion leads him to view Negro slavery in the Americas as "a single phenomenon, or *Gestalt,* whose variations were less significant than underlying patterns of unity."[16]

Older historical treatments of slavery in the United States proceed along the thesis that the status of the Negro in America as a member of a racial minority developed concurrently, because there was neither a tradition of slavery or racial prejudice in the colonies. But this, according to Sio, is an erroneous assumption, because recent historical evidence indicates that discrimination against the Negro occurred before the slave status was fully defined.

The tie between race and slavery accounts for all other major differences between American and ancient slavery. First of all, it explains why the American slave, in contrast to the slave of ancient times, was considered *intrinsically* inferior. This supposed innate inferiority was in turn developed into an ideology, a rationalization for the tie between slavery and race. The restriction of slavery to the Negro made possible its existence in the United States, a country whose Declaration of Independence proclaimed that all men were created equal. This restriction rested on the principle that it was a position fit for Negroes, and not whites, because the first were innately inferior beings. Slavery in ancient times was not restricted to any particular group who "ought properly to occupy the legal status of slave." Thus there was no conception of the slave or former slave as innately inferior. But in America it was considered proper and fitting that Negroes be slaves because of their race.

The tie between slavery and race also accounts, to quote Sio, for "the creation of a hereditary, endogamous, and permanent group of individuals in the status of slaves." When we consider slavery in terms of the criterion of open-closed, we realize that the closure is not inherent in the norms of slavery. As Frank Tannenbaum noted, and he is quoted by Sio, slavery systems differ in terms of "ease and availability of manumission," of change from slave to free status. Manumission was a common phenomenon in the Greek world, and easy for the Roman slave but very hard for the Negro slave in America.

This joining of slave status with race also throws light on why the position of the freed Negro was low in contrast to the situation in Rome and Greece where the former slave could rise. Sio explains it in terms of "caste law as well as slave law" governing the status of the Negro in the ante-bellum South. (The fact that the law of the South restricted the status of slavery "to members of a particular group for whom slavery is defined as natural, inevitable, and permanent" makes him think of it as "caste law.") This writer prefers to formulate it differently, however: Slavery was joined with race and an ideology of inferiority developed to justify it. And these were the two seeds of the caste system that developed fully once slavery was abolished in the South. Prior to that there was the incipient caste of the small number of free Negroes in the North and South who were legally prohibited from intermarrying with the dominant group. The free Negro was a living denial that slavery followed "naturally and inevitably" from the fact of being Negro and was thus a symbolic threat to Southern slavery. This throws light on the growth of "caste laws" in the *later slavery* period. Because of them the "freedom" of the Negro turned out quite often to be limited. The caste laws and practices also strengthened pro-slavery feelings among nonslaveholders, even the

---

[16] Davis, *op. cit.,* pp. 223–262. Direct quotations are from pp. 224 and 229.

very poor ones whose economic opportunities were limited by slavery.[17] No matter how low his status the white person was higher than the Negro, by virtue of not being the property of another and not having the *potential* of being turned into property. It is the latter that sustained the strong commitment of the non-slaveholding free population to slavery, even if slavery was the source of economic disadvantage for many of them. The case in point is that of the unskilled laborer who had no place open for him for advancement under the system of slavery. But in the matter of prestige he was twice ahead of the slaves: he was neither a slave nor a potential slave.

The main factor in status variation among the whites was the relation to slaveholding. Among slaveholders, status varied directly with the numbers of slaves held. Among those with no slaves, "the immediacy of relationship or closeness of approximation to the goal of slaveholding was the primary relevant consideration." In the slave stratum, too, variations in prestige could be distinguished between substrata such as "house servants" and "field hands."[18]

Sociologists first became aware of caste through their studies of India. Much later came the interest in caste in the United States. When one reads detailed descriptions of caste stratification in these two societies, the similarities in codes of behavior and practices are glaring.[19] The sharp difference between them is that in the United States caste is pinned to race, whereas in India the caste line is not a color line. (Indians do seem to have skin color preferences, in that "fairness" is considered more beautiful, but this may be comparable to the present preference for blond hair in the United States).[20]

But then it is this sharp difference that has given rise to the controversy about whether the concept of caste fits the American condition. In our selection "Caste in India and the United States," Gerald D. Berreman summarizes the essential points of this controversy by defending the position that a caste structure exists in the South. The definition of the caste system with which he begins is a "hierarchy of endogamous divisions in which membership is hereditary and permanent," he adds that the "hierarchy includes inequality, both in status and access to goods and services." He then goes on to demonstrate how the system in the South is similar to that of India in the characteristics included in the definition, as well as in other features. It seems to me that it would prove useful as we read Berreman to think of how the caste system lines up on the criteria of relevance we proposed at the beginning of the introduction (p. 52) and how it differs on these from slavery.

The criterion that looms largest is the criterion of open-closed, for the norms of the caste system—in contrast to those slavery, let alone the other types of stratification systems—call for *absolute* closure of the strata. Next, in filling positions, the norms call for *exclusive* reliance on ascription. The mechanism that effectuates the preceding two norms is that membership in strata is *exclusively* hereditary. Endogamy is not necessary for assuring closure or ascription, because this could be

---

[17] Support for my reinterpretation is found in Wilbert E. Moore and Robin M. Williams, "Stratification in the Ante-Bellum South," *American Sociological Review,* Vol. 7, June, 1942, pp. 343–351; and in Klein, *op. cit.*

[18] *Ibid.,* Moore and Williams.

[19] John Dollard, *Caste and Class in a Southern Town,* New Haven: Yale University Press, 1957; Baidya Nath Varma, "The Caste System of India," in *Contemporary India,* London: Asia Publishing House, 1964. pp. 59–81; and Harold C. Isaacs, *India's Ex-Untouchables,* New York: John Day Company, 1965.

[20] Isaacs, *ibid.*

accomplished through a patrilineal or matrilineal inheritance of positions. I would suggest that the unconditional endogamy in the caste system is related to another criterion, that of degree of institutionalization of inequality. Of all the principal types of stratification systems, the caste system is most highly institutionalized. In the caste system the inequality between the strata is guaranteed not only by laws—which is also true of slavery—and by conventions—which is true of other stratification systems—but also by ritualism—which is not present elsewhere. If we recall our readings in theory, Max Weber drew our attention to ritualism as a characteristic feature of caste stratification. Elsewhere he spoke about ritual barriers as being essential for caste.[21] Berreman shows convincingly how this feature is present in the South as well as in India.[22] I want to suggest that unconditional endogamy is the logical consequence of the idea of ritualistic impurity just as are the "inviolable barriers against commensalism," to use Max Weber's expression. Endogamy is characteristic of all other types of stratification but is not unconditional even in slavery. American slavery departed in this respect from the ideal type and contained this feature of caste stratification.

Finally, we must consider which factor of inequality is the paramount one. It should be recalled that Weber spoke of caste as a closed status group, meaning that it was stratification in terms of prestige. The Weberian formulation can be modified by stating that prestige inequality is the most important factor from which all other inequality flows. There is a hierarchy of prestige in terms of *inherent* inferiority and superiority that applies to both the strata and the individuals who are found in them. This determines the economic and power position of the individuals in that stratum. It contrasts with slavery, where the predominant factor is the economic one. Thus it could be said that although the Marxist model of economic determinism fits slavery it does not fit the caste system. The crucial test of the weight of the status factor in caste stratification is that in those cases of discrepancy between one's economic standing and his status, states decides the caste placement. Furthermore, status in caste stratification, in contrast to the economic situation in slavery, as we already noted, is unchangeable. People of low caste who manage to advance economically, nevertheless cannot cross the caste line.

It is noteworthy that feudalism has been the subject of controversy among social scientists similar to that surrounding caste. Some historians insist that feudalism is a technical term that can be used only for Western European institutions of the Middle Ages and reject attempts to find feudalism in other places or at other times. Others, like Strayer and Coulborn, think of it as a highly abstract concept that describes a general method of political organization.[23]

To the latter belongs also Marc Bloch, even if in his book *Feudal Society*—and in the excerpt we are reprinting—he deals almost exclusively with Western European feudalism. His is a dynamic treatment of feudalism, for he deals with its emergence and its development. Bloch too sees the political aspect as primary, since power—or as he terms it, authority—is monopolized by a small group of

[21] Max Weber, *The Religion of India*, Glencoe: Illinois, Free Press, 1958, pp. 39–45.

[22] We find parallel descriptions of this phenomenon in Japan in regard to the *Eta* who today comprise about 2 per cent of the total populace and who physically are indistinguishable in any sense from the rest. See George De Vos and Hiroshi Wagatsuma, *Japan's Invisible Race*, Berkeley: University of California Press, 1966.

[23] Joseph R. Strayer and Rushton Coulborn, "The Idea of Feudalism," in *Feudalism in History*, Princeton, N.J.: Princeton University Press, 1956, p. 5.

military leaders. The main function of these leaders was as warriors, for fighting, as Bloch shows, was not merely an occasional duty, but their life's purpose. Whatever the sources of their income—mostly land, but sometimes shops and workshops—they always "Lived on the labour of other men." He therefore stresses that the characteristic feature of the top stratum was not the possession of wealth but "some form of exploitation." The men who had power also possessed important sources of wealth, but wealth alone did not confer power.

Neither did wealth confer status. Status was derived from power rather than ownership and was joined indivisibly to it. As Bloch expresses it, "If the possession of manors was the mark of a genuinely noble status . . ., the only form of wealth which seemed compatible with high rank, this was due in the first place to the authority over other men which it implied. (Could there ever be a surer basis of prestige than to be able to say: 'It is my will.')"

Bloch refers to the strata in the feudal order as classes, using the term in the generic sense that we noted in Marx. Contemporary sociological writing generally employs the term *estates,* a distinction derived from Toennies' dichotomous typology of estates as "communal and classes as societal collectives." [24] As we gather from the descriptions this fits the top stratum, if not during the period of the emergence of feudalism, certainly once it was solidified. It was "set apart by its power, by the nature of its wealth, its mode of life, by its very morals." Bloch describes in some detail the mode and style of life, the central values and code of behavior of this "dominant class" that eventually became transformed into a nobility. The facts could serve us well as points of comparison when we focus on comparable aspects of modern stratification. As far as the understanding of feudal stratification, we are now touching on the degree of institutionalization of inequality. Sociologists generally conceive of estate stratification as a system where the strata are clearly distinguished and set off from one another by *law.* [25] Bloch's treatment presses us to reconsider this point. He demonstrates that such laws did not exist during the "first feudal age" in Europe and explains the conditions under which they came into existence in the twelfth century. In that century a new power was born, the urban patriciates who aspired to noble status. The warriors recognized them as foreign to their own mentality and therefore as constituting a special threat, because their number would endanger the noble way of life. On the other hand they were farsighted enough not to exclude from their ranks the "new forces." Thus, according to Bloch, came about the transformation of the nobility into a legal class. The law did not impose a ban on new admissions, but rather subjected them to strict control. We see then that norms of the estate system call for relatively closed strata; only a limited number of new families can be admitted to the dominant stratum in accordance with firmly established rules. As Bloch picturesquely expresses it, "If the access to the circle of knights was not absolutely closed, the door was nevertheless only slightly ajar." In filling the positions, the norms stipulate chief reliance on ascription by means of inheritance but also pay heed to achievement. The enforcement of these norms may be through custom and tradition or, when these do not suffice, through formal laws.

Another common sociological formulation that requires critical scrutiny, in

[24] Ferdinand Toennies, "Estates and Classes," in Reinhard Bendix and S. M. Lipset, eds., *Class, Status and Power,* Glencoe, Illinois: 1953, p. 49.

[25] See Mayer, *loc. cit.*; see also Bernard Barber, *Social Stratification,* New York: Harcourt, Brace, 1957, p. 55.

light of Bloch's profound analysis of European feudalism, is the conclusion that the estate system consisted of "a *hierarchy* of several social strata," (italics supplied).[26] In his summary of the fundamental characteristic of European feudalism, Bloch stresses that it was an *unequal* society, rather than a hierarchical one.

Before proceeding to the discussion of the next selection it might be interesting to mention that Bottomore, basing himself on Bloch, considers, among the different types of stratification systems, feudalism as closest to Marx's model of a society because it is characterized by the rule of a warrior class that has in its hands the ownership of land and military force.[27]

But it is Marx's model of capitalist society that is subjected to thorough criticism in our last selection on types of stratification systems. Its author, Theodor Geiger, makes a distinction between stratification in capitalist society and contemporary highly industrialized society, which according to him is no longer capitalist. He sees Marx's theory as an adequate explanation of capitalist stratification but completely erroneous in relation to "postcapitalist" stratification. Geiger's distinction between capitalist and postcapitalist society is especially important because capitalism and industrial society are often treated by social scientists as if they were synonymous.[28] Capitalism is only one form of industrial society, whose distinguishing mark Geiger shows is the joining of ownership with control of the means of production. Thus the economic factor is decisive and power results from it. One might add, so does status result from it, as was noted by Max Weber, who pointed to the class situation (economic) in the society of his time (capitalist) as "by far the predominant factor, for of course the possibility of style of life expected for members of a status group is usually conditioned economically."[29]

Geiger's penetrating essay,[30] *Die Klassengesellschaft im Schmelztiegel* has exercised a profound influence on European sociological thought but is unknown in the United States.[31] I have translated parts of the book that seemed to me to convey the essential thoughts of Geiger on the differences between capitalist and postcapitalist stratification.

He puts forth clearly the thesis of the weakening of class in the Marxian sense, because in the postcapitalist society the existing interest groups are no longer determined by the social relationships within the system of production, that is, property. The old class society stands on the threshold of a new type of society that cannot be adequately understood in terms of class opposition and conflict. Certain new lines of development are taking place that were unanticipated by Marx and cannot be accounted for by his theory. The old middle class—contrary to Marx's prediction—did not become "proletarianized" and did not join the anticapitalist proletarian front. As a matter of fact it turned against it. In addition, a new propertyless middle class has arisen that has turned out to be largely aloof

[26] Mayer, *loc. cit.,* p. 7.
[27] T. B. Bottomore, see p. 160 of this volume.
[28] Ralf Dahrendorf, in *Class and Conflict in Industrial Society,* Stanford: Stanford University Press, 1959, especially pp. 36–41, is very critical of the failure to distinguish between the two. In his book he consistently uses the label postcapitalist to designate advanced industrial society.
[29] See p. 24–34 of this volume.
[30] T. H. Marshall, "General Survey of Changes in Social Stratification in the Twentieth Century," in *Transactions of the Third World Congress of Sociology,* Vol. III, London, 1956, p. 13.
[31] For example, among the prominent authors in the field of stratification the following European sociologists refer to Geiger: Ossowski, Marshall, Bottomore, Aron, and Dahrendorf. Not even in the most recent writings of Lipset, Lenski, and so on, has there been mention of the work of Geiger.

and even hostile to the proletarian front. Geiger sees fascism and Nazism as the outcome of this hostility of the middle class to socialism as well as to large capital.

The pauperization of the working class which, Marx foretold, has not taken place. On the contrary, a new line of development is evident: income distribution crosses class lines. With it comes the increasing importance of consumption. In the postcapitalist era, devoid of traditional symbols, status, according to Geiger, is determined by income. Consumption replaces ownership of the means of production as a status symbol.

Another new line of development is the "institutionalization" of class conflict, by which Geiger means the recognition by owners of the legitimacy of labor organization. The owners and trade unions face each other as two great powers of the economic structure. Galbraith's more recent concept of trade unions as a "countervailing power" resembles the Geiger formulation about the institutionalization of class conflict. So does Dahrendorf's "theory" of "institutional isolation of industrial conflict."[32]

Geiger also points to the "managerial revolution" (Burnham's thesis)[33] as a new line of development. Under this heading is found his very important analysis of the difference between ownership and control of the means of production. We are witnessing, says Geiger, the separation of control of property or the means of production from ownership. He maintains that, insofar as in the postcapitalist society of the West the owner is increasingly hampered in the control of the property, society becomes "socialist in substance," even though it has remained capitalist in name. This is largely a semantic problem, but I doubt that it is correct to think of such a society as "socialist in substance." Socialist implies both *collective ownership* and *collective control,* and the latter accounts for the fact that to this day socialism has been only possible in small groups. Because collective control is not a feature of advanced industrial society, a more appropriate designation is the one that is currently coming into usage, *welfare capitalism,* to distinguish it from the Soviet type of society. Geiger himself points out that in the latter societies, so called socialist countries, collective ownership is only a phrase, because not the public, but economic managers have control over the property. This places them in a position of power. Thus the analysis by Geiger suggests—and we shall be able to judge on the basis of empirical studies to what extent this holds true—that the stratification in contemporary Soviet-type societies and Western-type societies is essentially the same. Both are characterized by the primacy of the state over the economy, and in both a group of men controls the economic resources of the society. This group, says Geiger, is the ruling stratum of the future if society continues on the road of planned economy.

We gather from this account that power is emerging as the primary factor of inequality in advanced industrial society. If this is so—and we will be able to judge better later in light of the empirical studies in the next section of the book—then the stratification system of highly industrialized society will differ fundamentally from its predecessor capitalist stratification whose primary factor is economic. Mosca made the point that in capitalism, which he referred to as the bureaucratic state, "... wealth produces power just as political power has been producing

---

[32] John K. Galbraith, *American Capitalism: The Concept of Countervailing Power,* Boston: Houghton Mifflin, 1956, pp. 114–117; Dahrendorf, *op. cit.,* pp. 267–272.

[33] James Burnham, *The Managerial Revolution,* New York: John Day Company, 1941.

wealth" in feudalism.[34] Advanced industrial society would then resemble feudalism in the primacy of power.

It is fitting to conclude this introduction with a summary of how the principal types of stratification systems, about which you will be reading, line up on the criteria of relevance that were proposed at the beginning of the introduction. In terms of the first criterion—whether the norms call for open or closed strata—the caste system stands at one extreme and the capitalist and modern systems at the opposite extreme. The norms of the caste system ask for *absolute closure,* the norms for the latter for *absolute openness.* The norms of the estate system also prescribe closure, but not complete closure, for they provide an opening for the select few to move up to the higher estates. As for slavery, it seems to vary on this criterion.

Corresponding to the lineup on the first criterion is the lineup on the second criterion of normative reliance on achievement or ascription—and the reasons are clear, because each of the two criteria is the consequence of the other. Again the polar types are caste with its call for *exclusive reliance on ascription* and its opposite, class plus the advanced industrial system for *exclusive reliance on achievement.*

As for the third, the degree and nature of institutionalization, the highest degree corresponds to caste with its ritualistic impurity, for it imposes utmost control. Also quite binding are the laws of slavery and the customs, traditions, or laws of estates. The matter of institutionalization in capitalist and advanced industrial society is more intricate, as we shall discover from later readings. Because the norms call for absolute openness and exclusive reliance on achievement, we have to search the manner and degree to which these goals are guaranteed. Suffice it to say at this point that the factual order in caste, slavery, and possibly also the estate system comes closer to their respective normative order of closure and ascription than does the factual order of capitalist and advanced industrial societies to the norms of absolute openness and exclusive reliance on achievement.

In the matter of the fourth criterion, the actual predominant factor of social inequality from which all other inequality tends to flow, it is the economic component in the cases of slave and class stratification, status in caste, and power in the case of estate and modern stratification. Clearly, we are not implying that the economic factor in the first two stratification systems or the power factor in the two last ones is the same in nature, manifestations, or complexity. This also applies to the other factors in each stratification system: In all types of stratification systems economic, power, and status inequality are present, but they vary in their nature, manifestations, and complexity from system to system.

Where the difference lies between capitalist and modern on one hand, and the other stratification systems, on the other, is in the correlation between economic, power, and prestige inequality; although close, it is not equally tight. This is so because the relations among the three factors are considerably more complex in the first than in the latter systems.

But a common note in all stratification systems, as the readings show, is that the strata are not homogenous and in each of them substrata can be distinguished. It merits emphasis, because this characteristic is often seen as unique to the class system.

Finally, I should like to make clear that in this summary the most tentative generalizations are those concerning modern stratification in advanced industrial

---

[34] Gaetano Mosca, *The Ruling Class,* New York: McGraw-Hill Book Company, 1939, p. 57.

society. It resembles capitalist stratification on three of the four criteria, but this may be because it is an emerging system; new and different features may come forth in the course of its development. What the new features are or are likely to be is the subject of much controversy, as we shall learn later from the readings in the final part of this volume.

INTERPRETATIONS OF SLAVERY: THE SLAVE STATUS IN THE AMERICAS

Arnold A. Sio

Recent interpretations of slavery in the United States suggest that we may be entering a new phase of scholarship on slavery as new approaches and categories are introduced by historians, and as anthropologists and sociologists again take up the study of an institution that was of such concern to their nineteenth century predecessors.

As an assessment of these interpretations, the concern of this essay is with those aspects of the legal status of the slave which appear as problematic or neglected. The purpose is to reformulate, refocus, and clarify rather than to introduce an alternative interpretation or to present new materials.

Although the scholarship on slavery has tended to shift away from the strong moral bias as well as the categories of analysis carried over for so long from the pro-slavery and anti-slavery debates, those aspects of the slavery system traditionally at issue also constitute the problematic aspects in the more recent interpretations. These are the legal status of the slave, the relations of masters and slaves, and the relationship between these two facets of the institution.[1]

I.

The concept of slavery covers a considerable variety of social phenomena, but it is generally thought of as the practice of bring-ing strangers into a society for use in economic production and legally defining them in terms of the category of property. The complete subordination of the slave to the will of the master is regarded as a main defining feature of the institution.

Subordination implies and is an aspect of authority. Authority is the socially recognized right to direct, control or manage some or all of the affairs of a person, or group, or thing. In this sense there is an overlap between property as a bundle of rights over things and the authority which is invested in some person over others as their slaves, with the result that such types of authority are treated as property at law.[2]

Slavery involves the "legal assimilation of interpersonal rights to the norm of property rights over things".[3]

This definition of the legal status of the slave has been taken in many studies as a basis for an interpretation solely in terms of the property component in the status[4]. ... This conception obscures significant differences between the property and racial components in the status, and circumvents critical evidence pertaining to the personal component in the status.[5]

In this essay an attempt is made to distinguish between the property and racial components in the status of the ante-bellum slave through a comparison with Roman slavery where the status involved a property but not a racial component. This is followed by a consideration of the evidence for a personal component in the definition of the slave status in the United States. The essay concludes with some re-examination of the status of the slave in Latin America in terms of the three components.

The interpretations of Frank Tannen-

From *Comparative Studies in Society and History*, Vol. VII, No. 3, April, 1965, pp. 289–308. Reprinted by permission.

[1] See Stanley Elkins, *Slavery*, (Chicago, 1959), Chap. I; Kenneth Stampp, "The Historian and Southern Negro Slavery," *American Historical Review*, LVII, (April, 1952), pp. 613–24; Richard Hofstadter, "U. B. Phillips and the Plantation Legend," *Journal of Negro History*, XIXX, (April, 1944), pp. 109–25.

[2] M. G. Smith, "Slavery and Emancipation in Two Societies", *Social and Economic Studies*, III, Nos. 3 and 4 (1954), pp. 245–46.

[3] *Ibid.*, p. 246.

[4] The classic account is H. J. Nieboer, *Slavery as an Industrial System* (Rotterdam, 1910).

[5] Wilbert Moore, "Slave Law and the Social Structure", *Journal of Negro History*, XXVI April, 1941), pp. 171–202.

baum[6] and Stanley Elkins[7] exemplify the shift away from the moral approach to the institution of slavery and the introduction of new methods and categories. The treatment in both is comparative. Why did slavery in the United States differ in form and consequences from the kind of servitude developed in the Latin American colonies of Spain and Portugal? According to Tannenbaum, there were at least three traditions or historical forces in Latin America which prevented the definition of the slave there solely as property; namely, the continuance of the Roman law of slavery as it came down through the Justinian Code, the influence of the Catholic Church, and the long familiarity of the Iberians with Moors and Negroes.[8] Tannenbaum puts his emphasis on whether, "The law accepted the doctrine of the moral personality of the slave and made possible the gradual achievement of freedom implicit in such a doctrine" and on a universalistic religion, i.e. Catholicism, in preventing the definition of the slave solely as property.[9] In the United States slavery developed in a legal and moral setting in which the doctrine of the moral personality of the slave did not affect the definition of his status in the society. "Legally he was a chattel under the law, and in practice an animal to be bred for market."[10]

[6] *Slave and Citizen* (New York, 1947).

[7] *Slavery.* Chap. 2. This discussion is limited to his treatment of the legal status of the slave. Elkins proposes an alternative to the established approach to slavery in the United States which, taking its stance from the debates over slavery, has been concerned mainly with the rightness or wrongness of the institution considered in terms of categories pertaining to the health and welfare of the slaves. The historical study of slavery has alternated over the years between a pro-slavery and an anti-slavery position, but the purpose and the categories of analysis have remained unchanged. The result has been a continuing confusion of the historical study of slavery with moral judgments about slavery. Elkins proposes discarding this approach and adopting instead the method of comparison as followed by Tannenbaum. Slavery as an evil is taken for granted. Elkins' treatment of slavery as analogous to the concentration camp in its effects on Negro personality is discussed in Earle E. Thorpe, "Chattel Slavery and Concentration Camps", *The Negro History Bulletin*, XXV (May, 1962), pp. 171–76.

[8] Tannenbaum, pp. 43–65.

[9] *Ibid.,* p. 8.

[10] *Ibid.,* p. 82.

In comparing North American and Latin American slavery, Elkins adds to Tannenbaum's earlier treatment. The legal status of the slave in "the liberal, Protestant, secularized, capitalist culture of America" is contrasted with that of the slave in "the conservative, paternalistic, Catholic, quasi-medieval culture of Spain and Portugal and their New World colonies".[11] Elkins concludes that in the absence of such restraining institutions in the United States the search for private gain and profit was unlimited, and the law of slavery developed in such a way as to eliminate the slightest hindrance to the authority of the slaveholder over his slaves. The legal status of the slave developed exclusively in terms of property as the result of the demands of an emerging capitalism. Slavery in the United States was "a system conceived and evolved exclusively on the grounds of property."[12]

For Elkins and Tannenbaum the definitive feature of the legal status of the antebellum slave was the centrality of the property component. The rights of personality were suppressed by the law, and the legal subordination of the slave to the authority of the master in the areas of parentage and kinship, property and other private rights, and police and disciplinary power over the slave was developed to such an extent as to make slavery in the United States a unique system.[13] The entire institution became integrated around the definition of the slave as property.

Kenneth Stampp's *The Peculiar Institution*[14] has been viewed as one of the most important and provocative contributions since Ulrich B. Phillips' *American Negro Slavery.*[15] Although it is organized essentially in terms of the categories used by Phillips and other earlier students of slavery, Stampp's study exceeds the earlier work in comprehensiveness, in presenting the response of the slave to the institution, and in its use of the available scientific evidence regarding race. In contrast to Elkins and

[11] Elkins, p. 37.

[12] *Ibid.,* p. 55.

[13] *Ibid.,* p. 52. These categories are taken from Elkins, but they are also used by Stampp and Tannenbaum in describing the status of the slave.

[14] (New York, 1957).

[15] (New York, 1918).

Tannenbaum, Stampp takes up the social organization of slavery as well as its legal structure. His interpretation of the legal status of the slave is mainly in terms of economic values, and stresses the property component as do Elkins and Tannenbaum.[16] Unlike Elkins and Tannenbaum, however, he finds that the status also contained a personal element, which made for a certain degree of ambiguity in the status.[17]

In these interpretations, the initial status of the Negro is taken as having been neither that of a slave nor that of a member of a racial group against which discrimination was practised. The status of the Negro as a slave and his status as a member of a racial minority apparently developed concurrently, since there was no tradition of slavery or of racial discrimination in the colonies to inform the initial status of the Negro. The causal connection implied between slavery and racial discrimination is a widely held conception and needs to be reconsidered in the light of recent historical investigation and comparative evidence.

Much more difficult to grasp is the effect of racial discrimination on the definition of the slave status. Elkins refers to "the most implacable race-consciousness yet observed in virtually any society" as affecting the definition of the status, but the stress on economic values in his interpretation obscures any distinction that may have been intended between the property and racial components in the status[18]. . . .

Tannenbaum is clearly concerned with the consequences of racial discrimination for the legal status of the Negro as slave and as freedman. He stresses the fact that slavery in the United States meant Negro slavery. In contrast to Latin America, slavery in the ante-bellum South involved "caste", "by law of nature", or "innate inferiority".[19]

Slavery systems can be distinguished in terms of the ease and availability of manumission and the status of the freedman, as these indicate whether or not the law denied the moral personality of the slave.[20] In the United States the conception of the slave as a racial inferior led to severe restrictions on manumission and to a low status for free Negroes. At the same time, however, it is readily apparent from Tannenbaum's comparison with slavery in Latin America that in his view the conception of the ante-bellum Negro as innately inferior affected all the legal categories defining his status: the extent of the assimilation of his rights to property in law as well as manumission and the status of the freedman.[21] Racial discrimination accentuated the legal definition of the slave as property.

The slave as property is taken as the primary or exclusive component in these interpretations of the legal status of the slave in the United States. For Elkins and Stampp this is the consequence mainly of economic forces, while for Tannenbaum ideological forces are basic. The focus on the definition of the slave as property results in a tendency to fuse the property and racial components, and in a failure to consider the evidence bearing on the personal component in the legal status.

II.

While the assimilation to property in law of the rights of slaves was common to slavery in classical antiquity and the United States, slavery in ancient society "was a type unfamiliar to Europeans and Americans of the last two centuries. It had no color line. (Therefore, *pace Aristotle*, it had no single and clearly defined race or slave caste.)"[22] Moreover, the law of slavery in ancient society did not deny the moral personality of the slave as, according to Roman law, the institution of slavery was of the *Ius Gentium* but at the same time contrary to the *Ius Naturale*, for all men

---

[16] Stampp, Chap. 5.
[17] *Ibid.,* pp. 192–93.
[18] Elkins, p. 61.
[19] Tannenbaum, pp. 55–56.

[20] *Ibid.,* p. 69. See also William L. Westermann, *The Slave Systems of Greek and Roman Antiquity* (Philadelphia, 1955), p. 154.
[21] Tannenbaum, p. 69.
[22] William L. Westermann, "Slavery and Elements of Freedom in Ancient Greece", *Bulletin of the Polish Institute Of Arts and Sciences in America,* I (Jan., 1943), p. 346. See also M. I. Finley, "Between Slavery and Freedom", *Comparative Studies in Society and History,* VI (Apr., 1964), p. 246.

were equal under natural law.[23] A comparison with slavery in Rome . . . thus provides a method for distinguishing between the property and the racial components in the definition of the legal status[24]. . . .

As to marriage and the family in the antebellum South, marriages between slaves had no legal standing. "The relation between slaves is essentially different from that of man and wife, joined in lawful wedlock . . . with slaves it may be dissolved at the pleasure of either party, or by the sale of one or both, depending on the caprice or necessity of the owners."[25] The denial of legal marriage meant, in conjunction with the rule that the child follow the conditions of the mother, that the offspring of slaves had no legal father, whether the father was slave or free. The duration of the union between slaves depended on the interests of the master or those of the slaves. The union was subject at any time to being dissolved by the sale of one or both of the slaves. The children of these "contubernial relationships", as they were termed, had no legal protection against separation from their parents. In the law there was no such thing as fornication or adultery among slaves. . . .

Roman slaves were also legally incapable of marriage. Any union between slaves or between slaves and free persons was differentiated as *contubernium* as opposed to *conubium*. A marriage was terminated if either party became enslaved. Infidelity between slaves could not be adultery. Although a slave could be guilty of adultery with a married free woman, it was not possible for an enslaved female to commit the offense, or for it to be commited with her. The inheritance of slavery followed the rule that the child follow the status of the mother, whatever the position of the father. . . . The children of slaves were the property of the owner of the mother, and, since the economic use of slaves during the Republic was at the discretion of the master, slaves were bought and sold without regard for their families. . . .[26]

According to the legal codes of the antebellum South, a slave "was unable to acquire title to property by purchase, gift, or devise".[27] A slave might not make a will, and he could not, by will, inherit anything. Slaves were not to hire themselves out, locate their own employment, establish their own residence, or make contracts for any purpose including, of course, marriage. A slave "can do nothing, possess nothing, nor acquire anything but what must belong to his master".[28] He could engage in financial transactions, but only as his master's agent. A slave could not be a party to a suit, except indirectly, when a free person represented him in a suit for freedom. Slaves might only be witnesses in court in cases involving slaves or free Negroes. When the testimony of a slave was allowed, he was not put under oath as a responsible person. Teaching slaves to read and write was prohibited, and instruction in religion was also subject to legal restrictions.

"Of the slave's civil position", in Rome, "it may be said that he had none."[29] A slave could not make a contract, he could be neither creditor nor debtor, he could not make a will, and if he became free, a will made in slavery was void. Slaves could in no way be concerned in civil proceedings which had to be made in the name of the master. A judgment against a slave was null and void and the pact of a slave was likewise void.

At to his participation in commerce, "his capacity here is almost purely derivative, and the texts speak of him as unqualified in

---

[23] Westermann, *The Slave Systems*, pp. 57, 80; W. W. Buckland, *The Roman Law of Slavery* (Cambridge, 1906), p. 1. The consequent ambiguity in the status of the slave as property and as a person in ancient society is discussed at a later point.

[24] Materials for the description of the legal status of the ante-bellum slave are standard and taken from Elkins, Chap. 2; Stampp, Chap. 5; Tannenbaum, p. 69ff; and Helen T. Catterall, *Judicial Cases Concerning Slavery and the Negro* (Washington, 1926). Those for the Roman Republic are taken from the standard work by Buckland; R. H. Barrow, *Historical Introduction to the Study of Roman Law* (Cambridge, 1932); and Rudolph Sohm, *The Institutes* (Oxford, 1907).

[25] *Howard v. Howard*, 6 Jones N.C. 235, December 1858. Catterall, II, p. 221.

[26] Buckland, p. 77.

[27] Stampp, p. 197.

[28] The Civil Code of Louisiana quoted in John C. Hurd, *The Law of Freedom and Bondage in the United States* (Boston, 1858), II, p. 160.

[29] Buckland, p. 82.

nearly every branch of law".[30] Although the Roman slave could acquire possessions for the master, "the will of the slave and, in fact, his mental faculties in general, operate in principle, where they operate at all, for the benefit of the master".[31] Legally the slave did not have possessory rights in the property acquired by him or granted to him. The *peculium* assigned to him by the master . . . did not go with the slave upon manumission unless expressly given by the master. . . .

The slave codes of the South supported the "full dominion" of the master in matters of policy and discipline. The slave's relationship with his master was expected to be one of complete subordination. Generally, homicide was the major crime that could be committed against an enslaved individual. The owner of a slave, however, could not be indicted for assault and battery on his own slave. "The power of the master must be absolute to render the submission of the slave perfect."[32] Furthermore, the master was not held responsible for the death of a slave as a consequence of "moderate correction", for "it cannot be presumed that prepensed malice (which alone makes murder felony) should induce any man to destroy his own estate".[33] The master was to recover damages caused by an assault or homicide against his slave.

During the Roman Republic there was no legal limitation on the power of the slave-owner: "his rights were unrestricted".[34] "Except in cases of revolt which endangered the government the Roman state left the problem of the discipline and punishment of slaves to their masters."[35] Sohm writes that as against his master, "a slave had no legal rights whatsoever".[36] . . . In case of injury done to a slave "the master had cause of action for damages against the perpetrator".[37] If a slave was enticed into escaping or forcibly removed the owner might resort to both criminal and civil action.

These comparisons suggest that, on the legal evidence which defines the authority of the master in the areas of parentage and kinship, property and other rights, and police and disciplinary power over slaves, there is nothing sufficiently distinctive to distinguish the legal status of the slave as property in the United States from that in Rome.

Arnold Toynbee refers to the "Negro slave immigrant" as having been "subject to the twofold penalization of racial discrimination and legal servitude".[38] A society may extensively assimilate to property in law the rights of slaves, as indeed many have, but yet not restrict the status of slavery to members of a particular group for whom slavery is defined as natural, inevitable, and permanent as occurred in the United States. This was the introduction of caste into the status of the ante-bellum Negro, slave or free. The Negro as slave occupied both a slave status and a caste status.[39] He was subject to disabilities in addition to those connected with the legal categorization of him as property, and these disabilities continued to define his status as a freedman. Caste law as well as slave law governed the status of the Negro.

The restriction of slavery to the Negro rested on the legal principle that it was a status properly belonging to the Negro as an innately (racially) inferior being. If slavery was a status attaching to a racial inferior, then it was inheritable even where one parent was white. Intermarriage between Negro slaves and whites was prohibited. Racial inferiority, legalized inheritance, and endogamy were related to another principle; namely, that slavery was the presumptive status of every Negro or person of color. The slave status was to follow naturally and inevitably from Negro ancestry.[40]

Although the slave and caste statuses were coextensive for the preponderant majority of ante-bellum Negroes, there were

---

[30] *Ibid.*, p. 82.
[31] *Ibid.*, p. 82.
[32] *State v. Mann*, 2 Deveroux 263, (N.C.), December 1829, Catterall, II, p. 57.
[33] Virginia Act of 1669, Hurd I, p. 232.
[34] Buckland, p. 36.
[35] Westermann, p. 75.
[36] Sohm, p. 166.
[37] Westermann, p. 83.

[38] Arnold J. Toynbee, *A Study of History* (Oxford, 1934), II, p. 218.
[39] Moore, pp. 177–9.
[40] *Ibid.*, 184–88. See also Winthrop D. Jordan, 'American Chiaroscuro: The Status and Definition of Mulattoes in the British Colonies", *William and Mary Quarterly*, XIX, No. 2 (April, 1962), pp. 183–200.

free Negroes in the North and South who, however, continued to be members of the lower caste. Caste was inclusive of the slave and free status. Thus the rule that the child follow the condition of the mother made slaves of the majority of Negroes and members of the lower caste of all Negroes. Negroes, slave or free, were legally prohibited from intermarrying with members of the dominant group. All members of the lower caste were presumed to be slaves unless they could establish that they should be legally free. There was a definite strain in the legal structure to establish slavery and caste as coextensive for all Negroes. The status of the free Negro is evidence of this strain. Although legally no longer an object of property rights, he was legally and socially a member of a lower caste and as such his life chances, whether he lived in the North or South, were held within narrow limits.[41]

Slavery in Republican Rome was not restricted to any particular group who ought properly to occupy the legal status of slaves. The legal restrictions on intermarriage of slave and free, on manumission, and on the status of freedmen, though at times severe, were not the consequence of a conception of the slave or former slave as innately inferior. Those who were enslaved in Rome did not constitute a caste in the society for whom the proper and permanent status was conceived to be slavery.[42] . . .

Setting aside the conventional question as to "why slavery produced discrimination?" Carl Degler has separated the two elements, and, still treating the question historically, asks rather "which appeared first, slavery or discrimination?" His main argument is that from the beginning "the Negro was treated as an inferior to the white man, servant or free".[43] Caste or elements of caste antedated slavery, and as the legal status evolved "it reflected and included as a part of its essence, this same discrimination the white man had practiced against the Negro" from the outset in New England as well as the South.[44]

The colonists of the early seventeenth century not only were well aware of the distinction between indentured servitude and slavery, but they had ample opportunity to acquire the prejudicial attitudes and discriminatory practices against Negroes through the slave trade and from Providence, Bermuda, Barbados, Jamaica, and the Spanish and Portuguese colonies.[45] Moreover, there was the inferior status ascribed to the non-Caucasian Indians and even their enslavement almost from the beginning of English settlement.

The evidence summarized by Degler indicates that Negroes were being set aside as a separate group because of their race before the legal status of slavery became fully crystallized in the late seventeenth century. There was legislation (1) preventing interracial marriages and sexual union; (2) declaring that the status of the offspring of a white man and a Negro would follow that of the mother; and (3) establishing civil and legal disabilities applying to Negroes either free or in servitude.[46] As to the situation of the Negro in the North, "from the earliest years a lowly differentiated status, if not slavery itself, was reserved and recognized for the Negro—and the Indian, it might be added".[47] Degler concludes that "long before slavery or black labor became an important part of the Southern economy, a special and inferior status had been worked out for the Negroes. . . . it was a demand for labor which dragged the Negro to American shores, but the status he acquired cannot be explained by reference to that economic motive."[48] . . .

[41] John Hope Franklin, *The Free Negro in North Carolina* (Chapel Hill, 1943); Leon F. Litwack, *North of Slavery* (Chicago, 1961).

[42] Westermann, pp. 15, 23.

[43] Carl N. Degler, "Slavery and the Genesis of American Race Prejudice", *Comparative Studies in Society and History*, II (Oct., 1959), p. 52. Cf. Oscar and Mary F. Handlin, "Origins of the Southern Labor System", *William and Mary Quarterly*, 3rd. Ser., VI (April, 1950), pp. 199–222; Winthrop D. Jordan, "Modern Tensions and the Origins of American Slavery", *Journal of Southern History*, XXVII (Feb., 1962). pp. 18–33.

[44] Degler, p. 52.

[45] *Ibid.,* pp. 53–56. See also Winthrop D. Jordan, "The Influence of the West Indies on the Origin of New England Slavery", *William and Mary Quarterly*, XXVIII (April, 1961), pp. 243–250.

[46] *Ibid.,* pp. 56–62. See also Moore, pp. 177–86.

[47] Degler, p. 62.

[48] *Ibid.,* p. 62. Jordan, *The Influence of the West Indies,* pp. 243–44, 250.

Kingsley Davis has observed that "slavery is extremely interesting precisely because it does attempt to fit human beings into the category of objects of property rights. . . . Always the slave is given some rights, and these rights interfere with the attempt to deal with him solely as property."[49] Westermann found this to be a "constant paradox" in Greek and Roman antiquity, and "inherent in the very nature of the institution". "Theoretically", the slave was a chattel and subject only to the laws pertaining to private property, and in "actuality" he was "also a human being and subject to protective legislation affecting human individuals".[50] . . . Under the law in Greek, Roman, and Near Eastern society the slave had an ambiguous status: he was both an object of property rights and a rudimentary legal person.

As to the personal component in the status of the slave in the United States, Elkins argues that as a consequence of the requirements of capitalistic argriculture "to operate efficiently and profitably", through the rational employment of slaves as economic instruments, any ambiguity in the legal status of the slave as property could not be tolerated.[51] Any rights of personality that remained to the Negro at the end of the seventeenth century had been suppressed by the middle of the eighteenth.[52] However they may differ as to causation, Elkins and Tannenbaum are in agreement that the status of the slave was determinate as property.[53] . . . Stampp, on the other hand, found a "dual character" in the legal codes. The legal authorities "were caught in a dilemma whenever they found that the slave's status as property was incompatible with this status as a person".[54] In a much earlier and very careful treatment of the personal component, Moore found that initially the question as to whether a slave was a person or a piece of property was involved in the difficult issue as to the status of the slave after conversion and baptism.

Allowing the slave the privilege of salvation implied a recognition of him as a Christian person, and, by implication, as a legal personality. The idea that conversion and baptism altered the status of the slave as property was not easily changed, and the settling of the difficulty in favor of continued enslavement does not appear to have finally disposed of the matter.[55] . . .

There are three aspects to be considered in taking up the matter of the doubtful status of the slave before the law. The most obvious, of course, is that the dual quality is inherent in the status itself. Slaves are conscious beings defined as economic property. . . . The value of a slave as property resides in his being a person, but his value as a person rests in his status being defined as property.[56]

The second aspect involves the recognition in the law not only of the humanity of the slave, but also that he may be the subject of rights of his own. In this connection, Stampp has noted a significant juxtaposition of two clauses in the legal code of Alabama in 1853. The first defines the status of the slave as property and establishes the owner's rights to the slave's "time, labor, and services", as well as the slave's obligation to comply with the lawful demands of the master. The second contains the personal element and states the master's obligation to be humane to his slaves and to provide them with adequate food, clothing, and with care during illness and old age.[57] . . .

Cases clearly affirming that the slave was a person were also numerous during the ante-bellum period. One judgment in Tennessee held:

A slave is not in the condition of a horse . . . he is made after the image of the Creator. He has mental capacities, and an immortal principle in his nature . . . the laws . . . cannot extinguish

[49] *Human Society* (New York, 1949), p. 456.
[50] Westermann, p. 1.
[51] Elkins, pp. 49, 53.
[52] *Ibid.,* p. 42.
[53] Tannenbaum, p. 97.
[54] Stampp, pp. 192–93.

[55] Moore, pp. 195–96. See also Charles Sellers, "The Travail of Slavery", in Charles Sellers, ed., *The Southerner as American* (Chapel Hill, 1960), pp. 40–71.
[56] Talcott Parsons and Neil J. Smelser, *Economy and Society* (Glencoe, 1956), p. 12.
[57] Stampp, pp. 192–93. The following discussion is not intended to be comprehensive. For a detailed treatment of the definition of the slave as a person see Moore, pp. 191–202.

his high born nature, nor deprive him of many rights which are inherent in man.[58]

. . . .

Many of the laws also implied that a slave was a legal person in that he was capable of committing crimes and could be held to trial. . . .

. . . Again, however, there were limits on the extent to which the personality of the slave was recognized, and in defining these limits the courts frequently expressed the indeterminate character of the status:

Because they are rational *human beings*, they are capable of committing crimes; and, in reference to acts which are crimes, are regarded as *persons*. Because they are *slaves*, they are . . . incapable of performing civil acts; and in reference to all such, they are *things*; not persons.[59]

. . . The third aspect pertains to the cases of manumission by will, deed, and legislative action; the instances of successful suits for freedom; and the cases of self-purchase —all of which implied evaluation of the slave as a person with some legal capacity. . . .[60]

Moreover, the presence of free Negroes in the population from the beginning; manumission; suits for freedom; and self-purchase indicated that slavery did not follow naturally and inevitably from Negro ancestry. The intrusion of the values of liberty and individual achievement into the legal structure meant that race and slavery were not coextensive for all Negroes. The law sanctioned the possibility of slaves legitimately aspiring to and attaining in attenuated form the culture goals of the enslaving group having to do with freedom and individual achievement. The status of the free Negro was real and symbolic evidence of the indeterminacy resulting from the attainment of goals that were presumably denied to Negroes and applicable only to whites.[61]

III.

. . . As the preceding discussion has indicated, in the United States where slaves were conceived of as innately inferior they constituted a caste in the society and their rights were extensively assimilated to property in law. In Republican Rome where slaves were not conceived of as innately inferior to the enslaving group and did not form a separate caste an equally extensive assimilation of their rights to property occurred. In contrast to the United States, manumission was easily available to the Roman slave, and the freedman could look forward to assimilation into Roman society.

Although the slave status in Rome was not justified in terms of the innate inferiority of the slave, the assimilation of ownership in slaves to property was comparable to that in the United States. Roman law respected the moral personality of the slave, as reflected in the rules governing manumission and the status of the freed slave, but this did not prevent the assimilation of his rights to property in law.

In so far as the legal categorization of the slave as property is concerned we are dealing with a common social form in Rome and the United States. Caste produced the contrast between the legal structures of the two systems of slavery. The consequence of racial discrimination for the legal structure of ante-bellum slavery was the creation of a hereditary, endogamous and permanent group of individuals in the status of slaves who, moreover, continued as members of a lower caste in the society after freedom. Although the conception of the slave as innately (racially) inferior to the enslaving group had important consequences for manumission and for the status of freedmen, as Tannenbaum has indicated, the comparison with Rome suggests that it did not accentuate the assimilation of ownership in slaves to property. Racial discrimination does not appear to have

---

[58] *Kennedy v. Williams*, 7 Humphreys, Sept., 1846 (Tenn.) *Ibid.*, II, p. 530.

[59] *Creswell's Executor v. Walker*, 37 Ala. 229, January, 1861, *Ibid.*, III, p. 247.

[60] *Catherine Bodine's Will*, 4 Dana 476, October 1836, (Ken.), *Ibid.*, I, pp. 334–35.

[61] Wilbert Moore and Robin Williams, "Stratification in the Ante-bellum South", *American Sociological Review*, VII (June, 1942), pp. 343–51. Cf. Douglas Hall, "Slaves and Slavery in the British West Indies", *Social and Economic Studies*, II, No. 4 (December, 1962), pp. 305–18.

affected the legal status of the slave as property.

Now slavery in Rome was not a single social phenomenon historically. Not until the first two centuries of the Empire did significant changes occur in the authority of the master over the rights of slaves. "In their ultimate legal formulation the changes found expression in the Codes of Theodosius and Justinian."[62] Up to that time, although Roman law respected the moral integrity of the slave, the subordination of the slave to the authority of the master was comparable to that in the United States. The slave law that came down through the Justinian Code to influence the Iberian law of slavery, later to be transferred to Latin America, contained not only the doctrine of the moral personality of the slave, but also embodied those changes in later Roman law which had "loosened the strict controls by which the slave element had formerly been bound to the will of the master group".[63]

According to the interpretations of slavery in Latin America by Tannenbaum and Elkins, it was this body of law in conjunction with certain traditions and institutional arrangements that functioned to protect the slaves both from an extensive assimilation to property in law and from a caste status. Some reference will be made in the concluding portion of this essay to the need for a revision of this interpretation on the basis of more recent research.

Considerable variation occurs among slavery systems in the extent to which the slave is assimilated to property in law. Variations in this component are generally taken to be related to "the level of technical development and the accompanying institutional apparatus, including the economic system".[64] Where slavery was a domestic system, as in China and the Near East, the assimilation of the slave to property in law was less extensive than in Rome and the United States where slavery was an industrial system.[65]

[62] Westermann, p. 140.

[63] *Ibid.*, p. 140.

[64] Sidney W. Mintz, Review of *Slavery* by Stanley Elkins, *American Anthropologist,* 63 (June, 1961), p. 580.

[65] G. Martin Wilbur, *Slavery in China During the Former Han Dynasty* (Chicago, 1943), p. 243; Mendelsohn pp. 121–22.

The property component in the status of the ante-bellum slave was undoubtedly related to economic values and the labor needs of an emerging capitalism, as Elkins and Stampp have emphasized, but the entire status cannot be derived from the operation of economic values. On the one hand, the extensive assimilation to property in law of the Roman slave did not generate a conception of him as innately inferior and create a caste of slaves and freedmen. On the other hand, the absence of certain institutions and traditions embodying values respecting the moral personality of the slave does not account for the conception of the Negro as inherently inferior and for caste. If these were absent, then the assimilation of ownership in slaves to property in law must have caused racial discrimination and caste. The historical evidence indicates rather that discrimination against the Negro occurred before the slave status was fully defined and before Negro labor became pivotal to the economic system.[66]

In the conception of the legal status of the slave as determinate in terms of property the slave has neither a juridical nor a moral personality. The values of the dominant group in the United States that had a bearing on the law of slavery were, on the one hand, those which legitimatized slavery and the rigid system of stratification, and on the other hand, those values pertaining to freedom and individual dignity and worth. Although there was no complex of laws, traditions, and institutions pertaining to the institution of slavery as such that embodied

[66] That the essential features of a caste status for the Negro may have preceded the full development of the slave status does not alter the widely accepted proposition that the initial status of the Negro was not that of a slave but rather that of an indentured servant or free man. Some aspects of caste appear to have developed later than others, but the main defining features were fixed early and before the complete development of the status of slavery. Racial segregation, although obviously foreshadowed in the status of the free Negro, did not appear as a part of the caste system until the late nineteenth and early twentieth centuries. The system of restricted contacts between Negroes and whites, clearly based on the long-standing assumption of the innate inferiority of the Negro, was simply the latest feature of caste to develop. See C. Vann Woodward, *The Strange Career of Jim Crow* (New York, 1957).

these latter values, a significant element in the general value system of the South was an ethical valuation of the individual. The legal evidence indicates that these extra-legal values of the society were expressed in the legal definition and conception of slavery. The law of slavery shows the existence of an ethical norm, however vague and rudimentary, attaching value to the individual.[67]

The interpretation of the legal status of the slave primarily or wholly in terms of property has implications as well for the conception of the pattern of relations between masters and slaves. In discussing the connection between the legal structure and the master-slave relationship, David Potter has observed that "the human relationship within this legal context was complex and multiple". The relation between masters and slaves had "two faces—a paternalistic manorial one and an exploitative commercial one".[68]

In the interpretations of Tannenbaum, Elkins, and Stampp there is a close correspondence between the legal structure and the pattern of the master-slave relationship. Since, according to these writers, the slave status was governed by instrumental and economic values and not affected by the religious and ethical convictions of the dominant group attaching value to the individual, there was nothing to impede the rational use of slaves as economic instruments. The exploitative commercial pattern was expected to be followed in organizing the relations of masters and slaves. It was

normatively and numerically the predominant pattern in the South.

Given this conception of the connection between the legal structure and the relations of masters and slaves, the paternalistic manorial pattern can only be interpreted as a deviation from the expected and approved pattern of the master-slave relationship. It is not interpreted as an equally recognized and approved mode of organizing and managing the relations of masters and slaves, but rather as the result of fortuitous circumstances. It is attributed to the smallness of the plantation or to the "personal factor".[69] According to this interpretation there was nothing in the law to sanction the paternalistic manorial pattern, while the commercial exploitative pattern was clearly compatible with the instrumental use of slaves as sanctioned in the definition of the slave as an object of property rights. Yet, the paternalistic manorial pattern was widespread in the South as an accepted and approved mode of organizing the master-slave relationship and represented, as did the personal component in the legal status, the intrusion of the valuation of the individual into a categorized relationship.[70]

IV.

Since the contrast with slavery in Latin America is central to the interpretations of

---

[67] Moore, pp. 201–02. For another discussion of the alternative value systems and the resulting conflicts within Southern society and within individuals see Sellers, pp. 51–67. A similar ambiguity existed in connection with slavery in ancient society. In Roman law "slavery is the only case in which, in the extant sources . . ., a conflict is declared to exist between the *Ius Gentium* and the *Ius Naturale*". Buckland, p. 1. "No society", writes Finley, "can carry such a conflict within it, around so important a set of beliefs and institutions, without the stresses erupting in some fashion, no matter how remote and extended the lines and connections may be from the original stimulus." M. I. Finley, "Was Greek Civilization Based on Slave Labour?", in M. I. Finley, ed. *Slavery in Classical Antiquity* (Cambridge, 1960), p. 162.
[68] David M. Potter, Review of *The Peculiar Institution* by Kenneth Stampp, *Yale Review*, 46 (Winter, 1957), pp. 260–61.

[69] Elkins, pp. 137–38.
[70] . . . Franklin has pointed out that the bulk of the slaves were on small plantations. If so, then the paternalistic manorial pattern must have been exceedingly widespread. On the other hand, it has also been suggested that this pattern was to be found on the larger holdings. Phillips had this conception of the master-slave relationship on large plantations. It seems likely that both patterns were normative; that is, accepted and approved ways of organizing the master-slave relationship. If this was the case, then further investigation must be directed at ascertaining the determinants of these patterns on the concrete level. Size would be one among several determinants. See John Hope Franklin, *From Slavery to Freedom* (New York, 1952), pp. 185–86. Needless to say, the pattern of the master-slave relationship is significant for the impact of slavery upon the personality of the Negro. If the paternalistic manorial pattern was widely institutionalized in the ante-bellum South, then a very significant number of Negro slaves were able to escape the tendency for the system to absorb the personality. Cf. Elkins, pp. 137–138.

slavery in the United States by Tannenbaum and Elkins, some reference may be made to the more recent studies of slavery and race relations in Latin America and the implications for a comparison with North America. The results of these studies appear to be consistent with those of this essay.

In connection with the interpretations of slavery in Latin America by Elkins and Tannenbaum, Mintz questions whether slavery in Latin America can be treated as a single phenomenon historically.[71] He points out that once slavery became a part of the industrial plantation system in Cuba and Puerto Rico, for example, an extensive assimilation to property in law of the rights of slaves occurred in spite of an institutional framework protecting the moral personality of the slave. Slavery in Cuba "dehumanized the slave as viciously as had Jamaican or North America slavery".[72] Much the same thing happened in Puerto Rico. . . .[73]

As to the racial component in the slave status, investigations of race relations in Brazil, where most of the work has been done, indicate that during the colonial period slavery also involved a caste system between whites and Negro slaves, "based on white supremacy and the institutionalized inferiority of colored slaves".[74] Concubinage was widely practiced, but inter-marriage was rare, "as the system demanded the separation of the two castes and the clearcut distinction of superiors and inferiors".[75] Colonial legislation discriminated against the free Negroes who "were often coupled with enslaved Negroes in the laws".[76] They were prevented from acquiring possessions or participating in activities in the society "which might tend to place them on a level with whites".[77] Mulattoes who attained positions of importance in Brazil "did so in spite of the official and social prejudices which existed against them throughout the whole of the colonial period".[78]

It is readily apparent from these studies that a much greater similarity existed between slavery in the United States and Latin America than here-to-fore suspected. The status of slaves in Latin America, as well as in Rome and the United States, indicates that whether or not the law respected the moral personality of the slave, an extensive assimilation of his rights to property in law occurred under slavery as an industrial system. Moreover, contrary to the widely held conception, racial discrimination was present in Latin America and had the consequence of creating a duality in the status of the slave as property and as a member of a racial caste.[79] These elements were apparently combined to some extent with a respect for the moral personality of the slave in the law.

Further comparative study of slavery in the United States and Latin America will enable us to delineate more precisely the differences and similarities in the property, racial, and personal components of the slave status in these societies. We may also expect such study to reveal, as this essay has attempted to do, that economic and ideological forces were not mutually exclusive in their consequences for the legal structure of slavery.

---

[71] Useful summaries are to be found in Juan Comas, "Recent Research on Race Relations— Latin America", *International Social Science Journal*, XIII, No. 2 (1961), pp. 271–99; Oracy Noguiera, "Skin Color and Social Class", *Plantation Systems of the New World* (Washington, 1959), pp. 164–83; Roger Bastide, "Race Relations in Brazil", *International Social Science Bulletin*, IX, No. 4 (1957), pp. 495–512.

[72] Mintz, p. 581.

[73] *Ibid.,* p. 583, See also O. A. Sherrard, *Freedom from Fear* (London, 1959), p. 75. *The Golden Age of Brazil* (Berkeley, 1961), p. 173. Gilberto Freyre's *The Masters and the Slaves* (New York, 1946), on which much of the existing conception of slavery in Brazil is based, wrote mainly about domestic slaves.

[74] Harley Ross Hammond, "Race, Social Mobility and Politics in Brazil", *Race*, IV, No. 2 (1962), p. 477. See Charles Wagley, "From Caste to Class in North Brazil", in Charles Wagley (ed.), *Race and Class in Rural Brazil* (New York, 1963), pp. 142–156.

[75] *Ibid.,* p. 4.

[76] Boxer, p. 17.

[77] *Ibid.,* p. 17.

[78] *Ibid.,* p. 17.

[79] Noguiera, pp. 167–176, has attempted to distinguish race prejudice in Brazil from that in the Unites States. With reference to the origin of race prejudice in Brazil, James G. Leyburn, in his dicussion of Noguiera's paper, questions whether it was slavery which produced race prejudice. *Ibid.,* p. 181.

CASTE IN INDIA AND THE UNITED STATES[1]

Gerald D. Berreman

Many writers who have contributed to the vast literature on the caste system in India have emphasized its unique aspects and ignored or denied the qualities it shares with rigid systems of social stratification found in other societies. Others have claimed to find caste systems or caste groups in such widely scattered areas as Arabia, Polynesia, Africa, Guatemala, and Japan.[2] Some observers refer to Negro-white relations in the United States, and particularly in the South, as being those of caste,[3] a usage which others, including C. S. Johnson, Oliver C. Cox, and, more recently, G. E. Simpson and J. M. Yinger, have criticized. This paper will compare the relationship between "touchable," especially twice-born, and "untouchable" castes in India with that between Negroes and whites in the southern United States.

Caste can be defined so that it is applicable only to India, just as it is possible to define

Reprinted from the *American Journal of Sociology*, Vol. LXVI, September, 1960, by permission of the University of Chicago Press. Copyright 1960 by the University of Chicago.

[1] Delivered in abbreviated form before the Fifty-eighth Annual Meeting of the American Anthropological Association in Mexico City, December, 1959, and based partly on research carried out in India under a Ford Foundation Foreign Area Training Fellowship during fifteen months of 1957-58 (reported in full in my "Kin, Caste, and Community in a Himalayan Hill Village" [unpublished Ph.D. dissertation, Cornell University, 1959]). I am indebted to Joel V. Berreman and Lloyd A. Fallers for their helpful comments.
[2] E. D. Chapple and C. S. Coon, *Principles of Anthropology* (New York: Henry Holt & Co., 1942), p. 437; S. F. Nadel, "Caste and Government in Primitive Society," *Journal of the Anthropological Society of Bombay*, New Series VIII (September, 1954), 9–22; M. M. Tumin, *Caste in a Peasant Society* (Princeton, N.J.: Princeton University Press, 1952); J. D. Donoghue, "An Eta Community in Japan: The Social Persistence of Outcaste Groups," *American Anthropologist*, LIX (December, 1957), 1000–1017.

[3] E.g., Allison Davis, Kingsley Davis, John Dollard, Buell Gallagher, Gunnar Myrdal, Kenneth Stampp, Lloyd Warner.

narrowly almost any sociocultural phenomenon. Indianists have traditionally held to specific, usually enumerative, definitions. Indeed, the caste system in India has several unique features, among which are its religious aspects, its complexity, and the degree to which the caste is a cohesive group that regulates the behavior of its members. Within India there is considerable variation in the characteristics of, and the relations among, the groups to which the term "caste", is applied.

However, caste can be accurately defined in broader terms. For many purposes similar social facts may be usefully categorized together, despite differences which, while not denied, are not crucial to the purposes at hand. For purposes of cross-cultural comparison this is necessary: for the study of social process, and with the aim of deriving generalizations, caste is a concept which might well be applied cross-culturally. For these purposes a caste system may be defined as a *hierarchy of endogamous divisions in which membership is hereditary and permanent*. Here hierarchy includes inequality both in status and in access to goods and services. Interdependence of the subdivisions, restricted contacts among them, occupational specialization, and/or a degree of cultural distinctiveness might be added as criteria, although they appear to be correlates rather than defining characteristics.

This definition is perhaps best viewed as describing an ideal type at one end of a continuum along which systems of social stratification might be ranged. There can be little doubt that the systems in India and the southern United States would fall far toward the caste extreme of the continuum.[4] It now becomes necessary to look at the differences cited as crucial by those who object to use of the term "caste" in both societies. The objections raised by those interested in structure, relationships, and interaction will be discussed here; the objections of those interested in specific content will be ignored —not because the latter objections are less cogent, but because they are less relevant

[4] The Tira of Africa, for example, would not fall so far toward this extreme (cf. Nadel, *op. cit.*, pp. 18 ff.).

to the comparison of social systems.[5]

Johnson sees many similarities in the two systems but objects to identifying both as caste, since "a caste system is not only a separated system, it is a stable system in which changes are socially impossible; the fact that change cannot occur is accepted by all, or practically all, participants. . . . No expenditure of psychological or physical energy is necessary to maintain a caste system."[6] Simpson and Yinger agree with Johnson and further object that, in the United States, "we lack a set of religious principles justifying a rigid system of social stratification and causing it to be willingly accepted by those at all levels."[7] Cox lists a number of features of a caste system (i.e., caste in India) which distinguish it from an interracial situation (i.e., Negro-white relations in America), important among which are its "nonconflictive," "nonpathological," and "static" nature, coupled with absence of "aspiration and progressiveness."[8]

Central to these distinctions is that caste in India is passively accepted and indorsed by all on the basis of religio-philosophical explanations which are universally subscribed to, while Negro-white relations in America are characterized by dissent, resentment, guilt, and conflict. But this contrast is invalid, resulting, as it does, from an idealized and unrealistic view of Indian caste, contrasted with a more realistic, pragmatic view of American race relations; Indian caste is viewed as it is supposed to work rather than as it does work; American race relations are seen as they do work rather than as they are supposed, by the privileged, to work. The traditional white southerner, asked to describe relations between the races, will describe the Negro as happy in his place, which he may quote science and Scripture to justify. This is similar to the explanations offered for the Indian system by the advantaged.

The point here is that ideal intercaste behavior and attitudes in India are much like those in America, while the actual interaction and attitudes are also similar. Commonly, ideal behavior and attitudes in India have been contrasted with real behavior and attitudes in America—a fact which has led to a false impression of difference. Similarly, comparisons of race relations in the rapidly changing urban or industrial South with caste relations in slowly changing rural or agrarian India lead to erroneous conclusions. Valid comparison can be made at either level, but must be with comparable data. The impact on intergroup relations of the social and economic changes which accompany urban life seems to be similar in both societies. Recent literature on village India and on the changing caste functions and caste relations in cities and industrial areas presents a realistic picture which goes far toward counteracting traditional stereotypes of Indian caste.[9]

---

[5] As a matter of fact, ignorance of the details of content in the patterns of relations between whites and Negroes in the United States has prevented many Indianists from seeing very striking similarities. Two contrasting views of the cross-cultural applicability of the concept of caste have appeared since this paper was written: F. C. Bailey, "For a Sociology of India?" *Contributions to Indian Sociology*, No. 3 (July, 1959), 88–101, esp. 97–98; and E. R. Leach, "Introduction: What Should We Mean by Caste?" in *Aspects of Caste in South India, Ceylon and North-west Pakistan* ("Cambridge Papers in Social Anthropology," No. 2 [Cambridge: Cambridge University Press, 1959]), pp. 1–10.

[6] C. S. Johnson, *Growing up in the Black Belt* (Washington, D.C.: American Council on Education, 1941), p. 326.

[7] G. E. Simpson and J. M. Yinger, *Racial and Cultural Minorities* (New York: Harper & Bros., 1953), p. 328.

[8] O. C. Cox, "Race and Caste: A Distinction," *American Journal of Sociology*, L (March, 1945), 360 (see also his *Caste, Class and Race* [Garden City, N.Y.: Doubleday & Co., 1948]).

[9] See, for example, the following community studies: F. G. Bailey, *Caste and the Economic Frontier* (Manchester: University of Manchester Press, 1957); Berreman, *op. cit.*; S. C. Dube, *Indian Village* (Ithaca, N.Y.: Cornell University Press, 1955); Oscar Lewis, *Village Life in Northern India* (Urbana: University of Illinois Press, 1958); McKim Marriott (ed.), *Village India* (American Anthropological Association Memoir No. 83 [Chicago: University of Chicago Press, 1955]); M. E. Opler and R. D. Singh, "The Division of Labor in an Indian Village," in *A Reader in General Anthropology*, ed. C. S. Coon (New York: Henry Holt & Co., 1948), pp. 464–96; M. N. Srinivas *et al.*, *India's Villages* (Development Department, West Bengal: West Bengal Government Press, 1955). See also, for example, the following studies of caste in the contemporary

In a study of caste functioning in Sirkanda, a hill village of northern Uttar Pradesh, India, I was struck by the similarity of relations between the twice-born and untouchable castes to race relations in the southern United States.[10] In both situations there is a genuine caste division, according to the definition above. In the two systems there are rigid rules of avoidance between castes, and certain types of contacts are defined as contaminating, while others are non-contaminating. The ideological justification for the rules differs in the two cultures, as do the definitions of the acts themselves; but these are cultural details. The tabooed contacts are symbolically rather than literally injurious as evidenced by the many inconsistencies in application of the rules.[11] Enforced deference, for example, is a prominent feature of both systems. Lack of deference from low castes is not contaminating, but it is promptly punished, for it implies equality. The essential similarity lies in the fact that the function of the rules in both cases is to maintain the

caste system with institutionalized inequality as its fundamental feature. In the United States, color is a conspicuous mark of caste, while in India there are complex religious features which do not appear in America, but in both cases dwelling area, occupation, place of worship, and cultural behavior, and so on, are important symbols associated with caste status. The crucial fact is that caste status is determined, and therefore the systems are perpetuated, by birth: membership in them is ascribed and unalterable. Individuals in low castes are considered inherently inferior and are relegated to a disadvantaged position, regardless of their behavior. From the point of view of the social psychology of intergroup relations, this is probably the most important common and distinct feature of caste systems.

In both the United States and India, high castes maintain their superior position by exercising powerful sanctions, and they rationalize their status with elaborate philosophical, religious, psychological, or genetic explanations. The latter are not sufficient in themselves to maintain the systems, largely because they are incompletely accepted among those whose depressed position they are thought to justify. In both places castes are economically interdependent. In both there are great differences in power and privilege among, as well as class differences within, castes and elaborate barriers to free social intercourse among them.

Similarities in the two caste systems extend throughout the range of behavior and attitudes expressed in relations among groups. An important and conspicuous area of similarity is associated with competition for certain benefits or "gains" which are personally gratifying and/or socially valued and which by their nature or under the circumstances cannot be enjoyed by all equally. Competitive striving is, of course, not unique to caste organization; it is probably found to some extent in all societies. It is subject to a variety of social controls resulting in a variety of forms of social stratification, one of which is a caste system as defined here. However, the genesis of caste systems is not here at issue.[12]

---

setting: Bailey, *op. cit.,* N. K. Bose, "Some Aspects of Caste in Bengal," *American Journal of Folklore*, LXXI (July-September, 1958), 397–412; Leach, *op. cit.,*; Arthur Niehoff, *Factory Workers in India* ("Milwaukee Public Museum Publications in Anthropology," No. 5 [1959]); M. N. Srinivas, "Caste in Modern India," *Journal of Asian Studies*, XVI (August, 1957), 529–48; and the several articles comprising the symposium on "Caste in India" contained in *Man in India*, XXXIX (April–June, 1959), 92–162.

[10] The following discussion is based not exclusively on the Sirkanda materials but on observations and literature in non-hill areas as well. The hill area presents some distinct regional variations in caste structure, important among which is the absence of intermediate castes—all are either twice-born or untouchable. This leads to a dichotomous situation, as in the United States, but one which differs in that there are important caste divisions on either side of the "pollution barrier" (cf. Bailey, *op. cit.,* p. 8; Berreman, *op cit.,* pp. 389 ff.). Relations across this barrier do not differ greatly from similar relations among plains castes, although somewhat more informal contact is allowed—pollution comes about less easily—in the hills.

[11] The symbolic acts—the "etiquette" of caste relations—in India and in America are often remarkably similar. The symbolism in America is, of course, not primarily religious as much as it is in India, although the sacred aspects in India are often far from the minds of those engaging in the acts and are not infrequently unknown to them.

[12] Cf. Nadel, *op cit.*

The caste system in India and in the United States has secured gains for the groups established at the top of the hierarchy. Their desire to retain their position for themselves and their children accounts for their efforts to perpetuate the system. John Dollard, in his discussion of "Southerntown," identifies their gains as economic, sexual, and in prestige.

In the economic field, low-caste dependence is maintained in India as in America by economic and physical sanctions. This assures not only greater high-caste income but a ready supply of free service and cheap labor from the low castes. It also guarantees the continuing availability of the other gains. In India it is the most explicitly recognized high-caste advantage.

The sexual gain for the southern white caste is defined by Dollard, quoting whom I will substitute "high caste" and "low caste" for "white" and "Negro," respectively. In this form his definition fits the Indian caste system equally well.

In simplest terms, we mean by a "sexual gain" the fact that [high-caste] men, by virtue of their caste position, have access to two classes of women, those of the [high] and [low] castes. The same condition is somewhat true of the [low-caste] women, except that they are rather the objects of the gain than the choosers, though it is a fact that they have some degree of access to [high-caste] men as well as men of their own caste. [Low-caste] men and [high-caste] women, on the other hand, are limited to their own castes in sexual choices.[13]

This arrangement is maintained in the Indian caste system, as it is in America, by severe sanctions imposed upon any low-caste man who might venture to defy the code, by the toleration accorded high-caste men who have relations with low-caste women, and by the precautions which high-caste men take to protect their women from the low castes.

High-caste people gain, by virtue of their caste status alone, deference from others, constant reinforcement of a feeling of superiority, and a permanent scapegoat in

the lower castes. Dollard has stated the implications of this gain in prestige, and, again substituting a caste designation for a racial one, his statement describes the Indian system perfectly:

The gain here . . . consists in the fact that a member of the [high] caste has an automatic right to demand forms of behavior from [low-caste people] which serve to increase his own self-esteem.

It must always be remembered that in the end this deference is demanded and not merely independently given.[14]

Ideally the high-caste person is paternalistic and authoritarian, while the low-caste person responds with deferential, submissive, subservient behavior. Gallagher might have been describing India rather than America when he noted: "By the attitudes of mingled fear, hostility, deprecation, discrimination, amused patronage, friendly domination, and rigid authoritarianism, the white caste generates opposite and complementary attitudes in the Negro caste."[15]

An additional high-caste gain in India is the religious tradition which gives people of high caste promise of greater rewards in the next life than those of low caste. People can increase their rewards in the next life by fulfilling their traditional caste duty. For high castes, this generally results in increasing the economic advantages and prestige acquired in this life, while it requires that the low castes subordinate their own economic gains and prestige in this life to the service and honor of high castes. Thus, for high-caste people, behavior leading to immediate rewards is consistent with ultimate rewards, while, for low-caste people, behavior required for the two rewards is contradictory.

These advantages are significant and recognized reasons for maintenance of the

[13] John Dollard, *Caste and Class in a Southern Town* ("Anchor Books" [Garden City, N.Y.: Doubleday & Co., 1957]), p. 135 (cf. Berreman, *op cit.*, pp. 470 ff.).

[14] Dollard, *op cit.*, p. 174. Nadel speaking of caste in general, has noted that "the lower caste are despised, not only unhappily under-privileged; they bear a stigma apart from being unfortunate. Converseley, the higher castes are not merely entitled to the possession of coveted privileges, but are also in some way exalted and endowed with a higher dignity" (Nadel, *op cit.*, p. 16).

[15] B. G. Gallagher, *American Caste and the Negro College* (New York: Columbia University Press, 1938), p. 109.

system by the privileged groups.[16] They are expressed in folklore, proverbs, and jokes; for instance, a story tells that, as the funeral procession of an old landlord passed two untouchable women going for water, one hand of the corpse fell from under the shroud and flopped about. One of the women turned to the other and remarked, "You see, Takur Singh is dead, but he still beckons to us." Other stories recount the avariciousness of Brahmins in their priestly role, the hard-heartedness of landlords, and the like.

The compensatory gains for low-caste people are cited more often by high-caste advocates of the system than by those alleged to enjoy them. They are gains common to authoritarian systems everywhere and are usually subject to the will of the dominant groups.

As noted above, India is frequently cited as an example of a society in which people of deprived and subject status are content with their lot, primarily justifying it by religion and philosophy. This is the characteristic of caste in India most often cited to distinguish it from hereditary systems elsewhere, notably in the southern United States. On the basis of my research and the literature, I maintain that this is not accurate and therefore not a valid distinction. Its prevalence is attributable in part, at least, to the vested interests of the advantaged and more articulate castes in the perpetuation of the caste system and the maintenance of a favorable view of it to outsiders. The same arguments and the same biases are frequently presented by apologists for the caste system of the southern United States.

In both systems there is a tendency to look to the past as a period of halcyon amity and to view conflict and resentment as resulting from outside disturbances of the earlier normal equilibrium. Alien ideas, or large-scale economic disturbances, or both, are often blamed for reform movements and rebellion. Such explanations may account for the national and regional reform movements which find their advocates and followers primarily among the educated and social elites; they do not account for the recurrent grass-roots attempts, long endemic in India, to raise caste status; for the state of mind which has often led to low-caste defections from Hinduism when the opportunity to do so without fear of major reprisals has presented itself; nor for the chronic resentment and tension which characterizes intercaste relations in even so remote a village as Sirkanda, the one in which I worked.

Among the low or untouchable castes in Sirkanda, there was a great deal of readily expressed resentment regarding their caste position. Specific complaints revolved around economic, prestige, and sexual impositions by the high castes. Although resentment was suppressed in the presence of people of the dominant high castes, it was readily expressed where there was no fear of detection or reprisal.[17] Low-caste people felt compelled to express village loyalties in public, but in private acts and attitudes caste loyalties were consistently and intensely dominant when the two conflicted.

Caste, as such, was not often seriously questioned in the village. Objections were characteristically directed not at "caste" but at "my position in the caste hierarchy."

In the multicaste system of India, abolition of the system evidently seems impossible from the point of view of any particular caste, and a change in its rank within the system is viewed by its members as the only plausible means of improving the situation. Moreover, abolition would destroy the caste as a group which is superior to at least some other groups, and, while it would give caste members an opportunity to mingle as equals with their superiors, it would also force them to mingle as equals with their inferiors. Abolition, even if it could be

---

[16] Cf. Pauline M. Mahar, "Changing Caste Ideology in a North Indian Village" *Journal of Social Issues*, XIV (1958), 51–65, esp. pp. 55–56; Kailash K. Singh, "Inter-caste Tensions in Two Villages in North India" (unpublished Ph.D dissertation, Cornell University, 1957), pp. 184–85; and M. N. Srinivas, "The Dominant Caste in Rampura," *American Anthropologist*, LXI (1959), 1–16, esp. p. 4.

[17] Elaborate precautions were often taken by informants to insure against any possibility that their expressions of feeling might become known to their caste superiors, which is very similar to behavior I have observed among Negroes of Montgomery, Alabama.

accomplished, would thus create an ambivalent situation for any particular caste in contrast to the clear-cut advantages of an improvement in rank.

In the dual system of the southern United States where the high caste is clearly dominant, abolition of the caste division may be seen by the subordinate group as the only plausible remedy for their deprived position. Furthermore, they have nothing to lose but their inferior status, since there are no lower castes. There are, of course, Negroes and organized groups of Negroes, such as the black supremacist "Muslims" recently in the news in the United States, who want to invert the caste hierarchy; conversely, there are low-caste people in India who want to abolish the entire system. But these seem to be atypical viewpoints. The anticaste religions and reform movements which have from time to time appealed with some success to the lower castes in India, for example, Buddhism, Islam, Christianity, Shiism, have been unable, in practice, to remain casteless. This seems to be a point of real difference between Indian and American low-caste attitudes, for in America objection is more characteristically directed toward the system as such.[18]

In Sirkanda those low-caste people who spoke most piously against high-caste abuses were likely to be equally abusive to their caste inferiors. However, no low caste was encountered whose members did not seriously question its place in the hierarchy. A sizable literature is accumulating concerning castes which have sought to alter their status.[19] Such attempts were made in Sirkanda. A more common reaction to deprived status on the part of low-caste people was what Dollard calls "passive accommodation" coupled with occasional ingroup aggression.[20]

In both America and India there is a tendency for the person of low caste to

"laugh it off" or to become resigned. In Sirkanda low-caste people could not avoid frequent contacts with their superiors, because of their proximity and relative numbers. Contacts were frequently informal, but status differences and the dangers of ritual pollution were not forgotten. An untouchable in this village who covered up his bitter resentment by playing the buffoon received favors denied to his more sullen caste fellows. The irresponsible, simpleminded untouchable is a widespread stereotype and one which he, like the Negro, has found useful. Similarly, sullen resignation, with the attendant stereotype of lazy shiftlessness, is a common response, typified in the southern Negro axiom, "Do what the man says." This, too, helps him avoid trouble, although it does little for the individual's self-respect. Aggression against the economically and numerically dominant high castes in Sirkanda was too dangerous to be a reasonable alternative. It was discussed by low-caste people in private but was rarely carried out. Even legitimate complaints to outside authority were avoided in view of the general belief that the high-caste's wealth would insure an outcome unfavorable to the low castes—a belief well grounded in experience.

Since they harbored indignation and resentment, a number of rationalizations of their status were employed by low-caste people, apparently as mechanisms to lessen the sting of reality. Thus, they often attributed their caste status to relative wealth and numbers: "If we were wealthy and in the majority, we would make the high castes untouchable."

Three more explanations of their caste status were consistently offered by low-caste people. These had the effect of denying the legitimacy of their low-caste position:

1. Members of the entire caste (or subcaste) group would deny that they deserved the low status to which they had been assigned. One example:

Englishmen and Muslims are untouchables because they have an alien religion and they eat beef. This is as it should be. We are Hindus and we do not eat beef, yet we, too, are treated as untouchables. This is not proper. We should be accorded higher status.

---

[18] Whether this difference in attitude is widely correlated with multiple, as compared to dual, caste systems, or is attributable to other differences in the Indian and American situations, can be established only by further comparative work.

[19] E.g., Opler and Singh, *op. cit.,* p. 476; B. S. Cohn, "The Changing Status of a Depressed Caste," in Marriott (ed.), *op. cit.,* pp. 53–77; and Bailey, *op. cit.,* pp. 220–26.

[20] Dollard, *op. cit.,* p. 253.

No group would admit to being lowest in the caste hierarchy.

2. People might grant that the caste of their clan, lineage, or family was of low status but deny that their particular group really belonged to it. I have not encountered a low-caste group which did not claim high-caste ancestry or origin. Thus a typical comment is:

Yes, we are drummers by occupation, but our ancestor was a Brahmin who married a drummer woman. By rights, therefore, we should be Brahmins, but in such cases the high castes here go against the usual custom and assign the child the caste of his low-caste parent rather than of his father, from whom a person inherits everything else.

3. A person might grant that his own caste and even his lineage or family were of low status, but his explanation would excuse him from responsibility for it. Such explanations were supplied by Brahmins who, as the most privileged caste and the recipients of religiously motivated charity from all castes, have a vested interest in maintenance of the system and its acceptance by those at all levels. An individual's horoscope would describe him as having been of high caste and exemplary behavior in a previous life and therefore destined for even greater things in the present life. However, in performing some religiously meritorious act in his previous existence, he inadvertently sinned (e.g., he was a raja, tricked by dishonest servants who did not give to the Brahmin the charity he intended for them). As a result he had to be punished in this life with a low rebirth.

Thus, no one said, in effect, "I am of low status and so are my family members and my caste-fellows, and justly so, because of our misdeeds in previous lives." To do so would lead to a psychologically untenable position, though one advocated by high-caste people and by orthodox Hinduism. Rationalizations or beliefs such as these form a consistent pattern—they are not isolated instances. Neither are they unique to the village or culture reported here: the literature reveals similar beliefs elsewhere in North India.[21] They evidently indicate something less than enthusiastic acceptance of caste position and, meanwhile, they perhaps alleviate or divert resentment.

That people remain in an inferior position, therefore, does not mean that they do so willingly, or that they believe it is justified, or that they would do anything in their power to change it, given the opportunity. Rationalizations of caste status which are consistent and convincing to those who are unaffected or who benefit from them seem much less so to those whose deprivation they are expected to justify or explain. Adherence to a religious principle may not significantly affect the attitudes and behavior to which logic would seem, or to which dogma attempts, to tie it. A comparison of the realities of caste attitudes and interaction in India and the United States suggests that no group of people is content to be low in a caste hierarchy—to live a life of inherited deprivation and subjection—regardless of the rationalizations offered them by their superiors or constructed by themselves. This is one of many points on which further cross-cultural comparison, and only cross-cultural comparison of caste behavior, might be conclusive.

It should be evident that the range of similarities between caste in India and race relations in America, when viewed as relations among people, is wide and that the details are remarkably similar in view of the differences in cultural context. Without denying or belittling the differences, I would hold that the term "caste system" is applicable at the present time in the southern United States, if it is applicable anywhere outside of Hindu India, and that it can be usefully applied to societies with systems of hierarchical, endogamous subdivisions whose membership is hereditary and permanent, wherever they occur. By comparing

[21] Cf. E. T. Atkinson, *The Himalayan Districts of the North-Western Provinces of India* (Allahabad: North-Western Provinces and Oudh Press, 1886), III, 446; B. S. Cohn, "The Camars of Senapur: A Study of the Changing Status of a Depressed Caste" (unpublished Ph.D. dissertation, Cornell University, 1954), pp. 112 ff.; and D. N. Majumdar, *The Fortunes of Primitive Tribes* (Lucknow: Universal Publishers Ltd., 1944), p. 193.

caste situations, so defined, it should be possible to derive further insight, not only into caste in India, but into a widespread type of relations between groups—insight which is obscured if we insist upon treating Indian caste as entirely unique.

FEUDAL SOCIETY
Marc Bloch

THE DISAPPEARANCE OF THE ANCIENT ARISTOCRACIES OF BIRTH

For the writers who first gave feudalism its name, for the men of the French Revolution, who worked to destroy it, the idea of nobility seemed inseparably linked with it. It would scarcely be possible, however, to find an association of ideas more palpably false— at least if we set any store by the exact use of historical terms. Certainly there was nothing egalitarian about the societies of the feudal era; but not every dominant class is a nobility. To deserve this name such a class must evidently combine two characteristics. First, it must have a legal status of its own, which confirms and makes effectual the superiority to which it lays claim. In the second place, this status must be hereditary —with the qualification, however, that a limited number of new families may be admitted to it, in accordance with formally established rules. In other words, actual power is not enough, nor is even that form of inheritance (effective though it is in practice) which consists as much in the advantages children enjoy through having parents of high status as in the wealth they may inherit; it is necessary, in addition, that social privileges as well as hereditary succession should be recognized by law. . . . In this sense—and it is the only legitimate one—nobility made its appearance relatively late in western Europe. The first linea-

Reprinted from *Feudal Society* by Marc Bloch by permission of the University of Chicago Press. Translated from the French *La Société Féodale*. English translation © Routledge & Kegan Paul Ltd., 1961.

ments of the institution did not begin to emerge before the twelfth century, and it took definite shape only in the following century when the fief and vassalage were already in decline. Throughout the first feudal age, and in the period immediately preceding it, it was unknown.

. . . .

The most striking feature of the history of the dominant families in the first feudal age is the shortness of their pedigrees—at least if we agree to reject not only the fables invented by the Middle Ages themselves, but also the ingenious though improbable conjectures which in our own day various scholars have founded on very hypothetical principles for the transmission of proper names. . . . To speak of nobility is to speak of pedigrees: in the case in point, pedigrees did not matter because there was no nobility.

DIFFERENT MEANINGS OF THE WORD *NOBLE* IN THE FIRST FEUDAL AGE

This is not to say, however, that from the ninth to the eleventh century the word "noble" (in Latin *nobilis*) was not to be found fairly frequently in the documents. But it had no precise legal meaning and simply indicated an actual or an accepted pre-eminence, in accordance with a variety of different criteria. Almost invariably it involved the idea of a certain distinction of birth; but it also implied a measure of wealth. Thus we find Paul the Deacon (an eighth-century writer who is usually more lucid than in this case), in a commentary on a passage of the *Rule* of St. Benedict, hesitating between, and confusing, these two interpretations.[1] From the beginning of the feudal era these uses of the word "noble," though too fluctuating to admit of precise definition, at least reflected some major trends, and their very vicissitudes are instructive.

In days when so many men had to agree to hold their lands of a lord, the mere fact of escaping such subjection was a sign of superiority. It is not surprising therefore that the possession of an allod (even if this was no more than a peasant property) should

[1] *Bibliotheca Casinensis*, vol. IV, p. 151.

have been sometimes considered a sufficient title to the name "noble" or *edel*. It is also worth noticing that in the majority of the texts in which petty allodialists appear with this designation, we see them parading it only to surrender it immediately by becoming the tenants or serfs of a more powerful man.

If from the end of the eleventh century onwards we come across scarcely any more "nobles" of this sort—in reality rather humble folk—the crystallization of the idea of nobility which was then taking place on altogether different lines was not the only reason. In a great part of the West practically the whole social class had disappeared; it had become extinct.

In the Frankish period a great number of slaves had received their freedom. Naturally these intruders were not readily accepted as equals by families which had never been sullied by the servile taint. With the "free man" (*liber*), who might be a former slave set free or the recent descendant of a freedman, the Romans had not so long before contrasted the pure *ingenuus*; but in the Latin of the decadence the two words had become almost synonymous. An unblemished line was nevertheless genuine nobility in the vague sense in which that word was ordinarily employed. "To be noble is to count among one's ancestors no one who has been subjected to slavery." Such was the definition still given, towards the beginning of the eleventh century, by an Italian gloss, systematizing a usage of which we find more than one trace elsewhere.[2] . . .

Nevertheless, in the course of the first feudal age, the word [noble] gradually lost its humbler uses and tended more and more to be reserved for those groups of powerful men who had been able to acquire a growing dominance in society as a result of the breakdown of government and the general extension of protective ties. In this sense the word was still loosely used, without any precise definition of status or caste; but not without a very strong sense of the supremacy of the rank so described. Certainly the strong sense of a hierarchic order was present in the minds of those parties to a peace pact in 1023 who swore to refrain

from attacking "noble-women"—no others were mentioned.[3] In short, if the concept of nobility as a legal class remained unknown, it is quite permissible from this period, by a slight simplification of terminology, to speak of a social class of nobles and especially, perhaps, of a noble way of life. For it was principally by the nature of its wealth, by its exercise of authority, and by its social habits that this group was defined.

THE NOBLE CLASS A CLASS OF LORDS

This dominant class has sometimes been described as a landed class, and if by that is meant that fundamentally its members derived their revenues from their control of the soil, we may agree. From what other source could they have looked for them? Yet it must be added that, when available, tolls, market fees, and fines levied on a local trade were not the least coveted of properties. The characteristic feature was some form of exploitation. Whatever the sources of the noble's income—agricultural land or, as was much more rarely the case, shops or workshops—he always lived on the labour of other men. In other words, he was above all a manorial lord. . . .

THE PROFESSION OF ARMS

If the possession of manors was the mark of a genuinely noble status and, along with treasure in money or jewels, the only form of wealth which seemed compatible with high rank, this was due in the first place to the authority over other men which it implied. (Could there ever be a surer basis of prestige than to be able to say: "It is my will"?) But another reason was that the very vocation of the noble prevented him from engaging in any direct economic activity. He was committed body and soul to his particular function—that of the warrior. This fact, which is of fundamental importance, explains the rôle of the military vassals in the formation of medieval aristocracy. They did not constitute the whole of it; the owners of allodial manors, quickly assimilated by social habits to the enfeoffed vassals and sometimes more powerful than they,

---

[2] *M.G.H., LL,* vol. IV, p. 557, col. 2, l. 6.

[3] Peace oath of Beauvais in C. Pfister, *Études sur le régne de Robert le Pieux,* 1885, p. lxi.

could hardly have been excluded. The vassal groups, nevertheless, formed the basic element in it. . . .

It was not only vassals, of course, who had the capacity or the duty to fight; nor were they the only ones with a love of fighting in that first feudal age, when society from top to bottom was imbued with the taste for violence or the fear of it. The laws which attempted to restrict or prohibit the bearing of arms by members of the lower classes did not make their appearance before the second half of the twelfth century, and they coincided both with the progress of legal differentiation between classes and with a relative abatement of disorder. But whether he was a vassal or even—where such still existed—an allodial lord, the "noble" of early feudal times, in contrast with all the temporary soldiers, had the special characteristic of being a better armed warrior and a professional warrior.

He fought on horseback; and though he might on occasion dismount during the battle, he always moved about on horseback. Moreover, he fought fully equipped; his offensive weapons were the lance and the sword, occasionally the mace, while for defence he wore a helmet and a garment made wholly or partly of metal, and he carried a round or triangular shield. Strictly speaking, it was not the horse alone which made the knight; his humbler companion, the squire, whose duty it was to look after the horses and arrange the change of mounts along the road, was also mounted. Sometimes in addition to the heavy cavalry of the knights, armies included the more lightly equipped horsemen usually known as "serjeants." The distinguishing mark of the highest class of fighting-man was the combination of horse and complete equipment.

. . . .

Now is it surprising that in the eyes of generations which had good reasons for exalting force in its crudest form the fighting-man *par excellence* should have been the most feared, the most sought-after and the most respected of men? A theory at that time very widely current represented the human community as being divided into three "orders": those who prayed, those

who fought, and those who worked. It was unanimously agreed that the second should be placed much higher than the third. But the evidence of the epic goes farther still, showing that the soldier had little hesitation in rating his mission even higher than that of the specialist in prayer. Pride is one of the essential ingredients of all class-consciousness. That of the "nobles" of the feudal era was, above all, the pride of the warrior.

Moreover, fighting was for them not merely an occasional duty to be performed for the sake of their lord, or king, or family. It represented much more—their whole purpose in life.

. . . .

A supple and muscular body . . ., it is almost superfluous to say, was not enough to make the ideal knight. To these qualities he must add courage as well. And it was also because it gave scope for the exercise of this virtue that war created such joy in the hearts of men for whom daring and the contempt for death were, in a sense, professional assets. It is true that this valour did not always prevent mad panics (we have seen examples of them in face of the Vikings), nor was it above resorting to crude stratagems. Nevertheless the knightly class knew how to fight—on this point, history agrees with legend. Its unquestionable heroism was nurtured by many elements: the simple physical reaction of a healthy human being; the rage of despair—it is when he feels himself "wounded unto death" that the "cautious" Oliver strikes such terrible blows, in order "to avenge himself all he could"; the devotion to a chief or, in the case of the holy war, to a cause; the passionate desire for glory, personal or collective; the fatalistic acquiescence in face of ineluctable destiny, of which literature offers no more poignant examples than some of the last cantos of the *Nibelungenlied*; finally, the hope of reward in another world, promised not only to him who died for his God, but also to him who died for his master.

Accustomed to danger, the knight found in war yet another attraction: it offered a remedy for boredom. For these men whose culture long remained rudimentary and who—apart from a few great barons and their counsellors—were seldom occupied by very heavy administrative cares, everyday life easily slipped into a grey monotony. Thus was born an appetite for diversions which, when one's native soil failed to afford the means to gratify it, sought satisfaction in distant lands.

. . . .

. . . it was undoubtedly considered that the finest gift the chief could bestow was the right to a share of the plunder. This was also the principal profit which the knight who fought on his own account in little local wars expected from his efforts. It was a double prize, moreover: men and things. . . .

. . . War in the feudal age was in no sense war in kid gloves. It was accompanied by actions which seem to us today anything but chivalrous; as for instance—a frequent occurrence, sometimes even in disregard of a solemn oath—the massacre or mutilation of garrisons which had held out "too long." It involved, as a natural concomitant, the devastation of the enemy's estates.

. . . .

THE NOBLE AT HOME

Favourite sport though it was, war had its dead seasons; but at these times the knightly class was distinguished from its neighbours by a manner of life which was essentially that of a nobility.

. . . .

Everything tended to induce him to live in the country. First, there was the habit, which was becoming more and more widespread, of remunerating vassals by means of fiefs, consisting in the vast majority of cases of rural manors; then there was the weakening of feudal obligations, which favoured the tendency among the retainers who had now been provided with fiefs to live each in his own home, far from the kings, the great barons, and the bishops, who controlled the towns; finally, a taste for the open air, natural to these sportsmen, played its part. . . .

Thus whatever modifications it may be necessary to introduce into the picture of a nobility exclusively rural from the outset, it remains true that, ever since knights existed,

a growing majority of them in the North and many even in the coastal regions of the Mediterranean ordinarily resided in a country mansion.

. . . .

OCCUPATIONS AND DISTRACTIONS

Though usually a countryman in the sense that his home was in the country, the noble was nevertheless no agriculturalist. To put his hand to the hoe or the plough would have been an indication that he had come down in the world—as happened to a poor knight whose history is known to us through a collection of anecdotes. And if he sometimes liked to contemplate the workers in the fields or the yellowing harvest on his estates, it does not appear that as a rule he took a very direct part in the management of the farm. The manuals of estate management, when they came to be written, were intended not for the master, but for his stewards; the "country gentleman" belongs to quite another age—after the economic revolution in the sixteenth century. Although the rights of jurisdiction which he possessed over his tenants constituted one of the essential sources of his power, the lord of the village as a rule exercised them much less frequently in person than through the agency of bailiffs, themselves of peasant extraction. Nevertheless the exercise of judicial functions was certainly one of the few peaceful occupations of the knight. As a rule he only concerned himself with judicial duties within the framework of his class, which meant that he either settled the lawsuits of his own vassals or sat as judge of his peers in the court to which he had been summoned by his feudal lord; but where public justice survived, as in England and Germany, he took his place in the court of the county or the hundred. There was enough of this activity to make the legal spirit one of the earliest cultural influences to be diffused in knightly circles.

The favourite amusements of the nobility bore the imprint of a warlike temper.

First, there was hunting. As has already been said, it was more than a sport. The people of western Europe were not yet living in surroundings from which the menace of wild beasts had been finally removed. Moreover, at a time when the flesh of cattle, inadequately fed and of poor stock, furnished only indifferent meat, much venison was eaten, especially in the homes of the rich.

. . . .

Then there were the tournaments. . . . The contests of young men are an almost universal feature of folklore. In the armies, moreover, the imitation of war at all times provided a training for troops as well as a pastime. . . . The distinctive contribution of the feudal age was to evolve from these contests, whether military or popular, a type of mock battle at which prizes were generally offered, confined to mounted combatants equipped with knightly arms; and hence to create a distinctive class amusement, which the nobility found more exciting than any other.

. . . .

Nevertheless, the passion for tournaments, as for genuine warfare, was not always disinterested. Since the victor frequently took possession of the equipment and horses of the vanquished and sometimes even of his person, releasing him only on payment of a ransom, skill and strength were profitable assets. More than one jousting knight made a profession, and a very lucrative one, out of his skil¹ in combat. Thus the love of arms inextricably combined the ingredients of "joy" and the appetite for gain.

RULES OF CONDUCT

It was natural that a class so clearly defined by its mode of life and its social supremacy should eventually devise a code of conduct peculiar to itself. But it was only during the second feudal age, which was in every sense the age of awakening self-consciousness, that these rules assumed a precise form and, along with it, a more refined character.

The term which, from about the year 1100, commonly served to describe the sum of noble qualities was the characteristic word "courtesy" (*courtoisie*), which is derived from *cour*. . . . It was in fact in the assemblies, temporary or permanent, which were formed round the principal barons and the kings, that these laws of conduct came to be evolved; the isolation of the knight in his "tower" would not have permitted their development. Emulation and social contacts were necessary, and that is why this advance in moral sensibility was bound up both with the consolidation of the great principalities or monarchies and with the restoration of a greater degree of intercommunication. Another term was *prudhomme,* and as "courteous" (*courtois*) gradually acquired a more commonplace meaning, this word was used more and more frequently to denote something higher: a name so great and so good that merely to pronounce it "fills the mouth," declared St. Louis, intending thereby to vindicate the secular virtues as against those of the monk.

. . . .

As we have seen, the nobility had never been completely illiterate; still less had it been impervious to the influence of literature, though this was listened to rather than read. But a great step forward was taken when knights themselves became literary men. It is significant that the *genre* to which they devoted themselves almost exclusively up to the thirteenth century was lyric poetry. The earliest of the troubadours known to us—it should be added that he was certainly not the first—ranked among the most powerful princes in France. . . .

Towards the pleasures of the flesh the attitude of the knightly class appears to have been frankly realistic. It was the attitude of the age as a whole. The Church imposed ascetic standards on its members and required laymen to restrict sexual intercourse to marriage and the purpose of procreation. But it did not practise its own precepts very effectively, and this was especially true of the secular clergy, among whom even the Gregorian reform purified the lives of few but the episcopate. . . .

. . . The noble's marriage, as we know, was often an ordinary business transaction, and the houses of the nobility swarmed with bastards. At first sight, the advent of "courtesy" does not seem to have effected any great change in these morals. Certain of the songs of William of Aquitaine sing the praises of sensual pleasure in barrack-room style and this attitude was to find more than one imitator among the poets who succeeded him. Nevertheless, with William, who was apparently the heir of a tradition whose origins elude us, another conception of love was already emerging—that "courtly" love, which was certainly one of the most curious products of the moral code of chivalry. Can we conceive of Don Quixote without Dulcinea?

The characteristic features of courtly love can be summarized fairly simply. It had nothing to do with marriage, or rather it was directly opposed to the legal state of marriage, since the beloved was as a rule a married woman and the lover was never her husband. This love was often bestowed upon a lady of higher rank, but in any case it always involved a strong emphasis on the man's adoration of the woman. It professed to be an all-engrossing passion, constantly frustrated, easily jealous, and nourished by its own difficulties; but its stereotyped development early acquired something of a ritual character. It was not averse to casuistry. Finally, as the troubadour Geoffrey Rudel said, in a poem which, wrongly interpreted, gave rise to the famous legend of Princess Far-away, it was, ideally, a "distant" love. It did not indeed reject carnal intercourse on principle, nor according to Andrew the Chaplain, who discoursed on the subject, did it despise minor physical gratifications if obliged to renounce "the ultimate solace". But absence or obstacles, instead of destroying it, only enriched it with a poetic melancholy. If possession, always to be desired, was seen to be quite out of the question, the sentiment none the less endured as an exciting emotion and a poignant joy.

Such is the picture drawn for us by the poets. For courtly love is only known to us through literature and for that reason it is very difficult to determine to what extent it was merely a fashionable fiction.

. . . .

That a knight should carefully calculate his booty or his ransoms and, on returning home, impose a heavy "tallage" on his peasants provoked little or no criticism.

Gain was legitimate; but on one condition —that it should be promptly and liberally expended. "I can assure you," said a troubadour when he was reproached for his brigandage, "if I robbed, it was to give, not to hoard."[4] No doubt we are entitled to regard as a little suspect the insistence with which the minstrels, those professional parasites, extolled above all other duties that of generosity, *largesse*, "lady and queen in whose light all virtues shine." No doubt also, among the nobles of middle or lesser rank and still more perhaps among the great barons, there were always miserly or merely prudent individuals, more inclined to amass scarce coin or jewels in their coffers than to distribute them. It is none the less true that, in squandering a fortune that was easily gained and easily lost, the noble thought to affirm his superiority over classes less confident in the future or more careful in providing for it. This praiseworthy prodigality might not always stop at generosity or even luxury. A chronicler has preserved for us the record of the remarkable competition in wasteful expenditure witnessed one day at a great "court" held in Limousin. One knight had a plot of ground ploughed up and sown with small pieces of silver; another burned wax candles for his cooking; a third, "through boastfulness," ordered thirty of his horses to be burnt alive.[5] What must a merchant have thought of this struggle for prestige through extravagance—which reminds us of the practices of certain primitive races? Here again different notions of honour marked the line of separation between the social groups.

Thus set apart by its power, by the nature of its wealth and its mode of life, by its very morals, the social class of nobles was toward the middle of the twelfth century quite ready to solidify into a legal and hereditary class. The ever more frequent use which from that time onwards seems to have been made of the word *gentilhomme*—man of good *gent* or lineage—to describe

[4] Albert de Malaspina, in C. Appel, *Provenzalische Chrestomathie*, 3rd ed., no. 90, v. 19 *et seq.*

[5] Geoffroi de Vigeois, I, 69 in Labbe, *Bibliotheca*, II, p. 322.

the members of this class is an indication of the growing importance attributed to qualities of birth. With the wide adoption of the ceremony of "dubbing" or formal arming of the knight the legal class of nobility took definite shape.

TRANSFORMATION OF THE NOBILITY INTO A LEGAL CLASS

It is true that when they expressly imposed the hereditary rule sovereigns and courts of law were hardly aware that they were doing anything new, since at all times the great majority of those who were knighted were descendants of knights. In the eyes of an increasingly exclusive group opinion, only high birth—"guarantee of the continuation of ancient honour," as it was called by Ramon Lull—enabled a man to observe the code of behavior to which he was committed by the delivery of arms. "Ah, God! how badly is the good warrior rewarded who makes the son of a villein a knight!" exclaims the poet of *Girart de Roussillon,* about 1160;[6] which, however, testifies to the fact that these intruders were by no means rare. No law, no custom, could altogether exclude them. Moreover, they appeared at times to be almost necessary for the recruitment of armies; for that same class prejudice produced a strong conviction that only knights had the right to fight on horseback fully armed. In 1302, on the eve of the battle of Courtrai, the Flemish princes, desiring to have a cavalry force, knighted a number of rich burghers whose wealth enabled them to provide themselves with the necessary horses and equipment.[7] The transformation of what had long been by mere convention a hereditary vocation, liable to many setbacks, into a legalized and jealously-guarded privilege was therefore of capital importance, even if contemporaries had no clear awareness of this development. The profound social changes which were in progress at that time on the

fringes of the knightly world had certainly done much to inspire these Draconian measures.

In the twelfth century a new power was born—the urban patriciate. In these rich merchants who frequently acquired manors and many of whom had aspired to "the baldric of knighthood", for themselves or their sons, the hereditary warriors could not fail to recognize elements much more foreign to their own mentality and way of life—much more disturbing also on account of their number—than the soldiers of fortune or the manorial officials who had hitherto provided most of the non-noble candidates for knighthood. We know, through Bishop Otto of Freising, the reactions of the German barons to the knighthoods which they considered were too freely distributed, in northern Italy, to "men in trades and crafts"; Beaumanoir, in France, has very clearly explained how the pressure of the new social classes, eager to invest their capital in land, led the kings to take the precautions necessary to prevent the purchase of a fief from making every *nouveau riche* the equal of a descendant of knights. When a class feels itself threatened it tends to close its ranks.

It would be a mistake, however, to imagine that there was, in theory, any insuperable obstacle. A class of powerful individuals could not transform itself completely into a hereditary caste without being compelled to exclude from its ranks the new forces whose inevitable emergence is the very law of life, thereby condemning itself, as a social group, to permanent enfeeblement. Thus the evolution of legal opinion during the feudal period tended much less to impose a strict ban on new admissions than to subject them to rigorous control. Formerly every knight could make a knight. . . . however, such action had become illegal, and a heavy fine was the just punishment for this anachronism. For a member of the knightly order no longer had the right to confer membership on others unless the aspirant was already of knightly lineage. When such was not the case he might indeed be knighted, but only by special permission from the sole authority who, according to contemporary notions, was entitled to exercise the extraordinary

---

[6] Raimon Lull, *Libro de la orden de Caballeria,* ed. I. R. de Luanco, III, 8; *Girart de Roussillon,* trans. P. Meyer, p. 28 (cf. ed. Foerster, *Roman. Studien,* vol. V, p. 940 *et seq.*).

[7] P. Thomas, *Textes Historiques sur Lille,* II, 1936, p. 237.

power of dispensing from customary rules: namely the king, the sole bestower, as Beaumanoir says, of "novelties." . . .

If access to the circle of knights by birth was not absolutely closed, the door was nevertheless only very slightly ajar. It was certainly very much less easy to enter than it had been before or would be in the future; hence the violent reaction against the nobility which, in France at least, broke out in the fourteenth century. What more striking proof can be found of the solidarity and exclusive spirit of a class than the fierceness of the attacks to which it is subjected? "Revolt of the non-nobles against the nobles"—the expression, which was virtually in official use at the time of the Jacquerie is revealing; and not less so is the list of combatants. Étienne Marcel, a rich burgess and the first magistrate of the first of cities, deliberately set himself up as the enemy of the nobles. Under Louis XI or Louis XIV he would have been one of them himself. In truth, the period from about 1250 to about 1400 was, on the continent, the period which witnessed the most rigid stratification of social classes.

THE DESCENDANTS OF KNIGHTS BECOME A PRIVILEGED CLASS

By itself, however, the restriction of knighthood to members of families already confirmed in that status or to the recipients of exceptional favours would not have sufficed to form a genuine nobility. For this would have meant that the privileges which according to the conception of nobility were inseparable from noble birth would have been made dependent on a ceremony which might or might not be carried out. It was not just a question of prestige. Increasingly the pre-eminent position which it was agreed to accord to knights, both as "ordained" warriors and as vassals charged with the highest responsibilities in war and counsel, tended to take concrete shape in a precise legal code. Now, from the end of the eleventh century to the first years of the thirteenth, the same rules were reproduced throughout feudal Europe. In order to enjoy these advantages it was necessary in the first place that a man should efficiently perform his duties as a vassal, "that he have arms and horses, that, unless prevented by age, he take part in the host and in the expeditions, in the assemblies and in the courts," say the *Usages* of Catalonia. It was also necessary that he should have been knighted. The general weakening of vassal services had the result that gradually the first condition ceased to be insisted on; the later texts pass it over in silence. The second, on the other hand, remained for a long time very much in force. As late as 1238, a private family regulation, the statute of the parceners who possessed in common the castle of La Garde-Guérin in the Gévaudan, gives priority to a younger son over the eldest, if the former has received knighthood and the latter has not.

. . . .

In the last years of the thirteenth century, the evolution was almost everywhere complete. What henceforth made the noble was not the old rite of initiation, now reduced to the status of a polite formality and neglected by the majority because as a rule it involved great expense; it was the hereditary right to be knighted, whether or not that right was exercised. One calls a nobleman, writes Beaumanoir, whoever is "of knightly lineage". And shortly after 1284 the earliest authorization of knighthood granted by the chancellery of the kings of France to a person not of noble birth raised at one stroke, without imposing any conditions at all, the entire posterity of the recipient "to the privileges, rights and franchises which the nobles are accustomed to enjoy by virtue of the two lines of descent".

THE LAW OF THE NOBLES

This body of private law (which with certain necessary modifications applied to women of noble birth as well as to men) varied considerably in its details from one region to another. Moreover it evolved only slowly, and in the course of time underwent important modifications. Military vassals had for a long time been governed by a law which differed from the common rules. They were not tried by the same courts as other dependents; their fiefs were not inherited in the same way as other properties. Their family status itself bore the marks of their rank. . . .

A number of other features underlined still more emphatically the social supremacy of the class as well as its character as a fighting order. If it was a question of maintaining purity of blood, there was obviously no more effective means than the complete prohibition of marriages with persons of inferior status. Only in the imported feudalism of Cyprus and the hierarchic society of Germany, however, did it come to that; and in the latter country, which was characterized, as we shall see, by a highly-developed system of gradations within the nobility itself, it was only the higher ranks and not the petty knights, sprung from former manorial officials, who were restricted in this way. Elsewhere the memory of the ancient equality of free men continued, so far as marriage was concerned, to be reflected in law, if not in practice. Everywhere, however, certain great religious communities, which hitherto had displayed their aristocratic spirit only in rejecting postulants of servile origin, decided now to admit them only if they were descended from the nobility. Everywhere also—earlier in one place, later in another—we find evidence that the noble was specially protected in his person against the non-noble; that he was subject to an exceptional penal law, with heavier fines, as a rule, than those exacted from the common people; that recourse to private vengeance, regarded as inseparable from the bearing of arms, tended to be reserved for him; that the sumptuary laws assigned to him a place apart. The importance attached to birth as the source of privilege was expressed in the transformation of the old individual signs of "recognition," painted on the knight's shield or engraved on his seal, into the armorial bearings, sometimes transmitted with the fief but more often handed down, even without the property, from generation to generation. The use of these symbols of continuity, first seen in the royal and princely dynasties, where pride of birth was particularly strong, and soon adopted by houses of lesser rank, was regarded henceforth as the monopoly of the families classed as noble. Finally, although tax exemptions were still far from being strictly defined, the military obligation—formerly the characteristic duty of the vassal, now the noble's duty *par excellence*—had henceforth the effect of relieving the nobleman of the usual

pecuniary burdens; these being in his case replaced by warlike services.

However strong the rights acquired by birth, they were not so strong that they might not be lost by the exercise of certain occupations deemed to be incompatible with high rank. It is true that the conception of derogation (*dérogeance*) was as yet far from being fully developed.[8] The rule which forbade nobles to engage in trade seems at that time to have been imposed on them above all by certain urban statutes, which were intended to protect the virtual monopoly of the merchant communities rather than to serve the pride of a hostile caste. But by universal consent agricultural labor was regarded as contrary to the honor of the military class. Even with his own compliance—so the *Parlement* of Paris decided —a knight who had acquired a tenement in villeinage could not perform rural labor services. "To plough, to dig, to carry a load of wood or manure"—these were actions which, according to a Provençal ordinance, automatically involved deprivation of knightly privileges. It was also in Provence that a noblewoman was characterized as one who goes "neither to the oven, nor to the wash-house, nor to the mill".[9] The nobility had ceased to be defined by the exercise of a function— that of the armed retainer. It was no longer a class of initiates. It remained, however, a class distinguished by its mode of life.

. . . .

HAS THERE BEEN MORE THAN ONE FEUDALISM?

In the eyes of Montesquieu, the establishment of "feudal laws" was a phenomenon *sui generis*, "an event which happened once in the world, and which will perhaps never happen again." Voltaire, less experienced, no doubt, in the precise formulation of legal definitions, but a man of wider outlook, demurred. "Feudalism," he wrote,"is not an event; it is a very old form which,

[8] [*Dérogeance* was an act on the part of a nobleman which constituted an impairment of his rank and led to its forfeiture.]
[9] *Olim,* I, p. 427, no. XVII (Chandeleur, 1255); F. Benoit, *Recueil des actes,* passages cited above, p. 326, n. 1; M. Z. Isnard, *Livre des privilèges de Manosque,* 1894, no. XLVII, p. 154.

with differences in its working, subsists in three-quarters of our hemisphere."[10] Modern scholarship has in general rallied to the side of Voltaire. Egyptian feudalism, Achaean feudalism, Chinese feudalism, Japanese feudalism—all these forms and more are now familiar concepts. . . . Since it is obvious that all these societies, separated by time and space, have received the name "feudal" only on account of their similarities, real or supposed, to Western feudalism, it is the characteristics of this basic type, to which all the others must be referred, that it is of primary importance to define.

. . . .

Let us therefore try to bring in broad outline what we have learned about European feudalism, in the strict sense of the word, from its history. . . .

The simplest way will be to begin by saying what feudal society was not. Although the obligations arising from blood-relationship played a very active part in it, it did not rely on kinship alone. More precisely, feudal ties proper were developed when those of kinship proved inadequate. Again, despite the persistence of the idea of a public authority super-imposed on the multitude of petty powers, feudalism coincided with a profound weakening of the State, particularly in its protective capacity. But much as feudal society differed from societies based on kinship as well as from those dominated by the power of the State, it was their successor and bore their imprint. For while the characteristic relationships of personal subjection retained something of the quasi-family character of the original companionage, a considerable part of the political authority exercised by innumerable petty chiefs had the appearance of a usurpation of "regalian" rights.

European feudalism should therefore be seen as the outcome of the violent dissolution of older societies. It would in fact be unintelligible without the great upheaval of the Germanic invasions which, by forcibly uniting two societies originally at very different stages of development, disrupted both of them and brought to the surface a

[10] *Esprit des Lois*, XXX, I; Voltaire, *Fragments sur quelques révolutions dans l'Inde*, II (ed. Garnier, XXIX, p. 91).

great many modes of thought and social practices of an extremely primitive character. It finally developed in the atmosphere of the last barbarian raids. It involved a far-reaching restriction of social intercourse, a circulation of money too sluggish to admit of a salaried officialdom, and a mentality attached to things tangible and local. When these conditions began to change, feudalism began to wane.

It was an unequal society, rather than a hierarchical one—with chiefs rather than nobles; and with serfs, not slaves. If slavery had not played so small a part, there would have been no need for the characteristically feudal forms of dependence, as applied to the lower orders of society. In an age of disorder, the place of the adventurer was too important, the memory of men too short, the regularity of social classifications too uncertain, to admit of the strict formation of regular castes.

Nevertheless the feudal system meant the rigorous economic subjection of a host of humble folk to a few powerful men. Having received from earlier ages the Roman *villa* (which in some respects anticipated the manor) and the German village chiefdom, it extended and consolidated these methods whereby men exploited men, and combining inextricably the right to the revenues from the land with the right to exercise authority, it fashioned from all this the true manor of medieval times. And this it did partly for the benefit of an oligarchy of priests and monks whose task it was to propitiate Heaven, but chiefly for the benefit of an oligarchy of warriors.

As even the most perfunctory comparative study will show, one of the most distinctive characteristics of feudal societies was the virtual identity of the class of chiefs with the class of professional warriors serving in the only way that then seemed effective, that is as heavily armed horsemen. . . .

In feudal society the characteristic human bond was the subordinate's link with a nearby chief. From one level to another the ties thus formed—like so many chains branching out indefinitely—joined the smallest to the greatest. Land itself was valued above all because it enabled a lord to provide himself with "men" by supplying the remuneration for them. We want lands, said in effect the Norman lords who refused the gifts of jewels, arms, and horses offered by their duke. And they added among themselves: "It will thus be possible for us to maintain many knights, and the duke will no longer be able to do so."[11]

....

A subject peasantry; widespread use of the service tenement (i.e. the fief) instead of a salary, which was out of the question; the supremacy of a class of specialized warriors; ties of obedience and protection which bind man to man and, within the warrior class, assume the distinctive form called vassalage; fragmentation of authority—leading inevitably to disorder; and, in the midst of all this, the survival of other forms of association, family and State, of which the latter, during the second feudal age, was to acquire renewed strength—such then seem to be the fundamental features of European feudalism. Like all the phenomena revealed by that science of eternal change which is history, the social structure thus characterized certainly bore the peculiar stamp of an age and an environment. Yet just as the matrilineal or agnatic clan or even certain types of economic enterprise are found in much the same forms in very different societies, it is by no means impossible that societies different from our own should have passed through a phase closely resembling that which has just been defined. If so, it is legitimate to call them feudal during that phase. . . .

CLASS SOCIETY IN THE MELTING POT

Theodor Geiger

. . . A united proletarian class front against the capitalist system has neither grown

From *Die Klassengesellschaft im Schmelztiegel*, Kiepenheuer & Witsch, 1949. Reprinted by permission. (Translated by Celia S. Heller.)

[11] Dudo of Saint-Quentin, ed. Lair (*Mém. Soc. Antiquaires Normandie*, XXIII), III, 43–4 (933).

stronger nor expanded in modern times. The new proletarian sections of society—for example, the impoverished petty bourgeois groups and considerable portions of the white collar stratum—have reacted entirely differently than the industrial workers to their social situation; at any rate, they do not perceive socialism as the target of their interests. How strange it is to see a supposedly scientific train of thought[1] first assert that this attitude, deviating from the class consciousness of the industrial workers, is precisely typical for the bourgeois-infected proletarian groups, and then go on to designate this objectively described typical attitude as a false consciousness!

Within the working class itself a cooling of proletarian class consciousness and a split has taken place. There is a cooling as considerable parts of this class have risen in their income level to lower middle-class conditions. Their social attitude and thinking follows much more this changed income status than their relation to the means of production. They have become, as one says, *bourgeois* (*verbürgerlicht*). They no longer see their interests lying in the collectivization[2] of the means of production, but rather in the preservation and further improvement of their socioeconomic position within the existing society. In connection therewith a split has opened between "consciousness" and interests. Large portions of the wage-working class have found their place and have established themselves within the existing society. This class as such is a multitude of linked substrata that live in quite different circumstances. Opposite interests have therefore evolved *within* the wage-working class.

On the other hand—unexpectedly—the interest of the so-called capitalist class in the preservation of capitalism is wavering. This is connected with the previously mentioned change in the organizational form of the economy. The individuals who are in key positions in the capitalist economy, the leaders of the big enterprises, are no longer the owners but big executives

[1] Marxist thought. (C. S. H.)
[2] Geiger uses the German term "*Sozialisierung*" and I shall refer to it throughout the text as *collectivization*. I consider it closer to the German meaning than *nationalization*. (C. S. H.).

who are salaried employees. They are not directly interested in the preservation of the rights of property. Their kind will not disappear in case of full collectivization. They would pass from serving the stockholders to serving the state, but their function would continue essentially unchanged. It is very doubtful whether the far-sighted among them still think in the categories of capitalism-socialism at all. The representatives of today's capitalism are not committed to capitalism.

The true capitalist attitude, the interest in preserving the right of private property, is to be sought among the real owners—but this means today among the smaller to medium businessmen. Outright anti-socialism, that is opposition to the idea of collectivization, is still widespread among the intellectuals. However, their anti-socialist posture has nothing to do with the "relationship to the means of production" and is altogether divorced from their economic position. They do not stress the right of property, but economic freedom. They distrust the political conditions that appear to follow in the wake of collectivization and distrust the dictatorship that does not tolerate personal and, especially, intellectual freedom. Precisely therein the intellectuals today have found allies in all strata, not last among the working class itself. The activization of the class struggle and sharpening of psychological class contradictions anticipated and foretold by Marxism have not materialized. The interest fronts regarding the future social structure have shifted in a direction for which there is no explanation based on Marxist social theory. *"Scientific" Marxism has failed, confronted with the social reality of the twentieth century.*

. . . The Marxist model of industrial class society was presumably not inappropriate for the period of high capitalism. To be sure, a series of phenomena did not fit this model of stratification and therefore, at no time did the model give a complete picture of society. But one must consider that society has been seized by deep unrest since the breakthrough of industrialization. The structural changes no longer occur as a series of distinct conditions, each of which has its typical appearance, but rather do they form a continuous stream within which the various structures barely have time to unfold but, so to speak, are intertwined. They do not appear as consecutive states separable from one another but rather as changing trends of development. The society of Marx's time, viewed statically, was in no way dominated by the class principle. . . . What Marx saw—and adequately described—was a tendency toward the abolition of the then structural lines. What he predicted—and in this he erred—was the full development of the class structure. Class stratification never really emerged as a dominant state of stratification. Long before it was able to penetrate the whole society, other structural trends broke into the picture, deflected the stratification of "capital and labor" and obscured it. These new structural trends came to the fore before the preceding ones could mature. . . .

. . . The class society of Marxist coloring is obviously in retreat. No one can tell as yet with confidence which direction the development will take. But we can point out a number of competing trends and, with caution, venture some suggestions as to the weight and force with which they will contribute to the future formation of society. . . .

NEW LINES OF DEVELOPMENT

The Middle Strata. The first shift in the stratification lines proceded from the propertied middle stratum. Marxism counted that the struggle between capital and wage labor would become the fate of the entire society and define its features. This prediction came true in fact but in a manner surprising to its authors. The expectation was that individual members of society would increasingly solidify around the two poles of capital and wage labor. . . . A minority of middle tradesmen would with energy and luck advance to the ranks of capital but the majority would sink, would become proletarianized, and would finally join the anticapitalist front in its struggle. In this manner the final point in the unfolding of capitalism would be reached; after the collapse and liquidation of that system, socialism would come into being. The actual run of events was different. The class struggle between the opposite poles of capitalism and wage labor did not by and by seize the entire society and did not divide it into two hostile camps. However, this class struggle did give rise to a new constellation of fronts on a different plane. Let us see how this came about.

The class struggle between capital and wage labor did indeed become also the fate of the propertied middle stratum. It was directly on its way to proletarianization. But those partially caught and partially threatened by it refused to draw what the Marxists considered the only "reasonable" conclusion from their social destiny. Their sociopolitical stand oscillated between dull resignation and desperate uproar. The blind hatred of the artisans and petty industrialists against the large enterprises with which they were competing and the struggle of the small traders against the department stores and the consumer organizations remind one in their reactionary-utopian absurdity of the corresponding phase in the labor movement: the attack on machines by the Luddites.[3]

The following phase almost coincided with ... the economic recovery of the middle stratum. At that time the middle-class movement began, the realistic political (*realpolitische*) efforts of which were partly directed toward the organization of solidary self-help and partly aimed at legislative measures for the protection of the middle class, for the restoration and strengthening of the economic position of the small artisans. This realistic political struggle was not directed against the capitalistic system as such but against its development beyond the point where, through the continuous concentration of [big] enterprises, it became dangerous to the small and middle-size entrepreneurs. In this the middle-class movement proved itself hostile to progress and conservative in a narrow bourgeois way.

Curiously contradictory tendencies were at work underneath the ideological struggle

[3] A quasi-insurrectionary movement of working people in England who between 1811 and 1816 smashed new labor-saving textile machinery in a protest against reduced wages and unemployment attributed to their introduction. For a penetrating analysis of this movement, see E. P. Thompson, *The Making of the English Working Class*, New York: Vintage Books, 1966, pp. 547–602. (C. S. H.).

of the movement. The threat to the smaller traders by the big enterprises was answered by a deep, even hostile, aversion against "capital." One protested against being considered as part of the capitalist class that one feared and hated. Here the fact that the word "capitalist" had assumed an odious sound because of the obtrusive agitation of the labor movement may have played a psychological part. The ancient talk about solid workmanship of handicraft and the cheap factory output—long since bare of its old validity—was nevertheless continued in ideological propagandist form. Pseudo-theoretical arguments were brought forth in favor of competitive morality, which recognized as proper methods of competition precisely those that the small tradesman could cope with and could himself apply, while the underbidding made possible through the higher efficiency of the big enterprises was labeled as dirty competition. In practice the then continual and heated agitation against the formation of the monopoly of big capital did not fail to make a certain impression on the public.

The repulsion against capital did not manifest itself, however, in a corresponding good will toward the class-struggling enemies of capital. On the contrary! The anticapitalism of the bourgeois middle stratum limited itself to the competitive superiority of the large enterprises, to the progressive concentration and monopolization of enterprises. In contrast, it defended with tooth and nail the right of private property of the means of production as an economic and moral article of faith. The attack of the labor movement against the right of private property was totally misunderstood by the middle stratum—it considered the idea of collectivization a real horror. In addition, other factors created a deep chasm between the middle stratum and the organized working class. The religiously conventional petit bourgeoisie was not negligibly offended by the religious hostility of the labor movement of that day. But above all it experienced as a shocking challenge the Marxist prediction of a proletarianization of the middle stratum that was then obtrusively stressed by socialist agitators. This was, from the standpoint of the labor movement, the worst possible psychology of recruitment. The middle stratum reacted to it in a fully paradoxical manner. Even though it lived in state of constant fear of actually becoming proletarianized through the development of large capitalism, it turned with deepset indignation against those who predicted this very proletarianization.

Insofar as the economic and realistic political struggle of the middle stratum was mainly directed against large capital, its socio-ideological struggle was above all directed against the labor movement and its proletarian socialism. The middle stratum flattered itself in its propaganda with the fact that it was a protective "buffer" between the fronts of the class struggle but actually it felt helplessly squeezed between these fronts. It conducted a two-front struggle against both. The situation further deteriorated when a little later, right after 1900, the class struggle entered a regulated phase, partly because of the governmental social policy, partly because of legislative recognition of the wage struggle and collective bargaining. The anxious feeling grew that both powerful fronts—on one side capital and on the other side the mass organization—would fight out their class struggle upon the back of the middle class and conclude their truce at its cost. The engagement of the middle class on two fronts against both parties to the class struggle became transformed into a struggle precisely against the class struggle that threatened to pulverize it between its two fronts. . . . The class principle itself, the class society as a structural model, was a thorn in the side of the middle stratum. It is significant that from this perspective the designation middle class was experienced as an insult. The spokesmen of the movement always talked about the middle estate and thus symbolically placed their flock outside the model of a class society.

After the end of the nineteenth century this attitude received strength because the propertied middle stratum gave way to the so-called new middle stratum—that is, the private employees whose number at that time grew like an avalanche. The socio-political attitude of this new stratum was at the beginning not uniform and was insecure. On the one hand the employees recognized

that their position as a paid work force demanded a mass organization corresponding to the labor movement. On the other hand, their behavior toward the "proletarian" class front was largely aloof and even hostile. Many of them stemmed from middle-class small businessmen. They were themselves victims of the proletarianization of the industrial middle stratum, but ideologically they reacted against this, contrary to their destiny, precisely because they felt *déclassé*. They had a prestige need to open and deepen a social gulf between themselves and the workers.

Another part of the salaried employees' stratum derived from working-class families. They appreciated their transition from the factory to the office, from blue-collar to white-collar clothes, from the machine to the desk as a social advance and because of this they experienced a need to maintain a distance. I omit, but do not forget, those among them who joined the socialist workers' front. There were many of them and their number grew in time, not least because of the fact that the socialist parties became socially acceptable (*salonfähig*). In terms of the class structure in Marx's sense, the salaried employee was doubtlessly closer to the worker than to anybody else in modern society. Because of his prestige need for detachment from the working class he coveted the status ideology of the industrial middle stratum.

Out of totally different—and partly directly opposite—motives the industrial middle stratum, as well as a large part of the officials, nourished an aversion against the class model as such. . . . The last result of this new front formation was the bourgeois revolution of fascism and hitlerism. The "folk community" (*Volksgemeinschaft*) and the "corporate" ideas[4] were slogans unmistakeably directed against the class struggle idea. It was among this dissatisfied industrial stratum, among the lower levels of salaried employees with their suppressed ambitions that Mussolini and Hitler—and their henchmen in all countries —recruited their first followers. Here they found that mixture of narrow-minded brutality and sentimental "idealism" that

[4] Fascist concepts. (C. S. H.)

made an impression on their half barbarian and half confused political goals. *It is the joke of history that Hitler in twelve years contributed more toward the ruin of the industrial middle stratum than capitalism during the entire past century could manage.*

The brief role of the middle strata in big politics is a paradox of social history: a class denies indignantly that it is a class and it carried on a bitter class struggle against the reality and idea of the class struggle.

Class Structure and Income. The second line of development that worked against the class structure came from the distribution of wealth. Marx emphasized that the size of income had nothing to do with class position. The worker may be as well rewarded as possible, he is still cut off from the means of production. The producer may be on the verge of bankruptcy—he still disposes of the production apparatus. The class difference rests on the relation of the individual to the means of production, not his position as a consumer. This is basically so, but Marx does not underestimate the importance of income distribution. How else could he have ascribed in his theory of the development and the collapse of capitalism such an essential role to the supposedly progressive pauperization? The pauperization would sharpen the class antagonism and the class struggle. . . .

How the income distribution crossed class lines is to be described in greater detail. No matter what the doctrinaires of pauperization may claim, the actual position of workers has improved in absolute terms as well as relative to other strata. The entire picture is, however, more complex. A small group of individuals still have tremendous incomes. Apart from these few, an increasing income equalization has taken place. This was primarily accomplished in many countries by a strongly progressive income tax. Furthermore, there is the wage policy that remains limited in its effects on the relations between workers, salaried employees, and officials. Within the realm of wage and salary earners, the workers have achieved a much more favorable position through the organized struggle for better wages. In addition, within the last thirty years, the lowest wages more or less coincided with the movement of prices, and in

part outstripped them, whereas the compensation of those with higher incomes did not keep up with the rising prices. . . . Inside the working class itself there was the parallel occurrence of an opposite development. Some seventy years ago all workers were at the lowest income level of society. Since then in the wake of the specialization of industrial work the wages of workers have considerably varied. On account of this, specific categories of workers have been placed in varied favorable positions as consumers. The top wage categories come near the salaries of higher employees and officials. The workers in toto are better off but there is considerable variation within. . . .

So much for the facts. In order to fully appreciate their social significance, a view into social history is indicated. The stormy development of industry and large cities in the past century disolved the old traditions of status but also broke up the traditional consumption habits. Up until then for each social position there was a corresponding standard of living. A person in a high position owed to his social appearance a certain expenditure of wealth. The same was also true the other way around: it did not behove persons in modest positions to "raise themselves above their position" in expenditures. The standard of living that one could afford was not determined primarily by the available means but by the social position. . . .

In a time that is without traditional status symbols, the income position, the position as consumer, determines social status. Next to it the Marxist "relation to production" turns pale. To be sure, one can hardly speak of an income stratum. . . . A person either has or has not a share in the means of production. Here there is a clear boundary—even if not in each case, nevertheless in principle. Income, however, divides itself along a sliding scale. There is a contrast between Croesus and the have-not. Between these two, however, lie a thousand grades, and the majority of wage and salary earners are neither Croesi nor have-nots. The income scale is a continuum. . . . Indeed, one can divide the population into poor, of low means, well-off, and rich, but the boundaries between adjacent categories are arbitrarily drawn and are in reality fluid. The lowest of those of moderate means is farther away from the highest in his category than from the highest among the poor. Thus the income distribution no longer corresponds to the former class boundaries ... because it has put workers on an equal footing with certain groups from other classes. With that the class relation has lost much of its divisive strength. Most workers are, in terms of purchasing power and consumer habits, *petits bourgeois*. Insofar as they are not *petits bourgeois* in their political and social attitudes, it is due more to the labor-movement creed of the past century and to a doctrine that persisted because of convulsive propaganda rather than to the fact the "social consciousness is determined by social existence."

The Institutionalization of Class Conflict. A fourth line of development, the tension that crosses all class fronts has its origin in late capitalism and is therefore more recent.[5] It derives from the *institutionalization of class conflict.*

The wage workers used the method of coalition in their class struggle. The basic thought was to fight monopoly with another monopoly. The propertied bourgeoisie enjoyed, thanks to the legal institution of property, a monopoly over the means of production. Counter to them, the wage workers sought to create a collective monopoly of labor power through trade-union organization. These two monopolies complemented each other. Labor could only create goods by the use of the means of production; the means of production lay fallow without labor power. Therefore capital tried during the entire nineteenth century to prevent the creation of a labor-power monopoly, but in about 1900 the struggle was decided and the trade-union movement held the palm of victory in its hand. ...

Since then private ownership of the means of production and the mass organization of wage labor stand facing each other as the

two great powers of the economic structure. The collective contract means that organized capital and organized wage labor confront one another as two closed parties of the labor market. Collective bargaining and arbitration, if necessary forced arbitration, are only the last logical steps on this road.

The invaluable significance of this process can be expressed thus: henceforth class conflict was declared respectable (*salonfähig*) and was expressed less dramatically, and the tension between capital and labor was recognized as a structural principle of the labor market and raised to a societal legal institution. I have therefore designated the aforementioned process as the "Institutionalization of Class Conflict." The weapons, the methods, and the tactics of the class struggle are recognized and thereby brought under control. The conflict proceeds in accordance with definite rules of the game. Thus class conflict is deprived of its worst sting, it is transformed into a legitimate tension between power factors that balance each other. Capital and wage labor wrestle with each other, arrive at compromises, negotiate and decide on wage levels, hours, and other conditions of work. ...

The Managerial Revolution.

. . . .

The connection between democracy and capitalism has been discussed for a long time and is possibly more fervently disputed today than ever before. By democracy we understand a political form of organization under whose banner the people as a whole possess the power of government so that all participate equally therein. By capitalism we mean an economic system that rests on the private initiative of the owners of enterprises. It is well known that in the eyes of some the highest task of democracy is to overcome capitalism. Others maintain that political democracy alone is a farce as long as it is not supported by economic democracy, and the latter is defined as the exact opposite of capitalism. No matter what one's attitude, however, the fact is that the democratic idea arose in its time in alliance with capitalism. Also another connection between the two may be pointed to:

[5] We omitted the third line of development, the conflict between town and country. As Dahrendorf explains, the conflict between town and country "... presumably figures so largely in Geiger's book because it was first published in and for Denmark." Dahrendorf, *op. cit.,* p. 98.

Capitalism signifies a free scope of action and therefore the abstention of government from interference in the economic sphere. Thus capitalism can only thrive in a liberal state that is assigned a minimum of functions. On the other hand, as a matter of experience, since 1914 the frictions in the operation of democracy grew with the increasing scope of functions that the state arrogated to itself. This is not surprising, because such an increase brings with it a growing number of issues of conflict in state politics. Therefore, apart from basic considerations we may assert that there is a positive connection, both in a historical and practical sense, between capitalism and political democracy.

Unmistakable signs indicate that a profound change is taking place in the social structure—and in this Burnham is surely right—in fact it is already far advanced.

The concept of social structure refers among other things and above all to the distribution of power in society. Which is the ruling stratum? From a political–institutional point of view all share equally in democracy. It has, however, correctly been objected that this formal equality is confronted with the fact that in capitalist society the capitalist class possesses superior actual power—more accurately: used to possess it. Superior power—to follow Burnham's argument—is held by those who control the access to the economic resources of society and therefore enjoy income privileges. Now then, a capitalist is the owner of the means of production. Facing him stand the broad masses who obtain access to these means of production only through the work contract with the owner. Thus the capitalists control the economic resources of society, the capitalists skim the cream from the society's income, the capitalists are the ruling class.

But even within the framework of capitalist society the preceding propositions are subject to certain limitations. To be sure, the capitalist stratum has a monopoly over the material means of production. And a counterweight was already created with the unfolding capitalist society when workers through their trade unions organized a collective monopoly of wage labor, an economic resource of no lesser signif-icance than the material means of production. In the developed capitalist society capital and wage labor thus face each other as two organized fronts. Both are economic powerblocks and their balance shifts with the economic changes. In addition, it should be noted that political democracy shifts its center of gravity more and more in the direction of labor because the latter, thanks to its large numbers, was not only able to soften but even to cancel the privileged economic position of capital. And this then was indeed the course of affairs during the short history of democracy. Capital's freedom of movement was being noticeably diminished. We learned to view this development as social progress.

. . . .

For a long time socialism was considered the opponent and heir of capitalism. If capitalism rests on private initiative, socialism signifies that society as such steers the economic life. If the private ownership of the means of production is capitalism then socialism is the joint ownership of the means of production. Collectivization according to Marx is the expropriation if the expropriators. The state abolishes private ownership of the means of production and thereby makes also impossible any kind of economically privileged position insofar as such advantage is based on the control of the access to the means of production by single individuals or groups of individuals. That the latter is fallacious will become clear later. First I invite you to consider the right to property and its relation to collectivization.

The capitalist age has committed idolatry with the concept of property, buttressed by the theory of natural rights. Three ideas became especially prominent in the process:

1. The right of property is conceived as the relationship of a person to a thing and the content of this relationship is the dominion of the owner over the property.
2. Property belongs to the original rights of man and is therefore regarded as independent from the legal order. The right of property is there *a priori*, and legislation must merely protect it.

3. Property is inherently an unlimited dominion and yet its exercise can be limited by law in order to preserve the human rights of others.

The newer theory of jurisprudence unmasks the preceding conception as a legend. I shall attempt to show why. Already Marx—perhaps he was not the first but nevertheless he was more impressive than his predecessors—has demonstrated that the property relationship is not a relationship of a person to a thing but a relationship between persons in regard to a thing. The property relationship is a social relationship. Paul's property is the authority to exclude Peter and John from the use of the object of property. . . .

The meaning of the concept of property consists of the guarantee by society that the owner may use the property object in certain ways and that others should not disturb him in this, especially not by their own use of the object. The meaning of the right of property is therefore, concisely expressed, the conception of the right to dispose of a thing that society guarantees to an individual. And here something quite decisive comes to light. These rights to dispose are not consequences or derivatives of the right of property but they constitute in their aggregate the entire content of the right of property. Without them nothing is left of the right of ownership.

This leads us to the question of the limits of the right of property. Nowhere is it unlimited. Even the liberalism based on the concept of natural law (*naturrechtlicher Liberalismus*) imposes limitations. But notice: it perceives the right of property as an absolute in itself, as complete dominion, and limits only its use in certain respects. Such a distinction becomes senseless once one recognizes that precisely this guaranteed right to control is the only constant of the right of property. If one limits that, one limits the very right of property.

But furthermore: according to the liberalism based on the concept of natural law, the proper understanding of the general rights of men automatically and compellingly indicates in which way and direction the exercise of the right of property is to be limited. It is, however, not possible to set up an objective and universally valid criterion as to the threshold beyond which A's exercise of his right of property would violate the presumed legitimate interests of B or the general welfare. Everything depends here on the social structure and the concept of law (*Rechtsauffassung*) in a given place and time. And indeed the right of property is very diverse and varying in societies of different times and in different lands. Because, however, as it was explained above, the meaning of the right of property is nothing else than precisely the sum of the rights to control, socially guaranteed, the preceding can be better expressed in the following way. Instead of saying that the exercise of the ("inherently absolute") right of property is variously limited, we may express it: the right of property is a concept that, in different societies, comprises different contents of the right to control things. . . . Thus the talk of governmental or legal interference with property is completely senseless. Without a positive governmental or legal order there is no right of property with which one could interfere.

What conclusions follow for the ideas of collectivization from this conception that diverges from the metaphysics of natural law? If the content of the property relation is not a mystic authority over a thing, but quite simply the totality of the rights of control that are guaranteed in a given society, then the formal abolition of the right of property is a completely unimportant gesture. It comes down to this: what right to dispose of property is guaranteed to what persons by the positive legal order of a society? On the other hand, it is quite unimportant what legal term we use to designate the formal source of this right to dispose. The right of property is one term—any other term would do just as well. Despite his attempt toward a sociological concept of law, Marx remained nevertheless a son of the nineteenth century and a disciple of the metaphysics of that time. Capitalist society is possessed by the ideal of the sanctity of private property—its opposite, socialism, is not less blinded by the notion that the right of property is the work of the devil. Both endow the concept of property with a mystic content of reality. The striking force of socialism is directed against the myth of property. Supposedly its existence keeps capitalism alive, and its abolition will result in the means of production being under the collective control of society. But when the right of property is deprived of its magic blind faith, clearly neither the former nor the latter is shown to be the case.

One can imagine a society in which the formal juridical right of property is completely maintained but where its exercise is visibly limited. This simply means that the number, scope, and intensity of the owner's rights to dispose are diminished through so called public interference. Intervention brought special restrictions in the rights to control the means of production and because of this the right of property took on a different and more modest meaning. This reduction in the content of the right of property can and has been continued through a policy of taxation, regulations, allocation of raw materials, and so forth. One can conceive of a society that remains capitalist in the sense that it formally and juridically maintains the right of property, but it is emptied of all content. It no longer guarantees, especially in regard to the means of production, any rights to dispose. Interventionism has limited only negatively the rights of control: whatever was not explicitly prohibited was allowed. However, extensive economic planning made positive decisions how and for what the owner is to use his production apparatus. He receives his directives from the outside (from above) or is driven to one kind of production and prevented from another by the allocation of raw materials, fuel, and labor as well as price regulation. What he retains then is the title of property, the designation of owner without any content to it and also that income that derives from the arrangements forced on him.

Part of this income provides for personal expenses. The owner is not a capitalist because of this income. It corresponds to the salaries of the managers in the service of a socialist society. One is a capitalist thanks to that part of the income that through savings is newly invested. In a socialist society this part of the yield of a given enterprise goes to the collective, in capitalist society it takes the form of accretion in the wealth of the owner. But also the right of ownership of this saved wealth becomes hollow in the planned society. The owner cannot invest his wealth according to his own discretion and calculation. The public authority decides through money, credit, and investment policy and through the regulation of the production of capital goods where and how newly acquired money is to be invested. Thus it is true that the capitalist is the formal owner but he is robbed of all his authority to control his property. This is plain collectivization. The right of ownership is maintained as a legal institution but no authority (*Befugnisse*) can be derived from it. One could just as well abolish the right of ownership as such. The only difference would be in the terms, not in the substance. The society is capitalist in name, socialist (*sozialisiert*) in substance.

Thus I would like to substitute another concept for Burnham's concept of socialism. He denies socialism any chance of a future because the workers are neither capable of collectivizing the societal production apparatus or of gaining by force the use of the corresponding income privilege. Socialism is thus implicitly defined as rule by workers. It seems to me that a more practical concept would be that of designating as socialism any socioeconomic arrangement in which the right to control the means of production is no longer vested in the owner but in society as such. Naturally this does not mean that the "public" exercises this control and in this Burnham was right: the expropriation of the means of production does not put the workers or the collectivity into the possession of economic power.

The analysis of the right of property and the right to control it has its reverse side. Similarly to the society in which the right of ownership is formally guaranteed but through comprehensive economic planning made hollow, the so-called collective ownership of the means of production is only a phrase. If the concept of ownership is to have any real meaning it can only be the one that the owners are guaranteed certain rights of control. The socialist society does not recognize any owners authorized to dispose of property. And yet somebody must exercise control. It cannot be the general public as such. The ones who are authorized to dispose in a socialist society are the economic officials of the commonwealth (*Gemeinwesen*). It is a different circle of persons than that in capitalist society but, as there, it is a minority. To those deprived of control it does not matter who has the legal title to control property, and on what basis. One could answer that it nevertheless does matter whether the capitalist controls in his own interest or whether the official in a socialist society controls on behalf of the public. But again these are only words. The capitalist also claims that he proceeds in the public interest. But who can actually make him do it? In a socialist society the owner is deprived of the right to dispose and therefore also of the possibility of uncontrolled misuse of that power. In his place the economic official of the commonwealth has the power to dispose—and who actually has authority over him? Higher officials and so on until the peak of the hierarchy is reached. But not the public. And it is part of human experience that the occupant of a position of power takes care to know how he can use it for his own advantage. Both the private owner in capitalist society and the economic official in socialist society enjoy a position of power because of their control of the production apparatus. Both are also privileged because of a superior share in the social product. The difference lies solely in the formal legal base of the privilege. The institutions are of a different juridical structure, the phenomenon is essentially the same.

The right of property without the right of control over it is but a phrase. But whoever is authorized to control it enjoys a superior position that corresponds to ownership even if the title of ownership is abolished.

From these conditions one can arrive at a certain picture of the structure of future society. It must be admitted that those who dispose over the means of production and control the access of others to them are the ruling social stratum. Thus far there is no doubt that the capitalists were the ruling class in nineteenth-century Western Europe, that their influence weakened in the first half of the twentieth century and that in the Soviet Union it was completely abolished.

It is theoretically conceivable but highly improbable that the Western world would return to a free economy; that is, one that is autonomously regulated by its own mechanisms. If this were to happen, the power position of the owners of the means of production would become strong again. It is much more probable that we will follow the beaten track and will move toward a more systematic governmental regulation of the economy. . . .

Burnham saw well through the hollowness, that is, the purely ideological meaning of the concept of the natural right of property. He also described in certain breadth how the right of the owners to control has diminished in favor of society and has become replaced by governmental regulation of the economy. He saw quite well that in this respect the difference between Soviet Russia and the West is not one in direction as such but in methods and degree of thoroughness. Burnham also calls special attention to the fact that collectivization, which was brought about in the Soviet Union through revolution and with a bang, is proceeding in Western Europe and in America as part of a slower development. The owner of the means of production is forced out of his position of power through regulation and other interference. . . .

The nineteenth-century period of governmental restraint is at an end, the political system of trade has gained the upper hand over the economic one. We designate it as the primacy of the state over the economy. Something else is closely linked with it. In the liberal economy the single enterprise with its production apparatus is an autonomous economic unit—within the framework of economic legality. In the government-controlled economy the single enterprise becomes a dependent organ of the entire economic machinery of society. What the single enterprise produces with the help of its apparatus, how much and how it produces, what qualities, and so on—all this is decided by political channels, either directly by means of directives and orders or indirectly by the manner in which the state controls the flow of raw material, fuel, labor power, and credit that keeps production going. The single enterprise is no longer a productive autonomy.

Thus the owner of the enterprise, even though he is left with this legal title, has been robbed of his position of power. But I do not see how this power is to be transferred to the production personnel of the plant. The whole enterprise and its apparatus are organized within the total economic apparatus of society. No person whose functions are confined to a single enterprise can henceforth be assigned the right to control the production apparatus or to control the access to it by others. Economic life becomes centralized and the authority to control the total economic apparatus of society passes over to the state. Burnham is quite correct in this: that the system of economic planning corresponds to the bureaucratic form of political rule. He describes these parallels in all their breadth. But curiously he fails to see that political buraucratism (*Bürokratismus*) absorbs the economy itself—yes, that it comes into being exactly through nationalization (*Verstaatlichung*) of economic life. . . .

Now, then, our government is democratic: that is, we live under the rule of the majority. If the economy is to be subordinate to governmental authority, this could mean that the growing democratic majorities gain respective authority to control the total societal production apparatus. Economic power, in the same sense as political democracy, would thus come into the hands of "the people."

But it is known that those in whom power is vested institutionally do not necessarily possess it in actuality. The absolute prince lost his power to the professional bureaucracy whose specialized knowledge he faced as a dilettante. In democracy political power lies with the people as a whole but there are complaints everywhere that it is being slid over more and more from the hands of the people to those of the professional politician. Political affairs have become gradually so complicated that the individual is no longer able to comprehend them. The broad masses can never have power in their own hands but must entrust it to special organs. The real power position of the general public can therefore only lie in its effective control over the use of power by its trusted organs. This is its proper sense in the political sphere. So will it also be in

the governmental economic sphere—probably to a more marked extent yet.

The group of individuals that controls the total economic apparatus of society can be properly designated as the governmental economic bureaucracy. This bureaucracy began to form during the period between the two world wars. Regulation of prices, allocation of raw materials and fuel, taxing investments through money and credit policy, and other measures brought new administrative bodies into being. So a whole hierarchy of employees arises . . . and grows in number with the spread of economic regulatory measures. . . . These employees manage the societal power to control the means of production. They do not lean, as capitalists do, on the legal title of ownership but on something else by the name of office mandate or office authority. If the names differ, the phenomenon is to a large extent the same. In the hands of a small group of people is concentrated the power to dispose over the economic resources of society. This group is the ruling stratum of the future if society persists on the road to a planned economy. Within this bureaucracy the production heads of single enterprises constitute only external organs, local executive organs of the central economic bureaucracy. Only through this peripheral belonging to the state economic bureaucracy do they participate in the latter's collective position of power. On the other hand, the above described development also signifies a strengthening of the hitherto existing administrative bureaucracy. First of all, the total number of the corps of officials grows with the rise of the new economic bureaucracy. Secondly, thanks to the similarity in education, status, and function a narrow solidary relationship is formed between the old and new bureaucracy. Thirdly, the hitherto existing administrative functions and the new functions of directing the economy become interlocked in such a manifold way that a sharp dividing line between the corresponding official hierarchies can hardly emerge.

One may object that the corps of officials in a democratic political system behave in accordance with the orders of the political channels; that, properly speaking, the economic bureaucracy does not decide but rather the government does, controlled by parliament that, in turn, is watched by the electorate. It has already been suggested that today there is less control by the people over parliament and government than the proponents of democracy must have wished. When the state also takes over the direction of the economy then even the position of professional politicians is diminished. The economy offers an abundance of complex connections and problems, the knowledge and mastery of which demand expert technical knowledge of the highest order. Most laymen hardly have a notion of the existence of some of these problems, let alone the capacity to solve them. To some smaller extent this also applies to professional politicians. Parliament may make its decisions, the government and each single minister may give their directives, but they become rather powerless when the technical experts of the economic bureaucracy invoke invincible economic principles. They will largely have the last word, especially because the directives can be manifoldly modified in their practical application. . . . In a centrally planned economic and social order (*Wirtschaftsgesellschaft*), power belongs to the economic officials, and if the name bureaucracy sounds too forbidding, one may substitute for it "the rule of experts."

In its peculiar, indeed impressive, course, the democratic-capitalist society transforms itself step by step. Democracy and capitalism are the offspring of the same historical hour. Political equality and economic freedom go together. The rule of the people —the governmental form of political equality—becomes, because of practical necessity, the representative rule of the majority. With the unfolding of capitalism, the propertyless strata grew in number. With the consistent application of the democratic principle of equality they win the political majority. As propertyless they seek to weaken the power of the propertied. The political power of labor as a majority built a counterweight, nearly outweighing the power of the capitalist minority: political equality thus becomes the rival of economic freedom. Through their control of the governmental power apparatus the propertyless masses clipped the owners'

power to dispose over the means of production and also their autonomous initiative. Capitalism is thus being liquidated by democracy.

But next, the bell also tolls for democracy. Under the pressure of the majority, the democratic state takes hold more and more of the economic sphere: first in the form of intervention, then with regulation of the scope of enterprises, and finally through comprehensive economic planning. Democratic government becomes strong government, takes on new tasks and more of them, and also casts itself as the master over the economy. . . . Mounting governmental power breaks down the public's actual control over the governmental organs' use of power. And yet with the control of these organs by the public, democracy stands or falls. First comes the weakening of the power of voters in favor of the professional politicians. But then, apparently through the nationalization (*Verstaatlichung*) of the economy, the position of the professional politicians is weakened in favor of economic bureaucracy. The circle has been completed, a new social era gets off to its start. . . .

This prognosis naturally fits only the case of the planned economy—but this case it fits well. . . . With the elevation of open economic planning into an institution, the position of officialdom, at least economic officialdom, becomes quite different. It is a position that in the place of private entrepreneurs disposes over the economic resources and therewith gets the chance of income privileges. It is undeniable that there has risen also in Soviet Russia, in this dictatorial bureaucracy, a new stratum of both the powerful and the relatively rich. Their prosperity expresses itself not only in their salaries; it consists much more and to a growing extent of consumer privileges, apart from salary, that are connected to their function. It would indeed be remarkable if the masters of the productive apparatus were not to enjoy a rich bonus in the process of distributing the social product. . . .

In yet another respect—and with this we may conclude our reflections— it behooves us to put forth in hypothetical form the consequences of a planned economy for social stratification and to contrast them with the class theory of Marx.

Material economic factors determine, according to Marx, the social structure and especially the class structure of a society. The conflict of classes, whose members are in solidarity because of the equality in their position and social status, determines political behavior. This means, however, that the respective power constellation of the classes that are anchored in the economic plane determines the political institutions and measures of a society. Differently expressed, the material economic factors (EF) determine the class structure (CS) and the latter through the respective power constellation determines the political superstructure (PSS). This relation is shown in Figure 9.

$$EF \dashrightarrow CS \dashrightarrow PSS$$

Figure 9

It follows logically, as far as I can see, that this scheme of relationships can apply validly only within the boundaries of a liberal economic and social order. One could imagine that the prevailing dynamic-dialectic course of events—according to Marx's conception of history—has at a given point of time brought about a constellation of political factors that made it possible for those momentarily in possession of power to establish economic planning. . . . The productive forces will be brought under political control. . . . Consequently, let us assume that the class disposed toward planning and politically dominant in a given historical period ushers in not only what it considers a planned economy but also proves capable of keeping the officials in the planned economy under control. In this manner the whole course of dialectic change would be brought to a halt and Marx's casual relationship turned upside down (Figure 10). The political superstructure moves from the end of the chain to its beginning.

$$(CS \dashrightarrow) PSS \dashrightarrow EF \dashrightarrow CS$$

Figure 10

A given class structure has brought about a constellation of political factors that makes possible the transition to a planned economy and is thus utilized. The authorities that, thanks to this condition (class structure and its corresponding political superstructure), control the apparatus of the planned economy therewith also direct the course of the future social structure that depends on the formation of material economic factors. Those who possess power naturally make an effort to protect their key positions and their control over the planned economy. They therefore arrange the economic and political affairs so as to preclude a shift in the material economic factors. Such a shift would, according to the doctrine, entail a change in the class structure, and thereby in the balance of power, and threaten the power position of the then ruling class. The dynamic unfolding of economic capacity is thus brought to a halt by economic planning. . . . The economic and social order is placed under a stationary legality, in any case, a legality whose change is regulated. By purposefully shaping it, the masters of economic planning are able to determine the class structure of society. Invalid would be the objection that the productive forces in Marx's sense consist not only of purely economic material factors but also of technology whose further development within the planned economy could lead to surprising changes. Technical innovations can only change the material economic structure, can only become new economic forces if they are put into service; that is, if they are utilized in the production process. Total economic planning, however, naturally also signifies the control of technical means and proceedings. Innovations become either recognized or suppressed; the degree of technical rationalization is determined by the authorities. Thus whoever controls and governs the planned economic apparatus prevents the mobilization of newly discovered technical opportunities insofar as they threaten his power position in society.

The historical dialectic materialism of Marx—if there is still a grain of truth left within its content—applies only so long as the productive forces continue to be permitted to unfold according to their internal dynamics. The material economic factors constitute the independent variable in the historical and philosophic thought of Marx. Conversely, in a society with a pervading planned economy, the political power constellation with its corresponding superstructure of political institutions becomes the independent variable, and those who possess power know how to prevent its variation.

Thus, the science of Karl Marx is nothing but the anti-ideology corresponding to the liberal social reality of his time. Its conceptual models were derived from the time-bound liberal social reality and their value is limited by it. If Marxist practice were to succeed in casting aside the remainder of the liberal reality, the Marxist theoretical principles on which such political practice is based would become valueless.

PART III
Major
Dimensions of
Social
Stratification

Social inequalities are diverse and intricate, especially in the highly complex societies of today and even in those where all people are considered equal before the law. The inequalities must therefore be categorized in order to be studied and understood. The basic division along which our selections in this section are organized is one that has its roots in Marx's thought—objective and subjective dimensions. The first refers to actual inequalities—their sources, extents, and forms—whereas the latter refers to the perception, interpretation, and evaluation by the society in general, as well as by the individuals variously located in it.

In presenting the readings about the objective side of stratification, we in turn utilize the scheme adopted from Max Weber and arrange them under the subheadings (1) economic inequality (2) power inequality and (3) status inequality. The scheme served us well in the last section where, in the introduction to the readings on the principal types of stratification systems we analyzed each type in terms of its predominant dimension or factor of inequality. In studying modern societies this analytical framework is especially useful, because its stratification systems are more complex and are not characterized by such a close and visible correlation between the three dimensions—economic inequality and differences in power and prestige—that marked feudal and caste stratification.

Most of the readings in this section are based on empirical studies of stratification in the twentieth century. They will therefore, among other things, provide us with some basis for judging to what extent Geiger's generalizations about "post-capitalist society"—the last selection in the preceding section—are borne out by systematic observation. In each grouping of the present we made an effort to include materials on Soviet-type as well as Western-type societies.

OBJECTIVE DIMENSIONS

Economic Inequality. Considering that the economic factor is the predominant factor in class stratification we must note that it has been—as was brought out in the introduction to the preceeding section and some of its selections—almost completely neglected as a subject of empirical studies by sociologists. This may be partly due to the fact that it is considered the domain of economists rather than sociologists. Whatever the reason, it does explain why our selections on this subject are mostly from the works by economists.

Economic inequality must be approached in at least two important ways: in terms of distribution of both income and wealth. Before doing so it is worth noting that the representatives, defenders or ideologists of capitalism never denied the inequality of income and wealth. They simply justified its existence as representing just rewards for initiative, effort, intelligence, frugality, etc.—qualities which they held in great esteem and considered as meriting rewards. But after World War II we witness in Western societies (which still tend to be called capitalist but for which social scientists are increasingly adopting the name "welfare capitalism", the designation of their structures as egalitarian and the claims of a trend toward leveling in income and wealth. The latter was based on both common sense observations of post-World War II "prosperity" and affluence as well as elaborate analyses of official statistics. In England, for example, until the 1960s a remarkable agreement existed among economists and statisticians about a continuous movement toward greater equality in incomes since 1938. Then Richard T. Titmuss raised the important issue—which has been posed again and again in regard to many other problems, starting with Durkheim's concern about the statistics on suicide—about the validity of official figures on income and wealth. Reexamining the data on which the conclusions about greater equality were based, Titmuss found that tax returns were mostly used. But tax returns, he says, do not provide a complete picture of income distribution. *Yearly income* in the traditional sense of disposable cash gives a delusive picture of the state of affairs of the upper class because of a number of widespread practices such as the transformation of cash into benefits in kind, the spreading of "income" over life and over the lives of a few generations, and the transformation of income into capital. As he expresses it, ". . . all these make 'cash in hand' less necessary for the business of daily life for certain classes and living on overdrafts, trusts, and other forms of command over resources more fiscally rewarding if, at times, perhaps a little irksome."[1]

After examining the statistics and the validity of the conclusions that economists and statisticians drew from them, he infers that less is known about economic inequality today than is generally thought or admitted. Inequality has according to him, assumed new and subtle forms and the old statistical tools are not adequate for measuring it. Thus he warns that one needs to be more hesitant in suggesting that long-range equalizing tendencies are operating in Britain.

To judge from the evidence presented in our first reading, "What's Happening to Our Income Revolution?" by Herman P. Miller, neither do we have any basis for asserting that such a trend exists in the United States. True, we have the indisputable facts that real incomes are higher today in the United States than anywhere else in the world and that they have been growing steadily. But these facts are often used as if they were indicative of reduced inequality, which they are not. To talk about the latter, one has to compare relative income through time. Miller does

---

[1] Richard M. Titmuss, *Income Distribution and Social Change*, London: George Allen and Unwin, 1962, p. 293.

that and comes up with the finding that although inequality was being reduced during the war years and the immediate postwar years, income distribution has remained stable during the last twenty years.

What is particularly interesting is the reason Miller gives for studying the gap between the poor and the rich even though conditions are improving in America. He gives as his reason the feelings of relative deprivation on the part of those who have less, although he does not use this expression. Proceeding from the theories of Marx, Toynbee, and Veblen, he assumes that these feelings are widespread. Looking critically at this, one must point out that it is largely an empirical question—that is, only empirical studies can ascertain to what extent such feelings prevail today. Theoretically one can hypothesize that feelings of relative well-being are just as extensive or even outweigh those of relative deprivation, because a generation has experienced a marked improvement in its standard of living and is reminding its children of this improvement. However, all this is in the realm of the subjective aspect of stratification and we want to deal with the objective factors first, keeping them analytically separate from the subjective. In studying the objective side of economic inequality, the basic question is what the actual extent of inequality is —not how do people perceive it or experience it.

The technique used by Miller for comparing income distribution through time would also be appropriate in this kind of approach. Also suitable are cross-societal comparisons, which Miller pursues in the opening chapter of his book, and they show that incomes are about as evenly distributed in the United States as in Great Britain and more evenly distributed than in most other countries for which such figures are available.[2] But one could go beyond that by introducing an equalitarian model and measuring the extent of inequality in a given society at a given time or through time, as well as by comparing different societies, against this model. Thus, for example, taking the data presented by Miller, we would see that the lowest fifth of families and individuals in the United States has been receiving since 1944 only one-fourth of the income that would be theirs if there were income equality, whereas to the top 5 per cent went four times the income that they would receive under income equality. Interestingly, the next to the highest fifth of families and individuals has been receiving the share (22–23 per cent) that approximately corresponds to the equalitarian model. (See Table 2, p. 13.)

After exposing as a myth the contention that incomes in general are becoming gradually more evenly distributed, Miller goes on to deal with other misrepresentations on the theme of "a trend toward equalization." He shows that in the last ten years the income gap between whites and nonwhites has not been narrowing: on the contrary, there is some evidence of its having widened again. The same applies to the income differentials between skilled and unskilled workers.

In the last part of his essay, subheaded "Where Do We Go From Here?", Miller raises the issues of technological unemployment, of the American economy being plagued by relatively high unemployment since late 1957, and of the unskilled finding it increasingly difficult to find jobs. And these issues are the main subject of the selection by Gunnar Myrdal, who sees a trend in America toward the

---

[2] Herman P. Miller, *Rich Man, Poor Man,* New York: Thomas Y. Crowell Co., 1964, chap. 1, and summary on p. 31.

development of an *underclass* that is really not an integrated part of the nation. It is composed of unemployed, unemployable and underemployed persons and families at the bottom, to whom opportunities are becoming more closed while they are growing more plentiful for the rest of the nation. They are generally referred to as the poor, but social scientists have variously designated them as lower class (distinguished from the working class), the lower-lower class and more recently "the unstable poor," "the clinically dependent," and "the disreputable poor."[3] Whatever the designation, the descriptions of the characteristics of this group resemble Marx's references to the *Lumpenproletariat*. Here one finds demoralization and social pathology on a grand scale and the root of it, Myrdal argues, is unemployment. The aid given to these people, such as unemployment compensation, may keep them alive, but it is not the solution to the problems of demoralization and pathology bred by unemployment; on the contrary, it breeds more pathology. As Myrdal expresses it, ". . . there is no real cure for unemployment," and this cure is not forthcoming on a large enough scale.

That this phenomenon is not unique to the United States we gather from studies in Great Britain. There too you find poverty ". . . confined to particular groups in the population—mainly old people and workers in certain occupations or regions that have been left behind as a result of technological progress," groups separated from the working class at large whose material conditions have improved in the last decades.[4] However, if an underclass of unemployed, unemployable, and underemployed is thought of as a characteristic feature of highly industrial societies then the proposition has to be confined to so-called capitalist countries, for this phenomenon is absent in the Soviet Union and Soviet-type societies. It could be argued that there is in the Soviet Union an underclass, but then one would have to make clear that its origin, in contrast to that of the West, is not primarily economic but political. I am referring to the large numbers in the forced-labor camps of Siberia—widely known as slave laborers. They are there because they are deemed politically or socially undesirable. They are not underemployed, but, on the contrary, they constitute a source of cheap labor for the Soviet authorities. The plight of these captive laborers has gained some new attention as a result of the lately published memoirs and autobiographical novels of former camp inmates.[5] But exact studies of this Soviet underclass are non-existant.

Such studies even if few, do exist about economic inequality among the population at large in the Soviet Union (excluding the forced laborers). In his article "The Soviet Income Revolution," which is reprinted here, Murray Yanowitch focuses on income inequality since 1956, since de-Stalinization. The extent of actual inequality in the Soviet Union is of particular interest, because the Soviet regime came into power on slogans of economic equality. But the equalization that was brought about by the revolution was soon reversed by differential wages

---

[3] S. M. Miller uses the term "unstable poor," Hyland Lewis "clinically dependent," David Matza "the disreputable poor" See David Matza, "The Disreputable Poor," in Neil J. Smelser and S. M. Lipset, *Social Structure and Mobility in Economic Development*, Chicago: Aldine Co., 1966, pp. 311–340. S. M. Miller "The American Lower Classes: A Typological Approach," *Sociology and Social Research*, Vol. 48, No. 3, April, 1964. Hylan Lewis "Child Rearing Among Low Income Families" Washington Center for Metropolitan Studies, 1961.

[4] T. B. Bottomore, *Classes in Modern Society*, New York: Pantheon Books, 1966, pp. 42–43.

[5] See, for example, Alexander Solzhenitsyn, *One day in the Life of Ivan Denisovich*, New York: E. P. Dutton & Co., 1963.

as incentives for increased production.[6] As the inequality grew so did the ideological rationalizations that denounced equalitarianism as non- or antisocialist by labeling it petty bourgeois, and so on. By 1931, and until de-Stalinization, Yanowitch tells us, every major statement of Soviet wage policy contained such denunciations.[7] Thus, a government that called itself socialist promoted inequality in its territories while its admirers abroad were criticizing the economic inequalities in their own countries.

With de-Stalinization came a new wage policy that put much emphasis on *narrowing* the income gap between high- and low-paid personnel (not on eliminating inequality). Yanowitch examines the extent to which this policy has been implemented since 1956. The measures that he used to ascertain the trends in Soviet wages, as he points out and as the reader will soon learn, are summary measures of wage dispersion that, in contrast to Miller's measures, tell nothing about the share of total income received by a given percentage of the working population. But in footnote 9 of his article we find some data, based on Soviet sources, that make it possible to derive rough estimates of the shares of total income and to compare them cautiously to the data on income distribution in the United States. On the basis of the figures found there we calculate that since 1934 the bottom fifth of the working population received 10.2 per cent; the second fifth 14.9 per cent; the third fifth 19.1, the fourth 24.6, and the top fifth 31.2 per cent of the total wages. If one compares it to the distribution in the United States (see Table 2, p. 134), there seems to be in this respect less inequality in the Soviet Union. One must however, be very cautious in making such a comparison, for a number of reasons. First of all, the figures are not strictly comparable. If the American figures are only conservative estimates of inequality, the Soviet figures are even more so. The monetary bonuses and nonmonetary supplements of the top-income group are way out of proportion to those of the lower groups. This leads us to a more fundamental and more difficult problem of comparing inequality in the Soviet Union and the United States, which has been well captured in another connection by Andreski. He points out that the difference between a family that has to live in a corner of a room that it shares with two others and a family that has one room per person is greater than the difference between the latter and a family that possesses one hundred rooms. The difference between freezing and having adequate clothing is larger than between having, let us say, three suits and three hundred. [8] Need we say

[6] The question of incentives is again arising today in such countries as China and Cuba. It seems that in the latter it is a source of controversy between Castro and the pro-Soviet old-guard Communists. The latter are for financial incentives, which Castro opposes as fostering inequality. To promote greater equality he proposed a plan to abolish rent by 1970. As harbingers of the future, the following are now free: public telephones, funerals, and admission to ballparks. Castro champions "moral incentives" for increasing production insisting that "Men are capable of responding to moral factors." See "Castro Assails Old-Guard Reds," *The New York Times,* September 30, 1966; Juan de Onis, "Castro's Migrant Labor," *The New York Times,* February 10, 1968. In an interview with Mr. Mathews, a former correspondent and editorial writer for the New York Times, Castro said, "Communist countries like Russia are becoming more capitalistic because they are relying on material incentives more and more." But in Cuba, "We do not believe in the materialistic concepts of capitalism and other types of communism in which money is the incentive." He added that "Men live for more things than money" and went on to explain that in Cuba the ". . . . economic system is being planned, gradually and with much success, to create a society in which money will become unnecessary." See "Castro, an Interview, Confirms Soviet-Cuban Rift," *The New York Times,* December 21, 1967, p. 17.

[7] For a general article on Soviet stratification under the reign of Stalin, see Alex Inkeles, "Social Stratification and Mobility in the Soviet Union: 1940–1950," *American Sociological Review,* Vol. 15, 1950, pp. 465–479.

[8] Stanislav Andreski, *The Uses of Comparative Sociology,* Berkeley: University of California Press, 1964, p. 347.

that the first alternatives symbolize the conditions in the Soviet Union and the second in America? Lest we should become too philosophical for the taste of some readers, let us finish on a note of certainty. Even on the basis of the official figures there is a considerable amount of inequality in the Soviet Union if measured against the equalitarian model we proposed as a heuristic device.

To return to the subject of new trends, which is the main theme of the Yanowitch article, it is particularly worth noticing that since 1956 a narrowing of wage differentials between skilled and unskilled workers has been taking place in the Soviet Union (in contrast to the United States). But then it seems that the USSR has a shortage of unskilled labor, as compared with its recent overabundance in the United States. As for his measures of general wage inequality, Yanowitch found since 1956 a reversal of the 1934–1956 trend of growing inequality, so that wage inequality has been decreasing but still has remained greater in 1959 (his last figures) than in the late 1920s and 1930s. If the planned changes were to be realized, he says, the inequality would be further reduced. Subsequent studies indicate that by 1965 it was less reduced than was anticipated for that date by Yanowitch on the basis of the Soviet government pronouncements.[9] However, even if the plans were realized, the Soviet Union, as Yanowitch underlines, would still be far from an equalitarian society. One could add that equalitarianism continues to be condemned in the Soviet Union as a goal for now. For instance, the March 4, 1966, *Izvestia* column, "Talks with Readers," was devoted to comments on "Ours and 'Mine' in Theory and Life." Here we find such statements as: ". . . there is not and cannot be yet complete equality here because people's labor is not equal. . . . There is not and cannot be as yet equality in income and in the amount of personal property here. The CPSU [Communist Party of the Soviet Union] has never assented and will never assent to the principle of leveling since it reflects petty bourgeois attitudes and operates against the interests of the working people. The Party is taking all possible steps to *reduce* the difference between high paid and low paid categories of workers. But this difference can be reduced to a minimum *only gradually*." (Italics supplied.)[10]

Whether or not the Party is "taking all possible steps," we gather from Yanowitch's objective analysis that the inequality in income distribution is being reduced. He finished, however, on an important note that it is not "at all clear . . . that inequality in the distribution of political power is moving in the same direction." And it is this inequality in power that, according to many sociologists, is the most significant factor of Soviet stratification.

Power Inequality. In the selection from his book, *The New Class,* Milovan Djilas maintains that in the Communist states a governing class exercises complete control over the society through power, ownership, and ideology. Of these three factors, power is the one that played and still plays the most important part: it constitutes "the basic characteristic of communism." What distinguishes Communist power is its being almost exclusively an end in itself "because it is both the source and guarantee of all privilege." This power is in the hands of a new class, a political bureaucracy resembling the ruling classes of other societies, except that its power is more complete and less subject to restraint. It developed gradually from the very

---

[9] See Janet G. Chapman, "The Minimum Wage in the USSR," *Problems of Communism,* Vol. XIII, No. 5, September-October, 1964, pp. 76–79.

[10] Condensed text reprinted in: *Current Digest of the Soviet Press,* Vol. XVIII, No. 9, March 23, 1966, p. 5.

narrow group of "professional revolutionaries" into a "class of owners and exploiters." Here Djilas pursues a Marxist analysis by arguing that the new class is the
actual owner of the means of production. Collective ownership is but a façade,
because the new class disposes with property and exercises exclusive control over it.
(Note the similarity to Theodor Geiger's analysis.) The monopoly it establishes in
the name of the working class turns out to be primarily a monopoly over the working class itself. Finally, Djilas predicts at the end of the excerpt that, as did other
ruling classes, this one will have its end. And when this occurs ". . . there will be less
sorrow over its passing than there was for any other class before it." It is
noteworthy that these words come from a person who helped to bring this
"class" into being in Yugoslavia and who was for some time one of its prominent members. This leading Communist, former vice-president of Yugoslavia
and friend of Tito, was expelled from the Party in 1954 and in 1956 sen-
tenced to serve a ten-year prison term for expressing the ideas contained in the
New Class.

When we shift our attention to power inequality in the United States, we are
struck by it complexity as compared with the Soviet type of power. Numerous
empirical studies have been conducted on the power structure of various American
communities and they present a far from uniform picture. Richard A. Schermerhorn
reviews under four headings the findings of these studies in the selection on "Power
in the Local Community." First comes the question of governmental versus
nongovernmental control, and here the findings are fairly consistent. American
communities that have been studied display more reliance on nongovernmental
rather than governmental control, on private rather than official leaders, on
business leaders rather than men from other walks of life. When it comes to the
second theme, the pattern of power distribution, the studies show wide differences.
Subsequent to the Schermerhorn analysis, Peter Rossi has nevertheless discerned
three main types of community power structure, the first two being very similar
and differing only in the number of decision makers who share power among
themselves. (1) Pyramidal—the ultimate source of power is in one man or a very
small number of men. He (or they) makes major policy decisions that are carried
out by the lower echelons. Examples are the Lynds' Middletown and Hunter's
Regional City. (2) Caucus rule—"Lines of power tend to end in a relatively large
group of men who make decisions through consensus. Decision making tends to
be a matter of manufacturing consent among the 'cozy few' who make up the
caucus." An example is Rossi's Mediana. (3) Polylith—there are separate power
structures for major spheres of community activity, such as local government in the
hands of professional politicians and community service organizations in the hands
of businessman and professionals.[11]

The third heading under which Schermerhorn reviews the findings of various
studies is, "What issues are decided at what levels in American Communities?"
Here the primary concern is with the nature of the issues that are kept out of the
arena of public discussion, as compared with those that are allowed to reach the
attention of the public. Again, there is no uniformity in the findings. And finally he
examines the role-images of the leaders in the communities. Public opinion, community confidence in leadership—he argues—may determine what can or cannot be

---

[11] Peter H. Rossi, "Power and Community Structures," in Lewis A. Coser, ed., *Political Sociology*,
New York: Harper & Row Publishers, 1966, pp. 132–145, especially pp. 142–143.

done by those who wield one type of authority or another. But the information on this score is far from conclusive.

One should add that the studies of community power have been criticized on methological grounds. Because many of them employed the reputational method in order to ascertain the distribution power, the issue has been raised whether reputations of power are an adequate index of its distribution.[12]

It is worth remembering that at first those who have studied the power structure in given communities were convinced that they were getting by this means at the power structure of the country at large. With time this optimistic view was challenged and voices were heard that the power distribution in the United States was not merely the sum of its distributions in local communities. After all, the focus of those studies was on community decisions, for the basic question about community power is who has more to say, or can have more to say, about things that affect people in that particular community. These decisions are quite minor as compared with those on the national scale that determines the future of the society at large.[13] Even if we had a thorough knowledge of community decision making, we would gain from it very little knowledge about the decisions that affect the whole nation. And yet despite the wide recognition that community and national power refer to different "orders of phenomena," few sociological studies of the national power structure have been made. Thus C. Wright Mills' *The Power Elite* remains the significant but highly criticized work in this area.[14] Mills interprets the American power system in terms of a power elite that makes the top decisions in the economic, political, and military spheres and a powerless mass at the bottom. His interpretation has been and continues to be subject to much controversy. It's validity has been challenged on both theoretical and factual grounds.

Talcott Parsons, for example, characterized C. Wright Mills' approach to power as a "zero-sum" conception and criticized it as not fitting the actual phenomenon of power in complex societies. According to this conception, Parsons explains, ". . . there is a fixed 'quantity' of power in any relational system and hence any gain of power on the part of A must by definition occur by diminishing the power at the disposal of the other units B, C, D." But, believes Parsons, this is not how power operates in "advanced" national societies. He conceptualizes power as a circulating medium, analogous to money, so that a "systematic extension of power spheres without sacrifice of the power of other units" often occurs.[15]

Suzanne Keller, on the other hand, criticizes the validity of the data and their interpretation in *The Power Elite*. According to her, there is a marked inconsistency between elaborate empirical documentation and sweeping generalizations without sufficient evidence. Where empirical evidence is presented it is not always thoroughly examined. She maintains that "Mills' own data do not firmly support his conclusions concerning the increasing social uniformity and ascending power of the leading elites in American society."[16] Perhaps most surprising of all criticisms is the one by Dahrendorf who designates *The Power Elite* as showing traces of a

---

[12] Raymond E. Wolfinger, "Reputation and Reality in the Study of 'Community Power'," *America Sociological Review*, 25, October, 1960, pp. 636–644.
[13] William Spinard, "Power in Local Communities," *Social Problems*, 12, Winter, 1965, pp. 335–356.
[14] C. Wright Mills, *The Power Elite*, New York: Oxford University Press, 1967.
[15] Talcot Parsons, "On the Concept of Political Power," Reinhard Bendix and Seymour Martin Lipsett, eds., *Class, Status and Power*, 2nd ed., New York: Free Press, 1966, pp. 240–265. Direct quotation from p. 261.
[16] Suzanne Keller, *Beyond the Ruling Class*, New York: Random House, 1963, p. 109.

conservative view. (This work, as well as many of Mills' other writings, has been often characterized as leftist in position). Dahrendorf labels it conservative in charging that Mills does not take full cognizance of the consequences of separation of ownership and control in American society.[17] But irrespective of the nature of critisicm, the striking fact remains that no serious sociological discussion of power in America or in modern society in general fails to refer to Mills' work.

Foremost among such discussions is T. B. Bottomore's *Elites and Society*. The excerpt here, "From the Ruling Class to the Power Elite," represents his much-applauded effort of clarifying and reconciling the two competing concepts of ruling class and power elite. In his critical examination of the two concepts he points to the work of Mills as exemplifying most clearly the difficulties in the concept of governing—or power elite. (As Bottomore rightfully reminds us, Mills was influenced by theories that are considered contradictory, on the one hand by Marx and on the other by Mosca and Pareto). In Mills' study of the power elite there is an explanation of the power position and its three principal components. The power position of business executives is explained by the growth in size and complexity of business corporations, of the military chiefs by the growth in scale and expense of the weapons of war, and of the national political leaders by the decline of the legislature. But, says Bottomore—and this writer does not entirely agree with him—Mills does not explain why there is not one but three power elites. I disagree because Mills does concern himself with the basis of its unity. He talks about their easy intermingling because of similarity in origin, education, and style of life. But what is perhaps even more compelling is Mills' contention that they have many "points of coinciding interest" and that at times their unity is that of "explicit coordination" for the purpose of common interests.[18]

However, if we return to the main aims of Bottomore's essay, we do find that he successfully solves for us the riddle of which way the two concepts—ruling class and governing or power elite—are alike and in which way they differ. Both, says he, emphasize the division between rulers and ruled as one of the most important facts of social structure. But the division is stated differently: ". . . the concept of a 'governing elite' contrasts the organized, ruling minority with the unorganized majority, or masses, while the concept of a 'ruling class' contrasts the dominant class with subject classes, which may themselves be organized, or be creating organizations." From these different conceptions, Bottomore adds, come the differences in the way of conceiving the relations between ruler and ruled. One could add that they are also the bases of contrasting views of the future. We noted the optimism of Djilas, which we can now see as being tied to his conception of the ruling group as a class rather than elite and the bottom as a subject class with the potential of becoming organized. In comparison, Mills' view of the future is a pessimistic one, for at the bottom is a mass of politically uninterested beings, shortsighted concerning events outside their immediate experiences.

But if we were to agree with all that Bottomore says we would have to conclude that Djilas' optimism has no basis in the reality situation, for his concept of new class does not fit the reality of Soviet-type societies. According to Bottomore the actual power structure of the Communist countries approaches the "pure type of a 'power elite'." It is regrettable that he does not deal at this point with the Djilas

---

[17] Ralf Dahrendorf, *Class and Class Conflict in Industrial Society*, Stanford: Stanford University Press, 1959, p. 43.
[18] Mills, *op. cit.*, p. 19.

argument, a crucial one: that the power group in these countries is a class because it exercises complete control over property.

Conceivably one could resolve the dilemma of whether the ruling group in a Soviet-type society is a class or an elite by concretely applying in the analysis of these societies an idea found in the conclusion of Bottomore's essay. I have in mind the thought that the ruling class and power elite "may be seen as complementary concepts which refer . . . to different aspects of the *same* political system" (italics supplied), as well as to different types of political systems. As far as I know, no one has pursued successfully this sort of analysis in regard to Communist countries.

Also worthy of being stressed in the conclusion is the author's explicit program of what can be accomplished with these two concepts. As he expresses it, "With their help we can attempt to distinguish between societies [a] in which there is a ruling class, and at the same time elites which represent particular aspects of its interests; [b] societies in which there is no ruling class, but a political elite which founds its power upon the control of administration, or upon military force, rather than upon property ownership and inheritance; [c] and societies in which there exists a multiplicity of elites among which no cohesive and enduring group of powerful individuals or families seems to discoverable at all."

Yes, we can attempt to classify in the above suggested manner and, in dealing with past societies, perhaps achieve some consensus. But when we deal with contemporary society, different social scientists, with perhaps equal devotion to objectivity, place the same society in different categories of this classification. This is vividly exemplified in the two contrasting pictures of the structure of power in American society drawn by two American sociologists writing in the 1950s—C. Wright Mills and David Riesman. Riesman's picture is not that of a power elite but of "'veto groups' among which power is dispersed."[19] Thus, according to him, there is no single unified power at the top of the structure, as asserted by Mills, but an "amorphous power structure." It consists of a ". . . series of groups, each of which has struggled and finally attained a power to stop things conceivably inimical to its interests and, within far narrower limits, to start things."[20] Riesman's picture of the American power structure resembles then type C, whereas Mills' is type B in the Bottomore classification. Which is right? Regrettably the question remains unanswered, for the evidence on both sides of the controversy is rather sketchy. Thus, one cannot do better than finish on the usual note that more disciplined historical and comparative research is needed as a solid empirical basis for evaluating who is right, Mills or Riesman.[21]

Status Inequality. Where the research is rather plentiful is on the dimension of status inequality. This becomes especially interesting if one holds the view that the power and economic aspects are more important factors of stratification. It is the position of Lenski, among others, who made little attempt in his book on stratification to examine prestige inequality. He justified it partly on the grounds ". . . that

[19] David Riesman, "The Images of Power," in *The Lonely Crowd,* New York: Doubleday Anchor Edition, 1953, pp. 239–271. Later, two books have appeared, continuing the controversy—the first is consistent with the thesis of Mills and the second with that of Riesman: G. William Dornhoff, *Who Rules America?,* New Jersey: Prentice Hall, 1967; Arnold M. Rose, *The Power Structure,* New York: Oxford University Press, 1967.

[20] *Ibid.,* p. 247.

[21] William Kornhauser, "'Power Elite' or 'Veto Groups'?" in S. M. Lipset and Leo Lowenthal, eds., *Culture and Social Character,* New York: Free Press, 1961, p. 267.

prestige can be understood more readily as a function of power and privilege than the other way around. " He holds that while ". . . there is a certain element of feedback, the major causal flow . . . [is] from power and privilege to prestige. " [22] Although we might take some issue with this generalization, based on the analysis of caste in the preceding section of this book, it nevertheless fits well the system of contemporary stratification in industrial society. The future historian of knowledge may be puzzled that the stratification studies of the most industrial country of our time concentrated so heavily on status to the neglect of power. The fact that empirical investigations of stratification in America began with small towns—and small towns in New England at that—may hold the key to this puzzle. (We use here and throughout this discussion the term *status* in Weber's sense or, as Mayer rephrased it, as ". . . the *differentiation* of prestige and deference among individuals and groups in a society. ")[23]

It was W. Lloyd Warner who opened the floodgates of empirical studies, to borrow Hodges' metaphor, [24] when he led a research team of social anthropologists into the New England seaport of Newburyport, a town of 17,000 inhabitants, which he called Yankee City. That is why, mindful of the methodological criticisms to which Warner's work has been subjected, [25] I nevertheless agree with Milton Gordon's conclusion that "All in all, American sociology owes more of a debt of gratitude to this social anthropologist who transferred his attention from the aborigines of the Australian bush to the good citizens of Yankee City than has hitherto been acknowledged."[26] Other studies of stratification in small towns in America by Warner and his colleagues followed the Yankee City series. He summarizes the findings of all in the excerpt from the book *Social Class In America,* which is reprinted here.

In the first part of the selection is found the theoretical orientation of Warner and his collaborators. They make clear that in talking about social class they refer to a status of rank hierarchy. (Later in the book from which this selection is taken, this is made even more explicit in the authors' formal definition of class as "two or more orders of people who are believed to be, and are accordingly ranked by all members of the community in socially superior or inferior positions.")[27] Then the authors proceed to a functional explanation of social class in America. It exists, according to them, because the social structure of complex societies "must have rank orders to perform certain functions necessary for group survival." The main function of stratification, they elaborate, is an integrative one. This is the very opposite of the view of class found in Marx: in Marx's conception, class divides society; in the above functionalist view, social class unites and solidifies society. But then one must recall that Warner's meaning of social class is different from that of Marx. This is especially worth noting because Warner claims to have

---

[22] Gerhard E. Lenski, *Power and Privilege*, New York: McGraw-Hill Book Company, 1966, p. 430.
[23] Kurt B. Mayer, *Class and Society*, New York: Random House, 1955, p. 24.
[24] Harold M. Hodges, *Social Stratification*, Cambridge: Schenkman Publishing Company, 1964. p. 63.
[25] See, for example, Harold P. Pfautz and O. D. Duncan, "A Critical Evaluation of Warner's Work in Community, Stratification," *American Sociological Review*, 15, April, 1950, pp. 205–215; Ruth Kornhauser, "The Warner Approach to Social Stratification," in R. Bendix and S. M. Lipset, eds., *Class, Status and Power*, Glencoe, Illinois: Free Press, 1953, pp. 224–255.
[26] Milton M. Gordon, *Social Class in American Sociology*, Durham, N. C.: Duke University Press, 1958, p. 123.
[27] W. Lloyd Warner, with Marchia Meeker and Kenneth Eells, *Social Class in America*, Chicago: Social Science Research Associates, 1949, p. 129.

begun his studies with an economic conception of class borrowed from Marx.

He explains that his concept was changed when he discovered in Yankee City that the divisions were not strictly along economic lines and that money alone did not guarantee high social position. And yet, when we examine critically what he tells us about the highest stratum among the six he delineates—the upper-upper, whose rank is determined by lineage,—we discern that the ultimate source of the status is nevertheless money, even if it is only a certain kind: "old money" that has been in the family for generations. What I am suggesting is that Warner's evidence, contrary to what he claims, shows wealth to be the basis of status in Yankee City and the other towns, but in order to be at the top of the status hierarchy one must either have old money or "translate new money" into socially approved behavior and possessions.

In this respect Yankee City and the *stetl* in prewar Poland bear some similarity, as can be observed in our next selection: "Social Stratification of the Jewish Community in a Small Polish Town," by Celia Stopnicka Heller. Wealth alone did not assure a person of status in the Jewish community. It was a source of prestige only insofar as it enabled a man to contribute to the welfare of the community, to do "good deeds" and to give to charity. But no matter how it was used, it was a source of power. Those wealthy individuals who did not use a part of their money in the prescribed manner were nevertheless accorded deference, even if it were spurious, in order to prevent them from exercising power against one. This suggests that, contrary to numerous sociological formulations, including the preceding definition of status by Kurt Mayer, deference is tied not only to prestige but also to power. Deference accorded because of power superiority may, however, be either real or spurious. It is likely to be only spurious if power ranks low in the normative system of a society, as it did in the Jewish culture of Poland.

The power of money and material goods also throws light on the pronounced manifestation of conspicuous consumption in the Jewish community. Since Veblen's formulation, conspicuous consumption has been largely seen by sociologists as a symbolic claim of status.[28] And yet in the small town Jewish community of Poland conspicuous consumption was more tied to power than status. First of all, by parading one's money in terms of conspicuous consumption one was not likely to win prestige because, as we have noted, money alone was not the source of it. Furthermore, ostentation was strongly discouraged in the process of home socialization on the grounds that it would make others jealous and would strengthen the hostile attitudes of the Gentiles. Despite this it was quite prominent. Conspicuous consumption performed two functions: it served notice that one was powerful enough to deal with the hostile outside world and that one was capable of dispensing favors.

Because money was considered an unstable commodity, it was expected that one would use it to obtain the greater and more lasting sources of status: lineage and learning. The traditional meaning of education in the *stetl* (small town) deserves special attention; it was very different from that in modern industrial society. In modern industrial society, education, perhaps even more than money, needs to be translated into socially approved behavior—proper occupation—to be a source of prestige. Thus the observation that Warner made about money and prestige in Yankee City applies, I think, even more to education. In contrast with

[28] Thorstein Veblen, *The Theory of the Leisure Class*, New York: Macmillan, 1899; new ed., New York: Mentor Books, 1953.

this, in the *stetl*, education needed no further validation to yield prestige: it was an unqualified source of it.

The pattern of stratification described in this article involved most of the Jews in prewar Poland, because three-fourths of the Jewish population lived in small towns. But the critics have increasingly questioned whether the small town represents America, a claim made by Warner and picturesquely expressed in his phrase "Jonesville is in all Americans and all Americans are in Jonesville. . . . To Study Jonesville is to study America."[29] After all, census data show that the big cities and their suburbia are increasingly more representative of America, and sociological analysis reveals that the dominant forces of society are located there, rather than in small towns.

Now, as Kurt Mayer explains, prestige rests on interpersonal recognition that always involves at least one individual who claims deference and another who honors this claim.[30] The description of status hierarchy in small towns, where every one knows everyone else, is therefore far from a description of prestige stratification of American society at large. How does it operate in the anonymous, impersonal city, with its fleeting social contacts and segmented activities? What about prestige and stratification in the metropolis or megalopolis? We do lack systematic studies that tackle such questions, but they are beginning to be explored.

Bensman points to the existence of status communities as the vehicle of prestige differentiation in urban society. These are not territorial communities but what he calls communities "of shared meanings."[31] Perhaps it is an awkward designation and *nonterritorial* would have sufficed, for what is most significant here is that in contrast to small towns, territory is not relevant.[32] As Bensman expresses it in terms of the musical community, his case study, the professional musician may be more at home in the concert halls of New York or Moscow than in the apartment of his next-door neighbor. It is a community in the sense that in it "the individual chooses to live out his major life interests."[33]

He talks about the "multidimensionality" of prestige or status in urban society. It refers to the contended fact that there are different sets of prestige values within the same society, each status community having its own set of prestige values. Thus there is a vast array of prestige values or sources of status that, in their totality, may be interrelated but often are in conflict. According to Bensman, the prestige one receives in the society at large is based on how one's status community rates in the society and on his imputed position in that status community.

Bensman maintains that in a complex urban society, status communities are not only the "basic vehicle" of prestige stratification, but also of "the total pattern of life for much of the urban population at large."[34] I would take issue with both of these, for I doubt that status communities are characteristic of the

[29] W. Lloyd Warner, *Democracy in Jonesville,* New York: Harper & Brothers, 1949, p. xv.

[30] Kurt B. Mayer, *op. cit.,* p. 24.

[31] Joseph Bensman, "Status Communities in an Urban Society: The Musical Community," paper delivered at the Annual Meeting of the American Sociological Association, August, 1967.

[32] Similarly, Charles Kadushin, tracing himself to Simmel, points to "social circles" as units of mass society. They are "nongeographical communities" of "like-minded persons." See his "The Friends and Supporters of Psychotherapy: On Social Circles in Urban Life," *American Sociological Review,* Vol. 31, December, 1966, pp. 786–802.

[33] Bensman, *loc. cit.,*

[34] *Ibid.*

working class. If anything, territorial communities are the pattern, as is reflected dramatically in the fights of juvenile gangs over the boundaries of territories. In contrast to the professional musicians who, the author tells us, draw their friends from among professional musicians and devoted amateurs and find their marriage partners among them, workers, and especially their children, tend to make friends among neighbors and marry the girl or boy next door or the high school sweetheart. Much of the social pathology of urban areas may, however, be the result of the breakup of lower-class territorial communities with no corresponding development of nonterritorial status communities.

But Bensman's contention (and my criticism of it), could only be settled through empirical research into the problem of how representative status communities are of the society at large or of certain layers of society. Such research is, of course, lacking, because the concept of the status community is a recent one. In contrast, the aspects of status stratification that has been thoroughly investigated is occupational ranking. As a matter of fact, the prestige hierarchy of occupations is probably the best-studied aspect of stratification systems of contemporary societies. Extensive empirical investigations have been conducted on this subject in different types of societies, so-called capitalist and socialist, developed and developing. A few studies have also appeared comparing the occupational hierarchies of different countries, starting with the pioneering and influential work of Inkeles and Rossi that appeared in 1956.[35] Inkeles and Rossi examined comparable occupations in six industrialized countries: (the only ones for which data were available then) the United States, Great Britain, New Zealand, Japan, Germany, and the Soviet Union, in order to test two contrasting positions—the *structuralist* and *culturalist*—on the relation between the standardized modern occupational system and the value system of a given nation. The structuralist position holds that the modern industrial occupational system is a highly coherent one, tied to the requirements of industrial society and little influenced by traditional values. In contrast, the culturalist position is that the particular values of a nation would result in a differential evaluation of modern occupations within that nation. Inkeles and Rossi found much evidence to support the structuralist position. There was remarkable agreement on the prestige accorded by popular opinion to comparable occupations in the six countries (twelve of the fifteen coefficients of correlation were above 0.9), despite differences in culture—especially pronounced between Japan and the rest—and differences in form of government—especially marked between the Soviet Union and the rest. Actually, the author's explanation of the similarity was expressed in terms of two causal factors: First, there "... is a relatively invariable hierarchy of prestige associated with the industrial system" and secondly, the countries compared have in common the characteristic of a national state.[36]

The influential and widely accepted thesis presented in this article was a bit shaken when studies in developing nations came forth, showing rankings of occupations similar to those in industrialized countries.[37] Subsequently Hodge, Treiman, and Rossi addressed themselves to an explanation of this uniformity in

---

[35] Alex Inkeles and Peter H. Rossi, "National Comparisons of Occupational Prestige," *American Journal of Sociology*, Vol. 61, January, 1956, pp. 329–339.

[36] *Ibid.*, p. 339.

[37] See, for example, on occupational ranking in Indonesia, Murray Thomas, "Reinspecting a Structural Position on Occupational Prestige," *American Journal of Sociology*, Vol. 67, March, 1962, pp. 561–565.

occupational ranking of industrialized and developing nations.[38] They examined data from twenty-four nations, underdeveloped as well as developed. Their findings show ". . . that it is impossible to argue at least for newly developing countries that similarities in levels of industrialization induced similarities in the hierarchical evaluation of occupations, since without any substantial progress toward industrialization many new nations have achieved a structure of occupational evaluations quite similar to that observed in the United States."[39] (This is noteworthy because it was precisely what was argued in the essay by Inkeles and Rossi, and because Rossi is the coauthor of the article we are now discussing). The data, as they make explicit, did not fall in a simple structuralist or a simple culturalist position. According to them, their data suggest that occupational evaluations may be a causal factor in industrialization, and not merely the effect of industrialization. The "appropriate" kind of occupational evaluations, either native or borrowed, may lead to economic expansion, "providing a necessary though not sufficient condition for development rather than being a simple consequence of it."[40] In other words, if occupations that are necessary to industrialization are valued, people are more likely to train for them, thus hastening industrialization.

Obviously the authors of the study were convinced that their data were valid, that the comparisons were valid despite the technical defects. They do mention that in light of the great heterogeneity of the occupational studies in various lands and the problems involved in matching occupational titles, there may be some question about the wisdom of comparing them at all, but they dismiss this question and move on to comparisons. The question has, however, subsequently been taken up by Archibald Haller and David Lewis.[41] They examined the statistical limitations of the data, including the deficiencies in comparability, and concluded that inferences about the similarities in the occupational prestige structures of different societies are not well established. First of all, the evidence of similarities is confined to translatable occupational titles. Then, too, the small and biased samples of both occupational titles and the people interviewed about them are subject to significant errors.

Whether the thesis of similarity of occupational prestige hierarchies from country to country has been substantially dented by Haller and Lewis awaits further scholarly appraisal. But what do we know about the stability of such hierarchies over time in the same country?

Hodge, Siegel, and Rossi address themselves to this question in our next reading, "Occupational Prestige in the United States, 1925–1963," and their data are from the various studies of occupational ranking conducted in the United States at different times. Such studies have a fairly long history in the United States. One of the first investigations was that by Counts, who, in 1925, asked a group of teachers and college and high school students to rate forty-five familiar American occupations.[42] Hodge, Siegel, and Rossi review this study, as well as the ones that followed it, and come out with the finding that no appreciable changes have

---

[38] Robert W. Hodge, Donald J. Treiman, and Peter H. Rossi, "A Comparative Study of Occupational Prestige," in Bendix and Lipset, *op. cit.,* 2nd ed., pp. 309–322.

[39] *Ibid.,* p. 320.

[40] *Ibid.,* p. 321.

[41] Archibald O. Haller and David M. Lewis, "The Hypothesis of Intersocietal Similarity in Occupational Prestige Hierarchies," *American Journal of Sociology*, Vol. 72, September, 1966, pp. 210–216.

[42] George S. Counts, "Social Status of Occupations," *School Review*, Vol. 33, 1926, pp. 16–27.

taken place in the prestige structure of American occupations in the last forty years.

Among these studies, the most systematic and influential was the one made by North and Hatt, shortly after World War II, of the nationwide ranking of ninety occupations.[43] And it is this study that the authors have replicated in 1963. They found an unusually high correlation of 0.99 between the prestige scores derived from the 1947 North and Hatt study and their replication. Thus, the authors conclude that few changes have occurred in the sixteen-year period. Their explanation of this stability is that there are many good reasons for its existence. However, when one examines these reasons, he finds that a number of them are not necessarily the reasons *for* stability, but merely functional consequences *of* occupational stability. We cannot simply deduce, as the authors do, that stability in occupational ranking exists because pronounced changes in the prestige structure would lead to such negative consequences as furthering ambiguities or status inconsistencies and altering fundamentally the meaning of achievement, career, seniority, and occupational prestige. (The reasoning seems circular.) Apart from these consequences, erroneously labeled reasons for stability in occupational ranking, they enumerate the following factors, which could be considered causal factors in prestige stabilty. The educational requirements and monetary rewards of occupations tend to be stable. Because prestige of occupations is largely determined by these two factors, the prestige tends to be stable.

In this connection we may recall that the North-Hatt study did attempt to find out why people ranked occupations the way they did. They discovered that *high income* was most frequently mentioned by the public as the most important criterion for an "excellent" rating.[44] Moreover, in his analysis of the North-Hatt data, Dudley Duncan shows a 0.91 correlation between occupational evaluations and a combined measure of the income and educational attainment of each of the occupations examined.[45] We get some further insight into how much importance is assigned to the income of an occupation from two questions asked in a Gallup Poll of 1951. They were, "Which of these two jobs would you personally prefer a son of yours to take, assuming he is equally qualified: a skilled laborer's job at $100 a week or a white-collar desk job at $75 a week?"; and, after the same beginning, ". . . a college professor's job at $4,000 a year or a factory foreman's job at $6,000 a year?" In answer to both of these questions, a majority of respondents, in both manual and nonmanual occupations, expressed a preference

---

[43] National Opinion Research Center, "Jobs and Occupations: A popular Evaluation," *Opinion News,* September 1, 1947, pp. 3–13, reprinted in Bendix and Lipset, *op. cit.,* pp. 411–426.

[44] *Ibid.,* p. 419. The study asked, "When you say certain jobs have 'excellent standing' what do you think is the one main thing about such jobs that gives this standing?" The answers were:

The job pays well	18%
It serves humanity; it is an essential job	16
Preparation requires much education, hard work & money	14
The job carries social prestige	14
It requires high moral standards, honesty, responsibility	9
It requires intelligence and ability	9
It provides security, steady work	5
The job has a good future; the field is not overcrowded	3
The job is pleasant, safe, and easy	2
It affords maximum chance for initiative and freedom	0 (less than 0.5%)
Miscellaneous answers; don't know, no answer	10
	100%

[45] O. D. Duncan, "A Socioeconomic Index for All Occupations," in Albert J. Reiss, *Occupation and Social Status,* New York: Free Press, 1961, p. 124.

for the manual job. In the case of the second question, where the majority was smaller, the preference for the foreman among manual respondents was 61 per cent as against 34 per cent and among nonmanual 52 per cent as against 44 per cent.[46] These figures read like a modern rendition of *Vico's* dictum ". . . by the eternal common civil nature, men first seek wealth, then honors. . . ."[47]

All this suggests, and casual observation supports it, that although at an given time there may be a discrepancy between the prestige and income of an occupation, in the long run there is a high consistency. A high-ranking occupation whose relative income falls substantially will eventually go down in rank. If the income of a given occupation increases substantially, it will eventually gain in rank. We are, of course, touching on the problem referred to by the various terms of *status consistency, congruence* and *crystallization*. It was for the first time, as far as we know, subjected to quantification by Gerhard Lenski in his article "Status Crystallization: A Non-Vertical Dimension of Social Status," which appeared in 1954. This was followed by a stream of research and discussion on the subject which continues to this day. Much of the research is cited and briefly summarized in "Status Consistency and Inconsistency" the pages reprinted here from Lenski's book, *Power and Privilege*. (The term *status* in this usage is broader than in the Weberian sense. It refers to position in general rather than prestige position.)

When Lenski undertook the task of conceptualizing status crystallization in his original article, he made clear that individual or family status is approached by him not as "a single position in a uni-dimensional hierarchy" but as a "series of positions in a series of related hierarchies."[48]

Lenski focused on the relative positions in the following four hierarchies: (1) the income hierarchy, (2) the occupational hierarchy, (3) the educational hierarchy, and (4) the ethnic hierarchy. Two logical possibilities flow from this: (1) status consistency or crystallization—positions of the individual rank more or less the same, as for example all high or all low and (2) status inconsistency—one or more positions of an individual rank much higher than another or others.

But Lenski conceptualized status consistency or crystallization in terms of a continuum ranging from high to low. He developed a technique, which he describes in the article, for comparing the relative positions of an individual in several hierarchies. High status crystallization occurs when the positions rank nearly the same; low crystallization when they rank quite differently in the different hierarchies.

At this point it would be well to mention that in a later article Warner Landecker —who conducted the research project jointly with Lenski—addressed himself in part to when high crystallization is more likely to occur by devising a crystallization index and then testing the hypothesis that status crystallization is strongest at the two extremes of the stratification system. He arrived at this hypothesis by reasoning that persons who rate highest in one hierarchy will have the most power to monopolize equivalent positions in the other hierarchies. On the other hand, to be at the bottom of one hierarchy handicaps one's access to higher positions in the other hierarchies. The latter part of the hypothesis was not confirmed by the results of

---

[46] Quoted in W. G. Runciman, *Relative Deprivation and Social Justice*, Berkeley: University of California Press, 1966, p. 234.

[47] The rest of the sentence reads "and lastly nobility." See Thomas Goddard Bergin and Max Harold Fisch, eds., *The New Science of Giambattista Vico*, New York: Anchor Books, 1961, p. 320.

[48] Gerhard E. Lenski, "Status Crystallization: A Non-Vertical Dimension," *American Sociological Review*, Vol. 19, August, 1954, p. 405.

the tests, but the first was. The hypothesis that crystallization would be particularly strong at the highest level was supported by the fact that the index of class crystallization showed a higher score at the top status level than at any other level.[49]

Lenski's main interest was different: He was concerned with the *utility* of the concept of status crystallization. His study was aimed at testing its utility by investigating whether it could account ". . . for some of the variance in political behavior which is left unexplained by traditional methods of stratification analysis." He then treated status crystallization as the independent variable and "liberal political tendencies" as the dependent one. The analysis of the data led him to the conclusion that such tendencies ". . . are associated with low degree of status crystallization."

Extrapolating from these findings, Lenski contended that one could predict that the greater the proportion of the population suffering from acute status inconsistencies, the greater the proportion supporting programs of social change. This has been criticized by Kenkel, who demonstrated that it has not always been the case.[50] It is noteworthy that in the reprinted pages from the book that appeared about a decade later than his article, Lenski states his hypothesis about the consequences of status inconsistency in more cautious terms. Since the appearance of the book, Kelly and Chambliss have reported on their attempt to resolve the discrepancy between the findings in Lenski's initial article and the findings by Kenkel. Their study, however, relied on a mail-back questionnaire sent to a sample of Seattle residents. The responses indicated that the ". . . social class membership and ethnic background of respondents are far more important determinants of political attitudes than the degree to which persons are status consistent or inconsistent."[51]

But other empirical studies that appeared about the same time or subsequently have provided some specification as to which kinds of status inconsistency lead to which kind of liberal tendencies. For example, in a later article Lenski showed that his secondary analysis of twenty-five national surveys of voting behavior in Australia, Britain, and the United States provides support for the thesis that status inconsistency between one's occupation and religious affiliation increases liberal or left-of-center tendencies.[52] On the other hand, Treiman's study shows that status inconsistency *per se* has no effect on prejudice against Negroes.[53]

The Polish sociologist Andrzej Malewski has given further thought to this problem. contending that although status inconsistency tends to lead to support of change, this does not necessarily mean support of liberal or leftist causes, as suggested by Lenski and others. He reasons that when an individual of incongruent

[49] Werner S. Landecker, "Class Crystallization and Its Urban Pattern," *Social Research*, Vol. 27, Autumn, 1960, pp. 308–320.

[50] F. W. Kenkel, "The Relationship Between Status Consistency and Politico-Economic Attitudes," *American Sociological Review*, Vol. 21, June, 1956, pp. 365–368. See also, Gerhard Lenski, "Comment on Kenkel's Communication," same issue, p. 369.

[51] K. Dennis Kelly and William J. Chambliss, "Status Consistency and Political Attitudes," *American Sociological Review*, Vol. 31, June, 1966, p. 381.

[52] Gerhard E. Lenski, "Status Inconsistency and the Vote: A Four Nation Test," *American Journal of Sociology*, Vol. 32, April, 1967, pp. 298–302.

[53] Its data were from a representative national sample of the adult white population in the United States, and its measures of consistency involved: (1) income and education as status variables and (2) education and education of spouse. See Donald J. Treiman, "Status Discrepancy and Prejudice," *American Journal of Sociology*, Vol. 71, May, 1966, pp. 651–669.

status cannot raise himself on those hierarchies where his position is low, he will tend to "reject the system of evaluation which justifies his humiliations" and join those who oppose that system.[54] If the only group rejecting this system of evaluation is the radical Left, such individuals will tend to accept its program. However, if there are radical Right groups, whose programs promise possibilities of raising one's position in the hierarchies where one ranks low, they show great readiness to accept such programs. Malewski supports his contention with evidence from empirical studies.[55]

Later than Malewski, however, Norbert Wiley put forth the interesting hypothesis that the consequences of status inconsistency may be different for individuals and different for the social system. He argues that although status inconsistent individuals may be more radical, their existence may have an overall conservative effect on the social system. According to him, "To the people at the bottom of the system, who are all too consistent, the possibility of social ascent—even though it be only on one dimension, into an inconsistent posture—may give them a certain amount of hope which prevents them from becoming more radical."[56] Thus he concludes that in the United States, status inconsistency ". . . may contribute to keeping the whole political system in the Democratic-Republican center, at the cost of pushing some inconsistents a bit to the right or left of the main line."[57]

As we can gather, the concept of status consistency has been given considerable attention since the initial article by Lenski. To what degree it represents an important addition to the hitherto pursued analysis of political behavior as a reflection of presence or lack of class consciousness will become clearer after we have studied the subjective dimension of class.

SUBJECTIVE DIMENSION

The study of the subjective dimension of inequality revolves around the query whether, to what extent and how, subjective awareness of stratification varies with one's objective position in the stratification system. Another central question is that of the consequences of different kinds of awaremess. In other words the problem is that of the origin, nature, forms and consequences of what is often labeled as class consciousness.

As we have learned from the readings in theory, Marx saw the objective conditions of inequality pressing for an awareness to develop. Even Marx's writings, however, imply that the objective position in the stratification system is not the only determinant of class consciousness. Basing ourselves on the work of later theorists, we can point to the other important factor, *the definition of the situation* by which the perception and thinking about the objective position, or situation is guided. Here, as is often the case when observing a wide variety of social phenomena, the W. I. Thomas theorem manifests relevance: "If men define situations as real,

---

[54] Andrzej Malewski, "The Degree of Status Incongruence and its Effects," *The Polish Sociological Bulletin*, Vol. 7, No. 1, 1963. Reprinted in Bendix and Lipset 2nd ed., *op. cit.*, pp. 303–308.

[55] For further support of the thesis that a relationship exists between status inconsistency and right-wing political extremism, see Gary B. Rush, "Status Consistency and Right-Wing Extremism," *American Sociological Review*, Vol. 32, February, 1967, pp. 86–92.

[56] Norbert Wiley, "The Ethnic Mobility Trap and Stratification Theory," *Social Problems*, Vol. 15, Fall, 1967, p. 159.

[57] *Ibid.*

they are real in their consequences."[58] And such definitions in regard to stratification are provided by ideologies. Thus the objective position may press for certain awareness but the prevailing ideology may constitute a counterforce against such awareness arising. All things being equal, persons who believe in the ideology that their society is classless are less likely to perceive actual class differences than the nonbelievers. For example, most observers well acquainted with both sides of the Atlantic maintain that Americans are less class conscious than Europeans. And this is often accounted for by the Americans' belief in the creed of equality.[59]

That the ideology about the stratification system as a whole is an important factor in coloring or distorting the perception of inequality is implied in the essay "Non-Equalitarian Classlessness" by the well-known Polish sociologist Stanislaw Ossowski. He concentrates on the ideologies of the two mutually opposed systems, the United States and the Soviet Union, and shows the similarities between them. Both interpret the objective social inequalities in their own system in another way than in terms of class. As a matter fact, in each ideology the rejection of the image of its own society as a class hierarchy goes hand in hand with a recognition of the existance of social inequalities and its approval as representing just rewards of merit. Ossowski draws this conclusion from a point-by-point comparison of the traditional American ideology, the American Creed, and the official Soviet ideology.

As one reads the details, the question arises in one's mind: How is it possible for such similar conceptions of social structure to be applied to countries with such different political and economic systems as the United States and the USSR? The author addresses himself to this question and answers that it is so because the two start with a different assumption, the assumption of each being incompatible with the assumption of the other. Communist doctrine assumes that the abolition of private ownership of the means of production is the necessary condition of a classless, harmonious society. The American Creed assumes that the rights guaranteed by the American Constitution are the necessary conditions.

In the beginning of the essay Ossowski shows how American sociology has been influenced by traditional ideology, by the American Creed, in its choice of problems for study, in its answers, in its concepts and interpretations. And yet toward the end he states that in the United States the American Creed can and is being questioned by sociologists and others as a valid representation of existing reality (even if rarely, I would add, as a valid set of values and goals), in sharp contrast to the Soviet Union where no conceptions at odds with the official ideology were found until 1954, when Ossowski wrote this essay. One could extend the generalization for the Soviet Union up to this day, although it would not apply to some Soviet-type societies. It is not inappropriate to mention that when Ossowski wrote the

[58] For a treatment of how ideologies in general provide definitions of situations, see Florian Znaniecki, *Cultural Sciences,* Urbana: University of Illinois Press, 1963, pp. 267–285. As for a sociological definition of ideology, a number are available. Many of them resemble in content the following definition of Talcott Parsons: "An ideology, then, is a system of beliefs, held in common by members of a collectivity, i.e., a society, or sub-collectivity of one—including a movement deviant from the main culture of the society—a system of ideas which is oriented to the evaluative integration of the collectivity, by interpretation of the empirical nature of the collectivity and the situation in which it is placed, the processes by which it has developed to its given state, the goals to which its members are collectively oriented, and their relation to the future course of events." *The Social System,* New York: Free Press, 1964, p. 349.

[59] See, for example, S. M. Lipset and Reinhard Bendix, "Ideological Equalitarianism and Social Mobility in the United States," *Transactions of the Second World Congress of Sociology,* Vol. II, London: International Sociological Association, 1954.

essay—as well as other parts of the book *Class Structure in the Social Consciousness* from which it is taken—he did not think it would be published in Poland. As he explains in the preface to the American edition of the translated book, "Its appearance in print was in a certain sense linked with the events of October 1956 in Poland, for these made it possible to publish the work on which I had been engaged for several years without hope of publication. . . . The book went to press in the post-October period of enthusiasm and hope, and the emotional climate was reflected in its final touches." Perhaps to these final touches reflecting overenthu-siasm belongs the note on which the book ends. One of the important consequences of the events that took place in Poland in October, 1956, says the author ". . . was the destruction of the official myths which concealed our reality" [Poland's actual conditions]. But although Polish sociologists may not have been as free to address themselves to certain questions as they were in the short period following the so-called Polish October, they nevertheless continued up to 1968 (when the cam-paign against "revisionism" and "Zionism" began) to investigate problems that remain untouched in the Soviet Union. This is exemplified in the article by Nowak to be discussed soon, and the articles by Wesolowski found in Parts VII and VIII of this book.

In the reprinted essay, Ossowski does refer to Richard Centers' influential work, *The Psychology of Social Classes.* But I would like to elaborate a bit on this book because it constituted at the time of its appearance in 1949 an important break-through in the study of the subjective aspect of class. I am not referring to its theoretical line, which is rather weak. Even though at the beginning of the book the author expresses his indebtedness to Marx, and throughout it he maintains that his evidence supports the interest theory of class, his very definition of class, as well as of other formulations, reflects a psychological, and what would be labeled by Marxists an idealistic, position. He states that ". . . *a class is no less than what people collectively think it is. It is a psychological structuring. . . .*"[60] This explicitly denies that class is an objective phenomenon which, as we recall, was Marx's position. The following widely quoted passage from Marx's writing expresses plainly his view of the general relation between objective reality and subjective experience: "As in private life one distinguishes between what a man thinks and says of himself and what he really is and does, so still more in historical struggles must one distinguish the phrases and fancies of the parties from their real organism and their real interests, their conception of themselves from their reality."[61] Marx spoke of objective class interests, not the psychological dispositions that Centers terms interests.

When we referred to Centers' work as a breakthrough in its time, we had in mind that his work in a sense exploded the ideological myth that Americans, irrespective of socioeconomic position, considered themselves as belonging to one class, the middle class. This myth was supported by various national polls conduc-ted prior to the Centers study which reported that 79 to 88 per cent of Americans placed themselves in the middle class. It led *Fortune Magazine,* a sponsor of one of these polls, to proclaim "America Is Middle Class."

In his book Centers explains how he came to doubt the validity of those findings.

---

[60] Richard Centers, *The Psychology of Social Classes,* Princeton: Princeton University Press, 1949, p. 78.
[61] Karl Marx, *The Eighteen Brumaire of Louis Bonaparte,* New York: International Publishers, n.d., p. 41.

His study demonstrated that they were a function of the alternatives that the people were given to choose from: upper, middle, and lower. Not many chose to place themselves in a class designated by the value-laden term *lower*. When given a fourth alternative by him, working class, about half placed themselves there. Centers refers to this self-placement in a specific class as *class identification* and shows that it correlates with one's occupation. Three-fourths of business, professional, and white-collar individuals placed themselves in the middle class while almost four-fifths of the manual workers placed themselves in the working or lower class. He considers the fact that most people placed themselves, as they were asked to do, in one of these four classes, and that it correlated with their occupation, as indicating class consciousness. Thus he came up with the finding that Americans are class conscious, which was contrary to the hitherto prevalent characterizations of Americans in general, and of American working class in particular, as lacking class consciousness when compared with Europeans, for example. [62]

But by now, through the discussion engendered by Centers and subsequent studies, social scientists recognize that their surveys both hide some of the ignorance that people have about their stratification system and encourage some ideological distortions. In which case they place themselves is partly an artifact of the alternatives they are given to choose from rather than the expression of their everyday way of thinking. Respondents may, for instance, for fear of appearing ignorant, hide the fact that they do not understand the question or do not know to which class they belong, and make a choice of one of the alternative answers. Then too, the different alternatives given in surveys may tap different ideologies. The three alternatives in the *Fortune* study—upper, middle, lower—may have tapped the American equalitarian ideology, discussed by Ossowski. The four-class alternatives in Centers' study may have tapped the "Work Is Good" ideology, the heritage of the Protestant Ethic. [63]

The empirical study conducted by Gross in Minneapolis, Minnesota has much bearing on what was discussed here. By administering different types of questions to the sample of respondents, he demonstrated that the degree of structuring of a question has an effect on how people "identify" themselves in terms of class. In response to the open-ended question "What class do you belong to?" every third respondent failed to place himself in a class (20 per cent answered they did not know and about 15 per cent replied that there were no social classes or that they did not belong to any class). He also used two types of closed questions: the one that appeared in the *Fortune* survey and the one from the Centers study. Having analyzed and compared the answers to the open-ended and the two closed-ended questions, Gross stated, "In short, the conclusions the investigator emerges with using upper-middle-lower or the upper-middle-working-lower forced choice questions, are of great variance with the conclusion that emerges from the use of an open-ended class identification question." [64]

Apart from class identification, Richard Centers saw the politicoeconomic orientation as the major aspect of class consciousness. The instrument that he

[62] Centers, *op. cit.*, pp. 30–38 and 78–106.
[63] Bernard Barber, *Social Stratification*, New York: Harcourt, Brace and Company, 1957, pp. 210–211.
[64] Neal Gross, "Social Class Identification in the Urban Community," *American Sociological Review*, Vol. 18, 1953, pp. 398–404.

employed for ascertaining the politicoeconomic orientation was a *conservatism-radicalism battery* of six questions. But his material by and large does not support his contention that class self-identification is the intervening variable between occupation and politicoeconomic orientation. Centers contends that not only do Americans readily identify the class to which they belong, but that the answers to the identification question are predictive of the answers to the ideology battery. His data showed that the highest percent of conservatives and ultraconservatives fall in the self-identified upper and middle classes, whereas the greater proportion of radicals and ultraradicals are in the self-identified working and lower classes. However, careful inspection of his data discloses that one gets a better prediction of the politicoeconomic orientation by varying occupation than by varying class self-identification.[65]

Subsequently Arthur Kornhauser reviewed the findings of the Centers study, as well as other public opinions studies up to 1950, and generalized that on economic issues there was a tendency for opinions to be based on class position. But questions on other issues—such as international questions, race relations, religious doctrine, and so on—". . . fail to support the conception of a neat general pattern of radicalism-conservatism in which social classes manifest consistent contrasts."[66]

This ties in rather well to our next reading, "Social Class, Ideology, and Voting Preference" by Gertrude Jaeger Selznick and Stephen Steinberg, which analyzes the 1964 presidential vote. The paper aims at two things: to clarify the relation between voting and general beliefs, which they term *ideology*, and to gain a better understanding of the reasons for Goldwater's overwhelming defeat in the 1964 election. As regards the first, they found that both objective class, indicated by occupation, and political beliefs are related to how people voted in that election. The question posed then was whether the relationship between objective class and the vote could be explained by class differences in political beliefs. But their data showed that political beliefs were not related to class. Ideological agreement and disagreement with Goldwater was fairly equally distributed throughout the class structure.

The authors then proceded to consider whether the relation between class and the vote could be explained by immediate economic interests as perceived by the voters, what they label pocketbook concerns. Among all classes, many voters displayed the discordant combination of fairly conservative political beliefs and a pro-welfare orientation. But in such cases, the pro-welfare orientation tended to take precedence as far as voting was concerned. A pro-welfare orientation was most prevalent among workers and this explains the overwhelming vote for Johnson.

Selznick and Steinberg underline that the pro-welfare stand of many Johnson voters was not backed up by a consistent set of liberal political beliefs. Such people, they point out, could respond favorably to reactionary movements if their economic interests were not threatened and, one could add, especially if they were promised an enhancement of their economic interests. The authors conclude that class in the United States has little relation to basic political ideology. Thus in the United States the workers continue to differ from the pattern of class consciousness

---

[65] Joseph A. Kahl, *The American Class Structure*, New York: Holt, Rinehart and Winston, 1957, p. 165.
[66] Arthur Kornhauser, "Public Opinion and Social Class," *American Journal of Sociology*, Vol. 55, January, 1955, p. 334.

as envisaged by Karl Marx. Does this imply that growing affluence will tend to reduce even this limited class consciousness of working people now related to economic issues? The claim that this is the case falls within the thesis of the *embourgeoisment* of the working class under welfare capitalism. (Recall the early formulation of this thesis by Theodor Geiger.) But some sociologists warn against such an assumption saying that working-class affluence may sharpen class consciousness if status differences increase or harden at the same time. They point out that ". . . the development of marked discrepancies between income and status hierarchies tends to be productive of radical attitudes on the part of those who are unable to secure a degree of social recognition commensurate with their economic standing."[67]

But whether class consciousness would increase, I would like to add, would depend on how people perceive and experience these status differences. A work that throws much light on this is the book by W. Runciman, *Relative Deprivation and Social Justice,* in which class consciousness is explored systematically and in depth in a manner and to a degree hitherto unencountered. The author does this using both the historical and survey methods.

Our selection from this book is limited to the findings of the survey he conducted in England in 1962. (A stratified random sample of the British population, consisting of 1415, was chosen, of which 1087 respondents were interviewed.)[68] The main problem to which he addresses himself here is, "What is the relation between institutionalized inequalities and the awareness or resentment of them?" It has particular relevance in Britain, because it is a country of the following contradictions which, as the author notes in his introduction to the book, have been "variously admired or deplored according to the observer's political taste." Here is the country where the Industrial Revolution began and one of the few that is currently described as affluent. Yet its social structure is, according to Runciman, the most traditional of any industrialized country in the world. It has a Socialist government, but its hereditary monarchy has survived with undiminished prestige. The class consciousness of the working class in England led Marx to the prediction that the proletariat in advanced capitalism would revolt, yet the British Labor movement is "notorious in its gradualism."[69]

The two concepts that Runciman employs, *relative deprivation* and *reference group,* are related, in that both derive from a truism that ". . . people's attitudes, aspirations, and grievances largely depend on the frame of reference within which they are conceived."[70] Throughout the selection, as one comes again and again across the term relative deprivation, one must bear in mind that the author uses it as a strictly subjective concept. It refers to the sense and feeling of deprivation.

---

[67] John H. Goldthorpe and David Lockwood, "Affluence and the British Class Structure," *The Sociological Review,* Vol. 11, July, 1963, p. 140; Gavin Mackenzie, "The Economic Dimensions of Embourgeoisement," *The British Journal of Sociology,* Vol. XVIII, March, 1967, pp. 29–45. Other researches show that such consciousness is present to a larger degree in certain sectors of the working class—notably the unemployed who express more militant views than the employed. See: John C. Legett, "Economic Insecurity and Working-Class Consciousness," *American Sociological Review,* Vol. 29, April, 1964, pp. 226–235; John C. Legett, *Class, Race, and Labor—Working-Class Consciousness in Detroit,* New York : Oxford University Press, 1968. For similar findings in Cuba, see Maurice Zeitlin, "Economic Insecurity and the Political Attitudes of Cuban Workers," *American Sociological Review,* Vol. 31, February 1966, pp. 35–52.

[68] Runciman, *op. cit.,* p. 151.

[69] *Ibid,* p. 4.

[70] *Ibid,* p. 9.

In accordance with this meaning a person who is relatively deprived is not necessarily *objectively deprived,* in the sense of lacking certain things. Thus relative deprivation may be greater or smaller than actual deprivation. In addition, the concept of relative deprivation means that the sense and feeling of deprivation come from a comparison with the perceived situation of another person or group, which is the reference group. [71] Poverty does not in itself necessarily lead to relative deprivation. As Durkheim noted long ago, what is needed for men to be content with their lot ". . . is not that they have more or less, but that they be convinced that they have no right to more." [72] And although it is true that today in societies that are no longer traditional men tend not to be satisfied with their lot, Runciman observes that only rarely are egalitarian resentments as militant or widespread as the actual structure of inequalities would suggest to be plausible. On the basis of his more systematic examination of historical materials from 1918 to 1962, he comes to a similar conclusion concerning Great Britain during that period. The magnitude and frequency of relative deprivation seldom corresponds to the facts of economic inequality.

In his survey of 1962, Runciman investigated separately the feelings of deprivation in regard to economic inequality and status or prestige inequality. His historical investigation led him to the hypothesis that the relation between inequality and relative deprivation in each of these two dimensions would be different. The survey data confirmed it: There is a difference between attitudes toward economic and status inequality of the kind that the historical discussion suggested. Working-class people are less likely to feel relatively deprived in respect to income than middle-class people who are earning the same. (The author uses the term working class as synonymous with manual occupations and middle class with nonmanual occupations.) The class in which people place themselves—which Centers called self-identification and which Runciman calls self-rated class—does not seem to have any significant effect on such attitudes. But it does correlate independently with attitudes toward inequalities of status. Manual workers who placed themselves in the middle class showed greater relative deprivation in status than those who designated themselves as working class. These differences, as well as others, are explained by the author in terms of reference group theory.

In the conclusion to our selection, Runciman explains that he is turning in the final section of the book to the problem of how far the relative deprivation which the English people were feeling in 1962 could be vindicated by the appeal to social justice. He considered this problem an integral part of the task he undertook in his book. In the final part of his book he poses then the nonsociological question: "Which, if any, of these inequalities ought to be perceived and resented—whether they are or not—by the standards of social justice." [73] We know that, to paraphrase Pareto, the subject of sociology is what *is,* not what *ought* to be. The book is concerned with both of these questions and no wonder therefore, that its author described it as a work at once of sociology and political philosophy. [74]

Although Runciman's concern with the social justice of inequalities is nonsociological, the problem of social justice and inequality can be approached

---

[71] The concept of reference group was first coined by Herbert H. Hyman. See his "The Psychology of Status," *Archives of Psychology,* Vol. 38, 1942, pp. 5–94.

[72] As quoted in Runciman, *op. cit.,* p. 25.

[73] Runciman, *op. cit.,* pp. 3–4.

[74] *Ibid,* p. 5.

sociologically, as demonstrated in the article by Stefan Nowak.[75] The author investigated whether in socialist Poland people perceive as just the social inequalities that exist. From this alone we can gather the originally of the article, for it is a subject to which sociologists have not been paying much attention.

It is also original because the subjective aspect of class has hitherto been unexplored *in* Poland, let alone *in* other Soviet-type societies. We only have some indirect knowledge about subjective awareness of class in the Soviet Union, such as from the earlier study conducted by Harvard University's Russian Research Center among Russian refugees at the end of World War II. That study showed that many respondents, irrespective of class, saw the interests of workers and peasants as opposed to that of the intelligentsia—the professional, managerial, and white-collar strata.[76] Of course, such indirect findings have to be approached with some caution, because the refugees differed in many ways from those who stayed behind.[77]

Stefan Nowak's article is based on a survey conducted *in* Poland in 1961 (comparable in recency to Runciman's study). The author begins the analysis of his data with the answers to the question of how respondents thought their social position ranked as compared with that of other people in Poland.

In looking at the distribution of answers that the author arranged along a seven-point scale ranging from very high to very low, it is especially interesting to note that in this socialist society only 6 per cent of the respondents were "unable" to answer how they ranked in their society. In Poland, where the official ideology maintains and insists that the workers are in power, more than half of the unskilled workers and almost one-third of the skilled workers feel relatively deprived as compared with 7 per cent of the professionals—categorized in Poland as "creative intelligentsia and free professions." (Nowak suggests that those who answered that they compared low or very low could be considered as expressing the feeling of deprivation.) Or take those who considered their position above average in this "workers' land": only 6 to 7 per cent of the workers, but half of the professionals did so.

Consistent with the above, are also the findings concerning the subjective aspect of social mobility. The higher the occupational group, the greater the proportion of those who consider themselves to have advanced to a higher position than that of their fathers. Still this might be a biased reading of the article, as well as of the Polish reality, if we fail to note the ingenious refinement in Nowak's analysis of the perception of self-advancement. He examined in turn the answers of those individuals who remained in their father's occupational category to discover how they evaluated their position in comparison with that of their fathers. The fact that a sizable proportion of workers whose fathers were workers see their position as higher than that of their fathers, Nowak interprets to mean that they thus ". . . express indirectly the conviction that the over-all position of the working class in the social structure has improved." Of course, one could easily inject a

[75] Another Polish sociologist who addresses himself to social justice and inequality is Adam Sarapata, "The *Iustum Premium* as a Criterion of Social Stratification," paper presented at the Sixth World Congress of Sociology, Evian, France, September, 1966.

[76] Alex Inkeles and Raymond Bauer, *The Soviet Citizen*, Cambridge, Mass.: Harvard University Press, 1959. The generalization here is based on the respondents' answers to the following question: "Below is given a paired list of classes in Soviet society. We would like to know for each of these pairs . . . do their interests coincide with or contradict each other? Check the condition you think correct for each group." See Tables 85 and 89.

[77] However, the authors of the study present evidence to support their contention that these difference were not extreme. See *ibid,* pp. 7–10 and 25–40.

note of doubt into this interpretation. It blurs the distinction between two areas that must be clearly distinguished from one another: first, an over-all improvement in the position of the working class and, second, an improvement in the position of individuals *within* the working class. The answers of the Polish workers could reflect the objective fact that they have *individually* advanced as compared with their fathers. Because Poland is becoming more industrialized, it is quite possible that many of these individuals have experienced upward mobility, although they have not moved out of the paternal occupational category. After all, skilled and even unskilled occupations have their own internal hierarchy. What we are suggesting is that, in contrast to Nowak's contention, the answers of those who said that they have advanced as compared with their fathers may reflect their perception of their own individual advancement, rather than the advancement of their class.

But let us turn to the important problem—with which we began this discussion of Nowak's article—of how people perceive the social inequalities existing in Poland. Again, a smaller proportion of manual workers than those in nonmanual occupations answered that the differences have diminished. (See Table 9T.) As a matter of fact, if we dichotomize the answers (Nowak does not) into those who think that social distinctions have diminished and those who do not think so, there is almost an even split among unskilled workers: 51.5 and 48.5 per cent, respectively. Still, it must not be omitted that a majority in each occupational category thought today's differences to be smaller than the prewar ones. Nevertheless, as the author states and demonstrates, the prevailing structure is "... regarded as marked by a fairly strong system of differentiation." The factor (among the ten enumerated in the questionnaire) on which there is most agreement as being the source of division and animosity in Poland is income and wealth inequality. (Over 80 per cent thought that it divides, and over 70 per cent that it is the cause of animosity.) But of all the ten factors, the smallest percentage pointed to differences in social origin, 21 and 17 per cent, respectively. I think the latter is especially noteworthy, because prewar Poland was marked by its aristocratic tradition. [78]

The author deepens the analysis by investigating the relationship between the perception of social animosity and the respondents objective social position. He shows that the higher the position the greater the chance that the respondent will perceive the structure as a *nonconflicting* one. Furthermore, the higher the position the more likely that he will see social animosity coming from the lower levels of society. In reverse, the lower the objective position the greater the tendency to see the animosity coming from the top levels.

We finally come to the crucial question of preferences concerning the continuation of social differences in Poland. Strikingly, over 80 per cent of all the respondents wanted to see an increase in equality, with almost half of the total sample coming out for the complete disappearance of social inequality. However, the proposition expressing the latter extreme equalitarian attitude had the smallest endorsement in the highest occupational group, the professionals.

It would be most interesting, especially in light of the Ossowski thesis, if we had comparable data from those Western-type societies marked by equalitarian ideologies, such as the United States or Australia. I cannot help but doubt that half of the population in such societies would express a desire for the complete

[78] Alexander Hertz, "The Case of an East European Intelligentsia," *Journal of Central European Affairs*, 1951, pp. 10–26; Jan Szczepanski, *Les Classes Sociales de la Société Polonaise Contemporaine*, *Cahiers Internationaux de Sociologie*, 1963, pp. 205–211.

disappearance of social inequality. But even if studies demonstrated that more people in Soviet-type societies than in Western societies wanted the complete disappearance of social inequality, we still could not conclude from it that the impact of socialist ideology on equalitarian attitudes is stronger. We must not forget that the Communist ideology posits a communist stage in the far-off future completely devoid of social inequality. In answering the question the way they did, the Polish respondents may have simply given back to the investigators that ideological line. One would have to ask two questions, one about the near future and one about the far-off future, to interpret with more confidence the answers on the preferences of the Polish people concerning the continuation of social inequalities.

INDEXES OF STRATIFICATION

Because the study of the subjective dimensions of class revolves around the queries whether, to what extent, and how subjective awareness or class consciousness varies with the objective position in the stratification system, it is most important to consider briefly in this introduction the methodological problem of indicators of objective position. In scientific study we seek an indicator that, in addition to being valid, is (1) standardized—capable of application in exactly the same way to all the things it is supposed to indicate or measure; (2) reliable—giving the same results no matter who uses it; and (3) preferably scalar—that it permit determination of different amounts or degrees of the given phenomenon for which it stands; (4) economical—giving maximum results with a minimum expenditure of time and effort. An indicator that has such characteristics is usually referred to as an *index*.[79]

Now many investigators of various aspects of American stratification have devised indexes of socioeconomic position that proved useful for their researches. A study of nineteen such major indexes found a high intercorrelation among these "standard measurement tools."[80] The relatively high correlations among the variables in these indexes suggested that they all may be measuring the same factor with varying accuracy. To test this Kahl and Davis, the authors of the above study, used the statistical technique of factor analysis. They discovered that the indexes were highly correlated, because they all measured, but in differing degrees, the same underlying dimension.

Because this underlying dimension was related to occupation, it may be well to add here that in contemporary industrial society when a single-item index is used it is most often occupation. And even though a single item-index may suffer in accuracy, it has the advantages of being easier to standardize, make reliable, scale, and use economically. An occupational index has the additional advantage in that it is relatively easy to ascertain a person's occupation, although his salary or the cost of his house may be harder to obtain.

To conclude this introduction to the readings on major dimensions of stratification, it should be said that even though the intercorrelation between them is considerable it is far from perfect. There is a certain amount of overlapping among them. Both because of the complexity of modern stratification and the discrepancies in positions along one or another dimension, the readings are arranged separately for each dimension.

[79] For a thorough treatment of indices, see "Indices of Social Class Position," in Barber, *op. cit.*, pp. 168–185.

[80] Joseph A. Kahl and James A. Davis, "A Comparison of Indexes of Socio-Economic Status," *American Sociological Review*, Vol. 20, June, 1955, pp. 317–325.

Objective Dimensions
Economic Inequality

WHAT'S HAPPENING TO OUR INCOME REVOLUTION?

Herman P. Miller

A myth has been created in the United States that incomes are gradually becoming more evenly distributed. This view is held by prominent economists of both major political parties. It is also shared by the editors of the influential mass media.

Arthur F. Burns, chief economist for the Eisenhower Administration, stated in 1951 that "the transformation in the distribution of our national income . . . may already be counted as one of the great social revolutions of history." Paul Samuelson, one of President Kennedy's leading economic advisers, stated in 1961 that "the American income pyramid is becoming less unequal. . . ."

In the preceding chapter, several basic facts were presented regarding trends in the inequality of income distribution in the United States. It was shown that there has been no appreciable change in income shares for nearly twenty years. This question will now be examined a little more intensively.

Despite the existence of much poverty in the United States, there is general agreement that real levels of living are much higher than they were only ten years ago and that the prospects for future increases are very good.[1] If $3,000 in 1962 dollars is used as

[1] We are here inserting the table, figures, and text from the preceding chapter to support this point (C. S. H.).

TABLE 1   Distribution of Families and Incomes by Income (in 1962 dollars) 1929, 1947, and 1962

Income Level	1929	1947	1962
Under $3,000	51%	30%	21%
Between $3,000 and $6,000	34	40	31
Between $6,000 and $8,000	7	14	18
Between $8,000 and $10,000	3	7	11
$10,000 and over	5	9	19

Jeanette M. Fitzwilliams, "Size Distribution of Income in 1962," *Survey of Current Business,* April, 1963, Table 3. Figures for the under $3,000 group are based on unpublished data.

the poverty line, it can be noted that thirty years ago about half of the families and individuals lived at levels that would be regarded as substandard today. This number may be somewhat overstated because of the inclusion of unrelated individuals, but it is not grossly out of line. Of course even today there are large numbers trying to get by on very little, but the proportion at this low level has been more than cut in half. In 1962 only about one-fifth of the families and individuals had incomes under $3,000.

The figures at the other end of the income scale show why ours is called an affluent society. In 1962 about one family out of every five had an income over $10,000. In many cases this high an income is achieved only because the wife and the husband are both out working; but the income is there nonetheless and it is available for air conditioners, dishwashers, second cars, and prestige schools. Thirty years ago an income over $10,000 (in 1962 terms; much less as dollars were counted then) was achieved by only one family out of twenty.[2] Since conditions are improving you may wonder why it is important to consider the gap between the rich and the poor. Isn't it enough that the *amount* of income received by the poor has gone up substantially? Why be concerned about their share? Many who

[2] We are now returning to the text of the chapter. (C. S. H.)

have thought about this problem seriously regard the *share* as the critical factor. When Karl Marx, for example, spoke about the inevitability of increasing misery among workers under capitalism he had a very special definition of misery in mind. Sumner Slichter, in summarizing the Marxian position on this point, states: " . . . Marx conceded that real wages *might* rise, but not the relative share of labor. Even if real wages rose, misery would grow, according to Marx, since workers would be worse off relative to capitalists. . . ."

In other words "needs" stem not so much from what we lack as from what our neighbors have. Veblen called this trait our "pecuniary standard of living" and modern economists refer to it as the "relative income hypothesis," but it all comes back to the same thing. Except for those rare souls who have hitched their wagons to thoughts rather than things, there is no end to "needs." So long as there are people who have more, others will "need" more. If this is indeed the basis for human behavior, then obviously the gap between the rich and the poor cannot be ignored, however high the *minimum* levels of living may be raised.

. . . .

Most opinions regarding changes in inequality, including those held by professional economists, are based on statistical measures of income rather than on philosophical concepts. With all their limitations, the income figures may well serve as a first approximation of changes in welfare.[3]

[3] We are inserting the figures and explanatory text from the preceding chapter. (C. S. H.)

During the depression of the thirties there was a distinct drop in the share of the income received by the upper income groups. In 1929, the last year of the prosperous twenties, the top 5 percent of the families and individuals received nearly one-third of the income. Their share dropped during the depression and amounted to about one-fourth of the income at the outbreak of World War II. During the war years there was a further decline and their share dropped to 21 percent in 1944. Since that time there has been no significant change in the percent of income received by the wealthiest group. The stability of income distribution during the past twenty years is a matter of some concern that has been generally overlooked by students in the field.

. . . The trend described for the top twentieth applies to the top fifth as well. But now let's look at the bottom groups. In 1935, the poorest fifth of the families and individuals received only 4 percent of the income. Their share rose to 5 percent in 1944 and has remained at that level ever since. The stability since 1944 of the shares received by each of the other quintiles is equally striking.[4] These figures show that the share of income received by the lower income groups has not changed for twenty years. Let us look at some other evidence that supports this view and then examine the implications of the findings.

[4] We are now returning to the text of the chapter. (C. S. H.)

TABLE 2   Percent of Income Received by Each Fifth of Families and Individuals and by Top 5%

Families and individuals ranked from lowest to highest	1959	1935	1941	1944	1961
Lowest fifth	13%	4%	4%	5%	5%
Second fifth		9	10	11	11
Middle fifth	14	14	15	16	16
Fourth fifth	19	21	22	22	23
Highest fifth	54	52	49	46	45
Top 5%	30	27	24	21	20

U.S. Bureau of the Census, *Historical Statistics of the United States, Colonial Times to 1957*, p. 166, and Jeanette M. Fitzwilliams; see Table III-2.

WHITE-NONWHITE INCOME DIFFERENTIALS ARE NOT NARROWING

The narrowing of income differentials between whites and nonwhites (92 percent of whom are Negroes) is sometimes cited as evidence of a trend toward equalization. . . .

The income gap between whites and non-whites did narrow during World War II. During the last decade, however, it shows some evidence of having widened again (see Table 3 . . .). The census statistics demonstrate this dismaying fact.

In 1947, the median wage or salary income for nonwhite workers was 54 percent of that received by the whites. In 1962, the ratio was almost identical (55 percent). Prior to

TABLE 3 The Income Gap: White vs. Nonwhite Male Workers Aged 14 and Over, in 1939, and 1947 to 1962[5]

Year	White	Nonwhite	Nonwhite as percent of white
All persons with wage or salary income:			
1939	$1,112	$ 460	41%
1947	2,357	1,279	54
1948	2,711	1,615	60
1949	2,735	1,367	50
1950	2,982	1,828	61
1951	3,345	2,060	62
1952	3,507	2,038	58
1953	3,760	2,233	59
1954	3,754	2,131	57
1955	3,986	2,342	59
1956	4,260	2,396	56
1957	4,396	2,436	55
1958	4,596	2,652	58
1959	4,902	2,844	58
1960	5,137	3,075	60
1961	5,287	3,015	57
1962	5,462	3,023	55

1947 there was a substantial reduction in the earnings gap between whites and nonwhites. In view of the stability of the earnings gap during the postwar period, however, the reduction during the war years cannot be

[5] These figures, as well as others throughout the selections, are expressed in terms of constant purchasing power so that the effects of inflation are eliminated. (C. S. H.)

viewed as part of a continuing process, but rather as a phenomenon closely related to war-induced shortages of unskilled labor and government regulations such as those of the War Labor Board designed generally to raise the incomes of lower paid workers, and to an economy operating at full tilt.

This conclusion is reinforced by details of the 1960 census which show that in the twenty-six states (including the District of Columbia) which have 100,000 or more Negroes, the ratio of Negro to white income for sales increased between 1949 and 1959 in two states (District of Columbia and Florida) and it was unchanged in two others (New Jersey and Oklahoma). In every other state there was a widening of the gap between the incomes of whites and Negroes and in some cases it was fairly substantial.

OCCUPATIONAL DIFFERENTIALS IN EARNINGS ARE NOT NARROWING

One of the most widely and strongly held misconceptions about income concerns the narrowing of the difference in earnings between skilled and unskilled workers. The prevailing view holds that the decrease in the earnings gap between the skilled and the unskilled in the United States is part of a historical process that has been going on since the turn of the century. The Department of Labor reports that in 1907 the median earnings of skilled workers in manufacturing industries was about twice that received by unskilled workers. By the end of World War I, it was only 75 percent greater, and by the end of World War II only 55 percent greater. Thus, during a forty-year period, this income gap was reduced by about 50 percent, an average of about 1 percent per year.

Recent trends in income differentials between skilled and unskilled workers are shown in Table 4. These figures represent the median wages and salaries received during the year in the major occupation groups for men. Women are excluded because their earnings are highly influenced by the fact that a large proportion of them work intermittently rather than full time.

There was not too much variation among occupation groups in the rate of income growth during the entire twenty-two-year period. The average income for most of the

TABLE 4   Men's Income by Occupation: Percent Change

Year	Professional and Managerial Workers	Craftsmen	Semiskilled Factory Workers	Service Workers and Nonfarm Laborers
1939–61	243%	322%	331%	314%
1939–50	96	160	172	180
1950–61	75	62	59	48

U.S. Bureau of the Census, *Current Population Reports—Consumer Income,* Series P-60, Nos. 9 and 39 (for Table 4).

occupations quadrupled. But an examination of the growth rate for two different periods, 1939–50, and 1950–61, reveals striking differences.

During the decade that included World War II, the lower paid occupations made the greatest relative gains in average income. Thus, laborers and service workers (waiters, barbers, janitors, and the like), two of the lowest paid groups among nonfarm workers, had increases of about 180 percent. The gains for craftsmen, who are somewhat higher paid, was 160 percent; professional and managerial workers, the highest paid workers of all, had the lowest relative gains —96 percent.

During the past decade the picture has been reversed. Laborers and service workers made the smallest relative gains, 48 percent; craftsmen had increases of 62 percent, and the professional and managerial workers had the greatest gains of all, 75 percent. The narrowing of the income gap between the skilled and the unskilled, the high-paid and the low-paid workers, which was evident up to and including the war years, has stopped during the past decade and the trend seems to be moving in the opposite direction.

The above figures are national averages in which all industries and regions are combined. They are very useful for identifying major trends, but they can also be very misleading because they average together so many different things. It is important to examine the figures for a particular industry in a particular region to get a better understanding of the underlying trends. The primary and fabricated metals industries have been selected for this purpose. The same analysis was also made for about

ten other major American industries and the results are generally the same as those presented below.

About 2,200,000 men were engaged in the production of metals or the fabrication of metal products in 1960. This employment was about equally divided between production and fabrication

. . . .

An examination of employment in this industry shows that the total number of workers increased by 24 percent between 1950 and 1960. Professional, managerial, and other white-collar workers increased 62 percent; skilled and semiskilled production workers increased by about 20 percent, but unskilled laborers decreased 9 percent. Thus, despite the general rise in employment and output in this industry, there was a drop in the demand for unskilled labor.

In view of these changes in the demand for labor in this industry, what happened to earnings? . . . In all states except Ohio and California, unskilled workers in this industry made greater relative gains than the semiskilled between 1939–49. Similar figures are not available for the higher paid "other" workers for 1939. Thus there was a tendency toward a narrowing of earnings differentials in this industry between 1939–49. But, during the decade 1949–59, the reverse was true. In every state there was a widening of differentials, with the highest paid "other" workers making the greatest relative gains, followed by the semiskilled workers and then the unskilled. . . .

WHERE DO WE GO FROM HERE?

There was a time, not too long ago, when economists did not look for changes in income distribution because they did not expect to find any. Indeed, the stability of the income curve was so striking that it was given a name, Pareto's Law, in honor of the economist[6] who conducted some of the earliest statistical inquiries in this field.

Pareto believed that the distribution of income is fixed and that regardless of changes in economic conditions, short of a revolutionary change from a competitive to a collectivist society, the distribution of income is the same in all places and at all times.

Statistical studies in recent years have so thoroughly demolished Pareto's notions that we have now come to look for change where no change exists. The facts show that our "social revolution" ended nearly twenty years ago; yet important segments of the American public, many of them highly placed government officials and prominent educators, think and act as though it were a continuing process. Intelligent public policy demands that things be seen as they are, not as they were.

The stability of income distribution, particularly during the fifties, could be related to the fact that the decade was dominated by a political philosophy committed to stability rather than change. In a different climate income differentials might narrow further. This could be accomplished through legislation designed to raise the levels of living of the poor: expansion of unemployment insurance benefits, federal aid to dependent children of the unemployed, liberalization of social security benefits, increase in the minimum wage and extension of its coverage, federal aid under the Area Redevelopment Act to revitalize the economies of areas with large and persistent unemployment.

In opposition to political factors that seem to favor equalization, there are some very stubborn economic factors that seem to be headed in quite the other direction. For many years now unskilled workers have been a declining part of the American labor force. This fact has been documented over and over again. Between 1940 and 1950 and again between 1950 and 1960 only one

nonfarm occupation group for men—laborers—declined in number at a time when all other groups were increasing. Their income changed erratically. Laborers had the greatest relative income gains during the forties and the smallest relative gains during the fifties. This could mean that unskilled labor was in very short supply during World War II, with millions of young men away in the armed forces and the economy working at full steam. This pressure, with a little help from the government, forced wage rates up more for unskilled workers than for other workers. Since the fifties, on the other hand, there is evidence that the supply of unskilled labor has far exceeded the demand. As a result the unskilled are finding it increasingly difficult to locate jobs and many who are employed live in constant fear of being replaced by machines. Moreover, the overabundance of these workers has prevented their wages from keeping pace with the others; thus the gap between the earnings of skilled and unskilled has widened.

The American economy has been plagued by relatively high unemployment since late 1957. According to the Joint Economic Committee, which has studied this problem in some detail, it is still premature to attribute this unemployment to the technological changes that are rapidly reshaping the economy. However, there can be no doubt that many thousands of unskilled workers in farming, manufacturing, mining, and railroads have been permanently displaced by machines and that this trend will continue. The labor-union leaders who represent these workers certainly tend to view the problem in this light. Even if they do not qualify as impartial observers, they know how these economic developments are interpreted at the grass-roots level. The leader of the Transport Workers Union of America, Michael Quill, is one among many who have spoken out sharply. His words carry a defiant ring that has been virtually absent from the American scene for over twenty years. He stated: "Unless something is done to put people to work despite automation, they may get rough in this country and this country may have a real upheaval, a real turmoil." The increase in racial tension and juvenile delinquency during

---

[6] Vilfredo Pareto, claimed by economists as well as sociologists. (C. S. H.)

the past few years may be early manifestations of trouble to come.

Labor-union leaders are not the only ones who have shown a keen awareness of both the bogey and the boon of automation. Many who have given the matter serious thought find it conceivable that, in the absence of remedial action, this nation may soon be faced with an increase in the disparity of incomes. We may then discover that our "social revolution" has not only been marking time for nearly twenty years, but that it is beginning to move backward. Justice William O. Douglas has spoken out eloquently on this subject in the pamphlet *Freedom of the Mind:* "We have a surplus of everything—including unemployed people; and the hundreds of unemployed and unemployable will increase if technology continues to be our master. We have a surplus of food and millions of hungry people at home as well as abroad. When the machine displaces man and does most of the work, who will own the machines and receive the rich dividends? Are we on the threshold of re-entering the world of feudalism which Europe left in the 15th and 16th centuries and which is fastened on much of the Middle East today?"

CHALLENGE TO AFFLUENCE—THE EMERGENCE OF AN "UNDER-CLASS" [1]

Gunnar Myrdal

The facts about unemployment and its immediate causes are well known in

Condensed from *Challenge to Affluence,* by Gunnar Myrdal. Reprinted by permission of Pantheon Books, a Division of Random House, Inc.

[1] The word "under-class" does not seem to be used in English. . . . Nevertheless, the term will be used in this book as the only one adequate to the social reality discussed.

America due to its excellent statistical reporting. . . . Less often observed and commented upon is the tendency of the changes under way to trap an "under-class" [1] of unemployed and, gradually, unemployable and underemployed persons and families at the bottom of a society, while for the majority of people above that layer the increasingly democratic structure of the educational system creates ever more real liberty and equality of opportunity, at least over the course of two generations.

The American self-image was, and is, that of a free and open society where anyone who is of a sound body and soul and has the drive can find work, at least when business is on the upturn, and where he can climb to the highest and most rewarding positions. It was this image, and the considerable degree of reality that actually corresponded to it, that induced millions of poor people in Europe to seek their opportunity in America right up to the First World War.

Reality never agreed entirely with that image. And over the last few generations a process has been under way that, while it opened more opportunities to more people, also closed ever more opportunities to some. Now in the end it threatens to split off a true "under-class" that is not really an integrated part of the nation but a useless and miserable substratum.

To start at the heights, the "self-made man" with great wealth and a supreme command over men and productive resources has been disappearing in America ever since the time when college education became so common that a man without a degree could hardly advance in business. Business itself has tended to become increasingly large-scale and highly organized. . . .

We have to remind ourselves, however, that to a considerable extent this American image was always something of a myth. Even leaving out the highest social and economic positions that have now been closed up to those starting without higher education, the opportunity to rise in society, or even to maintain a decent and respectable level of living and to participate in the nation's general culture and the solution of its problems, was not always that open in the old days. Great masses of people had no possibility of sharing in the American image of liberty and opportunity of rising economically and socially. This applied to the cotton farming Negro tenants in the South, the white hillbillies not far south of Washington, D.C., and similar groups of poor whites elsewhere in the country, the migrant workers on the big California farms, and to the workers in the sweatshops in the cities. Moreover, partly overlapping with the last category, there were the new immigrants in the city slums, handicapped in many ways, who often suffered miserable hardships before they came into their own.

Finally, in the periodic slowdowns in business activity a large number even of well integrated workers found themselves unemployed and without an income. The series of such reverses culminated in the Great Depression when up to 20 percent or more of the labor force was unemployed.

Abject destitution for millions of people is thus nothing new in America. The trend has definitely been to decrease the number suffering from it or even running a major risk of it. Major causes of this have been the rising productivity of the American economy and also the facts that educational facilities have been vastly improved and that good schools and college education have been placed at the disposal of an ever increasing portion of the people, earlier and more generously than in any other Western country.

THE NEW THREAT

Nevertheless, there is something threatening in the very recent changes and in the trend for the foreseeable future. The displacement of unskilled and even of much skilled labor has a definiteness that must compel us to stop and think. To take advantage of the expansion of demand for highly educated and trained labor, which is occurring and would do so even more rapidly if the growth rate of the economy were higher, would require such education and training of the displaced that he simply cannot think of jumping the gap, no matter how alert and enterprising he is. He needs to be helped to do it by society or he will not be able to do it at all.

What is happening is similar to the disappearance more than half a century ago of the "self-made man" from the highest positions as a result of the widening of college education and training for leadership in business as it increasingly became large-scale, organized, and stratified. This process has continued steadily downwards, first to middle positions and then to ever lower strata of employees in industry and commerce, until it is now beginning to make unskilled and many skilled workers redundant.

This is a new threat. For when the process has proceeded that far, without a parallel change for educating and training the *whole* labor force to correspond to the new demands, there is no longer any vast space left beneath for economic advance and social mobility as when the self-made man at the top disappeared. Those not needed are true "outcasts." They simply become unemployed, and indeed largely unemployable, or underemployed. It is almost as difficult for them to get and hold a good job as it long ago became to start as a shoeshine boy and end as the president of a big corporation.

This emergence of an American "underclass" of unemployed and largely unemployable and underemployed occurs at a time when almost the last batches of immigrants from Southern and Eastern Europe and their descendants have finally become integrated in the American nation. It happens when those educated and trained to fit the new direction of labor demand are experiencing a brisk demand for their work, and when the general levels of living of the majority of well employed Americans—and thereby the general conception spread by the mass-communication industry of what the American way of life is like—have risen high above what a few generations ago were considered comfortable standards. In society at large there is more equality of opportunity today than there ever was. But for the bottom layer there is less or none.

The disappearance of the self-made man was a slight change in society compared to that now under way, closing all good jobs and soon almost all jobs worth having in affluent America to those who have happened to be born in regions, localities, or economic and social strata where education and training for life and work in this new America are not provided as a normal thing. For the larger part of America there is social and economic mobility through the educational system. Beneath that level a line is drawn to an "under-class." That class line becomes demarcated almost as a caste line, since the children in this class tend to become as poorly endowed as their parents.

In a situation of high and rising unemployment even the trade unions often, unwillingly, become instrumental in hardening the line which excludes that substratum of workers from opportunities of getting jobs. The process of automation is particularly extensive in sectors of the American economy in which there are effective trade unions. These unions are thus forced to press for job security for their own members even when this creates incentives for the employers not to engage new workers. In a situation of high unemployment the unions also often feel their bargaining strength weakened and find it difficult to dissipate too much of it by taking a consistent and strong stand for what is the main interest from all the workers' point of view, full employment. . . . To an observer it seems almost a miracle that big units of the movement, particuarly the industrial unions in the C.I.O. wing, have found it possible to take such broadminded and progressive positions on national economic issues as they actually have.

The fact that the substratum is not very articulate in America and is, therefore, not much noticed by the ordinary, well educated Americans who are busily and happily enjoying both their work and their leisure, does not detract from the gravity of this development. On the contrary, it is fatal for democracy, and not only demoralizing for the individual members of this under-class that they are so mute and without initiative and that they are not becoming organized to fight for their interests. For its own health and even preservation an effective, full-fledged democracy needs movements of protest on the part of the underprivileged.

THE CURSE OF UNEMPLOYMENT

. . . It is discouraging but probably realistic when the Kennedy administration has redefined tolerable unemployment to be as high as 4 per cent, apparently not reckoning part-time unemployment and underemployment at low productivity levels.

There is even a probability that the level of unemployment may be higher still when a boom has to be broken, ultimately, because of the scarcity of educated and trained workers, if for no other reason. This will leave a hard core of unemployment that is uncomfortably high.

Unemployment is a damaging way of life. It is particularly damaging for the young in the nation, and even more particularly when their educational and cultural level is low. Crime, prostitution, and all sorts of shady ways of passing time will thrive as they did in the slums during the depression years in the thirties and as they increasingly begin to do today.

The well meaning proposals, put forward by progressive writers, for paying greatly increased unemployment benefits or sometimes even full wages without time limit to those who have been thrown out of work through no fault of their own, have, of course, little chance of being accepted by Congress. But apart from their lack of political realism, such proposals underestimate how unhealthy and destructive it is for anybody and particularly for young people without much share in the national culture to go idle and live more permanently on doles—this tenet of old fashioned Puritanism, I believe, is also fully borne out by recent social research. Work is not only, and not even mainly, a "disutility" as conceived by the classical economist. It is, if not always a pleasure, the basis for self-respect and a dignified life. There is no real cure for unemployment except employment, which does not mean, of course, that it is not important to make it possible for people to live when they have become unemployed.

A VICIOUS CIRCLE

The essential question when probing into the social impact of the formation of this under-class is the character of the selective process which determines whether a man comes above or beneath the dividing line. The selection operates on the criterion of education and training. When old people have failed, and young people are now failing, to get an education up to levels which correspond to national standards and the direction of the demand for labor, the explanation is usually that they have been living in an environment of poverty and squalor.

It has become customary to describe the situation in underdeveloped countries as one of a vicious circle where "poverty perpetuates itself." But the same vicious circle operates in an underprivileged class in the richest country. . . .[2]

They will become disheartened and apathetic. As parents they will not be able to pay toward such support of the education of their children that would be needed. Instead, they will have an incentive to take them out of school early if any employment, even at low wages and promising no secure future, offers itself. The home environment of the unemployed and poor will generally be less conductive for children and youth to become educated and trained for good jobs.

The unemployed will be forced to live in the slums or, more probably, they will always have lived in the slums. Whatever the regulations are, the schools will be bad in the slums as they will be in the districts where the backwoods farmer lives. And the whole way of life in the crowded slum quarters in the cities or the rural slum districts will be destructive for the will and ability to advance in life.

A remarkable tendency in America has been that parallel and prior to the rise in unemployment the efforts of slum clearance in the cities have mainly benefited the middle third of the nation who could afford to pay the rents in the new houses which only to a small extent have really been "low-cost housing." Those made homeless have been pressed into other already crowded slum districts or into districts which in this process of change became slum districts.

This perverted tendency in American housing policy has its parallel in almost all

[2] For an early statement of the theory of circular causation resulting in a cumulative process and of its application to an underprivileged category of people in a rich country, see *An American Dilemma* (New York, Harper, 1944), Chapter 3, Section 7, "The Theory of the Vicious Circle," pp. 78 ff., and Appendix 3, "A Methodological Note on the Principle of Cumulation," pp. 1035 ff.

other social policies. Various social security schemes as well as to an extent the minimum wage regulations happen to stop just above the very neediest groups of people. The voluntary health insurance schemes are much too expensive for the poorest who show the highest incidence of illness and ill health, both mental and bodily. In the same way agricultural policy has mainly aided the big and progressive farmers and has done little if anything for small farmers, small tenants, and agricultural workers. It is true that most of them should be moved out of agriculture, but little is done to speed the process, to prepare them not to end up unemployed or underemployed in the slums.

There is a political factor in this vicious circle of circular causation leading to a cumulative process. The poor in America are unorganized and largely mute. They exert no pressure corresponding to their numbers and to the severity of their plight. They are the least revolutionary proletariat in the world. As the studies of registration and election participation show, they are largely responsible for the comparatively low percentage of voters in America, and this not only in the South where the Negroes are still largely kept from voting even if they wanted to, but in the rest of the country, as well.

As they represent the big unutilized reserve of potential voters, the platforms of both Democrats and Republicans worked out before every election will regularly seem to imply a radical departure from policies pursued up till then—though most often couched in general and noncommittal terms. When the elections are over, however, and many of the poor are seen to have still stayed away from the polls, actual policies return to the routine of not doing much for them.

THE MINORITY GROUPS

Much of the rising unemployment falls upon minority groups and implies a serious setback in the process of national integration. The largest and still most handicapped minority group in America is that of the Negroes.

From about the beginning of the last war there has been a definite trend toward improved race relations in America, a development which is the more remarkable as for sixty years up till that time there had been no great change in the status of the Negroes in America. A very important cause among others of this encouraging trend was undoubtedly the rising level of labor demand from the beginning of the war and after the Great Depression. An increasing number of Negroes were allowed to acquire skills, join trade unions, and get seniority and job protection in new fields that were opening themselves for Negroes.

But the Negroes are still the "last hired and the first fired." Negro unemployment is presently about three times as high as the average rate, which means that close to a fifth of the Negro workers are unemployed. Apart from a tiny upper and middle class of professionals and business people, mostly thriving behind the remaining walls of prejudice, and now a considerably increased group of skilled and union protected workers, the majority of Negroes are much poorer and have had less education and training than the average white Americans. They are consequently more vulnerable in the present situation where labor demand is, and must be, turning towards those who have been educated and trained.

They are also directly discriminated against, legally and illegally, when seeking a home. Negro slums are getting the more overcrowded and dilapidated for this reason. . . . All other acts of prejudice and discrimination tend to press the Negroes down economically and socially. . . . The reforms are slow to work themselves out in terms of substantial changes in the Negroes' living conditions.

High and rising unemployment among Negroes is, on the one hand, an aggravating cause, in many ways hampering the rise in status of the American Negroes. On the other hand, these inferior living conditions, including inadequate education and training, tend to make it more difficult for Negroes to get and hold the good jobs. The greatest danger threatening the gratifying upward trend in race relations in America stems from this vicious circle, operating in a situation of generally high and rising unemployment. . . .

But to the large number of Negro workers —more than 10 per cent of the labor force— who more than others are hit by unemployment when it is high and rising, and to the Puerto Ricans, the Mexicans, and other minority groups affected in the same way, must be added poor white people everywhere in America who will be pressed down, and by the vicious circle held down, in this substratum which is excluded from the prosperity of the nation at large and the progress of the American way of life.

POVERTY

The Bureau of the Census, several of the departments in Washington and of the state administrations, university institutions, and other research outfits have in recent years done a commendable job of laying bare the facts of American poverty and of the causal relations behind this poverty. . . .

The summary condensation below of the results of these various studies is derived from *Poverty and Deprivation in the U.S.*, published by the Conference on Economic Progress (Washington, 1962), which has taken them all into consideration and properly accounted for the methods used to arrive at the figures.

If poverty is defined as having to live on an annual income under $4,000 for multiple-person families and $2,000 for unattached individuals, 38 million Americans, or more than one fifth of the nation, were poor in 1960. In deprivation, above poverty but short of the requirements for what in America is now considered a modestly comfortable level of living—from $4,000 to $6,000 for families and from $2,000 to $3,000 for unattached individuals—were more than 39 million people, or again more than one fifth of the nation. Utter destitution, estimated to be the situation of people with less than half of the income representing the poverty line, was the destiny of more than $12\frac{1}{2}$ million Americans, or nearly 7 per cent of the population in the United States.

The proportion of people in these different categories of deprivation, poverty, and destitution has been decreasing since the depression years, first rapidly and then slowly. The slowdown has become particularly marked during the last decade. The proportion of the destitute with incomes under half the level taken to be the poverty line has actually increased a little. . . .

Poverty is greater in the South. It is more than twice as common among the nonwhite population all over the country. More than three times as many nonwhites as whites have less than half of the income taken to demarcate the poverty line. .

Poverty is also greater in agriculture. It there afflicts the small farmers, the small tenants, and the hired workers who make up the majority of rural people. About two thirds of the latter group earned less than $1,000 a year.

Much more frequently poverty hits families whose head is female, whether they have lost a husband and father or never had one. People over sixty-five years of age are particularly poor in America. Of those aged sixty-five and having a family, close to two thirds lived in poverty and nearly one third were destitute, according to the definitions given above. Indeed, one tenth of the families had to live on less than $1,000 a year which means utter destitution. The lonely elderly persons were even worse off. Four fifths lived in poverty and nearly half were destitute. The median income of families with heads aged sixty-five and over was under $3,000 and of unattached individuals only a little over $1,000. This age group is now increasing almost twice as fast as ten years ago.

Low income is closely related to the amount of schooling people have had. . . .

More than 40 per cent of the families whose heads were unemployed lived in poverty. They constituted a fourth of the total population living in poverty. The other three fourths had occupations for which we have invented the new term "underemployed" when analyzing the development problems in underdeveloped countries in order to characterize people who have been stuck in localities and jobs on a low level of productivity and, consequently, of earnings.

To the underemployed in this sense belong the larger part of the agricultural population of which the progressive, and prosperous, mainly large-scale farm operators, are a minority. In the cities they have low-paid jobs, often of a casual nature.

INCREASED INEQUALITY IN THE MIDST OF GENERAL EQUALITY

It is perfectly possible for the majority of Americans to live, together with practically everybody they have primary contact with, in a situation of full and even overfull employment where there is brisk demand and competition for their labor, while they read in the newspapers that there is large and growing unemployment beneath them. That this can be so is the result of the nature of unemployment being to a large extent structural in character.

While this is happening at the bottom of American society it is perfectly possible that there is ever greater social mobility, liberty, and equality of opportunity and a generally rising economic and cultural level in majority America. More and more individuals and families may move further away from the neighborhood of the dividing line. Social welfare policies have, as I pointed out, been framed to give greater security especially for that middle group in the nation. And there might even be some successful passing of the poverty line by individuals coming from beneath it, which then gives a false assurance that America is still the free and open society of its cherished image and well established ideals.

But as less and less work is required of the type the people in the urban and rural slums can offer, they will be increasingly isolated and exposed to unemployment, to underemployment, and to plain exploitation. There is an ugly smell rising from the basement of the stately American mansion.

THE SOVIET INCOME REVOLUTION

Murray Yanowitch

A number of studies of income distribution have suggested that income inequality in the

From *Slavic Review*, Vol. XXII, No. 4, December, 1963, pp. 683–697. Reprinted by permission.

United States showed some tendency to decline during the 1930s and the war years. Although the extent and timing of the decline may be in dispute among specialists in this area, and some recent studies suggest that no significant changes in income shares have occurred since 1944, the American Income Revolution has nonetheless been widely accepted and acclaimed.[1] All the more reason, it would seem, that studies of changes in income inequality in Soviet Russia should prove of great interest. If income inequality has been reduced in the world's major capitalist economy, what has been happening to income distribution in the Soviet Union?

Until recently the kind of income data required to answer this question have been unavailable. Some reliance, however, could be placed on official policy statements on wage structure. For almost thirty years, beginning in 1931, every major statement of Soviet wage policy was accompanied by a denunciation of "equalitarianism." Wage-leveling was identified as a petty bourgeois and utopian socialist policy; at times it was linked with even more ominous associations.[2] Since wage structure was centrally controlled, it was logical to assume that a government which was combating equalitarianism was pursuing a policy designed to increase income inequality. Reports of extremely high incomes for individual scientists, literary figures, and composers reinforced this impression.

The anomaly of a self-proclaimed socialist government promoting and extending income inequality while inequality was being reduced in the United States provided an intriguing contrast. Some scholars, apparently uninhibited by the paucity of data, concluded that income inequality in Soviet Russia far exceeded anything existing in the Western world.[3] The fact remains, however, that there was little upon which to base such judgments other than official Soviet statements of wage policy and a scattering of wage and salary rate data.

The situation has changed markedly since 1956 in several important respects. Beginning with the 20th Party Congress in 1956 and culminating with the program adopted by the 22nd Party Congress in 1961, the main emphasis in Soviet wage policy has been placed on a narrowing of the income gap between high- and low-paid personnel. The theme was first enunciated by Mikoyan at the 20th Party Congress;[4] it was implemented at the 21st Congress in 1959, at which time a program of increasing minimum wages from their prevailing level of 27–35 rubles to 50–60 rubles per month by 1965 was announced;[5] and it was reasserted at the 22nd Congress, where it was declared in the program that in the next twenty years "the disparity between high and comparatively low incomes must be steadily reduced."[6]

Since 1956 these policy declarations have been accompanied by the issuance of new wage and salary schedules and by the publication of some earnings data which permit us to establish recent trends in Soviet income structure. Projected changes in the incomes of various groups of the population also make it possible to determine what extremes in Soviet income differentials will look like in the future if the policies enunciated at the last three Party Congresses continue to be implemented.

Our concern here is with the money incomes of those classified as "workers and salaried personnel" (*rabochie i sluzhashchie*). Thus we shall not consider the impact on wage structure of recent income tax changes and the ending of compulsory bond purchases in 1958. The broad effect of the first of these measures, however, seems reasonably clear. The suspension of the program to eliminate all income taxes on wages and

---

[1] . . . An effective presentation of a dissenting view appears in Gabriel Kolko, *Wealth and Power in America* (New York, 1962). . . .

[2] Thus in A. Ляпин, *Труд при социализме* (Moscow, 1951), p. 60, it was identified as a policy of "Trotskyites, Zinovievites, Bukharinites and other enemies of the people. . . ."

[3] One such example is the sociologist S. M. Lipset in *Socialist Call*, Summer, 1961, p. 12. However, he cites Italy as an exception.

[4] *Правда*, Feb. 18, 1956.

[5] All ruble figures in this paper are given in terms of the new rubles introduced in January, 1961. The original figures here were 270–350 rubles and 500–600 rubles.

[6] *Program of the Communist Party of the Soviet Union Adopted by the 22nd Congress of the CPSU, October, 1961* (New York, 1961), p. 95; hereafter cited as *Party Program*.

salaries after taxes had been ended on incomes up to 60 rubles per month (and reduced on incomes between 61 and 70 rubles per month) has certainly operated to narrow income inequality. It is possible, however, that the ending of compulsory bond purchases has worked in the opposite direction. Nor will we consider the increasing portion of income which is scheduled for distribution in the form of free goods and services in the future, except to note that it will reinforce whatever trend toward equalization is observed in the distribution of money income. Further, our comments apply only to the non-agricultural sector of the population.[7]

RECENT TRENDS IN SOVIET INCOME STRUCTURE

Wage Workers. It is now quite clear that the gap between the income of relatively high- and low-paid workers increased between the state of the anti-equalitarian campaign in the early 1930s and the holding of the 20th Party Congress in 1956. This can hardly occasion great surprise. What is perhaps of greater interest is the extent to which the trend toward greater income differences has been reversed since 1956 and how income inequality among workers in recent years compares with that prevailing in the past.

Trends in Soviet wage inequality over the last thirty years may be traced by observing changes in the ratio of the ninth to the first decile of the distribution of Soviet workers according to earnings and similarly the ratio of the third to the first quartile.[8] These are summary measures of wage dispersion, and it is in this sense that we shall refer to inequality here. They tell us nothing about the share of total income received by any percentage of the population.[9] But they are the best measures currently available for our purpose. We may refer to them henceforth (admittedly somewhat loosely) as the ratios of upper-to-lower tenth incomes (D9/D1) and upper-to-lower quarter

[7] Incomes of collective farmers are scheduled to rise more rapidly than those of workers (*ibid.*, p. 96).

[8] The ninth decile wage is the wage which was exceeded by the top 10 per cent of the workers; the first decile wage is the wage which the bottom 10 per cent failed to reach. The third and first quartiles may be defined similarly for the corresponding 25 per cent of workers. Changes in these ratios reflect not only changes in the relative wages of particular occupations but also changes in the relative importance of the various occupations. Hence, these ratios are more properly designated as measures of wage variation rather than of wage differentiation. See Abram Bergson, *The Structure of Soviet Wages* (Cambridge, Mass., 1946), p. 55.

[9] It is possible, reading from a Soviet chart, to derive rough estimates of the share of wage income received by different proportions of Soviet workers and on this basis to construct Lorenz curves of wage distribution for 1934, 1956, and 1959 (М. Можина, «Изменения в распределении промышленных рабочих СССР по размерам

заработной платы», *Бюллетень научной информации, труд и заработная плата*, No. 10, 1961, p. 24).

The chart shows the percentage of workers on the vertical axis and mid-points of income classes on the horizontal axis, with the mid-points expressed as percentages of the median wage. It is our judgment, however, that the values that may be read from this chart are of dubious value for observing changes in the size distribution of Soviet wage incomes. Portions of the chart are barely distinguishable, and there is particular uncertainty about the low- and high-income extremes. The Lorenz curves that may be derived from this chart (at least in our reading of the values) appear to be essentially the same for 1934, 1956, and 1959. Whether this reflects the actual state of affairs or the roughness of the chart (or our reading of it), we prefer to leave for future study. We may note, however, that the income shares estimated from the chart for 1934 exhibit less inequality than was suggested by Bergson's study of Soviet wages in that year (Bergson, *op. cit.*, p. 123):

Cumulative percentage of workers	10	20	30	40	50	60	70	80	90	100
Cumulative percentage of wage bill (Bergson)	3.4	8.7	15.0	22.3	30.5	39.9	50.5	62.7	77.7	100.0
Cumulative percentage of wage bill (Soviet chart)	4.8	10.2	17.5	25.1	34.0	44.2	55.6	68.8	82.0	100.0

For 1956 and 1959 the estimated shares of the wage bill differ altogether insignificantly from those read from the Soviet chart for 1934.

incomes (Q3/Q1) respectively. The results are shown below:[10]

YEAR	Decile Ratio (D9/D1 IN PER CENT)	Quartile Ratio (Q3/Q1 IN PER CENT)
1929	315	182
1934	317	182
1956	338	185
1959	328	184

The anti-equalitarian campaign was begun in the early 1930s, and its full impact would not yet have been apparent by 1934. Hence the figures show only a slight increase in wage inequality between 1929 and 1934 if the first of our measures is used, while no change is exhibited by the second measure. By 1956 however (before the decisions announced at the 20th Party Congress could be implemented), our indicators of wage inequality had risen by 21 percentage points as measured by the ratio of upper-to-lower tenth incomes, and 3 percentage points if the less sensitive ratio of upper-to-lower-quarter incomes is used. After 1956 there was a decline in dispersion, thereby reversing the earlier trend, but inequality remained greater in 1959 than it had been in the late 1920s and early 1930s.

What is particularly striking, however, is that almost one half of the increase in wage dispersion between 1934 and 1956 (as recorded by the more sensitive of these ratios) was wiped out in the brief period between the 20th and 21st Party Congresses (1956 to 1959).[11]

Where direct evidence exists of changes in

wage dispersion since 1959, it points in the same direction as the decile and quartile ratios cited above—to a narrowing of wage inequality in recent years. Changes in wage structure at the *Elektrosila* electrical machinery plant between 1959 and 1960 are cited as typical of those in this industry as a whole. They are presented below:[12]

YEAR	Decile Ratio (D9/D1 IN PER CENT)	Quartile Ratio (Q3/Q1 IN PER CENT)
June, 1959	228	159
June, 1960	213	154

There is every reason to believe that the decline in income differences among workers observed since 1956 has continued to the present (1963) and that upper-to-lower income ratios today are not much higher (if at all) than they were some thirty years ago. This seems evident from the continuing implementation of three policies: (1) Wage-rate differentials between skilled and unskilled occupations are being reduced in newly issued wage scales. The ratios of extreme rates in wage scales issued in 1960 and 1961 have generally been in the neighborhood of 2 to 1 or 1.8 to 1, compared to the 2.8 to 1 and higher that was typical of earlier scales. Although these ratios exclude premiums, the reduction of basic wage-rate differentials suggests at least the direction of change in actual earnings differentials. (2) Minimum wages were raised to 40–45 rubles per month in 1962 compared to the 27–35 rubles established in 1957. This change narrowed not only occupational but also inter-industry wage differentials, thereby reinforcing a process that began even before 1956.[13] (3) The piece-rate system of wage

[10] Можина, *op. cit.*, pp. 21, 25. The decile and quartile ratios given here for 1934 are below those which may be derived from Bergson's study (*op. cit.*, p. 128). The Bergson data imply decile and quartile ratios of 374 and 194 respectively, thus suggesting greater wage dispersion in 1934 than that indicated by the figures presented here (317 for the decile ratio and 182 for the quartile ratio). The discrepancies may possibly be explained by differences in coverage and Bergson's need to rely on interpolation of the required values.

[11] It should be noted, however, that the peak in wage inequality probably occurred before 1956. Wage rate differentials had been reduced after the war. Most of the increase between 1934 and 1956 in the ratios shown above may reflect the widening of wage differentials prior to the war.

[12] А. Агеева and А. Тыклин, «Анализ сокращения различии в оплате труда низко- и высокооплачиваемых работников электротехнической промышленности,» *Бюллетень научной информации, труд и заработная плата*, No. 12, 1961, p. 32.

[13] Between 1950 and 1956 wages in the most highly paid sectors (coal, oil, steel) increased less than average earnings in industry as a whole (Можина, *op. cit.*, p. 24).

payment is gradually being replaced by time rates. This is clear from the data presented in Table 1.

Although the bulk of Soviet workers are still on some form of piece rates (about two-thirds in 1961 compared to three-fourths in 1959), there is clear recognition that the measurement of individual output is increasingly incompatible with new technology, particularly that associated with automation.[14] Soviet writers expect the number of piece workers to decline to 45 to 50 per cent of all industrial workers within a decade.[15] The progressive piece-rate system has all but disappeared, with only 1 per cent of the workers in industry being paid according to this method in 1961.

If these policies continue to be pursued throughout the 1960s (and the current Soviet literature on the subject suggests that they will be), by the end of the decade income differentials among workers may be less than those which prevailed before the attack on equalitarianism.

Wage Workers and Salaried Personnel. Another aspect of the changing Soviet income structure may be observed by asking what happened to the earnings of workers compared to those of other groups, in particular to the salaried personnel category. Salaried personnel in Soviet industry fall into two categories: (1) "engineering-technical personnel," ranging from foreman to plant director and including also technicians, engineers, and shop superintendents; (2) "employees," which corresponds roughly to our white-collar office and accounting personnel. The results of such a comparison are quite revealing and are indicated below.[16]

These figures suggest a rather remarkable change in the Soviet income structure. While the average earnings of engineering-technical personnel exceeded those of workers by some two and one-half times in the early 1930s, their relative wage advantage over workers had fallen to 50 per cent by 1960. As for employees, their earnings fell below those of workers in the postwar period after having been 50 per cent above them in the early 1930s. The most striking aspect of this improvement in the relative income status of workers compared to salaried personnel is surely the narrowing of the average earnings gap between workers and engineering-technical personnel. This narrowing is apparent not only on an all-industry basis (the figures above) but also within those individual industries for which

[14] Г. Х. Гендлер, *Заработная плата и технический прогресс* (Moscow, 1961), p. 65.

[15] Е. И. Капустин, *Заработная плата в промышленности СССР и ее совершенствование* (Moscow, 1961), p. 98.

[16] А. Г. Аганбегян В. Ф. Майер, *Заработная плата в СССР* (Moscow, 1959), p. 202; ЦУНХУ, *Труд в СССР* (Moscow, 1936), p. 96; *Социалистический труд*, No. 10, 1961, p. 31. While the figures through 1955 clearly apply to earnings, including premiums, there may be some doubt as to the figure for 1960 cited in the latter source. The 1960 figure is referred to as "the relationship between average wages of workers and the average rate (*oklad*) of engineering-technical personnel." However, the same terminology is also used here for a 1932 figure which other sources make clear applies to earnings. In any case, the trend from 1932 to 1955 revealed in the figures above remains unaffected.

Year	Average Earnings of Engineering-Technical Personnel in Per Cent of Average Earnings of Workers	Average Earnings of Employees in Per Cent of Average Earnings of Workers
1932	263	150
1935	236	126
1940	210	109
1950	175	93
1955	165	88
1960	150	

TABLE 1   Distribution of Soviet Workers by Form of Wage Payment in
Selected Industries, 1956 and 1961 (in Per Cent)

Industry	1956		1961	
	Piece Work	Time Work	Piece Work	Time Work
Ferrous metallurgy	70.9	29.1	60.1	39.9
Coal	59.1	40.9	48.9	51.1
Oil extraction	51.1	48.9	17.7	82.3
Oil refining	65.0	35.0	8.9	91.1
Machine-building and metalworking	74.2	25.8	57.3	42.7
Chemical	68.5	31.5	39.0	61.0
Woodworking	87.6	12.4	76.9	23.1
Paper	87.4	12.6	58.7	41.3
Cement	80.1	19.9	64.7	35.3
Textiles	84.8	15.2	68.4	31.6
Food	82.0	18.0	58.4	41.6
Printing	67.2	32.8	59.5	40.5
Shoe	85.6	14.4	82.9	17.1
Glass and porcelain	81.2	18.8	65.1	34.9

Sources: Г. Х. Гендлер, *Заработная плата и технический прогресс* (Moscow, 1961). p. 65; *Вестник статистики*, No. 6, 1962, pp. 94–96. The 1961 figures apply to March 31.

the appropriate wage data are available for the 1930s and 1950s (see Table 2). The narrowing of these differentials seems all the more significant when it is realized that it apparently applies to earnings, inclusive of premiums, rather than to basic wage rates. At least this is suggested by the terminology used (*zarabotnaia plata* rather than *oklady* or *stavki*).

Where the data for individual sectors can be extended to 1960, they point in the same direction. Thus in 1960 the ratio of engineering-technical earnings to workers' earnings stood at 1.83 in nonferrous metallurgy and 1.58 in the cement industry as compared to 2.06 and 1.76 respectively before the wage adjustments made in the late 1950s.[17]

Part of the explanation of this phenomenon undoubtedly lies in the changing occupational composition of the workers and engineering-technical personnel categories. Among workers the relative importance of the more skilled and therefore the most highly paid occupations within the group increased markedly after the 1930s. These were also the groups that gained most from the anti-equalitarian wage

[17] Капустин, *op. cit.*, p. 41.

TABLE 2   Average Monthly Earnings of
Engineering-Technical Personnel in
Per Cent of Average Earnings of Workers,
1934 and 1956

Industry	1934	1956
Nonferrous ore mining	—	240
Iron ore mining	294	170
Coal mining	301	160
Logging	—	150
Machine-building	222	150
Cotton	290	160
Wool	302	140
Knitted goods	246	135
Fishing	—	200
Fruit production	—	180
Meat	277	160
Butter and dairy products	—	130
Electric power stations	257	180

Sources: 1934 figures for knitted goods and meat apply to October, 1934, while for other sectors they are based on average monthly earnings for the whole year. Figures for 1934 were calculated from ЦУНХУ, *Труд в СССР* (Moscow, 1936); ЦУНХУ, *Заработная плата рабочих крупной промышленности в октябре 1934 г.* (Moscow, 1935). Figures for 1956 are from А. Г. Аганбегян and В. Ф. Майер, *Заработная плата в СССР* (Moscow, 1959), p. 202; А. Я. Аврух, *Себестоимость электрической и тепловой энергии* (Moscow, 1957), p. 88.

policy. Among engineering-technical personnel, on the other hand, comparatively low-paid occupations increased in importance more rapidly than highly paid ones.

But even independently of changes in occupational composition within the two groups, Soviet wage policy since at least the end of the war has operated to narrow the earnings gap between workers and engineering-technical personnel. Thus, wage increases granted at the end of 1946—which were designed partially to compensate relatively low-paid personnel for price increases attendant on derationing—benefited primarily wage workers and office employees. Similarly, the wage increases announced for workers' occupations as a group since 1956 have exceeded those granted to engineering-technical personnel. Where the opposite trend has appeared in individual plants it has been treated as a "negative feature" in conflict with current Soviet wage policy.[18] Further, salary differentials within the engineering-technical category are also being reduced. In 1958 salary-scale revisions in some sectors were reported to have reduced the ratio of plant directors' to foremen's rates from 4–5 to 1 to 3–3.5 to 1. Between 1959 and 1965 the difference between the earnings of plant directors and engineers, is scheduled to decline by 50 per cent.[19]

In some industries the narrowing of the wage differential between workers and engineering-technical personnel has also been accompanied by a considerable overlapping of incomes received by personnel in the two groups. Thus in 1956 the wages of approximately 30 per cent of the workers in some sectors of the coal and machine-building industries exceeded the average earnings of the engineering-technical category as a whole in these sectors.[20] Basic wage rates authorized in recently issued wage scales for the most skilled workers' occupations exceed those set for the lower categories of engineering personnel.

The overlapping of worker and engineering-technical incomes is also related to the marked inter-industry wage differentials which have continued to characterize Soviet wage structure. Thus in the mid-fifties the average earnings of workers in coal mining exceeded those of workers in the food industry by more than 100 per cent, in the textile industry by about 95 per cent, in logging operations by more than 60 per cent, and in machine-building by almost 50 per cent.[21] Judging by the regional data available for 1959 (for the Ukraine) similarly large inter-industry wage differentials are still in effect.[22] Juxtaposing these figures with those given in Table 2 on the ratios of engineering-technical to workers' earnings it is clear that the average wages of workers in coal mining exceeded the average earnings of engineering-technical personnel in the food, textile, and logging industries, and approached them in machine-building. Workers' average earnings in such highly paid sectors as steel and nonferrous metallurgy also exceeded those of engineering-technical personnel employed in some consumer goods sectors.

The material reviewed here, particularly on the narrowing of the earnings gap between workers and salaried personnel, suggests the strong possibility that inequality in the distribution of *wage and salary income combined* diminished between the early 1930s and the late 1950s. Although the available measures of income inequality are not really adequate, it does seem significant that the only two measures available both point in the direction of reduced inequality:

(1) The only serious Western study of Soviet income inequality, that by Abram Bergson, found that in 1934 the top 10 per cent of wage and salary recipients in industry received 24.3 per cent of the total wage bill, while the bottom 10 per cent received 3 per cent. This 1934 ratio of

---

[18] Агеева and Тыклин, *op. cit.*, p. 38.

[19] *Социалистический труд*, No. 11, 1958, p. 20; Аганбегян and Майер, *op. cit.*, p. 228.

[20] В. Е. Комаров, *Экономические основы подготовки специалистов для народного хозяйства* (Moscow, 1959), p. 156.

[21] Аганбегян and Майер, *op. cit.*, p. 187; Можина, *op. cit.*, p. 24.

[22] Thus the average earnings of coal miners in the Ukraine in 1959 were about 260 per cent of the earnings of workers in the food industry, 250 per cent of those in light industry, and 220 per cent of those in the forestry, paper, and woodworking industries (Капустин, *op. cit.*, p. 197).

approximately 8 to 1 between the average earnings of the highest and lowest paid 10 per cent of wage and salaried personnel combined may be compared with a ratio of 5.8 to 1 announced in recent Soviet publications for 1959.[23]

(2) Soviet wage studies have found that the ratio of the third to the first quartile of the earnings distribution of wage and salaried personnel combined declined slightly between 1946 and 1956.[24]

Trends in income structure in Soviet industry over the last three decades may be summarized briefly as follows. Wage inequality among workers tended to increase over most of the period between the early 1930s and the late 1950s. This reflected the implementation of an anti-equalitarian wage policy by means of widening occupational wage-rate differentials between skilled and unskilled workers and the extensive application of the piece-rate system. Wage inequality declined between 1956 and 1959 but remained greater in 1959 than it was in the early 1930s. The period since 1956 has been marked by a narrowing of skill differentials in wage rates, substantial increases in minimum wages, and the declining importance of the piece-rate system. These policies promise to reduce wage inequality among workers below the level prevailing in the early 1930s, if they have not done so already.

While wage inequality among workers was increasing, the income gap between workers and the bulk of engineering-technical personnel was declining. Workers also improved their income position relative to that of office personnel.

SOVIET INCOME DIFFERENTIALS IN THE FUTURE

The new party program and the other documents of the 22nd Party Congress do not contain much in the way of precise quantitative material on planned changes in income structure. By 1970 the real incomes of "low paid" workers and employees are scheduled to approximately triple, while for all personnel they will be "almost doubled." These documents, however, frequently reaffirm the previously announced intention of further reducing income inequality. We may summarize some of the earlier announcements bearing on future trends in income inequality as below.

To complete the picture we may note one additional bit of information. The wages of those who earned more than 140 rubles per month in 1959 are to remain "basically unchanged" by 1965; the wages of those earning 60 to 140 rubles per month are to rise by an average of 20 to 25 per cent, while the average increase for those earnings below 60 rubles will be in the range of 45 to 60 per cent.[25]

In the West we have been accustomed to viewing marked changes in income structure as normally requiring a rather extended period of time. Considering the short period within which the Soviet program outlined above is to be achieved and the magnitude

---

[23] П. С. Мстиславский, *Народное потребление при социализме* (Moscow, 1961), p. 86. The data for 1934 are in Bergson, *op. cit.*, p. 123.

[24] Можина, *op. cit.*, p. 22.

[25] Мстиславский, *op. cit.*, pp. 85–86. The average wage figures above are estimated from data in С. П. Фигурнов, *Реальная заработная плата и подъем материального благосостояния трудящихся в СССР* (Moscow, 1960), p. 136.

	1959	1965
Ratio of average wages of top 10 per cent of workers and salaried personnel to bottom 10 per cent	5.8:1	3.8:1
Ratio of average incomes of top 10 per cent of families to bottom 10 per cent (including money and non-money incomes)	4.75:1	3:1
Minimum wages (in rubles per month)	27–35	50–60
Average wages of workers and salaried personnel (in rubles per month)	79	99

of the changes involved, the term Soviet "income revolution" does not seem like an exaggeration.[26]

However, even if the planned changes in income structure are actually realized, Soviet Russia will hardly approximate the vision of an equalitarian society. This is apparent if we observe how large the wage differentials which will separate the top from the bottom of the occupational ladder will be in 1965. Since we lack the necessary earnings data, reliance will have to be placed on basic salary rates (exclusive of bonuses and other supplementary income). To represent the upper extreme we may select the top rates of some of the highly paid occupations whose wages will remain essentially stable between 1959 and 1965. The bottom of the income ladder may be represented by occupations whose lowest rates were at or slightly above the prevailing minimum wage in 1959. The extremes in Soviet salary rates will look approximately as follows in the steel industry in 1965 as compared to 1959 (in rubles per month):[27]

	1959	1965
Director of scientific research institute	600	600
Director of steel plant	400	400
Elevator operator, janitor, watchman	35	60
Typist, secretary	41	60

Thus if the lowest 1959 rates increase to the extent implied by the minimum wage goal for 1965, while the top rates remain unchanged, the ratio of highest to lowest rates will still be 10:1 compared to 17:1 in 1959. Further, this ratio obviously understates the difference between extremes in actual money earnings as distinct from basic salary rates. The director of the steel plant is more likely to receive a bonus supplement than is the elevator operator or janitor, and the research institute director will probably receive royalties and additional pay for teaching at the local university. It is clear that whatever may be the share of monetary and non-monetary supplements in the incomes of the lowest paid occupations, differences between extremes in real incomes in Soviet society will remain considerable by any standards throughout the 1960s.

THE NON-EQUALITARIAN REDUCTION OF INCOME INEQUALITY

How are we to explain the reduction in workers' wage differentials since 1956 and the planned reduction of income inequality in the future? First, it is clear that these phenomena cannot be explained by the growth of equalitarian sentiments among the Soviet leaders. Indeed, it is a curious feature of the current Soviet scene that in the midst of what is obviously a serious attempt to narrow income differentials, great pains are taken to disassociate this policy from any equalitarian taint. Khrushchev's report to the 22nd Party Congress and the party program make this distinction time and

[26] It is hazardous but tempting to compare Soviet income inequality with that prevailing in the United States. We may simply indicate what some highly provisional findings reveal. Among workers the ratio of the third to the first quartile (Q3/Q1) of a wage distribution covering about two-fifths of non-farm wage earners in the United States in 1956 was 1.37; Paul T. Homan, Albert G. Hart, and Arnold W. Sametz, *The Economic Order* (New York, 1958), p. 285. As noted above, the corresponding Soviet figures in recent years have been in the neighborhood of 1.85. Although there are serious questions concerning the comparability of the data, the direction in which these figures point is unmistakable—wage dispersion among workers is greater in Soviet Russia than in the United States. However, comparisons of income inequality for the whole population of the two countries point in the opposite direction. In the United States the share of money income received by the highest 10 per cent of spending units in recent years has been approximately thirty times that received by the lowest 10 per cent (U.S. Bureau of the Census, *Statistical Abstract of the United States, 1961*, p. 315). The Soviet ratio of incomes—money and non-money—of the top 10 per cent of families to the bottom 10 per cent (4.75:1) is, of course, not comparable to these United States figures. But it seems quite unlikely that the necessary adjustments to the Soviet figures would raise the Soviet ratio to the United States level. The chief adjustments would require inclusion of the farm population's income and elimination of all non-money incomes. The latter adjustment alone would raise the Soviet ratio to no more than 6:1 or 7:1 (Фигурнов *op. cit.,* p. 94).

[27] С. М. Левин and М. Н. Тимошпольский, *Организация заработной платы в черной металлургии* (Moscow, 1959), pp. 194, 196–98.

again.[28] Thus for some thirty years now, beginning with Stalin's denunciation of anonymous equalitarians in 1931 and extending through periods of both increasing and decreasing wage inequality, equalitarianism has been a term of opprobrium in Soviet Russia. Why should this have been necessary in the past and why is this still the case? A brief examination of the shifting uses of this term casts a revealing light on the way in which both continuity and change may appear in Soviet policy-making.

When the attack on equalitarianism began in the early 1930s it was not immediately clear who or what was being attacked. There had been no widespread pressure—at least in print—for wage equalization from any section of the party or trade union leadership in the immediately preceding period. In any explicit discussions of equalitarianism that appeared in the more academic publications in the late 1920s, the main purpose was to distinguish it from what was viewed as the genuine socialist tradition.[29] It is true that in 1926 at the 7th Congress of Trade Unions (with Stalin and other party leaders present) a policy of reducing wage differentials had been adopted and M. P. Tomsky, the head of the Soviet trade unions at the time, referred to this as a matter of "elementary class justice." But this policy had not been carried very far by 1931 and there is no evidence that such statements were still being made. Who, then, were the equalitarians? Considering the vigor of the attack against them, one would expect that they represented an influential group of party or trade union leaders urging the immediate elimination or marked reduction of wage inequality. In this sense, the answer to the question, who were the equalitarians, must be that they were at least partly a myth.

Having decided on a policy of rapid industrialization, the Soviet leadership realized that this would require a similarly rapid change in the occupational composition of the industrial work force, in particular a sharp increase in the number of skilled workers. One instrument for achieving this goal was to be a rather prolonged policy of widening wage differentials between skilled and unskilled occupations. The attack on equalitarianism, then, was in reality less an attack on a specific group of opponents of party policy than it was a way of focusing attention on a crucial problem— the need to utilize monetary incentives to promote the development of scarce skills. But like any other major policy of the period it had to be pursued as a "struggle" against something, that is, against an anonymous, largely mythical group of wage-levelers.

To the extent that equalitarianism was not a myth but a real obstacle, it represented a general unawareness of this problem, an unawareness to which the socialist tradition had contributed. For the whole tradition of socialist thought, including its Marxian wing, had long been imbued with the vision of eliminating the income inequalities associated with capitalism. While there were differences within this tradition with respect to the timing and the extent of the increased equality expected under socialism, there was nothing in socialist thought to suggest that the new society would ever require a widening of income inequality among workers. Marx's concept of distribution in the first phase of the Communist society ("according to work performed") involved acceptance of income inequality. This inequality, however, reflected the defects of the old society from which the first phase of communism would emerge, not a feature which the new society should promote.

But if the Soviet leaders' attack on equalitarianism in the 1930s served a useful purpose, what function does the continued rejection of equalitarianism serve now that differences in income are being reduced? Erich Fromm has pointed to the ritualistic character of some Soviet statements, in which it becomes necessary to speak as an upholder of an old orthodoxy even while the latter is being rejected in practice. After thirty years it is possible that anti-equalitarianism has become such an orthodoxy. While this explanation may have some validity as applied to the statements of

---

[28] N. S. Khrushchev, *Report on the Program of the Communist Party of the Soviet Union* (New York, 1961), I, 130; II, 87–88; *Party Program* p. 93.

[29] В. Волгин, «Социализм и эгалитаризм,» *Вестник коммунистической академии,* XXIX (1928), 13–27.

lower-echelon officials and writers (among whom old habits of speech and thought seem particularly persistent) it seems to us too facile an explanation of the anti-equalitarian strictures voiced by Soviet leaders. Of all the Stalinist orthodoxies which are being abandoned why should this particular one be retained?

Another possibility is that the continuing criticism of equalitarianism is now directed against popular misconceptions of "distribution according to needs" and "Communist equality," both of which have been presented by Soviet leaders as the principles of income distribution in the future Soviet society. Thus some Soviet writers warn that these principles do not imply absolute equality of income for all or "equal shares" in the total product, conceptions which these writers link with equalitarianism.[30] But it is difficult to believe that much of the Soviet population envisions either the immediate or distant future in terms of "equal shares." Neither the Marxian tradition nor what we know of the Soviet people's aspirations point in this direction. If the warnings against equalitarianism were to be primarily aimed at such views they would be battling a largely nonexistent danger.

There is another explanation for these strictures which seems quite simple and which simultaneously focuses attention on the reasons for the policy of reducing income inequality. Income differentials are now being reduced largely because a substantial rise in the educational, and hence in the skill, level of new entrants into the labor force has made the wide differentials of early industrialization unnecessary. Not only are they unnecessary; in some economic sectors their retention would be clearly harmful. Although the typical new entrant into the labor force is probably capable of performing at least semiskilled work (if not immediately, then within a few months), there are still a considerable number of unskilled jobs that must be performed in Soviet industry. The reluctance of workers to accept such jobs when their training permits their employment in more skilled and therefore more remunerative work clearly makes reduced wage differentials for skill a desirable policy. The strange phenomenon (strange for Soviet industry) of a "shortage of unskilled labor" has been explicitly cited in Soviet discussions of labor and wage policy.[31] Where this is not a problem, the leveling of workers' skills and proficiency as a result of the broad extension of technical education is itself a factor which makes the reduction of income differentials appear advisable.

The relevance of all this to the continuing rejection of equalitarianism seems quite clear. The principal reasons for the policy of reducing income inequality are rooted in "objective factors," that is, in the changing relative scarcities of skilled and unskilled labor. They have little if anything to do with Tomsky's sentiments of "elementary class justice" (at least thus far). Equalitarianism, then, has come to signify a narrowing of income differentials that would go beyond the limits imposed by these "objective factors." Thus the Central Committee report to the 22nd Party Congress contrasts equalitarianism with the present policy of reducing wage differentials in conformity with the disappearance of the unskilled worker category. Looking ahead to the future when the principle of "distribution according to needs" will govern, the report emphasizes that attempts to introduce this principle prematurely "would be outright equalitarianism." Its introduction requires a much higher level of material abundance than presently exists and the transformation of work from a means of earning a livelihood to a "social calling, a moral duty" (or, in the more usual terminology, "the first necessity of life"). The point was made clearly in an article written more than a year before the latest Party Congress: "The first and foremost problem of the construction of Communism is not how to distribute justly but how to create an abundance of material values."[32]

While in the 1930s the strictures against

[30] С. П. Первушин, *Некоторые проблемы перехода от социализма к коммунизму* (Moscow, 1960), pp. 96–97.

[31] А. Каценелинбойген, «О редукции труда,» *Вопросы экономики*, No. 3, 1961, p. 57.

[32] М. Саков, «От каждого по способностям, каждому по потребностям,» *Политическое самообразование*, No. 8, 1960, p. 27.

equalitarianism were linked with a policy of increasing wage differentials for skill, today they serve to emphasize the limits within which the opposite policy may be pursued. In both the 1930s and 1960s, however, the primary concern is with increasing output, not with "how to distribute justly."

The latter question will come into its own when material abundance and changed attitudes toward work will have been achieved. When this occurs, the problem of equalitarianism will disappear and "Communist equality" in distribution will prevail, that is *equal access* by all to the goods and services required to satisfy rational human needs.

Whatever the possibility of realizing this vision of the future, it is clear that inequality in the distribution of income is currently being reduced. But this, of course, is only one form of inequality in Soviet society. It is not at all clear that inequality in the distribution of political power is moving in the same direction.

Power Inequality

THE NEW CLASS

Milovan Djilas

I.

Everything happened differently in the U.S.S.R. and other Communist countries from what the leaders—even such prominent ones as Lenin, Stalin, Trotsky, and Bukharin—anticipated. . . . The greatest illusion was that industrialization and collectivization in the U.S.S.R., and destruction of capitalist ownership, would result in a classless society. In 1936, when the new

From *The New Class*, by Milovan Djilas, Frederick A. Praeger, 1965. Reprinted by permission.

Constitution was promulgated, Stalin announced that the "exploiting class" had ceased to exist. The capitalist and other classes of ancient origin had in fact been destroyed but a new class, previously unknown to history, had been formed. . . .

This new class, the bureaucracy, or more accurately the political bureaucracy, has all the characteristics of earlier ones as well as some new characteristics of its own. Its origin had its special characteristics also, even though in essence it was similar to the beginnings of other classes.

Other classes, too, obtained their strength and power by the revolutionary path, destroying the political, social, and other orders they met in their way. However, almost without exception, these classes attained power *after* new economic patterns had taken shape in the old society. The case was the reverse with new classes in the Communist systems. It did not come to power to *complete* a new economic order but to *establish* its own and, in so doing, to establish its power over society.

In earlier epochs the coming to power of some class, some part of a class, or of some party, was the final event resulting from its formation and its development. The reverse was true in the U.S.S.R. There the new class was definitely formed after it attained power. Its consciousness had to develop before its economic and physical powers, because the class had not taken root in the life of the nation. This class viewed its role in relation to the world from an idealistic point of view. Its practical possibilities were not diminished by this. In spite of its illusions, it represented an objective tendency toward industrialization. Its practical bent emanated from this tendency. The promise of an ideal world increased the faith in the ranks of the new class and sowed illusions among the masses. At the same time it inspired gigantic physical undertakings.

Because this new class had not been formed as a part of the economic and social life before it came to power, it could only be created in an organization of a special type, distinguished by a special discipline based on identical philosophic and ideological views of its members. A unity of belief and iron discipline was necessary to overcome its weaknesses.

The roots of the new class were implanted in a special party, of the Bolshevik type. . . . To be more precise, the initiators of the new class are not found in the party of the Bolshevik type as a whole but in that stratum of professional revolutionaries who made up its core even before it attained power. . . . The new ruling class has been gradually developing from this very narrow stratum of revolutionaries. These revolutionaries composed its core for a long period. Trotsky noted that in pre-revolutionary professional revolutionaries was the origin of the future Stalinist bureaucrat. What he did not detect was the beginning of a new class of owners and exploiters.

This is not to say that the new party and the new class are identical. The party, however, is the core of that class, and its base. It is very difficult, perhaps impossible, to define the limits of the new class and to identify its members. The new class may be said to be made up of those who have special privileges and economic preference because of the administrative monopoly they hold. . . .

In loose terms, as the new class becomes stronger and attains a more perceptible physiognomy, the role of the party diminishes. The core and the basis of the new class is created in the party and at its top, as well as in the state political organs. The once live, compact party, full of initiative, is disappearing to become transformed into the traditional oligarchy of the new class, irresistibly drawing into its ranks those who aspire to join the new class and repressing those who have any ideals.

The party makes the class, but the class grows as a result and uses the party as a basis. The class grows stronger, while the party grows weaker; this is the inescapable fate of every Communist party in power.

If it were not materially interested in production or if it did not have within itself the potentialities for the creation of a new class, no party could act in so morally and ideologically foolhardy a fashion, let alone stay in power for long. Stalin declared, after the end of the First Five-Year Plan: "If we had not created the apparatus, we would have failed!" He should have substituted "new class" for the word "apparatus," and everything would have been clearer.

It seems unusual that a political party could be the beginning of a new class. Parties are generally the product of classes and strata which have become intellectually and economically strong. However, if one grasps the actual conditions in pre-revolutionary Russia and in other countries in which Communism prevailed over national forces, it will be clear that a party of this type is the product of specific opportunities and that there is nothing unusual or accidental in this being so. Although the roots of Bolshevism reach far back into Russian history, the party is partly the product of the unique pattern of international relationships in which Russia found itself at the end of the nineteenth and the beginning of the twentieth century. Russia was no longer able to live in the modern world as an absolute monarchy, and Russia's capitalism was too weak and too dependent on the interests of foreign powers to make it possible to have an industrial revolution. This revolution could only be implemented by a new class, or by a change in the social order. As yet, there was no such class. . . .

2.

The social origin of the new class lies in the proletariat just as the aristocracy arose in a peasant society, and the bourgeoisie in a commercial and artisans' society. There are exceptions, depending on national conditions, but the proletariat in economically underdeveloped countries, being backward, constitutes the raw material from which the new class arises.

There are other reasons why the new class always acts as the champion of the working class. The new class is anti-capitalistic and, consequently, logically dependent upon the working strata. The new class is supported by the proletarian struggle and the traditional faith of the proletariat in a socialist, Communist society where there is no brutal exploitation. It is vitally important for the new class to assure a normal flow of production, hence it cannot ever lose its connection with the proletariat. Most important of all, the new class cannot achieve industrialization and consolidate its power without the help of the working class. On the other hand, the working class sees in expanded industry the salvation from its poverty and despair. Over a long period of time, the interests, ideas, faith, and hope of the new class, and of parts of the working class and of the poor peasants, coincide and unite Such mergers have occurred in the past among other widely different classes. Did not the bourgeoisie represent the peasantry in the struggle against the feudal lords?

The movement of the new class toward power comes as a result of the efforts of the proletariat and the poor. These are the masses upon which the party or the new class must lean and with which its interests are most closely allied. This is true until the new class finally establishes its power and authority. Over and above this, the new class is interested in the proletariat and the poor only to the extent necessary for developing production and for maintaining in subjugation the most aggressive and rebellious social forces.

The monoploy which the new class establishes in the name of the working class over the whole of society is, primarily, a monopoly over the working class itself. This monopoly is first intellectual, over the so-called *avant-garde* proletariat, and then over the whole proletariat. This is the biggest deception the class must accomplish, but it shows that the power and interests of the new class lie primarily in industry. Without industry the new class cannot consolidate its position or authority.

Former sons of the working class are the most steadfast members of the new class. . . . In this case a new exploiting and governing class is born from the exploited class.

3.

When Communist systems are being critically analyzed, it is considered that their fundamental distinction lies in the fact that a bureaucracy, organized in a special stratum, rules over the people. This is generally true. However, a more detailed analysis will show that only a special stratum of bureaucrats, those who are not administrative officials, make up the core of the governing bureaucracy, or, in my terminology, of the new class. This is actually a party or political bureaucracy. Other officials are only the apparatus under the control of the new class; the apparatus may be clumsy and slow but, no matter what, it must exist in every socialist society. . . .

It is important to note the fundamental differences between the political bureaucracies mentioned here and those which arise with every centralization in modern economy—especially centralizations that lead to collective forms of ownership such as monopolies, companies, and state ownership. The number of white-collar workers is constantly increasing in capitalist monopolies, and also in nationalized industries in the West. . . .

While such functionaries have much in common with Communist bureaucrats, especially as regards "esprit de corps," they are not identical. Although state and other bureaucrats in non-Communist systems form a special stratum, they do not exercise authority as the Communists do. Bureaucrats in a non-Communist state have political masters, usually elected, or owners over them, while Communists have neither masters nor owners over them. The bureaucrats in a non-Communist state are officials in modern capitalist economy, while the Communists are something different and new: a new class.

As in other owning classes, the proof that it is a special class lies in its ownership and its special relations to other classes. In the same way, the class to which a member belongs is indicated by the material and other privileges which ownership brings to him.

As defined by Roman law, property constitutes the use, enjoyment, and disposition of material goods. The Communist political bureaucracy uses, enjoys, and disposes of nationalized property.

If we assume that membership in this bureaucracy or new owning class is predicated on the use of privileges inherent in ownership—in this instance nationalized material goods—then membership in the new party class, or political bureaucracy, is reflected in a larger income in material goods and privileges than society should normally grant for such functions. In practice, the ownership privilege of the new class manifests itself as an exclusive right, as a party monopoly, for the political bureaucracy to distribute the national income, to set wages, direct economic development, and dispose of nationalized and other property. This is the way it appears to the ordinary man who considers the Communist functionary as being very rich and as a man who does not have to work. . . .

To divest Communists of their ownership rights would be to abolish them as a class. To compel them to relinquish their other social powers, so that workers may participate in sharing the profits of their work—which capitalists have had to permit as a result of strikes and parliamentary action—would mean that Communists were being deprived of their monopoly over property, ideology, and government. This would be the beginning of democracy and freedom in Communism, the end of Communist monopolism and totalitarianism. Until this happens, there can be no indication that important, fundamental changes are taking place in Communist systems, at least not in the eyes of men who think seriously about social progress.

The ownership privileges of the new class and membership in that class are the privileges of *administration*. This privilege extends from state administration and the administration of economic enterprises to that of sports and humanitarian organizations. Political, party, or so-called "general leadership" is executed by the core. . . . Discrepancies between the pay of workers and party functionaries are extreme; this could not be hidden from persons visiting the U.S.S.R. or other Communist countries in the past few years.

Other systems, too, have their professional politicians. . . . However, there are fundamental differences between professional politicians in other systems and in the Communist system. In extreme cases, politicians in other systems use the government to secure privileges for themselves and their cohorts, or to favor the economic interests of one social stratum or another. The situation is different with the Communist system where the power and the government are identical with the use, enjoyment, and disposition of almost all the nation's goods. He who grabs power grabs privileges and indirectly grabs property. Consequently, in Communism, power or politics as a profession is the ideal of those who have the desire or the prospect of

living as parasites at the expense of others.

Membership in the Communist Party before the Revolution meant sacrifice. Being a professional revolutionary was one of the highest honors. Now that the party has consolidated its power, party membership means that one belongs to a privileged class. And at the core of the party are the all-powerful exploiters and masters. . . .

4.

. . . Behind Lenin, who was all passion and thought, stands the dull, gray figure of Joseph Stalin, the symbol of the difficult, cruel, and unscrupulous ascent of the new class to its final power.

After Lenin and Stalin came what had to come; namely, mediocrity in the form of collective leadership. And also there came the apparently sincere, kind-hearted, non-intellectual "man of the people"—Nikita Khrushchev. The new class no longer needs the revolutionaries or dogmatists it once required; it is satisfied with simple personalities . . . whose every word reflects the average man. The new class itself is tired of dogmatic purges and training sessions. It would like to live quietly. It must protect itself even from its own authorized leader now that it has been adequately strengthened. . . . Without relinquishing anything it created under Stalin's leadership, the new class appears to be renouncing his authority for the past few years. But it is not really renouncing that authority—only Stalin's methods which, according to Khrushchev, hurt "good Communists."

Lenin's revolutionary epoch was replaced by Stalin's epoch, in which authority and ownership, and industrialization, were strengthened so that the much desired peaceful and good life of the new class could begin. Lenin's *revolutionary* Communism was replaced by Stalin's *dogmatic* Communism, which in turn was replaced by *non-dogmatic* Communism, a so-called collective leadership or a group of oligarchs.

These are the three phases of development of the new class in the U.S.S.R. or of Russian Communism (or of every other type of Communism in one manner or another).

The fate of Yugoslav Communism was to unify these three phases in the single personality of Tito, along with national and personal characteristics. . . . The road which Yugoslav Communism has traveled—attaining a revolution, copying Stalinism, then renouncing Stalinism and seeking its own form—is seen most fully in the personality of Tito. . . .

The heroic era of Communism is past. The epoch of its great leaders has ended. The epoch of practical men has set in. The new class has been created. It is at the height of its power and wealth, but it is without new ideas. It has nothing more to tell the people. The only thing that remains is for it to justify itself.

. . . .

5.

. . . Since the hold of the new class on economic life and on the social structure was fairly precarious, and since it was fated to arise within a specific party, it required the highest possible degree of organization, as well as a consistent effort to present a united, balanced, class-conscious front. This is why the new class is better organized and more highly class-conscious than any class in recorded history.

This proposition is true only if it is taken relatively; consciousness and organizational structure being taken in relation to the outside world and to other classes, powers, and social forces. No other class in history has been as cohesive and single-minded in defending itself and in controlling that which it holds—collective and monopolistic ownership and totalitarian authority.

On the other hand, the new class is also the most deluded and least conscious of itself. Every private capitalist or feudal lord was conscious of the fact that he belonged to a special discernible social category. He usually believed that this category was destined to make the human race happy, and that without this category chaos and general ruin would ensue. A Communist member of the new class also believes that, without his party, society would regress and founder. But he is not conscious of the fact that he belongs to a new ownership class, for he does not consider himself an owner and does not take into account the special privileges he enjoys. He thinks that he belongs to a group with prescribed ideas,

aims, attitudes, and roles. That is all he sees. He cannot see that at the same time he belongs to a special social category: the *ownership* class.

Collective ownership, which acts to solidify the class, at the same time makes it unconscious of its class substance, and each one of the collective owners is deluded in that he thinks he uniquely belongs to a movement which would abolish classes in society.

A comparison of other characteristics of the new class with those of other ownership classes reveals many similarities and many differences. The new class is voracious and insatiable, just as the bourgeoisie was. But it does not have the virtues of frugality and economy that the bourgeoisie had. The new class is as exclusive as the aristocracy but without aristocracy's refinement and proud chivalry.

The new class also has advantages over other classes. Because it is more compact it is better prepared for greater sacrifices and heroic exploits. The individual is completely and totally subordinated to the whole; at least, the prevailing ideal calls for such subordination even when he is out seeking to better himself. The new class is strong enough to carry out material and other ventures that no other class was ever able to do. Since it possesses the nation's goods, the new class is in a position to devote itself religiously to the aims it has set and to direct all the forces of the people to the furtherance of these aims.

. . . .

In the new class, just as in other classes, some individuals constantly fall by the wayside while others go up the ladder. . . . The road to the top is theoretically open to all, just as every one of Napoleon's soldiers carried a marshal's baton in his knapsack. The only thing that is required to get on the road is sincere and complete loyalty to the party or to the new class. Open at the bottom, the new class becomes increasingly and relentlessly narrower at the top. Not only is the desire necessary for the climb; also necessary is the ability to understand and develop doctrines, firmness in struggles against antagonists, exceptional dexterity and cleverness in intra-party struggles, and talent in strengthening the class. Many present themselves, but few are chosen. Although more open in some respects than other classes, the new class is also more exclusive than other classes. Since one of the new class's most important features is monopoly of authority, this exclusiveness is strengthened by bureaucratic hierarchical prejudices.

Nowhere, at any time, has the road been as wide open to the devoted and the loyal as it is in the Communist system. But the ascent to the heights has never at any time been so difficult or required so much sacrifice and so many victims. On the one hand, Communism is open and kind to all; on the other hand, it is exclusive and intolerant even of its its own adherents.

6.

The fact that there is a new ownership class in Communist countries does not explain everything, but it is the most important key to understanding the changes which are periodically taking place in these countries, especially in the U.S.S.R. . . . All changes initiated by the Communist chiefs are dictated first of all by the interests and aspirations of the new class, which, like every social group, lives and reacts, defends itself and advances, with the aim of increasing its power. This does not mean, however, that such changes may not be important for the rest of the people as well. . . .

The Communist regime, in common with others, must take into account the mood and movement of the masses. Because of the exclusiveness of the Communist Party and the absence of free public opinion in its ranks, the regime cannot discern the real status of the masses. However, their dissatisfaction does penetrate the consciousness of the top leaders. In spite of its totalitarian management, the new class is not immune to every type of opposition.

Once in power, the Communists have no difficulty in settling their accounts with the bourgeoisie and large-estate owners. The historical development is hostile to them and their property and it is easy to arouse the masses against them. Seizing property from the bourgeoisie and the large-estate owners is quite easy; difficulties arise when seizure of small properties is involved. Having

acquired power in the course of earlier expropriations, the Communists can do even this. Relations are rapidly clarified: there are no more old classes and old owners, society is "classless," or on the road to being so, and men have started to live in a new manner.

Under such conditions demands to return to the old pre-revolutionary relations seem unrealistic, if not ridiculous. Material and social bases no longer exist for the maintenance of such relations. The Communists meet such demands as if they were jests.

The new class is most sensitive to demands on the part of the people for a special kind of freedom, not for freedom in general or political freedom. It is especially sensitive to demands for freedom of thought and criticism, within the limits of present conditions and within the limits of "socialism"; not for demands for a return to previous social and ownership relations. This sensitivity originates from the class's special position.

. . . .

Every real demand for freedom in Communism, the kind of demand that hits at the substance of Communism, boils down to a demand for bringing material and property relations into accord with what the law provides.

A demand for freedom—based on the position that capital goods produced by the nation can be managed more efficiently by society than by private monopoly or a private owner, and consequently should actually be in the hands or under control of society exercised through its freely elected representatives—would force the new class either to make concessions to other forces, or to take off the mask and admit its ruling and exploiting characteristics. . . .

This does not mean that the new class cannot make concessions to the people, even though it only considers its own interests. Workers' management, or decentralization, is a concession to the masses. Circumstances may drive the new class, no matter how monopolistic and totalitarian it may be, to retreat before the masses. In 1948, when the conflict broke out between Yugoslavia and the U.S.S.R., the Yugoslav leaders were forced to carry out certain reforms. But they stopped the process and even reversed it, as soon as they felt that they were in jeopardy. Something similar happened recently in other East European countries. . . .

The new class cannot avoid falling continuously into profound internal contradictions; for in spite of its historical origin it is not able to make its ownership lawful, and it cannot renounce ownership without undermining itself. Consequently, it is forced to try to justify its increasing authority, invoking abstract and unreal purposes.

This is a class whose power over men is the most complete known to history. For this reason it is a class with very limited views, views which are shaky because they are based on falsehoods. Closely knit, isolated, and in complete authority, the new class must unrealistically evaluate its own role and that of the people around it. . . .

Having achieved industrialization, the new class can now do nothing more than strengthen its brute force and pillage the people. It ceases to create. Its spiritual heritage is overtaken by darkness.

While the revolution can be considered an epochal accomplishment of the new class, its methods of rule fill some of the most shameful pages in history. Men will marvel at the grandiose ventures it accomplished and will be ashamed of the means it used.

When the new class leaves the historical scene—and this must happen—there will be less sorrow over its passing than there was for any other class before it. . . .

FROM THE RULING CLASS TO THE POWER ELITE

T. B. Bottomore

The value of Marx's concept of the ruling class depends upon the truth of his general

From *Elites and Society*, by T. B. Bottomore, © T. B. Bottomore 1964, Basic Books, Inc., Publishers, New York.

social theory. If that theory is not universally valid a ruling class may be conceived as originating from military power, or in modern times from the power of a political party, just as well as from the ownership of the means of production. It may still be maintained, however, that the consolidation of a ruling class requires the concentration of the various types of power—economic, military and political—and that, as a matter of fact, in most societies the formation of this class has begun with the acquisition of economic power. But this raises a more fundamental question about the idea of a ruling class. Is it the case that in every society other than the most simple and primitive this concentration of power occurs, that a ruling class is formed? It should be said at once that the different types of society conform in varying degrees with Marx's model of a society which is clearly divided between a ruling class and subject classes. The most favourable case is probably that of European feudalism, characterized by the rule of a warrior class[1] which had securely in its hands the ownership of land, military force, and political authority, and which received the ideological support of a powerful Church. But even here, a number of qualifications are necessary. The idea of a cohesive ruling class is contradicted by the decentralization of political power which was characteristic of feudal societies,[2] and at the stage when this decentralization was overcome—in the absolute monarchies—the European societies were no longer ruled, in a strict sense, by a warrior nobility. Nevertheless, the nobility of the *ancien régime* does come close to the ideal type of a ruling class.

Another case which fits Marx's model well in many respects is that of the *bourgeoisie* of early capitalism. The development of the *bourgeoisie* as an important social class can well be explained by economic changes, and its rise in the economic sphere was accompanied by the acquisition of other positions of power and prestige in society— in politics, administration, the armed forces and the educational system. This conquest

[1] Marc Bloch, *Feudal Society*, Vol. II, Book III, Chap. I.
[2] Marc Bloch, *op. cit.*

of power in the different spheres of society was a long and confused process, which had many local variations in the European countries, and Marx's model was an abstraction from the complex historical reality, bringing together the experiences of the revolution in France—the most violent ideological and political expression of the rise of a new class—and those of the industrial revolution in England. Nevertheless, the pattern of events does conform broadly with Marx's scheme; in England, the Reform Act of 1832 gave political power to the *bourgeoisie*, and it produced changes in the character of legislation even if it did not, for some considerable time, change the social composition of Parliament or cabinets[3]; the reform of the Civil Service after 1855 opened the way for upper middle class aspirants to the highest administrative posts[4]; and the development of public schools created new opportunities for children from the newly rich industrial and commercial families to be trained for elite positions. The *bourgeoisie* also gained powerful ideological support, according to Marx's account, from the political economists and the utilitarian philosophers.

Nevertheless, the *bourgeoisie* appears in several respects a less cohesive ruling class than the feudal nobility. It does not actually combine in the same persons military, political and economic power, and there arises the possibility of conflicts of interest between the different groups which *represent* (as Marx says) the *bourgeoisie*. Furthermore, capitalist society is more open and mobile than was feudal society, and in the ideo-

logical sphere especially, with the development of secular intellectual occupations, conflicting doctrines may arise. Marx expected that the polarization of the two principal classes—the *bourgeoisie* and industrial working class—would accompany the development of capitalism, and that the rule of the *bourgeoisie* would become more manifest and more onerous. But this did not happen in the advanced capitalist societies: the different spheres of power appear to have become more distinct, and the sources of power more numerous and varied; the opposition between the "two great classes" of Marx's theory has been modified by the growth of the new middle classes and by a much more complex differentiation of occupation and status; and political rule has become altogether more mild and less repressive. One important element in this development has been the introduction of universal adult suffrage, which produces, in principle, a separation between economic and political power. Marx himself considered that the attainment of universal suffrage would be a revolutionary step, and that it would transfer political power to the working class.[5] Thus, whereas the connexion between economic and political power can easily be established in the case of feudal society, or in the case of early capitalism with its limitation of political rights to property owners, it cannot be so easily established in the case of the modern capitalist democracies, and the notion of a distinct and settled ruling class becomes dubious and unclear. Marxist fundamentalists, in their attempts to preserve Marx's social theory intact, have been obliged to argue that even in political democracies the *bourgeoisie* always effectively rules through

[3] See W. L. Guttsman, *The British Political Elite*, Chap. 3, "The changing social structure of the British political elite: 1868–1955."

[4] See J. Donald Kingsley, *Representative Bureaucracy*, especially Chap. III, "Middle Class Reform: the Triumph of Plutocracy." Kingsley concludes that "the middle classes had by 1870 destroyed the *ancien régime* on almost every front, [but] the chief gains had been made by the upper ranks of those classes. In the House of Commons wealthy merchants, bankers, industrialists, were displacing the landlords and would begin before many years to replace them in the cabinet. In the Civil Service a somewhat comparable change had occurred. Entrance to the higher posts was no longer a matter of aristocratic influence. The key that now unlocked the door was a costly education which . . . gave to the new system a 'plutocratic character'" (p. 76).

[5] Karl Marx, "The Chartists", *New York Daily Tribune*, 25th August 1852. ". . . Universal Suffrage is the equivalent of political power for the working class of England, where the proletariat forms the large majority of the population, where, in a long, though underground civil war, it has gained a clear consciousness of its position as a class, and where even the rural districts know no longer any peasants, but only landlords, industrial capitalists (farmers) and hired labourers. The carrying of Universal Suffrage in England would, therefore, be a far more socialistic measure than anything which has been honoured with that name on the Continent. Its inevitable result, here, is *the political supremacy of the working class.*"

the indirect influence of wealth, but this is more easily asserted than demonstrated.

These, in brief, are some of the principal difficulties in Marx's conception of the ruling class. . . .

The concept of the "governing elite" or "political class" was proposed as an alternative, partly, . . . in order to demonstrate the impossibility of attaining a classless form of society, but also to meet the theoretical difficulties which we have just considered. The concept of a governing elite avoids, in particular, the difficulty of showing that a particular class, defined in terms of its economic position, does in fact dominate all the spheres of social life; but it does so only at the cost of abandoning any attempt to explain the phenomena to which it refers. The governing elite, according to Mosca and Pareto, comprises those who occupy the recognized positions of political power in a society. Thus, when we ask, who has power in a particular society, the reply is, those who have power, i.e. those who occupy the specified positions. This is scarcely illuminating; it does not tell us how these particular individuals come to occupy the positions of power. Or else it is misleading; if, for example, those who appear to have power in the formal system of government are in fact subject to the power of other individuals or groups outside this system. . . .

The difficulties in the concept of a governing elite can be seen most clearly in a recent work which shows the influence of Marx on one side and of Mosca and Pareto on the other—the late C. Wright Mills' *The Power Elite*. Mills explains his preference for the term "power elite" rather than "ruling class" by saying: " 'Ruling class' is a badly loaded phrase. 'Class' is an economic term; 'rule' a political one. The phrase 'ruling class,' thus contains the theory that an economic class rules politically. That short-cut theory may or may not at times be true, but we do not want to carry that one rather simple theory about in the terms that we use to define our problems; we wish to state the theories explicitly, using terms of more precise and unilateral meaning. Specifically, the phrase 'ruling class,' in its common political connotations, does not

allow enough autonomy to the political order and its agents, and it says nothing about the military as such . . . We hold that such a simple view of 'economic determinism' must be elaborated by 'political determinism' and 'military determinism'; that the higher agents of each of these three domains now often have a noticeable degree of autonomy; and that only in the often intricate ways of coalition do they make up and carry through the most important decisions." [6]

Mills defines the power elite in much the same way as Pareto defined his "governing elite," for he says, "we may define the power elite in terms of the means of power—as those who occupy the command posts." [7] But the analysis which proceeds from this definition has a number of unsatisfactory features. In the first place, Mills distinguishes three major elites in the USA—the corporation heads, the political leaders and the military chiefs—and he is obliged to go on to inquire whether these three groups together form a single power elite, and if so, what it is that binds them together. One possible answer to these questions is to say that the three groups do form a single elite because they are representatives of an upper class, which has to be regarded, consequently, as a ruling class. But Mills, although he emphasizes that most of the members of these elites are in fact drawn from a socially recognized upper class, says initially that he will leave open the question of whether or not it is such a class which rules through the elites, and when he returns to the problem it is only to reject the Marxist idea of a ruling class in the brief passage cited above. In short, the question is never seriously discussed, and this is a curious failing in the particular case which Mills is examining, and in the context of the ideas which he is expressing. He has previously rejected the view that there is popular control of the power elite through voting or other means, and has emphasized the unity of the elite, as well as the homogeneity of its social origins—all of which points to the consolidation of a ruling class. The formulation which he actually gives is vague and

[6] *Op. cit.*, p. 277.
[7] *Op. cit.*, p. 23.

unconvincing: it is a reference to "the often uneasy coincidence of economic, military, and political power," a coincidence which he proposes to explain largely by thepressures of the international conflict in which America has been engaged.

These problems have frequently been raised in criticisms of Mosca and Pareto. Thus, Carl J. Friedrich observed that one of the most problematical parts of all elite doctrines is the assumption that the men of power do constitute a cohesive group: "In the light of the continuous change in the composition of the majority, it is not possible to say, under conditions such as prevail in a functioning democracy, that those who play some considerable part in government constitute a cohesive group."[8] This view of the elite in modern democracies has been widely held; it is stated boldly in the conclusions of a recent study of the upper strata of British society: ". . . the rulers are not at all close-knit or united. They are not so much in the centre of a solar system, as in a cluster of interlocking circles, each one largely preoccupied with its own professionalism and expertise, and touching others only at one edge . . . they are not a single Establishment but a ring of Establishments, with slender connexions. The frictions and balances between the different circles are the supreme safeguard of democracy. No one man can stand in the centre. for there is no centre."[9]

Mills rejects this fashionable liberal-minded doctrine, which he summarizes as follows: "Far from being omnipotent, the elites are thought to be so scattered as to lack any coherence as a historical force. . . . Those who occupy the formal places of authority are so checkmated—by other elites exerting pressure, or by the public as an electorate, or by constitutional codes—that although there may be upper classes, there is no ruling class; although there may be men of power, there is no power elite; although there may be a system of strati-

fication, it has no effective top."[10] As we have seen, he insists that the three principal elites—economic, political and military—are, in fact, a cohesive group, and he supports his view by establishing the similarity of their social origins, the close personal and family relationships between those in the different elites, and the frequency of interchange of personnel between the three spheres. But since he resists the conclusion that the group is a ruling class he is unable to provide a convincing explanation, as distinct from description, of the solidarity of the power elite. Furthermore, by eliminating the idea of a ruling class, he also excludes that of classes in opposition; and so he arrives at an extremely pessimistic account of American society. The real themes of his book are, first, the transformation of a society in which numerous small and autonomous groups had an effective say in the making of political decisions, into a mass society in which the power elite decides all important issues and keeps the masses quiet by flattery, deception and entertainment; and secondly, the corruption of the power elite itself, which he attributes primarily to a state of affairs in which it is not accountable for its decisions to any organized public, and also to the dominant value of the acquisition of wealth. Mills' account of the historical changes, which does indeed bring to light some important features of modern politics—the growing political influence of military chiefs, for example—is pessimistic in the sense that it suggests no way out of the situation which it describes and condemns. Like Pareto and Mosca, Mills seems to be saying that if we look at modern societies without illusions we shall see that, however democratic their constitutions, they are in fact ruled by an elite; and to be adding, in a devastating fashion, that even in a society so favourably placed as was the USA at its origins—without a feudal system of ranks, with very considerable equality of economic and social condition among its citizens, and with a strongly democratic ideology—the force of events has produced a governing elite of unprecedented power and unaccountability. Where Mills differs from the other Machiavellians is in condemning a

[8] Carl J. Friedrich, *The New Image of the Common Man*, pp. 259–60.
[9] Anthony Sampson, *Anatomy of Britain*, p. 624.
[10] *Op. cit.*, pp. 16–17.

state of affairs which they either praised or, in a spirit of disillusionment, accepted.

The concepts of "ruling class" and "governing elite" are used in descriptions and explanations of political happenings, and their value must be judged by the extent to which they make possible reasonable answers to important questions about political systems. Do the rulers of society constitute a social group? Is it a cohesive or divided, an open or closed group? How are its members selected? What is the basis of their power? Is this power unrestricted or is it limited by that of other groups in society? Are there significant and regular differences between societies in these respects, and if so, how are they to be explained?

The two concepts are alike in emphasizing the division between rulers and ruled as one of the most important facts of social structure.[11] But they state the division in different ways: the concept of a "governing elite" contrasts the organized, ruling minority with the unorganized majority, or masses, while the concept of a "ruling class" contrasts the dominant class with subject classes, which may themselves be organized, or be creating organizations. From these different conceptions arise differences in the way of conceiving the relations between rulers and ruled. In the Marxist theory, which employs the concept of a ruling class, the conflict between classes becomes the principal force producing changes of social structure; but in the elite theories—in spite of the fact that Pareto praised highly Marx's conception of class struggle, which he described as "profoundly true,"[12]—the relations between the organized minority and the unorganized majority are necessarily represented as more passive, and the resulting problem of how to explain the rise and fall of ruling elites, if it is confronted at all, has to be dealt with either by postulating a recurrent decadence in the elite (Pareto) or by introducing the idea of the rise of new

"social forces" among the masses (Mosca) which brings the theory close to Marxism.

A further difference between the two concepts lies in the extent to which they make possible explanations of the cohesion of the ruling minority. The "governing elite," defined as those who occupy the positions of command in a society, is merely assumed to be a cohesive group, unless other considerations, such as their membership of the wealthy class, or their aristocratic family origins are introduced (as they are consistently by Mosca, and occasionally by Pareto). But the "ruling class," defined as the class which owns the major instruments of economic production in a society, is shown to be a cohesive social group; first, because its members have definite economic interests in common, and, more importantly, because it is engaged permanently in a conflict with other classes in society, through which its self-awareness and solidarity are continually enhanced. Furthermore, this concept states in a precise form what is the basis of the minority's ruling position, namely its economic dominance, while the concept of the "governing elite" says little about the bases of the power which the elite possesses, except in so far as it incorporates elements from the Marxist theory of classes. In Mills' study of the "power elite," there is an attempt to explain the power position of the three principal elites taken separately—that of the business executives by the growth in size and complexity of business corporations; that of the military chiefs by the growing scale and expense of the weapons of war, determined by technology and the state of international conflict; and that of the national political leaders, in a somewhat less satisfactory way, by the decline of the legislature, of local politics and of voluntary organizations—but the unity of the power elite as a single group, and the basis of *its* power, are not explained. Why is there *one* power elite and not *three*?

The superiority of the concept of "ruling class" lies in its greater fertility and suggestiveness and in its value in the construction of theories. But I have pointed out earlier some of its defects, and it is now necessary to consider whether these can be overcome. The most important step in this

[11] "From the point of view of scientific research the real superiority of the concept of the ruling, or political, class ['political elite' in our terminology. TBB] lies in the fact that the varying structure of ruling classes has a preponderant importance in determining the political type, and also the level of civilization, of the different peoples". Mosca, *op. cit.*, p. 51.

[12] Pareto, *Les systèmes socialistes*, II, p. 405.

direction would be to give up the Marxist view of the concept as a description of a real phenomenon which is to be observed in all societies in the same general form, and to regard it instead as an "ideal type," in the sense which Max Weber gave to this term.[13] If we treat the concept in this way we can proceed to ask how closely the relationships in a particular society approach the ideal type of a ruling class and subject classes; and so employ the concept, properly, as a tool of thought and investigation. It is then possible to see clearly that the idea of a "ruling class" originated in the study of a particular historical situation—the end of feudalism and the beginnings of modern capitalism[14]—and to consider how far, and in what respects, other situations diverge from this ideal type, as a result of the absence or weakness of class formation, the influence of factors other than the ownership of property in the creation of classes, and the conflict between different forms of power.

There are two sorts of situation in which we can see especially plainly a divergence from the ideal type of a ruling class. One is that in which, although there is an "upper class"—that is to say, a clearly demarcated social group which has in its possession a large part of the property of society and receives a disproportionately large share of

the national income, and which has created on the basis of these economic advantages a distinctive culture and way of life—this class does not enjoy undisputed or unrestricted political power, in the sense that it is able to maintain easily its property rights or to transmit them unimpaired from generation to generation. This kind of situation has been discerned by many observers particularly in the modern democracies, in which, as I noted earlier, there is a potential opposition between the ownership of wealth and productive resources by a small upper class, and the possession of political power, through the franchise, by the mass of the population. . . .

In order to determine whether in such a case there is a "ruling class" it is necessary first to examine the degree in which the upper class has been successful in perpetuating its ownership of property. We shall have to note, on one side, that in the democratic countries during the present century a considerable number of restrictions have been placed upon the use of private property, and that there has probably been some reduction in the inequalities of wealth and income, as a result of progressive taxation, and of the growth of publicly owned property and publicly administered social services. On the other side we must note that the decline in the proportion of private wealth owned by the upper class has been modest and very slow, and that the redistribution of income through taxation has not proceeded very far. The situation in Britain was very carefully examined by John Strachey,[15] who concluded that "up to 1939 there had been little or no redistribution of the national income in favour of the mass of the population, either through trade union pressure or budgetary changes. . . ."[16] In the following period, up to 1951, there was some redistribution of income which resulted in transferring some 10 per cent of the total

---

[13] An ideal type concept "brings together certain relationships and events of historical life into a complex which is conceived as an internally consistent system . . . this construction itself is like a *utopia* which has been arrived at by the analytical accentuation of certain elements of reality . . . it *is* no hypothesis but it offers guidance in the construction of hypotheses. It is not a *description* of reality but it aims to give unambiguous means of expression to such a description. . . . An ideal type is formed by the one-sided *accentuation* of one or more points of view and by the synthesis of a great many diffuse, discrete, more or less present and occasionally absent *concrete individual* phenomena, which are arranged according to those one-sidedly emphasized viewpoints into a unified *analytical* construct". Max Weber, *The Methodology of the Social Sciences*, p. 90.

[14] As Croce observed of the whole theory of historical materialism: "The materialistic view of history arose out of the need to account for a definite social phenomenon, not from an abstract inquiry into the factors of historical life". B. Croce, *Historical Materialism and the Economics of Karl Marx*, p. 17.

[15] John Strachey, *Contemporary Capitalism*, Chap. VIII, "The Real Development". Strachey draws upon a number of other studies, including Douglas Jay, *The Socialist Case*; and Dudley Seers, *The Levelling of Incomes since 1938* and *Has the Distribution of Income Become More Unequal?*

[16] *Op. cit.*, pp. 137–8.

national income from property owners to wage-earners, but this trend was probably reversed again after 1951.[17] Strachey concludes: "All this is evidence that capitalism has in fact an innate tendency to extreme and ever-growing inequality. For how otherwise could all these cumulatively equalitarian measures which the popular forces have succeeded in enacting over the past hundred years have done little more than hold the position constant? Is it not clear that, if the workings of the system had not been continuously modified, it would have produced just that ever sharper polarization which Marx diagnosed as its essential tendency?"[18] It is evidence, to put the matter in another way, that the upper class in Britain has been able to resist with considerable success the attacks upon its economic interests, and that in this sense of having the power to defend its interests it has maintained itself during the present century as a ruling class. The situation in the other democratic countries, with the exception of the Scandinavian countries, does not differ greatly from that in Britain; in all of them, right-wing governments have been in power during most of the present century and the redistribution of wealth and income has occurred slowly, if at all. One must be sceptical, therefore, of the view that the extension of voting rights to the mass of the population can establish at once—or has in fact established in the short period of time in which modern democracies have existed—popular rule, and eliminate the power of a ruling class. What seems to have taken place in the democratic countries up to the present time is not so much a reduction in the power of the upper class as a decline in the radicalism of the working class.

The second type of situation in which there is a divergence from the "ruling class —subject classes" model is that in which the ruling group is not a class in Marx's sense. One instance is provided by those societies in which a stratum of intellectuals

or bureaucrats may be said to wield supreme power—in China under the rule of the *literati*, or in India under the rule of the Brahmins. Another instance is to be found in the present-day Communist countries where power is concentrated in the leaders of a political party. In these cases, however, we need to examine carefully how far the ruling stratum is clearly distinguishable from a ruling class. In India, the Brahmins during the ages when they were most powerful, were also substantial landowners, and they were closely allied with the land-owning warrior castes in the imperial and feudal periods of India's history. On occasion, they themselves founded ruling or noble houses, and there seems to have been, at times, an amount of movement of individuals and families between the Brahmin and Kshatriya (warrior) castes, which the doctrines of caste exclusiveness expounded in the classical texts do not indicate.

Again, in China, the *literati* were recruited, in the feudal period, from the principal landowning families, and at other times they came in the main from wealthy families[19]; so that they were always closely linked with an upper class. There is, moreover, another important economic aspect of the rule of these groups of intellectuals and administrators to which Karl Wittfogel has drawn attention.[20] One of the principal instruments of production in China and India (and in a number of other ancient societies)[21] was the system of irrigation, and the *literati* and the Brahmins, without owning this property upon which agricultural production depended, still exercised a more or less complete control over its use. Consequently they possessed, in addition to their ownership of land, a vital economic power which, according to Wittfogel, was the principal support of their political dominance.

But notwithstanding these qualifications the distinction between social strata of this kind and ruling classes which base their power directly upon the legal ownership of property remains. The possession of the

---

[17] *Ibid.,* p. 146. More recently, Richard M. Titmuss, in his *Income Distribution and Social Change,* has undertaken the most thorough study yet made in Britain of the sources of information about the distribution of income. . . .

[18] Strachey, *op. cit.,* pp. 150–1.

[19] See T. B. Bottomore, *Elites and Society,* New York, Basic Books, 1964, p. 65. (C. S. H.)

[20] Karl Wittfogel, *Oriental Despotism.*

[21] See Julian H. Steward *et al., Irrigation Civilizations: A Comparative Study.*

means of administration may be, as Max Weber argued, an alternative to the possession of means of economic production, as a basis of political power.[22] This distinction is perhaps more obvious in the case of the present-day Communist countries, in which there is no private ownership of the means of production, and in which the officials of the ruling party and the state control the economy. Wittfogel has attempted, in a very ingenious way, to assimilate this type of political power to the general category of "oriental despotism"[23] but I think the differences are too great—the existence of private ownership of land and other resources, and the intimate bonds between the officials and the property-owning classes in one case, and the specific characteristics of rule by a political party in the other[24]—for this attempt to be successful. The political system of the Communist countries seems to me to approach the pure type of a "power elite," that is, a group which, having come to power with the support or acquiescence of particular classes in the population, maintains itself in power chiefly by virtue of being an organized minority confronting the unorganized majority; whereas in the case of ancient China or India we have to deal with a system which combines the features of a ruling class and a power elite.

There is another element in the position of a ruling class, which has already been mentioned and which needs to be examined more fully in its bearing upon those situations in which the existence of such a class is doubtful. Since the power of a ruling class arises from its ownership of property, and since this property can easily be transmitted from generation to generation, the class has an enduring character. It is constituted by a group of families which remain as its component elements over long periods of time through the transmission of the family property. Its composition is not entirely immutable, for new families may enter it and old families may decline, but the greater part of its members continue from generation to

generation. Only when there are rapid changes in the whole system of production and property ownership does the composition of the ruling class change significantly; and in that case we can say that one ruling class has been replaced by another. If, however, we were to find, in a particular society or type of society, that the movement of individuals and families between the different social levels was so continuous and so extensive that no group of families was able to maintain itself for any length of time in a situation of economic and political preeminence, then we should have to say that in such a society there was no ruling class. It is, in fact, this "circulation of elites" (in the terminology of the elite theorists) or "social mobility" (in the language of more recent sociological studies) that has been fixed upon by a number of writers as a second important characteristic of modern industrial societies—the first being universal suffrage—which must qualify severely, if it does not altogether exclude, the assertion that there is a ruling class in these societies. By this means we may arrive at the view, which was formulated by Karl Mannheim among others,[25] that the development of industrial societies can properly be depicted as a movement from a class system to a system of elites, from a social hierarchy based upon the inheritance of property to one based upon merit and achievement.

This confrontation between the concepts of "ruling class" and "political elite" shows, I think, that, while on one level they may be totally opposed, as elements in wide-ranging theories which interpret political life, and especially the future possibilities of political organization, in very different ways, on another level they may be seen as complementary concepts, which refer to different types of political system or to different aspects of the same political system. With their help we can attempt to distinguish between societies in which there is a ruling class, and at the same time elites which represent particular aspects of its interests; societies in which there is no ruling class, but a political elite which founds its power upon the control of the

---

[22] The characteristics of bureaucratic societies have been examined at length in a recent study: S. N. Eisenstadt, *The Political Systems of Empires.*
[23] Wittfogel, *op .cit.*
[24] See T. B. Bottomore, *op. cit.,* see pp. 77–80. (C. S. H.)

[25] See especially, *Man and Society,* Part II, Chap. II.

administration, or upon military force, rather than upon property ownership and inheritance; and societies in which there exists a multiplicity of elites among which no cohesive and enduring group of powerful individuals or families seems to be discoverable at all. In order to establish such a classification we need to examine more closely ... the circulation of elites, the relations between elites and classes, and the ways in which new elites and new classes are formed.

POWER IN THE LOCAL COMMUNITY

Richard A. Schermerhorn

... Social research on the power structures of local communities is somewhat more advanced than inquiry into the national patterns. Though not yet detailed enough to supply answers to many specific questions, these findings nevertheless suggest an outline the details of which can be specified locally. The following review will focus on four major themes: governmental versus non-governmental controls, patterns of power distribution, selection of issues for decision-making, and role images of leaders.

GOVERNMENTAL VERSUS NON-GOVERNMENTAL CONTROLS IN THE COMMUNITY

In every town or city certain decisions are made outside the city council or mayor's office, others are referred to the government only when they have substantial support, and still others at least appear to be initiated and carried through by government personnel alone. It is hard to be sure that decisions of the last type are not the result of invisible community pressures.

Arthur Vidich and Joseph Bensman speak

From *Society and Power* by Richard A. Schermerhorn. © Copyright 1961 by Random House Inc. Reprinted by permission.

of the "minimal non-surrenderable functions of police control, street maintenance, water supply and elections" as areas where publicly visible decisions are absolutely required.[1] At the same time, many decisions appear to be made by extra-governmental means while the government plays the role of registering those that require political action to make them legal. At the informal or non-governmental level, leaders, cliques, and associations exercise power through networks of social groupings that form temporary alliances or, in other cases, more permanent coalitions. Some of these may include members of the city council or the mayor so that networks of communication are constantly kept open.

These informal clusters of power may have their source of legitimacy in the folkways, some of which may be unique to the community. As J. S. Coleman remarks, "the outcome of one dispute loads the dice in favor of a similar outcome the next time. Only a few such incidents may be necessary to fix the path of community disputes for fifty or a hundred years to come."[2] However, research is still needed to determine whether the sources of legitimacy are community-wide or whether they are restricted to limited groups whose prestige or coerciveness enables them to impose their views upon others. Further probes are also required to discover whether legitimacy in the community is restricted to highly limited spheres of decision-making. There probably is a good deal of variability from one community to another on such matters.

A pervasive value-system may reflect the national ethos and affect many communities. American individualism, for example, commands widespread attachment in the United States. One feature of individualism, the priority of informal over formal controls, forms the motif of freedom and laissez-faire in social life by tending to establish extra-governmental forms of activity as preferable to governmental action. As Robin Williams puts it, "a major implicit cultural premise

[1] Arthur J. Vidich and Joseph Bensman, *Small Town in Mass Society: Class, Power and Religion in a Rural Community*, p. 135 (Princeton, Princeton University Press, 1958).

[2] James S. Coleman, *Community Conflict*, p. 2 (Glencoe, Ill., The Free Press, 1957).

in the dominant valuation of freedom has been the equating of freedom with control by diffuse cultural structure rather than by a definite social organization. Thus it has seemed to make a great difference whether the individual receives a certain income or has a certain type of occupation as a result of impersonal, anonymous, diffuse competitive process as against being forced to accept that employment or remuneration by law or by the command of a visible social authority." [3]

In like fashion, individualism, growing out of the American experience of subduing the wilderness, exploiting the vast resources of a continent, and establishing new communities where none had been before, relegated the task of social coordination to the background of attention. Government often enough, became an afterthought, subordinate to the "real" concerns of men, which were largely economic. In many ways legitimacy for government became ceremonial and symbolic while business and agriculture attained a higher value priority.

Local communities reflect these individualistic values when they choose community leaders who are not political officials to make weighty decisions. Vidich and Bensman document this pattern for a rural village in upstate New York and they speak of the invisible government. [4] Floyd Hunter reports that in a large Southern city, a small number of influential citizens dominate community policy-making by acting in concert through informal business cliques while political leaders occupy lower echelons of power. [5] Norton Long, in a study of several metropolitan centers, maintains that when the press and broadcasters ask for leaders to solve crises, their demand is for private rather than official public leaders. In his judgment, when citizens posit the existence of such leaders, this action furnishes them with a kind of psychic security which fills the vacuum left by the absence of the more absolutistic rulers of the past. The mass media often credit such informal leaders with both running things and neglecting things; "the idols are both worshipped and beaten, at least verbally . . . This belief in part creates the role of top leadership and demands that it somehow be filled." [6] Vidich and Bensman comment similarly on a dominant leader behind the scenes in Springdale: "All groups and individuals over-estimate his authority, but by this very fact they increase his power since they act on the basis of their estimation." [7]

Research has established the fact that the top leaders in the informal structure are likely to be businessmen. Delbert Miller makes this point clear by comparing the nature of leadership in American and English communities. His study shows that business leaders form 67 per cent of the key influentials (those at the apex of the power structure) in Pacific City, 75 per cent in the Southern metropolis studied by Hunter, but only 25 per cent in a comparable English city. In the latter, professional persons in education, religion, civic organizations, and cooperatives, as well as prominent figures in trade unions and the Labor Party are abundantly represented; the English city has a more diversified group of leaders than is characteristic of the American communities studied. [8]

Although it is yet uncertain how widespread the pattern is, the American communities that have been carefully investigated show a decided preference for nongovernmental controls, private rather than official leaders, and business leaders rather than men from other occupations. These findings require independent verification for other communities and must be balanced by inquiry into the way power structures are organized.

[3] Robin M. Williams, Jr., *American Society, A Sociological Interpretation*, p. 419 (New York, A. A. Knopf, 1951).

[4] Vidich and Bensman, *op. cit.*, pp. 146ff.

[5] Floyd Hunter, *Community Power Structure, A Study of Decision-Makers*, pp. 62, 90ff. (Chapel Hill, N. C., University of North Carolina Press, 1953).

[6] Norton E. Long, "The Social Community as an Ecology of Games," *American Journal of Sociology* 64: 251–261, pp. 255–256 (November, 1958).

[7] Vidich and Bensman, *op. cit.*, p. 277.

[8] Delbert C. Miller, "Decision-Making Cliques in Community Power Structures: A Comparative Study of an American and an English City," *American Journal of Sociology* 64: 299–310 (November, 1958).

PATTERNS OF POWER DISTRIBUTION

Is there a typical "shape"for the power structure in American communities? It has been common for students of the problem to think of such a pattern as a pyramid having a small oligarchy of highly influential leaders at the top, a larger group of lesser figures at middle levels, and numerous followers at the base. Hunter's study undoubtedly did much to disseminate this view since he pictured a group of financial and corporation executives in Regional City at the apex of power, with their decisions possessing great weight even though such men had no formal authority. Policy decisions were made in private sessions and passed down to the second echelon of power (professional and political leaders) where a larger group of subordinates mobilized public opinion on behalf of policies already adopted. Being assured of support from the top echelons, secondary leaders were usually quite successful in carrying out the plans already formulated. Although Hunter disclaims the use of the pyramidal pattern, students of his findings conclude that it is difficult to interpret his research conclusions in any other way.[9]

Subsequent studies have shown wide differences in community power distribution. Roland J. Pellegrin and Charles H. Coates report, for example, that the leaders of Bigtown, a Southern city of 200,000 population, spoke approvingly of Regional City (the scene of Hunter's research) where things were "done right" and a small compact group "controls civic affairs with a firm hand." The same Bigtown leaders were pessimistic about their own community, deploring its lack of unity, the conflict between business cliques, and the failure to carry out many plans of community development.[10] On the basis of Pellegrin and Coates's observations, Bigtown appeared to have not a pyramidal or hierarchical pattern but a series of elongated, finger-like structures extending downward from upper levels of power.

The studies of Robert Schulze, C. W. M. Hart, and James McKee reveal power configurations of even greater diversity. Schulze investigated an industrial suburb where major industrial plants had been absorbed by absentee-owned corporations. The managers of these plants maintained a strictly hands-off policy in local affairs, leaving their direction to men who were not economic dominants.[11] This neglect appeared to leave a unique power vacuum at the top where several large companies were involved. It seemed that local managers did not agree on this permissive policy beforehand but adopted it singly in response to national company directives separately issued. These different directives converged in the local community.

It is quite obvious that policies made outside the community narrow the range of decisions made within it, or, in extreme cases determine what will be done locally. Roland Warren, whose provisional study of this problem has opened up important avenues for exploration, shows the existence of various types of control from outside the community—informal control through culture patterns and formal control through governmental regulations at the state level affecting taxation and education, working conditions, and wage deductions. Frequently there are economic units that are parts of organizations, which set forth policies or regulations to govern operations of these units in each city or town. Finally there are national or international organizations, such as the Red Cross, American Legion, and the Roman Catholic Church, which, while allowing a certain leeway for local variations, often enough formulate broad programs and policies that are binding on their sub-units.[12] Vidich and Bensman provide specific examples of how larger organizations restrict community action in various ways.[13] Small towns and one-industry cities seem to

[9] Herbert Kaufman and Victor Jones, "The Mystery of Power," *Public Administration Review* 14: 205–212, p. 207 (Summer, 1954).

[10] Roland J. Pellegrin and Charles H. Coates, "Absentee-Owned Corporations and Community Power Structure," *American Journal of Sociology* 61: 413–419 (March, 1956).

[11] Robert O. Schulze, "Economic Dominants in Community Power Structure," *American Sociological Review* 23: 3–9, pp. 6–8 (February, 1958).

[12] Roland L. Warren, "Toward a Typology of Extra-Community Controls Limiting Local Community Autonomy," *Social Forces* 34: 338–341 (May, 1956).

[13] Vidich and Bensman, *op. cit.*, p. 113.

be particularly vulnerable in this respect.

The organizational drift from local to national scope has led to increased decision-making in central headquarters; this is true of both large-scale corporations and unions. Similarly the increase of federal functions and controls in government has progressively narrowed the choices of local officials and leaders. In some cases this development has led more citizens to vote in national elections than in local community contests,[14] because, perhaps, they realize the greater importance to them of the issues involved. At any rate it is now important to learn what decisions are left to the local community and to whom they are vitally significant. One thing seems certain and should be kept in mind: community decisions are only partly autonomous.

The apparent power vacuum at the top in Schulze's example of the community with absentee-owned corporations may be a consequence of the fact that the local community is no longer in a position to make decisions significantly affecting corporate interests. On the other hand, this situation may represent a power potential rather than a power vacuum. Corporations with local branches may decides not to throw their weight around in smaller communities, but these firms hold in reserve a weapon of great effectiveness, namely the ability to move any local plant to a different location. In towns where employment is mainly dependent on one or two large companies, a decision to relocate manufacturing units can disrupt the entire economic base of the community. Although such decisions depend on national and international market and supply conditions, they are related to local political factors also. Absentee-owned corporations pay a disproportionate share of taxes in small towns; as a result the local government refrains from changing the tax structure drastically upward for this would kill the goose that lays the golden egg. As long as this tax situation continues, corporations can afford to maintain the kind of hands-off policy noted by Schulze. But such abdication of power is conditional rather than fixed policy.

Hart, in his study of Windsor, Ontario, presents quite a different power configuration from those sketched above. As he reports it, this community is dominated by four major groups: big business (Ford and Chrysler), the Roman Catholic Church, the unions, and finally the local business group including the Chamber of Commerce. So discrete and cohesive do these groups appear that Hart can find no trace of a general public. Its absence engenders conflicts that are naked and overt. Commenting on the lack of a power pyramid, Hart declares that it may not be clear who "runs the town," but at least "it is not the top management of Ford or Chrysler nor 'stooges' for those managements."[15] McKee, in a similar study, notes the central role of the CIO in Lorain, Ohio, and sees community power in terms of multiple groups combined differently on separate issues. He insists that the familiar pyramidal model seriously distorts many relationships in that city.[16]

Realistic analysis requires more than cross-sectional study of the local community; it must not neglect changes through time. For example, founder-owners of rapidly growing industries have often established family dominance of a corporation, which has gone hand in hand with almost monopolistic power in the local community. Robert and Helen Lynd documented this pattern in their second Middletown volume, showing that the "X family," which founded the local glass jar industry, extended its control into banking, real estate, retail business, education, recreation, religious institutions, charities, the press, and, to a considerable degree, local government.[17] Such dynastic control changes markedly as industry passes from family to managerial dominance. Any power shifts within industry bring in their train other shifts in community

[14] V. O. Key, Jr., *Politics, Parties and Pressure Groups*, 4th ed., p. 627 (New York, Crowell, 1958).

[15] C. W. M. Hart, "Industrial Relations Research and Industry," *Canadian Journal of Economics and Political Science* 15: 53–73, pp. 59–60, 66, 68 (February, 1949).

[16] James B. McKee, "Status and Power in the Industrial Community: A Comment on Drucker's Thesis," *American Journal of Sociology* 58: 364–370, p. 369 (January, 1953).

[17] Robert S. Lynd and Helen M. Lynd, *Middletown in Transition, A Study in Cultural Conflicts*, Chapter 3 (New York, Harcourt, Brace & Co., 1937).

power as local familial controls are replaced by specialized management and as labor unions develop; further changes result when local plants are sold outright to absentee-owned corporations.

Consequently any attempt to assess the organization of power in the local community must take into account the stage of maturation of its industry. It is perhaps too early to agree with Daniel Bell that "by and large, the system of family control is finished."[18] For example, one reason that Hunter's Regional City reveals such a marked hierarchical power pattern seems to be that hereditary wealth dominates business activity in that Southern metropolis; at least twenty-five out of Hunter's top forty leaders were so assisted in gaining positions of economic prominence.[19] There may be important regional differences in this respect; Schulze hints that the prevalence of family control in the South seems to be greater than it is elsewhere.[20]

Studies of changing power configurations over time would also probably show an increasing prominence of formerly submerged groups in American community life. Arnold Rose, commenting on this historic shift in the power balance, says that "now a significant proportion of the lower classes is organized into labor unions and a significant proportion of ethnic minorities have organized into reform groups; and both are participating in political organizations. Thus both the lower classes and the ethnic minorities today have a significant measure of power."[21] This change should be investigated in its relation to industrial maturation in different types of cities.

Generalizations such as Peter Rossi's statement, "the less diversified the economic base of the community, the more clustered is the power,"[22] do not appear to be applic-

able to all types of American communities. As we have seen, this proposition neglects those cases where absentee-owned corporations abdicate their power or where the rapid growth of unions in other industrial towns broadens the base of power distribution patterns.

While a good many American communities are notably similar in preferring nongovernmental to governmental controls, the plurality of power distribution in the wider societal area seems to preclude any uniform pattern. In some cases a commonly shared value system may impose a good deal of uniformity; in other situations the economic organization results in multiple power configurations for which as yet no adequate classification has been made. At the present stage of knowledge, social scientists are limited, for the most part, to searching out and reporting the unique power distribution in each community investigated. Yet structural similarities, as well as differences, are revealed in these community studies. This fact suggests that it may soon be possible to work out a typology of communities in terms of economic and social structure, including their functional relationships with the wider society. If this happens it will transcend the traditional distinctions of urban sociology which classifies communities into the broader and less useful categories of institutional cities, trading centers, metropolitan cities, and resort towns.[23] The use of local power patterns will be helpful to sharpen our analysis and furnish a new typology.

THE SELECTION OF ISSUES

What issues are decided at what levels in American communities? George Belknap and Ralph Smuckler found in a Midwest city that the top leadership remains constant, whatever the issue, while lower echelon leaders change in accordance with the problem.[24] Miller, on the other hand, reports considerable fluidity among key

[18] Daniel Bell, "The Power Elite—Reconsidered," *American Journal of Sociology* 64: 238–250, p. 248 (November, 1958).

[19] Miller, *op. cit.*, p. 307.

[20] Schulze, *op. cit.*, p. 8.

[21] Arnold Rose, "Power Distribution in the Community Through Voluntary Association," *Problems in Social Psychology, An Interdisciplinary Inquiry*, J. E. Hulett and Ross Stagner, eds., p. 80 (Urbana, Ill., University of Illinois, 1952).

[22] Peter H. Rossi, "Community Decision-Making," *Administrative Science Quarterly* I: 415–443, p. 440 (March, 1957).

[23] Svend Riemer, *The Modern City*, pp. 41–44 (New York, Prentice-Hall, 1952).

[24] George Belknap and Ralph Smuckler, "Political Power Relations in a Mid-West City," *Public Opinion Quarterly* 20: 73–81, p. 81 (Spring, 1956).

influentials as issues change.[25] Research into the reasons for this conflicting evidence should uncover more basic factors affecting community issues. Hunter, for example, mentions the fact that many issues are bandied about by subleaders; in due time they emerge for top level policy consideration.[26] The initiation of issues and the decisions about them may occur at quite different levels in the power structure.

James Coleman has furnished a trenchant analysis of community issues when they become matters of controversy or conflict. He distinguishes between the initiation of conflict and its perpetuation. In the initiatory phase, three major areas of life provide what Coleman calls bases of response to controversial issues. The first is the economic area, where conflicts arise over items like taxes or the movement of a factory to town; the second is the area of authority, where disputes about such things as city-manager plans and proportional representation arise; the third area consists of cultural values or beliefs, as when disagreements arise over the educational philosophy of school superintendents or about desegregation. Coleman notes that conflicts over cultural values take place especially in cities where there is a rapid influx of inhabitants with different styles of life, suburban communities, and in Southern towns.[27]

Throughout his discussion, Coleman observes two additional bases of response in the perpetuation stage: attachments or identifications with individuals or groups already involved in the dispute ("psychological") and associational membership that limits word-of-mouth discussions by restricting communication to specific channels ("sociological"). Associational ties seem to have greater influence on middle and upper class persons than on those of lower status; personal attachments play a greater role in small towns than in larger ones. In both the initiatory and later stages of controversy, the national climate of opinion may be pivotal, as it was during the McCarthy era when labor unions took no stand on the issue because of divided opinion within the membership. Coleman also observes that people who are weakly identified with the community at large (found especially among the lower classes and newer migrants) are apt to overstep the bounds of legitimate methods more quickly when aroused.[28]

Coleman has advanced our general knowledge about the operation of controversial issues in the community; power analysis raises additional questions. What issues are kept out of the arena of public discussion and what problems are allowed to reach the attention of the community? Is there a mechanism for keeping sensitive issues away from the public, and is it used by the private leaders who already possess significant power? This problem is important because the selection of issues—at least public issues—precedes the making of decisions. Often the local newspaper plays a significant role by accenting or exaggerating some problems while minimizing others or eliminating them entirely. Not only does the average citizen perceive the issues as they are revealed in the organs of public opinion, he has a tendency to accept the assigned importance of the issues themselves. Value preferences of the editor or publisher (sometimes related to his clique position) may be a key to the community perception of issues as presented in his newspaper, and these may reflect the views of top-level leaders.

Community issues thus furnish an important lead to two significant questions: How do these issues serve as channels for the operation of power structures already firmly set in the community? How do they supply focal situations for change in the community power balance? Hunter and his associates suggest how this problem may be approached when they indicate that a new issue raises three questions in the minds of community leaders: (1) who is behind this thing? (2) how much is it going to cost? (3) what will it do to my business or my agency or my reputation?[29]

[25] Miller, *op. cit.*, pp. 306, 310..

[26] Hunter, *op. cit.*, p. 225.

[27] James S. Coleman, *Community Conflict*, pp. 6–7 (Glencoe, Ill., The Free Press, 1957).

[28] Coleman, *op. cit.*, pp. 13, 21.

[29] Floyd Hunter, Ruth Connor Schaffer and Cecil G. Sheps, *Community Organization, Action and Inaction*, p. 33 (Chapel Hill, N.C., University of North Carolina Press, 1956).

ROLE IMAGES OF LEADERS

Public opinion, changeable and vacillating as it may be, has a definite bearing on the way in which power is exercised in the community. Community confidence in its leadership, both formal and informal, often determines what can or cannot be done by those who wield one type of authority or another. Assume for a moment that in a given community the role of private leaders has more legitimacy than that of public leaders in the local government. What happens when the public loses confidence in its private top leadership? Probably one of two things will occur: the public will raise its estimation of public authorities and demand that they do something or it will minimize the present mistakes of private leaders and laud them for what they have achieved for the community in the past. The issue will die down, and eventually the public will restore its belief in top leadership as a kind of prop for security feelings.

However there is not one public but many. Will people at different levels in the class structure have the same role images of their leaders? David Riesman and Nathan Glazer declare that "only the more disabused folk in the lower strata nourish the myth that there is an inner circle which knows how to manage them and to manage events."[30] Is this statement true or does it reflect certain assumptions about the class structure that are unproved?[31] Riesman and Glazer make their assertions confidently without the use of supporting evidence, so it is only natural for doubts to appear. At any rate, further research is definitely needed to determine how much difference there is in the way people at various socio-economic levels perceive both public and private authorities. This would furnish an invaluable clue to the way in which such leaders could or could not manipulate the masses.

On the other hand, the self-images of leaders have a great deal to do with the way they exercise their authority. Norton Long distinguishes the self-images of governmental and non-governmental leaders in the following way: "The politicians who hold the offices do not regard themselves as governors of the municipal territory but largely as mediators or players in a particular game that makes use of the other inhabitants." Informal leaders, on the other hand, are often "genuinely reluctant, fearful, and even morally shocked at their positions' becoming that of a recognized territorial government."[32] If this applies to all communities, we would have to conclude that even though power is desired, responsibility may not be. It seems likely that there is greater variability from one city to another on this issue than Long suggests. At any rate, a more thorough assessment of the way community power-holders view themselves will furnish a clue to the way they exercise their leadership.

Finally, how do community leaders view the public? Riesman and Glazer speak of upper-level leaders as feeling "mastered by vague events" and of how often they claim that public opinion will not "stand for" this or that policy; frequently such leaders "take refuge behind public opinion for their own inability to act."[33] Here again we may have an insight rather than the statement of a trend. But the issue has crucial significance; what are the images of the public held by dominant community leaders and what are the reciprocal role images of the leaders entertained by their followers? This sort of information can single out important factors in the climate of public opinion that have special relationship to the way different forms of power may be exercised.

In this final chapter we have reviewed enough of the literature on community power studies to give the reader a few salient points of reference which he can apply to his own city or town. It is hoped in this way to furnish not a mere intellectual exercise but a method of analysis that will help him to see the political process in sociological terms. In summary, some of the questions that may be found useful are: Who are the formal and informal leaders and what is their relationship to each other? What is the shape of the power structure? What is the stage of industrial maturity locally? What is

---

[30] David Riesman and Nathan Glazer, "Criteria for Political Apathy," *Studies in Leadership*, A. W. Gouldner, ed., p. 517 (New York, Harper & Bros., 1950).

[31] Leonard Reissman, *Class in American Society*, pp. 196–202 (Glencoe, Ill., The Free Press, 1959).

[32] Long, *op. cit.,* pp. 255, 259.

[33] Riesman and Glazer, *op. cit.,* p. 514.

the tradition of past decision? Who are the people most committed and least committed to the community as a focus of loyalty? What are the modes of formal and informal control? What is the role of the political party in joining the two? What types of decision depend chiefly on forces outside the community? How are issues selected for community decision and at what level? How do newspaper policies and the treatment of issues in the press affect the public? How much confidence is invested in both formal and informal leaders? How do members of the community at different socio-economic levels view the community leaders? How do the leaders see their own role and the role of the public?

Questions like these will perhaps reveal more than asking how many Democrats or how many Republicans there are in the city. At any rate, answers to such questions will help the reader to understand the enlargement of perspective, the excitement of exploration, and the satisfaction at reaching even tentative conclusions that motivate the social scientist in his study of power.

Status Inequality

WHAT SOCIAL CLASS IS IN AMERICA

W. Lloyd Warner with Marchia Meeker and Kenneth Eells

THE AMERICAN DREAM AND SOCIAL CLASS

In the bright glow and warm presence of the American Dream all men are born free and

From *Social Class in America*, by W. Lloyd Warner, Harper & Row, Publishers. Copyright 1949 by Science Research Associates, Inc., Chicago. Reprinted by permission.

equal. Everyone in the American Dream has the right, and often the duty, to try to succeed and to do his best to reach the top. Its two fundamental themes and propositions, that all of us are equal and that each of us has the right to the chance of reaching the top, are mutually contradictory, for if all men are equal there can be no top level to aim for, no bottom one to get away from; there can be no superior or inferior positions but only one common level into which all Americans are born and in which all of them will spend their lives. We all know such perfect equality of position and opportunity does not exist. All Americans are not born into families of equal position; some are born into a rich man's aristocracy on the Gold Coast; some into the solid comfort of Suburbia's middle classes; and others into a mean existence among the slum families living on the wrong side of the tracks. It is common knowledge that the sons and daughters of the Gold Coasts, the Main Lines, and Park Avenues of America are more likely to receive recognition for their efforts than the children of the slums. The distance these fortunate young people travel to achieve success is shorter, and the route up easier, than the long hard pull necessary for the ambitious children of the less fortunate middle class. Though everyone has the common right to succeed, it is not an equal "right". . . .

When some men learn that *all* the American Dream does not fit *all* that is true about the realities of our life, they denounce the Dream and deny the truth of *any* of it. Fortunately, most of us are wiser and better adjusted to social reality; we recognize that, though it is called a Dream and though some of it is false, by virtue of our firm belief in it we have made some of it true. Despite the presence of social hierarchies which place people at higher and lower levels in American communities, the principles of democracy do operate; the Christian dogma that all men are equal in the sight of God because He is our Father and we are His spiritual children, buttressed by the democratic faith in the equality of men and the insistence on their equal rights as citizens, is a powerful influence in the daily life of America.

. . . .

Most of us know from novels such as those of Sinclair Lewis of the Main Streets that run through all our towns and cities, populated by Babbitts, or, more explicitly stated, by "the substantial upper-middle class"; and by now, thanks to another group of novelists such as Erskine Caldwell, we know there is a low road, a Tobacco Road, that runs not only by the ramshackle houses of the poor whites of the South, but by the tarpaper shanties of the slums and river bottoms or Goat Hills of every town and city in the United States.

The "superior people" of Marquand's New England, "the North Shore crowd," divided into a top level of "old families" with a set of values and a way of life rated above those of the "new families," are matched by Philadelphia's "Main Line" families in Christopher Morley's *Kitty Foyle* and by similar groups in many other novels which report on the dominance of "the upper classes" in all regions of the United States. Reading them, together with similar novels reporting on Suburbia and Main Street for the middle classes and those on the Tobacco Roads and the city slums for the lower levels, gives one the understanding that throughout the towns and cities of America the inhabitants are divided into status levels which are ways of life with definite characteristics and values. . . .

Although well aware of social class, social scientists have been more concerned with their theories and with quarreling among themselves about what social class is than with studying its realities in the daily lives of the people. Until recently, they have lagged behind the novelists in investigating what our classes are, how they operate in our social life, and what effect they have on our individual lives. . . .

The researches on social class in the several regions of the United States make it possible to fill in much of the missing knowledge necessary to give Americans such explicit understanding of social class and to answer some of the important questions we raise about it when adjusting to the realities of our existence.

. . . .

THE STRUCTURAL IMPERATIVE— WHY WE HAVE A CLASS SYSTEM

. . . Just as students of comparative biology have demonstrated that the physical structure of the higher animals must have certain organs to survive, so students of social anthropology have shown that the social structures of the "higher," the more complex, societies must have rank orders to perform certain functions necessary for group survival.

When societies are complex and service large populations, they always possess some kind of status system which, by its own values, places people in higher or lower positions. Only the very simple hunting and gathering tribes, with very small populations and very simple social problems, are without systems of rank; but when a society is complex, when there are large numbers of individuals in it pursuing diverse and complex activities and functioning in a multiplicity of ways, individual positions and behaviors are evaluated and ranked.[1] This happens primarily because, to maintain itself, the society must co-ordinate the efforts of all its members into common enterprises necessary for the preservation of the group, and it must solidify and integrate all these enterprises into a working whole. In other words, as the division of labor increases and the social units become more numerous and diverse, the need for co-ordination and integration also increases and, when satisfied, enables the larger group to survive and develop.

Those who occupy co-ordinating positions acquire power and prestige. They do so because their actions partly control the behavior of the individuals who look to them for direction. Within this simple control there is simple power. Those who exercise such power either acquire prestige directly from it or have gained prestige from other sources sufficiently to be raised to a co-ordinating position. . . .

[1] L. T. Hobhouse, G. C. Wheeler, and M. Ginsberg, *The Material Culture and Social Institutions of the Simpler Peoples*, London: Chapman and Hall, 1915. This exhaustive study of hundreds of communities and societies of the world demonstrates how social stratification and rank are highly correlated with technological advancement and the increase in social complexity. See in particular pages 228–237.

The studies of other societies have demonstrated one other basic point: the more complex the technological and economic structure, the more complex the social structure; so that some argue (the Marxians and many classical economists) that technological advancement is the cause of social complexity and all class and status systems. It cannot be denied that economic and technological factors are important in the determination of class and status orders. We must not lose sight of the fact, however, that the social system, with its beliefs, values, and rules, which governs human behavior may well determine what kind of technology and what kind of economic institutions will survive or thrive in any given tribe or nation. In any case, social complexity is necessary for economic advancement. Furthermore, social complexity is a basic factor determining the presence or absence of class.

The Marxians have argued that the economic changes our society is undergoing always result in a class war in which "the proletariat" will be triumphant and out of which a "classless society" will result. The authors do not agree with them for several reasons. The principal reasons are: (1) the presence of a class order does not necessarily mean class conflict—the relations of the classes can be and often are amiable and peaceful; (2) classless societies (without differential status systems) are impossible where there is complexity for the reasons previously given. Russia's communistic system, supposedly designed to produce a pure equalitarian society, necessarily has citizens who are ranked above and below each other. Generals, there, outrank privates; commissars, the rank and file; and members of the Politburo, the ordinary comrade. Occupants of these higher ranks in Russia tend to associate together; those of the lower ranks form their own groups. Their children are trained according to the rank of their parents. This means that the younger generation learns these status differences, thereby strengthening status differences between levels and fostering the further development of social class in Communistic Russia.

All this has occurred despite the fact the Russians have removed the means of production from private hands and placed them under the control of the State ("the people"). The economic factor which by Marxian doctrine produced social classes is largely absent; yet social hierarchies and social classes are present for the reason that Russia is a complex society and needs them to survive. . . .

But let us return to the United States. We, too, have a complex, highly diverse society. We, too, possess an elaborate division of labor and a ramified technology. And we, too, possess a variety of rank orders built on the need of maintaining unity and cohesion in making our common enterprises successful. . . . Children are always born to their families' position. Through life they may increase or decrease their status. The family thereby strengthens and helps maintain our class order. Social status in America is somewhat like man's alimentary canal; he may not like the way it works and he may want to forget that certain parts of it are part of him, but he knows it is necessary for his very existence. So a status system, often an object of our disapproval, is present and necessary in our complex social world. . . .

CLASS AMONG THE NEW ENGLAND YANKEES

Studies of communities in New England clearly demonstrate the presence of a well-defined social-class system.[2] At the top is an aristocracy of birth and wealth. This is the so-called "old family" class. The people of Yankee City say the families who belong to it have been in the community for a long time—for at least three generations and preferably many generations more than three. "Old family" means not only old to the community but old to the class. Present members of the class were born into it; the families into which they were born can trace their lineage through many generations participating in a way of life characteristic of the upper class back to a generation marking the lowly beginnings out of which their family came. Although the men of this level are occupied gainfully, usually as large merchants, financiers, or in the higher professions, the wealth of the family, inherited

[2] . . . New and poorly organized towns sometimes have class systems which have no old-family (upper-upper) class.

from the husband's or the wife's side, and often from both, has been in the family for a long time. Ideally it should stem from the sea trade when Yankee City's merchants and sea captains made large fortunes, built great Georgian houses on elm-lined Hill Street, and filled their houses and gardens with the proper symbols of their high position. They became the 400, the Brahmins, the Hill Streeters to whom others looked up; and they, well-mannered or not, looked down on the rest. They counted themselves, and were so counted, equals of similar levels in Salem, Boston, Providence, and other New England cities. Their sons and daughters married into the old families from these towns and at times, when family fortune was low or love was great, they married wealthy sons and daughters from the newly rich who occupied the class level below them. This was a happy event for the fathers and mothers of such fortunate young people in the lower half of the upper class, an event well publicized and sometimes not too discreetly bragged about by the parents of the lower-upper-class children, an occasion to be explained by the mothers from the old families in terms of the spiritual demands of romantic love and by their friends as "a good deal and a fair exchange all the way around for everyone concerned."

The new families, the lower level of the upper class, came up through the new industries—shoes, textiles, silverware—and finance. Their fathers were some of the men who established New England's trading and financial dominance throughout America. When New York's Wall Street rose to power, many of them transferred their activities to this new center of dominance. Except that they aspire to old-family status, if not for themselves then for their children, these men and their families have a design for living similar to the old-family group. But they are consciously aware that their money is too new and too recently earned to have the sacrosanct quality of wealth inherited from a long line of ancestors. They know, as do those about them, that, while a certain amount of wealth is necessary, birth and old family are what really matter. Each of them can cite critical cases to prove that particular individuals have no money at all, yet belong to the top class because

they have the right lineage and right name. While they recognize the worth and importance of birth, they feel that somehow their family's achievements should be better rewarded than by a mere second place in relation to those who need do little more than be born and stay alive.

The presence of an old-family class in a community forces the newly rich to wait their turn if they aspire to "higher things." Meanwhile, they must learn how to act, fill their lives with good deeds, spend their money on approved philanthropy, and reduce their arrogance to manageable proportions.

The families of the upper and lower strata of the upper classes are organized into social cliques and exclusive clubs. The men gather fortnightly in dining clubs where they discuss matters that concern them. The women belong to small clubs or to the Garden Club and give their interest to subjects which symbolize their high status and evoke those sentiments necessary in each individual if the class is to maintain itself. Both sexes join philanthropic organizations whose good deeds are an asset to the community and an expression of the dominance and importance of the top class to those socially beneath them. They are the members of the Episcopalian and Unitarian and, occasionally, the Congregational and Presbyterian churches.

Below them are the members of the solid, highly respectable upper-middle class, the people who get things done and provide the active front in civic affairs for the classes above them. They aspire to the classes above and hope their good deeds, civic activities, and high moral principles will somehow be recognized far beyond the usual pat on the back and that they will be invited by those above them into the intimacies of upper-class cliques and exclusive clubs. Such recognition might increase their status and would be likely to make them members of the lower-upper group. The fact that this rarely happens seldom stops members of this level, once activated, from continuing to try. The men tend to be owners of stores and belong to the large proprietor and professional levels. Their incomes average less than those of the lower-upper class, this latter group having a larger income than any other group, including the old-family level.

These three strata, the two upper classes and the upper-middle, constitute the levels above the Common Man. There is a considerable distance socially between them and the mass of the people immediately below them. They comprise three of the six classes present in the community. Although in number of levels they constitute half the community, in population they have no more than a sixth, and sometimes less, of the Common Man's population. The three levels combined include approximately 13 per cent of the total population.

The lower-middle class, the top of the Common Man level, is composed of clerks and other white-collar workers, small tradesmen, and a fraction of skilled workers. Their small houses fill "the side streets" down from Hill Street, where the upper classes and some of the upper-middle live, and are noticeably absent from the better suburbs where the upper-middle concentrate. "Side Streeter" is a term often used by those above them to imply an inferior way of life and an inconsequential status. They have accumulated little property but are frequently home owners. Some of the more successful members of ethnic groups, such as the Italians, Irish, French-Canadians, have reached this level. Only a few members of these cultural minorities have gone beyond it; none of them has reached the old-family level.

. . . Ten per cent of the population belongs to the upper-middle class, and 28 per cent to the lower-middle level. The upper-lower is the most populous class, with 34 per cent, and the lower-lower has 25 per cent of all the people in the town. . . .

The upper-lower class, least differentiated from the adjacent levels and hardest to distinguish in the hierarchy, but clearly present, is composed of the "poor but honest workers" who more often than not are only semi-skilled or unskilled. Their relative place in the hierarchy of class is well portrayed by comparing them with the classes superior to them and with the lower-lower class beneath them in the category of how they spend their money.

A glance at the ranking of the proportion of the incomes of each class spent on ten items (including such things as rent and shelter, food, clothing, and education among others) shows, for example, that this class ranks second for the percentage of the money spent on food, the lower-lower class being first and the rank order of the other classes following lower-middle according to their place in the social hierarchy. The money spent on rent and shelter by upper-lower class is also second to the lower-lower's first, the other classes' rank order and position in the hierarchy being in exact correspondence. To give a bird's-eye view of the way this class spends its money, the rank of the upper-lower, for the percentage of its budget spent on a number of common and important items, has been placed in parentheses after every item in the list which follows: food (2), rent (2), clothing (4), automobiles (5), taxes (5), medical aid (5), education (4), and amusements (4–5). For the major items of expenditure the amount of money spent by this class out of its budget corresponds fairly closely with its place in the class hierarchy, second to the first of the lower-lower class for the major necessities of food and shelter, and ordinarily but not always, fourth or fifth to the classes above for the items that give an opportunity for cutting down the amounts spent on them. Their feelings about doing the right thing, of being respectable and rearing their children to do better than they have, coupled with the limitations of their income, are well reflected in how they select and reject what can be purchased on the American market.[3]

The lower-lower class, referred to as "Riverbrookers" or the "low-down Yankees who live in the clam flats," have a "bad reputation" among those who are socially above them. This evaluation includes beliefs that they are lazy, shiftless, and won't work, all opposites of the good middle-class virtues belonging to the essence of the Protestant ethic. They are thought to be improvident and unwilling or unable to save their money for a rainy day and, therefore, often dependent on the

[3] The evidence for the statements in this paragraph can be found in W. Lloyd Warner and Paul S. Lunt, *The Social Life of a Modern Community*, Vol. I, "Yankee City Series" (New Haven: Yale University Press, 1941), pp. 287–300.

philanthropy of the private or public agency and on poor relief. They are sometimes said to "live like animals" because it is believed that their sexual mores are not too exacting and that pre-marital intercourse, post-marital infidelity, and high rates of illegitimacy, sometimes too publicly mixed with incest, characterize their personal and family lives. It is certain that they deserve only part of this reputation. Research shows many of them guilty of no more than being poor and lacking in the desire to get ahead, this latter trait being common among those above them. For these reasons and others, this class is ranked in Yankee City below the level of the Common Man (lower-middle and upper-lower). For most of the indexes of status it ranks sixth and last.

CLASS IN THE DEMOCRATIC MIDDLE WEST AND FAR WEST

Cities large and small in the states west of the Alleghenies sometimes have class systems which do not possess an old-family (upper-upper) class. The period of settlement has not always been sufficient for an old-family level, based on the security of birth and inherited wealth, to entrench itself. . . . The family, its name, and its lineage must have had time to become identified in the public mind as being above ordinary mortals.

While such identification is necessary for the emergence of an old-family (upper-upper) class and for its establishment, it is also necessary for the community to be large enough for the principles of exclusion to operate. For example, those in the old-family group must be sufficiently numerous for all the varieties of social participation to be possible without the use of new-family members; the family names must be old enough to be easily identified; and above all there should always be present young people of marriageable age to become mates of others of their own class and a sufficient number of children to allow mothers to select playmates and companions of their own class for their children.

When a community in the more recently settled regions of the United States is sufficiently large, when it has grown slowly and at an average rate, the chances are

higher that it has an old-family class. If it lacks any one of these factors, including size, social and economic complexity, and steady and normal growth, the old-family class is not likely to develop. . . .

When the old-family group is present and its position is not recognized as superordinate to the new families, the two tend to be co-ordinate and view each other as equals. The old-family people adroitly let it be known that their riches are not material possessions alone but are old-family lineage; the new families display their wealth, accent their power, and prepare their children for the development of a future lineage by giving them the proper training at home and later sending them to the "right" schools and marrying them into the "right" families.

Such communities usually have a five-class pyramid, including an upper class, two middle, and two lower classes.[4]

Jonesville, located in the Middle West, approximately a hundred years old, is an example of a typical five-class community. The farmers around Jonesville use it as their market, and it is the seat of government for Abraham County. Its population of over 6,000 people is supported by servicing the needs of the farmers and by one large and a few small factories.

At the top of the status structure is an upper class commonly referred to as "the 400." It is composed of old-family and new-family segments. Neither can successfully claim superiority to the other. Below this level is an upper-middle class which functions like the same level in Yankee City and is composed of the same kind of people, the only difference being the recognition that the distance to the top is shorter for them and the time necessary to get there much less. The Common Man level, composed of lower-middle- and upper-lower-class people and the lower-lower level are replicas of the same classes in Yankee City.

The communities of the mountain states and Pacific Coast are new, and many of them have changed their economic form from mining to other enterprises; consequently, their class orders are similar to

---

[4] It is conceivable that in smaller communities there may be only three, or even two, classes present.

those found in the Middle West. The older and larger far western communities which have had a continuing, solid growth of population which has not destroyed the original group are likely to have the old-family level at the top with the other classes present; the newer and smaller communities and those disturbed by the destruction of their original status structure by large population gains are less likely to have an old-family class reigning above all others. San Francisco is a clear example of the old-family type; Los Angeles, of the more amorphous, less well-organized class structure.

CLASS IN THE DEEP SOUTH

Studies in the Deep South demonstrate that, in the older regions where social changes until recently have been less rapid and less disturbing to the status order, most of the towns above a few thousand population have a six-class system in which an old-family elite is socially dominant.

For example, in a study of a Mississippi community, a market town for a cotton-growing region around it, Davis and the Gardners found a six-class system.[5] Perhaps the southern status order is best described by Chart I . . . which gives the names used by the people of the community for each class and succinctly tells how the members of each class regard themselves and the rest of the class order.

The people of the two upper classes make a clear distinction between an old aristocracy and an aristocracy which is not old. There is no doubt that the first is above the other; the upper-middle class views the two upper ones much as the upper classes do themselves but groups them in one level with two divisions, the older level above the other; the lower-middle class separates them but considers them co-ordinate; the bottom two classes, at a greater social distance than

the others, group all the levels above the Common Man as "society" and one class. An examination of the terms used by the several classes for the other classes shows that similar principles are operating.

The status system of most communities in the South is further complicated by a color-caste system which orders and systematically controls the relations of those categorized as Negroes and whites. . . . Color-caste is a system of values and behavior which places all people who are thought to be white in a superior position and those who are thought of as black in an inferior status.

Characteristics of American Negroes vary from very dark hair and skin and Negroid features to blond hair, fair skin, and Caucasian features, yet all of them are placed in the "racial" category of Negro. The skin and physical features of American Caucasians vary from Nordic blond types to the dark, swarthy skin and Negroid features of some eastern Mediterranean stocks, yet all are classed as socially white despite the fact that a sizable proportion of Negroes are "whiter" in appearance than a goodly proportion of whites. The members of the two groups are severely punished by the formal and informal rules of our society if they intermarry, and when they break this rule of "caste endogamy," their children suffer the penalties of our caste-like system by being placed in the lower color caste. Furthermore, unlike class, the rules of this system forbid the members of the lower caste from climbing out of it. Their status and that of their children are fixed forever. This is true no matter how much money they have, how great the prestige and power they may accumulate, or how well they have acquired correct manners and proper behavior. There can be no social mobility out of the lower caste into the higher one. (There may, of course, be class mobility within the Negro or white caste.) The rigor of caste rules varies from region to region in the United States.[6]

The Mexicans, Spanish Americans, and

---

[5] Allison Davis, Burleigh B. Gardner, and Mary R. Gardner, *Deep South* (Chicago: University of Chicago Press, 1941). Also read: John Dollard, *Caste and Class in a Southern Town* (New Haven: Yale University Press, 1937); Mozell Hill, "The All-Negro Society in Oklahoma" (Unpublished Ph.D. dissertation, University of Chicago, 1936); Harry J. Walker, "Changes in Race Accommodation in a Southern Community" (Unpublished Ph.D. dissertation, University of Chicago, 1945).

[6] See St. Clair Drake and Horace R. Cayton, *Black Metropolis* (New York: Harcourt, Brace & Co., 1945), for studies of two contrasting caste orders; read the "Methodological Note" by Warner in *Black Metropolis* for an analysis of the difference between the two systems.

CHART 1

The Social Perspectives of the Social Classes*

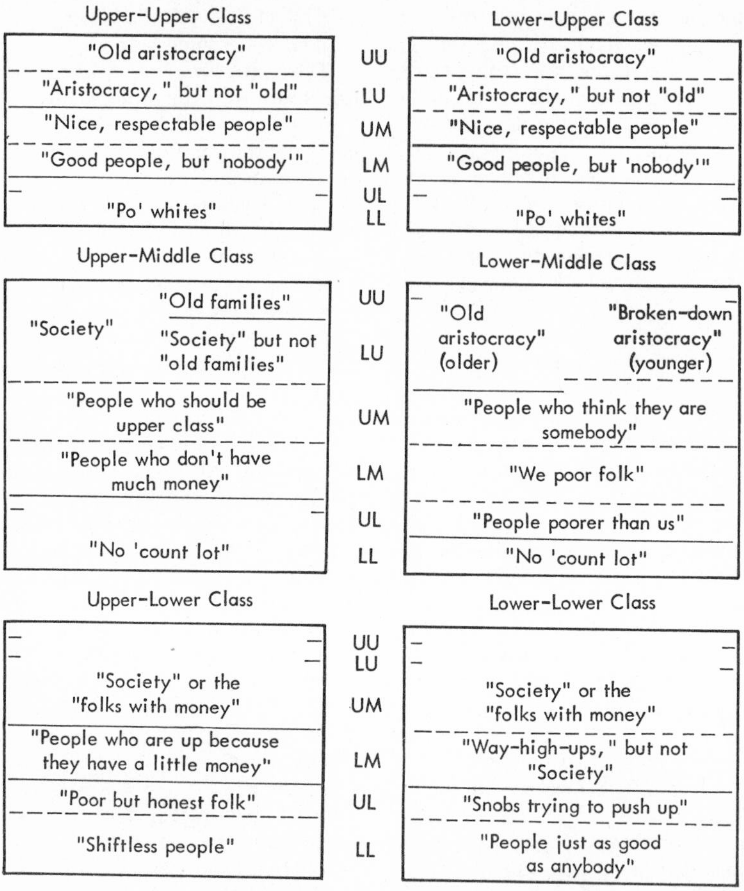

Upper–Upper Class		Lower–Upper Class
"Old aristocracy"	UU	"Old aristocracy"
"Aristocracy," but not "old"	LU	"Aristocracy," but not "old"
"Nice, respectable people"	UM	"Nice, respectable people"
"Good people, but 'nobody'"	LM	"Good people, but 'nobody'"
	UL	
"Po' whites"	LL	"Po' whites"

Upper–Middle Class			Lower–Middle Class	
"Society"	"Old families"	UU	"Old aristocracy" (older)	"Broken–down aristocracy" (younger)
	"Society" but not "old families"	LU		
"People who should be upper class"		UM	"People who think they are somebody"	
"People who don't have much money"		LM	"We poor folk"	
		UL	"People poorer than us"	
"No 'count lot"		LL	"No 'count lot"	

Upper–Lower Class		Lower–Lower Class
	UU	
	LU	
"Society" or the "folks with money"	UM	"Society" or the "folks with money"
"People who are up because they have a little money"	LM	"Way–high–ups," but not "Society"
"Poor but honest folk"	UL	"Snobs trying to push up"
"Shiftless people"	LL	"People just as good as anybody"

* Allison Davis, Burleigh B. Gardner, and Mary R. Gardner, *Deep South* (Chicago: University of Chicago Press, 1941), p. 65.

Orientals occupy a somewhat different status from that of the Negro, but many of the characteristics of their social place in America are similar.[7]

The social-class and color-caste hypotheses, inductively established as working principles for understanding American society, were developed in the researches which were reported in the "Yankee City" volumes, *Deep South*, and *Caste and Class in a Southern Town*. . . .[8]

THE GENERALITIES OF AMERICAN CLASS

It is now time to ask what are the basic characteristics of social status common to

[7] See W. Lloyd Warner and Leo Srole, *The Social Systems of American Ethnic Groups*, Vol. III, "Yankee City Series" (New Haven: Yale University Press, 1945). Chapter X discusses the similarities and differences and presents a table of predictability on their probable assimilation and gives the principles governing these phenomena.

[8] . . . For an early publication on color-caste, see W. Lloyd Warner, "American Caste and Class," *American Journal of Sociology*, XLII, No. 2 (September, 1936), 234–37, and "Formal Education and the Social Structure," *Journal of Educational Sociology*, IX (May, 1936), 524–531.

the communities of all regions in the United States and, once we have answered this question, to inqure what the variations are among the several systems. Economic factors are significant and important in determining the class position of any family or person, influencing the kind of behavior we find in any class, and contributing their share to the present form of our status system. But, while significant and necessary, the economic factors are not sufficient to predict where a particular family or individual will be or to explain· completely the phenomena of social class. Something more than a large income is necessary for high social position. Money must be translated into socially approved behavior and possessions, and they in turn must be translated into intimate participation with, and acceptance by, members of a superior class. . . .

To belong to a particular level in the social-class system of America means that a family or individual has gained acceptance as an equal by those who belong in the class. The behavior in this class and the participation of those in it must be rated by the rest of the community as being at a particular place in the social scale.

Although our democratic heritage makes us disapprove, our class order helps control a number of important functions. It unequally divides the highly and lowly valued things of our society among the several classes according to their rank. Our marriage rules conform to the rules of class, for the majority of marriages are between people of the same class. No class system, however, is so rigid that it completely prohibits marriages above and below one's own class. Furthermore, an open class system such as ours permits a person during his lifetime to move up or down from the level into which he was born. Vertical social mobility for individuals or families is characteristic of all class systems. . . . Although economic mobility is still important, it seems likely now that more people move to higher positions by education than by any other route. We have indicated before this that the mere possession of money is insufficient for gaining and keeping a higher social position. This is equally true of all other forms of mobility. In every case there must be social acceptance.

Class varies from community to community. The new city is less likely than an old one to have a well-organized class order; this is also true for cities whose growth has been rapid as compared with those which have not been disturbed by huge increases in population from other regions or countries or by the rapid displacement of old industries by new ones. The mill town's status hierarchy is more likely to follow the occupational hierarchy of the mill than the levels of evaluated participation found in market towns or those with diversified industries. Suburbs of large metropolises tend to respond to selective factors which reduce the number of classes to one or a very few. They do not represent or express all the cultural factors which make up the social pattern of an ordinary city.

Yet systematic studies . . . from coast to coast, in cities large and small and of many economic types, indicate that, despite the variations and diversity, class levels do exist and that they conform to a particular pattern of organization.

SOCIAL STRATIFICATION OF THE JEWISH COMMUNITY IN A SMALL POLISH TOWN[1]

Celia Stopnicka Heller

Various bases for social stratification existed in Stoczek. The old biblical classification was still adhered to but served only

American Journal of Sociology, "Social Stratification of the Jewish Community in a Small Polish Town," by Celia Stopnicka Rosenthal, Vol. LIX, No. 1, July, 1953. Reprinted by permission of The University of Chicago Press, Chicago, Ill. Copyright 1953 by the University of Chicago.

[1] This paper is part of a study of a small-town Jewish community in central Poland in the period between the two world wars. The town is called Stoczek and is located fifty-five miles from

for religious purposes and at times tended to play havoc with the existing status pattern. According to the biblical classification, the Jews were divided into priests (*Cohanim*), Levites (*Leviim*), and Israelites (*Israelim*). The priests had the function of blessing the congregation on holidays. Before the blessing ceremony those members of the community who enjoyed the greatest prestige served the priests by pouring water over their hands. It often happened on holidays that the "beautiful Jews," men of highest status, poured water on the hands of some "plain Jews" who were priests.

The existing status pattern was based on classifications in terms of occupation, money, learning, and lineage. This was recognized by the culture, which evolved special terms to designate each category. It is the aim of the writer, however, to show that, no matter which of the above dimensions one uses, one will find the same people with slight variations on the same point of the social scale.

Occupationally, the community was divided into three groups. At the bottom of the scale were the "men of labor," wage laborers and craftsmen. Among the manual occupations there existed a hierarchy of preference extending from watchmakers down to such lowly occupations as barbers, porters, and shoemakers. Above the men of labor stood the "businessmen," who ranged from small storekeepers to owners of forests and mills. Although no statistics are available, it is safe to estimate that about

---

Warsaw. In 1938 . . . the town's population was 4,000, out of which 2,500 comprised the Jewish community.

The paper is based on interviews with ten survivors on seven biograms received from Stoczek people now living in Israel. . . . Unfortunately, those interviewed do not constitute a representative sampling of the population, since so few survivors remain. Furthermore, the generalizations made are not based on direct observation of the community, but rather on recollection. Ideally, a study such as this should be made on the spot. . . . This, of course, is impossible as far as the Jewish communities in Poland are concerned, for they no longer exist. Apart from literary sources, the only way that their culture can be reconstructed is by interviewing persons who once lived in the small towns of Poland. This approach must, of course, be used with caution, since recollection is not identical with the facts of life as they once were. . . .

30 per cent of Jewish men were businessmen while about 69 per cent were workers. The third category, "learners," less than 1 per cent of the population, devoted all their time to learning, from which they derived no material benefit. No one looked down on them for not occupying themselves with making a living. On the contrary, they were treated with great respect. Usually the wife was the economic provider, and she was highly respected for being married to a man who devoted his life to learning. Parents-in-law often supported such a learner and his family.

Even though there was stigmatization of manual labor, an impoverished businessman who resorted to such labor was not looked down upon but pitied. It was assumed that no *balebatisher mensh,* man of middle-class respectability, would resort to manual labor unless he had no other alternative. On the other hand, a worker who became a businessman did not automatically gain in status but had to start living "respectably" in order to reach higher status.

The classification in terms of money presents a more complicated picture than that in terms of occupation. When former residents of Stoczek were asked to identify the source of prestige in their town, they invariably answered "not money." And yet, when they were asked to name the most highly esteemed people in Stoczek, they named those with much money, good lineage, great learning, or a combination of these. This apparent inconsistency becomes clear when one looks at the particular meaning ascribed to money in Stoczek.

In observing the people in Stoczek, one is impressed with their great desire to have money. This desire was expressed vividly in everyday conversation and in stock phrases. Even the poorest would start a sentence with "I should have as many millions as" and finish in a variety of ways, such as "the pairs of shoes I made" or "the number of chickens I sold." To an outsider it may have sounded strange that a man in rags who did not have enough money to buy bread spoke in terms of millions. In Stoczek it was the accepted way of talking and was never questioned or analyzed. Colorful terminology existed in reference to various gradations of wealth ranging from the very rich *magnates* and *gvirim*, through the rich *oishers,* to the poor *orime lait* and the very poor *kaptzunim.* . . .

Why was there such great emphasis on money in Stoczek? Did it represent the longing for food and material comforts of an impoverished community? It did represent that, but not that alone. As we shall see from the subsequent analysis, the material benefits of money, although recognized and enjoyed, were not its most significant ends. There were rich people who were envied for having money but who commanded no respect. By comparing the moneyed people who commanded respect with those who did not, we find one outstanding difference. Respected people used part of their money to do good deeds, *mitzvos,* for the needy. And, indeed, the common denominator of all good deeds was that they flowed from the haves to the have-nots.

The culturally favored response in the giving pattern was to the situation rather than to the individual. As one informant put it, "The man who did not look to see whether he would get his money back but rather whether the borrower needed it was considered to be good." Thus, one was required to help a person in need no matter who he was. This manner of help marked the donor as having a true "Jewish heart."

The point that was emphasized most in describing a man was his charitableness. "He is a man of great charity (*baal tzdokoh*)," was a description in itself which would bring a definite picture of the man to the listener's mind. In addition to charity, performing a *gmilus khesed,* act of loving kindness, that is, lending money to people in need without charging interest or demanding notes and securities, was considered a good deed. Aid to a sick person also ranked high as a good deed. The phrase "to save a Jewish soul" was used without additional elaboration. Well-to-do women sent the best food and delicacies to poor people who were sick and to destitute mothers who had just given birth. It was a good deed to visit the sick and people in mourning. The greater the social distance, the higher did the deed rank. Bringing peace to the community or to a divided family also ranked very high as a

good deed, and a man who was known as a peacemaker earned much prestige in Stoczek. Moreover, an individual who did a good deed for an orphan received greater credit than if he had performed a similar deed for any other person in the community.

The one who performed good deeds for the needy overcame his initial human failing of not being able to project himself into the position of the needy. "The well-fed does not believe the hungry one," went the saying. His returns for doing good deeds were, therefore, very high. The belief was prevalent that, when a man died and was called before God to be judged, his good deeds came forth to testify for him. Men at funeral processions chanted, "Charity prevents death." Thus, using money to do good deeds meant storing up credit for the afterlife. However, one also received high earthly rewards in terms of honor and respect.

Although giving brought prestige, taking when in need was shameful. An event which vividly illustrates the shame connected with taking occurred when the city council voted a substantial sum of money for milk to be distributed in school to needy children. The neediest of Jewish children did not accept the milk, while Polish children stood in line for it, even if they were not from the most destitute families. This shame of taking is especially puzzling in view of the fact that the one who took afforded the giver the opportunity to do a good deed. Therefore, it might seem that giving and taking was a reciprocal relationship. Why, then, was shame felt? The fact is that the culture did not recognize the giving and taking pattern as a reciprocal relation. Rather, the act of giving was phrased as an unselfish deed which originated in the giver's being a man of mercy and good heart. Only when we remember this particular phrasing, do we come to understand the role of shame.

Because taking was so shameful, the ideal pattern for an individual who gave charity was to deposit the gift with the needy person without confronting him and without his knowing the source of help. On the one hand he thus showed that he did not give to gain prestige and, therefore, bore testimony to the culture's phrasing of giving. On the other hand, he spared the taker the shame of facing the giver. The ideal pattern is understandable when we recall that, although charity and good deeds bring a person benefits in his afterlife and assure him of honor in this world, individual motivation for doing good is supposed to be induced not by those rewards but by the person's "Jewish heart." Actually, however, very few acted in terms of the ideal pattern, preferring to reap the earthly benefits of prestige for their good deeds.

A mechanism was developed whereby the taker was spared the shame of confronting the giver, and yet the giver could have the satisfaction of being known as such. There were persons, often children of good families who went from house to house to collect money for specific needy people. This was considered a noble act which brought much admiration for both grown-ups and children who engaged in it.

Where neither of the above methods of giving was used, and the giver confronted the taker, the giver was expected to make the shame bearable by setting into motion the mechanism of "beautification." Beautification, the process of making the taker feel equal, was used to remove the shame of the have-nots. The feelings of shame were not only characteristic of the poor but also of those who lacked any of the things that the culture valued highly. Although the culture did not recognize that the lack of possessions which it held significant, such as parents, children, money, and health, was in itself shameful, nevertheless, people so deprived were considered more sensitive and more easily shamed.

One of the acts of beautification was to ask a needy stranger—a wanderer, beggar, or soldier who happened to be passing through the town—to a Sabbath or holiday meal. To beautify him, such a man was called a "guest" and was, indeed, treated like a very worthy guest of the family. He was given an honorable place at the table, served the choicest foods, asked to lead in the after-meal prayer, to sing a hymn, and invited to relate some news. Even the stylized conversation between the head of the house and the guest becomes meaningful when one understands the mechanism of shame and beautification. The guest did not start the conversation, for he was imbued

with shame. He was constantly approached by the host, who, in addressing him, substituted the expression "a Jew" for "you." Thus, the head of the family would ask: "From where does a Jew hail?" "What is a Jew's name?" "Perhaps a Jew will sing a hymn?" In acting thus, it was as though the host were saying to the man: "You are poor; you cannot spend the holiday with your family, and you are, therefore, ashamed. But we are both Jews. I will make you forget your shame and make you feel like an equal."

To marry off an orphan or a girl from a very poor family ranked high as an act of beautification. A certain man in Stoczek attained the pinnacle of prestige by arranging a double wedding for his daughter and an orphaned girl. Since it was shameful for a bride-to-be not to have a trousseau, a person who supplied such a girl with a trousseau performed a good and beautifying deed. Adoption of an orphan also ranked high as an act of beautification. To make an orphan feel that he belonged and was not deprived, by providing him with parents and home, was indeed a *mitzva* ("good deed").

In order to understand the particular function of shame in the charity pattern, it is worth while to look at a situation in which shame did not exist. Professional beggars who came to Stoczek were insolent and arrogant. They seldom expressed thanks for the alms they received and often insulted the donor into giving more. The word *shnorer* ("beggar") was charged with much negative meaning and was used as an insult by both adults and children. The contempt and dislike of the beggar is explained by his behavior. The beggar discovered, and capitalized upon his discovery, that he was actually doing the donor a favor. He seemed to serve notice that he did not owe anyone thanks and honor for the donation given him, since he was thereby helping the donor reach salvation. Consequently, since the beggar did not feel shame, there was no need for the giver to exert himself in order to beautify him, and indeed he did not.

Yet, even these lowly outcasts, the beggars, were supposed to be imbued with the Jewish characteristic of shame during the

Sabbath and holidays. And, because it was assumed that they experienced shame on those days, the donor tried to beautify them. As was shown earlier, the beggar who was invited to a Sabbath or holiday meal was not referred to as a beggar but as a guest. Looking back on her memories of the beggar, the writer feels that during the Sabbath and holiday he abandoned his insolence and arrogance and conformed with the general pattern of behaving in a manner befitting one who receives charity. . . .

Just as a man who beautified a deprived person performed a good deed and was greatly respected for it, so the man who shamed such a person committed a sin and was looked upon with contempt. All members of the community were thought to be imbued with the Jewish susceptibility to shame, and it was, therefore, considered evil to do anything that would tend to shame another person. "One is not allowed to shame a human being," was the stock phrase. One was not supposed to point to a person's lowly occupation, state of deprivation, bad health, or misfits in the family, for that would produce shame. "As a child I had a friend from that family in which there was a *shmadke* (woman who changed her faith). My mother warned me that I should never mention the word 'convert' or anything similar in her presence so as not to hurt her," related one informant.

In both beautification and shaming it was presupposed that the act flowed from a man of higher status to a man of lower status. It was not conceivable that a man could beautify a person who stood higher than himself in the social scale. Such a man could afford honor but never beautify. The same was true of shaming. A man might be looked down upon by the community for being "insolent" to one of higher status but never for having "shamed" him.

Shame performed important functions in the culture of which the people in the community were not aware. On the one hand, it prevented people from asking for help, which the culture defined as highly dishonorable. This tended to perpetuate the belief that those who were able to help would move forward without being asked by the needy. Shame also averted refusal, which

was painful for both the person who refused and the one who was refused. Furthermore, it tended to prevent abuses in taking, for one would not expose himself to the shame of taking unless he were in great need. There were, of course, deviants who asked for help without needing it and took advantage of the good hearts of others, but they were considered to be very lowly people. On the other hand, shame helped to set in motion the whole mechanism of beautification. By using beautification, the giver would emerge feeling like a giver and not as in the beggar situation, where the giver was made to feel that he was taking as much as giving. Furthermore, he received part of his reward immediately in the form of honor and thanks from the man to whom he gave rather than having to wait for his return until the afterlife.

The purpose of this detailed discussion of the giving-taking pattern is to show that wealth alone did not assure a person of status in the community. Wealth was a source of prestige only in so far as it enabled a man to contribute to the welfare of the community, to do good deeds, and to give charity. Consequently, money was greatly valued, since with it one could obtain status. As the sayings went: "The rich man has this world and the next world" and "With money you can buy *yikhus* (lineage) and *koved* (honor and respect)." The substance of these sayings is that, by doing good deeds, the rich man not only assured himself of honor but also secured a "seat in heaven" for himself.

Just as a man did not gain status by virtue merely of obtaining money, his status did not diminish if he lost his money. An impoverished man of high status was pitied for not being able to live in the manner befitting him, but he did not suffer in prestige. . . .

However, it must not be deduced that money was valued only in so far as it enabled a person to do good deeds. The role of money in enabling a person to eat well, dress well, and have pleasure in so doing was clearly recognized. But the man who used his money only to satisfy his physical needs was lacking in Jewishness. Such a man would be referred to as a pig and the Polish saying, "Maciek (popular Polish given name) made it; Maciek ate it," was applied to him.

Nevertheless, the mere possession of money, even when it was not used in the socially prescribed manner, gave one a sense of power. A wealthy man who did not use part of his money to do good deeds did not receive *koved,* and people spoke badly of him, but he was accorded deference even if this was spurious. The reason for such deference was tied to Jewish experience with the outside world. Money was the only Jewish value that non-Jews appreciated. Hence, men of wealth had more contact with city officials than the rest of the community. It was assumed that a man who had money and did not "behave the way a Jew should," that is to 'say, did not give charity, was low enough to cause trouble with the officials for anyone who did now show him deference. "It is better not to start with such a one," went the saying, and people tried to keep out of his way.

Having examined the meaning of money in Stoczek, we can turn to the problem of conspicuous consumption. People were very much afraid of other people's jealousy. It was pointed out endlessly that "you are not allowed to take out other people's eyes," that is, that one should avoid making others jealous. Thus, ostentation was discouraged from childhood on, and society called for private enjoyment of the items of consumption. Ostentation was condemned also because of the effect it had on strengthening the hostile attitudes of the Polish population. Despite conscious discouragement in terms of the above two factors, however, ostentatiousness tended to flourish. Evidently, conspicuous consumption must have exercised an important latent function, since it persisted despite all verbal attacks. The explanation lies in the meaning of money in Stoczek. Display of wealth served notice of two things: (1) the displayer was in a position to dispense favors and (2) he was powerful enough to deal with the outside world.

Since the value of money was unstable, it was expected that the person who had it would use it to obtain more lasting sources of status, such as learning and lineage. Thus the dictum was to educate one's sons and marry one's daughters into *yikhus* ("lineage").

We have previously discussed learning as part of the social stratification in terms of occupation. We now come to a discussion of learning as a separate basis of social stratification. Before describing the status that went with learning, however, it is necessary to clarify the nature of Jewish learning. Learning was not considered a process which stopped at any given time or point but was conceived to go on throughout one's life. "The Torah (learning, teaching, and doctrine) has no bottom," went the saying. This concept of learning as a continuous process is reflected in the terms applied to a learned man. He was never referred to as a "learned man" when one spoke of his absorption with Jewish learning. The expression "He is an educated man" applied to secular education. "He knows how to learn" and "He is a great learner" designated a man's standing in Jewish learning. The words *talmid khokhom* denoted a man of highest Jewish learning and not merely a "smart student."

Learning was considered so valuable that it needed no validation in terms of good deeds. To be sure, a man who shared his learning with others received additional prestige, but the fact alone that "he knew how to learn" assured him status. Thus, even if he did not share his learning or give charity, he was never "common" or a "pig," terms which referred to a man of wealth who did not share his wealth. It was quite conceivable that a man could have much wealth and yet not behave properly, but it was unimaginable that a man of learning could behave improperly. Learning was equated with refinement, and the term *aydele Yid* ("refined Jew") meant a learned man. The rich man, even if he were charitable and did good deeds but had no learning, did not reach his maximum status until he married his children into *yikhus*. The learner needed only to be greatly learned to reach highest status. Thus, the learner created his own *yikhus* and did not need ancestral support.

Just as learning did not need validation in terms of other things, so it was not supposed to be used as a means of obtaining material benefits. Learning was a goal in itself, and one pursued it with love and joy. Persons who devoted their spare time to learning and were known to sit up until late at night studying were talked about with reverence. "He cannot tear himself away from learning," went the saying. The learned man would often be turned to for advice and opinions on community and world affairs. Men used to come to a learner's house on Saturday afternoon so that he "should learn with them." With them, he posed questions, answered difficult questions, and interpreted the text. Children were sent to such a man to be tested in their learning. It was inconceivable that he would accept money as a reward, and no one dared to offer it to him. The learner's rewards were great respect and joy from the fulfillment of one of the most important commandments of Jewish law, teaching the people.

However, not only status went with learning but a sense of power as well. The learners felt so powerful that a case once occurred wherein a learned man opposed the rabbi on a certain issue. Only someone highly powerful, highly honored and esteemed, would dare to do so. This power is also borne out by the fact that the learners were not bound by the same pattern of behavior as the rest of the community. As we have seen, taking was shameful, and yet the learner could be supported without shame by his wife or even by strangers. Children and youths who went to out-of-town *yeshivas* (schools of higher learning) ate in other people's houses without feeling shame. There is a striking similarity between the learner at the top of the social pyramid and the beggar at the bottom, neither of whom was ashamed to take. It would be inconceivable of course for somone in the culture to compare the two, since they were on opposite sides of the social scale. However, this comparison helps to reinforce our hypothesis concerning the functions of shame. The learner was very much aware that by devoting himself to learning he was doing the community a great favor. He kept the heritage of the Torah alive. Similarly, the beggar knew that he was the actual giver and could, therefore, receive without shame.

There remains to be discussed, among the sources of status, that which was called in Stoczek *yikhus*. *Yikhus* was a very important concept and yet was so elusive that it is hard to define. A notable fact is that each person knew the other's *yikhus*. It was one of the first things to be established when two strangers talked to each other or when two people spoke about a third. *Yikhus* is pedigree, lineage in terms of learned, wealthy, and charitable ancestors, that is, in terms of ancestors of high status. However . . . each person considered himself to be a man of *yikhus*, although he might not have been recognized to be so by others. He merely traced back to some ancestor, no matter how far removed, who was learned or prosperous and generous and leaned on him for self-esteem. The people whom the whole community considered to be of great *yikhus* were those whose families traced themselves back to revered rabbis, greatly learned men, and very rich persons who were community-conscious and gave *tzdokoh*, justice, meaning charity.

Yikhus, like learning, was based on solid and permanent foundations. However, a man of *yikhus* had to live up to his position. If he was not learned and charitable, he did not receive honor and respect, although it was never forgotten that he came from a good family. In fact, he was looked upon as having squandered his inheritance.

We have now completed the analysis of status in Stoczek in terms of occupation, money, learning, and lineage. What we find is a convergence of status so that, for example, the workers, the poor, and the uneducated were likely to be the same people. The community divided itself into three classes. . . . At the top of the social pyramid in Stoczek were the beautiful Jews. It is interesting to note that beautiful Jew never referred to physical beauty but to endowment which the culture valued. To the class of beautiful Jews belonged people of great *yikhus,* much learning, and those who combined wealth with much charity giving. Occupationally, they were usually men of independent means or learners. The middle class were the *balebatim.* To them belonged the shopkeepers and traders who had some means and some learning. At the bottom of the scale were the plain Jews, workers and craftsmen, who had little learning, no *yikhus,* and little or no money.

However, there were exceptions, people who fitted into one category occupationally and into another in terms of money or learning. There were a few workmen in Stoczek who spent all their spare time learning and were known to "know how to learn a little." Thus, occupationally they were at the bottom of the scale, but they were in the center of the learning scale. Such men were talked about in the following manner: "He is a worker but he is a *balebatisher mensh* (man of middle-class respectability)." On the other hand, there were some wealthy men of no education. One man in town who was known for his wealth and charity was spoken of by the learners as barely knowing how to read the Hebrew prayers. He was nevertheless respected because he gave bountifully. Men of great wealth who neither were charitable nor knew "how to learn" were referred to in the lowest terms.

The chief role of the beautiful Jews was to devote themselves to the welfare of the community and to be at the community's disposal. The members of the community came to them for help and advice on family, business, and religious matters. People of high status did not receive any material advantage from playing their role of community-minded, learned, and charitable individuals. They derived honor and respect and a good name in the community. "A good name is better than money," went the saying. Honor was, indeed, conceived to be something distinct from material possessions. The Jews often employed the following Polish saying: "I do not possess money, but I have honor." *Koved* ("honor") lived on, even after a person died. The beautiful Jew was long remembered after his death, and, when one talked about his son, one always mentioned that the father "gave much charity" or that the father was "a great learner."

Class distinction in Stoczek was very definite, and the people below owed deference to the people above. A man who did not behave with proper respect toward the man above was known to be "insolent" and was looked down upon by the whole community. If a man of the lower class used obscene language in the presence of people of the upper class, and that occurred very rarely, he was talked about as a "fellow from the streets." The man of high status did not argue with a man from the lower class who behaved disrespectfully to him. It was below his dignity to do so. Although there was much contact between the classes, as when persons of higher status attended weddings, funerals, circumcisions, and *bar mitzvahs* of the poor, the relationship was never that of equality but that of the man higher up beautifying the man below. There were no friendships between adults of different classes. The culture held that men of higher status could not mix with men of lower status because in the end the people below would not remember "who you are and who they are," that is, would behave disrespectfully. Where attempts at social intercourse between individuals of unequal status ended with the person of lower status behaving disrespectfully, people quoted the Polish saying: "Do not mix with slops, and the pigs will not eat you."

There was strong condemnation of faking status, and a man who "pretended to be big" was spoken of with great contempt and derision. The cultural concept existed that one could not hide his social background, for sooner or later one's behavior would reveal it. To bear out this conception, two Polish proverbs were often quoted: "You can tell a gentleman by his boots" and "The awl slips out of the bag."

Since a man's true social standing was easily discernible, one was supposed never to boast about it. A person who bragged was characterized as "he blows from himself." One was not supposed to talk about the good deeds he performed, and people were very careful not to transgress in this matter. People of the upper class were also expected not to engage in gossip. A beautiful Jew who heard members of his family speaking of another, even if not in a derogatory manner, after admonished them with the following saying: "Our teachers say that one should not discuss another person, for even if one starts with good words, one finishes with evil ones." Neither did a beautiful Jew engage in "empty words," which embraced small talk as well as gossip. He was supposed to talk about worthy matters and, if he had nothing worthy to say, to remain silent. A beautiful Jew would not laugh excessively, since this was considered to be a sign of stupidity and merited the observation, "Why do you laugh so much? Is stupidity pushing you?"

The members of the upper class were expected more than others to live up to the ideal cultural ways prescribed for the whole community. A man who broke a vow would lose face, and particularly so if he were from the upper class. All men were supposed to act with justice, especially the beautiful Jews. Obscene language was never used by the upper class.

The culture recognized appropriate behavior in accordance with the class to which one belonged. Such fitting behavior was nurtured from childhood. A mother whose son or daughter did not behave properly admonished her child by saying, "It does not befit a child of so-and-so (here she mentioned the full name of the husband) to behave thus."

Membership in a class was, for the most part, hereditary. Theoretically, higher status could be achieved by every Jew. The two "elevators," to use Sorokin's terms, were money and learning. A boy from the lower class who was talented and ambitious could become a learner, and, if he had luck, he could become well to do. However, a man who rose from the lower class, unless he were a learner, was on shaky ground. Money alone did not bring prestige to an individual. In order to be eligible for prestige, a newly rich man had to begin to behave in a "respectable manner." But even if he gave charity and tried to behave respectably, every misstep, no matter how trivial, caused people to refer to his lowly origin. It was also implied in Stoczek that a man of the lower class who became wealthy grew bad in the process of attaining wealth. "Woe, oh, woe, when a beggar becomes a lord," was the often employed Polish saying. In contrast to the newly rich, the position of a learned man who came from the lower class was not different from that of other learned men. The fact that his father was a worker was mentioned only to point to his great personal worth, for in spite of such an obstacle he had risen to be a learner. It was inconceivable that he could behave in any

other way than properly, since the culture equated learning with refinement.

There was actually little movement upward in the social scale. On the contrary, there was mass descent in terms of money and occupation. This descent, however, was not marked by loss of prestige. The wave of organized anti-Semitism and planned boycotting of Jewish stores made it almost impossible for a poor Jewish man to make good. Advancement in terms of learning was also hampered by great economic obstacles. It is true that a poor youth who was capable and devoted himself to learning could always be accepted in a *yeshiva* and did not have to starve. But a poor family could ill afford to relinquish the little money that a boy would bring in if he worked.

It was generally recognized that opportunities for advancement were meager. Although to be smart, *klig*, was highly valued in the culture, nevertheless, there was no attempt to correlate smartness with specific class, occupation, or status. Nowhere in the people's sayings or in their actions do we find an attempt to place wisdom in a certain class or claim that it is more prevalent in any group. It is inconceivable that a man who did not advance in Stoczek could have said of himself, "I guess I am stupid."

The social status of the Jew determined his seat in the synagogue. All seats were oriented to the east, for when a Jew prayed, he always faced east toward Jerusalem. The men of highest prestige occupied places nearest to the eastern wall. At the western wall sat the lower class, and in between the beautiful Jews and plain Jews sat the people from the middle class, the *balebatim*.

Status was also expressed in marriage. It happened occasionally that an impoverished good family made arrangements for a son to marry the daughter of a rich man who had risen from the lower class. This was considered a tragedy for the *yikhus* family and a highly significant event for the wealthy family. The community definitely thought the first to be the loser and the seond the gainer. This further bears out the generalization that the values of lineage and learning were placed far above that of money.

OCCUPATIONAL PRESTIGE IN THE UNITED STATES, 1925–63

Robert W. Hodge, Paul M. Siegel, and Peter H. Rossi

The prestige hierarchy of occupations is perhaps the best studied aspect of the stratification systems of modern societies. Extensive empirical studies have been undertaken in a variety of nations, socialist and capitalist, developed and underdeveloped. Intensive analyses have been undertaken of results of particular studies searching for the existence of disparate prestige hierarchies held by subgroups within nations.[1] Despite rather extensive searches conducted by a variety of techniques, it appears that occupational-prestige hierarchies are similar from country to country and from subgroup to subgroup within a country. This stability reflects the fundamental but gross similarities among the occupational systems of modern nations. Furthermore, knowledge about occupations and relatively strong consensus on the relative positions of occupations are widely diffused throughout the populations involved.

The consensus within and among populations on the prestige positions of occupations leads one to expect that there will be

Reprinted from the *American Journal of Sociology*, Vol. 70, November, 1964, by permission of the University of Chicago Press. Copyright 1964 by the University of Chicago.

[1] See, e.g., Kaare Svalastoga, *Prestige, Class and Mobility* (Copenhagen: Gyldendal, 1959), pp. 43–131; C. A. Moser and J. R. Hall, "The Social Grading of Occupations," in D. V. Glass (ed.), *Social Mobility in Britain* (London: Routledge Kegan Paul, 1954), pp. 29–50; and Albert J. Reiss, Jr., Otis Dudley Duncan, Paul K. Hatt, and C. C. North, *Occupations and Social Status* (New York: Free Press of Glencoe, 1961). The last mentioned volume contains the major analysis, the 1947 North-Hatt-NORC study of occupation prestige.

considerable stability over time in the positions of particular occupations. Industrialization has proceeded to different points in the several countries whose prestige hierarchies have been studied without seriously affecting the relative positions of occupations in the countries involved. Cross-sectional comparisons between different countries at different stages of industrial evolution suggest that it would be erroneous to expect any considerable change in the *prestige* structure of a single country over time, even though that country might be experiencing appreciable changes in *occupational* structure. We can only expect to observe changes on the order of those previously found between two nations at different stages of economic development.

On the other hand, there are cogent reasons for expecting that changes in occupational structure will be reflected, at least ultimately, in corresponding changes in the prestige positions of occupations. The prestige position of an occupation is apparently a characteristic generated by the way in which the occupation is articulated into the division of labor, by the amount of power and influence implied in the activities of the occupation, by the characteristics of incumbents, and by the amount of resources which society places at the disposal of incumbents. (Other factors are undoubtedly at work, but these are the most obvious.) Hence, as occupations shift in these respects over time, corresponding adjustive shifts in prestige positions can be anticipated.

Considerable changes have occurred since 1947 in the occupational structure and labor force of the United States. The long-term trend in the growth of professional and scientific occupations persisted and was even accelerated during this period. Governmental and popular concern over the numbers and quality of our professional and technical manpower was expressed in a great expansion of our universities as well as in more attention being given lower levels of schooling. The proportion of the labor force devoted to agricultural pursuits declined along with unskilled and heavy labor components. This was also the period during which automation continued to expand, raising a serious question as to whether the American labor force could absorb both workers freed from jobs eliminated by technological progress and the large cohorts of postwar births now beginning to enter the labor force. Mention must be made of the stepped-up drive for equality on the part of Negroes, although we cannot tarry here to examine it. The question at issue is whether changes in the occupational structure have been reflected in shifts in the prestige of occupations between the two points in time.

On the basis of our empirical knowledge concerning the stability under a variety of conditions of the hierarchy of occupational prestige, we can support an expectation that there will be relatively few changes in the positions of occupations as we proceed from the 1947 to the 1963 study. On the basis of what seems to be a reasonable model of how these prestige positions have been generated, we expect somewhat more in the way of changes. Neither point of view produces very precise expectations for we need to know what is an acceptable level of stability (or change) either to conform to or to negate each expectation.

One further problem plagues interpretation of any comparisons such as this study envisages: Consider a set of occupational titles for which we have an aggregate prestige rating at two points in time; the difference between these ratings can be attributed either to a general increase in the amount of prestige in the occupational system or to an increase in the prestige of the aggregate of occupations in the set and a corresponding decrease in the prestige of some occupations not in the set. There is no conceivable way of choosing between these interpretations with the present data.

In view of the large number of professional occupations included in the NORC list, it may well be the case that in the aggregate the ninety occupations stood higher in the prestige hierarchy in 1963 than in 1947. If prestige is regarded as a "commodity" that behaves like the payoff in a "zero-sum" game, then, to be sure, what one set of occupations gains another must lose. But the NORC titles might get higher ratings in 1963 than 1947 because

there is, all told, a greater amount of prestige in the system. If the latter is the case, the ninety NORC titles may get higher ratings and at the same time a smaller share of all prestige and a lower place in the total prestige hierarchy.[2]

These remarks are perhaps sufficient to alert the reader to the ambiguities which characterize the study of occupational prestige. Indeterminacies encountered in the study of a set of occupations are, of course, duplicated when the focus is upon a single occupation. It is for this reason that our focus is largely on the ordering of the ninety NORC occupational titles in two time periods and not upon changes in the prestige of particular occupations. All indications of changes in occupational prestige revealed here are of necessity relative to the set of ninety titles under consideration. These occupations exhaust our universe, and changes in their prestige are assumed to indicate restructuring of the relative prestige of the occupations under consideration.

METHODS AND PROCEDURES

A small-scale replication of the 1947 study was undertaken in the spring of 1963. In order properly to compare the replication with the original, it was necessary to replicate the study using procedures as nearly identical as possible with those of the earlier study. . . .

Because of the stability of prestige positions of occupations from subgroup to subgroup in the 1947 study, it was felt that a relatively small national sample would be sufficient for the replication. In all a total of 651 interviews was collected according to quota sampling methods from a national sample of adults and youths.[3]

As in the 1947 study, occupational

[2] This point is perhaps more clearly illustrated with a more familiar commodity: money income in dollars. It is fairly easy to see how a group could receive a smaller proportion of all income over time, but at the same time have greater income because there is more income to spread between groups.

[3] Justification for our claim that 651 cases suffice to give a reliable intertemporal comparison can be derived from examination of sampling error estimates based on the assumption of a random sample. . . .

TABLE 1. Distributions of Prestige Ratings, United States, 1947 and 1963

Occupation	March, 1947 PER CENT								June, 1963 PER CENT							
	Excellent*	Good	Average	Below Average	Poor	Don't Know†	NORC Score	Rank	Excellent‡	Good	Average	Below Average	Poor	Don't Know§	NORC Score	Rank
U.S. Supreme Court justice	83	15	2	=	=	3	96	1	77	18	4	1	1	1	94	1
Physician	67	30	3	=	=	1	93	2.5	71	25	4	=	=	1	93	2
Nuclear physicist	48	39	11	1	1	51	86	18	70	23	5	1	1	10	92	3.5
Scientist	53	38	8	1	=	7	89	8	68	27	5	=	1	2	92	3.5
Government scientist	51	41	7	1	=	6	88	10.5	64	30	5	1	=	2	91	5.5
State governor	71	25	4	=	=	1	93	2.5	64	30	5	1	1	1	91	5.5
Cabinet member in the federal government	66	28	5	1	=	6	92	4.5	61	32	6	1	1	2	90	8
College professor	53	40	7	1	=	1	89	8	59	35	5	=	=	1	90	8
U.S. representative in Congress	57	35	6	1	=	4	89	8	58	33	6	2	=	2	90	8
Chemist	42	48	9	1	=	7	86	18	54	38	8	=	=	3	89	11
Lawyer	44	45	9	1	1	1	86	18	53	38	8	=	=	=	89	11
Diplomat in the U.S. foreign service	70	24	4	1	1	9	92	4.5	57	34	7	1	1	3	89	11
Dentist	42	48	9	=	=	=	86	18	47	47	6	1	=	=	88	14
Architect	42	48	9	1	=	6	86	18	47	45	6	1	=	2	88	14
County judge	47	43	9	1	=	1	87	13	50	40	8	1	=	1	88	14
Psychologist	38	49	12	1	=	15	85	22	49	41	8	1	=	6	87	17.5
Minister	52	35	11	1	1	1	87	13	53	33	13	1	1	1	87	17.5
Member of a board of directors of a large corporation	42	47	10	1	=	5	86	18	42	51	6	1	=	1	87	17.5
Mayor of a large city	57	36	6	1	=	1	90	6	46	44	9	1	=	=	87	17.5
Priest	51	34	11	2	2	6	86	18	52	33	12	2	1	6	86	21.5
Head of a department in a state government	47	44	8	=	1	3	87	13	44	48	6	1	1	1	86	21.5
Civil engineer	33	55	11	1	=	5	84	23	44	48	8	1	1	3	86	21.5
Airline pilot	35	48	15	1	1	3	83	24.5	41	52	11	1	=	2	86	21.5
Banker	49	43	8	=	=	1	88	10.5	39	51	10	1	=	6	85	24.5
Biologist	29	51	18	1	1	16	81	29	38	50	11	1	=	6	85	24.5
Sociologist	31	51	16	1	1	23	82	26.5	35	48	15	1	1	10	83	26
Instructor in public schools	28	45	24	2	1	1	79	34	30	53	16	1	=	=	82	27.5
Captain in the regular army	28	49	19	2	2	2	80	31.5	28	55	16	2	=	1	82	27.5
Accountant for a large business	25	57	17	1	=	2	81	29	27	55	17	1	=	=	81	29.5
Public school teacher	26	45	24	3	2	=	78	36	31	46	22	1	=	=	81	29.5

Occupation																
Owner of a factory that employs about 100 people	30	51	17	1	=	2	82	26.5	28	49	19	2	=	1	80	31.5
Building contractor	21	55	23	=	1	1	79	34	22	56	20	1	=	=	80	31.5
Artist who paints pictures that are exhibited in galleries	40	40	15	3	2	6	83	24.5	28	45	20	5	2	3	78	34.5
Musician in a symphony orchestra	31	46	19	3	1	5	81	29	25	45	25	3	1	2	78	34.5
Author of novels	32	44	19	3	2	9	80	31.5	26	46	22	4	2	5	78	34.5
Economist	25	48	24	2	1	22	79	34	20	53	24	3	1	12	78	34.5
Official of an international labor union	26	42	20	5	7	11	75	40.5	21	53	18	5	3	5	77	37
Railroad engineer	22	45	30	3	=	1	77	37.5	19	47	30	3	1	1	76	39
Electrician	15	38	43	4	=	1	73	45	18	45	34	2	1	=	76	39
County agricultural agent	17	53	28	2	=	5	77	37.5	13	54	30	2	1	4	76	39
Owner-operator of a printing shop	13	48	36	3	=	2	74	42.5	15	51	34	3	1	2	75	41.5
Trained machinist	14	43	38	5	1	2	73	45	16	50	32	5	1	1	75	41.5
Farm owner and operator	19	46	31	3	1	1	76	39	16	45	33	3	1	3	74	44
Undertaker	14	43	36	5	2	2	72	47	17	46	33	5	2	5	74	44
Welfare worker for a city government	16	43	35	4	2	4	73	45	10	44	38	4	2	2	74	44
Newspaper columnist	13	51	32	3	1	5	74	42.5	16	49	38	3	1	1	73	46
Policeman	11	30	46	11	2	1	67	55	7	38	37	8	2	1	72	47
Reporter on a daily newspaper	9	43	43	4	1	2	71	48	9	45	44	7	1	1	71	48
Radio announcer	17	45	35	3	=	2	75	40.5	9	42	44	9	1	1	70	49.5
Bookkeeper	8	31	55	6	2	1	68	51.5	11	40	45	10	=	=	70	49.5
Tenant farmer (one who owns livestock and machinery and manages the farm)	10	37	40	11	=	1	68	51.5	6	37	42	11	2	1	69	51.5
Insurance agent	7	34	53	4	2	2	68	51.5	7	40	47	5	2	2	69	51.5
Carpenter	5	28	56	10	2	1	65	58	3	36	49	8	1	1	68	53
Manager of a small store in a city	3	40	50	4	1	1	69	49	8	40	48	7	=	4	67	54.5
A local official of a labor union	7	29	41	14	9	11	62	62	7	36	42	9	5	4	67	54.5
Mail carrier	8	54	54	10	1	1	66	57	6	29	53	10	1	2	66	57
Railroad conductor	8	30	52	9	9	1	67	55	4	33	48	10	3	3	66	57
Traveling salesman for a wholesale concern	6	35	53	5	2	2	68	51.5	6	33	54	7	2	2	66	57
Plumber	5	24	55	14	1	1	63	59.5	5	29	54	9	1	3	65	59
Automobile repairman	5	21	58	14	1	1	63	59.5	6	25	56	12	4	2	64	60
Playground director	7	33	48	10	2	4	67	55	4	29	46	15	4	3	63	62.5
Barber	3	17	56	20	1	1	59	66	6	24	56	13	2	1	63	62.5
Machine operator in a factory	4	20	53	20	2	2	60	64.5	4	25	51	15	4	1	63	62.5
Owner-operator of a lunch stand	4	24	55	14	4	3	62	62	6	25	57	11	3	1	63	62.5
Corporal in the regular army	5	21	48	20	3	6	60	64.5	4	22	47	15	6	2	63	65.5
Garage mechanic	4	21	57	17	6	3	62	62	6	18	56	15	3	3	62	65.5
Truck driver	2	11	49	29	9	1	54	71	3	11	54	19	9	5	59	67

195

TABLE 1. Distributions of Prestige Ratings, United States, 1947 and 1963 (continued)

Occupation	March, 1947								June, 1963							
	PER CENT						NORC Score	Rank	PER CENT						NORC Score	Rank
	Excellent*	Good	Average	Below Average	Poor	Don't Know†			Excellent‡	Good	Average	Below Average	Poor	Don't Know§		
Fisherman who owns his own boat	3	20	48	21	8	7	58	68	3	19	51	19	8	4	58	68
Clerk in a store	2	14	61	20	3	‖	58	68	1	14	56	22	6	‖	56	70
Milk route man	2	10	52	29	7	1	54	71	3	12	55	23	7	1	56	70
Streetcar motorman	3	16	55	21	5	2	58	68	3	16	46	27	8	2	56	70
Lumberjack	2	11	48	29	10	8	53	73	2	16	46	29	7	3	55	72.5
Restaurant cook	3	13	44	29	11	1	54	71	4	15	44	26	11	‖	55	72.5
Singer in a nightclub	3	13	43	23	18	6	52	74.5	3	16	43	24	14	3	54	74
Filling station attendant	1	9	48	34	8	1	52	74.5	2	11	41	34	11	‖	51	75
Dockworker	2	7	34	37	20	8	47	81.5	2	9	43	33	14	3	50	77.5
Railroad section hand	2	9	35	33	21	3	48	79.5	3	10	39	29	18	2	50	77.5
Night watchman	3	8	33	35	21	1	47	81.5	3	10	39	32	17	1	50	77.5
Coal miner	4	11	33	31	21	2	49	77.5	3	13	34	31	19	2	50	77.5
Restaurant waiter	2	8	37	36	17	1	48	79.5	2	8	42	32	16	‖	49	80.5
Taxi driver	2	8	38	35	17	1	49	77.5	2	8	39	31	18	1	49	80.5
Farm hand	3	12	35	31	19	1	50	76	3	12	31	32	22	‖	48	83
Janitor	1	7	30	37	25	1	44	85.5	1	9	35	35	19	1	48	83
Bartender	1	6	32	32	29	4	44	85.5	1	7	42	28	21	2	48	83
Clothes presser in a laundry	2	6	35	36	21	2	46	83	1	7	31	38	22	1	45	85
Soda fountain clerk	1	5	34	40	20	2	45	84	2	5	30	44	20	‖	44	86
Sharecropper—one who owns no livestock or equipment and does not manage farm	1	6	24	28	41	3	40	87	1	8	26	28	37	2	42	87
Garbage collector	1	4	16	26	53	2	35	88	2	5	21	32	41	1	39	88
Street sweeper	1	3	14	29	53	1	34	89	1	4	17	31	46	1	36	89
Shoe shiner	1	2	13	28	56	2	33	90	‖	3	15	30	51	2	34	90
Average	22	31	30	11	7	4	70	....	22	32	29	11	6	2	71	....

* Bases for the 1947 occupational ratings are 2,920 less "don't know" and not answered for each occupational title.

† Base is 2,920 in all cases.

‡ Bases for the 1963 occupational ratings are 651 less "don't know" and not answered for each occupational title.

§ Base is 651 in all cases.

‖ Less than 0.5 per cent.

Source of 1947 distributions: Albert J. Reiss, Jr., and others, *Occupations and Social Status* (New York: Free Press of Glencoe, 1963), Table ii-9.

ratings were elicited by asking respondents to judge an occupation as having *excellent, good, average, somewhat below average,* or *poor* standing (along with a "don't know" option) in response to the item: "For each job mentioned, please pick out the statement that best gives *your own personal opinion* of the *general standing* that such a job has."

One indicator of prestige position is the proportion of respondents (among those rating an occupation) giving either an "excellent" or a "good" response. Another measure which can be derived from a matrix of ratings by occupation requires weighting the various responses with arbitrary numerical values: We can assign an excellent rating a numerical value of 100, a good rating the value of 80, an average rating the value of 60, a somewhat below average rating the value of 40, and a poor rating the value of 20. Calculating the numerical average of these arbitrarily assigned values over all respondents rating the occupation yields the NORC prestige score. This latter measure has received rather widespread use despite arbitrariness in the numerical weights assigned to the five possible ratings.

The ratings and derived scores for each of the ninety occupations obtained in 1947 and in 1963 are shown in Table 1. We present the findings in such detail because of their intrinsic interest. However, the bulk of the analysis contained in this paper is more concerned with characteristics of the distributions of these ratings than with the positions of particular occupations.

CONGRUITIES IN OCCUPATIONAL PRESTIGE: 1947–63

The major result of the 1963 restudy is dramatically summarized in the product-moment correlation coefficient of .99 between the scores in 1947 and the scores in 1963. The linear regression of the 1963 on the 1947 scores is given by

$$Y = 0.97 X + 2.98,$$

a result which indicates that there are very little regression toward the mean and a slight net upward shift in scores.[4] (Here

and elsewhere in the text boldface symbols are used to represent regression estimates.)

The high over-all correlation in the total set of occupations is matched by high correlations within subsets of occupations. If we group occupations into professional occupations, other non-manual occupations, and manual occupations, as in Table 2, we can see that the regression lines within the three groups are quite similar.[5]

The very slight effect of grouping occupations is shown again in Figure 1, where the three within-group regression lines are plotted over the range of the 1947 NORC scores contained within each group. The three lines nearly coincide over the observed range of the NORC scores and do not appreciably depart from the line $Y = X$ (where the 1963 and the 1947 scores are equal).

The gross similarity between the 1947 and the 1963 NORC scores tends to overshadow some interesting small changes revealed by the data. Thus, in Figure 1 the regression line for blue-collar occupations lies above (and, in fact, parallels) the line $Y = X$. Consequently, one infers that all blue-collar occupations had slightly higher scores in 1963. For professionals and other white-collar workers, however, the picture is more complex, since the within-group regression lines for these two broad groupings cross over the line $Y = X$. Consequently, in the case of professionals, those particular occupations with the highest prestige scores in 1947 (largely scientific and free professional occupations) slightly increased their scores, whereas those professional occupations with relatively low prestige in 1947 (marginal professional occupations such as "singer in a nightclub") receive somewhat lower scores. Among "other white-collar occupations" the situation is reversed. That is, from the within-group regression line we see that the other white-collar occupations with highest prestige in 1947 (largely managerial and political occupations) tended on the average to decline slightly, whereas lower white-collar

---

[4] When the NORC scores are ranked, we find a Spearman rank-order correlation of .98 between the 1947 and 1963 ranks.

[5] The hypothesis that a common regression line fits all groups may be rejected at the 0.07 level of confidence, as indicated by the F-ratio resulting from an analysis of covariance.

occupations slightly increased in prestige.[6]

One other point is brought out sharply by Figure 1 and deserves mention. Since the within-occupational-group regression lines are plotted only for the range of 1947 scores observed within the group, one can easily see the appreciable overlap in scores between professional, other white-collar, and blue-collar occupations. Although these divisions are often employed by social

[6] There is a slight increase in the ability of the within-group regression lines to predict the direction of changes in scores between 1947 and 1963, as compared with the regression line for the total set. Correct predictions about the directions of change can be made by the over-all regression in 60.5 per cent of the cases and by the within-group regression lines in 62.8 per cent of them, an increase in efficiency of 5.8 per cent.

TABLE 2   Regressions Within Subsets of Occupations

Occupation Group	Regression Coefficient	Regression Constant	Correlation
Total, all occupations ($n=90$)	0.97	2.98	.99
Professional, including one title duplicated for validation purposes ($n=33$)	1.05	−3.61	.96
One non-manual occupation ($n=21$)	0.92	5.85	.98
All manual occupations, including one craft occupation duplicated for validation purposes and two military titles ($n=21$)	1.00	2.00	.99
Farm occupations ($n=4$); not computed			

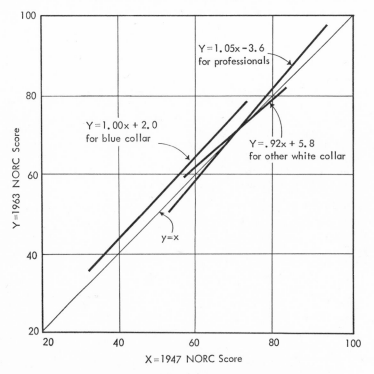

Figure 1. Regressions of 1963 NORC score on 1947 NORC score within occupational groups.

scientists as though they represented fundamental class barriers,[7] Figure 1 makes clear that no such barrier can be detected on the basis of occupational prestige. The cleavage between white-collar and blue-collar—if it exists at all—is based not so much upon matters of societal evaluation as perhaps upon the character of dress and work in the three groups.

All in all the preceding results indicate a striking similarity between the structure of the 1947 and the 1963 NORC scores. While we shall subsequently document a number of systematic shifts in the prestige of specific occupational groups, it is abundantly clear that these shifts are small and did not produce any substantial reordering of the relative prestige of the ninety occupations under consideration here.

There are several good reasons for this observed stability. First, relative differential educational requirements, monetary rewards, and even something as nebulous as the functional importance of occupations are not subject to rapid change in an industrial society.[8] Second, any dramatic shifts in the prestige structure of occupations would upset the dependency which is presumed to hold between the social evaluation of a job, its educational prerequisites, its rewards, and its importance to society. Finally, instabilities would further ambiguities or status inconsistencies if the prestige structure were subject to marked and rapid change. Indeed, the meaning of achievement, career, seniority, and occupational mobility would be fundamentally altered if occupational prestige were subject to large-scale changes. No small amount of intragenerational mobility between prestige classes would, for example, be induced

solely by the changing structure of occupational prestige *even though individuals did not change their occupations over time.*

. . . .

OCCUPATIONAL PRESTIGE SINCE 1925

Since the appearance of George S. Counts' pioneering 1925 study of occupational prestige, a number of readings have been taken on the distribution of occupational prestige. These studies have utilized a variety of different measurement techniques and different types of samples of raters, college students being quite popular. However, there is evidence that the over-all structure of prestige is invariant under quite drastic changes in technique.[9] Furthermore, one of the major findings of the original 1947 NORC survey was that *all* segments of the population share essentially the same view of the prestige hierarchy and rate occupations in much the same way.[10] With these findings in mind, we may utilize selected prestige studies conducted since 1925 to ascertain whether any substantial changes in the prestige structure of occupations have occurred since that date.

A pre-World War II and post-Depression bench mark is provided by the investigations of Mapheus Smith, who provides the mean ratings of one hundred occupations as rated by college and high-school students in the academic years 1938–39, 1939–40, and 1940–41. The rating technique used by Smith differs considerably from that employed in the NORC study. Respondents were originally required to *rank* occupations according to how far an average incumbent would be seated from the guest of honor at a dinner honoring a celebrity and then to *rate* the occupations on a 100-point

---

[7] This is, e.g., the major distinction employed in a recent comparative study of occupational mobility (Seymour Martin Lipset and Reinhard Bendix, *Social Mobility in Industrial Society* [Berkeley: University of California Press, 1959]).

[8] For a discussion of this point see Otis Dudley Duncan, "Properties and Characteristics of the Socio-economic Index," in Reiss *et al., op. cit.,* pp. 152–53. A correlation of .94 was found between an aggregate measure of the income of an occupation in 1940 and a similar indicator in 1950; a correlation of .97 was found between the proportion of high-school graduates in an occupation in 1940 and the same measure in 1950.

[9] One study, e.g., requested respondents to sort seventy of the occupations in the NORC list into groups of *similar* occupations. The respondent was then asked to order the groups of similar occupations he had formed into social levels. Nevertheless, a rank-order correlation of .97 was found between scores derived from this study and scores obtained from the 1947 NORC study (see John D. Campbell, "Subjective Aspects of Occupational Status" [unpublished Ph.D. thesis, Harvard University, 1952], chap ii).

[10] Reiss *et al., op. cit.,* pp. 189–90.

scale of prestige (according to the rater's personal estimation).[11]

A pre-Depression bench mark of occupational prestige is provided by Counts' study, which provides rankings of forty-five occupations according to their "social standing." The data were collected from high-school students, high-school teachers, and college students.[12] Unlike the NORC and Smith studies, rankings rather than ratings were obtained by Counts. Counts provides rankings for six groups of respondents, and a continuous type variable can be derived by taking the average rank of an occupation over the six groups, weighting for the number of respondents in each group.

These four studies, then, provide an opportunity to examine occupational prestige since 1925. A fairly large number of titles are shared in common between each pair of studies, so that the number of titles utilized in any given comparison is larger than the total number of titles that have been rated in many prestige studies.[13]

Product-moment correlations between the prestige ratings of occupations common to each pair of studies are presented in

[11] Mapheus Smith, "An Empirical Scale of Prestige Status of Occupations," *American Sociological Review*, VIII (April, 1943), 185–92.
[12] George S. Counts, "The Social Status of Occupations: A Problem in Vocational Guidance," *School Review*, XXXIII (January, 1925), 16–27.
[13] See, e.g., the national studies cited by Alex Inkeles and Peter H. Rossi, "National Comparisons of Occupational Prestige," *American Journal of Sociology*, LXI (January, 1956), 329–39.

Table 3, together with the number of matching titles. It is evident from the data presented in Table 3 that *there have been no substantial changes in occupational prestige in the United States since 1925*. The lowest correlation observed is .934, and this occurs between the 1963 NORC scores and the mean ranks derived from the 1925 study of Counts. In view of the high correlation between 1947 and 1963 NORC scores, it is not particularly surprising that high correlations are found between any pair of studies from adjacent points in time. That no substantial changes are observed over a span of approximately 40 years is a bit more surprising and is further evidence of constraints toward the stability of prestige hierarchies.

Slight though the variation in correlations in Table 3 may be, it is noteworthy that the observed variation is apparently a function of elapsed time. The longer the elapsed time between any two studies, the smaller tends to be the correlation between them. Although this point is readily apparent on inspection of Table 3, we can provide a convenient quantitative summary by correlating the squares of the correlations between the ith and jth time periods and the elapsed times between the ith and jth time period, yielding a coefficient of $-.85$, a value significantly different from zero at the 0.025 level despite the fact that only six observations are involved.

Small changes in occupational prestige can be obscured by the very high degree of intertemporal stability. Although the techniques used in the studies by NORC,

TABLE 3   Correlations Between Occupational Prestige Ratings at Selected Time Periods, 1925–63*

Study and Time Period	C	S	X	Y
C (Counts' mean ranks, 1925)		.968	.955	.934
S (Smith's mean ratings, *ca.* 1940)	23		.982	.971
X (NORC scores, 1947)	29	38		.990
Y (NORC scores, 1963)	29	38	90	

* Correlations placed above diagonal in Figure 1; no. of matching titles placed below diagonal.
   Sources: George S. Counts, "The Social Status of Occupations: A Problem in Vocational Guidance," *School Review*, XXXIII (January, 1925), 20–21, Table 1; Mapheus Smith, "An Empirical Scale of Prestige Status of Occupations," *American Sociological Review*, VIII (April, 1943). 187–88, Table I; National Opinion Research Center, "Jobs and Occupations: A Popular Evaluation," *Opinion News*, IX (September 1, 1947), 3–13. See text for details.

Smith, and Counts make direct comparisons precarious, regression analysis permits us to follow changes in the prestige of nineteen occupations common to all studies over the span 1925–63. . . .

. . . There is little evidence of any particular pattern to the small changes in prestige observed between the studies and no evidence whatsoever of any substantial changes in the over-all structure of prestige.

The residuals from the three regression equations linking the four studies in a time sequence can be examined in another way. . . . Although the patterns of change indicated by these residuals are highly irregular and do not lend themselves to an over-all interpretation, changes observed for particular occupations invite speculation. For example, the residuals indicate that the prestige of physicians increased slightly between 1925–40 and 1940–47, but declined in the period 1947–63. Increases in the two initial periods might be attributed to concomitant progress in medical technology, while the medical profession's attitude toward Medicare and other public medical plans might account for the recent decline in the prestige of physicians. Some corroboration of this interpretation can be derived from unpublished tabulations from the 1947 study and its replication of ratings by age cohorts. While the reader familiar with previous reports of prestige ratings will recall that subgroup differences are small, shifts in the prestige rating of physicians by age cohorts—small though they are—tend to indicate that older persons, more likely to be affected by health plans, were responsible for the relative decline in the prestige of physicians. This interpretation remains, however, an *ad hoc* one and has little but plausibility to support it.

. . . .

CHANGES IN OCCUPATIONAL PRESTIGE, 1947–63

The major occupation groups of the Census are far from homogeneous, and the allocation of NORC titles to these groups tends to obscure a number of important differences in the patterns of change observed within various occupational situses. . . .

In order to surmount this difficulty and to highlight some of the systematic, if small, prestige changes that were taking place, a classification of NORC titles was expressly designed to illuminate the changes; its chief virtue is the economy of presentation which it facilitates. The groups used in the classification are given in the stub of Table 4 and the specific NORC titles allocated to each group are shown at the bottom of the table. Some titles are dubiously classified and the classification clearly employs several dimensions of occupational structure ranging from class of worker to the kinds of interpersonal contact most frequently encountered on the job.

Several important points emerge on consideration of the classification of NORC titles into occupational situses. . . . The free professions, including occupations like physician and civil engineer, increased in prestige, while cultural or communication-oriented professions, such as "musician in a symphony orchestra" and "radio announcer," declined in standing. Perhaps the most dramatic change is among the scientific occupations, which, with the single exception of "economist," enjoyed positive score differences. A second change . . . was the slight decrease in prestige experienced by political and governmental occupations. One major exception to the rule for other governmental titles was "policeman," which experienced an upswing in prestige. However, such a change is difficult to interpret since there are no other governmental titles of fairly low prestige. Whether it represents regression toward the mean or a genuine increment in respect for law-enforcement officers is difficult to say. The remaining situses in Table 4 are more loosely identified, and we are loath to place any interpretation upon the directions of change observed in them (with the exception of "artisans," largely a craft occupation). They may, however, provide useful guidelines for other researchers seeking to classify the NORC titles into more meaningful categories than those currently available. Taken as a whole, the classification is, however, more closely related to the score differences and the percentage change in score than are the major occupation groups. Correlation ratios of .50

TABLE 4 Selected Measures of Prestige Change, 1947–63, by Occupational Situs*

Occupational Situs	No. of NORC Titles	Average Score Differences	Average Percentage Change
Total, all occupations	90	+0.8	+1.4
Free professionals	13	+1.5	+1.8
Cultural/communication-oriented professions	7	−2.0	−2.4
Scientific professions	8	+2.6	+3.1
Political/government occupations	10	−0.7	−0.6
Big businessmen	4	−0.8	−0.8
Customer-oriented occupations	11	+0.1	+0.4
Artisans	8	+1.6	+2.4
Outdoor-oriented occupations	10	+1.7	+3.2
Dead-end occupations	5	+2.8	+7.2
All farm	4	−0.2	0.0
Other	10	+1.0	+1.5

* NORC titles are classified into occupational situses as follows:

Free professionals: physician, college professor, minister, architect, dentist, lawyer, priest, civil engineer, accountant for a large business, instructor in the public schools, public school teacher, undertaker, welfare worker for a city government.

Cultural/communication-oriented professions: artist who paints pictures that are exhibited in galleries, musician in a symphony orchestra, author of novels, radio announcer, newspaper columnist, reporter on a daily newspaper, singer in a nightclub.

Scientific occupations: scientist, government scientist, chemist, nuclear physicist, psychologist, sociologist, biologist, economist.

Political/government occupations: U.S. Supreme Court justice, state governor, cabinet member in the federal government, diplomat in the U.S. foreign service, mayor of a large city, U.S. representative in congress, county judge, head of a department in a state government, county agricultural agent, policeman.

Big businessmen: banker, member of the board of directors of a large corporation, owner of a factory that employs about 100 people, building contractor.

Customer-oriented occupations that require face to face contact with the public in the ordinary course of a day's work: manager of a small store in a city, railroad conductor, owner-operator of a lunch stand, barber, clerk in a store, streetcar motorman, taxi driver, restaurant waiter, soda fountain clerk, bartender, filling-station attendant.

Artisans: owner-operator of a printing shop, electrician, trained machinist, carpenter, automobile repairman, plumber, garage mechanic, restaurant cook.

Outdoor-oriented occupations in which an ordinary day's work is typically performed either outside or in an outdoors setting: airline pilot, mail carrier, railroad engineer, fisherman who owns his own boat, milk route man, truck driver, lumberjack, coal miner, railroad section hand, dock worker.

Dead-end occupations which have no possibilities of future advancement: night watchman, janitor, garbage collector, street sweeper, shoe shiner.

All farm: farm owner and operator, tenant farmer (one who owns livestock and machinery and manages the farm), farm hand, sharecropper (one who owns no livestock or equipment and does not manage farm).

Other: captain in the regular army, official of an international labor union, bookkeeper, insurance agent, traveling salesman for a wholesale concern, playground director, local official of a labor union, corporal in the regular army, machine operator in a factory, clothes presser in a laundry.

Some of the titles in the "other" category might be reclassified into the remaining categories at some expense in homogeneity; such a reclassification does not affect the results presented in this table.

and .51 were found between the classification and, respectively, the score differences and percentage changes in scores.

A few other changes not previously noted and still obscured by the classification of NORC titles into occupational situses should be mentioned. Among the more important of these are the increases in scores observed for "a local official of a labor union" and "official of an international labor union." That these titles should experience increasing prestige, despite the sensational government investigations into the conduct of labor officials during the past decade, is perhaps indicative of the extent to which unions have been assimilated by, and have themselves adopted a more accommodating attitude toward, the established order.

The two military titles in the NORC list, "captain in the regular army" and "corporal in the regular army," remained much the same in the two time periods. Similarly, the two occupations rated twice under slightly different titles for reliability purposes, "public school teacher" (instructor in the public schools) and "automobile repairman" (garage mechanic), received nearly identical ratings under both stimulus titles in the replication, as had been the case in 1947. The reader will notice in Table 1 that one- and two-point differences in NORC scores can be produced by simply rating the same occupation under slightly different titles. It seems likely, therefore, that changes of one or two points in the NORC score of an occupation could hardly be adequate for establishing a real change in prestige or even the direction of change in prestige (if any). The results for the duplicated titles indicate, therefore, that many of the observed changes in prestige scores discussed above are quite negligible and might possibly have been reversed if a slightly different phrasing of the occupational title had been employed.

One other point is worthy of mention before turning to a summary. Duncan has recently used regression techniques to extend the 1947 NORC scores to all occupations in the detailed classification of the U.S. Bureau of the Census. In the course of presenting his results, Duncan had occasion to discuss the temporal stability of his index and the implication that changes in occupational socioeconomic status might have for the validity of his results. On the basis of comparisons between aggregate education and income of occupations as observed in the 1940 and 1950 censuses, Duncan suggested that "changes—albeit minor ones for the most part—were indeed occurring in the socioeconomic status of occupations during the decade 1940–50," adding that "such evidence as we have suggests a rather high temporal stability of occupational prestige ratings, although the time periods concerned have not been lengthy ones."[14] Surely there is nothing in the present study to alter these conclusions (which, indeed, provide a fair summary of the results of this paper). As the 1960 Census data become available for detailed occupations it will, of course, be possible to revise Duncan's index on the basis of the present replication, but barring any dramatic shifts in the aggregate income and education of occupations over the period 1950–60, there is no reason to believe that such a revision would alter in any appreciable way the socioeconomic scores which Duncan assigned to occupations on the basis of the 1947 NORC study and the 1950 Census data.

CONCLUSIONS

The theme of this paper has been accurately captured by an eminent pathologist who remarked of biochemical phenomena: "Universal instability of constituents seems to be compatible with a stability and even monotony of organized life."[15] Such is the picture one gleans of occupational structures from the present endeavor. Between 1947 and 1963 we are fully aware that many *individual* changes in occupation were under way as men advanced in their career lines, retired, or entered the labor force. Yet, despite the turnover of incumbents, occupational morphology, at least insofar as prestige is concerned, remained remarkably stable. To be sure, systematic patterns of change could be detected, but one would miss the import of this paper if one failed to recognize that

[14] Duncan, *loc. cit.*
[15] René Dubos, *The Dreams of Reason: Science and Utopias* (New York: Columbia University Press, 1961), p. 124.

these changes were minor relative to the over-all stability. The view developed here is that a stable system of occupational prestige provides a necessary foundation to which individuals may anchor their careers.

System maintenance is, however, only part of the story. Small, but nevertheless systematic, changes can be detected between 1947 and 1963. In some cases these changes appear to be attributable to increasing public knowledge of occupations, but it was suggested that any complete understanding of prestige shifts and their causes would require a time series pertaining to the standing of particular occupations. The present study is a step in that direction. Our purposes will be adequately accomplished if others are stimulated to make periodic readings of, as it were, the occupational weather.

STATUS CONSISTENCY AND INCONSISTENCY

Gerhard E. Lenski

When one takes a multidimensional view of distributive systems he soon finds himself confronted with another interesting problem involving men's reactions to the unequal distribution of power and privilege. . . . This is the question of *men's reactions to the phenomenon of status inconsistency.*

The recognition of this problem is largely a modern development because unidimensional views of stratification had such a strong hold on men's minds until recently that the very existence of the problem passed almost unnoticed. Even the few who did note it, such as Cooley and Sorokin, gave it scant attention.

More recently, however, a body of theory and research has developed which suggests that pronounced status inconsistencies of certain kinds tend to be a source of stress

and give rise to distinctive reactions which are not predictable simply from a knowledge of the rank of the individual in each of the respective status systems.[1] This theory is based on the postulate that individuals strive to maximize their satisfactions, even, if necessary, at the expense of others. This means that an individual with inconsistent statuses or ranks has a natural tendency to think of himself in terms of that status or rank which is highest, and to expect others to do the same. Meanwhile others, who come in contact with him have a vested interest in doing just the opposite, that is, in treating him in terms of his lowest status or rank.

One can see how this works, and the consequences of it, by imagining the interaction of a Negro doctor and a white laborer in a situation where neither the racial nor occupational status system alone is relevant. The former, motivated by self-interest, will strive to establish the relation on the basis of occupation (or perhaps education or wealth), while the latter, similarly motivated, will strive to establish the relationship on the basis of race. Since each regards his own point of view as right and proper, and since neither is likely to view the problem in a detached, analytical fashion, one, or both, are likely to be frustrated,

[1] Unfortunately, there is still no good summary of the relevant literature on this subject and no definitive treatment. Among others, the following have given special attention to the stress hypothesis: George Homans, "Status Among Clerical Workers," *Human Organization*, 12 (1953), pp. 5–10; Gerhard Lenski, "Status Crystallization: A Non-vertical Dimension of Social Status," and "Social Participation and Status Crystallization," *American Sociological Review*, 19 and 21 (1954 and 1956), pp. 405–413 and 458–464; Irving Goffman, "Status Consistency and Preference for Change in Power Distribution," *ibid.*, 22 (1957), pp. 275–281; A. Zaleznik *et al., The Motivation, Productivity, and Satisfaction of Workers* (Cambridge, Mass.: Harvard University Press, 1958); Elton Jackson, "Status Consistency and Symptoms of Stress," *American Sociological Review*, 27 (1962), pp. 469–480. Methodological problems have been a source of difficulty in this area, but two recent papers point the way to their resolution. These are Lenski, "Comment," *Public Opinion Quarterly*, 28 (1964), pp. 326–330, and Elton Jackson and Peter Burke, "Status and Symptoms of Stress: Additive and Interaction Effects," *American Sociological Review*, 30 (1965), pp. 556–564.

and probably angered, by the experience.

The practice of "one-upmanship," as this pattern of action has sometimes been called, is so common in everyday life that most who indulge in it hardly give it any thought. The net effect, however, is to create considerable stress for many persons of inconsistent status. As a result, such persons are likely to find social interaction outside the bounds of the primary group (where others tend to be like themselves) somewhat less rewarding than does the average person. . . .

CLASS AND STATUS CONSISTENCY

Considering the diversity of resources which affect the distribution of rewards in modern industrial societies, the question inevitably arises as to how they are inter-related. This, in turn, gives rise to questions of how discrepancies in an individual's statuses affect his actions, and how his actions affect the society of which he is a part. . . .

With respect to the first problem—the degree of relationship between dimensions—census data, as well as data from other sources, make it clear that the rank of individuals and families in one dimension is never a simple function of rank in another. Correlations between property holdings, political status, occupational status, educational status, status-group rank, age status, and sex status are never perfect, and usually are far from it.

One of the closest relationships is that between education and occupation, but studies in the United States have produced correlation coefficients no higher than .77, and in some instances as low as .30.[2] At the other extreme there are certain relationships where the correlation is almost .00. This is clearly the case in the relationship

between age and sex, and also with respect to relations between the following pairs: sex status and property holdings; age and occupational status; and finally, both age and sex on the one hand and status-group rank and educational status on the other. Other relationships tend to fall in the middle range.

In a few rare instances, the correlations between resources are actually negative. This is true with respect to age and sex because women now outlive men. More important, it is true of age and educational status where the younger generation has more years of schooling than the older generation because of rising educational standards.

The low correlations between the various types of resources indicates that there are substantial numbers of persons who find themselves confronted with inconsistent statuses of every type. . . . On grounds of deductive logic a good case can be made for the hypothesis that discrepancies between major status dimensions can be a source of stress, first of all for the individuals affected and, through them, for the society of which they are a part. As yet there is only a limited amount of systematic research on this subject, but, such as it is, it tends to support the hypothesis. For example, data gathered in two sample surveys of Greater Detroit in the early 1950s showed that persons with discrepant statuses were more likely to support the Democratic Party and take liberal positions on issues than persons of consistent status.[3] This was especially true in cases where racial-ethnic status was inconsistent with occupational status, and was most pronounced when the inconsistencies were substantial. To a lesser degree, the same pattern prevailed when there were inconsistencies between occupational and educational statuses. In a study based on a

[2] The highest coefficient comes from Warner's study of "Jonesville." See W. I. Warner, *et al., Social Class in America* (Chicago: Science Research, 1949), table 13, p. 172. Godfrey Hochbaum *et al.* report a correlation of .65 from Minneapolis, in "Socioeconomic Variables in a Large City," *American Journal of Sociology,* 61 (1955) p. 34. Robert Angell reports a figure of .39 for Detroit and .30 from Samuel Stouffer's national survey on communism and civil liberties, in "Preferences for Moral Norms in Three Problem Areas," *ibid.,* 67 (1962), pp. 651–652.

[3] For an earlier examination of one of these samples, using a not completely satisfactory methodology, see Gerhard Lenski, "Status Crystallization: A Non-vertical Dimension of Social Status," *American Sociological Review,* 19 (1954). For data on both samples using a better methodology, see Gerhard Lenski, "Comment," *Public Opinion Quarterly,* 28 (1964), especially tables 2 and 3. See also Werner S. Landecker, "Class Crystallization and Class Consciouness," *American Sociological Review,* 28 (1963), pp. 219–229, which analyzes the first of these samples from a different perspective but obtains essentially similar results.

national sample, similar results were obtained. Persons with discrepant statuses (involving occupation, education, and income) were more favorably disposed to changes in the distribution of power within American society than those with consistent statuses.[4]

The number of persons affected in this way by status discrepancies does not appear to be large, at least compared with the total population. More important than numbers, however, may be the fact that discrepant status brings into the ranks of the discontented, persons with many badly needed skills and other resources. In other words, such persons are singularly well equipped to provide the leadership and other resources which uneducated members of the working and nonpropertied classes are unable to provide for themselves. As noted previously, status discrepancy and the reactions it produces may well be a major source of the revolutionary leadership which Marx and Engels predicted (without explaining) would come from the ranks of the more privileged classes.

On the basis of limited studies like those cited above, one would hesitate to say that this hypothesis is much more than interesting speculation. However, there is also a considerable body of unsystematic evidence to support it. The role of ethnic and racial minorities in radical movements has long been noted, and it has also been observed that even the successful members of these minorities are attracted to such movements; in fact, they often provide much of the leadership.[5]

[4] Irwin Goffman, "Status Consistency and Preference for Change in Power Distribution," *American Sociological Review,* 22 (1957), pp. 275–281.

[5] See, for example, Robert Michels on the role of the Jews in the Socialist movement in Europe, *Political Parties: A Sociological Study of Oligarchical Tendencies in Modern Democracy,* translated by Eden and Cedar Paul (New York: Dover, 1959, first published 1915), pp. 258–262, or S. M. Lipset on the role of ethnic minorities in Canada's Socialist Party, in *Agrarian Socialism* (Berkeley, Calif.: University of California Press, 1950), p. 191. See also Stanislaw Ossowski, *Class Structure in the Social Consciousness,* translated by Sheila Patterson (New York: Free Press, 1963), p. 53, on the role of impoverished members of the Polish nobility in the early revolutionary movements in that country.

Obviously not all forms of status discrepancy generate political discontent. For example, one finds little of it among wealthy women or young members of the managerial class. One of the tasks for both theory and research in coming years is to specify the conditions under which this type of reaction occurs, and those under which some alternative reaction, or none at all, is more likely.

Subjective Dimension of Inequality

NON-EGALITARIAN CLASSLESSNESS— SIMILARITIES IN INTERPRETING MUTUALLY OPPOSED SYSTEMS

Stanislaw Ossowski

We believe that further research and writing on social stratification must be prepared for inequality to resurge in many particular guises.

N. N. FOOTE

This Chapter was written in 1953 and 1954. The comparison which it draws between the interpretation of the structure of United States society that is popular in certain American circles and the official interpretation of the structure of the Soviet

From *Class Structure in the Social Consciousness,* by Stanislaw Ossowski, 1963. Reprinted by permission of the Macmillan Company and also of Routledge & Kegan Paul Ltd.

Union is in general based on material available in 1953 at the latest. Thus it deals with the period in which the social structure of the Soviet Union was relatively stable and provided the model followed by the people's republics, particularly after 1948.

Our discussions do not therefore cover the changes that have occurred in the Soviet Union in recent years. . . . Nor do they cover the recent changes which have occurred in the United States. . . .

The subject-matter of this chapter has in my opinion a wider significance in that it provides an illustration of the way of conceiving the social structure which was outlined in the foregoing chapter; it also provides a particularly striking example of the application of a similar interpretation of social relationships in mutually opposed systems.

THE PROBLEM OF CLASS CONSCIOUSNESS IN THE UNITED STATES

It is generally accepted, not without some grounds, that in the consciousness of the mass of the population the "class" aspect of one's own society plays a much smaller role in the United States than it does in the capitalist countries of Europe. Such factors as the absence of estate-traditions,[1] the long-drawn-out territorial expansion to the West, the turbulent development of the country's industry, the dizzy careers made by individuals, the opportunities for upward social mobility (so much greater than in Europe), the heterogeneous ethnic composition of the working class, and finally the Negro question—these are the circumstances which have repeatedly been cited as reasons for the differing social attitudes of the American and the European worker, and for the feeble development of the Communist and Socialist movement in the country where private capital is at its most powerful, industrial production greatest and the income-range widest.

This state of affairs is also reflected in American sociology. Except for a small number of sociologists whose attitudes are somewhat "un-American", American

sociology has been isolated from Marxian problems and from Marxian methods of social analysis to a far greater degree than sociology in Western Europe. Just before the Second World War Robert Lynd accused American sociologists of avoiding the term "class" and the problems connected with it.[2] After the war, this charge was repeated by R. Centers.[3] The Swedish investigator of American social relationships, Gunnar Myrdal, though he drew attention elsewhere and in a different context to the recent interest shown in the problem of social class by the group of investigators led by Professor Lloyd Warner, also wrote in 1944: ". . . American sociology (which generally must be given the highest ranking in the world) is weak and undeveloped in regard to the problems of social stratification."[4]

Since these comments were made, studies of the class structure of American society have attained a leading place in the set of problems with which American sociology is concerned. . . . Today there is a growing body of field-research devoted to the class structure of the United States, and particularly of research which has as its common assumption recognition of the psychological criterion of social class, and has as its subject-matter people's opinions about the class-system in which they participate. This sort of approach to social structure is supported by the conviction that in social relationships the only things that matter are those which are immediately predominant in the consciousness of the participants.

As we already know, the American class structure is rather rarely interpreted otherwise than in terms of a scheme of gradation, whether we consider the statements of people representing various American milieux or the findings of field-researchers. Usually a synthetic gradation is involved: the synthesis is achieved in the social consciousness, whereas the theoretician

---

[1] In the legal sense of this term, passing over the *quasi*-estate culture of the Southern States.

[2] *Knowledge for What?* 1939: third edition, Princeton University Press, 1947, p. 227.

[3] "Perhaps no area of social and psychological research has been so neglected by American scientists as that of class conflict and class consciousness." *The Psychology of Social Class*, Princeton University Press, 1949, p. 8.

[4] *An American Dilemma*, New York, 1944, p. 670.

endeavours at best to define the role of the different elements in the synthesis.

THE STRATIFICATION OF AMERICAN SOCIETY IN AMERICAN SOCIOLOGY

It is first and foremost within this framework—the scheme of gradation and the psychological criteria of class membership—that discussions of the actual stratification of American society or of its trends of development are carried out amongst American sociologists or political commentators. In discussions of the actual situation, differences of opinion are usually differences in assessing the degree to which certain features of the social structure should be regarded as characteristic of American society. In discussions concerned with trends of development, opposing standpoints clash with each other: destratification or restratification? polarization or the extension of the middle class? Does the class system become more rigid or do rigid class barriers gradually disappear?[5] Nevertheless these opposing standpoints are for the most part not formulated too sharply. In their article *Patterns of American Stratification as Reflected in Selected Social Science Literature*,[6] Paul Hatt and Virginia Ktsanes surveyed the different modes of conceiving the structure of American society found in the work of twenty American social scientists over a quarter-century (1924–1949). They were concerned firstly with the degree of the stratification and distances between classes; secondly with the amount of individual mobility; and thirdly with the emphasis on economic factors in class stratification.

Another subject of discussion in the United States is the importance of the middle class in the American social structure. Until recently it was generally held that the vast majority of people in the United States regard themselves as members of the middle class. This conviction was supported by the Gallup findings of 1939, by the *Fortune* survey and by Can-

tril's work in 1943.[7] These showed that between 79 and 88 per cent of the population of the areas included in the surveys regarded themselves as belonging to the middle class. Because a certain percentage of respondents did not answer the questions, the percentage of middle class members amongst those who had a definite opinion about their class affiliation was still higher. For instance, 88 per cent of the respondents in the Gallup Institute Poll described themselves as members of the middle class, while only 6 per cent admitted to membership of the upper or lower classes.

Later studies, including the work of Centers, showed that the percentage of persons admitting middle class membership varies according to the manner in which the questions are formulated. For instance, the figure decreases considerably if, instead of giving the respondent a choice between upper, middle and lower classes an open-ended question is asked. The figure decreases still more if the term "working class" is included amongst the possible answers. In the latter case, Centers got a response of 43 per cent for "middle class" and 51 per cent for "working class." In any event, even when these differences are taken into account, the percentage of respondents admitting middle class affiliation clashes sharply with the Marxian prediction of polarization in capitalist societies.

The differing opinions expressed by American writers about the social structure of the United States are concerned not only with the stratification as defined by people's attitudes but also about the objective economic relationships which condition this subjective stratification.[8] Despite all the reservations which I made in Chapter III with regard to the simplification of the American picture of social structure, one should not forget the lively American

---

[5] N. N. Foote, "Destratification and Restratification". *A.J.S.* Jan. 1953; A. B. Hollingshead: *Trends in Social Stratification A.S.R.* Dec. 1952; G. Sjoberg: *Are Social Classes in America Becoming More Rigid? A.S.R.* Dec. 1951.
[6] *A.S.R.* Dec. 1952.

[7] G. Gallup and S. F. Rae, *The Pulse of Democracy*, New York, 1940; "The People of the United States—a Self Portrait", *Fortune*, 1940; H. Cantril, "Identification with Social and Economic Class", *Journ. Abnorm. and Social Psychology*, 1943, cited from Centers, *The Psychology of Social Class*, Princeton University Press, 1949, pp. 30–31 and 237–40.
[8] Cf. J. J. Spenger, "Changes in Income Distribution and Social Stratification", *A.J.S.*, Nov. 1958.

interest in a simple economic gradation; that is to say, the classification of people according to their income-level and the distinction of various income-groups is a common phenomenon, while terms such as "five thousand dollar men" or "twenty-five thousand dollar men" have become everyday currency.

THE CONCEPTION OF THE CLASSLESS SOCIETY IN THE UNITED STATES

In these American discussions of the social structure of the United States we may distinguish an extreme point of view. This is the "democratic optimism" that questions the whole reality of social classes in American society, thereby shifting the subject of discussion. Here we reach the model of social structure which in the last chapter I called the concept of a classless and inegalitarian society.

In an article published in 1952, G. H. Lenski contrasted two viewpoints held by different American sociologists. He noted that the American social classes on the one hand are regarded as statistical categories which can have only a heuristic significance,[9] on the other as social groups based on a psychological bond.[10] Supporters of the first approach claim that in America the social-status scale from top to bottom closely approximates to a continuum[11] and that the concept of class is alien to American society.

The view that the concept of class is alien to American society is based on the conviction that the social attitudes of the average American are formed by the traditional ideology—the so-called American Creed. Is it not true that there are no second or third class compartments in American trains in order that railway installations should not conflict with the principle that there are no classes within

the bosom of the great American nation, as William Archer ironically observed at the beginning of this century. For an additional payment one can of course travel in a pullman compartment or a drawing-room, but these are not compartments of a different class. In America, Daumier could not have conceived his lithographs in which the classes on the railway-coaches became symbols of the social structure.

As Ralph Bunche once wrote,

Every man in the street, white, black, red or yellow, knows that this is the land of the free, the "land of opportunity", the "cradle of liberty", the "home of democracy", that the American flag symbolises the "equality of all men"...[12]

One argument adduced to support the view that there are no distinct social classes in America is the way in which those sociologists who do not regard classes as a "heuristic concept" but consider the social-class system as a real phenomenon in the social consciousness fail to agree as to the number of classes which they differentiate. S. A. Hetzler wrote,

The Usemovs and Tangent found three distinct social classes, Centers found four, Hollingshead found five and Warner found six. In view of these discrepancies it is quite important that we ascertain whether contemporary society consists of clearly delineated classes or of a composite of statuses and roles arranged loosely on a continuum.[13]

In the town of Danielson in Connecticut, where Lenski conducted his field-research he found that different people divided the population of Danielson into three, four, five, six and even seven social classes.[14] Lasswell, reporting his findings with regard to the social stratification in a small town in Southern California, stated that the number of social strata mentioned by respondents varied from one (i.e. from a negation of class differentiation) to seven, no one category obtaining more than 17 percent of the total response. He also pointed to the lack of uniform criteria of class affiliation.

[9] "American Social Class: Statistical Strata or Social Group", *A.J.S.* Sept. 1952. Elsewhere we find the same opposition expressed in different terms: namely, that of the "substantive" and "classificatory nature of class". P. Hatt, "Stratification in the Mass Society", *A.S.R.* April 1950.
[10] Cf. O. Cox: *Caste, Class and Race*, New York, 1948.
[11] G. C. Homans, *English Villagers of the XIIIth Century*, Harvard University Press, 1941.

[12] Myrdal, *op. cit.*, p. 4.
[13] "An Investigation of the Distinctiveness of Social Class", *A.S.R.* Oct., 1953, p. 494.
[14] G. Lenski, "Status Crystallization", *A.S.R.*, 1954, p. 143.

These were some of the findings on which he based his conclusion that social strata in Citrus City are not rigorously distinguished by the general population.[15]

The view that there are no classes in American society is frequently encountered in investigations carried out in various American milieux, even when the questionnaire mentions class divisions. "I don't believe in classes" is a statement expressed by quite a number of American citizens when asked about their class affiliation or inter-class relationships.

As one might have anticipated, this conviction is class-determined, statistically speaking. During an investigation carried out in four districts of Minneapolis, the question was put: "What social classes do you think there are in Minneapolis and which one of these classes are you in?" In the wealthiest district 19 per cent of respondents replied that there were no social classes at all, whereas only 6 per cent gave the same response in the poorest district.[16] In this type of enquiry it is, of course, difficult to determine how far one is dealing with the repetition of ideological formulae and at what point one is confronted with genuine convictions.

What is in the minds of those who talk of the "American belief in classlessness"[17] or the American "tradition that class divisions are un-American"?[18] What is in the minds of those American citizens who say that they "do not believe in classes"?

From the commentaries on such statements we may deduce that those Americans who believe or would like to believe that they live in a classless society have in mind the sort of "classlessness" which we have been considering. This involves an image of society which meets the following conditions:

1. The social and economic status of individuals is not determined by descent; the road to the highest positions is open to all, even though they may not have an equal start.[19]
2. The social-status scale is not broken by any distinct barriers which could transform the continuum-like status order into a gradation of different strata.
3. In accordance with the last condition no definite privileges are attached to the various segments of that scale, nor do any permanent conflicts of interest exist between higher and lower levels of social status.[20]
4. There is no separation or restriction in social contacts between strata.

Civic equality, which is a tenet of the American Creed, is supposed to be based precisely on such classlessness, and not on a levelling-out of social status or income. Each citizen has equal rights and in a certain sense equal opportunities to aspire to lower or higher positions. It is assumed that inequalities of economic or social status are determined not by class affiliation but by personal qualifications, but nobody denies the existence of these inequalities. The great range of achievements is in accordance with the demands of free competition.

Those who rejected this optimistic image of American society did not need to appeal to a Marxian line of argument. . . . At the beginning of this century, William Archer wrote that the lack of class divisions in American trains was just as much a fiction as the classlessness of American society. Forty years later McGuire wrote: "Social class is a reality of American social stratification if the primary data of contemporary

---

[15] T. E. Lasswell: "A Study of Social Stratification", *A.S.R.* June 1954, p. 313. A similar conclusion is suggested in a rather less obvious manner by some material on the attitudes of textile workers in Patterson, New Jersey (cf. J. G. Manis and B. N. Meltzer: "Attitudes of Textile Workers to Class Structure", *A.J.S.* June 1954).

[16] N. Gross: "Social Class Identification in the Urban Community", *A.S.R.*, August 1953, p. 402.

[17] G. Sjoberg, *op. cit.*, (see p. 115, n. 2).

[18] Centers, *op. cit.*, p. 8.

[19] Parsons maintains that an equal start is impossible in a society in which an "occupationally-differentiated industrial] system and a significantly solidary kinship system" are combined. *The Social System*, Free Press, Glencoe, p. 161.

[20] "The bourgeoisie are not obviously set apart from the proletariat", wrote M. Rosenberg in a passage contrasting American and European relationships, "by virtue of owning a car. The differentiation is continuous rather than polar. One man owns a newer or better car than another but this will not induce a feeling of class consciousness in his slightly less fortunate fellow." "Perceptual Obstacles to Class Consciousness", *Social Forces*, Oct. 1953.

community studies are to have any meaning".[21] A little earlier Robert Lynd[22] had compared American society to an arena in which elephant and chickens have an equal chance to dance.

The characteristics of the various classes seen as distinct component elements of American society are to be found in the work of various field-researchers who did not confine themselves to questionnaires but followed Lynd's methods.[23] The characteristics of the poor white class in the Southern States as outlined by L. W. Doob remind one of the comparison between social classes and nations made by Disraeli and Engels.[24] Centers spoke of class solidarity and class interests. And in his reference to the great coal strike and President Truman's address to the American people on 24 May, 1946, he speculated whether the class struggle in the United States "had reached a stage where one could not help but wonder if men were not finding loyalty to a class a bigger and nobler thing than loyalty to a Government".[25]

THE CONTRASTING BACKGROUND

Independently of the degree to which the conception of a classless society actually finds support in the social consciousness and of the sectors of American society in which this occurs, we should remember that in America this image of the social structure is set against the background of the caste-like relationships between white and black, and that this system of caste relationships is marked by characteristics which are a radical negation of all four conditions mentioned earlier. For caste membership and caste-bound social status are decided exclusively by descent; caste-membership is determined for life before a child is born, and the barrier dividing the two classes cannot in principle be crossed. Between

white and coloured there is no intermediate status. In the United States, unlike South America, a light-coloured mulatto remains a Negro in his relations with the white caste. There is caste endogamy and social separation, and the Deep South has strictly enforced institutional separation between the castes. Finally, there are caste privileges, caste etiquette and caste discrimination, masked by the "Jim Crow" formula of "separate but equal" but fooling nobody.

This separation of the castes makes it easy to overlook the existence amongst the white population of exclusive clubs which are open only to individuals from the upper social brackets, or of such institutions as the *New York Social Register*. This is an annually-published list of the names of a few hundred distinguished individuals. . . .[26] Against a background in which caste membership is absolutely determined from birth, the influence of the parents' property and income-level on the class status of their children becomes less apparent, and the frequency with which class status is inherited less striking.

There is one further circumstance which helps Americans to feel this democratic optimism about the social structure of their own country. This is the old tradition of rejecting the class-divisions of Europe, a tradition which goes back as far as the eighteenth century. Americans see these class-divisions chiefly in terms of the relics of feudalism—estate distinctions, aristocratic exclusiveness, the privileges attached to descent from a good family.[27] America banned aristocratic titles in the dawn of its independence, and the good American citizen has been accustomed to compare his country with class-divided Europe, with its dukes, lords, counts and its primitive peasantry, whose representatives he could see in the East and South European immigrant districts of America's cities. And when the son or grandson of such an uneducated immigrant achieved high office in the United States, as a mayor, governor or the owner of a large business, this provided a forceful argument in favour of

---

[21] McGuire, "Social Stratification and Mobility Patterns", *A.S.R.*, April 1950.

[22] Lynd, *Knowledge for What?* 1939; 3rd ed., Princeton Univ. Press, 1947, p. 111.

[23] R. S. Lynd and H. M. Lynd: *Middletown*, New York, 1929; *Middletown in Transition,* New York, 1937.

[24] "Poor Whites: a Frustrated Class", Appendix to J. Dollard, *Caste and Class in a Southern Town,* ed. 1949, pp. 445–484.

[25] Centers: *op. cit.*, p. 7.

[26] G. Gorer, *The American People,* New York, 1948, p. 217.

[27] Cf. Myrdal, *op. cit.*, p. 670 and p. 1375.

the fundamental tenets of the American Creed.[28]

This dual background—that of the Negro caste and that of the European "old countries"—has made it easier for good Americans to see the system of social relationships within white society in the United States as a harmonious, dynamic and classless structure: harmonious in respect of the absence of class antagonism and polarising tendencies and also in respect of the number and prestige of the middle strata; dynamic in respect of the degree of mobility of individuals on the rungs of the social ladder.

In all these respects this image of social structure is opposed to the Marxian vision of the capitalist society, the vision of class antagonisms. Nor should we be misled by the use of the term "dynamic". The image of American society is dynamic in quite a different sense than is the Marxian theory of classes.

THE PROBLEM OF CLASSLESSNESS IN SOVIET SOCIETY

Looking at the social structure of the United States with eyes accustomed to observe reality through the prism of the class struggle, an East European Marxist is bound to regard American modes of conceiving American social stratification, even those that lay stress on a class hierarchy and on relatively rigid class boundaries, as a sort of mystification aimed at masking the essential class conflicts. The American conception of a classless society must appear absurd to him, for it combines classlessness with capitalism.

Nevertheless, there is one reason why this American conception should not strike a Marxist as absurd. For this extreme, optimistic and democratic view of society, combining classlessness with the maintenance of great differences in the share in the national income, which is contained in a

certain version of the American Creed, is by no means alien to the Soviet Union and the People's Democracies in relation to their own societies.

How did the Soviet society of the Stalinist period, described as being "the second stage of the development of the Soviet state, and which came after the victory of socialism and the transformation of the class structure",[29] appear from the viewpoint of the Communist Creed?

From the phrase just quoted about the transformation of the class structure, it would follow that the Soviet society of this period was not classless. And indeed, according to the Stalinist conception, classes do still exist in the Soviet Union, but they are "non-antagonistic classes", none of them being in a position to appropriate the labour of another class.[30] These classes are the workers and the *kolchoz* peasants—that is to say, the classes whose differentiation is based on the distinction between two forms of socialist property, state property and co-operative property. This differentiation remains in a certain correlation with the differentiation between town and country. The great Soviet Encyclopaedia also links the differentiation with the concept of the two sectors of socialist production. The intelligentsia is mentioned as a third component of Soviet society, but in accordance with Stalin's arguments it is not accorded the name of "class", but only of "stratum".[31]

Seen from the viewpoint of Marx and Lenin, "non-antagonistic classes" constitute a *contradictio in adiecto*. The authors of *Historical Materialism* appear to realize this; after citing Lenin's definition of class they write: "In this sense one can no longer call our society a class-society".

But the Stalinist conception of "non-antagonistic classes" breaks away from the concept of class found in Marx and Lenin in favour of a concept that is closer to Adam Smith's idea of classes (different

---

[28] "How always have men's hearts beat", wrote Woodrow Wilson in 1913, "as they saw the coast of America rise to their view. How it has always seemed to them that the dweller there would at last be rid of kings, of privileged classes, and of all those bonds which had kept men depressed and helpless". *The New Freedom*, New York, 1914.

[29] *Istoricheski materializm* (*Historical Materialism*), ed. Professor F. B. Konstantinov, Moscow, 1951, pp. 363–402.
[30] V. I. Lenin, "A Great Beginning" (1919), from *The Essentials of Lenin*, London, Lawrence & Wishart, 1947, Vol. II, p. 492.
[31] Cf. for instance, Konstantinov, *op. cit.*, p. 402

types of property, different sources of income). In relation to the basic concept of social class in Marxist doctrine the qualification "non-antagonistic" has a modifying and not a specifying function; but in relation to Adam Smith's concept of class it has a specifying function, because Smith acknowledged the existence of class antagonisms, although he did not deduce them from his definition of class.

The conception of "non-antagonistic classes" arose out of certain requirements of Soviet internal policy. The official recognition of the class of workers and the *kolchoz* peasantry as the only classes still existing in the Soviet Union, distinguished according to objective economic criteria, provided in advance a negative answer to the question whether privileged and underprivileged classes existed in the new social structure. The traditional meaning of the term "classless society" . . . was probably also involved. This associated the "classless society" with the Communist system, which is to be attained only in the future. But a spokesman for the ruling ideology, while acknowledging that classes still exist in Soviet society, will not call it a "class society" because of the term's old associations: for Soviet society is opposed to such class societies. Therefore it is stated that the fundamental class differences (*korennye klassovye razlicyiha*) have already been altogether overcome in the Soviet Union in consequence of the victory of Socialism.[32]

Quite apart from such terminological complications, the official Soviet image of contemporary Soviet society—an image which is part of the ideological training programme for the whole population—is of a society without class stratification, not only from the Marxist and Leninist viewpoints, but also from the viewpoint derived from the American criteria of the concept of class. In this society there is no exploitation of man by his fellow man, nor are there upper classes and lower classes in the sense in which we encountered them in the American scheme of gradation. The

superiority of the working class in relation to the peasantry is, according to Soviet ideology, a superiority of merit and not of privileges. This class occupies the leading place on the common road to Communism and not a higher level in the social structure. The often repeated expression concerning the "moral and political unity of the Soviet nation" is also a certain way of asserting the classless character of Soviet society, particularly when we consider the Marxist traditions concerned with the ideological superstructure.

This society without class privileges and class antagonisms is not of course an egalitarian society. No Soviet Marxist will deny that the share of individual Soviet citizens in the national income differs considerably. The tendency to *uravnilovka* (equalization or levelling of wages) which characterised the early phase of Soviet society was condemned as incompatible with the principles of Socialism. In the Polish People's Republic, too, President Bierut more than once spoke publicly of progress "in the direction of putting an end to the so-called *uravnilovka*" and of the need for a further campaign against *uravnilovka,* since private ownership of the means of production had been abolished.

In the Soviet Union economic privileges and discriminations have, in accordance with Soviet doctrine, nothing in common with class divisions. Even large differences of income are not associated with any sort of relationships such as could transform the extensive social-status scale into a class hierarchy. Instead, the individual's place in the scale is determined by his merits.

The idea that a new privileged class may be created as a result of the increasing range of income-differentials is not considered at all. In this respect the Soviet theory of the social structure in the land of socialism differs fundamentally from American conceptions. In judging whether a society is a "class society" or not, an American is thinking of a gradation of classes based above all, though not exclusively, on income-differences. In the Soviet Union and the People's Democracies this scheme of class structure is not applied at all. Soviet ideology employs only two conceptions of class: the Marxian in relation to other

---

[32] T. Gubariew, *O priodolenii klassovykh razlichii v SSSR* ("About the overcoming of class differences in the U.S.S.R."), *Bolshevik,* 1951, No. 5, p. 19.

countries, and Adam Smith's conception—in a certain sense—in relation to its own society. The transition from the present socialist system to the classless society is to be accomplished not by a levelling-off of wages but by the abolition of the fundamental differences between towns and countryside and by the merging of the two sectors of the economy—state and *kolchoz*—into one production sector.[33] This conception is linked with the thesis that the present class system in the socialist state is horizontally and not vertically structured.

SIMILARITIES AND DISSIMILARITIES

In contrast to the United States, where the American Creed and the conception of "classlessness" are the subject of analysis and dispute, no variants of the conception of Soviet society were as a rule to be found in Soviet publications before 1954. In comparison with the American optimistic view of American society, the Soviet conception of a harmonious and dynamic society, without antagonistic classes and without *uravnilovka,* was formulated in a more definite and radical manner. The similarities are however sufficiently apparent, despite the basic difference over the requirements for human cooperation: there the cult of private enterprise is stressed, here the subordination of individual activity to social planning on the widest scale.[34]

The Socialist principle "to each according to his merits" is in harmony with the tenets of the American Creed, which holds that each man is the master of his fate, and that a man's status is fixed by an order of merit.[35] The Socialist principle allows of the conclusion that there are unlimited opportunities for social advancement and social demotion; this is similar to the American concept of "vertical social mobility". The arguments directed against *uravnilovka* coincide with the arguments put forward on the other side of the Atlantic by those who justify the necessity for economic inequalities in a democratic society. "The maximisation of effort in an achievement-oriented society calls for considerable inequality"—wrote Spenger in 1953.[36] This sentence could equally well have been uttered by a statesman in the Soviet Union or the Peoples' Democracies. In the United States this "optimistic" conception of the system of relationships within the white population has as its background the old countries of Europe and the Negro caste situation within the country. In the Soviet case, the background consists of the relationships that prevailed in pre-revolutionary Russia, and of the capitalist world that today encircles the socialist countries. Stalin wrote,

The feature that distinguishes Soviet society today from any capitalist society is that it no longer contains antagonistic, hostile classes; that the exploiting classes have been eliminated, while the workers, peasants and intellectuals, who make up Soviet society, live and work in friendly collaboration.[37]

Communist doctrine assumes that a necessary condition of the development towards a harmonious society—a society in which everyone has an equal start, and there are no antagonistic classes—is the abolition of the private ownership of the means of production. But the American Creed does not accept this assumption at all. On the contrary, it regards the system guaranteed by the American Constitution as the one that offers the most favourable conditions for achieving just this kind of society. These incompatible assumptions enable similar conceptions of social structure to be applied in countries with such widely varying economic systems.

In comparing the official conception of Soviet society with the most optimistic and

---

[33] See the *Great Soviet Encyclopaedia,* under the heading *Classes.*

[34] For the changes which have been taking place recently in this connexion in American society see W. Friedmann, "Changes in Property Relations," *Transactions of the Third Sociological Congress in Amsterdam,* vol. II, 1956.

[35] "... An order of merit in terms of which men differ with respect to their rights and duties". J. J. Spenger, "Changes in Income Distribution and Social Stratification", *A.J.S.,* November, 1953.

[36] *Ibid.,* p. 258.

[37] J. Stalin, "Report on the Work of the Central Committee to the Eighteenth Congress of the C.P.S.U. (B.)", delivered March 10, 1939, published in J. Stalin, *Problems of Leninism,* Moscow, Foreign Languages Publishing House, 1947, p. 621.

extreme American viewpoints, we should not forget that this similarity refers only to images of the present situation. For both on one side and on the other the trends of development are presented in quite a different manner. The American Creed does not envisage a more perfect system, although it foresees progress in some respects within the present system. The Communist Creed, on the contrary, holds that the socialist society of today is only a stage on the road to a communist society.

This transition to a communist society should, however, according to the prospects outlined by Stalin himself be achieved not by means of upheavals—as is to be expected of all transitions from one "formation" to another—but via "the continuous expansion and perfecting of socialist production on the basis of higher technique".[38] This means by way of evolution, in the same sort of way in which Americans who, while taking the "optimistic" view, do not yet regard the American society of today as a "classless society", visualize the further democratization of the United States.[39] When the future of their own society is concerned, the ruling groups in both the capitalist and the socialist countries always take an evolutionary attitude.

Meanwhile the evolutionary processes are not necessarily proceeding in the predicted direction. The difficulties with which Communist ideology has to cope in connexion with the changes which have taken place in the socialist society are no less than those which the American Creed has encountered in its collision with the American reality. In the United States it was easier to believe in classlessness amongst the white community before the end of the expanding Western frontier with the unlimited possibilities which it offered to enterprising individuals, before the disappearance of the

"no-man's land", and before the great industrial concerns destroyed over large areas the free economic competition that is one of the tenets of the American Creed. And in the Soviet Union it was easier in 1918 to justify the ratios of the differential state wage scale ranging from 100 to 175 than it was in 1950 to justify the ratios of 1 to 40 which prevailed at that time.

THE MARXIST ANALYSIS AS A WEAPON OF STRUGGLE

The application of the Marxian scheme of social structure exclusively to the capitalist societies is entirely justified from the viewpoint of the Marxian theoretical approach, since the Marxian analysis referred solely to the class-system prevailing in a social order where class antagonisms were the result of private ownership of the means of production. Neither Marx nor Engels undertook to analyse the structure of a society in which the means of production were nationalized, and indeed such a society did not exist anywhere at that time. Thus in the Soviet image of Soviet society there is no relinquishing of Marxian assumptions, despite the introduction of the non-Marxian concept of "non-antagonistic classes". It would, on the other hand, be possible to say that there has been a relinquishing of Marxian methods of sociological analysis.

Because of the propaganda functions of the social sciences, Marxian methods—and in general all sociological methods that threaten stereotypes and social fictions—are rarely found suitable from the viewpoint of the ruling or privileged groups for the analysis of their own society. On the other hand, they are a useful weapon against outside enemies.

So it is the Soviet Union's opponents in the United States or Western Europe who attempt to use these methods in relation to the Soviet Union. A particularly active part in this is played by Russian émigré intellectuals, who are better acquainted with Marxism and with Russia than are their Western colleagues. In place of the "non-antagonistic classes" arising from different types of socialist property, they try to detect the formation of a new class structure based on economic privileges and on the

[38] J. Stalin, *Economic Problems of Socialism in the U.S.S.R.,* Moscow, Foreign Languages Publishing House, 1952, p. 45.
[39] Cf. for instance this passage from C. Sjoberg: "Although it can hardly be denied that, measured by objective criteria, some kind of class system exists in the United States, historical changes in the social structure may well give substance to the American creed of 'classlessness.'" "Are Social Classes in America Becoming More Rigid?" *A.S.R.*, Dec. 1951, p. 783.

exploitation of the labour of others by a privileged class composed of institutionally-established groups: this exploitation being carried out not directly but by means of the state administration and the state treasury, as was done by the court aristocracy in France under the last Bourbons. Those who like to apply Marxian methods to Soviet society in the Stalinist period stress the wide range of wage-scales and the importance of such economic privileges as were not included in the total of monetary rewards. They try to emphasize the tendency to stabilize class differences, citing such features as the great reduction in death duties and the sliding scale for income tax introduced in 1943; the reintroduction of fees for secondary and higher education in 1940, which was confirmed by the amendment of the 121st article of the Stalinist constitution in 1947; the institutionalization of "class barriers" evidenced by the whole system of rights, subsidies, privileges and so on. In general, they attempt to apply the Marxian theory of the state to the Soviet state, and the Marxian theory of "opium for the masses" to the ideology propagated in the socialist states.

In the last two chapters I examined the conception of classlessness in the light of certain social tendencies, namely the tendencies to soften the "class" aspect of the social structure. It emerged that the concept of the classless non-egalitarian society—the concept, not the term—within the frame of differing theories of social class is used for the characterization of one's own society in the leading countries of both the socialist and the capitalist world. In one case this conception is part of the official ideology in which the mass of citizens are reared, while in the other it may rather be said to constitute an extreme expression of a trend which is characteristic of the civic training propagated in that country. In both countries the view of their own society is based on the assumption that even widely ranging shares in the national income are not sufficient to establish social stratification, nor do they necessarily cause either class antagonisms or other symptoms characteristic of a class structure. The differences in economic system prevailing in the two countries are responsible for the fact that this assumption is interpreted in one way on the Western side of the Atlantic and in a different manner in Eastern Europe.

The similarity between the two interpretations of a non-egalitarian social structure is linked with a wider question: that of the causal determination of the various important phenomena of social life which, despite appearances and despite the theoretical simplifications convenient for polemical purposes, do exist in each of the two contemporary opposing forms of economic system. The similarity is also linked with the following threefold problem: in what respects do the institutions and ideologies of the contemporary states which have nationalized the means of production and established a new political order constitute the opposite of the capitalist system; in what respects do they form a continuation of it; and in what respects are the new stages of this new system, now in the process of stabilization, accompanied by a revival of the institutions, relationships, psychological attitudes, and ideas of pre-socialist, socio-economic formations?

SOCIAL CLASS, IDEOLOGY, AND VOTING PREFERENCE:

An Analysis of the 1964 Presidential Election

Gertrude Jaeger Selznick and Stephen Steinberg

The pervasiveness of social class as a factor in voting behavior is a well-documented

This is a revised version of a paper read at the 1966 Annual Meeting of the American Sociological Association. The data for this analysis are derived from a larger study supported by the Anti-Defamation League. Printed by permission of the authors.

fact.[1] In every presidential election since 1936, when polling data first became available, blue-collar or working-class voters have voted for Democratic candidates in far greater proportions than have white-collar or middle-class voters. From one election to another the proportions have varied. Nevertheless, in every election social class has predicted voting preferences.[2]

The *fact* that social class predicts vote is well-established. The *concept* of social-class voting, however, goes beyond the bare empirical relation between class and vote to include the idea that there are social-class reasons for social-class voting. In other words, there is a theory of social-class voting, although it is rarely put to an empirical test. According to this theory, much voting is rather directly inspired by immediate social-class interests, as these are perceived by the voter. Workers who vote Democratic are presumed to be doing so to further their pocketbook interests, just as the more privileged vote Republican to further theirs.

Past research has also demonstrated that political beliefs or ideology predict vote. Stated simply, some people take their basic ideological convictions into account when deciding their vote. But the problem arises of how to distinguish between ideological and social-class voting. A pro-welfare stand on economic issues can and frequently does have its roots in the urgencies of economic disprivilege, but it can be grounded in political philosophy, belief, or ideology as well. Similarly, an anti-social welfare stand can have its roots in the prerogatives of privilege, but it too can be ideologically determined. Clearly, until

social class, political ideology, and opinion on pocketbook issues are analyzed *simultaneously,* we cannot determine to what extent the relation between social class and vote is explained by social-class differences in ideology or by social-class differences in pocketbook concerns.[3]

These considerations are crucial for an understanding of social-class voting. It is one thing if workers vote Democratic because they are committed to both liberal political principles and a liberal economic policy. But it is another thing if they are conservative in their broad political outlook, but vote Democratic simply out of immediate economic self-interest. If this second possibility holds up in fact, then workers might in the future switch their political allegiance to a conservative or reactionary political party that makes an appeal—genuine or demagogic—to their economic interests.

This paper has two related purposes. First, it seeks a conceptual clarification of the concepts of social-class and ideological voting. Even though both have been discussed in past studies,[4] there has been little effort to assess the extent to which, and the conditions under which, each occurs. Secondly, this paper attempts a better understanding of the reasons for Goldwater's overwhelming defeat in the 1964 election. It is easy to show that both social-class and ideological agreement with Goldwater predict the Goldwater vote. If our reasoning is correct, however, this does not tell us whether the overwhelming vote against Goldwater stemmed primarily from ideological rejection of Goldwater's reactionary political philosophy, or merely from rejection of his stand on specific bread-and-butter issues of particular concern to workers.

From the outset it should be noted that

[1] See, for example, A. Campbell, G. Gurin, and W. E. Miller, *The Voter Decides,* Evanston, Ill.: Row, Peterson, 1954; A. Campbell, P. E. Converse, W. E. Miller, and D. E. Stokes, *The American Voter,* New York: Wiley, 1960; P. Lazarsfeld, B. Berelson, and H. Gaudet, *The People's Choice,* New York: Duell, Sloan and Pearce, 1944. For a summary and analysis of the results of many voting studies, see S. M. Lipset *Political Man,* New York: Doubleday, 1964, especially chap. 9.

[2] R. R. Alford, "The Role of Social Class in American Voting Behavior," *The Western Political Quarterly,* Vol. 16, No. 1, March, 1963, pp. 180–194.

[3] Numerous studies have demonstrated that voting is statistically related to social class, political ideology, and opinion on pocketbook issues. However, these variables are themselves interrelated. Little or no effort has been made to use multivariate analysis to factor out the ideological and the pocketbook elements in the social-class vote.

[4] Especially Philip Converse's essay in D. E. Apter, ed., *Ideology and Discontent,* New York: Free Press, 1964, chap. 8.

this study may have a basic limitation stemming from the peculiar character of the 1964 election. Both economic and ideological issues were particularly salient because of Goldwater's open attacks on social welfare programs and his outspoken advocacy of conservative principles. For this reason it is problematic to what extent the findings in this paper would apply to other elections, past or future. This, however, is a question that can be resolved only through replication.

THE DATA

The data for this analysis are derived from a national survey conducted during the weeks preceding the 1964 election. The survey was not designated as an election study. In effect, this is a secondary analysis, subject to the usual limitations.

The sample is a modified probability sample of almost 2000 cases.[5]

Certain groups are excluded from the analysis, reducing the working sample to just under 1400 cases. Negro and Jewish respondents are omitted because their voting behavior was obviously predicated on special factors, and they voted for Johnson with virtual unanimity. Also omitted are respondents who said they definitely would not vote, as well as the 5 per cent who refused to indicate their voting intentions. Otherwise, the sample is representative of white voters in the last election.

SOCIAL CLASS AND VOTE

In the 1964 election, as in other elections in the recent past, high social status is strongly associated with a tendency to vote Republican. Table 1 examines the Gold-

[5] The sample design and interviewing were conducted by the National Opinion Research Center. The sample combines probability and quota techniques. Comparisons with census materials indicate that it has a high degree of representativeness. Our prediction of the election result compared favorably with that of the final Gallup Poll. Gallup reported that 32 per cent of the electorate would vote for Goldwater, and that 7 per cent was undecided. In our survey 31 per cent definitely favored Goldwater and an additional 5 per cent were undecided. Both estimates were low; in the actual election Goldwater received 39 per cent of the vote.

water vote by occupation, education, and income. Compared to past elections, the Republican vote was sharply reduced at every occupational level. In 1964, people classified as managers, officials, and proprietors, or as farm managers or proprietors—the traditional backbone of Republican support—gave Goldwater at best half their votes. Among the lower occupations, in which the great bulk of the working force is found, support for Goldwater was at a virtually unprecedented low. He received just 39 per cent of the vote among clerical workers, and only a quarter of the vote among the four categories of manual workers.

Much the same picture emerges when the vote is inspected by education and income. Only those who finished college gave Goldwater a majority; among postgraduates the Goldwater vote decreases somewhat. The majority of Americans still have a high school education or less; yet below the college level Goldwater got less than a third of the votes. The relation between income and vote is less consistent, but in no income category did Goldwater receive a majority, except among that relative handful who earned $15,000 or more.

To facilitate analysis, education, income, and occupation are combined into an index of social class. Three criteria of social class were used: having four years of high school or more, a family income of $8000 or more, and a white-collar job. Persons with all three of these characteristics (19 per cent of the sample) are referred to as upper middle class. Persons with none of the three defining characteristics (31 per cent of the sample) are referred to as working class; the remaining 50 per cent are called middle class.

Using this index of social class, the figures in Table 2 document once again the systematic relation between social class and vote. The per cent voting for Goldwater ranges from 26 per cent in the working class to 47 per cent in the upper middle class, a spread of 21 percentage points. These figures confirm what was implicit in the magnitude of Goldwater's defeat and evident in Table 1. For the first time since 1936, when survey data first became

TABLE 1ᵃ   Per Cent Voting for Goldwater by Occupation, Education, and Income
(White Voters Only)

	Per Cent for Goldwater
OCCUPATION (OF THOSE PRESENTLY EMPLOYED)	
Sales workers	54% (74)
Managers, officials, and proprietors	49 (97)
Farm managers and proprietors	48 (83)
Professionals	45 (85)
Semiprofessionals	40 (52)
Clerical	39 (131)
Service workers ⎤	30 (104) ⎤
Craftsmen and foremen ⎟ Manual workers	29 (167) ⎟ 26% (431)
Operatives ⎟	24 (135) ⎟
Laborers ⎦	8 (25) ⎦
EDUCATION	
Grade School	28% (363)
Some high school	29 (254)
Finished high school	36 (449)
Some college	44 (172)
Finished college	56 (104)
Postgraduate	47 (55)
INCOME	
Less than $3000	34% (245)
$3000 to $4999	35 (252)
$5000 to $6999	26 (261)
$7000 to $9999	37 (298)
$10,000 to $14,999	42 (233)
$15,000 or more	53 (62)

ᵃ In this and subsequent tables, the number of cases is always less than the total of 1,397 in the working sample. This occurs because respondents occasionally failed to answer a question or because some responses could not be classified.

available, the Republican Party failed to win a clear-cut majority among the more privileged segments of our society. The proportion of the working class voting

TABLE 2   Per Cent Voting for Goldwater by Social Class (White Voters Only)

Social Class	*Per Cent for Goldwater*
Working	26% (405)
Middle	37 (656)
Upper middle	47 (253)

Democratic is also virtually unprecedented, and matches only the working-class vote for Truman in 1948.

Our task now is to analyze the basic relation between social class and vote in terms of both political ideology and opinion on concrete pocketbook issues.

POLITICAL IDEOLOGY AND VOTE

When the interview schedule was written, no study of the election result was contemplated. However, five questions included in the interview can be said to tap ideological agreement with Goldwater. The items and the marginal distributions are presented in Table 3. The term *ideology* as it appears in the literature, has different and frequently highly specialized meanings. In this paper it is used simply to refer to rather general political beliefs, in contrast to opinion on concrete pocketbook issues. It is important to note that none of the items in Table 3 deals with a concrete policy issue of a bread-and-butter character.

TABLE 3   Distribution of Responses on Items Measuring Ideological Agreement
with Goldwater[a] (White Voters Only)

The Federal government is gradually taking away our basic freedoms.

Agree	47%
Disagree	48
Don't know	5

In the past 25 years this country has moved dangerously close to socialism.

Agree	45%
Disagree	41
Don't know	14

Which of the statements on this card comes closest to expressing how you feel about the state of morals in this country at the present time?

They are pretty bad, and getting worse	42%
They are pretty bad, but getting better	13
They are pretty good, but getting worse	21
They are pretty good, and getting better	16
Don't know, or the same as ever	8

How great a danger do you feel that American Communists are to this country at the present time—a very great danger, a great danger, some danger, hardly any danger, or no danger?

A very great danger	18%
A great danger	23
Some danger	39
Hardly any danger	12
No danger	5
Don't know	3

Do you feel the United States is losing power in the world or is it becoming more powerful? *If Losing Power:* How much does this disturb you—a great deal, somewhat, or very little?

Losing power and disturbed a great deal	15%
Losing power and disturbed somewhat	10
Losing power and disturbed very little	5
Becoming more powerful	41
Staying the same	24
Don't know	5

---

[a] Responses in italics are considered in ideological agreement with Goldwater.

Goldwater repeated the traditional Republican charges that the Federal government is usurping individual freedoms and that the United States is drifting down the road to socialism. Agreement with Goldwater's position on these issues was widespread: almost half the voters agreed with each. With regard to the state of contemporary morals, an issue which Goldwater highlighted during the campaign, 42 per cent of the voters in our sample chose the statement that morals are pretty bad and getting worse. Almost the same proportion agreed with Goldwater's position concerning the threat of internal Communism; four out of ten said that Communists are a great or very great danger. Of the five issues examined, it is only on the issue of American power abroad that Gold-

water received relatively little support. Just a quarter of the sample believed that the United States is losing power in the world and said that this disturbed them a great deal or somewhat.

These five items were combined into a cumulative index by assigning one point for every instance of agreement with Goldwater. Column A of Table 4 shows that the index powerfully predicts the Goldwater vote. (This in itself is a persuasive validation of the index.) Among those who agreed with Goldwater on none of the five issues, 6 per cent voted for him. Percentages steadily rise until, among those in complete agreement, 87 per cent voted for him. The distribution across the index can be seen in column B of Table 4. When the figures in column A are combined with those in

TABLE 4   Per Cent Voting for Goldwater by Ideological Agreement
(White Voters Only)

Score on Index of Ideological Agreement	A Per Cent for Goldwater		B Per Cent of Total Sample
0	6%	(265)	19%
1	18	(330)	24
2	34	(295)	21
3	56	(225)	16
4	64	(180)	13
5	87	(90)	7
Total			100%
			(1,385)

column B, the arithmetic of Goldwater's defeat becomes clear. Only among those who agreed with Goldwater on three or more issues did the Republican vote reach a majority. But only a third of the sample— 36 per cent—expressed this level of agreement. This leaves 64 per cent who agreed with Goldwater on no more than two issues, and here the Goldwater vote fell far short of a majority. It thus appears that, despite fairly high levels of agreement on individual items, Goldwater's political beliefs were *consistently* accepted by only a minority. This was true quite apart from his stand on pocketbook issues.

It has just been observed that both social class and political ideology are related to how people voted in the last election. One might expect, then, that social class is also related to ideology. This is not the case, however. As can be seen in Table 5, social class is only mildly related to agreement with Goldwater. Differences between the three class levels are small, whether measured by the proportions at each level of ideological agreement or by mean scores on the index, shown at the bottom of Table 5. At best there is an 11 percentage-point difference between the working and upper middle class when the percentages scoring 4 and 5 on the index are combined. This compares to a difference of 21 percentage points in the proportions who actually voted for Goldwater. In short, ideological agreement and disagreement with Goldwater were fairly equally distributed

throughout the class structure, yet workers were much less likely to vote for him.[6]

Table 6 now examines social class and ideology simultaneously in their relation to vote. This table lends itself to two important conclusions. First, at extremes of ideological agreement, social class bears no relation to voting behavior. Among those who strongly disagreed with Goldwater (that is, had scores of 0 or 1 on the index) and among those who strongly agreed with him (score of 5), social class had virtually no effect on how people voted. This indicates that some people determined their vote on the basis of their ideological convictions, and did so regardless of their social class. Little or no tendency can be seen for the more privileged to vote Republican when they were in sharp ideological disagreement with Goldwater. Nor was there a pull toward the Democratic Party among those few working-class voters with very strong right-wing convictions.

The second conclusion to be drawn from Table 6 is that where opinion is not sharply polarized and is perhaps inconsistent, social class has a powerful influence. Among those who partially agreed with Goldwater, people were much less likely to vote

[6] Of the five items that comprise the index of ideological agreement, social class has no relation to two (decaying morals and the internal Communist danger), a weak relation to two (excessive Federal expansion and creeping socialism), and a fairly strong relation to one (loss of American power abroad). Where there is a relationship, workers were slightly less likely to be in agreement with Goldwater.

TABLE 5   Ideological Agreement with Goldwater by Social Class
(White Voters Only)

Score on Index of Ideological Agreement	Social Class		
	WORKING	MIDDLE	UPPER MIDDLE
0	20% } 45%	18% } 44%	20% } 37%
1	25	26	17
2	23	21	21
3	18 } 50	15 } 50	17 } 55
4	9	14	17
5	5	6	8
	(399)	(648)	(251)
Mean Score	1.97	2.00	2.12

for him if they were working class. This was true whether individuals had a score of 2, 3, or 4. Taking partial agreers as a whole (bottom row, Table 6), 63 per cent of the upper middle class voted for him. In striking contrast, among the working class only half as many—32 per cent—did so. This is a difference of 31 percentage points. In other words, the impact of social class on voting is limited to those with inconsistent political philosophies, and here the impact is great. This finding makes

good sense: When people have no clear-cut and consistent ideological grounds on which to form an opinion, they necessarily have to bring other considerations into play. Voting under these conditions becomes strongly influenced by social class.

SOCIAL CLASS, POLITICAL IDEOLOGY, AND OPINION ON POCKETBOOK ISSUES

We have yet to determine whether there were distinctive social-class reasons for the

TABLE 6   Per Cent Voting for Goldwater by Social Class and Ideological Agreement
(White Voters Only)

Social Class	WORKING	MIDDLE	UPPER MIDDLE	PERCENTAGE DIFFERENCE
Score on Index of Ideological Agreement	Per Cent for Goldwater			
0 ⎤	6%	5%	8%	2
⎱ Strongly	(81)	(116)	(51)	
⎰ Disagree	16	19	19	3
1 ⎦	(98)	(168)	(42)	
2 ⎤	24	37	42	18
	(92)	(135)	(52)	
3 ⎱ Partially	40	56	76	36
⎰ Agree	(72)	(98)	(42)	
4 ⎦	38	68	75	37
	(37)	(90)	(44)	
5 ⎱ Strongly	86	86	85	−1
⎰ Agree	(21)	(42)	(20)	
2–4	32%	51%	63%	

social-class vote among partial agreers. It has just been observed that persons who were somewhat sympathetic with Goldwater's political ideology tended not to vote for him when they were working class. To what extent was their rejection of Goldwater a reaction to his anti-social welfare stand?

Respondents were asked whether or not they thought the Federal government should pass a law to provide medical care for the aged, a crude paraphrase of the Medicare program. As the bottom row of Table 7 shows, there is a direct relation between socioeconomic status and favoring Medicare: 84 per cent of those classified as working class approved of Medicare as compared to 53 per cent of the upper middle class. Despite this class difference, it should not be overlooked that even among the most privileged segment of the population considerable support for Federal programs exists, at least in the area of Medicare for the elderly.

The body of Table 7 shows, not surprisingly, that those who agreed more strongly with Goldwater were more likely to disapprove of Medicare. This was true at every class level. As with vote, however, the impact of social class on favoring Medicare is greatest among those who partially agreed with the Goldwater ideology. Among this group, fully 80 per cent of the working class favored Medicare, whereas

only 40 per cent of the upper class did so.[7] This makes for a difference of 40 percentage points. Among strong agreers and strong disagreers, on the other hand, the percentage point differences are just 12 and 18, respectively. This again shows the small impact of social class where people have well-defined political convictions.

We can now turn to the final question: Does the impact of social class on opinions on Medicare help to explain why the working class tended to vote for Johnson even when they were in partial ideological agreement with Goldwater? Table 8 brings together all of the variables considered in the analysis. As observed before, social class has no impact on people who either disagreed or agreed strongly with Goldwater. The effect of social class is still confined to the partial agreers. It is also immediately apparent that people who

[7] Three-quarters of those in the working class favored Medicare even when they agreed that "the Federal government is gradually taking away our basic freedoms" or that "in the past twenty-five years this country has moved dangerously close to socialism." Even among those who indicated they strongly or somewhat approved of the John Birch Society, the overwhelming majority —89 per cent—approved of Medicare. Once again, this points to the tendency among workers to take a stand on pocketbook issues that is incongruent with their general political beliefs. Indeed, when their bread-and-butter interests are involved, political ideology seems to count for little.

TABLE 7   Per Cent Who Favor Medicare by Ideological Agreement and Social Class (White Voters Only)

Ideological Agreement with Goldwater	WORKING	MIDDLE	UPPER MIDDLE	PERCENTAGE DIFFERENCE
	% Favoring Medicare			
Strongly disagree	92% (179)	84% (323)	74% (93)	18
Partially agree	80 (200)	62 (323)	40 (138)	40
Strongly agree	57 (21)	38 (42)	45 (20)	12
Total	84% (400)	71% (649)	53% (251)	31

TABLE 8 Per Cent Voting for Goldwater by Social Class, Ideological Agreement, and Opinion on Medicare (White Voters Only)

Social Class	WORKING			MIDDLE			UPPER MIDDLE		
Ideological Agreement	STRONGLY DISAGREE	PARTIALLY AGREE	STRONGLY AGREE	STRONGLY DISAGREE	PARTIALLY AGREE	STRONGLY AGREE	STRONGLY DISAGREE	PARTIALLY AGREE	STRONGLY AGREE
Opinion on Medicare[a]					*Per Cent for Goldwater*				
Favor Medicare	10% (165)	26% (159)	75% (12)	12% (239)	38% (202)	81% (16)	6% (69)	40% (55)	78% (9)
Oppose Medicare	36 (11)	57 (35)	100 (9)	21 (38)	75 (110)	88 (25)	35 (20)	79 (80)	91 (11)
Total	12% (179)	32% (201)	86% (21)	13% (284)	51% (323)	86% (42)	13% (93)	63% (138)	85% (20)

[a] The 39 white voters who had no opinion on Medicare are excluded.

favor Medicare were much less likely to vote for Goldwater no matter what their social class or the extent of their ideological agreement or disagreement. However, the key question is whether opinion on Medicare helps to explain the social-class vote among those who partially agreed with him. The answer is yes: Among those who expressed partial agreement, the effect of social class is now reduced. The original difference between the working class and the upper middle class was 31 percentage points among partial agreers. It is now 22 percentage points among those who are against Medicare and only 14 percentage points among those who favor Medicare. The original 12 percentage point difference between the middle and upper middle class is now reduced to 2 and 4 percentage points.

It is apparent that at every social-class level, many voters were in conflict between a fairly conservative political ideology and a pro-social-welfare orientation. When this was the case, the likelihood was that their social-welfare orientation would take precedence and they would vote Democratic. However, a social-welfare orientation was most prevalent among workers, and this helps to explain their overwhelming vote for Johnson, even when they were in partial ideological agreement with Goldwater.[8]

CONCLUSIONS

What descriptive statements can be made concerning the reasons for Goldwater's

[8] It was thought that the remaining percentage point difference between the working and middle classes might be explained by the traditional loyalty of workers to the Democratic Party. Even though party identification powerfully predicted the Goldwater vote, particularly among partial agreers, it does not improve the interpretation of the relation between social class and vote.

Party identification has been given little attention here for two reasons. For one thing, like voting preference it is strongly predicted by political ideology and opinion on pocketbook issues. Secondly, our main concern has not been to explore all of the factors that enter into the voting decision, but to explain the *relation* between social class and vote. In this respect, party identification is not an important factor when political ideology and opinion on pocketbook issues are controlled.

crushing defeat? The data have shown that both social-class and ideological voting occurred on a wide scale in the 1964 election and together they account for the magnitude of Goldwater's defeat. About four out of ten voters at every class level agreed with Goldwater on no more than one of the five issues examined, and when this was the case only about 12 per cent voted for him. Most of these people also disagreed with Goldwater's position on social welfare, as represented by the Medicare issue. Hence, enough voters strongly disagreed with Goldwater on *both* economic and non-economic issues to guarantee his defeat. Significantly, the upper class was just as likely as the lower classes to vote against Goldwater when they were in ideological disagreement with him.

However, about half at every class level were on the ideological fence. They agreed with Goldwater on 2, 3, or 4 of the 5 issues, and when this was the case, social-class voting was very marked. The working class tended overwhelmingly to vote for Johnson, the upper middle class to vote for Goldwater. This rather strongly suggests that the less privileged were voting their perceived economic interests, and this interpretation holds up in fact. Opinion on Medicare went a long way toward wiping out social-class differences. Thus although Goldwater's defeat was made inevitable by widespread disagreement with his political ideas, it was worsened when he failed to win the votes of potential ideological supporters because of his economic conservatism.

What are the implications of these data for some reactionary political movement in the future? On one side it can be said that large proportions of voters at every class level rejected Goldwater's political ideology as well as his economic conservatism. On the other side, it is significant that the social-welfare liberalism of large numbers of Johnson's voters was unsupported by a consistent set of liberal political beliefs. The danger of opportunistic voting, when it is accompanied by conservative ideological tendencies, is that such people are vulnerable to a reactionary movement, especially one that does not threaten their economic interests.

Finally, what general conclusions might

be drawn about the nature and prevalence of ideological and social-class voting? It appears that, in the United States at the present time, social class has little relation to basic political ideology. Approval of social-welfare programs appears to be widespread, but it often occurs under an umbrella of at least verbal agreement on basic principles of a rather conservative character. Social class is significant, however, if only because it modifies the relation between political ideology and opinion on concrete issues. It determines to some extent whether people will draw policy conclusions congruent or incongruent with their basic political beliefs. In general, where political beliefs are consistent and strong, social class has little or no impact, and ideological voting occurs. On the other hand, among those with inconsistent or weak political beliefs, the impact of social class both on policy opinions and on voting is very strong.

RELATIVE DEPRIVATION— ATTITUDES TO CLASS AND STATUS INEQUALITY IN ENGLAND

W. G. Runciman

THE HISTORICAL BACKGROUND, 1918–1962

From this summary of the decades leading up to 1962, it is clear that the magnitude and frequency of relative deprivation has seldom been in close correlation with the facts of inequality of class. Each of the two world wars has set off a disturbance of reference groups and an upsurge of expectations. But after both of them, other influences have inhibited the mounting

egalitarianism which had been aroused. After the First World War, the Depression and its apparent irremediableness prevented manual workers and their families from seeing it as feasible that they should demand comparable rewards to those for non-manual work. After the Second, relative deprivation was damped down by the achievement of some gradual amelioration of the class-situation of manual workers and the conviction that a greater redistribution was taking place than did in fact occur. If the account which I have given is correct, then we should expect the evidence of the 1962 survey to show that in terms of inequalities of class, the respondents least likely to express relative deprivation will be those at the top of the manual stratum; working class reference groups will not often be taken from the other side of the manual/non-manual line; and an awareness, or even disapproval, of the greater prosperity of others will be more frequent among middle-class people looking at working-class people than the other way round. There is not yet, however, any conclusion to be drawn as to whether a similar relationship will hold between inequality and relative deprivation of status. . . .

REFERENCE GROUPS AND INEQUALITIES OF CLASS

The analysis of survey evidence on relative deprivation of class is in principle straightforward. If, for example, people are asked who (if anyone) they think of as better off than themselves, this information can then be related to the extent of their own wealth and the wealth of the comparative reference group which they have given. There are not the difficulties which bedevil even ordinal comparisons of status, and the actual discrepancy between inequality and relative deprivation can be expressed in quantitative terms. . . . I have used people's stated incomes (or, in the case of married women, their husband's income) rather than household income or sub-category of occupation, as my criterion. . . . The form of question used in the present survey was "Could you give me an idea roughly how much you (your husband) earn(s) each week after deductions?". . . . For the purpose of assessing relative deprivation . . . people's

TABLE 1   Satisfaction with Own or Husband's Present Income; by Stated Income Within Occupational Stratum

	Non-Manual			Manual		
	HIGH %	MEDIUM %	LOW %	HIGH %	MEDIUM %	LOW %
Yes	63	50	56	72	57	47
No	37	50	41	27	41	51
Don't know	0	0	3	1	2	2
Total	100%	100%	100%	100%	100%	100%
	(N = 160)	(N = 107)	(N = 75)	(N = 99)	(N = 278)	(N = 368)

estimates of their incomes are if anything more important than their actual incomes. . . . In the subsequent discussion I shall refer simply to either "high," "medium" and "low" or "top," "middle" and "bottom" levels of income. . . .

The questions asked about income . . . confirm the expectations suggested by the earlier discussion. Not merely are comparative reference groups among manual workers and their wives so far restricted as to result in a marked discrepancy between relative deprivation and actual inequality; their retention of working-class standards of comparison means that manual workers and their wives are consistently less likely to feel relatively deprived than are non-manual workers and their wives who are earning the same (or at the top level probably a great deal more). Only among the poorest does this conclusion need to be qualified at all; and even here, it can only be said that manual workers and their wives are less often avowedly satisfied, not that they more often feel relatively deprived.

It is not surprising that at the top level of incomes the standards of non-manual workers should be very much higher. A wage that would satisfy a skilled artisan is unlikely to satisfy a managing director or a high court judge. But the relation between relative deprivation and inequality is more complex than can be inferred from this predictable contrast by itself. The survey not only confirms that the comparative reference groups of the two strata are different. It also confirms how many qualifications must be made to the suggestion that prosperity has made manual workers and their wives "middle-class". Those few who

are in the top third of the overall income distribution are . . . likelier than the less prosperous manual respondents to have members of the non-manual stratum in mind. But even when they describe themselves as "middle-class" and have, therefore, in some sense a different reference group from almost all of those who describe themselves as "working-class", they are no more likely to see others as doing better. The influence of the reference group is strong only when they are asked whether they agree that manual workers are doing much better than white-collar; only then are those who think of themselves as "working-class" very much less likely to agree. Without some external stimulus powerful enough to dislodge the hold of traditional standards of comparison, the relative deprivations of manual workers, including even the most prosperous, will derive from very different reference group comparisons from those of non-manual workers and their families.

. . . .

There is no way of ascertaining in detail from the survey just what influences underlie this restriction of comparisons. If the normal response to economic inequality is to make comparisons only to those closest to oneself rather than to those by contrast with whom one is most unequally placed, then these results need, perhaps, no explanation whatever. But since it is clear that this is not universally true, the question remains to what extent and for what reasons reference groups are so restricted. A glance over the social history of Britain since 1918 reveals some, at least, of the reasons why on matters of economic class—but not status—there has not been a cumulative spiral of aspiration and prosperity since the collapse of the militant radicalism which followed the First World War. But the principal interest of the 1962 survey lies not in demonstrating what influences are at work—this must rest on the historical evidence for the period before the survey was taken—but in revealing to what extent the reference groups of the less well placed are limited in scope, unspecifically defined, and mildly expressed. Several different forms of question were used to elucidate the reference group comparisons made, and each served only to reinforce the same impression. Both the magnitude and frequency of relative deprivation among manual workers and their wives are very much lower than would accord with the facts of economic inequality. The lack of "class-consciousness" which is sometimes attributed to the British working class is in this sense, at least, amply confirmed. . . .

Within the manual stratum, income does not affect the choice of reference groups in any consistent pattern. . . . None of the differences which are not uniform with income—where, that is, a higher percentage of those at the middle level give a particular reply than those at either the top or the bottom—are at all large. But if all the differences of 3% or over are looked at together, they seem to confirm the picture of this group as the "fraternalists" of the manual stratum, who do not aspire in any sense to rise out of the working class but who do not yet have what they now see as attainable for manual workers as such. Within the manual stratum, those at the middle level of incomes are likelier than those at either the top or the bottom to have the following characteristics or attitudes: to say that they want or need something not mentioned on either of the two lists of goods; to think that manual workers are not doing "much better" than white-collar workers; to be dissatisfied with their (or their husband's) present income on the grounds of being worth more pay; to think that manual workers ought to be doing as well as they are doing by comparison with white-collar workers; to want, if they do not have, a car, a refrigerator, ownership of a house, a spare room and foreign holiday travel; if assigning themselves to the "working class" to define this by reference to manual work; to belong to a trade union; to think that the state should provide unemployment pay at full rate without a means test for as long as a man is unemployed; and to support the Labour Party. Given the inadequacy of the figures for the distribution of incomes, these differences cannot be pressed too hard. But they furnish a marked contrast to those results which suggest that where inequalities of status are at issue relative deprivation is more frequent among manual workers and their wives at the top level of incomes, and that this relative deprivation is of an "egoistic" rather than a "fraternalistic" kind.[1] This, however, is to anticipate the argument. For the moment, the main conclusion to have emerged is the restricted and even illogical choice of comparative reference groups, particularly in the manual stratum, on matters of economic class.

REFERENCE GROUPS AND INEQUALITIES OF STATUS

If my argument about inequalities of status is correct, then the questions in the survey which bear on it should disclose a very different pattern from those concerned with differences in income or resources. . . . The topics raised in the survey on inequalities of status are more ambiguous and less precise than those raised on inequalities of wealth or income. But if questions can be asked which it is legitimate to interpret as reflecting attitudes towards the hierarchy of status, as opposed to class or power, these can furnish at least some further evidence for or against the view that relative deprivation of status among the less well placed has been progressively increasing with the advance towards some greater measure of equality.

There are, however, two important differences from the discussion of class. The

[1] Egoistic is when one is dissatisfied with his present situation but not in a way that gives him a common cause with others like him. It designates one who feels deprived within his class but not on behalf of his class. Fraternalistic is a feeling of relative deprivation on behalf of the class of which one is a member. (C. S. H.) See Runciman, *op. cit.,* pp. 33–34.

first is that we are now considering "egoistic" as well as "fraternalistic" relative deprivations. I have argued that higher aspirations of status have been steadily spreading among manual workers and their families throughout the period since 1918; but these have in some ways been "egoistic" aspirations as much as a sense of relative deprivation on behalf of the working class as such, and they have been accompanied by a decline in the sort of intensely fraternalistic feelings characteristic of the traditional working-class militant. Such feelings are still common among some sections of the manual stratum, and particularly those workers who are socially isolated by the nature of their work and for whom an increase in prosperity may well exacerbate feelings of relative deprivation of social esteem. Miners and dockers should both be expected from any generalization about the spread of a wish on the part of manual workers to rise out of their status-group rather than with it. But the relative deprivation of status felt by manual workers and their families was probably less often and also less intensely fraternalistic in 1962 than in 1919. Even if this could be statistically demonstrated, it still would not mean that the manual workers of 1962 could properly be described as having "become middle-class". But as more and more manual workers and their families came to feel heightened aspirations of status, this tended to detach them from those whose more "traditional" working-class attitudes involved a relative deprivation of status—if any—only on behalf of all manual workers as such.

The second difference is that the questions asked with a view to elucidating feelings about status were mostly asked in terms of how respondents felt about the education and careers of their children (or hypothetical children). This is one of the most obvious ways in which changing aspirations of status are expressed, but it is a very different form of question from those used in asking about attitudes relevant to relative deprivation of class. Many people, when they are asked about their children, will express higher aspirations on their behalf than they would for themselves, and if the respondents in the survey had been asked

what they hoped that their children would earn, they might have given a much more extravagant answer than they did when asked about the "proper" standard of living for "people like themselves". The questions about education, therefore, cannot be interpreted as strictly comparable to the questions about income. . . .

It should, however, be possible to show whether normative reference groups, as suggested by self-rated "class", have an influence on the attitudes of manual workers and their wives towards education and careers for their children. A manual worker may, of course, think of himself as "middle-class" and still feel that manual workers as such should be given better educational facilities by comparison with those enjoyed by the entrants into white-collar occupations. But for him to want higher education for his son implies a willingness that the son should rise out of the status group of his birth into another—a willingness which, as we have seen, was probably much less common a generation before.

In the same way, a manual worker's preference that his son should have a non-manual job, particularly if it is no better or even less well paid, can be plausibly interpreted as an attitude to status as much as to class. During the Depression, the attraction of a clerical job to working-class families was, as the Pilgram Trust investigators commented, its security more than anything else. After the Second World War, this was no longer so. There might be in the minds of some working-class parents a residual fear of unemployment which would lead them to prefer a white-collar occupation for their sons. Some also might be aware of just those reasons cited earlier why the ostensible equality between upper manual and lower non-manual earnings should not be taken to demonstrate a genuine equality in the class-situation of the two. But in an enquiry conducted in 1962 it is plausible to interpret a manual worker's preference for a non-manual job for his son as indicating a wish that the son should rise out of, rather than with, the status-group of manual workers. A preference that the son should take a manual job need not, of course, always mean an attitude of militant fraternalism;

it may mean an acceptance of the subordinate status of the manual worker, or a complete indifference to considerations of status, or even a conviction that the manual worker is not accorded any less prestige by society than the non-manual. In any such case, the person belongs to the category which was labelled Type A—the person who feels relatively deprived neither as a member of his group nor on behalf of it. But given the social structure of Britain in 1962, it seems safe to assume that the manual worker who would prefer his son to have a manual job does not do so because he regards it as enjoying higher status. He either does not resent the subordinate status attached to manual work, or, while feeling that manual work is accorded too little status, still does not want a son of his to achieve higher status by "abdicating" from the working class. If, on the other hand, he would prefer a non-manual job for his son, then this can be plausibly interpreted as some sense of relative deprivation of status of an "egoistic" kind.

The evidence which can be drawn from the survey about attitudes to inequalities of status is not entirely confined to the questions about education or career for a son. There have already been some implications to be drawn from the analysis of self-assigned "class", and in addition two further questions were introduced as having some possible implications for attitudes to status. The questions which must, however, bear the brunt of interpretation on this elusive topic are those about attitudes to a hypothetical son.

The actual extent of educational inequality, as opposed to the frequency of relative deprivation aroused by it, can be measured in terms of the proportion of each stratum leaving school at the minimum age, the proportion remaining in secondary school and the proportion going on to higher education. Of the manual respondents in the sample, only 9% had stayed on at school beyond whatever was the minimum statutory age at the time; of non-manual respondents, the proportion was 49%, of whom 22% had had some university or college education. The advance towards actual equality is reflected in the answers given by those respondents with children

under 15 when they were asked at what age they expected their children to leave school. Of non-manual parents, only 7% said that they expected their children to leave at the minimum age, while the proportion among manual parents was 36%. The difference is still a large one; but the figure of 36%, even if it reflects some over-optimism among working-class parents, is still evidence of a radical change from the actual experience of the working-class parents in the sample. Furthermore, the proportion rises with income: over two-thirds of working-class parents at the top level of incomes expected at least one of their children to stay on beyond the minimum age. These figures not only provide ample confirmation that in this respect, at least, inequality of status between the manual and non-manual strata is very much less than it was, but suggest at the same time that the frequency of relative deprivation has been rising.

The survey also provides ample evidence for the extent to which the aspiration for higher education is shared by both strata. When asked the question, "Would you like any son of yours to have a university education?", 82% of manual respondents said "yes". . . . The figure for non-manual respondents is only 6% higher than the figure for manual. This question, however, is perhaps too loosely phrased to afford evidence of genuine aspirations; it may be a little too much like asking "would you like any son of yours to have a lucrative job?" in order to elucidate attitudes to inequalities of class. But the expectations of the working-class parents in the sample who have children under 15 furnish more tangible evidence of the extent to which educational aspirations have spread. Only at the top level of incomes do as many as half of the manual parents in the sample expect at least one of their children to have some form of education beyond school, and only a further half of these expect this further education to be at a university. But this reflects a large increase in the pre-war pattern not merely of hopes but of expectations of what is seen to be feasible. Furthermore, the replies show an effect made not only by income, but by self-rated "class". . . .

A better indicator, however, might be not what parents expect their children to achieve so much as whether they are prepared to contribute fees in order to help their children up the educational ladder. As on all these questions, it cannot be unerringly assumed that such a willingness implies an ambition of status for the children. . . . But the link between education and status is sufficiently close for it to be plausible to make some inferences about attitudes to status from attitudes about private education. . . .

The proportion of working-class parents with children who attended, or are expected to attend, a fee-paying school at any stage of their educational careers is, predictably, extremely small—6% (and only 8% even at the top level of incomes) as compared to 35% of non-manual parents. But a difference is made by self-rated "class" even among the handful of manual parents: 9% of those describing themselves as "middle-class" have children who either have attended, attend, or are expected to attend fee-paying schools, as against 5% of those describing themselves as "working-class". A similar difference is visible in the answers to the question "Do you have (or, would you like to have) private education for your children?" A number of people said that they did not know, which is obviously a reasonable response for those to whom the question was an entirely unreal one. These "Don't Knows" to some extent confuse the analysis of the answers by income and self-rating; but when both are held constant it is clear that both have an independent influence among manual respondents. The majority do not (or would not) want any form of private education for their children. But the proportion drops between the middle and top levels of income,

whatever the "class" to which the respondents assign themselves, and at all three levels of income a clear difference is made by self-rating. The figures are shown in Table 2.

Self-rated "class" thus shows a clear influence on the answers to a question which can be plausibly linked to attitudes to inequality of status. Indeed, those manual workers and their wives who describe themselves as "middle-class" are if anything less likely to reject the idea of a private education for their children than non-manual workers and their wives at the bottom or middle levels of income. Only at the top level of incomes, where nearly half the non-manual respondents would either like or, if they are parents, already have a private education for their children is there a marked difference from the manual respondents. Once again, these figures cannot demonstrate by themselves that there has been a steady spread of status-aspirations among the manual stratum during the postwar period; perhaps just as many manual workers and their wives would have said in 1938 that they would, in principle, like a private education for their children. But this is on the face of it implausible, and the difference between the attitudes of older and younger manual respondents suggests, as we shall see, a considerable change in attitudes. Furthermore, the influence of self-rated "class" on attitudes to status (unlike attitudes to income) is so far confirmed.

Since, however, questions about education may be misleading as a guide to attitudes to inequality of status, two questions were asked about the job which people would prefer for a hypothetical son. The respondents were first of all asked if they

TABLE 2   Proportion of Manual Respondents Who Do Not (Would Not) Want a Private Education for Their Children; by Self-Rated "Class" Within Income

High		Medium		Low	
SELF-RATED MIDDLE	SELF-RATED WORKING	SELF-RATED MIDDLE	SELF-RATED WORKING	SELF-RATED MIDDLE	SELF-RATED WORKING
46% (N = 41)	57% (N = 56)	55% (N = 101)	66% (N = 176)	54% (N = 91)	65% (N = 276)

would prefer a manual or non-manual job, assuming that they had a son who was at the moment choosing a job; they were then presented with the hypothetical alternative of a job with higher pay but lower status—a factory foreman—or a job with lower pay but higher status—a schoolteacher. . . . Where the question is put in terms of an unqualified manual/non-manual choice of job, then there may be no warrant for inferring that a preference for a non-manual job is based on status rather than class. But where the choice is weighted against the non-manual job in terms of income, then it does seem legitimate to draw some inference about attitudes to the hierarchy of status.

When manual workers and their wives were asked "If a son of yours was actually choosing a job at the moment, would you rather he chose a manual or a non-manual job?", almost a quarter said that they didn't know, or that it would be up to him, or that they would have no personal preference in the matter; of the remainder, 32% said "manual" and 49% said "non-manual". When, however, they were asked "If he had the choice of a foreman's job at £20 a week or a schoolteacher's job at £15, which would you prefer him to choose?" the proportion of Don't Knows . . . would prefer the school teacher to the foreman than vice versa—41% as against 40%. Of the non-manual respondents, more than four times as many expressed a preference for a non-manual job as for a manual, and at the top level of incomes more than eight times as many. When the choice of foreman or schoolteacher was put to them, the proportion choosing the foreman rose to 25%, but this is still less than half as many as chose the schoolteacher.

These results are of sufficient interest to call for a slight digression. If I am right about the changes which occurred in Britain in the decades preceding the survey, then this was a period in which relative deprivation of status was rising in both magnitude and frequency as equality of status came closer to being achieved. This period, in other words, corresponds to the rising slope of the hypothetical curve depicted in Chapter Two—the point at which equality has not yet been so far attained that the frequency of relative deprivation starts once again to fall. What, therefore, would happen if equality of status were in fact to be achieved? We can safely assume that the status of the teacher was higher than that of the foreman by the standards of English society in 1962. This difference of status is clearly reflected in the preferences expressed by respondents when confronted with the choice for their sons. A generation or more earlier, however, fewer manual workers and their wives would have chosen the schoolmaster's job for their son, since there was then still less equality of status between the manual and non-manual strata, and the reference groups of the manual stratum were still more limited. Conversely, if equality of status were to progress still further, then the frequency of preference for the schoolteacher ought to fall once again. Since the status of the two is not yet equal, there is no way of testing this for Britain. . . .

It requires to be demonstrated, however, that there is a difference between older and younger manual workers and their wives. If it is true that there has been a marked change in the forty years preceding the survey, then we should expect to find that older manual workers are less likely to express a preference in favour of a non-manual job for their sons. But since there should also be an effect shown by self-rated "class", it is necessary to test the effect of both together in order to insure against an overlap. On the initial question about an unspecified choice between a manual and non-manual job for a son, it turns out that self-rating makes the difference rather than age. Age does, however, show an effect independent of self-rating, particularly among those who describe themselves as "working-class". Manual workers or their wives who are aged between 21 and 45 are more likely to choose a non-manual than a manual job for a son, even if they describe themselves as "working-class", and so are those over 45 who describe themselves as "middle-class". But those who are over 45 and also describe themselves as "working-class" are no more likely to express a preference for the non-manual than for the manual job. The figures are given in Table 3.

When the specific alternatives of schoolmaster and foreman are suggested, the

TABLE 3 Choice for Son of Manual or Non-Manual Job; Manual Respondents
by Age Within Self-Rated "Class"

	Self-Rated Middle		Self-Rated Working	
	21–45 %	46 + %	21–45 %	46 + %
Manual	26	28	33	36
Non-manual	51	57	45	36
Don't know	23	15	22	28
Total	100%	100%	100%	100%
	(N = 125)	(N = 178)	(N = 254)	(N = 356)

pattern is slightly different. The effect of both self-rating and age is more marked: those of 45 or under, whatever their self-rated "class", are likelier to prefer the schoolteacher than the foreman, and so are those over 45 who describe themselves as "middle-class". But those who describe themselves as "working-class" and are over 45 are a good deal more likely to prefer the foreman than the schoolmaster. The figures are shown in Table 4.

This table provides clear evidence that first, there has been a significant change in attitudes to the hierarchy of status among manual workers and their wives, and second, these attitudes are influenced by normative reference groups as implied by self-rated "class". Indeed, the effect of self-rated "class" persists when either age or sex or education or income or father's occupation is held constant. It does not account for all the variation; each of these other attributes shows an independent effect, and sometimes quite a marked one. But the effect of self-rating is persistent and un-

mistakable, quite unlike its negligible effect on the questions related to inequalities of class. On questions of income it showed a distinct effect only where those describing themselves as "working-class" were found to be a good deal less likely to agree to the general suggestion that "manual workers are doing much better nowadays than white-collar workers"—a question on which the bearing of self-rated "class" seemed more closely analogous to its bearing on party choice than on direct perceptions of comparative reference groups who are seen to be better off. But on the question which of all those in the survey it is safest to interpret as indicating attitudes to status, self-rated "class", despite the diversity of meanings which underlies it, shows a strong independent effect.

A corollary of this is that some categories of manual workers and their wives who described themselves as "working-class" were a good deal more likely to prefer the foreman than the schoolteacher. When a working-class self-rating is combined with

TABLE 4 Choice for Son of Foreman's Job at £20 a Week or Schoolteacher's at £15;
Manual Respondents by Age Within Self-Rated "Class"

	Self-Rated Middle		Self-Rated Working	
	21–45 %	46 + %	21–45 %	46 + %
Foreman	24	40	33	49
Schoolteacher	61	47	47	28
Don't know	15	13	20	23
Total	100%	100%	100%	100%
	(N = 125)	(N = 178)	(N = 254)	(N = 356)

either an age over 45, or a father who was in a manual job, or a stated income at the bottom of the three levels, then the person concerned is more likely to prefer the foreman than the schoolteacher. These categories, moreover, comprise a substantial proportion of the manual stratum, and it is they who explain why the preference for the schoolteacher among the manual respondents taken as a whole is so narrow as to be almost negligible. . . .

There are two categories of manual respondents among whom a middle-class self-rating shows a particularly strong effect. The first is women, and the second those at the top level of incomes. . . . On the choice of jobs for a son, women who are manual workers or are married to manual workers and describe themselves as "middle-class" are particularly likely to express a preference for the schoolteacher rather than the foreman. . . . But women in the manual stratum who describe themselves as "middle-class" are more than twice as likely to prefer the schoolteacher than to prefer the foreman. . . .

Self-rating also makes a particularly marked difference at the top level of income. Here, those manual workers and their wives who describe themselves as "working-class" are likelier by 12% to express a preference for the schoolteacher than a preference for the foreman—a difference which is the same, within a few per cent., as among those at the middle level of income, whether they describe themselves as "middle-" or "working-class". Among those at the top level who describe themselves as "middle-class", however, the difference is 49%. From the size of this difference, it would appear that manual workers who reach the top level of income will be likely to feel a fraternalistic relative deprivation of status only if they retain as their normative reference group the "working class" (whatever this may mean to them). If, on the other hand, they think of themselves as "middle-class" this will make them anxious to distinguish themselves in status from other manual workers. The two are for obvious reasons likely to be bound up together—a middle-class self-rating and a preference for a higher-status job for a son are presumably both manifestations of an attitude to the

status hierarchy which, whatever its determinants, is different from that of the majority of those manual workers and their wives who prefer to call themselves "working-class". But it would seem that those who have reached the top level of income are not only more likely to describe themselves as "middle-class" but more likely, if they do, to have attitudes to the hierarchy of status which imply a divergence from the fraternalistic relative deprivations of status of the traditional proletarian.

. . . .

Self-rated "class" is a persistent correlate of attitudes to status, and the correlation—whether or not it can be properly described as a cause—is particularly marked among the richest manual workers and their wives. The correlation is not, perhaps, remarkable, once it has been shown that what manual workers and their wives mean by assigning themselves to the "middle class" can, despite the diversity of meanings, be generally interpreted as some sort of self-differentiation in terms of status. But there is a further conclusion to be drawn. Whereas the feelings of relative deprivation of class experienced by manual workers and their wives are a function of the comparisons which most readily present themselves to them, their relative deprivations of status are a function of normative as well as of comparative reference groups. It may be that if a question could be devised to show what comparative reference groups people choose when they have inequalities of status in mind, these would be found to correlate both with aspirations of status and with the choice of normative reference groups. But even if so, this would not alter the finding that the choice of self-assigned "class" has an effect on attitudes bearing on inequalities of status in a way that it does not on attitudes bearing on inequalities of class.

. . . .

It hardly needs saying that these questions do no more than touch on a few small facets of people's feelings about the inequalities in the social structure. It is possible not only that these are quite different on other topics which were not included in the questionnaire but also that within any one of the three dimensions of social inequality the same people may hold inconsistent or conflicting views. But it can, I think, be claimed on the evidence of the survey both that there is a clearly visible difference between attitudes to class and to status of the kind that the historical discussion suggested, and also that the influence of comparative and normative reference groups is demonstrably different in each case. It is in the light of these differences, therefore, that we must turn to the question how far the relative deprivations which English people were feeling in 1962 could be vindicated by appeal to social justice.

CHANGES OF SOCIAL STRUCTURE IN SOCIAL CONSCIOUSNESS

Stefan Nowak

The objective transformations effected by a socialist revolution in the social structure of a capitalist or pre-capitalist country are well known both from the theoretical literature and empirical research, or as well from official data and political programs.[1] . . . Comparatively less is known about the subjective aspects of these historical processes, i.e., the psychological concomitants of the changes in the social structure, and of psychological correlates of the newly shaped social stratification . . . with which

*This is a slightly revised version of the article that appeared in the *Polish Sociological Bulletin*, Vol. 2, 1964. Reprinted by permission of the author.

[1] See e.g. W. Wesołowski, A. Sarapata, *Prestiż zawodów i stanowisk* (*The Prestige of Occupations and Jobs*), "Studia Socjologiczne" 1961, No. 2; A. Malewski, *Czynniki determinujące postawy egalitarne* (*Factors Determining Egalitarian Attitudes*) Mimeographed; S. Nowak, *Social Views of Warsaw Students*, "The Pol. Soc. Bull.", 1962, No. 3–4 (5–6); A. Sarapata, *Iustum Pretium*, "The Pol. Soc. Bull." 1963, No. 1 (7).

this article is concerned. It is based on a questionnaire survey carried out in 1961 by the Chair of Sociology I of Warsaw University and the Public Opinion Research Centre at the Polish Radio. The survey was conducted on a quota sample of a male urban population above 18 years old.[2]

. . . .

FACTORS DETERMINING SOCIAL STATUS PERCEPTION

The first question of the questionnaire reads, "Is your position in society high or low as compared with that of other people in Poland?" The pre-categorized answers were classified on a seven-point scale, running from "very high" to "very low," and supplemented by the answer "hard to say."[3] The distribution of the answers is shown in Table 1.

Table 1 calls for a few remarks. The distribution of the subjective assessment of one's own social status approximates the shape of a normal curve biased "downward." But the largest percentage of answers falls into the "average" position. Furthermore, if it were possible to indicate some

[2] The survey was conducted both on a rural and on an urban quota sample of male population, but I omit in this report the rural data. The variables taken into account were: age, educational category and occupation (manual, non-manual) for the urban sample and age, occupational group and size of the farm for the rural sample.

After having fixed necessary proportions for the sample I realized that it comprised only few representatives of persons with university education (upper stratum of "intelligentsia") so I decided to bias the sample by adding 270 persons belonging to this social group so that both descriptive generalizations and multivariate analysis would be possible for this group. The questionnaires and the punch cards of the "overrepresentation" were marked in a special way and some of the analyses were done for the representative sample (tables marked by "R") and some for the total biased sample and these are marked by "T".

[3] The interviewer's instructions did not make more precise the meaning of the concepts "position in society" and aspects of social stratification which should be taken into account in answering this question. On the contrary, they were told to limit to the minimum any suggestions on the content of the questions, relying entirely on the respondents' intuition. For the aim of that question was to get a kind of general feeling and general perception of one's social status.

kind of division classifying extreme groups, then I would be inclined to consider points 1 (very low) and 2 (low) as evaluations expressing the feeling of deprivation connected with one's own social status; while points 5 (better than average), 6 (high) and 7 (very high) would be classified as positive evaluations. Finally, evaluations 3 and 4 would be treated as "emotionally neutral" positions. Thus, 28 per cent of the polled sample would be counted in the category feeling deprivation because of their social status, about 12.5 per cent—a positive evaluation and 54 per cent—a neutral evaluation. It is interesting that only 6 per cent were unable to answer the above question concerning their social status. . . .

TABLE 1 (R)

Is Your Position in Society High or Low as Compared with that of Other People in Poland?	%
7. Very high	0.5
6. High	4.5
5. Higher than average	7.4
4. Average	39.6
3. Lower than average	14.0
2. Low	21.8
1. Very low	6.0
Hard to say	6.2
Arithmetic mean of scores from 1 (very low) to 7 (very high) for the total sample	3.39

It was to be expected that differentiation by occupational groups would not be without significance here. And Table 2 shows this to be so. As can be seen, the occupational groups could be ordered on the basis of their "status evaluation". A number of additional conclusions flow from Table 2. First, in the category of unskilled workers more than half of the subjects expressed the feeling of deprivation connected with their social status, i.e., as evaluating their status as low or very low. At the same time, more than half of the creative intelligentsia and free professional group clearly belong to the privileged-feeling category, i.e., their evaluations being higher than average. As far as the skilled and non-manual workers are concerned, more than half of them fall into the intermediate, emotionally neutral category, while the decidedly dominant proportion of both groups define their status as average.

Both the percentage breakdown of the answers and the arithmetical mean of the corresponding scores seem to suggest still another conclusion: the distance dividing the skilled and non-manual workers is smaller than that separating these two from extreme groups.

Since our sample showed much educational differentiation, it would be reasonable to expect that the assessment of one's position in society would vary with education. The empirical findings, omitted here, proved this to be the case. The higher the

TABLE 2 (R)   Relationship Between the Perception of One's Social Status and Occupation (%)

Status Perception OCCUPATIONAL CATEGORY*	*7. Very high and 6. high*	*5. Higher than average*	*4. Average*	*3. Lower than average*	*2. Low and 1. very low*	*1. Mean score*
Unskilled workers	3.1	2.8	21.1	14.1	52.3	2.65
Skilled workers	2.7	4.2	42.8	14.9	30.2	3.25
Non-manual workers	7.1	11.9	46.0	14.0	15.0	3.78
Creative intelligentsia and free professions	24.3	25.7	31.4	7.1	7.2	4.53

* I omitted in Tables 6, 7, 8 the handicrafts group as too small. But I would like to add here that the mean score for handicraftsmen has been reckoned at 3.56, i.e., between skilled workers and non-manual workers.

TABLE 3 (T) Relationship Between Negative Perception of One's Social Status and Both Occupation and Education (%)

Occupational Category	*Educational Category*					
	INCOMPLETE ELEMENTARY	ELEMENTARY	INCOMPLETE SECONDARY	SECONDARY	INCOMPLETE HIGHER	HIGHER
Unskilled workers	69.8	62.8	—	—	—	—
Skilled workers	58.0	44.3	40.1	29.0	—	—
Non-manual workers	—	41.9	33.4	26.2	25.1	12.8
Free professions and creative intelligentsia	—	—	—	—	—	9.3

Note: The cells of the Table present the percentage of the following answers: very low + low + lower than average.

TABLE 4 (T) Relationship Between the Perception of One's Status (Mean Scores) and Occupation, Education, and Income—Combined

Occupation	*Education*	*Monthly Earnings*			
		to 1100	*1101–1800*	*1801–2900*	*above 2901*
Unskilled workers	incomplete elementary	2.40	2.73	2.75	
	elementary	2.49	2.72	3.23	
Skilled workers	incomplete elementary	2.39	2.34	3.44	
	elementary	2.84	3.16	3.43	3.64
	incomplete secondary		3.12	3.65	
	secondary		3.44	3.90	
	elementary		3.44	4.68	
Non-manual workers	incomplete secondary	2.76	3.55	4.19	
	secondary	3.31	3.58	3.90	4.35
	incomplete higher		3.81	3.98	5.00
	higher		3.81	4.30	4.76
Professions and creative intelligenstia	higher	3.40	4.22	4.53	5.10

* Note: Small categories are joined to the nearest category.

TABLE 5 (R).   Inter-generational Social Mobility of Urban Males in Poland*

Subject's Occupation		A. Agricultural Labourer		B. Farmer		C. Unskilled Worker		D. Worker (without qualification)		E. Skilled Worker	
		NO.	%	NO.	%	NO.	%	NO.	%	NO.	%
1. Unskilled worker	No.	15	4.6	89	27.2	32	9.8	81	24.8	57	17.4
	%	37.5		22.1		26.4		30.3		14.8	
2. Skilled worker	No.	19	2.3	164	20.0	61	7.5	118	14.4	233	28.5
	%	47.5	—	40.7	—	50.4	—	44.2	—	60.6	—
3. Handicraftsman	No.	—	—	2	7.2	—	—	1	3.7	5	18.5
	%			0.5				0.4		1.3	
4. Non-manual worker without higher educ.**	No.	6	1.0	127	21.5	25	4.2	59	10.0	81	13.7
	%	15.0		31.5		20.7		22.1		21.0	
5. Non-manual worker with higher educ.	No.			13	13.0	3	13.0	5	5.0	5	5.0
	%	—	—	3.2		2.5		1.9		1.3	
6. Others and no answer	No.			8	22.9			3	8.9	4	11.4
	%	—	—	2.0		—	—	1.1		1.0	
Total father's occupation	No.	40	2.1	403	21.2	121	6.4	267	14.3	385	20.3
	%	100%		100%		100%		100%		100%	

* The following sub-groups have been counted in the category "upwardly mobile": A.1, 2, 3, 4, 5: B. 1, 2, 3, 4, 5: C. 2, 3, 4, 5: D. 3, 4, 5: F. 4, 5: G. 4, 5: H. 5. This gives jointly 798 persons, or 42% of the sample.

education of our respondents, the more likely they were to perceive their social status as very high, high, or at least above average. The same direction of relationships was found when income was treated as the independent variable.

Hence the conclusion might be drawn that the perception of the rank of one's status depends on occupation as on education and material conditions. But the data in our survey indicating a strong relationship between the objective parameters of the social structure would caution against such a hasty conclusion. Under these circumstances, as is known, at least some of the correlations represented here might be spurious or might have to be explained by some intervening variable.

It may be suspected that differences in the perception of one's status by individual occupational groups may be "reduced"

to the differences in income or education among them. Let us analyse this hypothesis.

Table 3 presents the dependence of the perception of one's own status on both occupation and education of our subjects. It shows that education and occupation determine status perception independently of each other, i.e., that within the framework of each occupational group there exists a separate definite interrelation between status perception and education. Table 3 suggests still another interesting conclusion: with education held constant, the interrelation is no less definite between status perception and occupation. Among individuals with incompleted elementary education one's status evaluation is as a rule lower among unskilled than among skilled workers. And even among those with completed higher education one's status evaluation is higher among the creative

F. Handicraftsman		G. Merchant (store keeper)		H. Non-Manual Worker Without High Educ.		I. Nonman. Worker with Higher Educ. and Free Profession		J. Capitalist and Landowner		K. Other and No Answer		Total Subjects' Occupation	
NO.	%	NO.	%	NO.	%	NO.	%	NO.	%	NO.	%	NO.	%
25	7.6	2	0.6	10	3.1	2	0.6	—	—	14	4.6	327	100%
	10.6		3.9		4.0		2.4				24.1		17.2
133	16.3	17	2.1	45	5.5	10	1.2	—	—	18	2.2	818	100%
56.4	—	33.3	—	18.1	—	12.0	—	—	—	31.0	—	43.1	
12	44.4	4	14.8	1	3.7	1	3.7	1	3.7	—	—	27	100%
	5.1		7.5		0.4		1.2		25.0				1.4
52	8.8	21	3.6	157	26.6	40	6.8	3	0.5	13	3.2	590	100%
	22.0		41.2		63.1		48.2		75.0		37.2		31.1
10	10.0	6	6.0	26	26.0	28	28.0			4	4.0	100	100%
	4.2		11.8		10.4		33.8	—	—		7.0		5.3
4		1		10	28.9	2	5.8			3	8.9	35	100%
1.1	11.4	2.0		2.9	4.2		2.4	—	—	5.2	—		1.9
236	12.4	51	2.7	249	13.1	83	4.4	4	0.2	58	3.1	189	
100%		100%		100%		100%		100%		100%		100%	

** Respondents' occupations are categorized differently than in the previous tables. To obtain a category as close as possible to the category of the question on the father's occupation, the groups "non-manual workers" and "free professions" are combined, and then divided on the basis of completed higher education. Tables 5, 6, 7 data are calculated thus.

intelligentsia than among the non-manual workers category, although many of them undoubtedly occupy managerial positions in administration and in the economy. The same results were obtained when in multivariate analyses, first income and then occupation were each treated as independent variables.

Let us now see if we can grasp the interaction of all the three independent factors in determining the dependent variable (mean scores of social status perceptions). The necessary data are given in Table 4. They show that with any two of the independent variables held constant, the answers to the question on status perception are with clear regularity the function of the third variable.

The preceding paragraph hence may be summarised by the following conclusion: the perception of the rank of one's own social status in post-war Poland is independently determined by occupation, the economic situation and education; while these factors—which are in turn mutually interdependent—may either supplement or cancel the effects of each other.

THE PROCESSES OF SOCIAL MOBILITY AND THEIR REFLECTION IN SOCIAL CONSCIOUSNESS

. . . It is a well known fact that a large scale process of social mobility has taken place in Poland as a result of the social transformations. This has nevertheless been accompanied by only a fragmentary knowledge of the more precise course of this process.[4] Let us analyse the course and chief trends of

[4] See e.g. M. Pohoski, *Migracje ze wsi do miast* (*Migrations from the Rural Areas to the Cities*), Warszawa 1963.

the inter-generational social mobility by studying the relationships between occupational category of our respondents, and the occupation of their fathers.[5] The corresponding data are presented by Table 5. . . .

Let us now examine the pattern of inter-group movement. Lack of space precludes any detailed analysis, we can only signalise some of the most important conclusions.

(1) First of all it confirms the stereotypic knowledge about the extended social mobility in postwar Poland, predominantly upward mobility. But if we assume for the present that the transition from rural un-skilled to skilled labour, from manual to non-manual work and from clerks to "intelligentsia with a higher education" (as suggested by the notes to Table 5) represents the improvement of social status, then it must be said that 42 per cent of respondents hold higher positions than their fathers did at the same age.

The conclusion hence follows that under the above assumption 42 per cent of urban adult males must be reckoned in the category of "upwardly mobile."

(2) An analysis of the percentages in the vertical columns indicates that the parents' occupational status was not without its

[5] The wording of an open-ended question concerning fathers' occupation was as follows: "What was the occupation of your father when he was at your actual age?" The answers were coded in the way presented in Table 5.

effect on that of their sons. Whereas an average of 23 per cent of the sons of workers attained non-manual occupations, 34 per cent of the sons of peasants who moved to the cities did so. (Of course, this percentage would be much lower if we counted the whole population of peasants' sons.) The proportion of non-manual workers among the sons of non-manual workers without higher education amounted to 73 per cent and to 82 per cent among those of the free professions and intelligentsia with higher education. . . . Let us analyse now how the above objective changes in social status reflect themselves in social consciousness. (See Table 6.)

The lower marginals of Table 6 disclose that 44 per cent evaluate their status as "higher", while 22 per cent, or half as many, consider their status to have worsened as compared to that of their parents. It should be also noted that the higher the actual position of the given group, the more frequent are the convictions about their social advancement.

The 44 per cent figure of total advancement is quite close to the 42 per cent calculated by me on the basis of Table 5.

Table 7 establishes a fairly high contingency between the objective mobility on the social ladder and its subjective perception. The greater the distance between the occupations of father and son, the greater the chance of the corresponding change being reflected in the subject's evaluation—

TABLE 6 (T)   Relationship Between the Occupation and Perception of the Respondent's Own Social Mobility*

Occupational Groups	*Is Your Present Social Status Higher or Lower than That of your Father at the Same Age?*				
	MUCH HIGHER	HIGHER	ABOUT THE SAME	LOWER	MUCH LOWER
Unskilled workers	2.1	21.4	11.3	20.2	5.5
Skilled workers	5.4	33.0	33.4	17.7	4.3
Non-manual workers	13.3	42.3	19.2	16.7	4.7
Creative intelligentsia	15.9	40.3	20.1	14.4	5.7
Total sample	8.8	35.1	23.6	17.3	4.9

* The percentages do not add up horizontally to 100 because the "no answer" percentages are omitted. (C. S. H.)

TABLE 7 (R). Relationship Between Intergenerational Social Mobility and its Evaluation by the Respondent

Father's Occupation	Respondent's Occupation	Number of Persons in Given Group*	Is Your Present Status in the Society Higher or Lower than That of Your Father at the Same Age?						Evaluation of Status Changes in General		
			MUCH HIGHER	HIGHER	ABOUT THE SAME	LOWER	MUCH LOWER	HARD TO SAY	HIGHER	LOWER	DIFFERENCE HIGHER-LOWER
1	2	3	4	5	6	7	8	9	10	11	12
A. Agricultural laborer	1. unskilled worker	15	6.7	6.7	40.0	20.0	—	26.7	17.4	20.0	−2.6
	2. skilled worker	19	10.5	52.6	15.8	15.8	5.3	—	63.1	21.3	+41.8
B. Farmer	1. unskilled worker	89	1.1	28.1	37.1	16.9	5.6	11.2	29.2	22.5	+6.7
	2. skilled worker	164	5.5	43.3	28.0	12.2	3.7	7.9	48.8	15.9	+32.9
	4. non-manual worker**	127	15.0	50.4	12.6	13.4	1.6	7.1	65.4	15.0	+50.4
	5. non-manual worker with higher educ. and free profession	13	38.5	53.8	—	—	—	7.1	92.3	—	+92.3
C. Unskilled worker	1. unskilled worker	32	3.1	28.1	43.8	9.4	3.1	9.4	31.2	12.5	+18.7
	2. skilled worker	61	8.2	50.8	27.9	8.2	—	3.3	59.0	8.2	+50.8
	4. non-manual worker	81	32.0	40.0	20.0	2.0	—	—	72.0	2.0	+70.0
D. Worker without qualification	1. unskilled worker	118	—	17.3	60.5	14.8	3.7	3.7	17.3	18.5	−1.2
	2. skilled worker	59	5.9	33.1	38.1	16.1	2.5	4.2	39.0	18.6	+20.4
	4. non-manual worker	57	16.9	54.2	8.5	8.5	3.4	8.5	71.1	11.9	+59.2
E. Skilled worker	1. unskilled worker	23.3	5.3	17.5	35.1	24.6	10.5	7.0	22.8	35.1	−12.3
	2. skilled worker	81	5.6	31.3	36.1	16.3	3.4	7.3	36.9	19.7	+17.2
	4. non-manual worker	25	11.1	50.6	14.8	11.1	6.2	6.2	61.7	17.3	+44.4
F. Handicraftsman	1. unskilled worker	133	4.0	24.0	28.0	40.0	4.0	—	28.0	44.0	−16.0
	2. skilled worker	12	4.5	21.8	42.1	21.1	5.3	4.5	26.3	26.4	−0.1
	3. handicraftsman	52	25.0	16.7	25.0	25.0	8.3	—	41.7	33.3	+8.4
	4. non-manual worker	10	13.5	42.3	15.4	13.5	9.6	5.8	55.8	23.1	+32.7
	5. non-manual worker with higher educ. and free profession	17	30.0	60.0	—	10.0	—	—	90.0	10	+80.0
G. Merchant	2. skilled worker	21	—	5.9	47.1	41.2	5.9	—	5.9	47.1	−41.2
	4. non-manual worker	10	14.3	38.1	23.8	9.5	9.5	4.8	52.4	19.0	+33.4
H. Non-manual worker without higher education	1. unskilled worker	45	—	20.0	30.0	40.0	10.0	—	20.0	50.0	−30.0
	2. skilled worker	157	4.4	26.7	22.0	33.3	8.9	4.4	31.1	42.2	−11.1
	4. non-manual worker		3.8	29.9	31.2	24.8	6.4	3.8	33.7	31.2	+2.5
	5. non-manual worker with higher educ. and free profession	26	7.2	42.3	23.1	19.2	3.8	3.8	49.5	23.0	+26.5
I. Non-manual worker with higher educ. and free profession	2. skilled worker	10	—	10.0	20.0	30.0	40.0	10.0	—	70.0	−70.0
	4. non-manual worker	40	5.0	10.0	20.0	52.5	10.0	2.5	15.0	62.5	−47.5
	5. non-manual worker with higher educ. and free profession	28	3.6	17.9	42.9	25.0	14.3	—	21.5	39.3	−17.8

* We omitted the groups below 10 persons in number.

** Category "non-manual worker" refers to non-manual workers without higher education.

TABLE 8 (R)   Conviction of Advancement and Downgrading According to Father's and Son's Occupation (%)

Father's Occupation	Son's Occupation	Conviction of Advancement	Conviction of Downgrading	Difference
C. 1 Unskilled worker	unskilled worker	31.2	12.5	+18.7
D. 2 Skilled worker	skilled worker	39.0	18.6	+20.4
F. 3 Handicraftsman	handicraftsman	41.7	33.3	+8.4
H. 4 Non-manual worker	non-manual worker	33.7	31.2	+2.5
I. 5 Free profession and intelligentsia with higher education	free profession and intelligentsia with higher education	21.5	39.3	−11.8

in the form of a dominant conviction of advancement or downgrading. Nevertheless, the correlation between the objective mobility, as signified by Table 5, and the conviction that the subject's social status is higher or lower than his father's, was by no means a perfect one. Let us consider some of the deviations from it.

There is first of all the fact that the feeling of advancement was by no means dominant in all the groups characterized as "upwardly mobile" in Table 5.

An analysis of the last column of Table 7 shows that the sons of agricultural labourers or peasants being now unskilled workers were by no means convinced in majority that their status was higher than that of their parents. It hence follows that on a mass scale migrants from rural to urban areas have advanced socially only when they attain at least the position of skilled workers.

Secondly, among some of the groups we did not count in the socially advanced category, e.g., in which the father and son have the same occupation, there is a dominant conviction of social advancement. This question deserves a little more attention.

An analysis of the rows, with a convergence of father and son occupations, gives the figures shown in Table 8.

Reflected in these figures, in my opinion, are what may be called the advancement or downgrading of entire social groups. Thus workers—sons of workers locating their own and their parents' positions on the background of the corresponding social structures—evaluate their status as higher though they belong to "the same" occupational category. They thereby also express

TABLE 9 (T)   Perception of Changes in Social Structure by Occupational Group

Social-Occupational Groups	Are Social Distinctions Between People of Different Groups in Poland Generally Greater or Smaller Today than Before the War?*				
	MUCH SMALLER	A LITTLE SMALLER	ABOUT THE SAME	A LITTLE GREATER	MUCH GREATER
Unskilled workers	22.3	29.2	13.5	7.6	7.3
Skilled workers	28.2	29.6	13.9	5.7	7.3
Non-manual workers	37.9	31.2	10.8	4.3	5.2
Creative intelligentsia and free professions	30.9	36.0	16.0	2.2	3.6
Total sample	29.2	30.3	13.2	3.8	7.0*

* 14.1% of respondents answered: "hard to say." Most of them belonged to the younger age groups.

indirectly the conviction that the over-all position of the working class in the social structure has improved. It's significant that the handicraftsmen arrive at a similar conclusion, although perhaps in a more controversial manner. Among non-manual workers without higher education the percentage convinced of their advancement is just a little above those convinced of the opposite. Whereas those whose fathers before the war were in the free professions and intelligentsia with higher education category definitely evaluate their own status as worse, although they belong to the same category. They thereby express the conviction that the status of this group as a whole grew worse because of the changes in the social structure.

EVALUATION OF SOCIAL DISTANCE AND THE PERCEPTION OF DIFFERENTIATION IN THE SOCIAL STRUCTURE

Let us see now to what degree the transformations in the social structure of postwar Poland are reflected in the social consciousness.

According to the lower marginals of Table 9 the conviction is dominant that the changes effected a lessening of social differences. But the answers to this question are not independent of the respondents'

social position. As the data indicate, there is a definite tendency to the growth of optimism with regards to the egalitarian character of the changes, with the rise in the respondents' social status. As many as 38 per cent of non-manual workers and only 22 per cent of unskilled workers are convinced that social differences are much smaller today. It is worth noting that a certain decline of optimism (as compared with non-manual workers) in the evaluation of the egalitarian processes of the social structure is again observable among the creative intelligentsia and in the free professions.

The prevailing social structure is nevertheless regarded as marked by a fairly strong system of differentiation. In answer to the question what divides people in Poland, we obtained an interesting number of factors of division in the social structure. The relative data are presented in the first columns of Table 10.

The answers indicate that economic differentiation is regarded as the factor that divides people most. It is interesting that the factors which could be described as highly personal, such as political attitude or religious views, are considered weaker bases of social division than education or occupation, so clearly connected with social stratification. Also worthy of notice

TABLE 10 (R)   Perceived Factors of Social Division and Social Animosity (%)

Basis of Differentiation	WHICH IN YOUR OPINION DIVIDES PEOPLE IN OUR SOCIETY?		WHICH OF THE LISTED DIFFERENCES ARE IN YOUR OPINION THE CAUSE OF ANIMOSITY IN OUR SOCIETY?
	Very strongly	Rather strongly	
Differences in earnings or wealth	45.7	36.0	71.5
Differences in education	26.1	45.0	45.5
Differences between managerial and non-managerial positions	25.0	33.1	41.8
Division into manual and non-manual workers	15.9	41.1	35.4
Differences in manner of behaving in company	16.7	39.8	28.0
Differences in religious outlook	21.3	26.9	41.3
Differences of political views	13.8	27.4	43.6
Division between city and country	10.9	33.3	30.2
Differences of social origin	6.4	16.2	16.7

TABLE 11 (R)   Typology of Ways of Perceiving Social Animosity Along Different Dimensions of Social Stratification[6]

	BELIEVING THAT EITHER ALL OR AT LEAST MAJORITY OF THE GIVEN CATEGORY FEELS ANIMOSITY			
Basis of Differentiation	"At the top" as well as "at the bottom"	Only "at the top"	Only "at the bottom"	Neither "at the top" nor "at the bottom"
Education	19.8	18.1	18.9	31.4
Manual and non-manual work	17.9	11.8	22.7	38.2
Subordinates—authorities	21.6	10.1	19.8	34.3
Income	20.5	3.7	47.6	12.4
High or low positions	23.5	13.6	20.1	24.9
Country—city	19.8	11.0	13.4	41.0

is the fact that social origin is basically regarded as an entirely indifferent factor of social division.

Answers to the question as to which dividing factors cause social animosity are given in the last column of the same Table 10.

Let us now consider the rank order of different factors. Examining the columns of Table 10 we see that differences in earnings are clearly and uniformly given priority. Education is second in importance, while differences in social origin are definitely in the last place in both rank orders. It must be considered however that differences in religious or political views—among the lowest places as factors of social division—occupy considerably higher positions as factors of animosity among people.

The question on the source of animosity between people is to be found also at the end of the questionnaire, but in a different form. We asked for instance, if the educated dislike the uneducated and if the uneducated dislike the educated, if the high earners dislike the low paid, and vice versa, etc. This enabled us to study not only what, according

[6] The question, as it appeared in the Polish version of the article, read, "In your opinion which people in our country feel animosity? (a) educated toward uneducated: almost all, majority, minority, nobody or almost nobody, difficult to say. (b) uneducated toward educated: almost all, majority, minority, nobody or almost nobody, difficult to say." See Stefan Nowak, *Psychologiczne Aspekty Przemian Struktury Spolecznej, Studja Socjologiczne*, Vol. 2, No. 21, 1966, p. 101. (C. S. H.)

to our respondents, were the sources, but also the social location and the directions of social animosity.

On the basis of these answers we were able then to classify our respondents as to whether (within the given dimension of social stratification such as education for instance) they feel animosity to come only "from the top" (from the educated for the uneducated) or only "from the bottom" (from the uneducated for the educated) or from both at once, or if they are convinced that there is no conflict along the given stratification dimension. As a result we made the following typology of the manners of perceiving tension in the social structure by different occupational groups.

Table 11 shows certain interesting regularities. We first of all ascertain that the most numerous category consider the social system to be free of tension on both sides of the lines of social division. The next category sees the mutual animosity on both sides of mentioned lines of differentiation. We see furthermore that on all dimensions animosity is perceived more frequently as coming "from the bottom" than "from the top." This difference is most pronounced in dimension of income, 3.7 and 47.6, respectively. Hence when tension of a one directional character is perceived in our sample the tendency is to locate it more frequently in the lower social strata.

It could be expected that the attitude toward the social structure and toward the sources of tension within it would be

TABLE 12 (T) Perception of Sources of Division in Society by Respondents' Occupation

Occupational Groups	WHAT IN YOUR OPINION DIVIDES PEOPLE IN OUR SOCIETY? (% OF ANSWERS "VERY STRONGLY")					
	Education	Income	Political views	Kind of behaviour	Manual and non-manual work	Managerial and non-managerial position
Unskilled workers	34.2	54.1	18.3	16.8	23.3	32.1
Skilled workers	27.2	45.7	19.6	15.0	18.5	25.2
Non-manual workers	19.4	35.6	20.2	17.1	11.2	19.7
Creative intelligentsia and free professions	23.7	46.8	28.1	23.7	6.5	20.1

TABLE 13 How Different Occupational Categories Perceive the Patterns of Social Tension Along the Different Dimensions of Social Stratification (% Who Think Almost All or at Least a Majority Feel Dislikes)

Occupation	EDUCATION				MANUAL—NON-MANUAL				MANAGERIAL—NON-MANAGERIAL				INCOME				DIFFERENCE OF POSITIONS			
	1*	2	3	4	1	2	3	4	1	2	3	4	1	2	3	4	1	2	3	4
3. Unskilled workers	21.4	22.6	13.8	25.7	20.7	20.5	15.0	32.1	22.3	12.2	15.3	28.7	25.1	6.9	38.2	9.5	22.9	16.8	17.7	16.6
4. Skilled workers	20.2	22.8	13.0	31.3	22.4	13.9	16.8	36.8	22.4	11.0	16.7	35.8	22.2	3.9	44.4	14.3	23.6	13.8	17.6	26.5
5. Non-manual workers	16.2	10.3	29.6	35.3	11.7	5.2	35.9	39.4	17.6	7.5	26.9	36.4	16.0	3.2	58.3	11.6	20.5	11.3	27.4	27.1
6. Creative intelligentsia and free professions	12.9	7.2	43.2	28.8	9.4	2.2	39.6	40.4	17.3	6.5	36.7	28.8	20.1	0.7	60.4	7.9	20.9	5.0	25.3	23.0

* 1—at the top as well as at the bottom; 2—only at the top; 3—only at the bottom; 4—neither at the top nor at the bottom.

dependent on the place one occupies in the social system. That this is so is shown by the data in Table 12, in which the bases of social division are related to respondents' occupations.

What conclusions are suggested by Table 12? We observe first of all a definite tendency that the higher the respondents' social position the more rarely are they convinced that certain social differences create divisions among the people in Poland. This pertains to earnings, education, to the distinction between manual and non-manual labour, importance of positions or posts held, etc. But it must be noted that in 3 out of 4 cases the creative intelligentsia is more frequently convinced than are the non-manual workers that given differentiations definitely create divisions among people in Polish society.

The creative intelligentsia also seems to attach much greater importance than any other occupational group to . . . other sources of social distinction: differences in political views and in kind of behaviour ("good manners").

There is an interesting correlation between the perception and localization of social animosity and the respondent's social. position. Two different and complementary tendencies seen from Table 13 are to be noted here:

1. The higher is the social position, the greater the chance that the respondent will regard the structure as a non-conflicting one in both directions. And the converse: the lower the social position—the greater the chance of his perceiving mutual animosity between the groups.

2. The higher the respondent's position the greater the tendency to see the animosity as coming from the bottom. The lower the position—the greater is the tendency to see it as coming from the top, regardless of what line of dichotomic division is taken into account.

The first of the mentioned mechanisms is well known from other researches on psychological aspects of social stratification in different countries.

The cause of the latter mechanism might be seen perhaps in the fact that in Poland, owing to the widespread socialist patterns of egalitarian ideology and of harmonious images of the social structure, inter-group tensions are inhibited. Instead of being expressed in the direct answers they may occur rather in a "projective" form.

The combined action of the two mechanisms gives us a system of relationships in which a high social position increases the chances either to see the source of antagonism in the lower social strata, or to regard the structure as a whole as being harmonious. Conversely, the members of the lower social strata are inclined either to see animosity as coming only from those on top, or to perceive the structure as a conflicting one along the given dimension.

Let us now analyse another item of our questionnaire, namely, the demands for the egalitarianization of the social structure in the future.

We see from the lower marginals of Table 14 that over 80 per cent of the respondents demand the increase of equality in our social structure and almost half of them demand the complete abolition of all social differentiation. It's interesting that here too there is a relationship with the respondents' occupational status. As many as 53 per cent of skilled workers demand complete equality in that social structure as compared to 38 per cent of the creative intelligentsia.

CONCLUSIONS

Let us briefly summarize the main conclusions of the above preliminary analysis of the data of our survey. The social structure of the post-war Poland is characterized by a fairly large amount of upward social mobility with fairly high opportunities for social advancement. Both the inter-generational mobility and the advancement opportunities are fairly correctly "reflected" by social consciousness and there is a visible correlation between the changing of one's social position and its perception. At the same time a conviction prevails that there has been a reduction of social distance between the various social groups.

On the other hand, despite the sharp perception of all these social transformations, in the people's consciousness the egalitarian process is by no means regarded as completed. There are first of all clearly

TABLE 14 **Egalitarian Postulates for the Future as Related to Occupation**

Occupational Category	WOULD YOU WANT TO SEE IN THE FUTURE THE SOCIAL DIFFERENCES IN POLAND?			
	Entirely disappear	Diminish	Remain unchanged	Increase
Unskilled workers	44.0	38.2	4.0	3.7
Skilled workers	52.7	36.9	2.8	2.8
Non-manual workers	48.0	41.2	3.2	2.2
Free professions and creative intelligentsia	38.1	43.2	3.6	7.2
Total sample (R)	45.5	38.0	3.	2.8

differentiated feelings regarding social status, strongly correlated with one's occupation, income and education. At the same time a number of factors are still identified as sources of social division and tension in the social structure—with the economic differences in the first place among them. The perception of social differentiation combined with the acceptance of egalitarian ideals leads to the demand for the further reduction of, and, with almost half of the people, for the complete abolition of all social differences in the social structure.

The studied population seems to be influenced by two mechanisms shaping the image of the existing structure and the demand for the extension of social equality.

On the one hand, the population as a whole is under the strong influence of the egalitarian ideals of socialism with the demand for transformation of the social structure in the direction of the abolition of social differences. On the other hand, the well known sociological mechanisms continue to operate and they cause a decrease in the attractiveness of egalitarian ideals with the increase of social and economic position, while the egalitarian demands increase, as they are linked with hopes that they will lead to the improvement of social position. The interaction of both these mechanisms—interest group determinant of social consciousness and pressure of egalitarian ideals of socialist ideology—was presented above.

PART IV
Consequences of Stratification: Differential Life Chances and Ways of Life

---

In a complex society there is hardly an area of social life in which some aspects do not differ with social stratum. This is acknowledged in the methodological procedure of empirical sociological studies, almost automatic today, of statistically controlling the *class factor,* irrespective of the subject of study. Of all the variables that the sociologist employs in his analysis, few are as predictive as socioeconomic status. The vast number of specific areas, patterns, and nuances of behavior that vary with social stratum could perhaps be best subsumed under the concepts of *life chances* and *ways of life*. The first is easily recognized as derived from Max Weber. The second is a revision of Weber's *styles of life*. The word *style*, it seems to me, may not convey the breadth of the meaning of the concept because it carries the connotation of form, of manner of expression, rather than the substance of life. Way of life conveys an image of the total nature of social existence—including the general orientation to basic universal human problems, the goals and values, and the social organization—as well as its modes of expression.

To begin with life chances, the possibilities throughout one's life cycle, from the chance to stay alive during the first year after birth, through the school years—the chance to attend a scholastically adequate primary school, to finish high school, to go to college—to the chance of reaching a ripe old age, all are to some extent determined by the stratum to which one is born. The first selection in this Part deals with the basic chance to stay alive. In his "Social Class, Life Expectancy and Overall Mortality," Aaron Antonovsky surveys the statistical data of thirty studies ranging through the centuries and different Western nations. On the basis of this extensive survey he arrives at the general hypothesis—presented at the end of his article—that when mortality rates are very high or very low in a society, class differences tend to be small. As he expresses it, "when men are quite helpless before the threat of death or when men have made great achievements in dealing with this threat, life chances will tend to be equitably distributed." But when the achievements are only moderate, the class differences are substantial.

As for the data that suggested this conclusion, those *prior* to the nineteenth century are rather limited. They seem to indicate, however, that life expectancy, which was quite short in comparison with today's, did not differ with social stratum. The less-limited nineteenth-century data reveal a tendency toward the widening of class differences in mortality. This was probably the result of the rapid increase in the life expectancy of the middle and upper strata while that of the lower strata remained low. Toward the latter half of that century the class differences began to decrease, and by now they are narrow as compared to the past. But in the last three decades the trend toward the closing of the class gap "has been checked, if not halted." The large difference that exists is between the lowest level of the working class (Warner's lower lower) and the rest of the population.

Antonovsky poses the problem of forecasting future trends, always a delicate issue in sociology. He does not, however, go beyond stating (and, in light of present knowledge, he could not validly do so) the various logical possibilities of what might occur in the future : the narrow gap might remain; it might completely disappear; or it might widen. In a sense, the inability to foretell future trends in this area resembles very much the situation of class differentials in the fertility of Western countries. As national birth rates went down, class differentials in fertility were increased. But the trend that followed during the first decades of the twentieth century was one of a narrowing in the degree of inverse correlation between fertility and class. As for predicting the future trend, two alternative views are vying with each other: There are those who anticipate a complete disappearance of class differentials and those who predict the ultimate emergence of a positive correlation between fertility and status.[1] But then it would seem far harder still to forecast the future of differential class fertility than of mortality. Class variations in mortality, after all, depend primarily on access to public health and medicine. In fertility, family size preferences must be taken into account. The latter are surely more variable and uncertain than the former.

In moving from life chances to a discussion of our readings about the ways of life of different strata, it is important to state at the outset that two competing hypotheses run through the vast sociological literature on this subject. Ralph H. Turner labels them the *culture variation* and the *subculture* hypotheses. The first holds that there is a uniform system of values, common to all classes, and that class differences consist mainly of variations of these values, differential commitment to them, and differential rates of deviation from them. In contrast, the assumption behind the subculture approach is that each class is to some extent a "self-contained universe, developing a distinctive set of values which guides its members' way of life." And, although these class subcultures "are constrained by the necessity to maintain working relations with other classes within a general national framework," they are nevertheless fundamentally different from each other, even contradictory in many respects. [2]

For analytic purposes, these two positions can be stated as if they were mutually

[1] Dennis H. Wrong, "Trends in Class Fertility in Western Nations," *The Canadian Journal of Economics and Political Science,* Vol. XXIV, No. 2, May, 1958, pp. 216–229.
[2] Ralph H. Turner, *The Social Context of Ambition,* San Francisco: Chandler Publishing Company, 1964, pp. 9–10.

exclusive, but in reality they are not. As a matter of fact, the major exponents of each do not deny the other but rather give less importance to the other position. Those who stress the common value system, foremost among whom is Parsons, also recognize the existence of "secondary or subsidiary or variant value patterns."[3] On the other hand, those who stress that different values are held by different classes do not deny that a common core of values also exists. Thus, the disagreement is mainly over the relative importance of common values or different class values in a society. Nevertheless, attempts have been made to reconcile these views as if they were inherently contradictory. Among those attempting reconciliation, Hyman Rodman devised the concept of "lower-class value stretch" as a way of resolving the "contraditions, or apparent contradictions"[4] between the preceding two positions. The concept refers to a supposed lower commitment of the lower classes to the general values of society—they accept and even look with favor on certain deviations from these values—and a wider range of specific values. Its validity, it seems, could be questioned on the basis, among other things, of Sutherland's material on "white-collar" crime. He demonstrated vast areas of criminal behavior of persons not in the lowest strata.[5] All strata seem to accept certain deviations but those deviations accepted in one may not be accepted in another.

Herbert Gans, as will become evident to the reader, clearly leans heavily toward the subculture hypothesis. In our selection from his *Urban Villagers,* he addresses himself to the main class subcultures in contemporary America. His descriptions are based on the voluminous literature that exists on this subject, as well as on his own observations. Because his is a concise presentation that manages to capture the essence of each subculture, it can serve as a frame in which to place the remaining selections in this part of the book. Alas, what is lacking in his pages is a description of the upper-class subculture. Perhaps this reflects the comparatively meager knowledge that we have of it, for the upper class is not easily accessible for sociological study.[6] Still, what we do know suggests that, although it is at the opposite side of the social hierarchy, its subculture has a number of similarities with that of the lower class. For example, the family structure of each has certain

---

[3] Talcott Parsons, *The Social System,* New York: Free Press, 1964, p. 169.

[4] Hyman Rodman, "The Lower-Class Value Stretch," *Social Forces,* Vol. 42, December, 1963, pp. 205–215.

[5] Yes, criminal statistics consistently show that crime varies inversely with social class. But despite the challenge by Sutherland, over three decades ago, that official statistics are not a valid measure, sociological analysis to this very day proceeds largely as if they were. Sutherland challenged the conventional concept of crime, which is the taking-off point of the theories of crime. The theories are incorrect because their concept of crime is insufficient, a reflection of the popular notion of it, which omits white-collar crime. Basically white-collar crime does not differ from the crime of the lower strata: both are violations of the criminal laws. They differ mainly in the implementation of the criminal laws that apply to them, Sutherland argues. The upper class has greater influence in administering them in their own interests.

Once the concept of crime is clarified to include white-collar crime, it puts into question the presumptive high association between low socioeconomic status and crime. And yet today—so many years after Sutherland gave us this conceptual clarification—we still do not know the comparative rate of criminality (*including white-collar crime*) among the various classes. Thus we cannot say with confidence more than could be deduced from the Sutherland essay: the *type* of criminal behavior varies with social class. Whether the total amount differs with class is still an unanswered question. And this, I am convinced, could be extended to deviant behavior in general. See Edwin H. Sutherland, *White Collar Crime,* New York: Holt, Rinehart and Winston, 1949; Gildert Geis, ed., *White-Collar Criminal,* New York: Atherton Press, 1968.

[6] For some insight into the upper-class subculture, see Digby Baltzell, *Philadelphia Gentlemen,* Glencoe, Illinois: Free Press, 1958, and his *Protestant Establishment,* New York: Vintage Books, 1964. Also see August B. Hollingshead and Frederick C. Redlich, *Social Class and Mental Illness,* New York: John Wiley & Sons, Inc., 1958.

extended-family features, in contrast to the isolated nuclear type of the middle classes. The function of extension in each is, however, different: in the upper class it serves mainly to perpetuate advantages; in the lower, it serves as a mechanism of mutual aid. Another example is that both lack emphasis on upward mobility, so characteristic of the middle-class subculture. Upper-class people are already on top, whereas the lower class tends to view social advancement as beyond them.

Gans, however, talks of two subcultures in the lower strata. He separates sharply working-class subculture from the lower-class one (corresponding to Warner's lower-lower and to Myrdal's underclass), as well as from the middle-class subculture. But the fourth subculture that he describes, what he terms *professional upper-middle class,* he considers a "variant of the middle class." In addition to the basic description of each, we find an answer to an implicit question: Why these different subcultures? And this is especially important because many sociologists begin with subculture—usually in the narrow sense of values—as a given and explain specific differential class behavior in terms of it. In some of these treatments the differential class values appear as the prime movers, and one gets no indication of where they come from or why they exist. Gans explains the differential class subcultures as *responses* that have developed to a common life situation in which people of a given stratum find themselves. He expresses it, however, a bit differently: they are responses to "the opportunities and deprivations that they encounter"—the occupational opportunities of males being especially crucial.

The author carries his analysis beyond the explanation of the "why" of differential class subculture into what he terms the *evaluation* of the working-class and lower-class subcultures. He sees the first as "a generally satisfactory way of adapting to the opportunities which society has made available" but also points to some negative features. But the net effect of the lower-class subculture he evaluates as negative, as pathological. One could rephrase his presentation in more neutral terms—but in what some might consider the usual functional parlance—by considering the positive and negative consequences of each of these subcultures for its participants.

Gans points to the negative consequences of the *female-based family,* which is so prevalent in the lower class. Its socialization of male children is particularly inadequate: it produces people who can only work at unskilled jobs and these are becoming scarce. Subsequently to the Gans presentation, it has been shown that such families are on the rise in the United States.[7] It has also been argued that certain trends of modernization and reduction of family economic roles lead to an increase in *matrifocality.*[8] More recently, on the basis of a study of families in public housing, Helen Icken Safa advanced the hypothesis that the modern welfare state provides one more condition that weakens the economic role of the man in the lower-class household:

It is impossible to isolate any single factor of matrifocality—be it economic insecurity, the physical division of labor, or the modern welfare state. Any of these factors will hamper the man in his role as economic provider while the woman's role in caring for the household and children is left intact. Thus, whenever these factors operate, and

[7] Helen Icken Safa, "The Female-Based Household in Public Housing: A Case Study in Puerto Rico," *Human Organization,* Vol. 24, Summer, 1965, p. 135.
[8] Peter Kunstadter, "A Survey of Consanguine or Matrifocal Family," *American Anthropologist,* Vol. 65, No. 1, 1963, p. 64.

whenever the man is dependent largely on his economic role to maintain his position in the household, then matrifocal families are likely to develop.[9]

These studies suggest then that modern industrial society is working at a cross-purpose in this sphere. On the one hand, modernization and the welfare state lead to an increase in female-based households; on the other, it requires fewer of the type of males bred in such households, whose socialization makes them mostly fit for unskilled jobs that are diminishing. The implication is that a family structure is spreading in the lower class whose negative consequences for society as a whole may even outweigh such consequences for the lower-class individual.

A deeper insight into some negative consequences of the working-class subculture, as distinct from that of the lower class, is obtained from our next reading: "Blue-Collar Marriage—Barriers to Marital Communication" by Mirra Komarovsky. It is based on a study of fifty-eight marriages, using the case-study method, in a community of 50,000, with a heavy working-class population, which the author calls Glenton. These marriages are of people whom she designates the "stable blue-collar class" and that corresponds to Gans' working class, *not* his lower class. As Komarovsky explains in the book from which the selection here is taken, she set out to study the married life of what was intended to be a homogenous group of blue-collar workers: all husbands currently employed, native-born of native parents, not over forty years of age, with high school education or less, and parents of at least one child. But this restricted sample turned out to be not so homogenous with respect to the characteristics of their marriages. As the reader will gather from the selection, and it is true of most of the aspects of marriage studied by the author, the variation follows the level of education. (The major contrast appears between high school graduates and those who had not completed high school.) But, as she emphasizes, they are variations within the same subculture. The differences found between educational categories are "of degree, with considerable overlapping among them."[10]

Our selection from Komarovsky's book focuses on the socially structured barriers to communication between husbands and wives that are rooted in the working-class subculture. Very few shared interests are found between spouses. She traces back the sharp separation of male and female interests to the emphasis on male-female differences in early home socialization.[11] In addition, the home socialization results in a "trained incapacity to share," says the author. The subculture stresses the nonverbosity and reserve of men as distinct from the characteristics of women. Another factor, according to Kamarovsky, is "the impoverishment of the quality of life" among blue-collar people that severely limits their interests. It narrows the overlapping interests between husband and wife and also stunts personal development. There may be little or nothing to communicate. This, as the reader will gather, is quite different from the evaluation of the working-class subculture by Gans and resembles more his view of lower-class life. However,

[9] Safa, *op. cit.,* p. 139.

[10] Mirra Komarovsky, *Blue-Collar Marriage,* New York: Vintage Books, 1967, pp. 20–22.

[11] Relevant here is the subsequent analysis of working-class home socialization as failing to give individuals experience in role distance. See Julienne Ford, Douglas Young and Steven Box, "Functional Autonomy, Role Distance and Social Class," *British Journal of Sociology,* Vol. 18, December, 1967, pp. 370–381; for a thorough analysis of the findings of empirical studies in the United States over a 25-year period of social-class differences in child rearing, see Urie Bronfenbrenner, "Socialization and Social Class Through Time and Space," in E. E. Maccoby, T. M. Newcomb, and E. L. Hartley, eds., *Readings in Social Psychology,* New York: Henry Holt and Co., 1958, pp. 400–425.

we also get in the Komarovsky presentation a glimpse of some positive consequences of the working-class subculture. They are brought out indirectly when the author turns her attention to those couples in her sample whose communication is quite satisfying to each partner and who, nevertheless, in their values and behavior adhere to the working-class subculture. Despite the vulnerabilities inherent in that culture, these marriages function well because they benefit from *special supports* that are also rooted in the working-class subculture. These are the availability of close relatives and friends who fulfill for both, but primarily for the wife, functions lacking in marriage.

The crucial tie between family and stratification comes through not only in the readings by Gans and Kamarovsky but also in many of the theoretical and empirical articles throughout the book. What makes Kent Geiger's article, especially written for this volume, so pungent is that it deals with this family tie in the Soviet Union, a society that once made a determined effort to abolish it. First of all, in the Soviet Union, as elsewhere, there are the obvious differential chances and advantages that are automatically transmitted to children, because they live together with their parents, that can be subsumed under standard of living. The differences in such areas as housing and consumer goods and services may in a sense be sharper than in Western democracies because of the greater shortages of these goods in the Soviet Union.

Apart from the pronounced differences in the standard of living, there is the widespread pattern, discussed by Geiger, of persons in higher positions obtaining special access to opportunities and services for themselves and their families.[12] And even in the Soviet Union differential home socialization of the different strata plays an important part, despite the fact that socialization by agencies other than the family is unquestionably stronger there than in Western countries. The government, youth organizations, mass media, and so on, make a consistent effort to instill official values and approved modes of behavior in the entire population, irrespective of socioeconomic position. Nevertheless, we learn from the evidence presented by Geiger that such behavior varies from stratum to stratum. Take, for example, religious behavior in the Soviet Union, which is branded as a "survival" perpetuated by the family. There is a marked inverse relationship between religious practice and social stratum or what Geiger refers to as "social level." Parenthetically, this represents an opposite relation to that which exists in the United States. Numerous studies reveal a strong positive relationship between church participation and social class in America.[13] But then religious observance represents normative behavior in America and deviant behavior in the Soviet Union.

If religious and other behavior that is in conflict with the societal norms varies inversely with social position in the Soviet Union, the opposite seems to hold true for certain kinds of normatively approved behavior. Geiger tells us that evidence points to political conformity varying directly with *social level*. Also, the proportion

---

[12] For additional corroboration, see the impressive evidence on the advantages of Soviet children from the upper strata over their working-class competitors in seeking managerial positions assembled by David Granick, *The Red Executive*, Garden City: Doubleday Company, 1960, chap. 3. Also see Janina Markiewicz–Lagneau, "Les Problèmes de Mobilité Sociale en U.R.S.S.," *Cahiers du Monde Russe et Soviétique*, Vol. 7, No. 2, 1966, pp. 160–188.

[13] Eric Goode, "Social Class and Church Participation," *American Journal of Sociology*, Vol. 72, July, 1966, pp. 102–111; N. J. Demerath, III, *Social Class in American Protestantism*, Chicago: Rand McNally and Co., 1965.

of youngsters who graduate from high school and attend a university varies directly. There is, moreover, a positive association between parental societal status and the educational and occupational aspirations of youth, quite similar to the pattern found in the United States.

Some light is thrown on American class differences in educational and occupational aspiration by Mizruchi. In the selection here from his book, *Success and Opportunity,* he concentrates on the values of different classes, specifically values related to the American notion of success. The author set before himself the larger task of testing Merton's theory of anomie: that the social structure exercises pressure on lower-class individuals to engage in nonconforming behavior. To summarize Merton's well-known thesis: the goals of success are held out as legitimate objectives for all in the United States while the acceptable means of reaching these goals are largely unavailable to people in the lower classes. This results in a tendency in these classes toward practices that deviate from institutional norms. [14]

Some time ago Herbert H. Hyman questioned whether the goals of success have been uniformly assimilated in the American population. [15] Responding to this, Merton stated that ". . . among the problems calling for further research [is] the following: the extent to which Americans in different social strata have in fact assimilated the same culturally induced goals and values." [16] Mizruchi's work represents such research and it proceeds very much along the lines set by Herbert Hyman in his pioneering essay, "The Value System of Different Classes." The basic questions, quite similar to Hyman's, to which Mizruchi's empirical study addressed itself were: "What is the distribution of success values among the social classes?" "To what extent do members of different classes hold other values that aid or hinder them in their efforts to achieve success?" "To what extent do these members believe that opportunities for getting ahead are available to them?"

One of his findings is that education is more highly valued as an end in itself in the middle than in the lower strata. His contention is that the greater importance given to education as an end value by the middle classes provides them with greater opportunities for advancement.

If ability and formal education have long vied for first place as a means for advancement in American society, the latter has by now gained its victory. One must keep in mind that achievement in many positions that rank high in occupational status actually requires formal education. Occupational achievement is positively correlated with both amount and quality of education. In the words of Parsons, ". . . in our society experience in the course of formal education is to be regarded as a series of apprenticeships for adult occupational roles." [17]

That this kind of experience differs considerably with social class has been amply demonstrated by numerous empirical studies conducted in the last twenty years. [18] They consistently show a positive correlation between social class and academic achievement. Lower-class children tend to be poorer in school performance (in terms of grades, failures, and scholastic awards) and much higher in

[14] Robert K. Merton, "Social Structure and Anomie," in *Social Theory and Social Structure,* Glencoe, Illinois: Free Press, 1957, pp. 131–160.

[15] Herbert H. Hyman, "The Value System of Different Classes: A Social Psychological Contribution to the Analysis of Stratification," in Reinhard Bendix and Seymour Martin Lipset, eds., *Class, Status, and Power,* Glencoe, Illinois: Free Press, 1953, pp. 426–442.

[16] Merton, "Continuities in the Theory of Social Structure and Anomie," in *op. cit.,* p. 170.

[17] Parsons, *op. cit.,* p. 240.

[18] For a summary of their findings, see Robert E. Herriott and Nancy Hoyt St. John, *Social Class and the Urban School,* New York: John Wiley and Sons, Inc., 1966, pp. 4–12, 22–25, 203–211.

early withdrawal from high school (dropouts). In the newer studies the focus has shifted from that on the social class of the individual child to a focus on the social class composition of the school and its effects on learning. The essence of these effects is well captured in one sentence by Bernard Barber, "The public schools, then, do train a small number of their students for social mobility, but most of their students they train to keep pretty much the same class position as their parents have." [19]

Thus working-class children land overwhelmingly in working-class occupations as adults. How these people generally feel about their work comes through vividly in the Komarovsky selection discussed earlier. Her description of their disdain and boredom reads very much like the one by Harvey Swados, who, in "The Myth of the Happy Worker," exposed the worker's attitude toward his work as generally "compounded of hatred, shame, and resignation." [20] Considering that their kind of work produces feelings of powerlessness, meaninglessness, and self-estrangement—as contrasted with the self-actualization of "creative" work—it is not surprising that working-class people tend to view work simply as a means of getting things that one needs or desires and not as a virtue in itself.

[19] Bernard Barber, *Social Stratification*, New York: Harcourt, Brace and Company, 1957, p. 257.
[20] Maurice R. Stein, Arthur J. Vidich, and David M. White, eds., *Identity and Anxiety*, Glencoe, Illinois: Free Press, 1960, pp. 198–204.

SOCIAL CLASS, LIFE EXPECTANCY AND OVER-ALL MORTALITY*

Aaron Antonovsky

... recalling what happened when an "unsinkable" trans-Atlantic luxury liner, the *Titanic*, rammed an iceberg on her maiden voyage in 1912... The official casualty lists showed that only 4 first class female passengers (3 voluntarily chose to stay on the ship) of a total of 143 were lost. Among the second class passengers, 15 of 93 females drowned; and among the third class, 81 of 179 female passengers went down with the ship.[1]

Death is the final lot of all living beings. But, as the tragic experience of the *Titanic* passengers dramatically illustrates, the time at which one dies is related to one's class. The intent of this paper is to examine the evidence which bears upon the closeness of this relationship, ranging as far back as the data will allow. It will first focus on the question of life expectancy at birth, and subsequently turn to that of overall mortality.

STUDIES OF LIFE EXPECTANCY

The average infant born today in the Western world can look forward, barring unforeseen events and radical changes in present trends, to a life span of about 70 years. That this has not always been the case for the human infant—and still is not for by far most infants born today—is well known. Whatever the situation prior to the era of recorded history, for the greater part of this era, that is, until the nineteenth century, most men lived out less than half their Biblical span of years.

In what is probably the first study of

From The Milbank Memorial Fund *Quarterly*, Vol. XLV, No. 2, April, 1967. Reprinted by permission of the Millbank Memorial Fund.

[1] Hollingshead, August B. and Redlich, Frederick C., *Social Class and Mental Illness*, New York, John Wiley & Sons, Inc., 1958, p. 6, citing Lord, Walter, *A Night to Remember*, New York, Henry Holt, 1955, p. 107.

a total population, Halley, using data for the city of Breslau, Germany, for 1687 to 1691, calculated an average life expectancy at birth of 33.5 years.[2] Henry's estimate for the expectation of life of Parisian children born at the beginning of the eighteenth century was 23.5 years.[3] Half a century later, in the Vienna of 1752 to 1755, of every 1,000 infants born alive, only 590 survived their first year, 413 their fifth year, and 359 their fifteenth year.[4] ...

Ansell found a life expectation at birth for the total British population in 1874 of about 43 years.[5] At about the same time, the reported figures for Italy were somewhat lower: 35 years (1871 to 1880); 36.2 years for males, 35.65 years for females (1881–1882).[6]

Whatever the discrepancies and unreliabilities of these various sets of data, they consistently paint a picture of the Western world up to recent centuries which is quite similar to that of the world of presently "developing" societies until the last decade or two. Moreover, in the period of recorded history prior to the eighteenth century, no sizable increment had been added to the average life span. But if, from Greco-Roman times through the eighteenth or perhaps even the nineteenth century, the mythical "average" infant could anticipate living some 20 to 30 years, does any evidence indicate that dramatic class differences existed? Though the evidence

[2] Cited in Dublin, Louis I., Lotka, Alfred J. and Spiegelman, Mortimer, *Length of Life*, revised edition, New York, Ronald Press, 1949, pp. 34, 30–43. The book as a whole is one of the most detailed treatments of the subject of life expectancy.

[3] Henry, Louis, The Population of France in the 18th Century, *in* Glass, David V. and Eversley, D. E. C. (Editors), *Population in History*, London, Edward Arnold, 1965, p. 444.

[4] Peller, Sigismund, Births and Deaths Among Europe's Ruling Families Since 1500, *in* Glass and Eversley, *op. cit.*, p. 94.

[5] Ansell, C., Vital Statistics of Families in the Upper and Professional Classes, *Journal of the Royal Statistical Society*, 37, 464, 1874, cited *in* Titmuss, Richard, *Birth, Poverty and Wealth*, London, Hamish Hamilton Medical Books, 1943, p. 19.

[6] Cipolla, Carlo M., Four Centuries of Italian Demographic Development, *in* Glass and Eversley, *op. cit.*, pp. 578, 582.

is perforce limited, the answer would seem to be no.[7]

· ·

In other words, given a society which, though it manages to survive, does so at or near what might be called a rock-bottom level of life expectancy, one is not likely to find great differences among the strata of that society.

The data suggest the possibility that the trend in the nineteenth century, and perhaps even earlier, was toward a substantial widening of class differences. No report is available comparing the life expectancies of social strata of the population prior to the nineteenth century.

Can any conclusion be drawn from these data,[8] most of which are admittedly tenuous and not overly reliable? A crude picture . . . could be inferred which indicates the following. The bulk of recorded history was

[7] Dublin, Lotka and Spiegelman, *op. cit.*, pp. 31–32; Peller, *op. cit.*, p. 95.

[8] Pages reviewing the data are omitted. The studies containing the data are listed here (C. S. H.). Villerme, Louis R., *Tableau de L'état Physique et Moral des Ouvriers,* Vol. 2, Paris, Jules Renouard et Cie., 1840, pp. 251, 376–385; Farren, *Observations on the Mortality Among the Members of the British Peerage,* cited *in* Titmuss, *op. cit.*, p. 17; Morris, Jeremy N., *Uses of Epidemiology*, second edition, Edinburgh and London, E. and S. Livingstone, 1964, pp. 161–162; Titmuss, *op. cit.*, p. 18; Bailey, A. H. and Day, A., On the Rate of Mortality Prevailing Amongst the Families of the Peerage During the 19th Century, *Journal of the Institute of Actuaries*, 9, 305, cited in Collins, Selwyn D., *Economic Status and Health*, Washington, United States Government Printing Office, 1927, p. 14; Farr, William, *Vital Statistics. A Memorial Volume of Selections from the Reports and Writings of William Farr*, Humphreys, N. A. (Editor), London, The Sanitary Institute, 1885, pp. 393–394, also cited *in* Titmuss, *op. cit.*, pp. 17–18; Ansell, C., cited *in* Titmuss, *op. cit.*, p. 19; Mayer, Albert J. and Hauser, Philip, Class Differentiations in Expectation of Life at Birth, *in* Bendix, Reinhard and Lipset, Seymour M. (Editors), *Class, Status and Power*, Glencoe, Illinois, Free Press, 1953, pp. 281–284; Tietze, Christopher, Life Tables for Social Classes in England, Milbank Memorial Fund *Quarterly*, 21, 182–187, April, 1943; Yeracaris, Constantine A., Differential Mortality, General and Cause-Specific, in Buffalo, 1939–41, *Journal of the American Statistical Association*, 50, 1235–1247, December, 1955; Tayback, Matthew, The Relationship of Socioeconomic Status and Expectation of Life, *Baltimore Health News*, 34, 139–144, April, 1957.

one of high birth and high death rates, which offset each other and led to at most a very small increase in population. During the first 16 centuries of the Christian era, world population increased from about one-quarter to one-half billion people, an annual growth rate of about .005 per cent. Conceivably, throughout this period, no substantial differentials in life expectancy could be found among different social strata of the population. From 1650 to 1850 world population again doubled, most of the increase being in the Western world, representing an average annual increase of .05 per cent. These two centuries would seem to mark the emergence of an increasing class gap in life expectancy, starting slowly but gathering increasing momentum and reaching its peak about the time Malthus made his observations. On the one hand, the life expectancy of the middle and upper strata of the population increased at a rapid rate. On the other, the lowest strata's life expectancy may have increased much more slowly or, conceivably, even declined as an industrial proletariat emerged. At some time during the nineteenth century, probably in the latter half, this trend was reversed, and the class gap began to diminish. This is reflected in the doubling of the world's population, again mostly in the West, this time in the 80 years from 1850 to 1930. In recent decades, the class gap has narrowed to what may be the smallest differential in history, but evidence of a linear gradient remains, with a considerable differential, given man's life span.

This supposition—not claimed to be more than that—seems to be of more than historical interest. It is, for two important reasons, most germane to the concern of this paper. In the first place, the scientist, no less than the lay person, often seems, in considering the question of the relationship between class and health, to be beset by a nineteenth century notion of perpetual progress. Ideologically committed, in this area, to the desirability of the disappearance of the class gap, he tends to assume, with or without data, that the historical picture is unilinear; the history of mankind, in his view, shows steady progress in this respect. The realization that this may well be an inaccurate image, that the relationship is more complex, suggests a more cautious orientation. Such an orientation would suggest various possibilities: a narrowing gap being transformed into one which is widening; differing positions, on any given index of health, of different strata of the population at various times.

The second reason for stressing the possibility of a curvilinear relationship between class and life expectancy over time is that such a relationship may help in forming an adequate idea of the relationship between class and health, and, more broadly, an adequate theory of disease. Once the search begins for explanations of why, in a given period, one stratum seems to be making more health progress than another, and less so in another period, factors are uncovered which must be integrated into a theory of disease.

Thus, for example, McKeown and Brown, arguing that the increase in the population of England in the eighteenth century was overwhelmingly due to the decline in mortality, attribute that decline to improvements in the environment (housing, water supply, refuse disposal, nutrition) rather than to any advances in medical care.[9] Supposedly, such improvements first appeared in the upper strata of society, and only slowly percolated downward. This would explain the increasing class differences in life expectancy. Once the environmental sanitation gap began to narrow, some reversal in the trend could be expected which, however, might soon be offset by other factors; e.g., the malnutrition of poverty. The point is that a very careful collection of data over time and the search for ups and downs may serve to pinpoint the various factors, and their modes of interaction, which influence overall mortality or the course of any specific disease.

CLASS DIFFERENCES IN MORTALITY BEFORE WORLD WAR II

Twentieth century investigators have by and large focused on class differences in mortality rates. Chapin's study of Pro-

vidence, Rhode Island, probably provides the earliest relevant information. Using census and tax records of 1865, he located all but about 200 of the 2,000 taxpayers, covering a total of 10,515 individuals. Every deceased person in that year was assigned to either the taxpayer or non-taxpayer group. Chapin then calculated the death rates per thousand in each group. The crude annual death rate of the latter (24.8 per 1,000 living) was more than double that of the taxpayers (10.8). This disparity is found in all but the five- to nine-years age cohort, and is greatest in the productive years (30 to 49) and in the 70 and over cohort. Since the non-taxpayer group includes more than 80 per cent of the population, had Chapin been able to make a finer class breakdown he presumably would have found even greater differences between the top and bottom strata. . . .

The earliest data presented by Collins refer to Danish mortality rates from 1865 to 1874, the 1870 census having been used to obtain denominator information.[10] Individuals were assigned to high, middle or poor classes on the basis of the head of household's occupation. . . . The age-adjusted mean annual death rates, by sex, of the population aged 20 and over in Copenhagen and in other towns . . . the data show that class differences are greater in Copenhagen than in provincial towns, and greater among males than among females. More significantly, although the rates show primarily an inverse class gradient, the differences between the high and middle classes are relatively small compared to the gap between them and the poor class. . . .

The first of many ecological studies was Rowntree's well-known survey of York, England, in 1899.[11] Rowntree divided the wage-earner areas of the city of York into three levels. The overall death rates per thousand persons (not age-standardized) he reports for 1899 are: highest, 13.5; middle, 20.7; poorest, 27.8 (ratios of 100:153:206). In this case, unlike the earlier Danish data, the inverse gradient is quite regular.

[9] McKeown, Thomas and Brown, R. G., Medical Evidence Related to English Population Changes in the Eighteenth Century, *Population Studies*, 9, 119–241, 1955 (reprinted *in* Glass and Eversley, *op. cit.*, pp. 285–307).

[10] Collins, *op. cit.*, p. 13.
[11] Rowntree, Seebohm B., *Poverty and Progress: A Second Social Survey of York*, London, Longmans, Green & Co., 1941, p. 296.

In a paper focusing on later data, Britten calculates overall death rates for 1900 in the nine states and the District of Columbia, which then comprised the death registration area.[12] He compared white-collar rates to those for the "laboring and servant" class in three age groups. Taking the white-collar death rate as 100, the ratios for the lower class group were: for ages 15–24, 151; for ages 25–44, 165; and for ages 45–64, 159.

As a prologue to her analysis of 1950 death rates, Guralnick presents, without analysis, the full set of data upon which Britten evidently based his calculations, as well as similar date for 1890.[13] . . . The most striking fact about these data is the very sizable difference, at all ages, between the "laboring and servant" class and all other groups. In both 1890 and 1900, the ratio of this class is highest in ages 25–44 and 45–64, somewhat lower at ages 15–24, and lowest—though still relatively high—in the 65 and over category. An interesting pattern is shown by the clerical and official group: in the youngest age category its ratio is quite high, in 1900 approaching that of the lowest class; in each successive age category its ratio goes down, so that in the 65 and over category it has by far the lowest mortality rate. . . .

Huber[14] examined occupational mortality in France for 1907–1908, calculating death rates on the basis of the 1906 census. His figures are primarily for individual occupations, but he does give age-specific death rates for four broad groups. . . . Managers and officials consistently show the lowest rates. Clerical workers have, at ages 25–34, the highest rates, but thereafter craftsmen and kindred workers have higher rates. The rates of these two groups are, throughout, closer to each other than to those of the

managerial group. Class differentials are greatest at ages 45–54. Private household workers, presumably a low status group, have relatively low rates. Since the data refer only to males, who presumably served primarily in well-to-do households, such rates need not be inexplicable. . . .

In a relatively early review of morbidity and mortality data, Sydenstricker, one of the pioneers in the field, cites Bruno's study of 22,600 deaths among 1.3 million wage-earners in 1915–1916, with life insurance in 12 American companies, showing a clear inverse occupational gradient.[15] The death rates per 1,000 policyholders were: professional and semiprofessionals, 3.3; skilled workmen, 3.7; semiskilled workmen, 4.5; unskilled workmen, 4.8. Using the rate of the professional class as 100, the ratios of the other three were 112, 136 and 145.

· ·

Whitney's study using 1930 data was the first large-scale American study following the pattern which had been set by the British Registrar General.[16] Death certificate data were obtained from ten states: Alabama, Connecticut, Illinois, Kansas, Massachusetts, Minnesota, New Jersey, New York, Ohio and Wisconsin. These states contained 39 per cent of the gainfully employed. The census was used to obtain denominator information. Analysis was limited to males aged 15 to 64, in an attempt to limit the unreliability introduced by retirement. Age-standardized data are presented within the social-economic classification developed by Edwards and used standardly by the United States Census.

As can be seen in Table 1, mortality rates vary inversely with class in the total age group of 15–64. Only the proprietor group is out of line. If retail dealers, whose rate is 8.4, are excluded from this category, the

[12] Britten, Rollo H., Mortality Rates by Occupational Class in the U.S., *Public Health Reports*, 49, 1102, September, 1934.

[13] Guralnick, Lillian, Mortality by Occupation and Industry Among Men 20 to 64 Years of Age, U.S., 1950, *Vital Statistics, Special Reports*, 53, 56, Sepember, 1962.

[14] Huber, Michel, *Bulletin Statistique General de la France*, fasc IV, 1912, quoted *in* Daric, Jean, Mortality, Occupation, and Socio-Economic Status, *Vital Statistics, Special Reports*, 33, 175–187, September, 1951.

[15] Bruno, Frank J., Illness and Dependency, *Miscellaneous Contributions*, No. 9, The Committee on the Costs of Medical Care, Washington, 1931, cited *in* Sydenstricker, Edgar, *Health and Environment*, New York, McGraw-Hill Book Company, 1933, p. 94.

[16] Whitney, Jessamine S., *Death Rates by Occupation, Based on Data of the U.S. Census Bureau*, 1930, New York, National Tuberculosis Association, 1934, pp. 17, 32.

TABLE 1   Annual Death Rates per 1,000 Gainfully Occupied Males, Aged 15 to 64 Years (Age-Standardized) by Age Groups According to Socioeconomic Class, 1930[17]

Socioeconomic Class	Age Groups*							
	15–64		15–24		25–44		45–64	
	Rate	Ratio**	Rate	Ratio	Rate	Ratio	Rate	Ratio
All gainfully employed males	9.1	100	3.2	100	5.5	100	17.9	100
Professional men	6.7	74	2.3	72	3.5	64	16.2	90
Proprietors, managers and officials	7.9	87	3.1	97	4.2	76	15.8	88
Clerks and kindred workers	7.8	86	2.3	72	4.1	74	16.5	92
Skilled workers and foremen	8.3	91	3.0	94	4.9	89	17.1	96
Semiskilled workers	10.1	111	3.2	100	6.1	111	20.8	116
Unskilled workers	14.5	159	4.7	147	9.6	174	24.8	138

* The age-standardized figures for the age group 15–64 are based on the 53 occupational groups with 500 or more deaths (Whitney, Table 8, p. 32). These cover 79 per cent of the gainfully employed. This set of data was selected as more reliable than the figures for all deaths, given by Whitney in Table 1, p. 17. The trends in the two sets of data are very similar. The age-specific data are only available in Whitney's Table 1, and cover the entire surveyed population.
** Rate for all gainfully employed males = 100.

rate would be 7.0, making a linear relationship. The curve, however, is not smooth, as can be seen clearly from the ratios presented in the table. The largest difference is found between unskilled and semiskilled workers, with a sizable difference between the latter and skilled workers. Beyond this level the differences, although existent, are relatively small.

The same general pattern appears in each of the three age-specific sets of data. The spread, however, is greatest in the 25–44 age group and least in the oldest group. In the latter, differences among the four occupational categories from skilled workers and up are almost nonexistent. This study indicates, then, that class is most intimately related to mortality rates among the unskilled and, secondarily among the semiskilled workers, and during middle age.[17]

Sheps and Watkins[18] sought to overcome the weakness of ecological studies by utilizing information obtained in careful sociological study which grouped areas in New Haven, Connecticut, into "natural areas." The boundary lines of these areas were such that information about census tracts could be used for purposes of setting denominators and standardizing for age. ... The seven areas were ranked from best to worst, based on a composite of factors including rental, delinquency rates, social standing and financial dependency. All data were age-adjusted.

Taking the average annual death rate over the five-year period of the best area (8.0 per 1,000 persons) as 100, the ratios of the other six areas, going down the socioeconomic scale, were: 111, 110, 128, 136, 145, 148. Other than the fact that the rates for the second and third highest areas are almost identical, a clear inverse linear relationship is found. When the authors combined the seven areas into three, the range was substantially narrowed (100:114: 134). The strongest relationship between mortality rates and economic level were found at ages 0–5 and 25–64.

[17] Whitney's data are quoted and discussed by Britten, *op. cit.,* and Guralnick, *op. cit.*
[18] Sheps, Cecil and Watkins, J. H., Mortality in the Socio-Economic Districts of New Haven, *Yale Journal of Biology and Medicine,* 20, 51–80, October, 1947

. . . .

WORLD WAR II TO THE PRESENT

. . . .

Mortality rates in the Netherlands are among the lowest in the world. In this context, determination of social class differences becomes of particular interest. DeWolff and Meerdink[19] studied the mortality rates of gainfully employed males, aged 15–64 in Amsterdam in 1947–1952, using the 1947 census to provide denominator information. . . . The difference between the most favored group and the workers (117:100) barely reaches statistical significance. In contrast to the findings of all other studies, unskilled workers do not differ from skilled workers. Only the clerical group is relatively high (though a death rate of 5.1 is, as such, quite low). The authors suggest two reasons for this rate. First, the clerical workers do not reach the standards of physical fitness required to obtain civil service employment, which would have placed them in the top level. Second, many are probably children of manual workers and are not sufficiently fit to work.

By the 1950s, the number of studies of socioeconomic mortality differentials had increased considerably. . . . Tayback[20] divided Baltimore's 168 census tracts on the basis of the 1950 median tract rentals, grouping them into equal-sized population quintiles. . . . In overall terms, a clear inverse class gradient is seen, the male slope being somewhat steeper than the female slope, with very few figures being out of line. The gap tends to be quite large in the younger age groups, where the death rate is low. Class differences in middle age (35–54) are very sizable. At this age, the major differences seem to be at the top and bottom, between the highest and next-highest and between the lowest and second-lowest economic levels. Differences remain considerable at ages 55–64, but tend to become much smaller thereafter.

Ellis conducted a very similar study in Houston.[21] The index used to rank census tracts was a modification of the index of social rank developed by Shevky and Williams, which utilizes measures of education, occupation and median family income. Tracts were grouped into quintiles, each of which contained 12 or 13 tracts. . . . Although class differentials do appear, they differ from those in other studies. The range of differences is smaller, though still substantial. The two top groups of tracts, for males, and the three top, for females, are quite similar in their death rates. Most puzzling, perhaps, is the fact that males in the lowest tract level have a lower rate than do those in the adjacent level. Ellis suggests as a possible explanation the availability of free medical treatment for the lowest group. Group 4, not having such an advantage but having a limited income, may utilize funds for the females, who do have a lower rate than the females in group 5, whereas the males go on working and refrain from using such funds for themselves. . . .

Stockwell, whose concern was methodological as well as substantive, presents data exactly parallel to the above. . . . He also used a modified form of the Shevky-Williams index, studied deaths in 1949–1951, and included about one-fifth of the number of tracts in each socioeconomic level. Stockwell's data pertain to Providence and Hartford. The class differentials in these two cities are quite similar to those in Houston. In Providence, little difference is found among the top three levels of males or the top two levels of females. Hartford females do not differ among all five strata; levels 2 and 3 and levels 4 and 5 have almost identical rates.

Stockwell proceeded to compute rank order correlation coefficients between the census tracts in each city ranked by age-sex-standardized death rates and each of eight socioeconomic variables (occupation, two education variables, two income variables,

[19] DeWolff, P. and Meerdink, J., Mortality Rates in Amsterdam According to Profession, *Proceedings of the World Population Conference*, 1954, Vol. I, New York, United Nations (E/Conf. 13/413), pp. 53–55.

[20] Tayback, *op. cit.*, p. 142.

[21] Ellis, John M., Socio-Economic Differentials in Mortality from Chronic Diseases, *Social Problems*, 5, 30–36, July, 1957. Reprinted in expanded form in Jaco, E. Gartly (Editor), *Patients, Physicians and Illness*, Glencoe, Illinois, Free Press, 1958, p. 32.

two rent variables, crowding). In all cases, the correlation coefficients were significant.[22]

Since the British Registrar General system of social classification is the richest source of data on mortality differences over time among different socioeconomic levels, a number of attempts have been made to construct a comparable ranking in the United States. Breslow and Buell,[23] using the 1950 census for denominator data, classified all deaths of California males, aged 20–64, from 1949 to 1951, in one of five occupational classes. . . .

For the entire age group, a rough inverse gradient is seen between class and mortality. . . .

A more ambitious attempt along the same lines was conducted by Guralnick, who analyzed all male deaths in age group 20 to 64 in the United States in 1950.[24] In view of the fact that one primary purpose was to compare the United States data with the British, Guralnick collapsed classes II to IV to make this intermediate group comparable in the two countries. . . . For the entire age group, the picture is quite similar to that presented in the California study: a linear inverse gradient, with the intermediate occupational level being closer to class I, and the major gap occurring between class V and the intermediate group. Another publication by Guralnick,[25] in which standard mortality ratios are given separately for the five classes, presents figures almost identical with the California figures. The standardized mortality ratios for all United States males aged 20–64, in 1950, from class I to class V, are: 83, 84, 96, 97, 120. These ratios are for whites only, except for class I, which contains a few nonwhites. Once again classes I and II do not differ, nor do classes III and IV.

Examination of the age-specific rates . . . shows the largest class gap to lie in the 25 to 44 age group, with classes II to IV being closer to class I than to class V. A considerable gap remains at ages 45–54, but it is substantially narrowed by ages 55–64.

Guralnick also analyzed the same 1950 data along more traditional American lines, using the occupational classification developed by Edwards for the United States Census.[26] This scheme seeks to rank occupations by socioeconomic levels. The standardized mortality ratios presented in Table 2, for white males aged 25–59, shows an inverse gradient, but one which does not distinguish among all of the eight occupational groups. The lowest ratios are found among the top three groups; they are followed closely by sales, skilled and semiskilled workers, whose ratios are identical. Service workers fare substantially poorer, and, finally, laborers have a considerably higher mortality ratio.

This pattern does not hold in all age groups. Prior to age 30, only the roughest

[22] Stockwell, Edward G., *Socio-Economic Mortality Differentials in Hartford, Conn. and Providence, R. I.: A Methodological Critique*, unpublished doctoral dissertation, Brown University, 1960. Relevant papers published by Stockwell based on his dissertation include: ——, A Critical Examination of the Relationship Between Socioeconomic Status and Mortality, *American Journal of Public Health*, 53, 956–964, June, 1963; ——, Socioeconomic Status and Mortality, *Connecticut Health Bulletin*, 77, 10–13, December, 1963.

Stockwell investigated the difference made in the analysis of socioeconomic mortality data when different indices of class are used. He notes that the precise conclusions one draws will "vary considerably with the methodological conditions characterizing a particular study," however the overall patterns are sufficiently similar so that, for present purposes, it is adequate to refer to only one or two of his measures. Since many studies reported in the present paper used median rental, however, it is important to note that Stockwell's data indicate that, of all eight variables, this is the poorest predictor of mortality rates.

[23] Breslow, Lester and Buell, Philip, Mortality from Coronary Heart Disease and Physical Activity of Work in California, *Journal of Chronic Diseases*, 11, 421–44, April, 1960.

[24] Guralnick, Lillian, Socioeconomic Differences in Mortality by Cause of Death: United States, 1950 and England and Wales, 1949–1953, *in International Population Conference, Ottawa, 1963, op. cit.*, p. 298.

[25] ——, Mortality by Occupation Level and Cause of Death Among Men 20 to 64 Years of Age, U.S., 1950, *Vital Statistics, Special Reports*, 53, 452–481, September, 1963. For an earlier paper reporting provisional death rates in the same population by the five classes and seven age categories, *see* Moriyama, Iwao M. and Guralnick, Lillian, Occupational and Social Class Differences in Mortality, *in Trends and Differentials in Mortality*, New York, Milbank Memorial Fund, 1956, p. 66.

TABLE 2 Annual Death Rates per 1,000, and Ratios, White Males, by Age and Major Occupation Group, United States, 1950[26]

MAJOR OCCUPATION GROUP	25-29	20-24		25-29		30-34		35-44		45-54		55-59		60-64	
	SMR**	X	Y*	X	Y	X	Y	X	Y	X	Y	X	Y	X	Y
All occupations	93	1.7	100	1.6	100	2.0	100	3.9	100	10.1	100	19.4	100	28.8	100
Professional, technical, kindred	82	1.2	73	1.2	70	1.5	76	3.2	81	9.4	93	18.9	98	29.2	101
Managers, officials, proprietors, nonfarm	85	1.5	86	1.3	79	1.5	76	3.3	85	9.5	94	18.9	98	28.9	100
Clerical, kindred	83	0.9	54	1.3	78	1.5	76	3.3	86	9.6	95	18.2	94	26.9	93
Sales	94	1.1	62	1.1	66	1.7	82	3.6	94	11.0	109	21.7	112	31.8	110
Craftsmen, foremen, kindred	94	1.8	103	1.6	97	2.0	99	4.0	102	10.1	100	20.8	107	32.1	111
Operatives, kindred	94	1.8	106	1.8	108	2.2	107	4.1	106	10.3	102	19.4	100	28.6	99
Service, except private household	116	1.2	72	1.6	98	2.4	117	5.1	133	13.8	136	22.4	116	29.2	101
Laborers, except farm and mine	131	2.6	149	2.8	171	3.6	178	6.5	167	14.5	144	23.8	123	34.9	121

* X = death rate per 1,000. Y = ratio, computed on the basis of rate for all occupations in each age category = 100.

** Standardized mortality ratios are computed on the basis of the entire population. Since nonwhite are excluded in this table, SMRs can fall below 100.

[26] Guralnick, Lillian, Mortality by Occupation and Industry Among Men 20 to 64 Years of Age, U.S., 1950, *Vital Statistics, Special Reports*, 53, 59, 61, 84–86, September, 1962.

gradient appears, though laborers fare markedly worst. A clear gradient appears in the 30–34 groups, which is maintained in the next ten year cohort. In both cases, the ratios of the top three occupational groups are nearly identical. This pattern holds in ages 45–54 and 55–59 in part. Three mortality levels can be distinguished in these groups, which do not conform to the socioeconomic ranking: non-manual workers except sales workers; sales, skilled and semiskilled workers; and service and unskilled workers. In the oldest age category only laborers continue to differ from all other groups.

. . . .

Hansluwka's review of Austrian mortality data[27] begins with reference to a number of early studies which were based upon workers covered by social insurance, reflecting only a very small part of the population. He does, however, present data for the entire employed population for 1951–1953. . . . For the very gross categories of "middle and upper class" and "working class" occupations, few sizable differences emerge, though the latter's rates are higher. At ages 14–17, the former's rate is appreciably higher. At ages 60–64, however, the working class has a much higher death rate. Hansluwka also presents a bar chart showing mortality in Vienna in 1951–1953. The city's 23 districts were classified on the percentage of workers of the labor force in each district and grouped into four categories. The data, he concludes, show "a clearcut pattern of social grading of mortality."

A problem which has consistently bedeviled those who seek to study socioeconomic differentials on mortality by use of death certificates and census records is the frequent noncomparability of data in the two sources, which leads to overestimation of the denominator in some occupations and underestimation in others, or difficulty in making any calculations. The nature of the problem has been explored,

theoretically and empirically, by several writers.[28] Among these, Kitagawa and Hauser have sought to overcome the difficulties by individual matching of 340,000 death certificates from deaths occurring in the United States from May through August, 1960, with census information recorded for these individuals in the 1960 census. In addition, personal interviews were conducted with individuals knowledgeable about 94 per cent of a sample of 9,500 of the decedents.

A preliminary analysis of the data using education and family income for white persons has been reported, though not yet published.[29] Consideration of the education variable, which is broken down into four levels of completed education by persons 25 and older, shows an inverse gradient of mortality rates by amount of education for both sexes in ages 25 to 64. Interestingly enough, this gradient disappears for males 65 and over, but remains quite strong for females of this age.

The latest mortality study available is Tsuchiya's presentation of standardized mortality ratios for an occupational industrial categorization of Japanese males, age 15 and over, in 1962.[30] No clear occupational gradient emerges from the data. The ratios, ranked from low to high, are: "management," 58; "clerks," 67; "mechanics and simple," 88; "sales," 89; "professional and technical," 92; "transporting and communicating," 135.

[28] Buechley, Robert, Dunn, John E. Jr., Linden, George and Breslow, Lester, Death Certificate Statement of Occupation: Its Usefulness in Comparing Mortalities, *Public Health Reports*, 71, 1105–1111, November, 1956; Kitagawa, Evelyn M. and Hauser, Philip M., Methods Used in a Current Study of Social and Economic Differentials in Mortality, *in Emerging Techniques of Population Research*, New York, Milbank Memorial Fund, pp. 250–266; and ——, Social and Economic Differentials in Mortality in the U.S., 1960: A Report on Methods, *in International Population Conference, Ottawa*, 1963, *op. cit.*, pp. 355–367.

[29] Kitagawa, Evelyn M. and Hauser, Philip M., Social and Economic Differentials in Mortality, United States, 1960. Paper presented at the 1966 annual meeting of the Population Association of America.

[30] Tsuchiya, Kenzaburo, The Relation of Occupation to Cancer, Especially Cancer of the Lung, *Cancer*, 18, 136–144, February, 1965.

[27] Hansluwka, Harold, Social and Economic Factors in Mortality in Austria, *in International Population Conference, Ottawa*, 1963, *op. cit.*, pp. 315–344.

CLASS MORTALITY DIFFERENTIALS IN ENGLAND AND WALES

Since William Farr initiated the systematic study of occupational mortality statistics in 1851, the decennial reports of the British Registrar General for England and Wales have served as the outstanding source of information on the relationship of social class and mortality. For many years, the focus was on differential mortality risks of specific occupations. In the analysis of the 1910–1912 data, the various occupations were, for the first time, grouped together into five social classes. . . .

In 1930–1932 a further step was taken in moving from a concern with occupational hazards toward one with comparison of mortality risks of people sharing a given social environment: the mortality of married women classified according to husband's occupation was introduced as a systematic part of the data analysis. Since this time, despite reclassification of various occupations, the five-class scheme of the Registrar General has been maintained.[31]

. . . .

The five social classes are described as follows (the proportion of occupied and retired men aged 15 and over in 1951 is given in brackets):

Class I. Higher administrative and professional occupations and business directorships (3.3 per cent).

Class II. Other administrative, professional and managerial, and shopkeepers: persons responsible for initiating policy and others without this responsibility, but with some responsibility over others (15 per cent).

Class III. Clerical workers, shop assistants, personal service, foremen, skilled workers: skilled workers with a special name, special responsibility and adaptability (52.7 per cent).

Class IV. Semiskilled workers: persons who are doing manual work which needs no great skill or training but who are doing it habitually and in association with a particular industry (16.2 per cent).

Class V. Unskilled workers: laborers, cleaners and other lowly occupations (12.8 per cent). . . .

Farmers and farm managers are included in class II and agricultural workers in class IV. Also, class III, which includes more than half the population, is composed of both manual and non-manual workers.

From the great amount and variety of data available in the reports of the Registrar General and papers based on these reports, those that seem to be the most important have been selected for present purposes. These are presented in Table 3. Collins' analysis of the 1910–1912 data for occupied and retired males aged 15 and over, which refers to classes I, III and V and excludes textile workers, miners and agricultural laborers, shows a regular inverse gradient, with the largest gap being between class III and class V.[32] Stevenson's figures for the same period,[33] which also exclude the same three occupational categories, but refer to males aged 25–64 in the five social classes, show a similar gradient. The ratios for classes II, III and IV, however, are nearly identical, and not very much higher than for class I. Stevenson argued that about ten per cent of the laborers on the census are misclassified as class IV rather than class V, which tends to lower the rates for the former and increase those for the latter. Changing the denominators to this extent would, he notes, produce a smoother gradient, as

[31] . . . Registrar General's *Decennial Supplement, England and Wales, 1951, Occupational Mortality*, Part II, Vol. 1, *Commentary*, London, Her Majesty's Stationery Office, 1958, pp. 12–13. This system of classification is also described *in* Logan, W. P. D., Social Class Variations in Mortality, *in Proceedings of the World Population Conference, op. cit.*, pp. 185–188; and Brockington, Fraser C., *The Health of the Community*, third edition, London, J. & A. Churchill Ltd., 1965, pp. 325–334. The percentage distribution of the social classes is taken from Logan, p. 201. For further discussions of the antedecents and development of the Registrar General system of classification, *see* Greenwood, Major, *Medical Statistics from Graunt to Farr*, Cambridge, University Press, 1948; and ——, Occupational and Economic Factors of Mortality, *British Medical Journal*, 1, 862–866, April, 1939.

[32] Collins, *op. cit.*, p. 15.

[33] Stevenson, T. H. C., The Social Distribution of Mortality from Different Causes in England and Wales, 1910–1912, *Biometrika*, 15, 384–388, 1923; Logan, *op. cit.*, p. 204. Logan's paper was also published, with variations, under the same title, *in British Journal of Preventive and Social Medicine*, 8, 128–137, July, 1954, and *in Public Health Reports*, 69, 1217–1223, December, 1954.

TABLE 3 Standardized Death Rates per 1,000 and Standardized Mortality Ratios, England and Wales, for Selected Age–Sex Groups and Time Periods, by Social Class

Time Period	I	II	III	IV	V	Population Group
1910–12						
Death rate per 1,000	12.0	—	13.6	—	18.7	Occupied and retired
Ratio (I = 100)	100	—	114	—	156	males, age 15+, excludes textile workers, miners, agricultural laborers
Standardized mortality ratio	88	94	96	93	142	Males, age 25–64, excludes textile, miners, agricultural laborers
Standardized mortality ratio	88	94	96	107	128	As immediately above, modified by Stevenson
1921–23						
Death rate per 1,000	7.4	8.6	8.7	9.2	11.5	Males
Ratio (I = 100)	100	116	117	124	155	
Standardized mortality ratio	82	94	95	101	125	Males, 20–64
1930–32						
Standardized	90	94	97	102	111	Males, 20–64
mortality ratio	81	89	99	103	113	Married women, 20–64
1949–53						
Standardized	98	86	101	94	118	Males, 20–64
mortality ratio	96	88	101	104	110	Married women, 20–64
	100	90	101	104	118	Occupied males, 20–64, adjusted to control for occupational changes since 1930–32
Death rate per 1,000	6.6		6.4		9.5	Males, 20–64, excludes
Ratio (I = 100)	100		97		144	agricultural workers

shown in Table 3. Collins also took the 1900–1902 and 1890–1892 data for 100 specific occupations and classified them as they had been classified in 1910, adjusting the death rates for age. . . . Collins proceeded to analyze the age-specific rates, which show that class differentials were largest in the 25–54 age groups. This is supported by Stevenson's analysis.

A similar picture emerges from the data for 1921–1923, despite the significant changes in classification. The gap between classes I and II is somewhat greater than in the previous decade. Classes II and III have near-identical ratios and class IV a somewhat higher ratio, while class V is still widely distinct from the others. Britten's analysis[34] of the age-specific rates compares class I to class III and class III to class V. For the former comparison, the greatest gap is at ages 16–19, and declines with regularity at each succeeding age. The pattern of the class V : III ratio, however, is different. Here the greatest gap is at ages 35–44 and, though a bit less so, at 45–54.

By 1930, class differentials, though now presenting a regular inverse gradient, had narrowed, with standardized mortality ratios of 90 for class I and 111 for class V, for males, aged 20–64. The innovation introduced in the data analysis for these years

[34] Britten, Rollo H., Occupational Mortality Among Males in England and Wales, 1921–1923, *Public Health Reports*, 43, 1570, June, 1928.

shows that general socioeconomic differences rather than specific occupational hazards were crucial in the relationship between class and mortality. This is seen in the data for married women classified by husband's occupation, in which the gradient is somewhat more steep than for the males.

The latest available data, for 1949–1953, show a rather different picture than that of previous decades. Class V still has a substantially higher ratio than the other classes; for the males, it is even higher than in 1930. Class II, however, now has the lowest ratio, followed by classes IV, I and III, in that order. For married women, the inverse gradient persists, except that here too, as among the males, class II has a lower ratio than class I. The relatively low ratio of class IV may well be an artifact of classificational changes from one social class to another. Adjustment of the data for occupied males to take account of these changes "has had the important effect of raising the SMR of Social Class IV from 94, where it was second lowest, to 104, where it occupies the second highest position, as it did in 1921–1923 and 1930–1932." [35] Guralnick's analysis of the British data, [36] excluding all gainfully employed in agriculture, and collapsing classes II–IV, shows that this latter group had a very slightly lower death rate than class I, while class V remains very much higher.

Moriyama and Guralnick, [37] in their attempt to compare data for males from the United States and England and Wales, present age-specific ratios for the latter combining the three middle classes and excluding all engaged in agriculture, for 1950 only. For most age groups, little difference is seen between class I and classes II–IV; this is particularly true from age 45 upwards. Class V has consistently higher rates; but whereas this is the case to a moderate degree at ages 20–24, the differential increases thereafter, reaching a peak at ages 35–44, after which it declines again and nearly disappears at ages 60–64. (The respective ratios of the three class

groups I, II–IV and V, taking the rate of all occupations as 100, are: at ages 20–24, 102, 94, 122; at ages 25–34, 90, 95, 138; at ages 35–44, 83, 96, 143; at ages 45–54, 98, 97, 129; at ages 55–59, 99, 99, 115; and at ages 60–64, 100, 101, 106.)

Viewing the data for England and Wales in overall terms, class differentials in mortality in the twentieth century both have and have not declined. On the one hand, the differentials between the middle levels (among whom mortality rates differed little even in the earlier years) and class I have more or less disappeared. On the other hand, class V is still strikingly worse off than the rest of the population. Though indications are that its relative position improved in the earlier decades of the century, this does not seem to be the case between 1930 and 1950.

CONCLUSIONS

This statistical examination clearly provides no basis to reject the inference drawn from the figures of the *Titanic* disaster. Despite the multiplicity of methods and indices used in the 30-odd studies cited, and despite the variegated populations surveyed, the inescapable conclusion is that class influences one's chance of staying alive. Almost without exception, the evidence shows that classes differ in mortality rates. Only three such exceptions were found, indicating no or almost no class difference. Altenderfer, comparing 1939–1940 mortality rates of 92 United States cities classified into three mean income groups, shows a relatively small difference among them. Szabady, comparing nonagricultural manual and non-manual workers in Hungary in 1959–1960, shows the same. In both cases, the classification is so gross as to minimize differences which a finer analysis might reveal. Only DeWolff and Meerdink's study in Amsterdam in 1947–1952 can legitimately be regarded as strongly contradictory of the link between class and mortality. Their data, however, must be seen in the context of a population which has just about the lowest death rate ever recorded. This is not to dismiss the importance of their findings. On the contrary, it suggests the extremely important hypothesis that as the overall death rate of a population is

[35] Registrar General, *op. cit.*, p. 20.
[36] Guralnick, *op. cit.* (International Population Conference), p. 298.
[37] Moriyama and Guralnick, *op. cit.*, p. 69.

lowered, class differentials may similarly decline.

This hypothesis finds support in an overall trend reflected in the studies reported. In the earlier studies, the differential between the mortality rates of extreme class groups is about a 2:1 ratio, but later studies show a narrowing of this differential, so that by the 1940s, a 1.4:1 or 1.3:1 ratio is much more typical. As can be seen from studying the death rates, three years witnessed a progressive decline in the overall death rate. At the same time, a cautionary note must be exercised. Despite an undoubted overall decline in mortality in the past three decades, the trend in the earlier decades of the century toward the closing of the class gap has been checked, if not halted.

This indication focuses on the differences between mortality rates of the lowest class and other classes. A more accurate picture of the overall pattern would be to suggest that what has happened is a blurring, if not a disappearance, of a clear class gradient, while class differences remain. On the basis of the existent data—using, for the sake of convenience, a five-fold class distinction, this being the most popular—it is difficult to conclude whether classes I to IV now no longer differ in their mortality rates, or whether classes I and II have the lowest rates, and III and IV have higher rates, though not necessarily substantially so. What seems to be beyond question is that, whatever the index used and whatever the number of classes considered, almost always a lowest class appears with substantially higher mortality rates. Moreover, the differential between it and other classes evidently has not diminished over recent decades.

At this point discussion of the complex question of explanations for such patterns would not be appropriate. A possibility could be suggested, however. The truly magnificent triumphs over infectious diseases have been crucial in both narrowing the overall class differentials and in nearly eliminating differentials among all but the lowest class. In recent decades, however, access to good medical care, preventive medical action, health knowledge, and limitation of delay in seeking treatment have become increasingly important in combating mortality, as chronic diseases have become the chief health enemy in the developed world. In these areas, lower class people may well be at a disadvantage. As such factors become more and more important, as the historical supposition presented in the first pages of this paper suggests, increasing class differentiation may occur. This approach does not necessarily preclude consideration of genetic selection and what has commonly come to be called "the drift hypothesis."

The data reviewed lead to a further conclusion. With amazing consistency, the class differentials are largest in the middle years of life. This is no less true in the latest than in the earliest studies. Over and over again, the greatest gap is found in young and middle adulthood. The predominant pattern characterizing class differentials by age is that in which class differences are moderately high in the younger ages, rise to a peak at ages 30 to 44, begin to decline at that point and tend to disappear beyond age 65. Where a given set of data varies from this pattern, it is in one of two directions: in the former cases, class differentials are lowest in the younger and older groups; in the latter, the decline in class differentials only begins in late middle age.

This pattern of greatest class differences in middle adulthood may be linked to the two historical suppositions which have heretofore been presented. To hypothesize in more general terms, when mortality rates are extremely high or extremely low, class differences will tend to be small. In other words, when men are quite helpless before the threat of death, or when men have made great achievements in dealing with this threat, life chances will tend to be equitably distributed. On the other hand, when moderate progress is being made in dealing with this threat, differential consequences are to be expected. The crucial idea that may be involved here is that of preventable deaths, at any given level of knowledge, technique and social organization Where and/or when such deaths are concentrated, class differentials will be greatest, unless appropriate social action is taken This differential is not inevitable.

Much more, of course, could be said in summary, with reference to both substantive and methodological issues Needless to say, consideration of patterns of class differences by cause of death is essential for a full understanding of this relationship But this would have extended the paper into a book.

CLASS SUBCULTURES IN AMERICAN SOCIETY

Herbert J. Gans

· ·

The voluminous literature of class studies in America and elsewhere and the considerable similarity of the classes all over the industrialized world have made it possible to begin a delineation of the principal class subcultures. While I shall not attempt this task here, I do want to suggest what seem to me to be some of the major "focal concerns"[1] of four of the subcultures: working class, lower class, middle class, and professional upper-middle class. These brief outlines are based on observations made in the West End[2] and elsewhere, and on the research literature. For the most part, they describe the subcultures in America and in one period of the life cycle: that of the family which is rearing children.

Perhaps the most important—or at least the most visible—difference between the classes is one of family structure. *The working-class subculture* is distinguished by

Reprinted with permission of The Macmillan Company from *The Urban Villagers*, by Herbert T. Gans. © The Free Press of Glencoe, a Division of The Macmillan Company, 1962.

[1] I borrow this term from Walter Miller, who uses it as a substitute for the anthropological concept of value in his study of lower-class culture. See "Lower Class Culture as a Generating Milieu of Gang Delinquency," *Journal of Social Issues*, Vol. 14, 1958, p. 7. I use it to refer to behavior as much as to attitude, and to phenomena of social structure as well as culture.

[2] The Boston Italian-American community that is the main subject of the book from which this selection is taken. (C. S. H.)

the dominant role of the family circle. Its way of life is based on social relationship amidst relatives. The working class views the world from the family circle, and considers everything outside it as either a means to its maintenance or to its destruction. But while the outside world is to be used for the benefit of this circle, it is faced with detachment and even hostility in most other respects. Whenever feasible, then, work is sought within establishments connected to the family circle. When this is not possible—and it rarely is—work is primarily a means of obtaining income to maintain life amidst a considerable degree of poverty, and, thereafter, a means of maximizing the pleasures of life within the family circle. The work itself may be skilled or unskilled; it can take place in the factory or in the office—the type of collar is not important. What does matter is that identification with work, work success, and job advancement —while not absolutely rejected—are of secondary priority to the life that goes on within the family circle. The purpose of education is to learn techniques necessary to obtain the most lucrative type of work. Thus the central theme of American, and all Western, education—that the student is an individual who should use his schooling to detach himself from ascribed relationships like the family circle in order to maximize his personal development and achievement in work, play, and other spheres of life—is ignored or openly rejected.

The specific characteristics of the family circle may differ widely—from the collateral peer group form of the West Enders, to the hierarchical type of the Irish, or to the classic three-generation extended family. Friends may also be included in the circle, as in the West Enders' peer group society. What matters most—and distinguishes this subculture from others—is that there be a family circle which is wider than the nuclear family, and that all of the opportunities, temptations, and pressures of the larger society be evaluated in terms of how they affect the ongoing way of life that has been built around this circle.

The *lower-class subculture* is distinguished by the female-based family and the marginal male. Although a family circle may also exist, it includes only female relatives. The male, whether husband or lover, is physically present only part of the time, and is recognized neither as a stable nor dominant member of the household. He is a sexual partner, and he is asked to provide economic support. But he participates only minimally in the exchange of affection and emotional support, and has little to do with the rearing of children. Should he serve as a model for the male children, he does so largely in a negative sense. That is, the women use him as an example of what a man should not be.

The female-based family must be distinguished, however, from one in which the woman is dominant, for example, the English working-class family. Although this family may indeed revolve around the "Mum," she does not reject the husband. Not only is he a member of the family, but he is also a participant—and a positive model—in child-rearing.

In the lower class, the segregation of the sexes—only partial in the working class—is complete. The woman tries to develop a stable routine in the midst of poverty and deprivation; the action-seeking man upsets it. In order to have any male relationships, however, the woman must participate to some extent in his episodic life style. On rare occasions, she may even pursue it herself. Even then, however, she will try to encourage her children to seek a routine way of life. Thus the woman is much closer to working-class culture, at least in her aspirations, although she is not often successful in achieving them.

For lower-class men, life is almost totally unpredictable. If they have sought stability at all, it has slipped from their grasp so quickly, often, and consistently that they no longer pursue it. From childhood on, their only real gratifications come from action-seeking, but even these are few and short-lived. Relationships with women are of brief duration, and some men remain single all their lives. Work, like all other relationships with the outside world, is transitory. Indeed, there can be no identification with work at all. Usually, the lower-class individual gravitates from one job to another with little hope or interest of keeping a job for any length of time. His hostility to the outside world therefore is quite intense, and its attempts to interfere with the episodic

quality of his life are fought. Education is rejected by the male, for all of its aims are diametrically opposed to action-seeking.

The *middle-class subculture* is built around the nuclear family and its desire to make its way in the larger society. Although the family circle may exist, it plays only a secondary role in middle-class life. Contact with close relatives is maintained, but even they participate in a subordinate role. Individuals derive most of their social and emotional gratifications from the nuclear family itself. One of the most important of these is child-rearing. Consequently, the middle-class family is much more child-centered than the working-class one and spends more of its spare time together. Outside social life takes place with friends who share similar interests. The nuclear family depends on its friends—as well as on some caretaking institutions—for help and support. Relatives may also help, especially in emergencies.

The middle class does not make the distinction between the family and the outside world. In fact, it does not even see an outside world, but only a larger society, which it believes to support its aims, and in which the family participates. The nuclear family makes it way in the larger society mainly through the career of its breadwinner. Thus work is not merely a job that maximizes income, but a series of related jobs or job advances which provide the breadwinner with higher income, greater responsibility, and, if possible, greater job satisfaction. In turn his career enhances the way of life of the rest of the family, through increases in status and in the standard of living.

Education is viewed, and used, as an important method for achieving these goals. The purpose of education is to provide the skills needed for the man's career and for the woman's role as a mother. In and out of school, it is also used to develop the skills necessary to the maintenance and increase of status, the proper use of leisure time, and the occasional participation in community activities. Thus, much of the central theme of education is accepted. But the idea that education is an end in itself, and should be used to maximize individual development of the person, receives only lip service.

The subculture I have described here is a

basic middle-class one; a more detailed analysis would distinguish between what is currently called the middle-middle class and the lower-middle class. The upper-middle-class subculture is also a variant of the basic middle-class culture. There are at least two such subcultures, the managerial and the professional. Since I shall be concerned with the latter in subsequent sections of this chapter and the next, it is of primary interest here.

The *professional upper-middle-class culture* is also organized around the nuclear family, but places greater emphasis on the independent functioning of its individual members. Whereas the middle-class family is a companionship unit in which individuals exist most intensely in their relationships with each other, the upper-middle-class family is a companionship unit in which individuals seeking to maximize their own development as persons come together on the basis of common interests. For this subculture, life is, to a considerable extent, a striving for individual development and self-expression, and these strivings pervade many of its relationships with the larger society.

Therefore, work is not simply a means for achieving the well-being of the nuclear family, but also an opportunity for individual achievement and social service. Although the career, income, status, and job responsibility are important, job satisfaction is even more important, although it is not always found. Indeed, professional work satisfaction is a focal concern not only for the breadwinner, but often for the woman as well. If she is not interested in a profession, she develops an alternative but equally intense interest in motherhood, or in community activity. Child-rearing, moreover, gives the woman an opportunity not only to maximize her own individual achievements as a mother, but to develop in her children the same striving for self-development. As a result, the professional upper-middle-class family is not child-centered, but adult-directed. As education is the primary tool for a life of individual achievement, the professional upper-middle-class person not only goes to school longer than anyone else in society, but he also accepts its central theme more fully than do the rest of the middle class.

This concern with individual achievement and education further enables and encourages the members of this subculture to be deliberate and self-conscious about their choices. They are a little more understanding of the actions of others than the members of less educated strata. Their ability to participate in the larger society, plus their high social and economic status, also gives them somewhat greater control over their fate than other people, and makes the environment more predictable This in turn facilitates the practice of self-consciousness, empathy, and abstraction or generalization.

The possession of these skills distinguishes the upper-middle class from the rest of the middle class, and even more so from the working and lower classes. For the latter not only live in a less predictable environment, but they are also detached from the outside world, which increases their feeling that it, and, indeed, all of life, is unpredictable. In turn this feeling encourages a pervasive fatalism that pre-empts the optimism or pessimism of which the other classes are capable. The fatalism of the working and lower classes, as well as their lack of education and interest in personal development and object goals, minimizes introspection, self-consciousness, and empathy for the behavior of others.

CLASS: OPPORTUNITY AND RESPONSE

The subcultures which I have described are *responses* that people make to the *opportunities* and the *deprivations* that they encounter. More specifically, each subculture is an organized set of related responses that has developed out of people's efforts to cope with the opportunities, incentives, and rewards, as well as the deprivations, prohibitions, and pressures which the natural environment and society—that complex of coexisting and competing subcultures—offer to them. The responses which make up a subculture are compounded out of what people have retained of parental, that is, traditional responses, the skills and attitudes they have learned as children, and the innovations they have developed for themselves in their own encounters with opportunity and deprivation.

These responses cannot develop in a vacuum. Over the long range, they can be seen as functions of the resources which a society has available, and of the opportunities which it can offer. In each of the subcultures life is thus geared to the availability of specific qualitative types and quantities of income, education, and occupational opportunities. Although I have used occupational labels to distinguish between the major subcultures,[3] a man's job does not necessarily determine in which of these he shall be placed. In the long run, however, the existence of a specific subculture is closely related to the availability of occupational opportunities. For example, the functioning of the family circle and the routine-seeking way of life in the working class depend on the availability of stable employment for the man. The lower-class female-based family is a response to, or a method of coping with, the lack of stable male employment. The goals of middle- and upper-middle-class culture depend on the availability of sufficient income to finance the education that is necessary for a career, and on the availability of job opportunities that will allow middle-class individuals to find the type of job satisfaction for which they are striving.

When these opportunity factors are lacking, the cultural responses made by people are frustrated. Should opportunities be deficient over a long enough period, downward mobility results. Should they disappear entirely, the subculture will be apt to disintegrate eventually. For example, working-class culture can function for a time in a period of unemployment, but if no substitute sources of stability are made available, people initially resort to protest. Eventually, the family circle begins to break up under the strain, and its members adopt many if not all of the responses identified with the lower-class subculture.

[3] It is relevant to note that the words I have used to label the class subcultures are somewhat misleading. For example, I describe the middle class not as a group in the middle of the economic and power structure, but as a subculture focally concerned with the nuclear family. Likewise, the working class obviously works no more or less than any other group. Only the lower-class label fits well, since this subculture is in so many ways a response to the deprivations to which it is exposed.

Similar reactions take place in the other subcultures, although the ways in which they are expressed may differ. If job opportunities are lacking so as to frustrate the career desires of the middle class, or the professional desires of the upper-middle class, one reaction is to transfer aspirations elsewhere, for example, into non-work pursuits. Since upper-middle-class people are able and willing to act in the larger society, they may also develop social and political protest movements in order to create these opportunities, or to change society. Bourgeois socialist movements in America, taking their lead from the Marxist aim to "humanize" work so that it will provide quasi-professional job satisfaction to all people, are examples of such a reaction. Although downward mobility in the working class results in the adoption of lower-class responses, middle-class downward mobility does not bring about a working-class response. People may depend more on relatives as adversity strikes, but other differences between middle- and working-class subcultures remain in effect.

. . . .

THE EVALUATION OF WORKING- AND LOWER-CLASS SUBCULTURES

It should be evident from the description of the West Enders in the previous chapters that I believe the working-class subculture to be a generally satisfactory way of adapting to the opportunities which society has made available. Even so, it does have a number of negative features that constitute disadvantages both to working-class people and to the larger society.

One of these is the inability to participate in formal organizations and in general community activity. Although the lack of interest in voluntary associations is relatively unimportant, the inability to organize per se deprives working-class people of a method of political representation that is very important in a pluralistic society. Generally less well represented in the political arena than the economically more powerful, and socially more skillful groups, they are thus hampered in expressing their point of view, and in defending their interests. Consequently, they delegate the political representation function to others, yet only at some cost. Urban political machines and labor unions defend their interests, but the leadership of these organizations is not always fully representative. Moreover, when these agencies are not responsive, working-class people may turn to authoritarian and occasionally violent forms of protest—more out of desperation than choice. But such solutions are not always desirable or effective.

A related drawback is the general inability to understand bureaucratic behavior and object-orientation. This encourages the development of a conspiracy theory to explain the outside world, and breeds suspicions that are frequently inaccurate. As a result, the already existing gap between the working class and the larger society is widened.

Much of the time, the working class can protect itself from real or imagined injury by minimizing its dependence on the larger society. But this solution, which may work in prosperous times and in periods of social stability, is not always effective. In depressions, emergencies, and periods of rapid social change, however, the many indirect relationships to the larger society become apparent, mainly as they are being interrupted or altered. It is at these times that normal methods of class conflict over the distribution of opportunities go awry, and the gap between the working class and the larger society—notably the government—threatens to become harmful to both. The former is hurt by its inability to understand and deal with the changes that are taking place; the latter, by its inability to develop methods to solve the resulting problems even when it wants to do so. This state of affairs was illustrated only too well by the redevelopment of the West End. . . . The West Enders could not defend their interests, and the redevelopment agency was unable to understand their needs. Similarly, as automation and other technological changes alter the labor market, and reduce the need for semiskilled and unskilled workers, the working-class subculture's detachment from the larger society hampers the adjustment to changing conditions. Fortunately, the belief in education as a means to occupational success has allowed many working-class people to train themselves for the new job types that are now needed, and the problem is not as severe as it is in the lower class.

Another disadvantage of the working-class subculture is its rejection of certain types of caretakers, especially those whose services cannot be provided by the family circle. I am thinking here especially of the unwillingness to use medical specialists and psychotherapists. Although such caretakers may treat their clients as if they were middle class—which explains why they are so often rejected even when cost is no problem—the health goals which they further are sought by the working class as much as by any other. The family circle does provide a considerable amount of advice and emotional support to its members, but not always of the right kind. Indeed, some forms of care cannot be given by laymen, especially if the latter share the patient's mistaken beliefs. In dealing with mental illness, for example, the aid given by the family circle can even be harmful.

Finally, the emphasis on group life, the low value placed on privacy, and the general conservatism of the working-class culture all penalize those who deviate. For most people, this is no problem. Those who deviate by being mobile, for instance, are able to leave. But for people who are not mobile and who are different without wanting to be—such as those with neuroses that detach them from the group—the sanctions against deviance are harsh.

More intensive research of the dominant cultural patterns would undoubtedly indicate other patterns with deleterious consequences. For example, the impulsive child-rearing methods may have undesirable effects for some children who, for one reason or another, do not learn to cope with them. Only a highly detailed and longitudinal study of the subculture, however, will be able to unearth such patterns.

My limited observations suggest that, on the whole, the advantages of working-class subculture do outweigh the disadvantages. The latter are real, and ought to be removed, but they are not overwhelming. Thus, given our present knowledge, there is no justification for planning and caretaking programs which try to do away with the working-class subculture. John Seeley has suggested why it should not be done away with in his description of a Polish working-class group with whom he once lived:

... no society I have lived in before or since seemed to me to present so many of its members . . . so many possibilities and actualities of fulfillment of a number at least of basic human demands: for an outlet for aggressiveness, for adventure, for a sense of effectiveness, for deep feelings of belonging without undue sacrifice of uniqueness or identity, for sex satisfaction, for strong if not fierce loyalties, for a sense of independence from the pervasive omnicompetent, omniscient authority-in-general which at that time still overwhelmed to a greater degree the middle-class child. . . . These things had their prices, of course—not all values can be simultaneously maximized. But few of the inhabitants whom I reciprocally took "slumming" into middle-class life understood it or, where they did, were at all envious of it. And, be it asserted, this was not a matter of "ignorance" or incapacity to "appreciate finer things," but an inability to see one moderately coherent and sense-making satisfaction-system which they didn't know as preferable to the quite coherent and sense-making satisfaction-system they did know.[4]

Although his evaluation puts the case a little more enthusiastically than I might, it says very well that working-class culture is a positive response to the opportunities and deprivations which it encounters.

This is not true, however, of the lower-class subculture. Like all other cultures, it too tries to cope with the existing opportunities and deprivations, and to make life as bearable as possible. That it fails to succeed is largely the result of the intense deprivations with which it is saddled. Moreover, the response to these deprivations has consequences which make it difficult for lower-class people to accept opportunities for improvement if and when they are available.

Although lower-class culture has innumerable problems, perhaps the basic one is occupational. It seems to produce people who can work only in unskilled jobs. These jobs, however, are becoming more and more scarce, and they may virtually disappear in the not so distant future—

surely to no one's sorrow. But while lower-class women have developed working-class or quasi-working-class aspirations, the female-based family seems to raise men who find it difficult to develop the skills and the motivations that are necessary for obtaining and holding the jobs that will be available. In addition, these men are ambivalent about themselves and their role in society, and thus have considerable problems in achieving some sort of personal stability even when they want it, and even when they have gained some measure of economic stability. At present, then, lower-class culture breeds men who find it increasingly difficult to survive in modern society, and who, in a more automated future, will be unable to do so.

Lower-class women seem to be able to achieve some measure of stability—however problem-laden it may be—within and through the family. Even so, they are content neither with the subculture, nor with the female-based family, and try to see that their children escape it. This in itself suggests a major difference between the lower class and the other subcultures. The people within other subcultures are by and large satisfied with them and pass them on much more willingly to their children, at least to the extent that culture is ever transmitted deliberately. Lower-class women may not often succeed in raising their children to reject the culture they live in, but the mere fact that they try illustrates the absolute qualitative difference between the lower-class subculture and all the others.

There are more persuasive illustrations of this difference. Many lower-class children grow up in homes ravaged by alcoholism, drug addiction, and mental illness, and the subculture that they inherit is overlaid with pathology, for besides the comparatively more functional elements of lower-class subculture, there are many that are the result of pathological conditions, such as being raised by mentally ill parents. For example, many of the focal concerns of lower-class culture described by Walter Miller are useful methods of coping with the environment,[5] but there are some forms

---

[4] John R. Seeley, "The Slum: Its Nature, Use and Users," *Journal of the American Institute of Planners*, Vol. 25, 1959, pp. 7–14, at p. 10.

[5] "Lower Class Culture as a Generating Milieu of Gang Delinquency," *Journal of Social Issues*, Vol. 14, No. 3, 1958, pp. 5–19.

of action-seeking that reflect desperation more than adaptation. The episodes of riotous pleasure do not make up for the depression and self-destruction that accompany them. Significantly, the lower class not only has higher rates of mental illness than the others, but these rates are considerably higher than those of the working class.[6] Indeed, the difference in rates between these two classes is so great as to suggest that many elements of lower-class life are not merely culturally different from other ways of life, but that they are in fact pathological.

. . . .

BLUE-COLLAR MARRIAGE —BARRIERS TO MARITAL COMMUNICATION

Mirra Komarovsky

One of every three marriages in this study falls short of the prevailing American ideal of psychological intimacy between married partners. These reserved couples are examined in order to discover the barriers to communication. The emphasis upon barriers unfortunately reinforces the common assumption that high rapport in marriage is natural and requires no explanation. The ability of two individuals to share fully their inner lives is no more natural, however, than their failure to do so. Rapport and the breakdown of interaction are two facets of the same riddle, the solution of which ultimately requires a comparison of both

Condensed from *Blue-Collar Marriage*, by Mirra Komarovsky. © Copyright 1962, 1964 by Random House, Inc. Reprinted by permission.

[6] August B. Hollingshead and Fredrick C. Redlich, *Social Class and Mental Illness*, New York: Wiley, 1958, Chap. 7. The authors also note that male rates in the lower class (Class V) are higher than female ones, a disparity not prevalent in other classes. *Ibid.*, p. 200.

kinds of relationships. But barriers to communication are more visible than conditions which facilitate it.

Socially structured barriers, those rooted in shared values and conditions of life, will be considered. . . .

SHARP DIFFERENTIATION IN THE INTERESTS OF THE SEXES

Husbands and wives need not share identical mental worlds to understand one another, but their two separate worlds must be in contact at some points. This overlapping of interests is so narrow for a number of Glenton[1] couples that neither partner can serve as a satisfactory audience for the other. . . .

The upbringing of working-class children undoubtedly contributes to this separation of the sexes. Working-class parents make sharper distinctions than do the middle classes between the social roles of boys and girls. One investigator concludes that "middle-class mothers' conceptions of what is desirable for boys are much the same as their conceptions of what is desirable for girls. But working-class mothers make a clear distinction between the sexes. . . ."[2]

In another inquiry, working-class boys and girls were found to be aware of sex roles earlier and more clearly than both boys and girls of the middle-class group, as indicated by the recognition of "appropriate" toys and behavior.[3] Whatever the role of their upbringing, the gulf between the sexes does exist. The following excerpts from the interviews illustrate a variety of reactions to this situation—the boredom of the wives, the contempt and exasperation of the husbands, the resignation of some and the yearnings of others.

A 23-year-old husband, a grammar school graduate, married three years, declared:

[1] Fictitious name of a community of fifty thousand, heavily working class, located five miles from a city of about half a million and less than twenty miles from a metropolis. (C. S. H.)

[2] Melvin L. Kohn, "Social Class and Parental Authority," *American Sociological Review*, Vol. 24, June, 1959, p. 365.

[3] Meyer Rabban, "Sex-Role Identification in Young Children in Two Diverse Social Groups," Genetic Psychological Monograph, Vol. 42, August, 1950, pp. 140–141.

"What is it about women that they want to talk about things when there is really nothing to talk about? Why do they have to hash it over? They talk about screwy things. Keep quacking, like beating a dead horse." He and his buddies agreed that "it seems to be this way all around."

. . . .

Similar dissatisfactions were expressed by a wife who was trying to explain why talking with girl friends frequently proved more satisfying than conversations with her husband. When she once told her husband about a young woman in the community who had an illegitimate baby, he ended the discussion with: "It happens all the time." But with her girl friends she can talk over such matters in detail. (Does the girl really want to give up her baby? Should she? Would she marry the father of her baby if he asked her to? And so on.)

This pattern was detected in case after case.

. . . .

Generally, having neither competence nor interest in the mate's topic of conversation, each complains that the other "goes on and on about boring things" in unnecessary detail. One of the conditions causing this gulf between the interests of husbands and wives is the exclusion of the wives from their husband's world of work.

THE WIFE AND HER HUSBAND'S JOB

There is scarcely a couple among these Glenton families who does not occasionally discuss the husband's job or his occupational plans. But these matters head the list of topics which the husbands admittedly disclose least to their wives. The interviews reveal several grounds for this reserve.

The Monotonous Nature of the job. This is one reason for limited conversation. "There is nothing to elaborate about my job," said a 36-year-old steeplejack, "I just mix paint all day and put it on. It is monotonous." The men frequently note that if something humorous or unexpected takes place during their work day, they are apt to tell their wives about it. . . .

A 33-year-old hand truckman's testimony is characteristic "I'm glad enough to

be away from there. When I get away from the plant, I'd rather just let that rest till the next day. After all, it's no great fun; it's just something I got to make a living by. That's all." When asked "Does your wife take an interest in your job?" another husband replied: "I don't take much interest in it myself so I wouldn't expect her to if I couldn't."

The Job Is Usually Felt to Be Too Technical for Woman. Every husband was asked whether his wife understood the problems he encountered during his working day. Although a few of the husbands claimed that anyone, including their wives could easily understand their work, the great majority, many of whom held semi-skilled jobs of low technical level, agreed with the man who said, "She'd have to work alongside of me to understand. I don't expect her to." They often felt that only a man in the same line of work could comprehend the technical problems, the irritations, and the satisfactions of the daily routine. The social relationships on the job were seldom discussed at home and social contacts with co-workers were extremely rare. . . .

Talk About the Job Carries the Connotation, for the Husband, of "Griping," Which Is Thought to Be Unmanly. Our repeated question, "Can you talk to your wife about your job?" brought forth an unmistakable expression of a value: "I don't believe in bringing my job home." To talk about the job meant to "gripe about it." A 40-year-old sash fitter said apologetically, "Sometimes things go wrong and you come home and you got to get it out of your system and you can't help it if it spills over a little bit." A 23-year-old sanitation worker, in answer to the question about talk (a question which made no reference whatsoever to complaints), said, "Yes, I guess I do blow my stack sometimes: I try not to, but sometimes it sort of busts out of me."

The wives also tend to equate talk about the job with "griping." The item "tells wife about what happens on the job" was included in the schedule of "What makes a good husband?" Only 18 per cent of the women rated it as an important quality. And even this minority endorses conversation about the husband's work because of its presumed mental health function—"Let him talk if he has to get it off his chest." A more prevalent attitude is expressed by another woman who said, "When the hours is done, that is the end." In fact, the only women who complain that their husbands do not tell them enough about the job are a few unhappy wives for whom this silence seems to be another manifestation of the general withdrawal of the husbands.[4]

However self-critical their attitude towards "griping" about the job, we estimate about one-fifth of the husbands wished nevertheless that their wives were more interested in their work problems. On occasions when they wanted to share their work experiences they found their wives preoccupied with the children or uninterested.

Work and Home Should Be Kept Separate. The great majority of the wives, some 80 per cent, have no social contact with their husband's work-mates. The friendships husbands may form on the job do not include their wives. Indeed, in more than one-half of the cases the wives either never met their husbands' co-workers or saw them only once or twice when the latter delivered messages to, or called for, the husbands. In about 30 per cent of the cases, the wife did meet one or more fellow workers at some social gathering, a Christmas party or an outing. And in the remaining one-fifth of the cases, wives had more frequent contacts with co-workers. In several instances co-workers were relatives of the couple.

The feeling that work-mates do not belong in one's home was expressed by a 32-year-old painter: "It isn't nice to bring work people home. Homes are not for that. At home you raise children and relax. If you have friends from work, you're going to talk things over with them, and not want to have to hear babies crying or to go out shopping. When you're home you want to ease up and not have to keep on your toes." The idea that the home is too "pure"

for masculine comradery was also expressed by several men who noted that the talk among the fellows at work is too rough and vulgar for women. Thus a 38-year-old cable layer said to us, "Nah, they ain't got no call to come on home with me, what would they do there? We might feel like having a drink, or raising a ruckus, and you ought not to do that at home. It is a lot better in the tavern, or the dog-wagon or hanging around the street someplace."

Some Husbands Opt for Reciprocal Reticence. Instead of mutual sharing of daily experiences, some husbands recommend reserve. Thus a 31-year-old truck driver declared: "It don't do no good to go home and belly-ache to your wife. If you don't want to know about what happens with the washing and with the neighbors' kids, you shouldn't ought to tell her about what goes on at the plant either." And another husband: "The only things we don't tell each other are things the other don't want to hear. She don't want to know what I did in the warehouse and I don't want to know if the baby is sick, so long as it ain't really sick." . . .

The working-class situation stands in sharp contrast to the frequently reported involvement of the "corporation wife" in her husband's career.[5] The daily assessment of office politics, the prudent entertaining of superiors and associates and the resulting feeling of personal participation in a husband's career are all lacking here. If the workingman, in contrast to the corporation careerist, misses the opportunity to share his world of work, he enjoys a greater immunity from his wife's scrutiny of his daily performance. In any case, for better or worse, the husband's job is not an area of active common interest for the large majority of our couples.

In all social classes, to be sure, the sexes are bound to have some separate interests because their social roles differ. Neither husband nor wife can be expected to be interested in the purely technical aspects of the other's daily tasks. A woman friend, confronted with similar problems, will

[4] The wives, as well as the husbands, were questioned about the job as a topic of conversation. This served as a safeguard against the possibility that husbands minimized the extent of their talk because, in their own minds, this was "griping."

[5] See, e.g., William H. Whyte, Jr., "The Corporation and the Wife," *Fortune*, Vol. 44, October, 1951, 86 ff; and "The Wives of Management," *Fortune*, Vol. 44, November, 1951, 109 ff.

naturally have a more lively interest than the husband in the baby's diet, a new recipe or a bargain. Similarly, a fellow worker will be more competent than one's wife to discuss the technical problems of the job. Insofar as the husband is drawn into the domestic sphere or the wife gets involved in her husband's career, their interests converge. Neither of these conditions obtained for most of Glenton's families.

Men and women, however, may have their separate tasks and still share common interests in the psychological problems of child rearing, in their personalities, in social life and aspirations for the future. But it is only a slight exaggeration to say that for many of Glenton families life contains little else apart from the immediate daily tasks. The impoverishment of life and of personality curtails the development of shared interests.

THE IMPOVERISHMENT OF LIFE

Writers concerned with the meagerness of marital communication sometimes imply that it would flow abundantly were we only able to open the floodgates. However, the impoverishment of the quality of life not only narrows the overlapping of interests and consequent sharing of experiences, but also stunts personal development. There may be little or nothing to communicate. Speaking of television, for example, typical comments by the respondents were: "We both see it, why talk about it," and "What's there to talk about other than to say it's good or bad." In more general terms, one woman put it this way: "We tell each other things, but I don't know as how we talk about them. He'll tell me or I'll tell him something has happened, but there ain't nothing much to say. . . ."

If external life is restricted for these families, so is their inner world. For example, the meagerness of joint social life deprives the couples of conversation about mutual friends, gossip, planning of social affairs and "party post-mortems." Over one-third of these couples either never visit with another couple apart from relatives or do so only very infrequently, a few times a year on some special occasion of an anniversary or a New Year's celebration. Low level of interest in reading, in current events and in cultural subjects has a similar impoverishing effect.

Couples who are exposed to the middle-class values of companionship, but whose mode of life does not stimulate common interests, are sometimes acutely aware of this discrepancy. They know that husbands and wives are supposed to talk with one another, but they do not have anything to say. Characteristically, one young husband, a high school graduate, said: "I wish we had more things to talk about, but when I try to think of something I don't know anything to talk to her about. I wish we could get out and see the shows or something like that." And another man expressed a similar dissatisfaction: "If my wife and I had a little more education maybe we'd have what you call it—more interests? Maybe we could come together better, maybe life would be more interesting for us."

The barriers to communication described so far derive from the meager content of common interests. Deficient skills of communication, especially on the part of the less-educated husbands, also hinder the sharing of experiences.

THE TRAINED INCAPACITY TO SHARE

The phrase "trained incapacity to share" aims to convey a certain view about the men's inarticulateness. The ideal of masculinity into which they were socialized inhibits expressiveness both directly, with its emphasis on reserve, and indirectly, by identifying personal interchange with the feminine role. Childhood and adolescence, spent in an environment in which feelings were not named, discussed or explained, strengthened these inhibitions. In adulthood they extend beyond culturally demanded reticence—the inhibitions are now experienced not only as "I shouldn't," but as "I cannot." In explaining instances of reserve in marriage many more husbands than wives say: "It is hard to talk about such things." . . .

I used to try to ask him when we were first married, said a 26-year-old woman about her husband, why he gets into those real flippy moods, but he used to say nothing was wrong, and asking seemed to make him worse. The more I tried, the worse he'd get. So I found out that if you just don't bother him, it wears off. Another young woman described her husband: Sometimes he could get real black and quiet and you'd just better keep out of his way and not say anything.

The wives endorse the therapeutic value of talk more frequently than the husbands. Thus a 30-year-old woman:

Lots of people say it's not good to go around shooting off your lips about what's eating them, but I think the good thing is to talk it out and get it out of your system. But I have to leave him alone because if I try to get him to talk he'll get really sore, or he'll go off the deep end and walk out of here. Or maybe he'd tell me something else, lying like, just so I wouldn't get at the thing that makes him sore. He is strictly hands-off if something hurts him. . . . It makes it rough . . . not knowing what's eating him hurts you worse than it hurts him.

. . . These comments are not exceptional. Twenty-six per cent of the wives, but only 9 per cent of the husbands, in answer to questions about dissatisfactions with communication, complain that their mate "does not reveal worries." The responses to the projective story about the husband who doesn't talk enough . . . convey the same idea. Although the story contained no reference whatsoever to worry, 11 per cent of the respondents agreed: "He might not want to talk because something is wrong." Of 23 qualities of a good husband, the women ranked "speaks his mind when something is worrying him" as the second most important quality. These rankings reflect current deprivations—not merely ideals. The wives value the trait of speaking out precisely because they miss it in their husbands.

The ideal of masculinity accepted by the men is certainly one factor in their meager disclosure of stressful feelings. To gripe about the job .carries the connotation of weakness. A strong man bears his troubles in silence and does not "dump his load on the family"; he does not ask for solace and reassurance. Indeed, an adult male does not even experience hurt, much less admit it. "When I don't feel good," said one husband, "I light out and don't dump my load on them." Speaking of his wife, a 40-year-old carpenter (with eight years of school)

described the masculine norm quite explicitly: "Sure she gets hurt. Men are supposed to be braver than women, but women is bound to get hurt, it's in their nature, ain't it?"

The strength of such norms is demonstrated in the section of the interview dealing with feelings of hurt and of anger. When asked for sources of hurt feelings, almost twice as many men as women expressed disapproval of the very experience of hurt in an adult: "After a man gets on his feet, he shouldn't be hurt deeply about anything"; "You ought to outgrow it." More men than women say, "Nothing can hurt me anymore," or "Don't know what could reach me anymore." They generally add that at some earlier time—in childhood, "before the army," "before marriage," their feelings were hurt. Among the less-educated, 30 per cent of the men, but only 15 per cent of the women, denied completely that they experienced hurt at present. The sexes, however, report the experience of anger with nearly identical frequency: only 5 per cent of the women and 8 per cent of the men maintain that they are never angry.

It may be argued that the men experience hurt feelings less frequently (thus not merely concealing such feelings) than the allegedly more sensitive females. But the testimony of the high school graduates weakens this argument because the difference by sex in the reporting of hurt feelings narrows: 12 per cent of women and 17 per cent of the men in this educational category deny feelings of hurt. The high school men may have a less rigid norm of masculinity and be more willing to admit being hurt than the less-educated men. Consistent with this idea is the similarity between the two groups of men in their admission of anger: only 8 per cent of the less-educated and only 6 per cent of the high school graduates denied the experience of anger. Unlike the experience of hurt, anger does not carry the connotation of weakness to the less-educated men.

Socialized to identify the expression of certain emotions with a lack of masculinity, the men inhibit self-disclosure. Lack of education plays an independent role in limiting the capacity to identify, interpret and express feelings. . . . Of the four subgroups (high school and less-educated husbands and wives) the less-educated husbands are consistently the most withdrawn. They reveal less of themselves to their wives, are less inclined to find relief by openly expressing emotion, and tend to react to marriage conflict by withdrawal. Of all the aids in overcoming emotional stress listed by the uneducated husbands, only 28 per cent involve interaction with others, as against 42 per cent of such aids for the less-educated wives. These men seek relief in action rather than in talk.

The reticence of the less-educated husbands is also apparent in the relative scantiness of their replies to the section of the interview on self, personality and psychological relationships. The questions called for sources of feelings of hurt, happiness, worry, self-satisfaction and guilt, and for assessments of one's strong points and shortcomings. The less-educated husband lists fewer items per person than any of the other respondents. For example, in describing his strong and weak traits, he lists 5.4 fewer traits than does the less-educated woman. But among the high school graduates the sex difference is narrowed to only 2.1 items in favor of women. The inhibitions of the less-educated men are further revealed by the fact that, of all the four subgroups, the less-educated husbands are the only ones who list fewer items about their own personality than about the personality of their mates.

. . . .

THE EDUCATIONAL FACTOR IN COMMUNICATION

The foregoing pages have dealt with socially structured . . . barriers to marital communication. We have seen that communication between husbands and wives is hindered by certain traditional values. Having embraced these values, some men contemptuously relegate conversation about persons to "old women's gossip," and attribute self-disclosure of painful emotions to lack of self-sufficiency. Question: "Do you talk to your wife about this?" Answer: "Yes, once in a while I might *cry on her shoulder*" (emphasis ours), they admit shamefacedly. The separation between the masculine and the feminine spheres of interest also thwarts communication. The humdrum or the technical nature of the man's job makes it of little interest to the wife. The husband wants some "peace and quiet" upon his return home. . . .

The above analysis helps to account for the fuller self-disclosure of the high school graduates. Better education and associated social conditions help to lower a number of the barriers. Role differentiation in marriage is not so sharp among the better-educated as among the less-educated families. The high school fathers are somewhat more active in child care. And there is more discussion of the husband's job: of 18 high school graduates, 39 per cent and of 40 less-educated men, only 15 per cent discuss their jobs with their wives "quite a lot."[6] In the former group, an overlap in activities promotes communication by supplying a common content of experience. The high school graduates also exceed the less-educated in the extent of shared leisure-time activities. . . . Furthermore, the better-educated husbands admit feelings of hurt and describe their personalities in fuller detail than the less-educated men. Economic failure of the husband affects adversely the freedom of communication, and there are more such failures among the less-educated men. . . . The high school wives have more power in marriage in comparison with the less-educated women. . . . It is our impression that enjoying this power they are able to control the relationship more effectively and to give expression to their interest in sharing experiences. Finally, the high school graduates have relatively fewer very unhappy marriages in which marital conflict leads to a breakdown of communication. All such circumstances combine to raise the level of self-disclosure to mate among the high school graduates.

It should be stressed, however, that higher education by no means guarantees effective marital communication. To be sure, the marital dialogue of the high school graduates is, on the whole, fuller than that of the

[6] Robert O. Blood, Jr., and Donald M. Wolfe, however, found that low blue-collar husbands were more likely than high blue-collar husbands to report happenings on the job to their wives. *Husbands and Wives*, Glencoe, Illinois: Free Press, 1960, p. 168.

less-educated couples, but the overlap between the self-disclosure ratings of the two educational groups is substantial. Some better-educated couples are characterized by moderate or meager self-disclosure for a variety of psychological reasons. Conversely many less-educated couples enjoy deep and close relationships. Some of the latter are the poorly educated, who, apart from their few years of formal schooling, resemble the high school graduates in their values and mode of life. Some less-educated respondents, for example, expressed "middle-class" values on the projective stories.

More interesting, because more revealing of new insights, are the less-educated couples who enjoy satisfying communication and at the same time hold values and display the mode of life typical of the less-educated in general. We shall examine such a case.

EXISTENCE OF CLOSE, HAPPY MARRIAGES AMONG THE LESS-EDUCATED

Mr. and Mrs. King are both 26, married for eight years and expecting their fourth child. Both had ten years of schooling. They share few general interests and spend much of their leisure separately. They express many working-class norms of marriage. Do cases of this kind imply that social factors are, after all, unimportant—that perhaps "love" does conquer all?

The clue to the paternal role played by Mr. K. in this marital relationship was provided by his wife, who, the youngest of six siblings, found her marital role congenial.

He is no older than I am but he sure knows how to handle me if I get a head of steam on, said Mrs. K. He can steady me sometimes by just looking at me in a very nice way with his real blue eyes. She described an argument about making the boy eat his breakfast. Her husband slammed his hand on the table and told her not to discuss it in front of the children. That made me mad enough to cry. So she got up and started washing up, slamming dishes and pots around. Well, he came over and put his arm around me and he made me hold still and just looked at me and he said he had to go out and he hoped I'd be over this when he came back. So then I began to cry and he kissed me a little and left. All of a sudden I started to laugh at myself crying into the dishpan.

The K.'s gave typical working-class responses on the test stories. Their interests are sex-linked, and each (especially the wife) is deeply involved in their respective relationships with same-sex groups.

Both Mr. and Mr. K. felt that the wife who wanted her husband to give up evenings with his male friends was unreasonable and so was the husband who resented his wife's intimacy with her mother. The husband who comes home and does not talk to his wife should be left in peace by his "selfish" wife. . . .

Mrs. K. is the youngest of six children and Mr. K. has five siblings—the parents of each are living in the same community and none of the siblings is far away. The extraordinary closeness of family and in-law relations is a fact of great significance in the life of this couple. Economically, emotionally, recreationally—their daily lives are interwoven with the lives of their parents and siblings.

Mr. and Mrs. K. described a typical working-class division of interests. They talk little of his job. He discusses politics, sports and hobbies with men because she is not interested in these subjects. Mrs. K. on her side described most eloquently how "women should stick together and men should stay by themselves because they don't understand some things." She is in constant and intimate communication with mother, sisters, sisters-in-law and girl friends. Although she is shy and modest about sex, this subject is also discussed among the girls.

Mrs. K. gives the impression that she is more at ease in her female world. Her great respect for her husband and the desire to please him makes her cautious: "If he is feeling dopey I don't want to talk to him because he might get mad at me and I'd feel terrible."

Many an evening a week, Mr. K. goes out for a walk, to see his brother or to the tavern. He often does not tell his wife where he is going or when he expects to return.

Mr. K. does not help with housework or the care of children. Though sometimes he "sticks around" and wipes the dishes and baby-sits if Mrs. K. has something special she wants to do, the task allocation is traditional. Mr. K. is a devoted father. He can "make them mind him better" than their mother, but child care and discipline is Mrs. K.'s responsibility.

Mr. K. describes the typical male difficulty in expressing unhappy emotions and tends to withdraw when he is depressed. Mrs. K. said that she is not quite sure how her husband overcomes his bad moods: "He never bawls me out and he doesn't talk to me." Perhaps, "when he goes out he talks things over with his brother. I used to ask him why he was 'flippy' but it seemed to make him worse. . . . So I found out if you just don't bother him it wears off."

Mr. K. dislikes his job, despite its adequate pay, but does not reveal the full extent of his unhappiness so as not to worry his wife. He feels depressed at times, does not always understand the reason for these moods, and does not discuss them with his wife. She wishes that he did: "It would make it a lot easier for me if he'd explain why he felt the way he did sometimes when he comes home. I'd know if I had to shut up or if I could go on. This way I keep wondering what's the matter with him."

Despite many features which might be expected to estrange the couple, the marriage is close and deeply satisfying to both.

The personality needs of each are fulfilled at the emotional core of the marriage. Sex relations are satisfactory also.

Mrs. K., as the baby of the family, was always teased affectionately and is still easily hurt. "They sometimes called me a dumb Dora—it's on account of I can't talk sometimes. He bawls me out for minding what the others say and he says I'm not so dumb." Her husband gives her a combination of support, protection and appreciation which makes her say fervently, "Oh, he's the most!" He always compliments her when she cooks an especially good meal. His praise matters, she said, because unlike the in-laws who praise out of politeness, he doesn't say things he doesn't mean. He is the stronger of the two; she tries to please him and he rewards her adequately: "Whenever she's done a good job, I tell her so."

In his interview Mr. K. said: "I don't know if she'd tell you because she's kind of bashful but she's real good in bed. . . . I think you might call it ideal: a woman who is bashful and keeps to herself with every-

body else and who's better than anybody with you." . . .

Mr. K. is, in turn, fulfilled in marriage. He had a vulnerable spot of his own. He never cared for school and his brothers used to "ride him about being a dummy." His "wonderful mother" would tell them to lay off him. Now he enjoys the deep respect of his wife—"I am the skipper of this marriage." She often tells him how very patient he is. His wife sums up this aspect of their marriage with deep insight: "He ain't stuck on himself at all. Him and me is a little bit alike that way. We have to tell each other not to mind things and that we're better than we think we are. Only he bawls me out more than I do him because he's a man." And Mr. K.: "When I got something to say she listens. She didn't sit there and wish I'd stop or be thinking about something else. Sometimes she'll be talking about the babies that aren't my work, but I listen to her."

Both Mr. and Mrs. K. have patience and capacity to get along with people. Mrs. K. said that both have good dispositions. One of his brothers was teasing them and said, "There goes the patient couple." Mr. K. said in discussing her moods, "She is too nice to get furious, but she gets upset."

To return to the question posed at the outset of this analysis: do occasional marriages like this one indicate that the lower-class norms of marriage—segregation of interests along sex lines, reticence, and separate leisure-time pastimes—do not impair communication after all?

For one thing, a marriage which is so deeply satisfying can apparently affect behavior even in the absence of certain norms. The gratification derived from the relationship leads to mutual concern—"It isn't that I'm that much interested in the neighbors, I am interested in her," explains Mr. K. in describing their conversations. It appears also that the content of shared experiences must be distinguished from the scope of sharing. The sense of closeness is apparently compatible with a very specialized pattern of sharing: *what* specifically is shared may be more important for the feeling of intimacy than *how much* of one's life is shared.

But if "love" does offset the potentially estranging social factors, it isn't love alone that does it. These factors do create typical vulnerabilities. To maintain its happy equilibrium this type of marriage requires some special supports.

The equilibrium of this marriage is maintained by the shared ability of close relatives and friends who fulfill for both, but especially for the wife, functions lacking in marriage. "No [Mr. K.] don't give a hoot," said Mrs. K. about many things which are very important to her, and about which no man, she added, could be expected to care. If Mrs. K. were isolated or, like some of the other women in Glenton, not on good terms with her relatives and in-laws, and had to depend upon her husband to be her audience, the marriage probably would be strained. As it is Mr. K. is somewhat irritated by his wife's "gossip." Mr. K., in turn, spends much of his lesiure in masculine company and his wife suspects that, in his "flippy moods," his brother is more of a help to him that she is.

Mrs. K.'s deep involvement with her mother and sister is tolerated by her husband partly because he likes his in-laws and they like him. Mr. K. was asked, "Do women have more need than men for heart-to-heart talk?" and he replied, "Well my wife sure in hell does and that's for sure. I could go for a month without talking to anybody but she's gotta talk to them just about every day." It is easy to imagine how this mild irritation would be aggravated were his relations with his in-laws less satisfactory or his position in marriage less secure.

Moreover, satisfactory economic conditions and common economic aspirations add to the assets of the marriage. The K.'s have recently purchased a house with some help from their families, but also as a result of joint planning and effort. "I feel real happy and real proud," said Mrs. K., "I had a lot to do with it, working between having babies and living cheaply and saving up." Their satisfaction in this accomplishment was revealed when in answer to a question, "When did Mr. K. last tell you he loved you?" Mrs. K. replied, "He don't do it regular like a school kid but a couple of nights ago we were watching T.V. and the kids had gone to bed. We were feeling kind of good about the house and he just up and said he loved me."

The case of Mr. and Mrs. K. illustrates how close and satisfying marriage can be despite a very specialized pattern of sharing. Even within the strictly personal sphere (her hurts, enthusiasm and problems) Mrs. K. makes a sharp distinction between what is appropriate to share with her husband, on the one hand, and with her girl friends and female relatives, on the other. Deeply satisfied in their emotional needs, Mr. and Mrs. K. live large segments of their lives apart from one another.

This chapter has specified social . . . factors that tend to limit the sharing of experiences with the spouse. Being more prevalent among the less-educated than among the high school graduates, many of these factors account for the relatively meager self-disclosure of the poorly educated respondents. The final case study advances the analysis further. The close and happy marriage of the poorly educated Kings reveals some conditions offsetting the estranging factors. Deep psychic congeniality, for instance, can create mutual concern even in the absence of the social norm of companionship. This case demonstrates still another fact—that satisfaction with communication and a sense of closeness do not, apparently, require that the totality of one's experiences be shared with the mate. Such emotions may co-exist with a very specialized pattern of sharing. But we have indicated some other factors as, for example, availability of congenial relatives and friends and satisfactory economic conditions, which, apart from emotional complementarity, support this type of marriage.

SOCIAL CLASS DIFFERENCES IN FAMILY LIFE IN THE USSR*

H. Kent Geiger

Many of a society's most poignant discrepancies between its ideology and social

*Printed by permission of the author.

reality come to a head in the question of stratification. This is especially the case in the USSR, where the old order was overthrown in the name of the oppressed and where the building of a classless society is held as a national goal. In this and in related issues Soviet society exhibits some relatively unique features of great interest. The various groups and strata in the Soviet population have suffered or prospered in ways not commonly found in the history of other societies. There has been sustained intervention and control exerted by political authority over the structures and processes allowed more spontaneous development in other lands. Special attention has been accorded to the upgrading of women, but success in bringing them full equality with men cannot as yet be granted. And so on.

Many of the characteristics of Soviet social stratification are germane to our topic, social level differences in family patterns, but two are of particular consequence. It is widely recognized that the Soviet population is quite stratified, but the precise nature and extent of differentiation is little known, and least of all perhaps in respect to family life. In Part I, a number of the most important of these differences are identified. In Part II, I discuss the relevance in family life of dimensional inconsistency or, more precisely, inconsistency in the distribution of status elements. This is the tendency for the political, economic and social dimensions or orders of the Soviet system of stratification to be less highly correlated than in other societies.

THE NATURE AND EXTENT OF STATUS DIFFERENTIATION

The Standard and Style of Living. Comprehensive data describing the income or property of different categories of the population have not been published, but Soviet sociologists have in the recent past contributed statistical information for selected areas and groups which is well worth our attention. Some important aspects of the living standard and style of life are presented in Table 1, for the population of Terpenie, a Ukrainian village. When the families studied are grouped by occupational type and level of heads of households, such indicators of living

standard as masonry rather than log construction of walls, wood rather than dirt floors and number of cows owned per family (considerably less than one) suggest the important items and range of variation found in Soviet villages.

In one respect, at least, the rural family does not fare poorly in relation to the urban family. In Terpenie housing is primitive but most families in the village can boast of three separate rooms. In Soviet cities the ordinary family must live in a single room and share a kitchen with others.[1] The elite, of course, generally enjoy several rooms in a well-heated and furnished flat, and may even have the luxury of hot and cold running water and a private bath. Another feature of the family life of the Soviet urban elite is that many own country houses or *dachas* to which they can retire for vacations and week-ends. While typically small and simple, these are much cherished, and probably serve as important status symbols as well as a source of restorative escape from the city.

Table 2 shows differences among officials, employees and workers in enterprises of the Leningrad machine-building industry for a recent year. The differences in monthly pay at different job levels seem quite small, although the top category includes directors of "shops" and "departments" as well as enterprises, which doubtless considerably depresses the average pay for the group. Such an interpretation is supported by the fact that the variation for entries in that category is considerably larger than for the other categories. In general, Soviet factory directors, scientists, artists, etc., enjoy a standard of living which is low compared with similar elites in Western democratic societies but noticeably higher than their own less distinguished fellow citizens.

In the USSR the members of families must not only engage in a struggle for income but often must search vigorously for effective and enjoyable ways to spend it.

[1] At the end of 1961 urban housing conditions were comparable to those of 1926. Per capita living space at that time was only about a third of the amount available to the population of the USA. See Timothy Sosnovy, "The Soviet City," pp. 321–45 in Joint Economic Committee of the U.S. Congress, 87th Session, *Dimensions of Soviet Economic Power*, Washington, D.C., 1962.

TABLE 1   Representative Status Characteristic. Differences by Type of Labor of
Household Head, Village of Terpenie, Uk. SSR, 1964

Type of Labor	Per Cent of Houses with Masonry Walls	Per Cent of Houses with Wooden Floors	Cows per Hundred Families	Average No. of Years of Education	Per Cent of Houses with Religious Icons
	(1)	(2)	(3)	(4)	(5)
Skilled non-manual	75	100	75	12	7
Other non-manual	20	100	20	9	24
Skilled manual	37	86	33	7	34
Other manual	16	70	31	4	57

Source: Iu. V. Arutiunian, "The Social Structure of the Rural Population," *CDSP* 18.25:20–25, trans. from *Voprosy Filosofii*, No. 5, 1966, pp. 51–61.

The figures are adapted from Tables 3 and 4 and from the text. The first three columns refer only to kolkhoz families (N = 161). Columns (4) and (5) refer to the families of workers employed in state institutions and enterprises (N = 189) as well as those of the collective farmers in the village. Figures were rounded to the nearest even number.

The notorious weakness of retail distribution compounds the already short aggregate supply of consumer goods and services, so that the "opportunity to spend" has become itself an important component in the Soviet living standard. This is one reason why many people are so eager to leave the countryside to live in the city.

Residential location is extraordinarily important as a determinant of status in the USSR. Three distinctions are commonly made, probably of about equal importance. Siberia, the Far North and Central Asia contrast with the preferred European areas; the countryside contrasts with settled urban areas; and smaller, "provincial" towns and cities contrast with the central metropolitan areas, especially Moscow, Leningrad, and Kiev. The former in each of the paired categories suffers from more primitive conditions of life, greater scarcity of cultural, educational and recreational facilities, more inaccessibility, greater extremes of climate and topology, and so on. Those who reside in such areas suffer a corresponding status degradation.

The Soviet Government has in the past gone quite far in designating certain retail stores as special access or "closed distribution" institutions, thus reserving the chance to buy items desired but in short supply as a privilege. Other such services and privileges are at times reserved for the elite—dispensation from having to stand in line, allocation of a special lane on broad thoroughfares for the use of officials' cars, and so on.[2]

Typically Soviet are the state-operated public dining facilities and recreational or "cultural" clubs. The evidence suggests that eating outside the home in cafeterias and restaurants is positively associated with social level, and that the use of clubs is inversely associated with it. For example, one study reported from Leningrad that 25 per cent of the young people from worker family backgrounds but only 2 per cent of those from intelligentsia families visited a club during the preceding year.[3]

Certain patterns of public facility use are differentiated by social level for special reasons or involve distinctive implications. Placing a young child in a public institution such as an infants home for temporary care on a voluntary basis would seem to increase on higher social levels, because of the need for long trips connected with the job, field work to gain the practical experience required for a higher degree, and the like. But the surrender of a young child by its parent or parents on a permanent basis is more frequent on lower social levels. Much

[2] Joseph Novak, *The Future Is Ours, Comrade: Conversations with the Russians*, New York: Doubleday, 1960, pp. 38–39.

[3] A. G. Kharchev, "A Sociologist's Notes: A Free Evening," *CDSP* 17.46: 14–15, trans. from *Nedelia*, No. 42, Oct. 10–16, 1965, pp. 8–9.

TABLE 2   Selected Status Characteristics at Different Levels of Job Skill in Enterprises of the Machine-Building Industry, Leningrad, 1965

Occupational Group	Monthly Pay in Rubles	Years of Education	Per Cent Members of Party or YCL	Per Cent Participating in Public Activity	Per Cent Fully Satisfied with Occupation	N
	(1)	(2)	(3)	(4)	(5)	
Directors and organizers	173	14	61	84	n.a.	(92)
Technical and scientific	127	14	40	70	63	(135)
Skilled non-manual	110	12	43	82	n.a.	(287)
Semi-professional	129	9	38	79	80	(67)
Skilled manual workers	120	8	37	61	n.a.	(1002)
Semi-skilled non-manual	84	9	27	55	n.a.	(353)
Semi-skilled manual	107	8	39	54	61	(837)
Unskilled manual	98	6	14	35	25	(115)

Source: O. I. Shkaratan, "Social Differentiation in the Soviet Working Class," *CDSP* 19.12::3–8, trans. from *Voprosy Filosofi*, No. 1, 1967, pp. 28–39. This is an adaptation of Table 2 . . . and information reported in the text. Figures are rounded to the nearest even number.

the same has been true of attendance at Soviet boarding schools. Since the time when these institutions originated in 1956, they have been populated mainly by so-called "difficult children" or by children whose families did not adequately look after them. The tendency to use the boarding school like a corrective institution has brought them low esteem among the population at large and caused them to be widely considered a failure.[4]

Soviet sociological research has always paid a lot of attention to patterns of time usage, and studies almost always reveal that the higher status urban occupational groups work longer hours than do members of the working class.[5] We do not always know how to relate such knowledge to the comparative standard of living, since the variation by social level of relevant preferences is not entirely clear. Thus, higher status persons typically also display a substantially higher level of job satisfaction. See Table 2 for one example. Consequently, we do not know which group is better off; most probably this is an area where value consensus is lacking, and length of working day is not a decisive differentiating factor in respect to welfare.

How do the members of Soviet families spend their free time? In 1965 a representative national sample of 2730 urban adults was polled by the Public Opinion Institute of *Komsomolskaia Pravda*, the Soviet youth newspaper. Respondents were asked to describe their activities in terms familiar to Western survey researchers. The results suggest, among other things, that the Soviet urban population is highly literate. Eighty-two per cent of the sample reportedly read a newspaper each day, 71 per cent listen to

the radio, 70 per cent read books at least several times a week, and 38 per cent watch a television program several times a week.

Of some 24 different activities investigated, there were sizable social group differences (more than 10 per cent between the high category, "intelligentsia," and the low category, "workers") for eight of them. These are gathered under three more general rubrics supplied by the present writer in Table 3. The most striking difference between intelligentsia and worker respondents concerned an activity rather uniquely Soviet, attending to one's "political education." Although it is not made clear precisely what this means, reading Marx, Engels, Lenin, studying the history and program of the CPSU, etc., would probably qualify, as would attendance at lectures on political affairs. The social group difference confirms the important fact that political conformity varies directly with social level.

Other patterns of educational activity also reveal social group differences. Self-directed study is more common for intelligentsia families, whereas in the working-class family, study during the hours free from work is more likely to be formal in nature, outside of the home, as would be the case for instruction in night school. The inverse association between social level and formal instruction joins other evidence suggesting that education in the working-class is strongly vocational.

In the case of friendly visiting and attending "social functions" the worker adults are more active. The differences are sufficiently large to be significant and this is an important result, for it contradicts the pattern usually found in the United States. Perhaps it is connected with the fact that the traditional Russian national character appears to be highly loaded on the traits of gregariousness and affiliation,[6] and that the higher social levels are constrained to sacrifice this source of pleasure in order to maintain their positions. An interpretation

---

[4] For a revealing discussion, see Boris Izyumski, "Reflections on Boarding Schools: Just Like Home," *CDSP* 18.46:31–2, trans. from *Pravda*, Nov. 13, 1966, p. 3.

[5] The best evidence found is in *Komsomolskaia Pravda* for February 24–26, 1966. Table 1 on p. 3 of the Feb. 24 issue gives a breakdown of the length of the working day in the national sample for four different categories of urban occupational positions. Thirty-nine per cent of the professional intelligentsia and 17 per cent of the technical intelligentsia work nine hours or more per day, but only 12 per cent of the lower-status "employee" and 6 per cent of the "worker" categories work that long.

[6] For more detail see Alex Inkeles, *et al.*, "Modal Personality and Adjustment to the Soviet Socio-Political System," *Human Relations* 11:3–22, 1958, especially "Social Class Differentiation," pp. 17–19.

TABLE 3   Major Social Group Differences in Use of Free Time: Percentages of
Soviet Urban Adults Engaging in Different Activities, National Sample, 1965

| | *Educational* | | |
SOCIAL GROUP	POLITICAL STUDY SEVERAL TIMES WEEKLY	SELF-DIRECTED STUDY SEVERAL TIMES WEEKLY	NIGHT SCHOOL AND CORRESPONDENCE STUDY DAILY
Intelligentsia	67 (347)	53	18
Employees	56 (516)	37	25
Workers	38 (1092)	38	30

| | *Friendly Social* | |
	VISITING AND ENTERTAINING SEVERAL TIMES A MONTH	ATTENDING PARTIES, DANCES SEVERAL TIMES A MONTH
Intelligentsia	57	12
Employees	62	19
Workers	68	29

| | *High Culture* | | |
	READ MAGAZINES SEVERAL TIMES A MONTH	ATTEND THE THEATER SEVERAL TIMES A YEAR	ATTEND SYMPHONIC CONCERTS, LITERARY RECITALS SEVERAL TIMES A YEAR
Intelligentsia	87	55	34
Employees	86	44	18
Workers	67	39	13

Source: Adapted from information published by Boris A. Grushin in three articles in *Komsomolskaia Pravda*, February 24–26, 1966. The cross-tabular data are presented separately for two groups of the intelligentsia, the "technical intelligentsia" and the "professional" or "intelligentsia not engaged in material production (teachers, physicians, scientific workers, etc.)." I collapsed them into a single category and recomputed the percentages to provide a simpler comparison by status level of the three major urban occupational groups.

of this nature would be buttressed were we to find that the direction of the social level differences is reversed in response to the question: "How would you *like to spend* your free time?" for this would suggest the presence of pertinent dissatisfaction on the part of persons occupying higher social levels. While this does turn out to be the case for responses indicating a desire to spend free time visiting, the difference, which favors the intelligentsia, is only about one per cent in magnitude.[7]

The final difference shown in use of free time, concerning patterns labeled "high culture," reading magazines and attending theater, concerts, etc., are all strongly associated with the economic resources and

[7] Table 7, p. 3, in *Komsomolskaia Pravda*, Feb. 26, 1966.

educational training of persons in families on each social level.

The members of Soviet families do not all enjoy the same opportunities to strive for welfare and happiness. While children from families on all social levels seem to share high occupational aspirations, the fact is that the achievement of such aspirations is much more likely on the part of children who have a good start in life in the sense of coming from families from higher-ranking social levels. Recently in the city of Gorky 80 per cent of the children in the lower grades of school were of worker background and 20 per cent were children of members of the Soviet intelligentsia. As a result of the typical school drop-out pattern, most pronounced in the working class, the ratio was reversed among those graduating from secondary school, leading to what a Soviet commentator terms "inadequate social mobility."[8] See also Table 4 and accompanying comment below.

Patterns of Deviance and Conformity. The Soviet regime is committed to a thorough reconstruction of society by planned, occasionally forcible, intervention in social affairs. The family, however, is not a public institution. As a legally defined private grouping, it is minimally eligible for control by political authority. This fact has always been viewed by the Communist Party as somewhat of a defect, because the family harbors many of the patterns labeled "survivals" in the Soviet lexicon. Thus, "It is hardest of all to eliminate the survivals of harmful ways and hoary traditions in the sphere of family and everyday life. But it is very important for society that this sphere develop in step with the general progress."[9]

Soviet writers have been generous in their charges that the family breeds deviant behavior and have written at length about it. But they have been very reluctant explicitly to identify by social level the location or frequency of particular types of these undesired patterns. It will be our purpose here to make such an effort and to sample in the realm of social conformity as well.

Five important types of deviance seem to be inversely associated with social level: crime and delinquency, drunkenness, petty theft of public property, illegitimacy and religious activity. Research design and techniques of analysis and reporting leave a lot to be desired, but Soviet accounts of criminal behavior and drinking bouts, and the relevant though sparse statistics generally indicate that the participants are of low status. Drinking vodka on social occasions plays an important role in the Russian peasant tradition, and it must be reckoned as one of the main current diversions of men in these and worker families.[10]

I make special note of petty theft of state property and of illegitimacy because both are linked in much the same way to the problem of families with few resources. Poverty has led in each case to a semi-institutionalized pattern. A letter to *Izvestiia* from a young worker who objects to the pattern expresses the idea: "If you borrow a few kopecks from someone, woe be to you if you don't return every last kopeck. But we can steal from the state, can't we? One day I saw a mechanic wrapping up some pieces of pipe to take them home. I said to him: 'Why do you steal things from the plant?' He stared at me as if I had fallen from the moon. . . . Today pieces of pipe, tomorrow paint, next, who knows? The result is that our public property is pilfered without a thought."[11]

Illegitimacy has been tremendously inflated as a result of Soviet divorce policy. From 1944 until 1965 the law placed major obstacles in the path of those seeking divorce. Great numbers of unhappy unions were simply dissolved without legal recourse. Often the partners subsequently entered into new relationships which could not be registered as legal marriages because of the law prohibiting bigamy. Children born to persons in such families were technically illegitimate, and on occasion so identified publicly. There are disproportionate numbers of such children in the lower levels of the status system.

The Soviet population maintains religious interests, but in strong inverse association with social level. For example, the

---

[8] Vladimir Kantorovich, "Reflections on What Has Been Read: A Science Kindred to Us," *CDSP* 18.26:14–16, trans. from *Literaturnaia Gazeta*, May 5, 1966, pp. 1–2 and May 14, 1966, pp. 1–2.

[9] F. Konstantinov and V. Kelle, "Historical Materialism—Marxist Sociology," *CDSP* 17.8:3–9, trans. from *Kommunist*, No. 1, 1965, pp. 9–23.

[10] For a sampling of the kind of evidence from which these generalizations are drawn see D. M. Aptekman, "Causes of the Vitality of the Ceremony of Baptism Under Modern Conditions," *Soviet Sociology* 4.2:10–16, 1965, trans. from *Voprosy Filosofii*, No. 3, 1965; G. M. Minkovski, "Problems of Criminology: Some Causes of Juvenile Delinquency in the USSR and Measures to Prevent It," *CDSP* 18.30:9–13, trans. from *Sovetskoe Gosudarstvo i Pravo*, May, 1966, pp. 84–93; K. Kostenko, "On False Manliness and an Indifferent Province Committee," *CDSP* 6.29:6–7, trans. from *Komsomolskaia Pravda*, July 17, 1954, p. 2.

[11] Yu. Feofanov, "Reflections on Letters: Are You Holding Out Your Hand to Him?" *CDSP* 18.46:24–25, trans. from *Izvestiia*, Nov. 18, 1966, p. 6.

lower the social level the more likely is the Soviet parent to baptize his child.[12] Similarly, as Table 1 reveals, the lower the social level the more likely is the family to display holy icons.

Some survivals are directly correlated with social level. Divorce, a mild form of deviance since the mid-thirties, has in its legally constituted form almost certainly been distributed in positive association with social level simply because it has been expensive. How much of the association has been due to capacity to pay as opposed to the absence of traditional prejudice against divorce, still strong among the peasants, is not known.

A pattern of deviance peculiar to more affluent circles in cities has been exceptionally disturbing to the Soviet leaders. It is a complex of dissidence among the youth, probably the closest Soviet version to a rebellious youth culture. Some young persons refuse to follow the standards of behavior prescribed for a patriotic member of the Young Communist League. They refuse to work, cultivate personal appearance, seek out objects and styles of art, music, conversation, and clothing originating abroad, search for adventure and fun, fail to volunteer for recommended civic activities, and assume skeptical, disrespectful attitudes toward the Communist Party, older persons and much of the established Soviet way of life. They are variously identified and pilloried in the USSR as "stylists," "social parasites" or "nihilists."[13]

Another mode of deviant behavior derives from efforts made by upper level persons to obtain scarce goods, services and opportunities. The Soviet press has many complaints about collusion, nepotism, mutual protection and, above all, bribery, by which people seek to protect and enhance their economic and social interests in a society of perennial shortages. This is treated below under Part II.

Patterns of social conformity tend also to vary by social level. The bulk of virtuous patterns are manifested increasingly or predominantly in individuals and families of the higher-ranking social levels. Some of the most important are displayed in Tables 1 and 2. Completing a large number of years of formal education, taking a positive attitude toward work (shown here in the form of job satisfaction), participating in public activity, being a member of the Communist Party or YCL. are all patterns associated positively with social level. Others are easy to name or hypothesize. For instance, the general link between social level and political loyalty or ideological orthodoxy is manifested in the greater likelihood of the portrait of Marx, Lenin and the current First Secretary of the CPSU to be found in the home.

One of the few ways in which conformity varies inversely with social level is found in the production of children. I take "conformity" in this case to refer exclusively to the standards expressed by the party and state. In the official view there is a certain value in the production of children, and there are indeed more children per family in peasant than worker families, more in the latter than in intelligentsia families, and the inverse relation with social level holds for both urban and rural populations separately.[14] Because of government fertility policy, the lower the social level the more likely is the Soviet mother to merit special rewards for such conformity, to earn an honorary title ("Mother Heroine," etc.), receive a medal, and gain substantial monetary support for the many children she has borne.

Family Roles. Patterns of social conformity in the larger society constitute a proper starting point for the characterization of class differences in family roles. Responsible and efficient discharge of occupational, political, school, etc., duties tend to vary in direct association with the social level of the incumbent's family. The same is true in respect to most behavior

[12] See, for one report, p. 31 in V. B. Olshanski, "The Individual and Social Values," *Soviet Sociology*, 5.2:11–45, 1966, trans. from *Sotsiologiia v SSSR*, Vol. 1, Moscow, 1965, pp. 471–530.

[13] Of the many items published on this subject, one of the most absorbing is Lev Kassil, "Youth and the Young Without Youth (A Writer's Notes)," *CDSP* 9.27:12–14, trans. from *Literaturnaia Gazeta*, May 25, 1957, p. 2.

[14] Data on fertility and on family size resulting from a 1960 study of 37,000 families and 54,500 women over 17 are presented in A. Vostrikova, "Nekotorye dannye o rozhdaemosti v SSSR," *Vestnik Statistiki*, No. 12, 1962, pp. 42–46.

and attitudes displayed within the family. Thus, though higher level parents have fewer children, they or delegated relatives or servants spend more time with them and attend to their needs more carefully than parents on lower social levels.[15]

Soviet researchers note an important trend in family life, namely, increasing emphasis on achievement rather than ascription as a standard for status determination inside the family. In one report on the contemporary Turkmen worker family it is stated that "the position of each adult member of the family, regardless of age and sex, is determined by the work record on the job, and the moral qualities manifested in family and public life."[16] There has been a phenomenal rise in the number and level of opportunities in the larger social system made available to Soviet women in the years since the Revolution. There is good evidence that they have responded vigorously to these, and that their rise in general status is paralleled by an increase in their status inside the family.

Since there is a tendency for old and new ways of life on the one side to correspond with lower and higher social levels on the other, achievement as a basis for status recruitment to particular roles inside the family probably increases with higher social standing. Thus, the rate of intermarriage between persons of different ethnic background, a rough index of the lack of importance of this particular ascriptive factor, varies directly with social level, just as it finds more favor in the eyes of youth than amongst their elders.[17] Similarly,

holding to the principle of sex equality or, perhaps more accurately, opposition to social inequality based on sex varies directly with social level. The patriarchal tradition still enjoys some esteem among the peasantry and even more among the less assimilated Muslim portions of the population.

There is some variation by social level in the modes of feeling and styles of expressing emotion. Sentiments of hostility and anger appear more openly in lower level family life. Indeed, men who beat or assault their wives are not infrequently exposed in the daily press, and it seems that such scandals take place most frequently in peasant or working-class families. In contrast, open displays of tenderness or love tend to be subject to a norm of "masculine restraint" (*muzhskaia sderzhannost*) by which men are reluctant to reveal such feelings. I would assign more prominence to such a norm and accompanying behavior in lower level families. Correspondingly, the lower the level the less importance is attached to love as an experience; peasants, for instance, are said to choose marital partners in an impersonal way, without anticipation of a love relationship to aid in the selection.[18]

The picture of Soviet family life would not be complete without reference to interpersonal conflict. There is more conflict in the peasant families which retain features of the traditional way of life. Such conflict focuses on the problem of authority and differences in outlook between the older and younger generations. The young people frequently demand more say in the conduct of family life and their own affairs than their parents are willing to grant, and fail to share some of their parents' orientations, most notably their religious and political values.

II. REFLECTIONS OF INCONSISTENCY IN THE DISTRIBUTION OF STATUS ELEMENTS

I noted earlier the pronounced inconsistency in the way social honor, economic

[15] H. Kent Geiger, "The Soviet Family," in M. F. Nimkoff (ed.), *Comparative Family Systems*, Boston: Houghton-Mifflin Co., 1965, pp. 301–328.

[16] Shikhberdy Annaklychev, "The Life of the Oil Workers of Nebit-Dag and Kum-Dag (Part IV)," *Soviet Sociology*, 4.2:34–57, 1965, trans. from the Russian edition of 1961, published in Ashkhabad, TSSR.

[17] A review and discussion of Soviet studies may be found in A. G. Kharchev, *Brak i semia v SSSR*, Moscow, 1964, pp. 192–196. The main thesis argued is that the Soviet social order has decreased racial and ethnic prejudice and that intermarriage rates have gone up. Data on marriages and divorces registered for different years and different places also suggest that the non-Slavic partner is more likely to be male than female, but that when the non-Slavic partner is female, she is apt to be of the intelligentsia (p. 193).

[18] A village-community study quotes a young collective farmer: "We don't look for a great friendship. You like the girl, so you marry her." P. I. Kushner (ed.), *Selo Viriatino v proshlom i nastoiashchem*, Akad. Nauk SSSR, Trudy Instituta Etnog. imeni Miklukho-Maklaia, Novaia Seriia, Tom 41, Moscow, 1958, p. 226.

reward and political power are distributed in the Soviet system of social stratification. The fact is that there is a lot of *social* equality in the USSR which coexists in uneasy relation with a good amount of *economic* inequality. Effective performance in work is expressed in the functional or incentive reward system chiefly in the form of differentiated wage and salary levels, but also in terms of differentials in occupational prestige which are quite similar to those found in Western societies. Continuing devotion to equalitarianism by the ruling regime is expressed in the realm of the modest but widely available rewards provided by recreational and cultural facilities, opportunity for education and social mobility, accessible medical care, and the strongly fostered ideology of the dignity of labor and other aspects of what is sometimes referred to as Soviet humanism. In political life the degree of inequality is greatest. This is probably the best-known feature of Soviet society, a phenomenon reaching its most extreme form during the Stalin era, but which is still of paramount significance in Soviet society today.

In brief, then, Soviet society offers an unusual amount of social equality, a degree of economic differentiation quite ordinary or typical in modern societies, and an extraordinary level of political inequality. Taken together these facts are termed inconsistency in the distribution of status elements (or "distributive" or "dimensional" inconsistency) to refer to a property of the Soviet system of stratification as a whole. In reference to the individual citizen and his family they suggest widespread status inconsistency.

How is this situation reflected at different status levels of Soviet family life? The discrepancy between social equality and economic inequality is experienced in the upper level family as lack of opportunity for appropriate status display, and produces corresponding efforts in that direction. These are not considered legitimate channels for initiative, and from time to time the press prints exposés of persons manifesting such unworthy sentiments. A certain high ranking Soviet officer, for example, was reported as quite indignant, unable to reconcile himself, with the thought that he, a lieutenant colonel, had to live ". . . under the same roof with a former sergeant, now an ordinary worker."[19] A professor and his wife also revealed themselves to be snobs. They displayed coats-of-arms and diplomas in their home to call attention to their social importance, and were also brought to account for their frantic effort to discredit the wife of their son. She was of low social origin, the daughter of a miner, and they were opposed to the marriage.[20]

A more serious problem stems from the temptation for higher status persons to use their money unscrupulously, in effect to reduce social equality in consumption and the provision of equal opportunity. If they succumb, the sharpest resentment is aroused in regime and people when parents seek to guarantee access for their children to the limited places available for study in institutions of higher learning by bribing educational administrators.[21]

Families on lower social levels are faced with quite a different situation. Confronted by an immense gap between their economic ranking on the one side and the doctrine of social equality on the other, they commonly react in either or both of two ways. One involves selective cognitive stress on formal social equality irrespective of occupational differentiation. This tendency typically involves the denial of differences in occupational prestige, is officially encouraged, and receives suitable publicity from time to time. For instance, when N. Vikhrov told his former school teacher that he had become a mechanic, she expressed regret: "You had such talent. You could have become an engineer." Similar

[19] "Sovetskaia semia," *Pravda Ukrainy*, Sept. 16, 1959, p. 4.
[20] L. Likhodeyev, "Social Notes" (feuilleton), *CDSP*, 13.32:25–26, trans. from *Literaturnaia Gazeta*, July 1, 1961, p. 2.
[21] On April 19, 1958, N. S. Khrushchev was quoted in *Pravda* as follows: ". . . it sometimes happens that a person is admitted to a higher educational establishment not because he is well prepared, but because he has an influential papa and mama who can help him to get in." For further discussion of the problem, see "Entrance Requirements, Supply and Selection of Applicants in Soviet Higher Education," pp. 242–274 in Nicholas DeWitt, *Educational and Professional Manpower in the USSR*, Washington, D.C.: National Science Foundation, 1961.

sentiments are reported by him to be held by others. Vikhrov is critical of them. He asks, "Why doesn't a grandmother say proudly, 'My son drives a truck'?" Further, he queries, with apparent naiveté, "It is understandable that a person with a diploma has a higher position in any work collective, but will a good, highly skilled worker really enjoy any less respect?"[22]

A more common lower class reaction, we may suppose, though not necessarily always dislodging the first, goes in the contrary direction. It is to acknowledge the gap between the two status dimensions, find it distressing, consciously depreciate the significance of "social equality," and aspire strongly to occupational mobility. As we shall see, the strength of the aspiration does not guarantee the success of the enterprise, but the reflection within the family consists essentially in the appearance of articles of faith asserting that a good husband is one who constantly improves his occupational qualifications, perhaps by going to night

[22] N. Vikhrov, "Looking into the Mail: What Does 'Getting on in the World' Mean?" *CDSP* 18.12:19, abst. from *Komsomolskaia Pravda*, Dec. 21, 1965, p. 2.

school, that a good parent is one who ensures the successful education of his children, and that a good child is one who does well in school.

Some support for this interpretation is given by Table 4, where the aspirations for higher education and the actual fates of a 10 per cent sample of secondary school graduates for the year 1963, Novosibirsk Region, are compared for different social levels. The per cent wishing to continue studying past secondary school (column 1) is impressively high on all levels, suggesting, if we grant that the link between educational achievement and occupational mobility is well known, how eagerly sought after the latter must be.

Another story is told by the positive association between social level and actual achievement. A follow-up survey at a later date to see how many actually continued their studies established the association seen in column 2 of the table. I subtracted the figures in column 2 from those in column 1 to produce a measure of discrepancy between aspiration and achievement for each social group.

As the Soviet reporter notes, ". . . the

TABLE 4 Secondary School Graduates' Desire to Continue Formal Education and Actual Outcome by Social Group of Parental Family, Novosibirsk Region, 1963

Social Group of Parental Family	Per Cent Wishing to Continue Full-time Study	Per Cent Actually Continuing Full-time Study	Discrepancy
	(1)	(2)	(3)
Urban non-manual	93	82	11
Rural non-manual	76	58	18
Non-agricultural manual	80	55	25
Agricultural manual	76	10	66
Entire sample	83	61	22

Source: V. N. Shubkin, "Youth Starts Out in Life," *Soviet Sociology,* 4.3:3–15, 1966, also in *CDSP*, 17.30:3–9, trans. from *Voprosy Filosofii,* No. 5, 1965, pp. 57–70.

This is an adaptation of the original data. It excludes all respondents who envisaged combining work and study, excludes the residual social group category "others" and presents a single mean percentage figure for the three categories of non-agricultural manual workers—industry and construction, transport and communication, and service—analyzed separately in the original table. Social group is judged by father's occupation, or mother's if there was no father. The total and subgroup sample sizes are not revealed. However, a previous publication dealing with the same study indicates that the 10 per cent sample of eight year school 1963 graduates is "around 9,000," and that in autumn of the same year the researchers gathered information about the actual fate of "several thousand of the graduates we had studied." (Page 18 in V. N. Shubkin, "Vybor professii v usloviakh kommunisticheskogo stroitel-stva," *Voprosi Filosofii,* No. 8, 1964.)

paths through life taken by young people from various social groups show significant divergences."[23] We might add that the really massive discrepancy, which we can also provisionally interpret as a measure of frustration, is that for the "agricultural manual" group—Soviet peasants working as collective and state farmers. In their high hopes and disadvantaged chances in life, these parts of the Soviet population seem to be suffering the fate of lower class and less developed people throughout the world, immersion in a tide of rapidly rising ex-expectations unaccompanied by equivalent increases in opportunity.

One also finds in the Soviet scene an unusual discordance between the distribution of economic rewards and the distribution of political power. Soviet society, far from democratic, concentrates power in the top hierarchy. The local area is often a replica of the national picture: a few officials of the party and government enjoy extraordinary power.

The chief reflection of this in high level circles arises out of the chance for officials to abuse power in order to achieve personal or family goals. Family loyalty continues to be strong, opportunities for consumption not always responsive to the ruble, and Soviet politicians are subject to wishes and demands for special favors emanating from their wives and own dear children. The case of Sergei, a high party official, is most instructive. In the course of a short period, his wife or his mother made the following specific "requests" of him: (1) speak to the director of the agricultural experimental station about buying some currants, bigger, firmer, available in thick clusters and cheaper than those bought through the usual channels; (2) telephone the manager of a store about the purchase of a wool blouse for his wife, to avoid the "frightful waiting-in-line"; (3) telephone the director of the theatre for the favor of seats without previous purchase of tickets; (4) arrange an exception to the hospital rule so his wife could stay there with their sick daughter. Some of these requests were granted by

Sergei; others were refused, but elicited vigorous reproaches from his wife: "I am not inciting you to crime, after all!" or "You're no father, you're a walking moral code! Prude!" How, wonders this would-be model Communist, can he explain to his wife that ". . . a high official has less of a moral right than anyone else to use his official position, even in trivial matters?"[24]

How is the situation seen at the other end of the status continuum? For an answer, we turn to a case . . . of an influential father who went even further in exploiting his political position. He made a mockery of the notion of social equality by rescuing his hoodlum son from the constituted processes of Soviet justice. A drunken brawl during the summer of 1966 in the town of Iglino, Bashkir ASSR, was broken up by a militiaman. One of the participants, Fakhretdinov, was the son of an important local official. The father turned up at the station house, had his son released from custody, and the case was never brought to trial. When the affair became known to the townspeople, among other developments there was a letter sent to *Izvestiia*:

Everything is allowed to someone like Renat Fakhretdinov, for he is the son of the chairman of the district executive committee! He'll get away with everything, he can do anything, his daddy will fix it all up. But if he were the son of a worker, he would catch it quickly enough.[25]

Abuse of power produces resentment, antagonism and apathy at the bottom levels of society. While there has been curtailment of such abuse at the national level since the demise of Stalin, we cannot be certain of similar adjustments on the local scene nor that highly concentrated power will not be again abused in the future. Whether still largely present or only fresh in memory, it seems quite likely that such exploitation plays a significant role in the lives of Soviet working-class and peasant families as targets of recrimination and hostility.

On all levels of Soviet society there is

[23] V. N. Shubkin, "Youth Starts Out in Life," *Soviet Sociology* 4.3:3–15, 1966; also in *CDSP* 17.30:3–9; trans. from *Voprosy Filosofii*, No. 5, 1965, pp. 57–70.

[24] A. Volkov, "Incorruptible Conscience" (short story), *CDSP* 14.3:30–31, trans. from *Izvestiia*, Jan. 16, 1962, p. 4.
[25] F. Chernetski, "Kreslo ne pomoglo," , Aug. 20, 1966, p. 3.

some consciousness of the contradiction between the social and the political dimensions of stratification, between what I have termed unusual social equality and extraordinary political inequality. Alongside it one finds a standard tendency for cognitive separation of peoples' images of Soviet social structure into two parts. One stresses the social equality side of things—interpersonal and intergroup harmony, equality, cooperative labor and service to society—and is a fully legitimate image, fit for open admission and public display. The other part focuses squarely on the dimension of unequal power. It sees Soviet society as divided into "we" and "they." Which groupings qualify as "we" and which are lodged in the other category depends upon the political level of the viewer, but in any case, this is not a legitimate image. It is not usually revealed publicly, but like other sensitive issues in Soviet life it does attract some attention in discussion within the family.

....

SOCIAL CLASS AND SUCCESS

Ephraim H. Mizruchi

Our specific task . . . is to launch our exploration of Merton's hypothesis that differential access to the various means of achieving success in American society leads to greater anomie in the lower classes compared to the relatively high classes.

....

Merton's study is primarily concerned with types of individual reactions to

Reprinted from *Success and Opportunity*, New York: Free Press, 1964.

anomie, particularly deviant reactions. . . .[1]

Merton's theory consists of two approaches. On one hand, there is the discrepancy between aspiration and achievement; on the other, attempts to cope with this situation among different segments of the social structure. The notion of discrepancy is derived from Durkheim's theory that widespread aspiration for what is unattainable reflects anomie in the social structure. The typology of reactions to structured strain is Merton's own theoretical formulation. Srole, Bell, Hyman, and the other writers . . . are in reality attempting to test Durkheim's theory as Merton has applied it to American society, rather than Merton's theory of individual reactions. Our own study may also be placed in the category of assessments of the Durkheimian theory within the Mertonian framework. . . .

SUCCESS VALUES

Our major concern in this work is to test hypotheses systematically by utilizing empirical data gathered for that specific purpose. . . . Questions "concerning the objectivity of values [or] . . . their quality of absoluteness or lack of it," as Williams points out (1960, p. 402),[2] need not concern us here. . . . From our point of view, then, a value is z group's conception of the desirable (Williams, 1960, p. 402). The specific nature of the value-referent, although we will make extensive references to it, is not crucial to the test of our hypotheses. In our analysis, we use care in distinguishing between what are often referred to as values —the reified referents of the process of valuation—and the underlying conception that influence our judgments of these values.

[1] Writers who have dealt with this aspect of Merton's theory are, to name only a few, Robert Dubin, "Deviant Behavior and Social Structure," *American Sociological Review*, 24 (April, 1959), pp. 147–164; Richard A. Cloward, "Illegitimate Means, Anomie, and Deviant Behavior," *American Sociological Review*, 24 (April, 1959), pp. 164–176; Albert K. Cohen, "The Study of Social Disorganization and Deviant Behavior," in Robert K. Merton et al., *Sociology Today* (New York: Basic Books, Inc., 1959), pp. 461–484; and Talcott Parsons, *The Social System* (New York: The Free Press of Glencoe, 1951), Chapter 7.

[2] Robin H. Williams, Jr., *American Society*, New York: Alfred A. Knopf, 1960. (C. S. H.)

It is only in the latter case that we are truly dealing with values. . . .

The specific values, indices of which we are attempting to analyze, are those associated with the American notion of "success."

. . . .

Although there are several possible ways of approaching the study of values empirically, we use only one, an indirect approach to verbal value responses. We have asked a series of questions designed to elicit descriptions of behavior and possessions that reflect basic value systems. Although we are attempting to tap as broad a range of values as possible, we do not attempt to describe a total value system or even a sub-system. . . .

We begin our empirical analysis by examining the distribution among the several social classes of selected values pertinent to our problem. . . .

An attempt will be made here to answer the following questions: What is the distribution of success values among the classes? To what extent do members hold values that aid or hinder them in their efforts to achieve success? To what extend do members believe that opportunities of getting ahead are available to them?[3]

. . . .

SOCIAL CLASS AND "GETTING AHEAD"

In Merton's essay, "Continuities in Social Structure and Anomie," he attempts to evaluate several studies designed to test his hypothesis. In commenting on Hyman's findings that differences *do* exist among classes, in terms of values related to success in American society, he makes the following statement:

The survey data available to Hyman do not discriminate between the *degrees* of commitment to the goal but indicate only the relative *frequency* with which individuals in the samples drawn from the several social strata express some unknown degree of acceptance of the success goal and of related values . . . it appears

that subsequent inquiry might be usefully directed toward studying the intensity as well as the extent to which these values are held in diverse groups, social strata, and communities. (1957, p. 171).

In order to test the Merton hypothesis, we selected what seemed a well designed question to elicit the kind of response necessary for adequate assessment of the distribution of success values in American society. Morris Rosenberg has used a measure of the degree of importance placed upon striving for success in American society.[4] . . .

Rosenberg's question is phrased, "How important to you, personally, is it to get ahead in life?" Of the 226 respondents to Rosenberg's question in our survey, 174 (77%) answered that "getting ahead" is important, while only fifty-two replied that "getting ahead" is unimportant to them. Rosenberg found that 88% of his respondents thought "getting ahead" was important (1957, p. 159). His subjects were, however, college students, whom we should expect to be more involved in striving for success than our respondents, many of whom have already achieved some of their life goals.

Not only do *most* of our respondents feel that getting ahead is important, but our data indicates that it is slightly more important to the lower-class segments of the population.[5] The lower-class respondents

---

[3] Data were gathered in 1958 in a small upstate New York town (population about 16,000).

[4] Morris Rosenberg, *Occupations and Values* (New York: The Free Press of Glencoe, 1957); Robin M. Williams, Jr., ed. *Friendship and Social Values in a Suburban Community* (Eugene: Dept. of Sociology, U. of Oregon, 1956, Mimeographed); and Rose K. Goldsen, Morris Rosenberg, Robin M. Williams, Jr., and Edward Suchman, *What College Students Think* (New York: Van Nostrand, 1959). I should like to thank Professor Robin M. Williams, Jr., for permission to use questions that he has developed in connection with his research on values and for a number of important suggestions about the kinds of problem associated with research on the relationship between aspiration for success and anomie.

[5] Chi-square = 4.7, 2 degrees of freedom, P = .10. Although we are suggesting an arbitrary limit to acceptance or rejection of a probability statement as support for a particular finding, we want to avoid holding ourselves to any limit. We shall be content if the reader interprets the findings as they are presented, using his own judgment of whether or not they appear *theoretically* significant.

show a greater "degree of commitment," in Merton's terminology, as well as greater frequency of acceptance of success goals.

These data, if taken alone, might provide additional support for the findings of Srole and others that anomie is greater in the relatively low classes. It could then be argued that, since success is apparently more important to lower-class respondents and since anomie is already known to be higher among the lower classes, the greater degree of importance placed on success is a cause of anomie. In order to make a more complete assessment of the theory, however, it is necessary to relate anomie to class when acceptance of success goals is constant among all classes. . . .

SOCIAL CLASS, SUCCESS, AND RELATED VALUES

Our second question about the relationship between social class and values is, To what extent do members of the different classes have values what aid or inhibit them in their efforts to achieve success? What is success from the point of view of the respondent, how is it attained, and what part does his conception of success and its corollary values play in his opportunities for achievement? . . .

Social Class and Success Symbols. One method of exploring Americans' conception of the nature of success is to analyze the importance attributed to the symbols they associate with it. In an effort to uncover

these symbols, we asked, "Could you list, in order of importance, those things which you believe to be signs of success in our society?" Six possible responses were read by the interviewer, and the respondent stated an order of preference. The six elements were based on a code taken from open-ended replies to the same question in an earlier study. It is sufficient for our purposes to present only the first choices. The class categories, from the highest (I) to the lowest (V), are taken from Hollingshead's Two-Factor Index of Social Position. . . . The basis for our classification is occupational and educational attainment of the male head of the household in which the respondent resides.

As Table 1 indicates, there are several tendencies associated with the selection of success symbols among our respondents. The symbols rated first in importance by the greatest proportion of our sample (31%), was home ownership. "Having a good education" was ranked most important by 29% and "having a good, steady job" by 23%. When we review the distribution by class, we notice certain trends. Home ownership tends to be selected more frequently as class declines. There is also a slight similar tendency in selection of job security. Education, however, tends to be selected more frequently as we ascend the class structure.

A closer examination of the data suggests that these relationships are not simply the

TABLE 1   Class and Most Important Symbol of Success as Selected by Respondent (in Percentages)

| | Class | | | | | Total | |
	I	II	III	IV	V	PER CENT	N
Education	61	37	30	26	21	29	63
Many friends	0	10	17	5	3	7	16
Prestige	8	10	4	6	5	6	13
Job security	15	21	17	27	24	23	51
Home ownership	8	16	32	31	41	31	70
Money	8	6	0	5	6	4	10
Totals	100	100	100	100	100	100	223
N	(13)	(19)	(47)	(81)	(63)		
	Chi-square = 12.6, 3 d.f., P = .01.						

result of chance. By grouping job security, home ownership, and money into a category designated "material-economic symbols," as contrasted with "non-material-economic symbols," we find that class and category of success symbol are associated. A chi-square analysis yields a probability of .01, a much greater concentration of "material-economic" responses in the lower classes than we would expect by chance alone. It is clear, then, that symbols of the attainment of success are different for respondents in the several classes.

There are at least three possible interpretations of this finding that are worthy of consideration. First, the data may reflect the degree of awareness, that is, the limited range of experience, among the lower classes, of certain symbols and their referents. This reflection is analogous to the oft-noted suggestion that those at the bottom of the class structure know very little about those at the top. This observation is particularly true of life styles, tastes, and other class-related symbolic behavior. The symbols of success in the lower classes are limited, then, to the attainments they have had opportunities to see, particularly the most conspicuous. These goals are concrete and easily identified.[6]

A second possible interpretation is that people value most what they have least. On the lower levels, therefore, people still strive for the basic necessities, and only after attaining them do they seek other goals (*cf.* Inkeles, 1960).[7] The process of attainment in a society in which products are constantly being introduced and improved and goals are frequently reformulated—a society that tends toward a great deal of anomie in its sub-systems—involves reaching goals and then seeking still other goals,

endlessly. This process has been called the "escalator process." The mass media of communication, children and neighbors, and a host of other influentials encourage people to continue accumulating and trading in the old model for the new. In the middle classes, goals have shifted beyond the material, which presumably anyone can attain, to more intangible goals.

Finally, and this explanation provides a broad enough framework for incorporation of our first two, there are elements—reflected in their choices of symbols—of Williams's distinction between "achievement" and "success." He has written:

Whereas achievement refers to valued accomplishments, success lays the emphasis upon rewards. Amoral success-striving may not have gone to the lengths suggested by some observers, but the important point is that once success goals are divorced from the ultimate values of society, the way is opened for a corrosion of regulative norms. In the United States, the available evidence suggests that . . . the success pattern is still linked to achievement, achievement is still associated with work, and work is still invested with an almost organic complex of ethical values. Thus, success is still not a primary criterion of value in its own right, but rather a derivative reward *for* active, instrumental performance (1960, p. 419).

. . . The lower-class symbols are clearly *success* symbols as contrasted with the middle-class *achievement* symbols.[8] Occupational pursuits in the lower-class groups, for example, are much less likely to lead to achievement. Even the skilled technician has difficulty thinking of his work in such terms, as does the clerk in the same class category (Class IV). In contrast, the engineer, the scientist, or the small business owner who constantly speaks of "building" his business demonstrates a broader dimension of aspiration. It is not until the minimal *success* symbols have been attained that *achievement* becomes a goal in contemporary American society. In this respect, the lower classes do not suffer from structured

[6] James Beshers has suggested that secrecy about symbols is a means of maintaining a status group intact and keeping lower status groups in subordinate positions. See *Urban Social Structure* (New York: The Free Press of Glencoe, 1961). Note also that this suggestion explains why socially mobile groups grasp the symbols that are most concrete and conspicuous, those that they recognize as associated with higher status, only to find that they are not the symbols that count.

[7] Alex Inkeles, "Personality and Social Structure," in Merton, *et al.*, ed., *Sociology Today*, New York: Basic Books, Inc., 1959. (C. S. H.)

[8] Robert and Helen Lynd have made a similar observation, pointing out that the lower classes are concerned in their jobs with *things* while the middle classes are concerned with *people*, *Middletown*, New York: Harcourt, Brace & World, Inc., 1929, p. 22.

strain so much as those in the higher classes. There is comparatively little struggle for abstract goals, which are difficult to attain, among those in the lower classes. Their problem is the attainment of goals that are inherently more limited. The middle-class American, however, does seek goals that are more difficult to attain—though he often does manage to attain them—and struggles also with questions about the relative legitimacy of his *success* or lack of *success,* as contrasted with *achievement.* It is on the higher-class levels that we observe the consequences of structured strain of a particular type. For certain occupational groups, particularly the intellectuals, the gap between success and achievement is wide. While many have achieved some degree of prominence in their occupational spheres, they have often not been rewarded with adequate symbols of success. From this group come many of the intellectual-political critics of industrial societies.[9] Furthermore, there is a tendency toward the converse as well. The groups that have attained *success* without having *achieved* tend to look upon themselves and be looked upon by others as not quite legitimate. Americans are reluctant to give power to those who have not earned their wealth—a prototype is the speculator who seeks control of a long established business enterprise —and they accord less status honor to the attainers of success alone than to those whose success is the result of their own achievements. . . .

Characteristics Associated with Success. In addition to asking more abstract questions about "getting ahead" and "signs of success," we attempted to reach much more concrete levels of perceived success. One type of question was designed to pro-

ject the respondent momentarily into his community setting, in order to describe a particular phenomenon (an element of this approach was embodied in our question on signs of success). One concrete example is the question, "If you were asked to describe a successful person in your community how would you do it?" Response categories to this question were precoded in order to classify the characteristics stressed. The question was, however, open-ended, and the coding was done after the interview was completed. . . .

Our data were grouped to combine cells in which there were very few cases into broader, yet meaningful categories. Most of our respondents stressed characteristics of success that fell into the prestige-recognition category. Of the 179 respondents, eighty-eight (49%) stressed factors associated with "good" reputation in the community. Sixty-two (35%) emphasized those associated with the accumulation of material goods and security. Only 16% described success in terms of factors associated with family welfare or personal happiness. A chi-square analysis of these results yields a value significant at the .05 level of probability. There is a marked difference in perceptions of success among the several classes, the lower classes stressing material symbols.

These data are consistent with those presented earlier and suggest that both sets reflect underlying value systems that influence the choice of value-referents. The data, as a result, support our distinction between success and achievement, as a reflection of different value configurations among the classes.

The Differential Significance of Money and Security. Since the foregoing analyses have suggested that money and security are preferences that characterized the responses of the lower-class subjects and since the several studies of social class and anomie have shown that anomie has a greater impact on these classes, we shall investigate the relationship between money and security, on one hand, and social class, on the other. In analyzing two types of response, we may be able to assess the relative valuation associated with each among the several social classes.

[9] That this criticism represents structured strain is supported by our findings, reported later, that only the college- and high school-educated tend to be anomic when their incomes are below $5000 a year (P=.001 and P .03, respectively). It has often been suggested that the late President Franklin D. Roosevelt organized groups of artists, writers, and scholars into workshops during the depression of the 1930s to avert organized criticism of the system by this influential and potentially radical segment of the population. This insight was suggested to the writer some years ago by Professor St. Clair Drake.

Hyman reports some findings of a 1942 Roper survey based on a national sample of high school students, who were asked "to express their preference for one of three types of job: a low-income but secure job, a job with good pay but with an even risk of losing it, or a job with extremely high income and great risk" (1953, p. 433). According to Hyman, "The poor youth cannot accept the risk involved in becoming less poor" (*op. cit.*). Another sample taken by Roper in 1947 is reported by Hyman and provides data on adult responses to this question, reflecting a similar class pattern. "Thus, for example, a low income but secure job is chosen by 60% of factory workers but only by 26% of professional and executive persons. In 1949, a question presenting a similar choice situation between a secure job and a risky but promising career in one's own business yielded parallel results" (*op. cit.*, p. 434). . . . Roper's findings do suggest that security is of more concern to lower-class respondents than is money.

Our own interest is in the relative significance of money as a goal, compared to security, since our over-all findings suggest that both are more highly valued in the lower classes than they are in the middle classes. The same question Hyman asked was used in our study.

Of the 222 respondents to this question, 145 (63%) indicated that their choice of occupation would be one that pays only a low income but is secure. Only thirty-three (16%) would choose jobs that pay extremely high salaries to the successful, with a high risk of dismissal for the unsuccessful. A chi-square analysis of the association between social class and occupational choice yields a value with a probability of .001. Our data clearly indicate that the segments of the population for whom security is more important are the Class IV and V respondents, which is consistent with our other findings. These data also clarify the *specific* values that seem most important to lower-class respondents and help to support our explanation for the absence of emphasis upon *achievement* in the lower classes. *Security* has been isolated as a major concern of lower-class respondents. . . .

Education as a Value. Because education has been found to be a relatively important symbol of underlying values and because it plays a major role in opportunity for advancement, we attempted to take a closer look at the part education plays in the evaluative perceptions of our respondents. Hyman has devoted a large part of his analysis to the value placed on formal education. As he points out, the degree to which education is valued is a significant factor in differential opportunities to achieve success. He suggests that:

Part of the ideology of American life is that important positions are not simply inherited by virtue of the wealth of one's parents, but can be achieved. Such achievement, however, requires for many types of important positions considerable formal education. One cannot, for example, become a physician or a lawyer or an engineer without advanced education. Consequently, insofar as the lower classes placed less value on higher education, this would constitute an aspect of a larger value system which would work detrimental to their advancement (1953, p. 429).

Hyman proceeds to show that there is differential preference among the classes for college education, increasing with higher class position. Even though our own data support Hyman's findings and generalizations, we should approach his interpretation with some caution. The use of indices of "preference for college education" as a means of assessing educational values seems to the writer to involve a middle-class bias on the part of the investigator. We believe that success in a lower-class position can be achieved with high school education alone. The skilled technician and the shop foreman, for example, have certainly attained modest degrees of success in an objective sense, and college education for them seems superfluous if not completely meaningless. For those of the middle classes whose aspirations include professional achievement, however, college education may be much more meaningful.

We are dealing here with *means-values* rather than with *ends-values*. College education is being viewed as a means toward other ends, one of several alternative means for achieving "success." Our earlier findings, however, suggest that education is more highly valued by the middle classes as an *end-value* than it is by the lower classes. We hypothesize that the greater importance of education as an *end-value* for the middle classes provides them with greater opportunities for advancement *because* they view it as an *end-value*. As Hyman suggested, the nature of the value systems themselves limits or expands opportunities for success.

Values can have consequences that are either compatible or incompatible with the objectives of the actors in a social system, and these consequences may or may not be known to actors or to group members generally. There may, in fact, be latent, i.e., unrecognized, consequences of values for particular groups. Education's role as an *end-value* for the middle classes for example has the latent consequence of providing relatively greater chances of attaining both success and achievement goals, while for the lower classes the *lack* of education as an important *end-value* has the latent consequence of limiting chances for reaching goals in skilled, commercial, or professional occupations.

We should, then, expect to find that education itself is evaluated differently among the several classes. In order to test this hypothesis, our respondents were asked the following question taken from Williams (1956, Appendix I, p. 11), "Here are some reasons different people have given for wanting to have their children finish a certain amount of education. Which one of these would you say is most important?" The responses were grouped into two categories: instrumental perception of education and noninstrumental perception of education.

Our findings are reported in Table 2.

There is a marked tendency for instrumental perception of education to increase inversely to social class. . . . Our middle class respondents, then, tend to see education, not only as a means of achieving a better job or income, but also as a source of personal satisfaction. We should guess that our lower-class respondents tend to view education as somethng that would have helped them in adulthood had they pursued it in childhood and adolescence. While they see it as a means to success, they do not evaluate it so highly as other symbols (see Table 1). Floud and his colleagues, in a study entitled *Social Class and Educational Opportunity,* also noted the lower evaluation of education among working-class parents in England (1957, p. 81).[10]

Our lower-class respondents are caught in a situation analogous to Merton's conception of anomie on the social structural level. In the rational or *cognitive* sphere, education is viewed realistically by the lower classes as a means for the attainment of success. In the nonrational evaluative sphere, education is not highly valued. There is thus a disparity between the cognitive and evaluative dimensions that fosters a greater tendency to limited achievement in the lower classes. This disparity reflects strain between the subcultural system and the requirements of the lower-class social structure, an additional source of structured strain.

[10] J. E. Floud, A. H. Halsey, and F. M. Martin, *Social Class and Educational Opportunity*, London: William Heinemann, 1957. (C. S. H.)

TABLE 2   Class and Instrumental and Noninstrumental Perception of Education (in Percentages)

	Class					Totals	
	I	II	III	IV	V	PER CENT	N
Noninstrumental	91	72	55	46	44	52	107
Instrumental	9	28	45	54	56	48	98
Totals	100	100	100	100	100	100	205
N	(11)	(18)	(47)	(68)	(61)		

Chi-square = 11.5, 3 d.f., P = .01.

Bronfenbrenner has made a similar observation:

Perhaps this very desperation, enhanced by early exposure to impulse and aggression, leads working-class parents to pursue new goals with old techniques of discipline. While accepting middle-class levels of aspiration he has not yet internalized sufficiently the modes of response which makes these standards readily available for himself or his children. He has still to learn to wait, to explain, and to give and withhold his affection as the reward and price of performance (1958, p. 423).[11]

It should be noted, however, that our data do not totally support Bronfenbrenner's assumption that the "levels of aspiration" are identical with those of the middle class.

In answer to our second question—To what extent do members of the several classes hold values that aid or hinder them in their efforts to attain success in American society?—we must conclude that, although our lower-class respondents are aware of the utility of education as a means for getting ahead, that they do not view it as a high *end-value* does limit their chances for even modest advancement. We must agree with Hyman that the lower-class population does thus share a self-imposed tendency to nonachievement of success goals.

SOCIAL CLASS AND PERCEIVED OPPORTUNITY

We have so far attempted to answer the first two of our three questions about class distribution of success values and the relationship between certain values and their roles in the process of striving for success. The third question is, To what extent do members of the various classes believe that opportunities for getting ahead are available to them? We turn again to Hyman for suggestions on what we may expect to learn from our data. In interpreting Roper's data, Hyman indicates that the lower classes believe that economic opportunities are

[11] Urie Bronfenbrenner, "Socialization and Social Class Through Time and Space," in Eleanor Maccoby, T. M. Newcomb, and E. L. Hartley, eds., *Readings in Social Psychology*, New York: Henry Holt and Company, 1958, 3rd edition, pp. 400–425. (C. S. H.)

limited for them in comparison to opportunities for higher classes (1953, p. 437). He also suggests that there are class differences in perceptions of the most important factors in job advancement. We should expect that such perceptions are an important factor in the study of effects of social structural anomie on group participants.

We asked three questions about perception of opportunities for success. . . . Specifically, the questions deal with perceptions of universalistic or particularistic criteria for advancement; implicit acceptance of the success ideology and the opportunities of the striver; perception of the respondent's own chances of getting ahead as indicator of a class determined reaction; and the discrepancy between sought and achieved occupational rank.

Ability as a Factor in Success. In order to gauge perception of the degree to which legitimate striving will be rewarded, we asked, "Do you feel that a person with ability has a good chance of achieving success in our society, or do you feel that ablity has little to do with it?" Of the 224 subjects who responded, only fourteen replied that ability had little to do with it. . . . It appears, then, that the American dream of equal opportunity for all who have ability remains a potent ideological force in American society.

We use the term "ideological" with a clear understanding of its implications. We believe that, since objective conditions demonstrate that success is limited for those born into lower-class families and since the vast majority of lower-class respondents in our study still believe that ability is a major factor in advancement toward success, there is a disparity between the cognitive and evaluative dimensions of class perception. It should be clear from their perspective that ability *is not* a major factor in achieving success in our society unless they are willing to admit that they, as members of the lower classes, are people of low abilities. One way to close the gap between objective social circumstances and the group's limited capacity to deal with them is through ideology, that is, a set of beliefs and sentiments that will provide the group with goals, realistic or not, to give life meaning. In the American ideology of success, if one remains faithful to his task, continues to strive and to hope, he too will be rewarded by advancement. We hold that the ideology provides support only as long as objective conditions do not cause too great a gap between aspirations and opportunities for achievement. As the gap widens, the supportive potential of the ideology lessens. This factor is one of several that may explain our observation that average anomia decreases with age, climbing sharply upward only after age 55.[12]

Perceived Chances of Getting Ahead. Our second finding supports this interpretation. As our data show, there is a class differential in the respondents' perceptions of their own chances of getting ahead. As class declines, we note an increase in responses that reflect awareness and expectations of limited success even though the over-all distribution of responses is relatively even. Fifty-three per cent saw their chances as excellent or fair, compared to 47% who saw them as limited or almost nonexistent. The data provide a sharper picture when we combine Classes I and II, our smallest groups. Then we find 83% giving responses of "excellent" or "fair" and 17% giving less hopeful replies. A chi-square analysis yields a probability of less than .01.

It can be concluded, from this finding, that the lower classes in our sample tend to see their objective chances of success as limited. How does this result fit with our finding that most respondents in the same class had, only moments before in the interview, replied that a person with ability has a good chance of achieving success? We should expect from these two replies that those on the lowest rungs of the social-class ladder believe themselves lacking the *ability* to get ahead. Yet these data may also be interpreted as providing support for our suggestion that the disparity between *cognitive* perception and *evaluative* perception—another instance of socially structured strain—creates a vacuum that is filled by the ideology of success.

[12] A class-controlled analysis indicates that, for lower-class groups, the curve rises after age 60, while, for the middle classes, the rise begins after age 55.

Merton is correct in pointing out that the system is not threatened by the failure of particular individuals to achieve their aspirations. The system, as our data show, is not put to the test. Instead, the individual continues to hope for eventual reaping of rewards, or he turns the blame for failure upon himself. If we compare those in the lower classes who feel their chances are fair or excellent to those in the lower classes who feel their chances are limited, anomia scores reflecting structured strain will be higher for the latter. On one hand, using perception of limited opportunities as an index to the malfunctioning of the success ideology, we should expect anomia to increase with the decrease in expectation of success. On the other, we should expect this relationship to be stronger in the lower classes because they are more likely to see their chances as limited. A controlled analysis suggests that this expectation is not borne out. Anomia is associated with perception of limited expectations for the *middle* classes only! How do we explain this unexpected finding?

We begin by noting that the middle-class respondents are more involved in the competitive struggle for success. They affirm the American dream, and, while their chances of attaining success or achievement, are greater, their chances of failure are greater too. Those in the lower classes do not have far to fall if they fail. The lower-class respondent, furthermore, sees about him others whose opportunities are circumscribed, and rationalization comes more easily under these circumstances. By contrast, the middle-class *milieu* is one of success and continuous striving. Among those who have had access to education and job opportunities, what excuses can be offered for failure? Our preliminary results, which indicate that income and anomia are significantly associated only for those respondents who have gone to high school and college, provide further support for this hypothesis. The college educated respondents who earned less than $5000 a year were more likely to become anomic than were members of any other educational group. . . .

Social Class and Aspiration for Achievement. The third general question we set out to answer in this chapter was, what is the relationship of disparity between aspiration and achievement to social class? Although this question is, in reality, a test of the Durkheim-Merton hypothesis, since such a disparity may be viewed as an index to anomie, we are treating it here in the limited context of the relationship between social class and social values.

In an effort to develop a measure of structured strain independent of Srole's anomia scale, we decided to combine two separate items into what is, for the time being, a crude index to the disparity between the respondent's past occupational preference and his current occupational rank. Both elements were ranked according to the Hollingshead scale of occupations, a part of his index of social position. We asked, "Do you wish you had gotten into another line of work when you were younger?" The respondents who replied "yes" were then asked to describe the occupation to which they had formerly aspired. Since some of the respondents selected occupations different from their own on a horizontal plane—occupations with the same rank—we excluded them from our analysis It is on the vertical plane that we should expect the effects of anomie to manifest themselves, since disparity in occupational level is our major concern.

Our findings are reported in Table 3. . . . The distribution of low disparity declines from Classes I, II, and III to Class V, and that for high disparity ascends com-

parably.[13] . . . Our findings, then, indicate specifically that there is a greater gap between earlier occupational aspiration and occupational achievement in the lowest class (V) and, more generally, that the Durkheim-Merton hypothesis is supported. . . .

SUMMARY

Our problem in this chapter has been to explore the distribution of success values among the several social classes as reflected in responses to questions dealing with the importance of getting ahead; symbols of success; perceived characteristics of successful people; the selection of occupations in terms of security and monetary compensation; and the quality of educational preferences. In addition, related questions were asked on the role that ability plays in achieving success and on differential perceptions of opportunities for advancement.

Several sociologically interesting themes are evident. The importance of getting ahead is stressed, not only by most of our respondents throughout the class structure, but most heavily by the lower classes. This finding is true for both the extent and intensity of belief in getting ahead and therefore satisfies Merton's criterion for an "adequate" test of his theory. This index to the importance of success clearly lends support to Merton, Srole, Bell, and others

[13] "High disparity" means that three or more rank levels separated the aspired and achieved; "moderate," two levels; and "low," one level.

TABLE 3   Class and Disparity Between Earlier Occupational Aspiration and Achievement (in Percentage)

DISPARITY	Class			Totals	
	I, II, III	IV	V	PER CENT	N
Low	44	35	18	31	26
Moderate	25	32	15	26	21
High	31	33	67	43	36
Totals	100	100	100	100	83
N	(16)	(40)	(27)		

Chi-square = 9.3, 4 d.f., P = 0.06.

who have assumed that Americans share similar life goals. We can report, then, at this stage of our analysis, that there is evidence to support the Durkheim-Merton hypothesis.

We have also found that, by using Williams's distinction between "success" and "achievement," we obtain a clearer understanding of the nature of values and greater insights into the differential aspects of striving for success in the several classes. The distinction leads us, for example, to explore and to explain middle-class anomie.

Our data, at the same time, indicate that the idea of limited opportunity for the attainment of life goals is more complicated than Merton recognized. The tendency for the lower classes to select material symbols and preferences supports Hyman's suggestion that those objects and activities they rank highest are those that contribute least to the attainment of success. There is, as Hyman has noted, a self-imposed tendency to anomie in the lower classes thanks to low evaluation of the cultural mechanisms—objects and activities—instrumental in the attainment of success. This low evaluation is particularly true of education. In the middle classes, where education is valued more highly, the pursuit of learning, no matter how minimal or superficial, furnishes by-products that become assets in later life. We have suggested that when the question of future achievement is assessed cognitively, the middle-class adolescent, for example, has already developed many of the social and intellectual skills necessary to movement up the ladder of success. For the lower-class respondent, it is often too late. Although he can recognize education and its concomitants as instruments for the climb, there is little he can do to recapture his formative years. The lower classes, as a result, are "boxed in" by the consequences of a kind of structured strain, the discrepancy between their evaluative and cognitive perceptions of education.

This process, combined with the limitations imposed by the social structure and, more specifically, by the objective requirements for occupational advancement, leads to a cyclical phenomenon analogous to a self-fulfilling prophecy (Merton, 1957,

pp. 421–38). Lack of education blocks advancement and opportunities to move out of the lower-class *milieu*. Furthermore, lack of opportunity to incorporate middle-class values reinforces the tendency to seek more available means for getting ahead. "To him that hath shall be given."

We have implied that the lower-class situation is very much like that of the minority group. The nature of the values that characterize the lower classes by themselves explain much of the failure to advance from those classes.

We generalize that the belief that a man with ability can get ahead in American society is uniformly held throughout the class structure. The American dream remains intact, in spite of the objective social conditions of the lower-class milieu. Nevertheless, a number of respondents see their own chances of getting ahead as limited. Purely rational self-analysis might be expected to lead to a corresponding belief that such limited chances are owing to low ability. The success ideology, which effectively fills the gap between the cognitive and evaluative spheres, however, provides solace and hope that sooner or later success will be won as a just reward for legitimate striving. That this ideology protects the social order from disruptive criticism has been demonstrated by Merton. We add that this particular ideology fills the gap between the objective conditions of the "working class," as Marx described them, and their lack of a revolutionary orientation. Marx assumed that the working class would eventually become aware of its condition and would overthrow the "capitalist" classes.

. . . Marx failed to take account of alternative ideologies in his analysis. The success theme is such an alternative. Our view is that lack of class identification is not in itself what is responsible for so-called "working-class apathy" but the specific quality of the American dream itself. As Merton has noted, the American who believes he has equal opportunity for advancement has only himself to blame if he fails to succeed. Our findings support this suggestion.

Finally, we assessed the disparity between earlier occupational aspiration and current achievement and found it greatest among the lower classes. This finding provides a test of the Durkheim-Merton theory and lends it at least initial support.

In sum, we have managed to isolate four sources of structured strain in the social-class system of the small city from which our data are taken.[14] One was suggested by Merton and may be designated "external" to particular classes. He focused on the limits imposed upon the lower classes by the middle classes, which place obstacles in the path of those attempting to attain culturally prescribed goals. Three sources that are reflected in our data arise from class value systems themselves and may be described as "internal." Our choice of these terms is based on the extent to which groups other than those acting to achieve a particular goal are a primary source of strain (external) and on factors within the group

that are primary sources of strain (internal).

Of the internal sources, there is first the disparity between the success ideology, particularly the belief that all can achieve success, and the objective conditions of American life, which limit achievement and success to relatively few at each level of the class structure. For example, only a few signers can join the Metropolitan Opera Company, even though there may be many who are capable. Second, there is a disparity between the lower-class value system and the requirements for attainment of success in American society. The values themselves tend to circumscribe opportunities among the lower classes. Finally, there is the distinction between achievement and success.

Whether or not these observations clarify processes at work in other communities can be determined only by systematic observation. It is our view that they represent significant focal points for the study of social structure and anomie in American society.

---

[14] See Leon Festinger, *A Theory of Cognitive Dissonance* (New York: Harper & Row, Publishers, 1957) for a discussion that offers a possible method of integrating the social psychological and sociological approaches to structured strain.

PART V
Social Mobility

Throughout this book we have encountered references to the concept of social mobility and numerous assertions about its manifestations. Where it figured most prominently was in Part II, major types of stratification systems. There we discovered that the norms concerning mobility, as well as the amount of actual mobility, are integral features of different types of stratification systems. (Recall that, although the norms of given systems call for it, in fact no society is completely open or completely closed.) Now, however, the focus is on social mobility.

The first selection here is from Pitirim Sorokin's pioneer work, *Social Mobility*, which appeared in 1927 and which marks the beginning of the systematic sociological study of this subject. For a while it was not given the deserved recognition by sociologists, but it is now being rediscovered and hailed as a work unequaled among the many on the topic of social mobility that have appeared since it was published. (It is no exaggeration to say that no area of social stratification has received more attention in the last two decades, judging by the quantity of studies, than has that of social mobility.)

Our selection from Sorokin's book contains the well-known terms he coined and their definitions: *vertical mobility* and *horizontal mobility*. It is important to note that Sorokin defines social mobility as the transition from one *social position* to another, but when he turns to the preceding two concepts, referring to types of mobility, he tends to abandon *position* in defining them. Instead he defines each as a certain kind of movement from group to group or stratum to stratum. I think that it is preferable to define horizontal and vertical mobility also in terms of the more basic element of position. This, besides making the definitions more consistent with one another, would perhaps open the door to the study of intraclass vertical mobility, which has been much neglected. Thus, I would suggest that we slightly modify the Sorokin definitions to read: (1) horizontal mobility—the transition of an individual from one social position to another of the same rank and (2) vertical mobility—transition of an individual from one social position to another of different rank, or the change of the same position from one rank to another.

Perhaps the latter part of the definition of vertical mobility that I spelled out needs some elaboration. What is meant is that an individual may experience social mobility while remaining in the same position if that position changes in rank from one time to another. For example, if, as we have learned from our previous readings, scientists rank higher today than they did twenty years ago, then the individual scientist of twenty years ago who is still practicing his profession has experienced social mobility even if he has not changed positions. The case falls within the category of social mobility because a change has taken place in the ranking of the same position.

The preceding formulation again has its origin, as the reader will soon discover, in Sorokin's conceptualization and simply translates his ideas, substituting the more basic element of position. I have in mind Sorokin's idea that vertical mobility, in addition to the movement of individuals, also refers to the change in the rank of a group or stratum. He utilizes it in his discussion of the two types of vertical mobility, which he terms *ascending* and *descending,* but which are better known today as *upward* and *downward.* One of his historical examples of the first type is the Brahmin caste in India, whose rank supposedly was not always as high as it has been in the last two thousand years.

Subsequent to Sorokin's work, J. H. Hutton, in his book *Caste in India* demonstrated that the characteristic form of mobility in India was not individual movement, but the collective splitting off by subcastes. He referred to this as the "fissiparous tendencies in Indian castes,"[1] and described its process. It involves the subcaste's establishing a claim to superiority, changing its name, and in the final step denying any connection with the caste of origin.

Other concepts employed by Sorokin have proved useful in the study of social mobility. Take, for example, his formulation concerning the factors that bring about mobility, presented in summary form at the end of the selection here. There is the general tendency for individuals in high positions to seek to transfer their priviliges to their offspring and kin. But there are also "permanent and universal" factors that counteract this trend and bring about mobility. He locates three such factors: the demographic, "change of environment," and "dissimilarity of parents and children." The last we are only rediscovering lately in our concern about the insufficient supply of talent. The first two figure prominently in contemporary discussions on the subject of social mobility, the second being termed now either as factors of technological change or structural factors. In regard to the demographic factors, his analysis of statistics and historical materials (not included in our selections) lead him to the conclusion that the rate of reproduction of the higher strata is often less than that of the lower ones. Thus vacant top positions have to be filled by people from below. As for the second type, on the basis of extensive historical material (omitted from our selection), he concludes that social change facilitates social mobility.

Regrettably, modern analysis has not gone far beyond the accomplishments of Sorokin. The most important attempt to *measure* the effect of technological change on mobility was made by Kahl.[2] Comparing data in the United States on the occupational distribution in 1920 and 1950, he equated the interperiod change with intergenerational mobility (changes in the occupational standing of sons relative to their fathers). He then proceeded to calculate how much of this change was the result of the four factors he isolated: technological, reproductive, immigration and "individual mobility." (The last is a rather vague concept, explained by

---

[1] J. H. Hutton, *Caste in India,* Cambridge: The University Press, 1946, especially pp. 41–61, 97–100.
[2] Joseph A. Kahl, *The American Class Structure,* New York: Holt, Rinehart and Winston, 1961, pp. 251–272.

the author thus: "Some people slip down and make room for others to move up."[3])
He concluded that about 7 per cent of the labor force had to be mobile in order
to compensate for differential fertility. According to his calculations, about one-
third of all cases of intergenerational mobility were the result of technological
change. Except for reproductive mobility, the rest largely represented "individual
mobility." He found that only about 1 per cent of the native-born men were up-
graded by immigration and concluded that in the generation preceding 1950 the
effect of immigration on the mobility of the native born was almost nil.[4]

Kahl's findings were subsequently reexamined by experts who questioned their
validity. Duncan characterized Kahl's statistical procedures as "ingenious uses of
defective materials," but his main attack was on Kahl's conceptual framework.
Kahl's estimate was based on the assumption that over a thirty-year period there
is a complete replacement of fathers by their sons, when in fact, says Duncan,
there is considerable overlap. Still, Duncan's article contains the following statement, which in a way praises Kahl's work: "Although . . . Kahl's effort was a
failure—and for fundamental reasons, not merely because of flaws in the data
available to him—it falls into the class of honorable failures which needed to be
made in order to force a re-examination of the problem."[5] And so, notwithstanding
Kahl's effort, other experts too were forced to conclude that the importance of
technological change in the mobility process is largely unknown.[6]

If one compares the conclusions about the positive and negative consequences
of mobility found in Sorokin[7] and the present state of knowledge concerning this
subject, he is again likely to find only small advances, for they are still scanty and
impressionistic.[8] To the limited degree that hypotheses on this subject have been
tested, they bear out Sorokin's statements. For instance, a panel-design research
on lower-class youth entering a high-status university was used to test three
competing hypotheses of the personal and social consequences of upward
mobility, including one by Sorokin. Their evidence supported what the authors
term the *dissociative hypothesis* formulated by Sorokin. In describing the negative
psychological consequences, Sorokin asserted that social mobility "diminishes
intimacy and increases psychosocial isolation and loneliness."[9] The authors
demonstrate that their data bear out the hypothesis that upward mobility is a
disruptive social experience that produces rootlessness in and lack of effective social
support for the individual.[10]

In light of this discussion, the following remarks by Smelser and Lipset, made
in 1966, concerning Sorokin's *Social Mobility* and the state of contemporary
knowledge on this subject assume special significance:

[3] *Ibid.,* p. 253.
[4] For a discussion of how immigration can be a factor in both upward and downward mobility, see
Elbridge Sibley, "Some Demographic Clues to Stratification," *American Sociological Review,* Vol. 7,
1942, pp. 322–330.
[5] Otis Dudley Duncan, "Methodological Issues in the Analysis of Social Mobility," in Neil J.
Smelser and S. M. Lipset, eds., *Social Structure and Mobility in Economic Development,* Chicago:
Aldine Press, 1966, pp. 54–55.
[6] Kaare Svalastoga, *Social Differentiation,* New York: David McKay Co., 1965, p. 142. Also see
pp. 105–143.
[7] Pitirim A. Sorokin, *Social and Cultural Mobility,* New York: Free Press, 1959, pp. 508–545.
[8] Melvin M. Tumin, "Some Unapplauded Consequences of Social Mobility in a Mass Society,"
Social Forces, Vol. 36, October, 1957, p. 32; Svalastoga, *op. cit.,* p. 143.
[9] Sorokin, *op. cit.,* pp. 522–526.
[10] Robert A. Ellis and W. Clayton Lane, "Social Mobility and Social Isolation: A Test of Sorokin's
Dissociative Hypothesis," *American Sociological Review,* Vol. 32, April, 1967, pp. 237–253.

This work first published in 1927, which is rarely cited today, is not only a rich source of comparative data, but contains highly sophisticated analyses of both causes and consequences of social mobility. Much of the recent work in this field touches precisely on the issues Sorokin dealt with, and often "rediscovers" processes he specified. Unlike some of the more recent writers, Sorokin recognized the difficulties involved in trying to be overprecise in comparative research, and did not draw precise conclusions from what was and is only roughly comparable data.[11]

The last sentence is particularly noteworthy because Lipset himself was involved in studies of comparative mobility in industrial societies.[12]

Subsequently a number of critics have pointed to errors—resulting from methodological difficulties—in the international comparisons of intergenerational occupational mobility from which international similarities or differences were inferred. One such critic, Harold L. Wilensky, terms the errors "grievous" and claims that the categories compared in these studies are "both heterogenous and non-comparable." According to him, the samples are also noncomparable because they are of populations that differ substantially in age distribution and therefore will result in a large sampling error. And last but not least, the data-gathering efficiency varies from country to country. Thus he urges more caution than is being manifested in discussing comparative mobility rates.[13]

Fully conscious of these recent criticisms, we have nevertheless reprinted a portion of S. M. Miller's influential *Comparative Social Mobility*, convinced that it is a cautious work and among the best done in this field. But his study, like most empirical studies to date, is confined to intergenerational mobility.

He found that in fewer than one-third of the nations studied did upward mobility exceed downward mobility. Thus, downward rather than upward movement is the more compelling fact about mobility in industrialized societies. (Studies that have appeared subsequent to Miller's book show that, contrary to the general impression, there is also extensive downward mobility in emerging industrializing societies.)[14] In examining both types in the seventeen nations studied, Miller found that high rates of upward mobility may be associated with either low or high rates of downward mobility. He considers this varied connection between upward and downward mobility the most important new finding of his study. But others have found therein additional important contributions. Kaare Svalastoga, a well-known student of mobility, asserts that Miller presents "the most important collection of mobility tables available at present."[15] Moreover, he says that one of the most striking analytic contributions is Miller's deliberate emphasis on the distance of mobility in contrast to its neglect hitherto in the studies of rates of mobility.

[11] Smelser and Lipset, *op. cit.,* p. 47, footnote 93.

[12] See, for example, S. M. Lipset and Reinhard Bendix, *Social Mobility in Industrial Society,* Berkeley: University of California Press, 1959, chap. 2, pp. 22–76; also S. M. Lipset and H. L. Zetterberg, "A Theory of Social Mobility," *Transactions of the Third World Congress of Sociology,* Vol. II, 1956, pp. 155–177.

[13] Harold L. Wilensky, "Measures and Effects of Social Mobility," in Smelser and Lipset, *op. cit.,* pp. 98–105.

[14] Smelser and Lipset, "Social Structure, Mobility and Development," in *Social Structure and Economic Development, op. cit.,* pp. 45–50. It is noteworthy that again we encounter a finding consistent with Sorokin's formulation. In his book, Sorokin presented considerable evidence from various studies in the late nineteenth and early twentieth centuries demonstrating that a considerable proportion of the manual force in then industrially developing Europe were sons of middle-class and even elite fathers. See Sorokin, *op. cit.,* p. 435–449.

[15] Svalastoga, *op. cit.,* p. 123.

It should be mentioned that the concept of *distance of mobility* is found in the Sorokin reading under the term *intensiveness*. He defined it as "the vertical social distance . . . crossed by an individual in his upward or downward movement in a definite period of time." Sorokin made clear that in order to have a measure of over-all mobility in a society, one would have to devise an index that would combine "intensiveness"—that is, distance—with the "generality of the vertical mobility." (By generality he meant the number or proportion of individuals who have moved up or down.)

Although Miller has not devised such an index, he does succeed in projecting a picture of over-all mobility by presenting in tabular form the *national profiles*, which include measures of both aspects. (See his Table 8.) It is worthwhile to note how similar the profiles of the United States and the USSR are. Both show a general pattern of upward mobility with limited downward mobility.

Now Miller arrived at his profile of mobility in the United States on the basis of two sets of data: USA I refers to the white male 1946 data of Richard Centers; USA II to the Survey Research Center's 1956 data for white and Negro males. From our next selection by Peter M. Blau and Otis Dudley Duncan, which utilized 1962 data, we gather that the mobility profile has not changed much. As the authors point out in their book based on the same data, in 1962 there was no immediate cause for concern that the American occupational structure was becoming more rigid. On the contrary, there seemed to be more upward and less downward mobility in 1962 than earlier. At the end of their book the authors convincingly argue that higher rates of upward mobility do not intrinsically signify fairness in allocation of rewards. There is nevertheless, as they point out, a fundamental difference between a stratification system with high mobility and one with low mobility. The first perpetuates a structure of differential positions but not their inheritance, the latter perpetuates both. [16]

The reprinted article by Blau and Duncan is the preliminary report of the findings of the 1962 survey. (These were later elaborated upon in their book, discussed above.) Note, this was the first comprehensively designed inquiry into social mobility in the United States; the sample consisted of 20,700 men. The findings presented in the article deal with education, ethnic background, community size, migration and parental family as factors in occupational mobility.

The next reading on "Sponsored and Contest Mobility and the School System" by Ralph H. Turner turns our attention from the extent of mobility to that of *modes* of mobility. That education in advanced industrial society is the predominant channel of upward mobility is a well-documented proposition. [17] This statement in no way contradicts what was said in the introduction to the preceding section about the educational system in its relation to the social stratification system being mainly a mechanism whereby social-class positions are stabilized across the generations. (Numerous studies show that the higher one's class, the more and better the education he receives.) The educational system nevertheless also serves as a

---

[16] Peter M. Blau and Otis Dudley Duncan, *The American Occupational Structure,* New York: John Wiley, 1967, pp. 424–441.

[17] One of the latest studies bearing it out is that by Thomas Fox and S. M. Miller, "Economic, Political, and Social Determinants of Mobility. An International Cross-Sectional Analysis," *Acta Sociologica* 9, 1966, pp. 76–93. Another is Otis Dudley Duncan and Robert W. Hodge, "Education and Occupational Mobility: A Regression Analysis," *American Journal of Sociology,* Vol. 68, 1963, pp. 629–644. For an article casting some doubt on it, see Arnold Anderson, "A Sceptical's Note on the Relation of Vertical Mobility to Education," *American Journal of Sociology,* Vol. 66, 1961, pp. 560–570.

mechanism of social mobility. Many studies have been conducted on the ways given school systems facilitate or impede such mobility. But Turner adds a new dimension by raising the problem of varying societal norms concerning the accepted mode of upward mobility, which he considers a crucial factor in shaping the school system.

Specifically, the author contrasts the English norm of *sponsored mobility* with the American norm of *contest mobility*. The English norm requires that the existing elite grant elite status to those not born to it but nevertheless deserving it. Under the American norm, elite status should be, and is thought to be, the prize in an open contest. Consistent with this, in America the final award tends to be delayed as long as is practicable and an effort is made to keep lagging contestants in the race until the climax in order to insure the fairness of the race. On the other hand, in England the recruits are chosen early, to control their proper training for elite status. The varied norms of the two countries account then to a large extent, according to Turner, for the divergence between the English and American systems of social control and education. He shows how the logic of each affects the secondary school system, the kind of value placed on education, the content of education, and the system of examinations—all of which differ in the United States and in England.

It seems to me that despite the lack of systematic study of the phenomenon, it is not incorrect to say that much *noninstitutionalized* sponsored mobility has long been present in the United States. Although the ideology does not take cognizance of it, there is considerable awareness in this country of the importance of "contacts" in moving up the social ladder. The lower strata are especially conscious of the prevalence of this mechanism, as exemplified in their often used expression "It's not what you know; it's who you know." But then there is good reason to think that this sort of sponsorship was not included by Turner in the concept of sponsored mobility. However, even if we focus on the *institutionalized* form that his concept stands for, it appears that America is now leaping in the direction of sponsored mobility, at least on the university level: Witness the great expansion of scholarships and fellowships.

Turner visualized that his scheme could be applied to further comparisons between other countries. A systematic comparison between England and the USSR could reveal the latter outdoing the former in the pattern of institutionalized sponsored mobility. As Turner explains, the governing objective of this mode of mobility is the best utilization of talents in society, "by sorting persons into their proper niches," whereas that of contest mobility "is to give elite status to those who earn it." To express it in another way, the main manifest goal of the first is collective and of the second individualistic. The theme of utilization of talents in the interest of society is much stronger in the Soviet Union and other Soviet-type societies than in England. It has been shown that most Soviet citizens who occupy the top of the social pyramid are there because the party has facilitated their rise, stage by stage, to a position of distinction and leadership. This holds true for scholars, scientists, and artists, as well as government officials and industrial managers.[18] Talent is sought out early and cultivated by special schooling.

As is suggested by Turner, the emphasis on ambition and on motivation goes hand in hand with contest mobility, whereas emphasis on intelligence or ability is more characteristic of sponsored mobility. Thus Turner also touches on the subjective factors in mobility, which is the main concern of the next selection from the

[18] Frederic C. Barghoorn, *Politics in the USSR*, Boston: Little Brown, 1966, pp. 184–185.

much acclaimed book *Social Mobility in Industrial Society,* by S. M. Lipset and Reinhard Bendix. One cannot help but wonder whether the usual designations of such factors as *subjective* or *psychological* are adequate; some explanation of what is meant by these terms is therefore in order. Earlier in this discussion we spoke about technological or structural factors in mobility. These concern the rise or fall of certain positions and the expansion or shrinkage of positions. In a sense they are the objective conditions for mobility. When turning to subjective factors, the central question is, Why, given the same structural conditions, are some individuals mobile while others who originated in the same stratum are not? Put differently, and more specifically, if there is room at the top of the social hierarchy for people below to move into, who among them is most likely to do so?

Now, provided there is room, achievement is dependent on at least two kinds of factors: (1) that one have the motivation to move up and (2) that one have the necessary resources, such as ability and "know-how" for reaching the goals. We have already gathered from previous selections that the goals and means of mobility are differentially distributed among the social strata. In the reading by Lipset and Bendix we encounter additional empirical materials on this theme.[19] What is new for us is the well-documented discussion found therein of the *intra-stratum* variation of these subjective factors in its relation to mobility. The authors pulled together in a concise presentation the extensive materials that bear upon this subject. They have organized the materials differently, but hopefully it will be convenient to think of them as contributions to the knowledge of the motivation and means for mobility.

The authors begin with the *means,* insofar as they start with the discussion of intelligence. But let me first make a few comments about achievement motivation, because it logically precedes the means. Also, recent evidence indicates that motivation affects the utilization of the means of mobility. For example, Jackson and Marsden have shown the great importance of motivation in determining the academic success of British working-class youth.[20] We find at the end of the Lipset and Bendix presentation a discussion of the achievement motivation of children of the same social class, being related to early home socialization. Those working-class parents whose reference group is middle class are likely to socialize their children in middle-class values. Working-class boys' anticipatory socialization in such values may, on the other hand, take place when those boys associate with middle-class peers, as studies conducted after the publication of the Lipset and Bendix book suggest. Thus, for example, one study shows that working-class boys with high aspirations interact more with boys higher in status than do those with low aspirations.[21] Another study found that such boys were more similar to ambitious middle-class boys than to working-class boys with low aspirations in their tendency to be members of organizations and clubs as well as in naming only middle-class boys as friends.[22]

[19] For a concise treatment of materials that have appared since—that, as the author makes explicit, follows the framework of the Lipset and Bendix presentation—see Harry Crockett, "Psychological Origins of Mobility," in Smelser and Lipset, *op. cit.,* pp. 291–309.

[20] Brian Jackson and Dennis Marsden, *Education and the Working Class: Some General Themes Raised by the Study of 88 Working-Class Children in a Northern Industrial City,* New York: Monthly Review Press, 1962.

[21] Gerald D. Bell, "Processes in the Formation of Adolescents' Aspiration," *Social Forces,* Vol. 42, December, 1963, pp. 179–186.

[22] Richard L. Simpson, "Anticipatory Socialization and Social Mobility," *American Sociological Review,* Vol. 27, August, 1962, pp. 517–522.

In proceeding to a few remarks concerning intelligence as a factor in upward mobility, attention should be drawn to the fact that the findings presented under this heading in the Lipset and Bendix selection are largely about variations in IQ distribution. And, as the authors mention at one point, the evidence from the study of IQ distributions does not allow any definite conclusions about the effect of intelligence on social mobility because of the difficulties of separating in the IQ measure, native intelligence from the effects of differential class socialization. Still, I would say, the kind of ability that goes into scoring well on an IQ test may be an even greater asset to upward mobility in the United States than native intelligence. This is precisely so, because, as has been widely shown, the IQ test does not measure intelligence alone but a good deal of obviously acquired knowledge and skill and special abilities distinct from intelligence. [23] Further support for this contention can be gained from Anastasi's demonstration that the criterion used in validating intelligence tests "has nearly always been success in our social system." [24]

In light of this, the evidence presented in the Lipset and Bendix reading that intraclass variation in IQ is greater than interclass variation assumes special significance. The high IQ's of some working-class youngsters could be considered indicators that they have acquired certain skills conducive to advancement. True, social class is a greater determinant than IQ of motivation to go to college, as is amply demonstrated in the reading by Lipset and Bendix. Nevertheless, if one focuses on the data they present about working-class boys, he will find that a larger proportion of those who rank high in IQ plan to go to college than those who rank low. And, if working-class boys manage to get into college, their educational achievement does not differ from students from other class backgrounds.

Now, given the same high IQ's, those working-class boys whose parents have more education are more likely to land in college than those who do not. Thus, apart from IQ, parents' influence is an important factor in securing the additional means for advancement that college education represents. Another important factor is size of family. The consistent finding of many studies is that better-educated and upwardly mobile children of the lower classes tend to be from small families. Lipset and Bendix also outline additional factors in the intraclass distribution of means of mobility.

In reading about the subjective factors in social mobility it is important to bear in mind that usually a number of these factors are operating simultaneously and that their effects on a given individual may either cancel out or reinforce each other. Thus individuals in the same class, given the same opportunities, still vary considerably in mobility achievement.

---

[23] Raymond B. Cattell, "A Culture-Free Intelligence Test," *Journal of Educational Psychology,* March 31, 1940, p. 162; Susan S. Stodolsky and Gerald Lesser, "Learning Patterns in the Disadvantaged," *Harvard Educational Review,* Vol. 37, Fall, 1967, pp. 546–593.

[24] She shows that "Scores on the test are correlated with school achievement or perhaps with some more general measure of success in our society. If such correlations are high, it is concluded that the test is a good measure of 'intelligence.'" See: Ann Anastasi, *Differential Psychology,* 3rd ed., NewYork: The Macmillan Company, 1958, pp. 566–567.

SOCIAL MOBILITY*

Pitirim A. Sorokin

CONCEPTION OF SOCIAL MOBILITY AND ITS FORMS

By social mobility is understood any transition of an individual or social object or value—anything that has been created or modified by human activity—from one social position to another. There are two principal types of social mobility, *horizontal* and *vertical*. By horizontal social mobility or shifting, is meant the transition of an individual or social object from one social group to another situated on the same level. Transitions of individuals, as from the Baptist to the Methodist religious group, from one citizenship to another, from one family (as a husband or wife) to another by divorce and remarriage, from one factory to another in the same occupational status, are all instances of social mobility. So too are transitions of social objects, the radio, automobile, fashion, Communism, Darwin's theory, within the same social stratum, as from Iowa to California, or from any one place to another. In all these cases, "shifting" may take place without any noticeable change of the social position of an individual or social object in the vertical direction. By *vertical* social mobility is meant the relations involved in a transition of an individual (or a social object) from one social stratum to another. According to the direction of the transition there are two types of vertical social mobility: *ascending* and *descending*, or *social climbing* and *social sinking*. According to the nature of the stratification, there are ascending and descending currents of economic, political, and occupational mobility, not to mention other less important types. The ascending currents exist in two principal forms: as an *infiltration* of the individuals of a lower stratum into an existing higher one; and as a *creation of a new group by such individuals, and the insertion of such a group into a higher stratum instead of, or side by side with, the existing groups of this stratum.* Correspondingly, the descending current has also two principal forms: the first consists in a dropping of individuals from a higher social position into an existing lower one, without a degradation or disintegration of the higher group to which they belonged; the second is manifested in a *degradation of a social group as a whole, in an abasement of its rank among other groups, or in its disintegration as a social unit.* The first case of "sinking" reminds one of an individual falling from a ship; the second of the sinking of the ship itself with all on board, or of the ship as a wreck breaking itself to pieces.

The cases of individual infiltration into an existing higher stratum or of individuals dropping from a higher social layer into a lower one are relatively common and comprehensible. They need no explanation. The second form of social ascending and descending, the rise and fall of groups, must be considered more carefully.

The following historical examples may serve to illustrate. The historians of India's caste-society tell us that the caste of the Brahmins did not always hold the position of indisputable superiority which it has held during the last two thousand years. In the remote past, the caste of the warriors and rulers, or the caste of the Kshatriyas, seems to have been not inferior to the caste of the Brahmins; and it appears that only after a long struggle did the latter become the highest caste.[1] If this hypothesis be true, then this elevation of the rank of the Brahmin caste as a whole through the ranks of other castes is an example of the second type of social ascent. The group as a whole being elevated, all its members, *in corpore,* through this very fact, are elevated also. Before the recognition of the Christian religion by Constantine the Great, the position of a Christian Bishop, or the Christian clergy,

Reprinted with permission of The Macmillan Company from *Social and Cultural Mobility* by Pitirim A. Sorokin. Copyright © The Free Press of Glencoe, a Division of The Macmillan Company, 1964.

[1] See Bouglé, C., "Remarques sur le régime des castes," pp. 53 *et seq.; The Cambridge History of India,* pp. 92 *et seq.*

was not a high one among other social ranks of Roman society. In the next few centuries the Christian Church, as a whole, experienced an enormous elevation of social position and rank. Through this wholesale elevation of the Christian Church, the members of the clergy, and especially the high Church dignitaries, were elevated to the highest ranks of medieval society.[2]

. . . .

The situation is summed up in the following scheme.

INTENSIVENESS OR VELOCITY AND GENERALITY OF VERTICAL SOCIAL MOBILITY

From the quantitative point of view, a further distinction must be made between the intensiveness and the generality of the vertical mobility. By its *intensiveness* is meant the vertical social distance, or the number of strata—economic or occupational or political—crossed by an individual in his upward or downward movement in a definite period of time. If, for instance, one individual in one year climbed from the position of a man with a yearly income

[2] See Guizot, F., *The History of Civilization*, Vol. I, pp. 50–54, New York, 1874.

of $500 to a position with an income of $50,000, while another man in the same period succeeded in increasing his income only from $500 to $1,000, in the first case the intensiveness of the economic climbing would be fifty times greater than in the second case. For a corresponding change, the intensiveness of the vertical mobility may be measured in the same way in the field of the political and occupational stratifications. By *the generality of the vertical mobility,* is meant the number of individuals who have changed their social position in the vertical direction in a definite period of time. The absolute number of such individuals gives the *absolute generality* of the vertical mobility in a given population; the proportion of such individuals to the total number of a given population gives *the relative generality of the vertical mobility.*

Finally, combining the data of intensiveness and relative generality of the vertical mobility in a definite field (*e.g.,* in the economic), *the aggregate index of the vertical economic mobility of a given society* may be obtained. In this way a comparison of one society with another, or of the same society at different periods may be made, to find in which of them, or at what period, the aggregate mobility is greater. The same may be said about the aggregate index

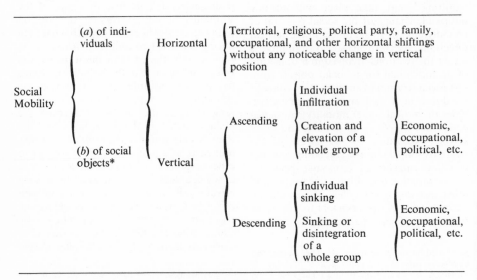

* The mobility of social objects and values and the horizontal mobility, in spite of the great importance of the problem, is not an object of this study.

of the political and occupational vertical mobility.

IMMOBILE AND MOBILE TYPES OF STRATIFIED SOCIETIES

On the basis of the above, it is easy to see that a social stratification of the same height and profile may have a different inner structure caused by the difference in the intensiveness and generality of the (horizontal and) vertical social mobility. Theoretically, there may be a stratified society in which the vertical social mobility is nil. This means that within it there is no ascending or descending, no circulation of its members; that every individual is forever attached to the social stratum in which he was born; that the membranes or hymens which separate one stratum from another are absolutely impenetrable, and do not have any "holes" through which, nor any stairs and elevators with which, the dwellers of the different strata may pass from one floor to another. *Such a type of stratification may be styled as absolutely closed, rigid, impenetrable, or immobile.* The opposite theoretical type of the inner structure of the stratification of the same height and profile is that in which the vertical mobility is very intensive and general; here the membranes between the strata are very thin and have the largest holes to pass from one floor to another. Therefore, though the social building is as stratified as the immobile one, nevertheless, the dwellers of its different strata are continually changing; they do not stay a very long time in the same "social story," and with the help of the largest staircases and elevators are *en masse* moving "up and down." *Such a type of social stratification may be styled open, plastic, penetrable, or mobile.* Between these two extreme types there may be many middle or intermediary types of stratification.

. . . .

GENERAL PRINCIPLES OF VERTICAL MOBILITY

1. *First Proposition.—There has scarcely been any society whose strata were absolutely closed, or in which vertical mobility in its three forms—economic, political and occupational—was not present.* . . . The nearest

approach to an absolutely rigid society, without any vertical mobility, is the so-called caste-society. Its most conspicuous type exists in India. Here, indeed, vertical social mobility is very weak. But even here it has not been absolutely absent. Historical records show that in the past, when the caste-system had already been developed, it did happen that members of the highest Brahmin caste, or the king and his family, were overthrown or cast out for crimes. . . . On the other hand, the outcasts, after a suitable repentance, might be reinstated, or individuals born in a lower social stratum might succeed in entering the Brahmin caste, the top of the social cone of India.

. . . .

. . . It is evident, therefore, that, in spite on the fact that the caste-society of India is apparently the most conspicuous example of the most impenetrable and rigidly stratified body, nevertheless, even within it, the weak and slow currents of vertical mobility have been constantly present. If such is the case with the India caste-society, it is clear that in all other social bodies vertical mobility, to this or that degree, must obviously be present. This statement is warranted by the facts. The histories of Greece, Rome, Egypt, China, Medieval Europe, and so on show the existence of a vertical mobility much more intensive than that of the Indian caste-society. The absolutely rigid society is a myth which has never been realized in history.

2. *The Second Proposition.—There has never existed a society in which vertical social mobility has been absolutely free and the transition from one social stratum to another has had no resistance.* This proposition is a mere corollary to the premises established above, that every organized society is a stratified body. If vertical mobility were absolutely free, in the resultant society there would be no strata. It would remind us of a building having no floors separating one story from another. But all societies have been stratified. This means that within them there has been a kind of "sieve" which has sifted the individuals, allowing some to go up, keeping others in the lower strata, and contrariwise.

Only in periods of anarchy and great

disorder, when the entire social structure is broken and where the social strata are considerably demolished, do we have anything reminding us of a chaotic and disorganized vertical mobility *en masse*.[3] But even in such periods, there are some hindrances to unlimited social mobility, partly in the form of the remnants of the "sieve" of the old régime, partly in the form of a rapidly growing "new sieve." After a short period, if such an anarchic society does not perish in anarchy, a modified "sieve" rapidly takes the place of the old one and, incidentally, becomes as tight as its predecessor. . . .

3. *The Third Proposition.—The intensiveness, as well as the generality of the vertical social mobility, varies from society to society (fluctuation of mobility in space).*

. . . .

4. *The Fourth Proposition.—The intensiveness and the generality of the vertical mobility—the economic, the political and the occupational—fluctuate in the same society at different times.* In the course of the history of a whole country, as well as of any social group, there are periods when the vertical mobility increases from the quantitative as well as from the qualitative viewpoint, and there are the periods when it decreases. . . .

Though accurate statistical material to prove this proposition is very scarce and fragmentary, nevertheless, it seems to me that these data, together with different forms of historical testimony, are enough to make the proposition safe.

The first series of corroborations is given by the great social upheavals and revolutions which have occurred at least once in the history of every society. It is certain that in the periods of such upheavals vertical social mobility in its intensiveness and generality is far greater than in periods of order and peace. Since, in the history of all countries, periods of upheaval have taken place, this means that the intensiveness and generality of the vertical mobility in every country has oscillated also. Here are a few examples. . . .

. . . .

The conquest by the Aryans of the native

[3] See Sorokin, P., *Sociology of Revolution,* Philadelphia, 1925, Pt. III.

population of Ancient India; by the Dorians, of the earlier population of Greece; by the Spartans, of Messenia; by the Romans of their "predia"; by the Spaniards of the native population of America and so on, have involved similar great depressions of the previous highest strata and the creation of a new nobility out of the people who had often been before very low. Even when a war is concluded without conquest or subjugation, it nevertheless calls forth similar results because of a great loss of the higher strata—especially political and military aristocracy—and because of the financial bankruptcy of some of the rich people and the enrichment of skillful swindlers from the new people. The "vacuum" in the nobility caused by the losses has to be filled, and this leads to a more intensive promotion of the new people to the higher positions.

For the same reason in such periods there is a greater occupational shifting, and, hence, a greater occupational mobility, than in a more normal time. The above considerations show the existence of a rhythm of static and dynamic periods in the vertical mobility within the same society at different periods.

. . . .

5. *The Fifth Proposition.—As far as the corresponding historical and other materials permit seeing, in the field of vertical mobility, in its three fundamental forms, there seems to be no definite perpetual trend toward either an increase or a decrease of the intensiveness and generality of mobility. This is proposed as valid for the history of a country, for that of a large social body, and, finally, for the history of mankind.* Thus, in the field of vertical mobility, the same conclusion of "trendless" change is reached which was met with in the field of social stratification.

In these dynamic times, with the triumph of the electoral system, with the industrial revolution, and especially a revolution in transportation, this proposition may appear strange and improbable. The dynamism of our epoch stimulates the belief that history has tended and will tend in the future toward a perpetual and "eternal" increase of vertical mobility. There is no need to say that many social thinkers have such an opinion. And yet, if its bases and reasons are investigated it may be seen that they are far from convincing.*

THE CHANNELS OF VERTICAL CIRCULATION

Since vertical mobility actually functions to some degree in any society, there must be in the "membranes" between the strata "holes," "staircases," "elevators," or "channels" which permit individuals to move up and down, from stratum to stratum. The problem to be discussed now is: What are these channels of social circulation?

Various Social Institutions Perform This Function.—Among them there are few especially important from our standpoint. Of these few, which may be in different societies or in the same society, at different periods, one or two are particularly characteristic for a given type of society. The most important institutions of this kind have been: army, church, school, political, economic, and professional organizations.

....

Of other channels of vertical circulation may be mentioned the family and marriage with a person of another social stratum. Such a marriage usually leads one of the parties either to social promotion or degradation. In this way some people have made their careers; some others have ruined them. In the past, a marriage to a slave or a member of the lower caste led to the degradation of a higher party and his offspring. . . .

At the present moment in our democratic societies, we see a mutual "gravitation" of rich brides and of the poor but titled bridegrooms. In this way both parties try: one to get a financial basis for keeping his titled position on a necessary level, the other to get a social promotion through money.

Besides these channels there undoubtedly are many others, but they seem to be not so important as the preceding ones. These have always been the most common and

* Many pages of historical facts which run counter to the reasons for assuming a perpetual trend follow this statement in Sorokin's book. C. S. H.

convenient elevators which have carried up and down the streams of people "traveling" in the vertical plane. Those who, like farmers and manual workers, have not tried to enter one of these elevators, have been doomed to stay in the lower strata, having very little chance either to go up or down. Playing in all periods to this or that degree the rôle of channels, each of the above institutions has played an especially important part in a definite society in a certain period. The army plays a great rôle in a period of war and social disturbances; a moderate one in a period of peace. The Church had a great importance in the Middle Ages and has a less one at the present time. Money making and political activity have great significance now and had less a few centuries ago.

Varying in their concrete forms and in their size, the channels of vertical circulation exist in any stratified society, and are as necessary as channels for blood circulation in the body.

....

THE FACTORS OF VERTICAL CIRCULATION

PRIMARY PERMANENT FACTORS

Since vertical circulation in some degree exists in every society it follows that among its factors, besides local, temporary, and specific conditions, there must be conditions which operate in all societies, in all periods. Correspondingly, the factors of vertical circulation may be divided into: (*a*) primary or general, and (*b*) secondary, or local and temporary, which facilitate or hinder mobility.

Among the primary factors are: (1) demographic factors. . . ; (2) dissimilarity of parents and children; (3) change of environment, especially of the anthropo-social environment; (4) defective social distribution of individuals within social layers.

DEMOGRAPHIC FACTORS OF VERTICAL CIRCULATION

Under this heading are meant all forces which call forth sterility, lower differential birth rate, or higher mortality of the upper classes. In the course of time they cause either an extinction of the aristocratic families, or a decrease of their proportion in the total increased population of a society. In both cases such a situation creates a kind of "social vacuum" within the upper strata. As the performance of the functions carried on by the upper strata continues to be necessary, and as the corresponding people cannot be recruited any longer from a diminishing upper population, it is natural that this "vacuum" must be filled by the climbers from the lower strata. Such in essence is this factor of vertical circulation.

It is not certain that the fecundity of the upper strata is always and everywhere lower than that of the lower strata. But it is possible to say that such a phenomenon has taken place within many societies and at different periods. Besides, it seems possible to contend that in some way, not exactly known to us, almost any aristocratic family sooner or later dies out either biologically or socially, in the sense that its descendants cease to be noticeable as the continuators of a given aristocratic family.

. . . .

If the figures are reliable, they show that within the royal families, fertility and sterility fluctuate considerably in time, and from dynasty to dynasty. Several other studies show similar oscillations. It follows from this that the difference between the fertility of the upper and the lower strata may fluctuate. It seems to be probable, nevertheless, that the lower fertility of the upper strata is, if not a permanent phenomenon, at least common for many societies and many periods.[4] . . .

Although, as we have seen, the mortality of the lower classes has been considerably higher than that of the upper strata, nevertheless, it does not compensate for the lower rate of increase of population of the upper strata. Some previously given data show this. The indicated sources give many additional corroborations of this statement. *In*

spite of lower mortality the members of the higher strata, owing to their lower fertility, increase often less rapidly than the members of the lower ones.

To the factor of lower fertility must be added that of a *high death rate by violence* which takes place in regard to some groups of aristocracy (royal, executive, and military), and which leads to the extinction of many aristocratic families, and, through that, creates a "social vacuum." Here are some illustrations of the statement.[5]

. . . .

The above sufficiently corroborates the statement concerning the demographic factors of social circulation. Whatever may be the concrete causes . . . these demographic conditions make social mobility necessary and inevitable. *And the greater the difference in the number of surviving children of the upper and the lower strata, the more intensive the vertical circulation caused by this factor will be*. . . . As this difference varies from time to time, it follows that, in the past, the periods of increase of the difference should have been the periods of an intensification of the vertical circulation, providing this factor were not checked by opposite factors.

DISSIMILARITY OF PARENTS AND CHILDREN AS A FACTOR OF VERTICAL CIRCULATION

Since the publication of the works of Francis Galton, especially of his *Hereditary Genius*, it has become customary to think that talented parents beget talented children, while stupid parents beget stupid children. The reason for this is seen in the factor of heredity. At the present moment, there seems to be no doubt that this rule is, in many cases, true. But is it a rule which is universal and does it not know any exceptions? It seems not. We certainly know many cases where the children of prominent parents happened to be below normal, and the children of quite average parents quite prominent. Dr. A. Marro rightly says

While one has seen children inheriting from their parents qualities by which parents have

---

[4] The exceptions to this rule seem to exist principally in polygamous societies where the chances for procreation of the upper classes are greater than in monogamic groups.

[5] Sorokin, P., "The Monarchs and Rulers," *Journal of Social Forces*, March 1926.

become eminent, other children, on the contrary, do not correspond at all to this expectation. One is painfully surprised to see the sons of Hippocrates quite stupid, and one is struck with astonishment in noting that from the race of Socrates and Aristotle there has not arisen the least spark of science, that Charles V, Peter the Great, and Napoleon I had only foolish sons.[6]

A similar admission is made by Francis Galton himself. "It has often been remarked that the men who have attained pinnacles of celebrity failed to leave worthy successors," says Galton.[7] It is possible to give hundreds of historical cases of this kind. . . . On the other hand, it is possible to indicate hundreds of historical cases where the children of quite average parents have turned out to be eminent men of genius: Shakespeare, Beethoven, Schubert, Faraday, Pasteur, Lincoln, and the greater part of the self-made men, achievers and climbers— these supply examples of this fact.

Whatever may be the causes of this phenomenon, the fact of the dissimilarity of the parents and the children in many cases is beyond doubt. And, it seems to me, the number of such cases is not so small as was formerly believed. . . . Meanwhile, the opposite is to be found in almost every study of heredity. I do not know a single investigation of such cases where the correlation between the qualities of the parents and the children would be perfect. In the best cases, even in such comparatively simple traits as stature, pigmentation, the color of hair or eyes, not to mention other traits, the correlation happens to be approximately 0.5.[8] In regard to other traits it was much lower. Similarly, there scarcely may be found any study of this kind which would not indicate the fact of "overlapping." The presence of overlappings and the indicated difference between the theoretically perfect and the actual coefficient of correlation are found in all statistical studies of heredity. This means that *the fact of dissimilarity of parents and*

children is also permanent and universal.[9]

. . . .

A common result of dissimilarity between fathers and children is the discrepancy between the social position of individuals and their inner and acquired qualities, necessary for a successful performance of the functions of the position. If a father is quite fitted for his position, his dissimilar son may be unsuitable for it. And the greater the dissimilarity, the more necessary becomes a voluntary or a compulsory vertical shifting of individuals.

The shifting of individuals is carried on in three principal ways. In the first place, *through the preventive shifting of individuals, performed through the machinery of social testing and selection of the individuals.* Its essence consists in the fact that the children, before obtaining their social position, are tested and are either barred or promoted, according to the results of the test. The stupid children from a family of high social standing cannot pass through school and be graduated (the cases of misuse are not interesting for us now). The profligate persons could not pass the test of the medieval Church, as a rule. The same may be said about an occupational test. As a result, in spite of their birth in a high stratum, many failures of this kind may be prevented from obtaining a high position. In this way many would-be successors to a throne have been eliminated; many would-be heads of industrial corporations have been put aside from a responsible position. Many sons of prominent scholars are barred from graduation or the position of a professor. Many candidates are beaten in elections. Many sons of high officials have been excluded from responsible official ranks. In brief, in any society there are many sieves which perform this eliminating function. It is true that in this way only a part—and sometimes a small one—of the unsuitable individuals are sifted and barred or promoted. But this part is enough to produce a strong or weak stream of vertical circulation.

In the second place, *there is a repressive way of shifting of individuals from the social*

[6] See Marro, A., "The Influence of the Age of the Parents upon the Psychophysical Character of Children," *Problems of Eugenics*, p. 119.

[7] Galton, Francis and Schuster, E., *Noteworthy Families*, p. xv, London, 1906.

[8] See Pearson, Karl, *The Scope and Importance to the State of the Science of National Eugenics* pp. 27–29, London, 1909.

[9] Cf. Conklin, E. G., *The Direction of Human Evolution*, pp. 128 *et seq.*, New York, 1922.

stratum in which they have been born. It is performed through a repressive social pressure. Their unsuitableness for the position leads to a failure in the fulfillment of duties. A poor performance calls forth either dismissal or degradation of such a person; or, if a man is a manager of his own business, his poor management causes its failure; the business is ruined, the man himself is put down. If the man is an executive of a church, a school, an army, or an empire, his failure leads to disorganization of the institution. Owing to the disorganization many people begin to suffer. Suffering urges them to get rid of such a leader. This creates a social pressure which often puts down the leader and promotes a lower-born person. In this way many failures from the upper strata have been put down, and many "risers" from the lower classes promoted.

In the third place, *individuals being placed by their birth in a position for which they are unsuited, become dissatisfied and begin to try to change it in the way which is dictated by their "natural proclivities."* An inborn ruler or a great thinker, born from slave parents, tries to obtain a position which permits an adequate expression. For many an inborn slave, born in the position of a ruler, power is a burden; such persons try to get rid of it or hold the power only nominally in the form of "reigning without ruling," or, at least, do not hold steadfastly to their position and easily give way to anybody who craves it. . . .

CHANGE OF ENVIRONMENT, AND ESPECIALLY OF THE ANTHROPO-SOCIAL ENVIRONMENT AS A FACTOR OF VERTICAL CIRCULATION

An individual or a group may be unfit for the successful performance of their social functions not only through their own fault but because of the change of the environment in which they act. A man with the specific talent for strategy may climb up very rapidly in time of war, and may not promote himself in time of peace. A fine artisan may rise in a society with a system of handicraft industry, and he may not have any chance in a society of machine production. A purely physical force often has been the cause of leadership in primi-

tive societies, but it has much less importance in present society. An exclusive honesty and asceticism led to a social rise in the Middle Ages, and the same qualities are likely often to ruin a man under existing conditions. . . . Any considerable change of it [of social environment] results in a social redistribution of individuals: those who, through the change, are put in a favorable position begin to rise or continue to hold their high positions; those who cannot or do not wish to adapt themselves to the change, are likely to go down.

As the social environment of human beings is always changing, and the rate of change is especially intensive now, this means that within social life there is a permanent factor of vertical circulation. It incessantly operates within a society and incessantly produces social redistribution of its members. Any invention, any change in the methods of production, in *mores,* beliefs, standards, literary and dress fashions, in science and arts, in the means of transportation—in brief, in any field of social life—may ruin one group of individuals, and promote another. . . . Some changes may be favorable for the promotion of honest men, some for dishonest; some for the ascetic, some others for the licentious; some for the conservative temperament, some others for the progressive. In short, the variety of changes of environment have caused a promotion of the most different types of human beings. Through this factor, whole social layers, fitted for their positions under certain conditions, may become quite unfitted under other ones, and *vice versa.*

A few historical examples are sufficient to illustrate this.

A change of social environment, which led to the legalization of the Christian Church by Constantine the Great, caused a social promotion of the Christians, who before had been persecuted, and a sinking of the non-Christians, who before had been promoted. An increased rôle of money since the thirteenth and fourteenth centuries in England called forth a social rise of the money-making class, and facilitated social sinking of the landed aristocracy. . . . *All factors which facilitate change are factors facilitating vertical social shifting, and vice versa.*

DEFECTIVE SOCIAL DISTRIBUTION OF INDIVIDUALS AND THE LAG IN SHIFTING AS A CAUSE OF THE EXTRAORDINARY VERTICAL CIRCULATIONS

Though the previous three factors of social circulation operate permanently, nevertheless, their work has been, it seems, not so intensive, nor so perfect qualitatively, in many cases, as it should be. From a quantitative viewpoint, its almost permanent defect has consisted in that only a part, and sometimes an insignificant part, of the "non-suitable" individuals have been shifted in time, while another part—and often the majority—of the non-suitable men have been left in positions for which they have not been fitted.

The institute of juridical or factual inheritance of social position, into which the individuals have been born, has always hindered timely and proper shifting of all non-suitable individuals to places corresponding to their innate and acquired qualities. It is certain that even in the United States, among present dwellers in the economic, occupational, or political strata, there is a considerable proportion of unsuitable individuals. It is not a very rare picture to see a mediocre man placed above a man of ability, and an incapable person giving orders to a more capable one. Such discrepancy between the social position of individuals and their physical and mental qualities has been shown above in the part devoted to the study of the population of the different strata. Though there is a correlation between social status and many physical and mental qualities of the social classes; yet, in regard to the physical and other traits everywhere, the fact of overlapping has been met. The characteristics of the upper strata are not common to all their members, and at the same time are found among the members of the lower classes. And, contrariwise, the traits typical for the majority of the lower classes are found also among a part of the upper classes. This is an evident manifestation of defectiveness in the social distribution of individuals or that of the existence of a lag.

Even in the most mobile society the membranes which separate one stratum from another are not so permeable as to permit an infiltration of all capable "newcomers," or an ousting of all "unsuitable" dwellers born within a stratum. The testing, selecting, and distributing agencies shift only a part of the unsuitable persons. Another part, owing to various causes, continues to stay where it was born. *In brief, one of the permanent defects of any society is a lag in the distribution of its members according to their qualities, and an existence within each social stratum of individuals not suited to their social position.* Such is the defect from a quantitative point of view.

From the *qualitative standpoint,* an almost permanent defect of social distribution of individuals has consisted in a looseness of correspondence between the type of the people desirable for each stratum at a certain period and the type of people who have really been selected for each stratum by the machinery of social distribution of individuals. . . .[10]

Besides these permanent factors of vertical circulation of individuals there are many other secondary conditions which may facilitate or hinder vertical mobility. . . .

COMPARATIVE SOCIAL MOBILITY

S. H. Miller

THE ADVANTAGES OF A CROSS-NATIONAL APPROACH

A cross-national, comparative approach to social mobility can contribute effectively to our understanding of society. A study of mobility in a particular nation, by itself, cannot reveal whether a rate of mobility is high or low. . . . With comparative data, it becomes possible to assert that the highest rate of mobility that has been attained in a

From "Comparative Social Mobility," by S. M. Miller, *Current Sociology,* Vol. IX, No. 1. Reprinted by permission.

[10] See Sorokin, P., *The Sociology of Revolution,* Pts. III and V.

given type of economic and social order is of a particular level, which may be deemed as one of the benchmarks of mobility. It may be used, then, in viewing rates of mobility in a society of similar or different characteristics.

More important, perhaps, is the possibility that comparative mobility analysis can lead to an isolation of the significant variables affecting mobility. The comparative method *approximates* an experimental method. Does a particular form and level of economic activity produce higher mobility than another? Are there significant differences in rates of mobility in nations of similar economic development so that non-economic factors must be introduced to explain them? The possibility then emerges after the variables are isolated of developing a general theory of mobility.

A comparative approach can also be important in analyzing the consequences of mobility. Where rates of mobility are similar, do similar attitudinal complexes emerge or do additional cultural factors intrude? . . .

Finally, comparative studies clarify the kind of data which are most useful for analysis and turn us back to the initial issue in the study of mobility, the collection of quality data.

COMPARATIVE DANGERS

In the previous section, we have reviewed some difficulties involved in studying social mobility. These difficulties are compounded in comparative analysis for the results of rather disparate investigations have to be molded into a form permitting them to be compared with one another. Distortion is inevitable. One must operate with the hazardous assumption that the distortion does not destroy the product. . . .

BASIC DATA

This monograph does not represent primary research. It is an effort to utilize available primary studies for the 18 nations where data are available.

The unit of the comparisons is basically though not exclusively the nation. . . . For four nations, data are reported on a city (in the case of Belgium, two towns); following the suggestion of the Sub-Committee on Social Stratification and Mobility of the ISA, I have included these data because of the possibility that they may be representative to some degree of the national facts, as discussed in Section I. In a fifth nation, we have also deviated from the practice of a national representative sample: for the Soviet Union the only available mobility information for the nation as a whole is the emigré study of the Russian Research Center of Harvard University. National samples and a Hungarian census are employed in the other 13 nations.

. . . .

Only two-step intergenerational (father-son) mobility is studied.

The time of the studies varies, although all are post-World War II studies with the exception of the report on the USSR. This report is as of 1940; the other reports range from 1946 to the middle fifties. Thus, there is no exact comparability in time.

. . . .

TYPES OF COMPARISONS

Despite all the difficulties with the manual/non-manual classification, it was decided to concentrate on comparisons of this sort. The lively interest in mobility still largely centers on crossing from manual to non-manual work even if the line between them is wavy and changing. Downward movement of the non-manuals as well as upward movement of the manual received special attention.

. . . .

THEIR FATHERS' SONS

The comparisons offered in this section are only a few of the many possibilities. . . . No one rate can be said to express *the* rate of mobility of a nation. Rather, it is perhaps most accurate to say—"Nation A has a higher rate of mobility *of this type* than does Nation B; Nation B has a higher rate *of this type*."

MANUAL TO NON-MANUAL

In many studies, urban workers are included with farm workers and cannot be separated out. This mixed category we have termed "manual" to distinguish it from

TABLE 1   Non-Manual Sons of Manual and Working-Class Fathers

	(1) Manual into Non-Manual	*(2)* Working Classes into Non-Manual
I. NATIONAL DATA	%	%
Denmark	24.1	*
Finland	11	*
France I	30.1	34.9
France II	29.6	32.9
Great Britain	24.8	*
Hungary	14.5	21.8
Italy	8.5	*
Japan	23.7	*
Netherlands	19.6	*
Norway	23.2	25.8
Puerto Rico	14.3	18.7
Sweden	25.5	29.3
USA I	28.8	*
USA II	28.7	*
West Germany	20.0	21.2
II. URBAN DATA		
Australia (Melbourne)	24.1	*
Belgium I (St–Martens–Latem)	5.7	6.4
Belgium II (Mont–Saint–Guibert)	30.9	*
Brazil (São Paulo)	29.4	*
India (Poona)	27.3	*
III. SPECIAL DATA		
USSR (emigrés)	*	34.9

* Unavailable.

the "working classes," which exclude farm workers and purport to represent those non-agricultural employees who work with their "hands." In Table 1 data are reported of the upward mobility of sons of fathers in the "manual" and in the "working-class" category.

Upward mobility for these two groups is defined as crossing into non-manual work, which includes all white-collar work, whether as employees, independent practitioners, and the self-employed in business.[1] Independent farmers are not included so that some upward movement of the manuals is excluded since movement into independent farming status is upward mobility for all who originate in farm-laboring families, and for some whose fathers were

[1] In some nations, artisans who are self-employed are classified as workers and were not reclassifiable because of coding procedures.

working men. . . . The mobility within the manual strata (e.g. from unskilled to skilled or semi-skilled) is ignored; obscured as well is the lack of consistency in rates within the classification—skilled, for example, having higher upward rates than farm workers or unskilled.

Column (1) shows that in France about 30% of the sons of manual fathers ended up in non-manual occupations. Among the nations, this is the highest rate, while the lowest rate for nations is Italy's 8.5%. The range, then, is considerable. Almost as many nations have rates under 20% as have rates over 20%, although if we include the city data, there is an increase in the number of nations in the over 20% group. Italy, Finland, Hungary, Puerto Rico and Belgium I lag behind all the others in having rates below 15%. Thus, about one quarter of the nations are distinctly low.

The differences among the high rate nations—France, USA, Belgium II, Brazil (São Paulo), India (Poona)—are minor, so that we have a group of nations with a decidedly higher rate than the rest.

WORKING CLASSES INTO NON-MANUAL

Column (2) of Table 1 presents the data on working-class mobility into non-manual occupations for the smaller number of nations where data are unavailable for the more traditional occupations of skilled, semi-skilled and unskilled non-agricultural labor.

The comparison between Columns (1) and (2) is instructive: in all cases, working-class mobility is greater than manual. . . . These findings are not surprising since it is well known that it is more difficult to enter white-collar work from a rural background than from urban origins. The order of differences suggests that if we add 3%–4% to figures for manual mobility into non-manual work, we shall not be far off the actual working-class upward mobility. . . .

What can be concluded about overall upward mobility from manual and working-class occupations?

1. The United States does not have the highest upward mobility rate out of manual/working-class occupations. France, the Soviet Union and the United States are rather similar.

2. There is a fair clustering of nations— 9 of the 18 nations (Belgium counted only once despite the two discrepant reports) range between 24% and 31% in the manual analysis and 4 of 8 between 24% and 35% in the working-class tabulation.

3. Several nations have distinctly lower rates of mobility than other nations for which data are available. These are Finland, Italy, Hungary (for the manual category only), Puerto Rico (for the manual category only) and Belgium I.

4. Whether industrial nations can be considered to have a similar rate of movement of manual/working class into non-manual depends upon the criterion employed and whether one wishes to emphasize similarity or diversity. The Soviet Union and French working-class figures are almost twice that of Puerto Rico, but the latter is not highly industrialized. If we exclude Puerto Rico, Hungary and Belgium I from the working-class comparisons, we have a range from 21.2 (West Germany) to the 35% of USSR and France I. The manual range, excluding Italy, Finland, Belgium I, Puerto Rico and Hungary, is from 19.6% (Netherlands, probably too high a figure for this nation) to 30+ % (France I, Belgium II). . . .

NON-MANUAL TO MANUAL

We assume for purposes of Table 2 that movement into manual work is downward mobility for all who originate in non-manual occupations. This assumption is especially dubious at the crossing over from lower-level non-manual to skilled manual work. . .

The willingness to discuss movement of non-manuals into manual and working-class occupations arises from the great concern with the presumably political implications of this movement. The economic differentials involved in such movement may indeed be slim and often may involve an income gain, but even those most aware of these discrepancies have an interest in this kind of movement.

The most startling element in Table 2 is the fact that in three nations more than 40% of sons of non-manual families end up in manual occupations. . . . Certainly, the differential economic and social effects of manual/non-manual may differ widely from nation to nation, but earlier estimates have not prepared us for such a drastic change in social fortunes. The relation of the drop from non-manual into manual occupations to concern with social status is a question that immediately arises: is it true that the easier the drop, the more the concern with status and social distance?

Almost equally striking is the range between the USSR's 15% and the highs of Great Britain, Netherlands and Puerto Rico. (The two Belgian studies, which differed markedly on up mobility, show great similarity in downward mobility.) There is no particular clustering: the three categories of under 25%, between 25% and 35%, and over 35% have fairly equal numbers of nations. While 12 nations are under 30% and six above, three of the former hover about the 30% mark.

TABLE 2   Manual Working-Class Sons of Non-Manual Fathers

	(1) Non-Manual into Manual	*(2)* Non-Manual into Working Classes
	%	%
I. NATIONAL DATA		
Denmark	36.8	*
Finland	24.0	*
France I	20.5	18.2
France II	26.9	25.9
Great Britain	42.1	*
Hungary	27.5	25.8
Italy	34.4	*
Japan	29.7	*
Netherlands	43.2	*
Norway	28.6	27.9
Puerto Rico	42.7	35.6
Sweden	27.7	25.7
USA I	19.7	18.6
USA II	22.6	*
West Germany	29.0	28.2
II. URBAN DATA		
Australia (Melbourne)	37.1	*
Belgium I (St–Martens–Latem)	8.9	7.1
Belgium II (Mont–Saint–Guibert)	3.4	*
Brazil (São Paulo)	18.5	*
India (Poona)	26.9	*
III. SPECIAL DATA		
USSR (emigrés)	15.0	12.8

* Unavailable.

NON-MANUAL INTO WORKING CLASSES

Only in the case of Puerto Rico does restriction to non-agricultural "hands" employment make a sizable difference (7.1 %). In the other nations, the restriction in analyzing downward movement involves 2.3 % or less. Non-manual downward movement is largely into industrial occupations rather than farm labor.

The Soviet Union has the extremely low rate of one of eight sons of non-manual origin terminating in working-class occupations. The USA and France (an average of the two figures) hover about the figure of one of five non-manual sons, while for Norway and Sweden, one of four non-manual sons have working-class occupations.

While we do not show the data here, a substantial part of the non-manual into working-class and manual employment is into the skilled labor category. And the overwhelming rate of all non-manual movement into manual is from the lower end of the non-manual category (e.g., clerks). Nonetheless, the size of "downward" movement raises a number of questions: among others are the purposes and practices of educational systems, the forces producing fluidity in society, the character of reactions to downward mobility in societies where it is frequent and where it is infrequent.

A TYPOLOGY OF MANUAL/ NON-MANUAL MOVEMENT

Bringing together rates of movement of manual into non-manual and non-manual into manual movement ... permits some very interesting comparisons. (See

Tables 1 and 2. C. S. H.) ... The manual category is used so that all the nations can be included in the analysis. The USSR (emigrés) figure for upward mobility is, however, for the working classes.

In only 5 of 17 nations (omitting Belgium where the two studies are inconsistent), does up-mobility exceed down-mobility. These 5 nations [France, USA, Brazil (São Paulo), India (Poona), and USSR (emigrés)] are all characterized by relatively high up-mobility, but in not all nations with high up-mobility does this latter rate exceed the downward movement of non-manuals into manual strata. *Downward movement is a more compelling fact about mobility than upward!* In Italy, Puerto Rico, Netherlands, Finland, and, to a lesser extent, Hungary and Great Britain, the downward rate is considerably in excess of the upward. (The · Dutch rate is probably high because of the coding problems of the data.)

Perhaps the most interesting aspect of manual movement into non-manual occu-

pations and non-manual movement into manual occupations is their complexity. Some nations are high on one, low or middle on another; others have a different pattern. A fourfold table makes possible the setting up of types or patterns of movement. If we dichotomize movement as high (over 24%) or low (24% or less), we have these four types of patterns. ...

Cell A represents a nation with high upward and downward mobility; Cell C, one with low rates of movement of non-manuals into manual occupations and high rates of manual movement into non-manual activity.

Below are grouped all the nations under the patterns which typify them:

A. *High Downward Non-Manual, High Upward Manual* (+ +): Denmark, France II, Great Britain, Sweden, Australia (Melbourne), India (Poona)

B. *High Downward Non-Manual, Low Upward Manual* (+ −): Hungary, Italy,

TABLE 3   Inequality of Opportunity

	(1) Non-Manual into Non-Manual *(Stability)*	*(2)* Manual into Non-Manual	*(3)* Index of Inequality *(1)* *(2)*
	%	%	%
Australia (Melbourne)	62.9	24.1	261
Belgium I (St–Martens–Latem)	91.1	5.7	1,598
Belgium II (Mont–Saint–Guibert)	96.6	30.9	313
Brazil (São Paulo)	81.5	29.4	277
Denmark	63.2	24.1	262
Finland	76.0	11.0	691
France I	79.5	30.1	264
France II	73.1	29.6	247
Great Britain	57.9	24.8	234
Hungary	72.5	14.5	500
India (Poona)	73.1	27.3	268
Italy	63.5	8.5	747
Japan	70.3	23.7	297
Netherlands	56.8	19.6	290
Norway	71.4	23.2	308
Puerto Rico	57.3	14.3	401
Sweden	72.3	25.5	284
USA I	80.3	28.8	279
USA II	77.4	28.7	270
USSR (emigrés)	85.0	34.9	244
West Germany	71.0	20.0	355

Japan, Netherlands, Norway, Puerto Rico, West Germany

C. *Low Downward Non-Manual, High Upward Manual* (− +): France I, USA I and II, Belgium II (Mont–Saint–Guibert), Brazil (São Paulo), USSR (emigrés)

D. *Low Downward Non-Manual, Low Upward Manual* (− −): Finland, Belgium I (St–Martens–Latem)

. . . The four patterns of mobility outlined here strongly suggest that rather than omnibus statements on gross similarities or differences in some overall rate of mobility, we need to develop explanations of *each* of these four different patterns in terms of their causes, processes and consequences.

To sum up, asymmetry exists among the mobility indicators: high rates of up-mobility may be associated with low or high rates of down-mobility. High rates of down-mobility may be associated with high or low rates of up-mobility. To describe the rate of upward mobility in a nation does not automatically give us an estimate of down-mobility. *The varied connections of upward and downward mobility form the most important new element in the present report.*

INEQUALITY OF OPPORTUNITY

In Table 3, the ability of non-manual sons to stay in the non-manual levels is compared with the ability of manual sons to move into these levels. The figures of column (3) are an index of inequality since they reflect the relative advantage of non-manual sons over manual sons in having non-manual positions.

. . . In no nation is the advantage of middle-class sons less than two to one (Great Britain: 234%). The most common advantage is between two and a half to one and three to one. The closeness of Denmark, France, Great Britain, Sweden, USA and USSR (emigrés) is particularly striking.

WORKING CLASSES AND MANUAL INTO THE ELITES*

In the preceding sections, there has been no concern with the height (or distance) of

* The author distinguishes two elites: Elite I— occupations "with the highest standing," and Elite II "with somewhat less standing but of distinctly higher standing than the other occupational groupings." (C. S. H.)

the mobility. The question has been: How much change of any extent has occurred? In light of the controversy concerning the advisability of considering all mobility into non-manual ranks as upward mobility for workers, it is particularly desirable to investigate mobility into the highest reaches of society.

Table 4 organizes the available data. . . .

1. As with movement into non-manual occupations, working-class mobility is higher into the elites than is manual mobility since the former excludes the farm workers with their low rates of entrance into the higher reaches of society. . . .

2. Movement into Elite I from the manual strata shows a small range from 0 in Italy to 3.9% in Japan. It *is* striking, however, that Britain has an extremely low movement from manual into elite occupations for its Elite I size; Britain's manual → elite movement is much lower than Sweden's and the Netherlands', although all three nations have the same elite size. Interesting also is the fact that Japan has a slightly higher rate than the USA.

3. Movement into Elite II shows a slightly greater range than does movement into Elite I. Puerto Rico is highest and the Netherlands has the second highest rate, but this may be at least partly attributable to our classification problems with that nation.

4. The bringing together of Elite I and II movement gives a very sizable range: from the Soviet Union (emigrés) figure of 14.5% to the low reports for West Germany, Italy and France II and Belgium I (St–Martens–Latem) and India (Poona). (France I is quite a bit higher.) The Soviet Union has a very large Elite I and II; Denmark, which follows Puerto Rico in movement, has a small Elite I and II. . . .

No clear-cut relationship exists between the rates for manual into non-manual movement, and for manual into elite mobility. The USSR (emigrés) and the USA have relatively high rates on both, but the USA (Elite I and II) is not so different from nations . . . with their smaller elites. In . . . the USA (Elite I), with its high manual into non-manual rate, is no higher than countries with low rates for such movement. Similarly, France (Elite I and II), another

TABLE 4 Working Classes and Manual into Elite I and II

	(1) Working Classes into Elite I	(2) Manual into Elite I	(3) Working Classes into Elite II	(4) Manual into Elite II	(5) Working Classes into Elite I and II	(6) Manual into Elite I and II	(7) Size of Elite I	(8) Size of Elite II	(9) Size of Elite I and II
	%	%	%	%	%	%	%	%	%
I. NATIONAL									
Denmark	*	*	*	*	*	1.1	*	*	3.3
France I	1.9	1.4	2.3	2.2	4.2	3.5	3.9	4.6	8.5
France II	*	*	*	*	2.0	1.6	*	*	6.1
Great Britain	*	0.6	*	1.7	*	2.2	2.9	4.6	7.5
Italy	*	0.0	*	1.5	*	1.5	0.9	5.7	6.6
Japan	*	3.9	*	3.1	*	7.0	7.1	4.6	11.7
Netherlands	*	1.2	*	5.5	*	6.6	2.9	8.2	11.1
Puerto Rico	2.6	1.5	8.9	7.1	11.4	8.6	2.7	11.0	13.8
Sweden	2.3	1.8	2.1	1.7	4.4	3.5	2.9	3.8	6.7
USA I	*	3.4	*	4.5	*	7.8	7.4	8.6	16.0
West Germany	*	*	*	*	1.6	1.5	*	*	4.6
II. URBAN									
Belgium I (St-Martens–Latem)	*	*	*	*	0.0	0.0	*	*	2.3
Brazil (São Paulo)	*	1.0	*	4.3	*	5.3	6.8	10.2	17.1
India (Poona)	*	0.7	*	0.8	*	1.4	1.7	2.4	4.1
III. SPECIAL DATA									
USSR (emigrés)	*	*	*	*	14.5	*	*	*	20.7

* Unavailable.

nation with a high rate for manual into non-manual movement, is no higher (and on the basis of France II data, lower) on manual into elite motion than nations with low rates of manual into non-manual when elite size is held constant.

These data support again the notion of asymmetry of mobility, for from one indicator of mobility (in this case manual into non-manual) we cannot indicate movement along another indicator (manual into elite).

Excluding the USSR data, what can be concluded about Elite I and II mobility of the manual strata when we disregard elite size?

1. No nation has considerable movement into the upper levels. Only a small part of the manual strata are able to obtain such positions.[2]

[2] This "small part" can be a large percentage of all those in the elite because of the disparity in size of the elite and manual strata. But from the point of view of the manuals . . . only a relatively few have made the big leap.

2. Nations with high overall upward movement (e.g., France) may not have, for the manual strata, high rates of access to the top positions.

3. The range is from less than 2% in 5 nations to almost 8% (USA) and 8.6% in Puerto Rico. It is possible to state that (a) the highest nation has five times the rate of upward movement into Elite I and II occupations that the lowest nation has, or that (b) the span between the highest and lowest nations is only 7 percentage points. Nonetheless, the differences may be important. I am particularly impressed by the fact that five nations have rates of movement into Elite I and II that are under 2.5% while the other rates are fairly well strung out.

4. The USA has a comparatively high rate for only Puerto Rico and the USSR (emigrés) exceed it. But Japan and the Netherlands, with considerably smaller

TABLE 5   Mobility of Manual Strata into Elite I and II Combined and into Non-Manual Strata

Size of Elite I and II	(1) Manual into Elite I and II	(2) Manual into Non-Manual	(3) Elite I and II Mobility as Percentage of Non-Manual Mobility (1) (2)
A. UNDER 4.6%	%	%	%
Denmark	1.1	24.1	4.6
West Germany	1.5	20.0	7.5
Belgium I (St–Martens–Latem)	0.0	5.7	0.0
India (Poona)	1.4	27.3	5.1
B. 6%–8.5%			
France I	3.5	30.1	11.6
France II	1.6	29.6	5.4
Great Britain	2.2	24.8	8.9
Italy	1.5	8.5	17.7
Sweden	3.5	25.5	13.7
C. 10%–15%			
Japan	7.0	23.7	29.5
Netherlands	6.6	19.6	33.7
Puerto Rico	8.6	14.3	60.1
D. OVER 15%			
Brazil (São Paulo)	5.3	29.4	18.0
USA I	7.8	28.8	27.1
USSR (emigrés)	14.5[1]	34.9	41.5

[1] This is a figure for the working classes, and therefore overstates manual movement into the elites.

percentages in Elites I and II, do not have much lower rates.

When the data for the Soviet Union (emigrés) are entered into the analysis, the differences are much greater and raise questions about (a) the similarity of rates in industrial nations, and (b) the validity of an explanation of mobility rates in terms of level of industrial development alone.

MANUAL INTO ELITE AND NON-MANUAL

. . . Another type of comparison which may influence attitudes toward the social structure is the ratio of the number of individuals who rise out of the working-class/ manual strata to those from the strata who move into the top-level positions. What are the chances of long-distance mobility, if there is *any* upward mobility at all? Table 5 presents these figures.

The high Puerto Rican figure is, of course, the most surprising for 6 out of 10 of the manual sons who end up in the non-manual strata move into the top brackets. The size of the overall manual to non-manual movement does not appear to be closely connected to the ratio computed. It does appear, though, that the size of elites affects the ratio of elites to non-manual movement, for categories C and D are uniformly higher than the two smaller elite categories. The

TABLE 6   Movement into Elites from Various Strata

Size of Elite	(1) Middle Classes	(2) Working Classes	(3) Manual Classes	(4) Inde-pendent Farmer	(5) Farm Worker	(6) (1) (2)	(7) (1) (3)
2.5%–4.6%	%	%	%	%	%	%	%
Denmark (Elite I and II)	4.6	*	1.1	*	*	*	418
France I (Elite I)	5.1	1.9	1.4	0.8	0.0	268	364
Great Britain (Elite I)	2.5	*	0.6	*	*	*	417
India (Poona) (Elite I and II)	6.2	*	1.4	*	*	*	443
Netherlands (Elite I)	2.6	*	1.2	*	*	*	217
Puerto Rico (Elite I)	6.1	2.6	1.5	2.0	0.9	235	407
Sweden (Elite I)	7.9	2.3	1.8	1.1	0.4	344	439
West Germany (Elite I and II)	8.3	1.6	1.5	2.1	0.6	519	553
6%–8.5%							
Brazil (São Paulo) (Elite I)	5.4	*	1.0	*	*	*	540
France I (Elite I and II)	12.3	4.2	3.5	1.9	2.0	293	351
France II (Elite I and II)	10.5	2.0	1.6	1.7	0.4	525	656
Great Britain (Elite I and II)	8.6	*	2.2	*	*	*	391
Italy (Elite I)	7.5	*	1.7	*	*	*	500
Japan (Elite I)	8.3	*	3.9	*	*	*	213
Sweden (Elite I and II)	18.1	4.4	3.5	2.6	1.0	411	517
USA I (Elite I)	9.5	*	3.4	*	*	*	279
10%–15%							
Japan (Elite I and II)	15.1	*	7.0	*	*	*	216
Netherlands (Elite I and II)	11.6	*	6.6	*	*	*	176
Puerto Rico (Elite I and II)	23.2	11.4	8.6	13.1	7.1	204	270
OVER 15%							
Brazil (São Paulo) (Elite I and II)	18.5	*	5.3	*	*	*	349
USA I (Elite I and II)	19.8	*	7.8	*	*	*	254
USSR (emigrés) (Elite I and II)	42.3	14.5	*	7.9	*	292	*

* Unavailable.

difference between USA I and USSR (emigrés) and Puerto Rico is intriguing; the high Dutch rate is also a surprise.

. . . Our concern so far has been with manual and working-class strata except for a brief examination of the downward movement of non-manual strata. Now, we turn to a closer examination of the largest part of the non-manual strata, the middle classes. . . .

MIDDLE CLASSES INTO ELITES

Table 6 continues the analysis of middle-class movement into the elites; in it nations are grouped by size of elite, as in some earlier tables, and data on similar working-class and manual mobility are also reported for comparative purposes.[3]

Column (1) shows that the middle-class movement into the elites is affected by the size of the elites, as one would expect. While there is some overlap among the four size groups into which elites are classified, there seems to be a fair break between them in

[3] A more complete analysis would also adjust for different sizes of the middle classes.

percentage moving into elites. Group A, those elites under 4.6%, shows a range from Britain's 2.5% (for Elite I) to West Germany's 8.3% (for Elite I and II). In Group B, a greater range exists between the 5.4% of the middle classes of Brazil (São Paulo) which moves into the elites (Elite I) to the 18.1% for the middle classes of Sweden (Elite I and II). The Swedish figure is very high, clearly higher than similar figures for its size elite and overlapping with those of nations with larger elites. France (Elite I and II) has a higher rate than the USA (Elite I). Britain (Elite I and II) is not very different from the United States, although for the smaller-size elites it was indeed low. In Group C, the high rate of Puerto Rico is pronounced. Group D produces the most interesting result—the extremely high figure for the Soviet Union (emigrés). Four of ten middle-class sons enter the elite according to the Harvard study. No other nation is near; the USA is closest with two of ten sons making this jump. As Table 7 shows even more sharply, the greatest opportunities for the middle-class sons are in the Soviet Union, the least in Denmark. (The

TABLE 7 Upward and Downward Movement of Middle-Class Strata

	(1) Into Working Classes	(2) Into Manual	(3) Into Elite I and II	(4) Into Independent Farmer	(5) (1)/(3)	(6) (2)/(3)	(7) (2)+(3)
	%	%	%	%	%	%	%
Belgium I (St–Martens–Latem)	7.9	9.9	7.2	*	110	138	17.1
Belgium II (Mont–Saint–Guibert)	*	3.4	*	0.9	*	*	3.4
Brazil (São Paulo)	*	24.1	18.5	*	*	130	42.6
Denmark	*	38.2	4.6	*	*	830	42.8
France I	20.1	22.8	12.3	6.2	163	185	35.1
France II	28.9	29.8	10.5	4.0	275	284	40.3
Great Britain	*	48.8	8.6	*	*	567	57.4
India (Poona)	*	28.1	6.2	*	*	453	34.3
Italy	*	32.5	7.5	*	*	433	40.0
Japan	*	31.6	15.1	*	*	209	46.7
Netherlands	*	49.2	11.6	*	*	424	60.8
Puerto Rico	40.2	45.1	23.2	6.1	173	194	68.3
Sweden	29.7	32.3	18.1	5.2	164	179	50.4
USA I	19.8	20.7	19.8	4.1	100	105	40.5
USSR (emigrés)	12.6	13.5	42.3	*	30	32	55.8
West Germany	29.6	30.5	8.3	2.0	357	368	38.8

* Unavailable.

Danish figure would be increased if elite size were in the same range as Britain.)

Columns (6) and (7) compare the rates of advance into the elites for the middle-class sons with those for the working-class and manual sons. The greatest comparative advantage of the middle-class sons is in France II (Elite I and II), but France I shows a much lower figure. West Germany has the next greatest advantage of middle-class sons. The USSR (emigrés) figure is not high on this index because manual sons also have a particularly good chance to rise into the elites. As a result the relative advantage of middle-class sons is not much different in USA I and in USSR (emigrés).

MIDDLE CLASSES: OUTFLOW

Table 7 provides a broad view of the outflow from the middle classes. Columns (1)–(4) show that the percentages of movement out of the middle classes range widely among the 16 studies reported. From the point of view of stability of position, the Belgium I (St–Martens–Latem) report indicates that over 90% of the middle-class sons remain in their class; in Puerto Rico, at the other extreme, only a quarter are immobile. The next lowest stability figure is for India (Poona), where 66% of the sons are stable, and this is probably a better figure than either Belgium figure to indicate the maximum stability which exists. Five nations—Great Britain, Netherlands, Puerto Rico, Sweden, USSR (emigrés)—are characterized by less than 45% stability for their middle-class sons. Overall middle-class sons are the most mobile group of the class structure.

The insecure hold of the middle classes is sharply evidenced by the comparison of column (2), the movement into the manual class, with column (3). the movement into Elite I and II, which is made in column (6). In only one nation—the USSR (emigrés)— do we find that the middle-class son, when he is mobile, has a better chance of terminating in the elites than in the manual strata. In Denmark, the chances are eight to one, that he will be downwardly mobile; in Britain, five and a half to one. In Japan the chances are two to one for downward mobility, while in the USA upward and downward movement are equally likely.

There does not seem to be any apparent relationship between the degree of stability of a nation and the likelihood of upward or downward movement of its middle-class sons; Germany with a rather stable middle class has a fairly high rate of downward relative to upward movement, while the Netherlands with an unstable middle class does not have a much greater possibility of downward movement for its middle-class sons. Small movement out of the middle class does not increase the chances of upward or downward movement.

A closer examination of columns (2) and (3) reveals that the range of movement into the manual strata is greater than the range for movement into the elites. In Britain, Netherlands and Puerto Rico, the middle-class son is as likely to move into manual occupations as to advance into the elites, to maintain a position in the middle classes or to assume an independent farming position.[4] The USA I and USSR (emigrés) offer the best chances, ignoring Belgium, for middle-class sons not to fall into manual strata. While, in general, a high rate of downward mobility means that the latter is likely to far exceed upward mobility out of the middle classes, this is not uniformly true, e.g. Puerto Rico. High downward movement can be associated with high upward mobility.

The rate of upward mobility for the middle classes is most striking for the USSR (emigrés) where over 40% of middle-class sons move up. Even deflating this figure quite a bit, as it probably deserves, would still give the USSR a high upward figure. Puerto Rico, the USA, Brazil (São Paulo) and Sweden come next in providing opportunities for the middle-class son. The high Swedish figure is in contrast with the low Danish figure; while the two nations were close in regard to non-manual movement of manual sons, here they are quite different.

---

[4] Since the "middle classes" is a broad category, we are ignoring what may be considerable mobility within the middle classes—movement of the sons of lower-level middle-class fathers to higher-level positions and the reverse movement, neither of which is captured by our wide categories. This is the same phenomenon as we had earlier with the manual and working-class strata which also represent broad groupings in which considerable and important internal motion can occur.

In general, though, there does appear to be a slight relation between upward movement of manual sons (Table 1) and upward movement of middle-class sons.

The movement into independent farming is not insignificant when compared with movement into the elites of the middle-class sons. The movement into the farm worker category—column (2) minus column (1)—is small except in Puerto Rico, where it is almost as great as the movement into independent farming. Overall, agriculture does not become the terminus of a great many middle-class sons.[5]

....

[5] Since in some nations, independent farmers are not separately categorized, but are included in the middle classes or, less frequently, the manual strata, it is not possible to portray the movement into the farmer position for all nations.

TABLE 8 National Profiles

	(1) Manual into Non-Manual	(2) Non-Manual into Manual	(3) Manual into Elite I and II	(4) Middle Classes into Elite I and II	(5) Total Movement Out of Elite I and II	(6) Middle Classes Downward to Upward Movement	(7) Elite I and II into Manual	(8) Index of Association
Australia (Melbourne)	H	H	*	*	*	*	*	I
Belgium I (St–Martens–Latem)	L	L	L	L	L	L	L	H
Belgium II (Mont–Saint–Guibert)	H	L	*	*	*	*	*	I
Brazil (São Paulo)	H	L	H	H	L	L	L	L
Denmark	H	H	L	L	H	H	L	I
Finland	L	H	*	*	*	*	*	H
France I (Bresard)	H	L	L	L	H	L	L	H
France II (Desabie)	H	H	L	L	L	H	H	H
Great Britain	H	H	L	L	H	H	H	L
Hungary	L	H	*	*	*	*	*	H
India (Poona)	H	H	L	L	L	H	L	L
Italy	L	H	L	L	H	H	H	I
Japan	L	H	H	H	H	L	H	I
Netherlands	L	H	H	L	L	H	H	I
Norway	L	H	*	*	*	*	*	H
Puerto Rico	L	H	H	H	H	L	H	I
Sweden	H	H	L	H	L	L	L	I
USA I (Centers)	H	L	H	H	L	L	L	L
USA II (SRC)	H	L	*	*	*	*	*	L
USSR (emigrés)	H	L	H	H	L	L	H	L
West Germany	L	H	L	L	L	H	L	H

Legend:
- (1) under 24—L, over 24—H
- (2) under 24—L, over 24—H
- (3) under 3.6—L, over 3.6—H
- (4) under 15.1—L, over 15.1—H
- (5) under 50% outflow—L, over 50% outflow—H
- (6) under 250%—L, over 250%—H
- (7) under 15.8%—L, over 15.8%—H
- (8) High, Low, Inconsistent

* Unavailable.

INTERPRETATIONS AND CONCLUSIONS

NATIONAL PROFILES

The data presented . . . have been complex and variegated; the only attempts at synthesis have been the two sets of typologies (relating rates of manual movement into non-manual levels with non-manual movement into manual and exit from the elites with entrance into the elites). A further attempt at synthesis has been made in Table 8 which brings into one table some of the more important indices which have been employed in the study. By looking across the rows, we obtain a brief profile of each nation.

The table shows, for example, that Great Britain has high up-mobility of the manual, high down-mobility of the non-manual, low long-range up-mobility of the manual, low long-range up-mobility of the non-manual, high movement out of the elites, high down-mobility of the middle classes (relative to the up-mobility of the same strata), high long-run down-mobility of elites and low indices of association for the various strata. It is possible from such information to develop new indices of total movement, of consistency of direction of movement, of distance of mobility by combining two or more columns.

What is particularly noteworthy is the close parallel of findings for USA, USSR (emigrés) and Brazil (São Paulo). The only divergence among them is in regard to column (7), Elite I and II into manual (the low of the USA is very close to the breaking point). This summary strengthens the earlier references to the similarities of movement in the USA and USSR (emigrés). It is an interesting pattern of high upward short and long distance manual mobility; high upward mobility of the middle classes and relatively low downward movement; low downward motion of the non-manual and the elites; low occupational inheritance with variation among the three in extent of long-range downward mobility of the elites. It is thus a general pattern of upward mobility with limited downward mobility.

Great Britain and India (Poona) have a somewhat similar pattern: high rates of movement, but with downward and limited upward movement much more pronounced than in the previous type.

Less clear as a group are Italy, Japan, the Netherlands and Puerto Rico. The dominant tendency seems to be downward mobility, although in Japan and Puerto Rico access to the elites is relatively high.

It is important to reassert the earlier warnings about the mixed quality of the data. Presenting materials in tabular form tends to "harden" them; the fact that numbers can be used obscures the weak procedures leading to the production of these numbers. I am acutely aware of the coercive manipulations of data which have necessarily occurred in this report and hope that all the comparisons here, as in other international analyses, will be viewed as "suggestive" of trends, rather than adequate descriptions of nations. Inevitably, we must build on shaky foundations, but awareness of the infirmities is important to the construction of a healthy structure.

These profiles, the culmination of the data of this report, must be taken as no more than suggestive of possibilities.

IMPLICATIONS OF THE DATA

Asymmetry. The point of departure of the monograph has been strongly supported by the data. Mobility is not a symmetrical phenomenon—perhaps better put, at least our knowledge at this time does not reveal its symmetry. A nation can be high in one measure of mobility and low in another. The patterns just suggested should not be assumed to have a definitive character. The profiles and typologies of this report are only limited ways of organizing the data.

The connections between mobility of one kind and mobility of another kind are unclear. We must, therefore, in making comparisons, specify the measure on which the comparison is based. *The* measure of mobility does not exist, only many measures tapping different dimensions of mobility which do not as yet at least form a smooth pyramid.

The Clear Result. The most striking result of the comparisons is that on both the simple comparison of working classes into non-manual and manual into elite strata, the Soviet Union (emigrés) has the highest rates. (France I has a similar working class into non-manual rate.) These rates are probably high, but even if reduced would probably still show the Soviet Union at the top of these comparisons. On the other hand, the Soviet Union had a rather low rate of downward movement out of the non-manual categories generally, and out of the elite strata specifically. Thus, the upward manual movement is not due to the decline of the middle classes and the elite, but to the expansion of these strata.

The United States has a high rate of manual movement into non-manual occupations, but not one that is distinctively higher than that of France or USSR (emigrés). On the other hand, it is distinctively higher in the manual movement into the elite strata than all nations other than the Soviet Union (emigrés).

Comparison with Lipset–Bendix–Zetterberg. Because of the forthright contentions of Lipset–Bendix–Zetterberg[6] in analyzing social mobility rates, there will be interest in comparing the results of the present analysis with theirs. In regard to their basic points, the scoreboard seems to be as follows:

(*a*) The United States is not distinctively higher on movement into non-manual from manual levels than are some industrial nations. On this account, Lipset and his colleagues are supported.

(*b*) The United States has a higher rate of movement into the elite strata from the manual strata than do all other nations except the Soviet Union (emigrés). This result does not support the L–B–Z thesis of the non-exceptionality of the United States which is based on one main type of measure, movement from manual into non-manual.

(*c*) The Lipset *et al.* thesis is that the rates of mobility are similar in industrialized nations. (1) The rates of manual into non-manual occupations seem to be the closest together, if we disregard the low Italian and Finnish figures and the high Soviet one. Even so, the range is not narrow, from 14+ % in Hungary and Puerto Rico to 30% in France. If we disregard the former two as not very industrialized, the lower limit is about 20% in the Netherlands and West

Germany. (2) The rates of non-manual into manual occupations show a spread between the under 20% of USA I and USSR (emigrés) on the one hand and the more than 30% of several nations. (3) The rates of movement of manual strata into the elite strata reveal a considerable range as well. (4) The rates of movement out of elite strata are widely varying.

It is difficult to summarize these findings. If we ignore nations at the extremes like the Soviet Union and Italy because of sampling and allied problems, we can see some convergence in rates of manual movement into non-manual. But if these nations had not appeared at the extremes, would we have been so ready to ignore them?

There probably is more convergence in rates than most people had believed. But that does not mean that the actual convergence is overwhelming; if we were able to approach the data without the background of decades of speculation, we would probably be concerned with the variation in the rates. Even if we were to accept the L–B–Z thesis of the similarity of rates, at some stage of analysis we have to turn attention to the reasons for the kind of divergences that have occurred. Here a great lack exists.

AN UNDERDEVELOPED AREA: DOWNWARD MOBILITY

As I have argued elsewhere, the concern with upward mobility has obscured the importance and amount of downward mobility. In the present study, it is striking how high the rate of movement from non-manual to manual is, and from elite strata to all other strata. A whole host of basic social issues arise, especially concerning the nature of education, which are not directly germane to the narrow focus of this monograph. But one aspect of this downward mobility is.

It may well be that downward mobility is a better indicator of fluidity in a society than is upward mobility.[7] The latter type of movement is a product of fluidity and opportunity, changes in the occupational

[6] Lipset, S. M., Bendix, R., *Social Mobility in Industrial Society*. Berkeley, University of California, 1959 : 301 pp.

[7] We use fluidity in the sense of the ease of movement from stratum to stratum in society that is not due to changes in the occupational structure.

distribution, as well as of demographic changes. Downward mobility is also a product of these factors, but here social fluidity is more important. In any case, a society which is dropping sons born in advantaged strata out of these strata has more openness than one which brings up talented manual sons but safeguards the privileges of the already advantaged.

Utilizing downward mobility as an indicator, then, the USSR, high on other indicators of mobility, does not show much movement. In many other nations, the down rate is much higher, e.g., France and Great Britain. The USSR may have more upward mobility, but not necessarily more fluidity in the social structure.

The psychological and social aspects of downward mobility are unclear. A society may have high downward mobility, high upward mobility and still lack a strong egalitarian ideology and even structural supports for facilitating up and down movement. The statement of rates does not exhaust the complicated relationships between mobility, ideology, structure and behavior. As Feldman[8] has indicated in his thoughtful analysis of Lipset and Bendix, there are many types of relations between ideology and rates to consider.

THE MEASURE OF MOBILITY

In interpreting results, it is not only important to be aware of the different measures of mobility and the varying quality of the data, but also of the basic definition of mobility which is involved. . . . the sociological study of mobility has been largely restricted to investigation of occupational mobility and to the prestige dimension of occupational mobility. Therefore, our comparisons of national rates of mobility are about this one slice of mobility. As Arnold Rose has indicated, if we were to study other aspects, such as political power of great masses of the citizenry or the degree of egalitarianism and social distance which prevails, then other results might be produced.[9] Rose feels,

for example, that nations which have already achieved high industrialization, e.g., the United States, are inevitably going to have lower rates of occupational mobility than nations at a lower stage of industrialization which necessarily have to upgrade many in order to fit them into the new technological demands of the economic structure. One way of meeting this problem would be to subtract the mobility due to changing occupational opportunities from the overall rates of mobility; where this has not been done, it is important to recognize that measures of mobility such as those reported in the present monograph, except for the index of association, are refractions to a considerable extent, although certainly not exclusively, of the occupational structure, a product of a stage of industrialization.

The measure of mobility affects the rate. The emphasis on occupational mobility may lower the rate of the already high industrial achievers relative to those nations striving to reach these levels. This point of Rose's is not an argument against using occupational data, but against using them as the sole dimension of mobility.

OCCUPATIONAL MOBILITY IN THE UNITED STATES

Peter M. Blau and Otis Dudley Duncan

This is a preliminary report from a study of occupational mobility in the United States. The objectives of the study are to describe the patterns of social mobility in some detail, to estimate the influence of various factors on occupational life chances, and to ascertain a few consequences of

---

[8] Feldman, A. S. "Economic Development and Social Mobility," *Economic Development and Cultural Change.* 8 (3), April, 1960: 311–321.

[9] Arnold M. Rose, "Social Mobility and Social Values," unpublished manuscript.

Original title: "Some Preliminary Findings on Social Stratification in the United States." Reprinted from *Acta Sociologica*, Vol. 9, fasc. 1–2, 1965, by permission.

socio-economic status and mobility, such as their implications for fertility. The present paper reports selected findings pertaining to factors affecting occupational achievement and the chances to move away from one's social origins. In particular, we shall examine the significance for occupational attainment of education, ethnic background, community size, migration, and parental family.

In addition to presenting preliminary substantive findings from our research, this paper also provides an opportunity for illustrating the analytical procedures we have used. The analysis relies to a large extent on the regression approach. Two major advantages of this approach which prompted our decision to adopt it are that it is a very efficient method of large-scale data reduction and that it permits, consequently, the simultaneous examination of the interrelations of fairly large numbers of variables, especially if computers are used. Contingency tables containing half a dozen or more variables and many hundreds of cells are too complex to be analyzed by inspection, whereas the regression method permits the analysis of these interrelations. To be sure, a limitation of regression analysis is that it makes restrictive assumptions about linearity and the absence of interaction effects, but the assumptions can be taken into account and hence removed in more complex analytical models. Simpler methods we use, such as comparisons of mean scores of occupational status, are complemented by regression analysis to determine not only the gross effects of various factors on socio-economic status but also the net effects with other variables held constant.

RESEARCH PROCEDURES

The data for this research were collected by the U.S. Bureau of the Census in March, 1962, partly in the course of its regular "Current Population Survey" interview, and partly in a supplementary self-administered questionnaire specifically designed for the purpose of our research. The sample of 20,700 American men between the ages of 20 and 65 represents the 45 million men in this age group who are in the "civilian noninstitutional population," that is, who are

neither in the Armed Forces nor in institutions. A subsample of those respondents who failed initially to return the supplementary questionnaire by mail was interviewed and appropriately weighted to make the sample highly representative. The present analysis, however, is confined to men whose fathers were *not* in farming occupations, which excludes a quarter of the total group. (In brief, the data derive from a representative sample of the 33 million American men with nonfarm backgrounds between 20 and 65 years old who are not in military service and do not live in institutions.[1])

Respondent's occupation and that of his father when the respondent was 16 years old were transformed into SES (socio-economic status) scores. The score, which ranges from 0 to 96, is based on the proportion of men in a specific occupation ("detailed occupational classification") who were, at least, high school graduates and the proportion reporting an income of over $3,500 in 1949, making adjustments for differences in age distribution between occupations.[2] The multiple correlation between these two predictors—the education and the income of the men in an occupation—and the N.O.R.C. prestige rating[3] for the 45 occupations that could be matched is +.91, and the regression equation that expresses this multiple correlation is used to determine the SES scores for all 446 detailed occupations. Respondent's education was transformed into an arbitrary score ranging from 0 to 8 which takes into account the special significance graduation from a

[1] All frequencies in the original tables, from which the analytical tables presented in this report are derived, refer to the estimated actual population in the United States in the given categories, reported in 1000's. The sampling ratio is, on the average, 1:2,173. To obtain the approximate numbers of actual cases from whom data were collected, therefore, the numbers reported in 1000's should be divided by 2.2.

[2] See Otis Dudley Duncan, *A Socio-Economic Index for All Occupations* in Albert J. Reiss, Jr., Occupations and Social Status, New York: Free Press, 1961. (This score was derived from the 1950 U.S. Census of Population, not from our sample.)

[3] National Opinion Research Center, *Jobs and Occupations*, Opinion News, Vol. 9 (1947), pp. 3–13.

given school level has.[4] Whereas socio-economic status and education are assumed to be continuous quantitative variables, no such assumption is made concerning the other factors used in the analysis, which are treated as qualitative attributes in terms of which individuals are classified into discrete categories.

To convey the meaning of the SES scores, the average scores of the conventional major groups of nonfarm occupations are presented below:

Professionals and technicians	75
Managers, proprietors, and officials	57
Sales and clerical occupations	47
Skilled workers and foremen	31
Semiskilled workers	18
Unskilled workers	7

The average difference between two adjacent categories is 13.6. Hence, the finding that an attribute affects the SES score by four or five points implies that, on the average, one third of the men with this attribute are one full step higher in this rank order (for example, are skilled rather than semiskilled workers) than those without this attribute. Fairly small differences in score are, therefore, of substantive significance, and given our large number of cases such small differences also are statistically significant.

EDUCATION AND ETHNIC BACKGROUND

The over-all correlation between father's and son's occupational status is +.38. This indicates that there is much occupational mobility in the United States; only one seventh of the variance in socio-economic status is attributable to the influence of father's socio-economic status. Nevertheless, this amount of mobility does not seem to be excessive compared to that in other Western countries. To make some rough comparisons, we computed the coefficient of association derived by Carlsson from the index earlier employed by Glass and Rogoff

to measure occupational inheritance.[5] Since the Swedish data, which otherwise are most comparable with ours, include persons of farm origins, we did so too in these computations. (The correlation coefficient for the total U.S. population, including men with farm background, is +.42.) Using ten categories of SES scores, this measure of inheritance is 1.51, and using ten occupational categories,[6] as required to make it comparable to the Swedish data, it is 1.95. The same measure applied to the Swedish data divided into ten occupational categories is 1.89 or 2.28, depending on the method used,[7] which implies that there is about as much occupational inheritance in the United States as in Sweden. One of our former associates, R. W. Hodge, has computed age-specific father-son correlations from the British data, using an arbitrary scoring of prestige categories. He finds coefficients varying between .44 and .50 over five age groups. This suggests a slightly higher degree of association between son's and father's status in Britain than in America, although lack of comparability in study design makes one loath to stress this conclusion. Svalastoga's correlations for Denmark are of the same order of magnitude.[8]

To examine the relative importance of social origins and of education for occupational attainments, the (nonfarm background) sample is first divided into five cohorts, providing a control for age (20–24, 25–34, 35–44, 45–54, 55–64). The multiple correlation of education and father's socio-economic status on son's SES increases from +.51 for the youngest group to +.66 for those 25–34 years old and then decreases again to +.59 for the oldest group (Table 1, row 1). This nonmonotonic relationship with age suggests that the influences of social background and of education on a man's career extend beyond its early phases

---

[4] Education is scored by the following system, which takes into account the special significance of graduation from one of the three main levels of schooling: 0 No School; 1 Elementary, 1 to 4 years; 2 Elementary, 5 to 7 years; 3 Elementary, 8 years; 4 High school, 1 to 3 years; 5 High school, 4 years; 6 College, 1 to 3 years; 7 College, 4 years; 8 Graduate school, 1 year or more.

[5] Gösta Carlsson, *Social Mobility and Class Structure*, Lund: Gleerup, 1958, pp. 74–75.

[6] The ten occupational categories are the six previously reported in the text, except that clerical and sales occupations are divided, service occupations are separately shown, and two categories of farm occupations are added, farmers and farm managers, and farm laborers.

[7] *Ibid.*, p. 114.

[8] Kaare Svalastoga, *Prestige, Class and Mobility*, Copenhagen: Glydendal, 1950, p. 351.

TABLE 1   Correlation Analysis: Respondent's Occupational SES on Education and Father's SES, for American Men with Nonfarm Backgrounds, Age 20 to 64, 1962

Item	20–24 Years	25–34 Years	35–44 Years	45–54 Years	55–64 Years
1. Multiple correlations (SES on education and father's SES)	.51	.66	.65	.61	.59
a. *Beta* coefficient, education	.46	.61	.57	.53	.52
b. *Beta* coefficient, father's SES	.09	.12	.15	.16	.13
2. Zero order correlation, SES and father's SES	.29	.37	.40	.38	.34
Components*					
a. Independent of education	.09	.12	.15	.16	.13
b. Mediated through education	.20	.25	.25	.22	.21

* For method of calculation, see O. D. Duncan and R. W. Hodge, "Education and Occupational Mobility: A Regression Analysis," *American Journal of Sociology*, 68 (May, 1963), 629–44.

and become increasingly pronounced for some years but that the significance of these factors eventually declines as they recede in time. An alternative explanation of this finding is that the influence of education has become increasingly important since the beginning of this century although a decline may now be under way. There has probably been little change in the significance of father's occupational SES for that of his son in this century.[9] The *beta* coefficients indicate that the net influence of education is at a maximum at about age thirty and then decreases, whereas that of father's SES continues to increase until about age fifty (rows 1a and 1b). Taking these partial regression coefficients in standard form (*beta* coefficients) as indications of the relative significance of the two antecedents, the data also show that the impact on occupational status of education independent of social origin is considerably greater than that of social origin independent of education.[10]

[9] Although we plan to investigate the problem of estimating time trends more thoroughly in the future, a re-analysis of Rogoff's data for the city of Indianapolis by Duncan indicates that there is no change in the father-son correlation between 1910 and 1940.

[10] Since the index used to score the status of an occupation is based on the amount of education and the amount of income that prevailed in the occupation, it is necessarily related to education to some degree. Experimentation, with an alternative index of occupational SES, not based explicitly on education levels, however, shows that the results are not dependent on the specific form of SES index used here.

This finding implies that the influence of father's socio-economic status on son's status is largely mediated in the United States by education. A man's chances of occupational advancement depend on his education (zero-order correlation, +.61), which, in turn, depends to a considerable degree on the socio-economic status of his father (+.41). These relationships can be further clarified by restating them in a slightly different way. Instead of asking how SES is affected by education and by father's SES separately, as we did above, we take now the (zero-order) correlation between father's and son's SES (Table 1, row 2) and ask to which extent this influence of father's SES on son's status is mediated through education (row 2b) and to which extent it is independent of education and thus due to other factors (row 2a). It is apparent from the data that education is the major means by which fathers affect the occupational chances of their sons. It should not be ignored, however, that social origins also have a definite effect on occupational opportunities that has nothing to do with educational qualifications. . . .

. . . .

Negroes have, of course, far less educational opportunity than whites in the United States. Whereas 18 per cent of the native whites have no more than eight years of schooling, fully 37 per cent of the nonwhites do.[11] The education of the second-generation Americans hardly differs from that of other native whites (21 per cent), but the foreign born are nearly as poorly educated as the Negroes, with 35 per cent not having gone beyond the eight years of elementary school. It is interesting that age affects educational attainment to an even greater extent than race. Among the native whites with native parents, only 8 per cent of the men 20–24 years old have no more than eight years of schooling, as compared with 39 per cent of those 55–64 years old. Among the Negroes, similarly, 22 per cent of the youngest age cohort in contrast to 70 per cent of the oldest one have not gone beyond elementary school. Discrimination notwithstanding, young Negroes in today's nonfarm population are better educated than old whites. Negroes, nevertheless, continue to suffer serious educational handicaps and these are, moreover, not the only handicaps that impede their occupational opportunities.

To ascertain the impact of various attributes, such as ethnic background, on occupational chances, the following procedure is used. The mean SES score for each age cohort is determined, and so are the deviations from this mean in various subgroups under consideration. Differences between these deviations from the mean indicate the gross effect of the attribute on SES, for example, the gross effect of being a Negro rather than a white with a given education on occupational status. The net effects the same attribute has on SES when father's SES is held constant are derived from a regression equation.[12] These net effects can be considered approximate indications of occupational mobility in the sense that they refer to average occupational achievements of groups whose point of social origin has been standardized. An interesting over-all

finding that emerges from our analysis is that controlling for father's occupation reduces the influence of various attributes but hardly ever alters the patterns of influence observed. In other words, the same factors that are associated with differential occupational status are also associated with differential achievements independent of level of origin.

Even when education is held constant, the occupational status of Negroes is far inferior to that of whites in the United States. Twenty independent comparisons between native whites of native parentage and nonwhites can be made in Table 2 (four educational groups in each of the five age cohorts). In all twenty, the score of whites is higher, and the average difference is 12.1, nearly a full step in the rank order of major occupational classes. This is a clear indication of the serious discrimination Negroes with the same educational qualifications as whites suffer in the employment market.[13] Moreover, controlling for father's occupation does not wipe out this difference. All twenty net effects favor the whites, an average of 10.2, notwithstanding the fact that Negroes, due to past discrimination, have much lower social origins than whites. In sum, Negroes are handicapped by having less education and by having lower social origins than whites. But even if these handicaps are controlled statistically—asking, in effect, what the chances of Negroes would be if they had the same education and social origins as whites—the occupational attainments of Negroes are still considerably inferior to those of whites.

[11] Our data actually refer to "nonwhites" but 92 per cent of all nonwhites in the United States are Negroes.

[12] For an explanation of the statistical model used, see Otis Dudley Duncan, *Farm Background and Differential Fertility,* paper presented to the Population Association of America at its June 1964 annual meeting. For a published discussion, see T. P. Hill, *An Analysis of the Distribution of Wages and Salaries in Great Britain,* Econometrics, Vol. 27 (July, 1959), pp. 355–381.

[13] It should be noted that some of the difference between Negroes and whites, though hardly all of it, may be due to the fact that holding constant the amount of education for the two groups does actually not hold constant their educational qualifications, since many of the schools to which Negroes go are inferior to those whites attend. Moreover, our broad categories do not even hold the amount of education fully constant, since, given the lower educational attainments of Negroes, there are undoubtedly fewer Negroes than whites near the upper end of the distribution within each category; for example, within the category, "one year of college or more," the proportion of college graduates is slightly smaller for Negroes than for whites.

TABLE 2 Ethnic Background, Education, and Occupational SES of American Men with Nonfarm Background, Age 20 to 64

Ethnicity by Education	20–24 Years	25–34 Years	35–44 Years	45–54 Years	55–64 Years
GRAND MEAN, ALL GROUPS	31.5	41.0	42.6	40.1	40.0
		Gross Effects			
Native white, native parentage					
8 years of schooling or less	−12.9	−18.1	−18.7	−13.8	−10.6
9 to 11 years of schooling	− 8.7	−13.6	−11.1	−5.6	0.3
High school graduate	0.2	−3.1	1.7	3.0	8.0
1 year of college or more	8.3	20.1	22.2	19.3	20.9
Native white, foreign parentage					
8 years of schooling or less	−12.9*	−18.0	−18.1	−14.6	−9.0
9 to 11 years of schooling	2.5*	−11.6	−14.3	−6.6	−0.9
High school graduate	4.7	−3.0	−0.8	6.4	6.7
1 year of college or more	12.3	21.2	20.3	24.1	21.2
Foreign-born white					
8 years of schooling or less	−12.9*	−15.5*	−19.4	−13.8	−10.8
9 to 11 years of schooling	0.3*	−9.6*	−12.8*	−3.0	1.5
High school graduate	1.1*	−13.2*	3.8	−2.9	4.9
1 year of college or more	5.4*	19.3	12.9	17.0	19.6
Nonwhite					
8 years of schooling or less	−20.3	−25.3	−23.8	−21.0	−19.5
9 to 11 years of schooling	−13.5	−23.4	−20.9	−17.7	−20.6
High school graduate	−7.5	−19.0	−18.3	−18.3	−2.8*
1 year of college or more	−1.4*	9.7	5.4	−3.9*	8.1*
		*Net Effects***			
Native white, native parentage					
8 years of schooling or less	−12.0	−16.8	−16.8	−12.1	−9.4
9 to 11 years of schooling	−8.0	−12.9	−10.4	−5.6	(−)0.0
High school graduate	0.1	−3.0	1.3	2.4	6.4
1 year of college or more	7.6	18.6	18.9	16.3	18.9
Native white, foreign parentage					
8 years of schooling or less	−12.2*	−17.2	−15.8	−12.8	−8.0
9 to 11 years of schooling	2.9*	−10.2	−12.8	−5.2	−0.7
High school graduate	4.8	−2.6	−0.2	6.3	6.3
1 year of college or more	11.6	20.2	20.2	21.7	20.0
Foreign-born white					
8 years of schooling or less	−12.4*	14.8*	−17.9	−12.1	−10.0
9 to 11 years of schooling	0.5*	−10.6*	−13.2*	−1.7*	1.7
High school graduate	0.7*	−13.4*	3.8	−2.6	3.7
1 year of college or more	4.8*	17.5	12.2	15.0	18.3
Nonwhite					
8 years of schooling or less	−18.8	−23.8	−20.6	−18.3	−17.5
9 to 11 years of schooling	−12.1	−21.7	−17.9	−15.4	−19.4
High school graduate	−6.2	−17.8	−16.5	−16.2	−4.9*
1 year of college or more	−0.5*	10.0	6.8	−1.7*	12.5*

* The cell frequency on which this value is based is less than 100.
** Father's occupational SES held constant.

Foreign-born Americans and their children, the second-generation Americans, in sharp contrast to Negroes, do not differ in occupational attainments from the native whites of native parentage on the same educational levels. The twenty comparisons of gross effects between native whites of native parentage and native whites of foreign parentage are inconsistent (averaging -1.1), and so are the twenty comparisons between the former and the foreign born (averaging 0.8). The various white ethnic groups in the United States apparently achieve occupational positions commensurate with their education. Whatever occupational discrimination may exist against some of these ethnic groups must be compensated for by other factors since it does not find expression in their over-all occupational chances.

Another perspective on the disadvantaged situation of the American Negro can be gained by examining the rewards he obtains for given educational investments compared to those a white person obtains. The average difference for the five age groups between native whites of native parentage who have some college education and those who have only an elementary school education is 33.0, whereas the corresponding average difference for Negroes is 25.6. In other words, roughly the same amount of educational investment has one and one third times as much payoff for a white man as for a Negro. The fact that Negroes obtain comparatively little reward for their educational investments, which robs them of incentives to incur these costs, might help explain why Negroes often manifest only weak motivation to pursue their education. The early school leaving that results from this lack of motivation further intensifies the disadvantaged position of the Negro in the labor market.

CITY SIZE AND MIGRATION

The discussion of the relationships between size of place, migration, and occupational opportunities will concentrate upon the urban areas, since the present analysis is confined to men whose fathers were not in farming occupations. Although data for nonfarm rural areas will be presented too, these must be interpreted with great caution,

inasmuch as all the sons of farmers living in these areas are excluded from consideration.[14] It should also be remembered that the large number of migrants from farms to cities is not reflected in the data that are now being analyzed.

The findings on size of community reveal few surprises. Table 3 presents the deviations from the mean socio-economic score in each age cohort by city size and by location in the central city or its suburban fringe. People who live in the urban fringe of cities have somewhat higher socio-economic status than those who live in the central cities, and this difference persists if their father's SES is controlled. Of the 15 possible comparisons (three city sizes by five age cohorts), 14 of the gross differences favor the fringe over the central city, an average of 4.1 points, and 12 of the net differences do so, an average of 2.7. The socio-economic status of men who live in suburbs is directly related to the size of the central city, at least for younger men, but the status of the inhabitants of the central cities is not monotonically related to city size.

Within the central city, socio-economic status is highest in cities with between one quarter and one million inhabitants It is somewhat lower in the largest cities of over one million (an average difference of 3.3 points from the former), as well as in the medium cities with 50,000 to 250,000 inhabitants (2.5) and in the small towns with 2,500 to 50,000 inhabitants (2.1). The average socio-economic status in the smallest American towns, however, is still higher than that in rural areas even when farm workers and their sons are excluded from the comparison (2.8). All these differences persist in slightly attenuated form when social origins are controlled, as the net effects in Table 3 show. In short, occupational opportunities are poorest in rural areas and best in fairly large cities, and they differ little on the average in the very large

---

[14] Since the criterion of nonfarm background is whether a man designated his father's occupation as being in farming, not whether he lives on a farm, there are a few farm residents in this nonfarm population. Wherever possible, these have been excluded from this analysis, but this was not possible in all cases. However, the numbers involved are so small that it is unlikely that these farm residents affect the results substantially.

TABLE 3 Size of Place and Occupational SES of American Men with Nonfarm Background, Age 20 to 64

Size of Place	20–24 Years Central City	20–24 Years Urban Fringe	25–34 Years Central City	25–34 Years Urban Fringe	35–44 Years Central City	35–44 Years Urban Fringe	45–54 Years Central City	45–54 Years Urban Fringe	55–64 Years Central City	55–64 Years Urban Fringe
Grand Mean, All Places	31.5		41.0		42.6		40.1		40.0	
Gross Effects										
Very large city (over 1 million)	1.8	4.3	−2.2	6.4	−3.7	5.7	−3.5	4.8	−0.5	3.4
Large city (¼–1 million)	1.1	0.0	2.7	5.6	1.2	5.4	3.4	5.8	0.2	4.0
Medium city (50,000–250,000)	−1.6	−1.0	−1.7	2.0	−1.5	3.0	−1.3	5.7	2.3	3.4
Small town (2,500–50,000)	0.0		−1.4		−0.8		0.6		−0.5	
Rural area (under 2,500)	−3.3		−2.8		−2.4		−4.1		−3.4	
Net Effects										
Very large city	1.9	2.6	−2.0	5.1	−2.6	4.5	−2.4	3.4	−0.1	3.3
Large city	0.5	−1.1	2.0	3.3	1.1	4.0	3.2	5.9	0.1	3.1
Medium city	−1.4	0.3	−0.4	−0.6	−1.8	1.4	−1.0	4.2	1.8	0.7
Small town	0.2		−0.2		−0.9		0.2		−0.8	
Rural area	−2.1		2.2		−1.6		−3.3		−2.6	

Note: No cell frequency is less than 100 and only one—fringe of medium cities for youngest age cohort—is less than 200.

cities and those that are medium or small.

The question arises whether this pattern of differences is the result of migration. The answer appears to be that although migration plays a role the basic pattern has not been produced by it. . . . The socio-economic status of the nonmigrants—the men who reached adolescence in the same community where they live now—reveals a pattern similar to that previously encountered for the total population.* For all five age groups of nonmigrants . . . average SES is higher in cities of at least medium size than in small towns (an average difference of 5.2), and it is higher in small towns than in rural areas (3.6), and the same is true for the net differences when father's SES is held constant (4.4 and 2.6). Since all cities with more than 50,000 inhabitants were combined for this analysis, as were the central cities and their urban fringe, it is not pos-

* We have omitted from the original text the table on which this conclusion is based and from which the following figures are taken. (C. S. H.)

sible to determine whether all specific differences observed in the total populations are reflected in parallel differences among nonmigrants. But the evidence does show that the over-all pattern is the same and that migration cannot account for the status differences between fairly large cities and small ones and between the latter and rural regions.

The socio-economic status of urban migrants is clearly superior to that of nonmigrants, though rural migrants are not superior to nonmigrants. In order to isolate the significance of migration as such from that of either living now or having lived previously in a certain environment, nonmigrants will be compared with only those migrants who reside at present in communities of the same size and who also lived as adolescents in communities of about the same size, that is, with those migrants who moved from as well as into communities of approximately the same size. . . . In all ten comparisons of urban nonmigrants with migrants who came from and are now in the same environment (two city sizes for five age cohorts), the socio-economic status of the migrants is superior, an average of 7.0 (net of father's SES, 5.4). The five comparisons between nonfarm rural migrants and nonmigrants yield no consistent results —two going in one and three in the other direction—and the average difference is very small (0.6; net, 1.3). Migrants within urban areas, then, tend to occupy superior occupational positions and enjoy higher achievements relative to their social origins than their nonmigrant counterparts, but there are no corresponding differences between the migrants within rural areas and the nonmigrants in these areas. These differences cannot be primarily due to the fact that migrants frequently move from smaller to larger communities where occupational opportunities are superior, because the influence of city size has been roughly controlled in this analysis. The inference therefore is that intra-urban migration is selective of men predisposed to occupational success, whereas this is not the case for intra-rural migration.

We turn now to examine the significance of the change in environment migration produces, which is the very factor we attempted to control in the preceding analysis of the significance of migration itself. What are the implications of the migrant's area of destination for his occupational chances? Regardless of geographical origins, men who move into urban areas tend to achieve higher socio-economic status than those who move into rural areas. Most pronounced is the difference between migrants to small cities and those to rural regions, with nine of ten comparisons indicating a higher SES for the men who moved to small cities, the average difference being 4.2 (and 3.5 if father's SES is held constant).[15] This difference parallels that between nonmigrants in small cities and rural areas. When cities over 50,000 are compared with

[15] Since only one value for migrants from the two urban to rural areas is given, the unweighted average of the two values for the migrants to small towns from large cities and those from small towns was used in computing the differences. In case of the youngest age group, for instance, 1.9 was subtracted from 5.4 (the average of 5.8 and 5.0).

smaller ones, however, the findings assume quite another pattern. Here point of origin makes a difference, and the situation of migrants differs from that of nonmigrants in the same type of place. Whereas nonmigrants tend to achieve *higher* occupational status in the relatively larger cities than in small ones, the status of migrants from rural areas does not differer consistently in the two localities, and migrants from other urban areas achieve lower status in the larger than in the small cities. . . . The SES of nonmigrants is *higher* in the larger than in the smaller cities in five instances out of five, the average difference being + 5.2 (net, + 4.4), but the SES of migrants from urban areas (rows 2 and 3) is *lower* in the larger than in the smaller cities in nine cases out of ten, the average difference being − 2.3 (net, − 2.0).

It seems paradoxical that the occupational chances of urban migrants are worse, and those of rural migrants are no better, in larger cities than in smaller ones, while the occupational opportunities of the natives are better in the larger than in the smaller cities. It must be remembered that the urban migrants to larger cities are somewhat superior in socio-economic status to the nonmigrants there, but their superiority is not as great as that of migrants over nonmigrants in small cities. One possible explanation of these findings is that the migrants to larger cities constitute a more heterogeneous group than those to smaller towns, including not only disproportionate numbers with good occupational qualifications but also very many with extremely poor qualifications. Thus the migrants who stream into the large Northern cities from the South can frequently only obtain the least desirable occupational positions, and these migrants take the place at the bottom of the industrial hierarchy that was once occupied by the recent immigrants from Europe. Another reason for the lesser superiority of migrants over nonmigrants in larger cities might be that being raised in large cities gives the natives an advantage in the struggle for occupational success that compensates for some of the other advantages the migrants have. The comparison of men reared in places of different size supports this interpretation.

Migrants who lived in larger cities when they were 16 years old tend to be superior in socio-economic status to those raised in smaller cities, and the latter tend to be superior to those who grew up in rural areas. . . . Of ten comparisons between migrants coming from larger and those coming from smaller cities, nine show that the former have a higher SES, the average difference being 4.0 (net, 2.9), and of 15 comparisons between migrants raised in small cities and those raised in rural areas, 14 show that the former have higher SES, the average difference being 8.6 (net, 5.5). The same difference is reflected in the finding that the SES of nonmigrants is directly related to the size of their present community, since in the case of nonmigrants the present community is, of course, identical with the place where they lived at age 16. Whether a man is a migrant or not, therefore, and regardless of the size of the community where he now works, the larger the community where he grew up, the better are his chances to achieve occupational success and to move up from the status of his father.

Since growing up in a large city is an occupational advantage, and so is being a migrant to a small city, the highest occupational status is achieved by migrants from larger to small cities, whose status is, on the average, 9.1 points above the mean (net, 7.1 points). One might speculate why men raised in large cities have greater chances of success in their careers. The advantage of the urban over the rural environment is undoubtedly in large part due to the superior educational facilities in the former, but it is questionable whether the superiority of the large-city environment over that in small cities can be attributed to differences in the educational system. It may be that at least part of this superiority is due to the greater sophistication about the labor market and occupational life generally that boys growing up in large cities tend to acquire.

PARENTAL FAMILY

A man's occupational chances are strongly affected by the size of his parents' family. The socio-economic status of men with three or fewer siblings is considerably sup-

erior to that of men with four or more siblings. The data in Table 4 permit 20 independent comparisons between men from small and from large families (excluding only children). All 20 indicate that the SES of men from smaller families is superior, the average difference being 8.0. Some of this difference is due to the fact that poorer couples tend to have larger families rather than to the influence of family size on the occupational chances of sons. But even if the former factor is controlled by holding father's socio-economic status constant, the socio-economic status of men from smaller families continues to be higher than that of men from larger families in all 20 comparisons, an average of 5.2 points. This net effect shows that a man's chances of occupational success are impeded by many siblings. Although in strictly economic terms only children must have an advantage over others, since they do not have to share their parents' financial resources with anybody, this economic advantage is not reflected in their careers. Only children do not achieve higher occupational positions than those from small families; the differences between the two groups are inconsistent, and the average approximates zero.

Sibling position as well as number of siblings influences occupational attainments. There are no consistent differences between oldest and youngest children, but the SES of both tends to be superior to that of middle children. Ten independent comparisons can be made between oldest children and middle children with an older brother (two sizes for five age cohorts). Eight of these indicate that the oldest child has a higher status, one that the middle child has, and one reveals no difference. The average difference is 3.7, which is reduced to 2.7 if father's SES is controlled. When youngest children are compared to middle children with an older brother, the youngest are seen to have superior SES in all ten cases, the average difference being 4.3, and this difference persists if father's SES is controlled (net, 4.0). (Comparisons with middle children without an older brother yield essentially the same results.) Both oldest and youngest children gain advantages from their positions compared to middle children, but perhaps for

TABLE 4   Parental Family and Occupational SES of American Men with Nonfarm Background, Age 20 to 64

Sibling Position and Number of Siblings	20–24 Years	25–34 Years	35–44 Years	45–54 Years	55–64 Years
Grand Mean	31.5	41.0	42.6	40.1	40.0
			Gross Effects		
1. Only child, no siblings	5.1	6.0	4.1	7.0	3.0
2. Oldest, 1 to 3 siblings	3.6	6.4	6.1	4.7	7.0
3. Oldest, 4 or more siblings	−2.1	−6.0	−6.0	−4.8	−0.3
4. Youngest, 1 to 3 siblings	5.3	3.6	6.5	5.3	5.6
5. Youngest, 4 or more siblings	−2.3	−2.4	−2.5	−2.3	−1.6
6. Middle, 2–3 s's, no older brother	−2.1	0.6	4.7	0.3	10.2
7. Middle, 2–3 s's, older brother	−2.3	−0.8	3.7	1.5	−0.1
8. Middle, 4 + s's, no older brother	−7.3	−4.3	−8.2	−4.8	−5.4
9. Middle, 4 + s's, older brother	−6.3	−7.6	−7.5	−3.6	−5.1
			*Net Effects**		
1. Only child, no siblings	3.8	3.9	2.9	4.2	3.0
2. Oldest, 1 to 3 siblings	2.6	4.0	4.2	2.6	4.4
3. Oldest, 4 or more siblings	−1.8	−4.5	−4.0	−3.1	0.8
4. Youngest, 1 to 3 siblings	4.4	2.3	4.0	3.5	4.6
5. Youngest, 4 or more siblings	0.1	−0.4	0.7	−0.6	−0.2
6. Middle, 2–3 s's, no older brother	−3.0	−0.1	3.8	0.3	8.4
7. Middle, 2–3 s's, older brother	−2.3	−0.5	1.9	1.1	−0.7
8. Middle, 4 + s's, no older brother	−5.6	−2.6	−7.1	−4.6	−3.8
9. Middle, 4 + s's older brother	−4.5	−5.1	−5.3	−1.9	−4.5
			*Residual Effects***		
1. Only child, no siblings	1.5	−1.2	−1.3	0.5	−0.9
2. Oldest, 1 to 3 siblings	1.0	1.0	1.4	0.5	1.3
3. Oldest, 4 or more siblings	0.3	−0.3	0.2	−0.8	1.7
4. Youngest, 1 to 3 siblings	2.4	−0.3	0.6	0.6	1.4
5. Youngest, 4 or more siblings	0.3	0.9	2.4	−2.5	0.5
6. Middle, 2–3 s's, no older brother	−2.7	0.5	2.0	−1.0	6.5
7. Middle, 2–3 s's, older brother	−3.4	−0.8	1.8	1.5	−1.2
8. Middle, 4 + s's, no older brother	−3.3	0.5	−3.2	−0.2	−1.1
9. Middle, 4 + s's, older brother	−1.0	0.0	−1.7	0.2	−1.7

Note: No cell frequency is less than 100 and only one—youngest in large families for cohort 20–24 years—is less than 200.

* Father's occupational SES held constant.

** First job, education, father's occupational SES, ethnic classification, region and place of birth and residence, and geographic mobility held constant.

different reasons. The fact that the occupational advantages of oldest children depend in part on the socio-economic status of their fathers while those of youngest children do not suggest that the latter are due to socio-psychological rather than economic factors. It may be that the occupational success of youngest children is primarily due to the greater social and emotional support they receive in their families rather than to the fact that their education pre-empts the economic resources of their parents.

Middle children with and without an older brother have been separated in order to examine the implications of having an older brother for occupational chances. The significance of an older brother for careers appears to be slight and confined to small families. Four of the five comparisons in small families (Table 4, rows 6 and 7) indicate that middle children without an older brother have higher SES than those with one, with an average difference of +2.3, but four of the five comparisons in large families go in the opposite direction and the average difference is zero. If father's SES is controlled, the difference in small families is +2.0 and that in large ones is −0.5. Having no older brother is a slight advantage for middle children in small families but not in large ones.

The bottom third of Table 4 presents the residual effects of size of parental family and sibling position when not only father's SES but also a number of other factors are controlled, namely, respondent's education, his first job, his ethnic background, the region where he was born and where he lives at present, the size of his place of birth and of his present community, and migration status. It is evident from the table that the residual effects of parental family on socio-economic status that remain after all these conditions have been held constant are small. This does not mean, however, that the effects of number of siblings and sibling position previously observed were spurious, because the factors that are now being controlled are not independent of a man's parental family. Some of these control factors are directly determined by the family into which a man is born, such as his ethnic affiliation and the area where he grows up, and others are strongly affected by the size of his family and his position in it, such as his education and his first job. The reduction in effects produced by the introduction of these controls indicates, by and large, the degree to which the initial effects of parental family were mediated by various social and economic conditions, for example, the training and experience a man obtained and the opportunities existing in the area where he was raised. If the initial (gross) effects are little reduced by introducing the controls, it suggests that they are not primarily due to the economic advantages children gain from their families, directly or indirectly, but to other, socio-psychological forces in the family.

Whereas the gross effects on SES of sibling position are considerably smaller than those of sib size, the former persist to a greater degree than the latter when economic conditions are controlled. Instituting these controls reduces the impact of family size on SES very much, it reduces the influence of sibling position a great deal, though not as much, and it reduces the interaction effect of having no older brother in small families hardly at all. The average gross difference in SES between men from small and from large families of 8.0 points is reduced to a residual average difference of merely 1.1 points in Table 4. In contrast to this decrease to one seventh of the original difference, instituting controls decreases the effects of sibling position on SES considerably less, only to about one third of their original size, from 4.3 to 1.3 for youngest (vs. middle) and from 3.7 to 1.3 for oldest (vs. middle) children. The case is more extreme for the interaction effect of having no older brother and family size on SES. The gross differences in SES between middle children with no older brother and those with an older brother are +2.3 in small families and 0.0 in large ones, and the residual differences are +1.5 in small and −0.6 in large families. Hence, the difference between these differences, which indicates the interaction effect, is virtually not affected by introducing controls, being 2.3 originally and still 2.1 for the residuals. Although the residual effects are very small, the reduction in gross differences effected by introducing controls varies so greatly that we are tempted to hazard some interpretations based on these variations.

The superior occupational achievements of children from small families are largely accounted for by the better economic conditions in which they find themselves compared to children from large families. The superior occupational achievements of oldest and youngest children relative to those of middle children, on the other hand, seem to be due to a combination of economic and psychological factors. The distinctive position the oldest and the youngest child occupy in the family may not only have the result that parents devote disproportionate resources to their training but also make it likely that these children receive more social and emotional support from other members of the family than do middle children. (Since the residual effects for oldest and for youngest child do not differ, we had to modify here an interpretation advanced earlier that distinguished the situation of the youngest from that of the oldest.)

The occupational advantages middle children with older brothers have in small families but not in large ones are apparently not due to economic factors. A possible explanation of this interaction effect is that an older brother is more likely to be the oldest child in a small than in a large family, and oldest children occupy, as we have seen, privileged positions, which means that not having a brother who is an oldest child is an advantage. One might also speculate whether older sisters are protective and supportive of younger brothers and thereby strengthen their potential for subsequent occupational success. If older sisters actually have such a beneficial influence on their younger brothers, it would explain the observed interaction effect, because the middle child without an older brother necessarily has an older sister, and the middle child with an older brother in a small family is unlikely to have also an older sister but in a large family he is likely to have also an older sister.

CONCLUSIONS

We have illustrated our procedures as well as some preliminary findings from our research in this paper. The complexity of the analysis required when several factors influence occupational success has undoubtedly become evident. Since the condensed discussion may well have been difficult to follow at various points, it might be useful to summarize in conclusion the main substantive findings.

There is much intergenerational occupational mobility in the United States, though probably not much more than in other Western countries such as Sweden and Britain. The correlation between father's and son's SES is $+.38$. The influence of father's on son's status is largely mediated through education, in apparent contrast to the situation in some other countries, but socio-economic origins also influence career chances independent of education.

It hardly comes as a surprise that racial discrimination in the United States is reflected in the Negro's inferior chances of occupational success, although the extent to which Negroes with the same amount of education as whites remain behind in the struggle for desirable occupations is striking. Negroes receive much less occupational return for their educational investments than whites do, and their consequent lesser incentive to acquire an education further disadvantages them in the labor market. What may be surprising, however, is that white ethnic minorities, on the average, appear to have as good occupational chances as the majority group. At least, the occupational achievements of foreign-born and second-generation Americans are no worse than those of native whites of native parentage with the same amount of education.

Urban migrants are more likely to occupy desirable occupational positions and to have moved up from the socio-economic status of their fathers than nonmigrants. Migration to urban areas brings occupational success more often than migration to rural areas (for the nonfarm population here under consideration), and migration from urban areas to small cities is particularly advantageous. The larger the place where a migrant grew up, the greater are the chances of his occupational success, regardless of the type of place where he ends up working. Indeed, for nonmigrants as well as migrants, there is a direct correlation between the size of the place where a man was reared and his occupational achievement.

Size of parental family and sibling position affect careers. The occupational attainments of men with many siblings, with whom they had to share parental resources, are inferior to those of men with few siblings, but only children do not achieve higher socio-economic positions than men from small families. Oldest and youngest children tend to have more successful careers than middle ones. In small families, though not in large ones, finally, having no older brothers appears to give a middle child a slight advantage in the struggle for occupational success, which suggests that older sisters improve future life chances.

SPONSORED AND CONTEST MOBILITY AND THE SCHOOL SYSTEM[1]

Ralph H. Turner

This paper suggests a framework for relating certain differences between American and English systems of education to the prevailing norms of upward mobility in each country. Others have noted the tendency of educational systems to support prevailing schemes of stratification, but this discussion concerns specifically the manner in which the *accepted mode of upward mobility* shapes the school system directly and indirectly through its effects on the values which implement social control.

Two ideal-typical normative patterns of upward mobility are described and their ramifications in the general patterns of stratification and social control are suggested. In addition to showing relationships among a number of differences between American and English schooling, the ideal-types have broader implications than those developed in this paper: they suggest a major dimension of stratification which might be profitably incorporated into a variety of studies in social class; and they readily can be applied in further comparisons between other countries.

THE NATURE OF ORGANIZING NORMS

Many investigators have concerned themselves with rates of upward mobility in specific countries or internationally,[2] and

with the manner in which school systems facilitate or impede such mobility.[3] But preoccupation with the *extent* of mobility has precluded equal attention to the predominant *modes* of mobility. The central assumption underlying this paper is that within a formally open class system that provides for mass education the organizing folk norm which defines the accepted mode of upward mobility is a crucial factor in shaping the school system, and may be even more crucial than the extent of upward mobility. In England and the United States there appear to be different organizing folk norms, here termed *sponsored mobility* and *contest mobility,* respectively. *Contest* mobility is a system in which elite[4] status is the prize in an open contest and is taken by the aspirants' own efforts. While the "contest" is governed by some rules of fair play, the contestants have wide latitude in the strategies they may employ. Since the "prize" of successful upward mobility is not in the hands of an established elite to give out, the latter can not determine who shall attain it and who shall not. Under *sponsored* mobility elite recruits are chosen by the established elite or their agents, and elite status is *given* on the basis of some criterion of supposed merit and cannot be *taken* by any amount of effort or strategy. Upward mobility is like entry into a private club where each candidate must be "sponsored" by one or more of the members. Ultimately the members grant or deny upward mobility on the basis of whether they judge the

[3] *Cf.* C. A. Anderson, "The Social Status of University Students in Relation to Type of Economy: An International Comparison," *Transactions of the Third World Congress of Sociology,* London, 1956, Vol. V, pp. 51–63; J. E. Floud, *Social Class and Educational Opportunity,* London: Heinemann, 1956; W. L. Warner, R. J. Havighurst, and M. B. Loeb, *Who Shall Be Educated?* New York: Harper, 1944.

[4] Reference is made throughout the paper to "elite" and "masses." The generalizations, however, are intended to apply throughout the stratification continuum to relations between members of a given class and the class or classes above it. Statements about mobility are intended in general to apply to mobility from manual to middle-class levels, lower-middle to upper-middle class, and so on, as well as into the strictly elite groups. The simplified expressions avoid the repeated use of cumbersome and involved statements which might otherwise be required.

From the *American Sociological Review,* Vol. 25, No. 6, December, 1960. Copyright 1960 by the American Sociological Association. Reprinted by permission.

[1] ... Special indebtedness should be expressed to Jean Floud and Hilde Himmelweit for helping to acquaint the author with the English school system.

[2] A comprehensive summary of such studies appears in Seymour M. Lipset and Reinhard Bendix, *Social Mobility in Industrial Society,* Berkeley and Los Angeles: University of California Press, 1959.

candidate to have those qualities they wish to see in fellow members.

Before elaborating this distinction, it should be noted that these systems of mobility are ideal types designed to clarify observed differences in the predominantly similar English and American systems of stratification and education. But as organizing norms these principles are assumed to be present at least implicitly in people's thinking, guiding their judgments of what is appropriate on many specific matters. Such organizing norms do not correspond perfectly with the objective characteristics of the societies in which they exist, nor are they completely independent of them. From the complex interplay of social and economic conditions and ideologies people in a society develop a highly simplified conception of the way in which events take place. This conception of the "natural" is translated into a norm—the "natural" becomes what "ought" to be—and in turn imposes a strain toward consistency upon relevant aspects of the society. Thus the norm acts back upon the objective conditions to which it refers and has ramifying effects upon directly and indirectly related features of the society.[5] . . .

Two final qualifications concerning the scope of this paper: First, the organizing folk norm of upward mobility affects the school system because one of the latter's functions is the facilitation of mobility. Since this is only one of several social functions of the school, and not the most important function in the societies under examination, only a very partial accounting of the whole set of forces making for similarities and differences in the school systems of United States and England is possible here. Only those differences which directly or indirectly reflect the performance of the

mobility function are noted. Second, the concern of this paper is with the current dynamics of the situation in the two countries rather than with their historical development.

DISTINCTIONS BETWEEN THE TWO NORMS

Contest mobility is like a sporting event in which many compete for a few recognized prizes. The contest is judged to be fair only if all the players compete on an equal footing. Victory must be won solely by one's own efforts. The most satisfactory outcome is not necessarily a victory of the most able, but of the most deserving. The tortoise who defeats the hare is a folk-prototype of the deserving sportsman. . . . Applied to mobility, the contest norm means that victory by a person of moderate intelligence accomplished through the use of common sense, craft, enterprise, daring, and successful risk-taking[6] is more appreciated than victory by the most intelligent or the best educated.

Sponsored mobility, in contrast, rejects the pattern of the contest and favors a controlled selection process. In this process the elite or their agents, deemed to be best qualified to judge merit, choose individuals for elite status who have the appropriate qualities. Individuals do not win or seize elite status; mobility is rather a process of sponsored induction into the elite.

Pareto had this sort of mobility in mind when he suggested that a governing class might dispose of persons potentially dangerous to it by admitting them to elite membership, provided that the recruits change character by adopting elite attitudes and interests.[7] Danger to the ruling class would seldom be the major criterion for choice of

---

[5] The normative element in an organizing norm goes beyond Max Weber's *ideal type*, conveying more of the sense of Durkheim's *collective representation; cf.* Ralph H. Turner, "The Normative Coherence of Folk Concepts," *Research Studies of the State College of Washington*, 25 (1957), pp. 127–136. Charles Wagley has developed a similar concept which he calls "ideal pattern" in his as yet unpublished work on Brazilian kinship. See also Howard Becker, "Constructive Typology in the Social Sciences," *American Sociological Review*, 5 (February, 1940), pp. 40–55.

[6] Geoffrey Gorer remarks on the favorable evaluation of the successful gamble in American culture: "Gambling is also a respected and important component in many business ventures. Conspicuous improvement in a man's financial position is generally attributed to a lucky combination of industry, skill, and gambling, though the successful gambler prefers to refer to his gambling as 'vision.'" *The American People*, New York: Norton, 1948, p. 178.

[7] Vilfredo Pareto, *The Mind and Society*, New York: Harcourt, Brace, 1935, Vol. 4, p. 1796.

elite recruits. But Pareto assumed that the established elite would select whom they wished to enter their ranks and would inculcate the attitudes and interests of the established elite in the recruits.

The governing objective of contest mobility is to give elite status to those who earn it, while the goal of sponsored mobility is to make the best use of the talents in society by sorting persons into their proper niches. In different societies the conditions of competitive struggle may reward quite different attributes, and sponsored mobility may select individuals on the basis of such diverse qualities as intelligence or visionary capability, but the difference in principle remains the same. . . .

Under the contest system society at large establishes and interprets the criteria of elite status. If one wishes to have his status recognized he must display certain credentials which identify his class to those about him. The credentials must be highly visible and require no special skill for their assessment, since credentials are presented to the masses. Material possession and mass popularity are altogether appropriate credentials in this respect, and any special skill which produces a tangible product and which can easily be assessed by the untrained will do. The nature of sponsored mobility precludes these procedures, but assigns to credentials instead the function of identifying elite members to one another. Accordingly, the ideal credentials are special skills that require the trained discrimination of the elite for their recognition. In this case, intellectual, literary, or artistic excellencies, which can be appraised only by those trained to appreciate them, are fully suitable credentials. Concentration on such skills lessens the likelihood that an interloper will succeed in claiming the right to elite membership on grounds of the popular evaluation of his competence.

In the sporting event there is special admiration for the slow starter who makes a dramatic finish, and many of the rules are designed to insure that the race should not be declared over until it has run its full course. Contest mobility incorporates this disapproval of premature judgments and of anything that gives special advantage to those who are ahead at any point in the race. Under sponsored mobility, fairly early selection of only the number of persons necessary to fill anticipated vacancies in the elite is desirable. Early selection allows time to prepare the recruits for their elite position. Aptitudes, inherent capacities, and spiritual gifts can be assessed fairly early in life by techniques ranging from divination to the most sophisticated psychological test, and the more naive the subjects at the time of selection the less likely are their talents to be blurred by differential learning or conspiracy to defeat the test. Since elitists take the initiative in training recruits, they are more interested in the latters' capabilities than in what they will do with them on their own. and they are concerned that no one else should first have an opportunity to train the recruits' talents in the wrong direction. Contest mobility tends to delay the final award as long as practicable to permit a fair race; sponsored mobility tends to place the time of recruitment as early in life as practicable to insure control over selection and training.

Systems of sponsored mobility develop most readily in societies with but a single elite or with a recognized elite hierarchy. When mutiple elites compete among themselves the mobility process tends to take the contest pattern, since no group is able to command control of recruitment. Sponsored mobility further depends upon a social structure that fosters monopoly of elite credentials. Lack of such monopoly undercuts sponsorship and control of the recruitment process. Monopoly of credentials in turn is typically a product of societies with well entrenched traditional aristocracies employing such credentials as family line and bestowable title which are intrinsically subject to monopoly, or of societies organized on large-scale bureaucratic lines permitting centralized control of upward social movement.

English society has been described as the juxtaposition of two systems of stratification, the urban industrial class system and the surviving aristocratic system. While the sponsored mobility pattern reflects the logic of the latter, our impression is that it pervades popular thinking rather than merely coexisting with the logic of industrial stratification. Patterns imported into an established culture tend to be reshaped, as they are assimilated, into consistency with the established culture. Thus it may be that changes in stratification associated with industrialization have led to alterations in the rates, the specific means, and the rules of mobility, but that these changes have been guided by the but lightly challenged organizing norm of sponsored mobility.

SOCIAL CONTROL AND THE TWO NORMS

Every society must cope with the problem of maintaining loyalty to its social system and does so in part through norms and values, only some of which vary by class position. Norms and values especially prevalent within a given class must direct behavior into channels that support the total system, while those that transcend strata must support the general class differential. The way in which upward mobility takes place determines in part the kinds of norms and values that serve the indicated purposes of social control in each class and throughout the society.

The most conspicuous control problem is that of ensuring loyalty in the disadvantaged classes toward a system in which their members receive less than a proportional share of society's goods. In a system of contest mobility this is accomplished by a combination of futuristic orientation, the norm of ambition, and a general sense of fellowship with the elite. Each individual is encouraged to think of himself as competing for an elite position so that loyalty to the system and conventional attitudes are cultivated in the process of preparation for this possibility. It is essential that this futuristic orientation be kept alive by delaying a sense of final irreparable failure to reach elite status until attitudes are well established. By thinking of himself in the successful future the elite aspirant forms considerable identification with elitists, and evidence that they are merely ordinary human beings like himself helps to reinforce this identification as well as to keep alive the conviction that he himself may someday succeed in like manner. To forestall rebellion among the disadvantaged majority, then, a contest system must avoid absolute points of selection for mobility and immobility and must delay clear recognition

of the realities of the situation until the individual is too committed to the system to change radically. A futuristic orientation cannot, of course, be inculcated successfully in all members of lower strata, but sufficient internalization of a norm of ambition tends to leave the unambitious as individual deviants and to forestall the latters' formation of a genuine subcultural group able to offer collective threat to the established system. Where this kind of control system operates rather effectively it is notable that organized or gang deviancy is more likely to take the form of an attack upon the conventional or moral order rather than upon the class system itself. Thus the United States has its "beatniks"[8] who repudiate ambition and most worldly values and its delinquent and criminal gangs who try to evade the limitations imposed by conventional means[9] but very few active revolutionaries.

These social controls are inappropriate in a system of sponsorship since the elite recruits are chosen from above. The principal threat to the system would lie in the existence of a strong group the members of whom sought to *take* elite positions themselves. Control under this sytem is maintained by training the "masses" to regard themselves as relatively incompetent to manage society, by restricting access to the skills and manners of the elite, and by cultivating belief in the superior competence of the elite. The earlier that selection of the elite recruits is made the sooner others can be taught to accept their inferiority and to make "realistic" rather than fantasy plans. Early selection prevents raising the hopes of large numbers of people who might otherwise become the discontented leaders of a class challenging the sovereignty of the established elite. If it is assumed that the difference in competence between masses and elite is seldom so great as to support the usual differences in the advantages accruing to each,[10] then the differences must

[8] See, e.g., Lawrence Lipton, *The Holy Barbarians*, New York: Messner, 1959.

[9] *Cf.* Albert K. Cohen, *Delinquent Boys: The Culture of the Gang*, Glencoe, Ill.: Free Press, 1955.

[10] D. V. Glass, editor, *Social Mobility in Britain*, Glencoe, Ill.: Pree Press, 1954, pp. 144–145, reports studies showing only small variations in intelligence between occupational levels.

be artificially augmented by discouraging acquisition of elite skills by the masses. Thus a sense of mystery about the elite is a common device for supporting in the masses the illusion of a much greater hiatus of competence than in fact exists.

While elitists are unlikely to reject a system that benefits them, they must still be restrained from taking such advantage of their favorable situation as to jeopardize the entire elite. Under the sponsorship system the elite recruits—who are selected early, freed from the strain of competitive struggle, and kept under close supervision—may be thoroughly indoctrinated in elite culture. A norm of paternalism toward inferiors may be inculcated, a heightened sensitivity to the good opinion of fellow elitists and elite recruits may be cultivated, and the appreciation of the more complex forms of aesthetic, literary, intellectual, and sporting activities may be taught. Norms of courtesy and altruism easily can be maintained under sponsorship since elite recruits are not required to compete for their standing and since the elite may deny high standing to those who strive for position by "unseemly" methods. The system of sponsorship provides an almost perfect setting for the development of an elite culture characterized by a sense of responsibility for "inferiors" and for preservation of the "finer things" of life.

Elite control in the contest system is more difficult since there is no controlled induction and apprenticeship. The principal regulation seems to lie in the insecurity of elite position. In a sense there is no "final arrival" because each person may be displaced by newcomers throughout his life. The limited control of high standing from above prevents the clear delimitation of levels in the class system, so that success itself becomes relative: each success, rather than an accomplishment, serves to qualify the participant for competition at the next higher level.[11] The restraints upon the behavior of a person of high standing, therefore, are principally those applicable to a contestant who must not risk the "ganging up" of other contestants, and who must pay some attention to the masses who are

frequently in a position to impose penalties upon him. But any special norm of paternalism is hard to establish since there is no dependable procedure for examining the means by which one achieves elite credentials. While mass esteem is an effective brake upon over-exploitation of position, it rewards scrupulously ethical and altruistic behavior much less than evidence of fellow-feeling with the masses themselves. . . .

Certain of the general values and norms of any society reflect emulation of elite values by the masses. Under sponsored mobility, a good deal of the protective attitudes toward and interest in classical subjects percolates to the masses. Under contest mobility, however, there is not the same degree of homogeneity of moral, aesthetic, and intellectual values to be emulated, so that the conspicuous attribute of the elite is its high level of material consumption—emulation itself follows this course. There is neither effective incentive nor punishment for the elitist who fails to interest himself in promoting the arts or literary excellence, or who continues to maintain the vulgar manners and mode of speech of his class origin. The elite has relatively less power to punish or reward a man for his adoption or disregard of any special elite culture. The great importance of accent and of grammatical excellence in the attainment of high status in England as contrasted with the twangs and drawls and grammatical ineptitude among American elites is the most striking example of this difference. . . .

This is not to imply that there are no groups in a "contest" society devoted to the protection and fostering of high standards in music, literature, and intellectual pursuits, but that such standards lack the support of the class system which is frequently found when sponsored mobility prevails. . . .

FORMAL EDUCATION

Returning to the conception of an organizing ideal norm, we assume that to the extent to which one such norm of upward mobility is prevalent in a society there are constant strains to shape the educational system into conformity with that norm.

---

[11] Gorer, *op. cit.*, pp. 172–187.

These strains operate in two fashions: directly by blinding people to alternatives and coloring their judgments of successful and unsuccessful solutions to recurring educational problems; indirectly, through the functional interrelationships between school systems and the class structure, systems of social control, and other features of the social structure which are neglected in this paper.

The most obvious application of the distinction between sponsored and contest mobility norms affords a partial explanation for the different policies of student selection in the English and American secondary schools. Although American high school students follow different courses of study and a few attend specialized schools, a major educational preoccupation has been to avoid any sharp social separation between the superior and inferior students and to keep the channels of movement between courses of study as open as possible. Recent criticisms of the way in which superior students may be thereby held back in their development usually are nevertheless qualified by the insistence that these students must not be withdrawn from the mainstream of student life.[12] Such segregation offends the sense of fairness implicit in the contest norm and also arouses the fear that the elite and future elite will lose their sense of fellowship with the masses. Perhaps the most important point, however, is that schooling is presented as an opportunity, and making use of it depends primarily on the student's own initiative and enterprise.

The English system has undergone a succession of liberalizing changes during this century, but all of them have retained the attempt to sort out early in the educational program the promising from the unpromising so that the former may be segregated and given a special form of training to fit them for higher standing in their adult years. Under the Education Act of 1944, a minority of students has been selected each year by means of a battery of examinations popularly known as "eleven plus," supplemented in varying degrees by grade school records and personal interviews, for admis-

[12] See, e.g., *Los Angeles Times*, May 4, 1959, Part I, p. 24.

sion to grammar schools.[13] The remaining students attend secondary modern or technical schools in which the opportunities to prepare for college or to train for the more prestigeful occupations are minimal. The grammar schools supply what by comparative standards is a high quality of college preparatory education. Of course, such a scheme embodies the logic of sponsorship, with early selection of those destined for middle-class and higher-status occupations, and specialized training to prepare each group for its destined class position. This plan facilitates considerable mobility, and recent research reveals surprisingly little bias against children from manual laboring-class families in the selection for grammar school, when related to measured intelligence.[14] It is altogether possible that adequate comparative study would show a closer correlation of school success with measured intelligence and a lesser correlation between school success and family background in England than in the United States. While selection of superior students for mobility opportunity is probably more efficient under such a system, the obstacles for persons not to be selected of "making the grade" on the basis of their own initiative or enterprise are probably correspondingly greater. . . .

This well-known difference between the British sorting at an early age of students into grammar and modern schools and the American comprehensive high school and junior college is the clearest application of the distinction under discussion. But the organizing norms penetrate more deeply into the school systems than is initially apparent. The most telling observation regarding the direct normative operation of these principles would be evidence to support the author's impression that major

[13] The nature and operation of the "eleven plus" system are fully reviewed in a report by a committee of the British Psychological Society and in a report of extensive research into the adequacy of selection methods. See P. E. Vernon, editor, *Secondary School Selection: A British Psychological Inquiry*, London: Methuen, 1957; and Alfred Yates and D. A. Pidgeon, *Admission to Grammar Schools*, London: Newnes Educational Publishing Co., 1957.

[14] J. E. Floud, A. H. Halsey, and F. M. Martin, *Social Class and Educational Opportunity*, London: Heinemann, 1956.

critics of educational procedures within each country do not usually transcend the logic of their respective mobility norms. Thus the British debate about the best method for getting people sorted according to ability, without proposing that elite station should be open to whosoever can ascend to it. Although fear of "sputnik" in the United States introduced a flurry of suggestions for sponsored mobility schemes, the long-standing concern of school critics has been the failure to motivate students adequately. Preoccupation with motivation appears to be an intellectual application of the folk idea that people should *win* their station in society by personal enterprise.

The functional operation of a strain toward consistency with the organizing norms of upward mobility may be illustrated by several other features of the school systems in the two countries. First, the value placed upon education itself differs under the two norms. Under sponsored mobility, schooling is valued for its cultivation of elite culture, and those forms of schooling directed toward such cultivation are more highly valued than others. Education of the nonelite is difficult to justify clearly and tends to be half-hearted, while maximum educational resources are concentrated on "those who can benefit most from them"—in practice, this means those who can learn the elite culture. The secondary modern schools in England have regularly suffered from less adequate financial provision, a higher student-teacher ratio, fewer well trained teachers, and a general lack of prestige in comparison with the grammar schools.[15]

Under contest mobility in the United States, education is valued as a means of getting ahead, but the contents of education are not highly valued in their own right. Over a century ago Tocqueville commented

[15] Less adequate financial provision and a higher student-teacher ratio are mentioned as obstacles to parity of secondary modern schools with grammar schools in *The Times Educational Supplement*, February 22, 1947, p. 241. On difficulties in achieving prestige comparable with grammar schools, see G. Baron, "Secondary Education in Britain: Some Present-Day Trends," *Teachers College Record*, 57 (January, 1956), pp. 211–221; and O. Banks, *Parity and Prestige in English Secondary Education*, London: Routledge and Kegan Paul, 1955. See also Vernon, *op. cit.*, pp. 19–22.

on the absence of an hereditary class "by which the labors of the intellect are held in honor." He remarked that consequently a "middling standard is fixed in America for human knowledge."[16] And there persists in some measure the suspicion of the educated man as one who may have gotten ahead without really earning his position. . . .

Second, the logic of preparation for a contest prevails in United States schools, and emphasizes keeping everyone in the running until the final stages. In primary and secondary schools the assumption tends to be made that those who are learning satisfactorily need little special attention while the less successful require help to be sure that they remain in the contest and may compete for the final stakes. As recently as December, 1958, a nationwide Gallup Poll gave evidence that this attitude had not been radically altered by the international situation. When asked whether or not teachers should devote extra time to the bright students, 26 per cent of the respondents replied "yes" and 67 per cent, "no." But the responses changed to 86 per cent "yes" and only nine per cent "no" when the question was asked concerning "slow students."[17]

In western states the junior college offers many students a "second chance" to qualify for university, and all state universities have some provision for substandard high school students to earn admission.

The university itself is run like the true contest: standards are set competitively, students are forced to pass a series of trials each semester, and only a minority of the entrants achieve the prize of graduation. This pattern contrasts sharply with the English system in which selection is supposed to be relatively complete before entrance to university, and students may be subject to no testing whatsoever for the first year or more of university study. Although university completion rates have not been estimated accurately in either country, some figures are indicative of the contrast. In American institutions of higher learning in 1957–1958, the ratio of bachelor's and first-professional degrees to the number of

[16] Alexis de Tocqueville, *Democracy in America*, New York: Knopf, 1045, Vol. I, p. 52.
[17] Reported in the *Los Angeles Times*, December 17, 1958, Part I, p. 16.

first-time degree-credit enrollments in the fall four years earlier was reported to be .610 for men and .488 for women.[18] The indicated 39 and 51 per cent drop-out rates are probably underestimates because transfers from two-year junior colleges swell the number of degrees without being included in first-time enrollments. In England, a study of the careers of individual students reports that in University College, London, almost 82 per cent of entering students between 1948 and 1951 eventually graduated with a degree. A similar study a few years earlier at the University of Liverpool shows a comparative figure of almost 87 per cent.[19] Under contest mobility, the object is to train as many as possible in the skills necessary for elite status so as to give everyone a chance to maintain competition at the highest pitch. Under sponsored mobility, the objective is to indoctrinate elite culture in only those presumably who will enter the elite, lest there grow a dangerous number of "angry young men" who have elite skills without elite station.

Third, systems of mobility significantly affect educational content. Induction into elite culture under sponsored mobility is consistent with an emphasis on school *esprit de corps* which is employed to cultivate norms of intra-class loyalty and elite tastes and manners. Similarly, formal schooling built about highly specialized study in fields wholly of intellectual or aesthetic concern and of no "practical" value serves the purpose of elite culture. Under contest mobility in the United States, in spite of frequent faculty endorsement of "liberal education," schooling tends to be evaluated in terms of its practical benefits and to become, beyond the elementary level, chiefly vocational. Education does not so much provide what is good in itself as those skills, especially vocational skills, presumed to be necessary in the competition for the real prizes of life.

These contrasts are reflected in the different national attitudes toward university

students who are gainfully employed while in school. More students in the United States than in Britain are employed part-time, and relatively fewer of the American students receive subsidies towards subsistence and living expenses. The most generous programs of state aid in the United States, except those applying to veterans and other special groups, do not normally cover expenses other than tuition and institutional fees. British maintenance grants are designed to cover full living expenses, taking into account parental ability to pay.[20] Under sponsored mobility, gainful employment serves no apprenticeship or testing function, and is thought merely to prevent students from gaining the full benefit of their schooling. L. J. Parry speaks of the general opposition to student employment and asserts that English university authorities almost unanimously hold that ". . . if a person must work for financial reasons, he should never spend more than four weeks on such work during the whole year."[21]

Under contest mobility, success in school work is not viewed as a sufficient test of practical merit, but must be supplemented by a test in the world of practical affairs. . . . By "working his way through school" the enterprising student "earns" his education in the fullest sense, keeps in touch with the practical world, and gains an apprenticeship into vocational life. Students are often urged to seek part-time employment, even when there is no financial need, and in some instances schools include paid employment as a requirement for graduation. As one observer describes the typical American view, a student willing to work part-time is a "better bet" than "the equally bright student who receives all of his financial support from others."[22]

Finally, training in "social adjustment" is peculiar to the system of contest mobility.

[18] U.S. Department of Health, Education, and Welfare, Office of Education, *Earned Degrees Conferred by Higher Education Institutions, 1957–1958*, Washington, D.C.: Government Printing Office, 1959, p. 3.

[19] Nicholas Malleson, "Student Performance at University College, London, 1948–1951," *Universities Quarterly*, 12 (May, 1958), pp. 288–319.

[20] See, e.g., C. A. Quattlebaum, *Federal Aid to Students for Higher Education*, Washington, D.C.: Government Printing Office, 1956; and "Grants to Students: University and Training Colleges," *The Times Educational Supplement*, May 6, 1955, p. 446.

[21] "Students' Expenses," *The Times Educational Supplement*, May 6, 1955, p. 447.

[22] R. H. Eckelberry, "College Jobs for College Students," *Journal of Higher Education*, 27 (March 1956), p. 174.

The reason for this emphasis is clear when it is understood that adjustment training presumably prepares students to cope with situations for which there are no rules of intercourse or for which the rules are unknown, but in which the good opinions of others cannot be wholly ignored. Under sponsored mobility, elite recruits are inducted into a homogeneous stratum within which there is consensus regarding the rules, and within which they succeed socially by mastering these rules. Under contest mobility, the elite aspirant must relate himself both to the established elite and to the masses, who follow different rules, and the elite itself is not sufficiently homogeneous to evolve consensual rules of intercourse. Furthermore, in the contest the rules may vary according to the background of the competitor, so that each aspirant must successfully deal with persons playing the game with slightly different rules. Consequently, adjustment training is increasingly considered to be one of the important skills imparted by the school system.[23] That the emphasis on such training has had genuine popular support is indicated by a 1945 *Fortune* poll in which a national sample of adults was asked to select the one or two things that would be very important for a son of theirs to get out of college. Over 87 per cent chose "Ability to get along with and understand people;" and this answer was the second most frequently chosen as the *very* most important thing to get out of college.[24] In this respect, British education may provide better preparation for participation in an orderly and controlled world, while American education may prepare students more adequately for a less ordered situation. The reputedly superior ability of "Yankees" to get things done seems to imply such ability.

To this point the discussion has centered on the tax-supported school systems in both countries, but the different place and emphasis of the privately supported secondary schools can also be related to the distinction between sponsored and contest mobility. Since private secondary schools in both countries are principally vehicles for transmitting the marks of high family status, their mobility function is quite tangential. Under contest mobility, the private schools presumably should have little or no mobility function. On the other hand, if there is to be mobility in a sponsored system, the privately controlled school populated largely with the children of elite parents would be the ideal device through which to induct selectees from lower levels into elite status. By means of a scholarship program, promising members of lesser classes could be chosen early for recruitment. The English "public" schools, in fact, have incorporated into their charters provisions to insure that a few boys from lesser classes will enter each year. Getting one's child into a "public" school, or even into one of the less prestigeful private schools, assumes an importance in England relatively unknown in the United States. If the children cannot win scholarships the parents often make extreme financial sacrifices in order to pay the cost of this relatively exclusive education.[25]

How much of a role private secondary schools have played in mobility in either country is difficult to determine. American studies of social mobility usually omit information on private *versus* tax-supported secondary school attendance, and English studies showing the advantage of "public" school attendance generally fail to distinguish between the mobile and the nonmobile in this respect. However, during the nineteenth century the English "public" schools were used by *nouveaux riches* members of the manufacturing classes to enable their sons to achieve unqualified elite status.[26] In one sense, the rise of the manufacturing classes through free enterprise introduced a large measure of contest mobility which threatened to destroy the traditional sponsorship system. But by using the "public"

---

[23] Adjustment training is not a necessary accompaniment of contest mobility. The shift during the last half century toward the increased importance of social acceptability as an elite credential has brought such training into correspondingly greater prominence.

[24] Reported in Hadley Cantril, editor, *Public Opinion 1935–1946*, Princeton: Princeton University Press, 1951, p. 186.

[25] For one account of the place of "public" schools in the English educational system, see Dennis Brogan, *The English People*, New York: Knopf, 1943, pp. 18–56.

[26] A. H. Halsey of Birmingham University has called my attention to the importance of this fact.

schools in this fashion they bowed to the legitimacy of the traditional system—an implicit acknowledgement that upward mobility was not complete without sponsored induction. Dennis Brogan speaks of the task of the "public" schools in the nineteenth century as "the job of marrying the old English social order to the new."[27]

With respect to mobility, the parallel between the tax-supported grammar school and the "public" schools in England is of interest. The former in important respects have been patterned after the latter, adopting their view of mobility but making it a much larger part of their total function. Generally the grammar schools are the vehicle for sponsored mobility throughout the middle ranges of the class system, modeled after the pattern of the "public" schools which remain the agencies for sponsored mobility into the elite.

. . . .

CONCLUSION: SUGGESTIONS FOR RESEARCH

The foregoing discussion is broadly impressionistic and speculative, reflecting more the general impression of an observer of both countries than a systematic exploration of data. Relevant data of a variety of sorts are cited above, but their use is more illustrative than demonstrative. However, several lines of research are suggested by this tentative analysis. One of these is an exploration of different channels of mobility in both England and the United States in an attempt to discover the extent to which mobility corresponds to the mobility types. Recruitment to the Catholic priesthood, for example, probably strictly follows a sponsorship norm regardless of the dominant contest norm in the United States.

The effect of changes in the major avenues of upward mobility upon the dominant norms requires investigation. The increasing importance of promotion through corporation hierarchies and the declining importance of the entrepreneurial path of upward mobility undoubtedly compromise the ideal pattern of contest mobility. The growing insistence that higher education is a prerequisite to more and more occupations is a similar modification. Yet, there is little

[27] *Op. cit.*, pp. 24–25.

evidence of a tendency to follow the logic of sponsorship beyond the bureaucratic selection process. The prospect of a surplus of college-educated persons in relation to jobs requiring college education may tend to restore the contest situation at a higher level, and the further possibility that completion of higher education may be more determined by motivational factors than by capacity suggests that the contest pattern continues within the school.

In England, on the other hand, two developments may weaken the sponsorship system. One is positive response to popular demand to allow more children to secure the grammar school type of training, particularly by including such a program in the secondary modern schools. The other is introduction of the comprehensive secondary school, relatively uncommon at present but a major plank in the labor party's education platform. It remains to be determined whether the comprehensive school in England will take a distinctive form and serve a distinctive function, which preserves the pattern of sponsorship, or will approximate the present American system. . . .

PSYCHOLOGICAL FACTORS IN SOCIAL MOBILITY: INTELLIGENCE AND MOTIVATION

Seymour Martin Lipset and Reinhard Bendix

In the preceding chapter we have demonstrated how structural analysis may help account for varying propensities for mobility. In this chapter, however, we shall deal with those basically psychological approaches which stress the effect of variations in ability and achievement motivation.

From Seymour Martin Lipset and Reinhard Bendix, *Social Mobility in Industrial Society*, University of California Press, 1962. Reprinted by permission.

Often unable to find structural determinants of deviation from group norms, many students of social mobility have dismissed or ignored the latter type of research, which, because it deals with individual differences, is presumed to be outside their legitimate sphere of interest.

THE ROLE OF INTELLIGENCE

Intelligence, as measured by various pen-and-paper intelligence-quotient examinations, has relevance for social mobility because, as we have seen, educational achievement is the main source of occupational achievement in a bureaucratized industrial society. . . . It may be expected that educational achievement will vary with intelligence, and that continuation in the educational system will depend, therefore, upon "above average" intelligence, especially when the student has a low-status background. However, students with middle- or upper-class backgrounds frequently continue in school despite their lack of scholastic aptitude.

It has proved exceedingly difficult to go much beyond this general conclusion, because the part played by "native ability" cannot be readily differentiated from that played by various environmental factors. For example, educational achievement not only depends upon intelligence and the financial resources of the family, but also upon a strong motivation to succeed in the school system. Students who come from well-to-do families will identify quite closely with the prevailing values of the school culture, partly because of parental urging and partly because parents, students, and teachers share the same middle-class values, and such sharing facilitates teacher-student communication. Students who come from lower-class families do not possess this cultural advantage and the question is, therefore, how they may overcome this handicap, provided that they have high intelligence[1]. . . .

[1] . . . Studies of intelligence tests reveal the influence of social bias. Allison Davis reports that by changing the vocabulary of test questions while retaining the logical operations which the question is supposed to test, the class differential in performance could be markedly reduced. See his "Education for the Conservation of Human Resources," *Progressive Education*, 27 (1950):221–224.

Yet it is possible to show the general character of the interrelationship between parental social class, intelligence, and orientation towards educational achievement. Boston high school students were asked to indicate whether or not they expected to go to college, and their answers to this question were then related to their fathers' occupations and their own I.Q.'s. . . . These data suggest that, although intelligence is important, parental social status provides more motivation for high school students to attend a university.[2] Most sons of high-status families declare their intention to go to college, and thus appear motivated—even those whose intelligence is quite low. On the other hand, only 29 per cent of the sons of unskilled and semi-skilled workers and 40 per cent of skilled workers' sons who ranked in the highest fifth on the intelligence test were planning to go to college. It is rather among those whose fathers are in the middle range of the class structure that intelligence appears to be particularly important as a factor affecting the intention of going to college.

But intention is one thing, action another. When one compares parental background, motivation, and I.Q., with the actual enrollment in college, it appears that intelligence does not necessarily determine who, among those motivated to do so, will actually go to college. Data from a study of the Cleveland area indicate that parental social class is much more significant than I.Q., although the latter seems to have some slight significance. However, after adolescents get into college their educational achievement does not seem to be affected

[2] Another study of the problem is William H. Sewell, *et al.*, "Social Status and Educational and Occupational Aspiration," *American Sociological Review*, 22 (1957):67–73. They found that in Wisconsin, the educational aspirations of high school seniors whose fathers' occupations were in the lower three quintiles in occupational prestige were about the same, while the top two quintiles were more highly motivated. On the other hand, both educational aspirations and aspirations for professional positions were directly and strongly related to intelligence quotients. The considerable difference between Sewell's and Kahl's results may be due to the fact that the Wisconsin study tested high school seniors, so that many with low aspirations may have been eliminated, while the Kahl study tested students earlier in high school. . . .

by their family background. The records of different colleges show, according to the Commission on Human Resources and Advanced Training, that, "after students get to college . . . the influence of socioeconomic differences disappears almost entirely. When college entrants are classified by the occupations of their fathers the percentages getting degrees are fairly constant . . . unless [the father] be a farmer."[3]

In contemporary Britain, where a great emphasis is placed on intelligence-testing, I.Q. is a prime determinant of educational achievement, and presumably of consequent social mobility. At age 10 or 11, all students in state schools are divided into two groups: one, those who are admitted to "grammar school," which prepares students for higher-status occupations and continuation in the school system as far as the university, and the other, those who will continue in schools designed to prepare them for lesser pursuits. A recent study of admission to these various schools reports that admission to the grammar schools is so highly correlated with I.Q. that, when intelligence of students is held constant, there is no difference in the proportion admitted from the different social classes.[4] That is, the intelligent child

from a middle-class family has the same opportunity of continuing on in grammar school as an equally intelligent working-class youth. Similar findings were reported in an earlier study, which indicated "very little overlap" in intelligence level between grammar and other schools.[5] There were few students not in grammar schools who were intelligent enough to qualify for it.

This is not to suggest that the classes have equal representation in English higher education. In fact sons of manual workers accounted for only 26 per cent of English males admitted to universities in 1955–56 although manual workers made up 72 per cent of the population at large.[6] This discrepancy can be accounted for only in part by the fact that both intelligence and achievement aspirations are differentially distributed among the social strata.

. . . .

The evidence does not permit any definite conclusion about the precise effect of intelligence as a factor in social mobility, largely because of the difficulties in isolating "native intelligence" from the effects of

---

[3] Dael Wolfe, *America's Resources of Specialized Talent* (New York: Harper's, 1954), pp. 160–161.

[4] Jean Floud, *et al.*, *Social Class and Educational Opportunity* (London: Heinemann, 1956), pp. 42–61. T. H. Marshall has described in somewhat greater detail how the English educational system attempts to eliminate social class discrimination by segregating pupils on the basis of performance in intelligence tests: "Equality of opportunity is offered to all children entering the primary schools, but at an early age they are usually divided into three streams—the best, the average and the backward. Already opportunity is becoming unequal, and the children's range of chances limited. About the age of eleven they are tested again, probably by a team of teachers, examiners and psychologists. None of these is infallible, but perhaps sometimes three wrongs may make a right. Classification follows for distribution into the three types of secondary school. Opportunity becomes still more unequal, and the chance of further education has already been limited to a select few. Some of these, after being tested again, will go on to receive it. In the end the jumble of mixed seed originally put into the machine emerges in neatly labelled packets ready to be sown in the appropriate gardens.

"I have deliberately couched this description in the language of cynicism in order to bring out the point that, however genuine may be the desire

of the educational authorities to offer enough variety to satisfy all individual needs, they must, in a mass service of this kind, proceed by repeated classification into groups, and this is followed at each stage by assimilation within each group and differentiation between groups. That is precisely the way in which social classes in a fluid society have always taken shape. Differences within each class are ignored as irrelevant; differences between classes are given exaggerated significance. Thus qualities which are in reality strung out along a continuous scale are made to create a hierarchy of groups, each with its special character and status. The main features of the system are inevitable, and its advantages, in particular the elimination of inherited privilege, far outweigh its incidental defects. The latter can be attacked and kept within bounds by giving as much opportunity as possible for second thoughts about classification, both in the educational system itself and in afterlife." T. H. Marshall, *Citizenship and Social Class* (Cambridge: Cambridge University Press, 1950), pp. 66–67.

[5] H. T. Himmelweit, A. H. Halsey, and A. N. Oppenheim, "The View of Adolescents on Some Aspects of the Social Class Structure," *British Journal of Sociology*, 3 (1952): 149 n.

[6] R. K. Kelsall, *Report on an Inquiry into Applications for Admission to Universities* (London: Association of Universities of the British Commonwealth, 1957), p. 9.

social class and educational environment. There can be no doubt, however, that the discrepancy between the distribution of intelligence in a given generation of youth and the distribution of social positions in the parental generation is a major dynamic factor affecting mobility in all societies in which educational achievement or other qualities associated with intelligence play an important role in status placement. That is to say, the correlation between high family status and the intelligence level of children, although strong,[7] is still compatible with the fact that a considerable number of lower-class youth have high I.Q.'s. According to Himmelweit, "previous research has shown that, except for the extremes of the occupational ladder, variations in I.Q. *within* occupation groups are generally greater than those *between* the groups. Very large occupational groups like those to which semiskilled and unskilled manual workers belong should, therefore, contain a larger absolute number of individuals of the requisite ability than some of the numerically much smaller middle-class occupational groups, despite the higher average intelligence level to be found among the latter."[8] Whatever the distribution of intelligence by class among the youth of a country may be it remains true that considerable upward and downward mobility will result from the discrepancies involved when children of lower-class parents are

high in intelligence, and offspring of middle-class families are low.

DIFFERENTIAL MOTIVATION

Studies of the influence of social background and intelligence on social mobility must deal with two related phenomena: the structure of opportunities to which the individuals are exposed, and their capacity to take advantage of these opportunities. Capacity consists of motivation or drive as much as it consists of intelligence. In a middle-class society the "bohemian" is, among other things, a person who has the intelligence but lacks the motivation to achieve. . . .

There can be little doubt, for example, that directly urging children to achieve plays a determining role. In the Boston area, among boys from the lower middle class and the skilled working class who had I.Q.'s in the top quintile, urging by the family to get further education for the sake of occupational advancement clearly differentiated those who intended to go to college from those who did not.[9] In England the same relationship was found between parental attitude and the admission of working-class children to grammar (preuniversity) schools, with the reservation that the parents' attitudes make the difference only among those who have real opportunities,[10] that is, live in a good working-class district. (Among those sons of workers who lived in slum areas, it was found that the income level of a working-class family made more difference in gaining admission to grammar school than did parental attitudes.)

[7] A comprehensive summary of the literature and bibliography on the relation of intelligence to the variable "socioeconomic status," as well as to the variables "size of family and order of birth," is found in Jean Sutter, "La Valeur de l'intelligence suivant le milieu: état présent des connaissances," *in* Institut National d'études Démographiques, *Le Niveau intellectuel des enfants d'âge scolaire*, No. 13 (Paris: Presses Universitaires de France, 1950), pp. 41–62.

[8] H. T. Himmelweit, "Social Status and Secondary Education Since the 1944 Act: Some Data for London," *in* D. W. Glass, ed., *Social Mobility in Britain* (Routledge and Kegan Paul, 1954), p. 145 (emphasis in original). Similar conclusions have been recently presented in an analysis of a mathematical genetic model of the distribution of high intelligence. Even when high intelligence is assumed to be completely inherited and of greater frequency in the high social stratum, it will exist in greater absolute numbers in the lower orders. A. H. Halsey, "Genetics, Social Structure and Intelligence," *The British Journal of Sociology*, 9 (1958): 15–28.

[9] J. A. Kahl, "Educational and Occupationa Aspirations . . .," pp. 186–203. This has also been confirmed by Elizabeth Cohen's study of working-class boys which found that "parents of mobile sons reported more deliberate encouragement of upward mobility through educational channels, starting in the boy's childhood," and that "parents of mobile sons were more likely to have a middle-class occupational aspiration for their sons." However, a surprising finding of this research was that there were no differences between parents of mobile and nonmobile sons in their concern with their children's high school performance. Elizabeth G. Cohen, *Parental Factors in Educational Mobility* (Unpublished Ph.D. dissertation, Harvard University, 1958), pp. 136–137.

[10] Jean E. Floud, *et al.*, *Social Class . . .*, pp. 93–95, 107–108.

One would expect that the higher the education of the parents, the more likely they would be to instill motivation for upward movement in their children. This is confirmed by a number of studies. In the Boston area, approximately 40 per cent of working-class high school pupils with high I.Q.'s whose fathers graduated from high school went on to college, compared to only 25 per cent of those high-I.Q. students whose fathers had less education.[11] In Denmark, if fathers in lower strata have more education than the class mean, their sons are likely to be upwardly mobile. Similarly, in England, working-class children who reach the grammar school are likely to have parents whose education is higher than the average for their class. A report on Belgian studies states that the cultural level of lower-status families, rather than their material situation, determines the tendency toward upward mobility.[12]

One would expect further that parents who are themselves downward mobile would attempt to compensate by encouraging their children to rise. Elizabeth Cohen confirmed this relationship in her study of 100 working-class high school boys. She matched the boys by I.Q., ethnicity, and school, into two groups of 50 boys who were going to college, and 50 who were not. Of those fathers who had been downward mobile, 64 per cent had sons planning college compared to only 45 per cent of the sons of stationary fathers. Downward mobility of the mother proved to be even more highly associated with a son's mobility potential.[13] . . .

Increased amounts of stimulation for achievement may also result from especially early and long-continued association with adults and their values, rather than with other children.[14] This may help explain the findings that the most successful persons in many fields occupied sibling positions which intensified their relations with their parents and weakened those with other children. The more successful among Methodist ministers,[15] top scientists,[16] and a sample of extremely gifted children in New York,[17] were all more likely to be only children, oldest children, or children with longer than average distance between themselves and the next older child, than could be explained by chance.[18] Studies of the determinants of intelligence-test scores consistently show

---

[11] Samuel Stouffer, "First Rough Draft of Summary Report on Some Statistics Collected in the Harvard Mobility Study" (Unpublished manuscript, Harvard University, 1958).

[12] K. Svalastoga, "An Empirical Analysis of Intrasocietary Mobility Determinants" (Working Paper Nine submitted to the Fourth Working Conference on Social Stratification and Social Mobility, International Sociological Association, December, 1957); J. E. Floud, F. M. Martin, and A. H. Halsey, "Educational Opportunity and Social Selection in England," in *Transactions of the Second World Congress of Sociology*, Vol. II, pp. 194–208; Paul Minon, "Choix d'une profession et mobilité sociale," *ibid.*, pp. 209–213.

[13] Elizabeth G. Cohen, *Parental Factors in Educational Mobility*, pp. 67–70.

[14] This does not imply, of course, that the attitudes of peer groups may not in some situations stimulate mobility aspirations. The lower-class youth of "Elmtown" whose sociometric choices showed high educational expectations were much more likely to attend college. R. J. Havighurst and R. R. Rodgers, "The Role of Motivation in Attendance at Post-High-School Educational Institutions," in Byron S. Hollinshead, *Who Should Go to College?* (New York: Columbia University Press, 1952), pp. 135–165.

[15] Phillip J. Allen, "Childhood Backgrounds of Success in a Profession," *American Sociological Review*, 20 (1955): 186–190.

[16] Anne Roe, *The Making of a Scientist* (New York: Dodd-Mead, 1953), pp. 70–74; and Francis Bello, "The Young Scientists," *Fortune*, June, 1954, pp. 142–148 ff.

[17] Paul M. Sheldon, "The Families of Highly Gifted Children," *Marriage and Family Living*, 16 (1954): 59 ff.

[18] The Scottish Intelligence Survey showed that in each size of family the *first-born* and the *last-born* had higher I.Q. scores than middle-born siblings. A plausible explanation is that both the oldest child and the "baby of the family" receive disproportionate amounts of parental attention. Sir Godfrey Thomson, "Intelligence and Fertility: The Scottish 1947 Survey," *The Eugenics Review*, 41 (1950): 168. Similarly, a British study found that a working-class boy had a greater chance of entering an upper school if he were an elder or eldest child. See A. H. Halsey and L. Gardner, "Selection for Secondary Education and Achievement in Four Grammar Schools," *British Journal of Sociology*, 4 (1953): 60–75, cited in Floud, Martin, and Halsey, "Educational Opportunity . . . ," p. 208. More evidence that the middle sibling position is a handicap comes from the Harvard mobility study, which found that with occupation and size of family held constant, middle children are considerably less likely to go to college. See S. Stouffer, "First Rough Draft . . . ," p. 21.

that those from larger families do less well than children from small families.[19] Both the study of scientists and the study of gifted children show that the families of those who become exceptional have kept them isolated from other children,[20] and Robert E. L. Faris found that isolation in childhood was a very common experience of the "geniuses" he studied.[21] Available evidence also indicates that the degree of adult contact may be the most important single factor in linguistic development.[22] One might summarize the implications of these studies for social mobility by saying that all factors which intensify the involvement of a child with his parents or other adults, and reduce his involvement with other children, increase the likelihood that he will be upwardly mobile.

These findings which indicate a relationship between "isolation from contact with other children" and upward mobility tie in with the historic association between social advancement and a small family of orientation: restricted fertility has recently been discussed as a factor in the long-term process which enabled certain French bourgeois families to enter the nobility in the *ancien régime*.[23]

Modern studies of social mobility from six Western European countries—England, France, Belgium, Denmark, Sweden, and Italy—all indicate that the upwardly mobile and better-educated children from lower-status groups are likely to come from small

families.[24] Evidence from Italy and England suggests that a restricted family may be an important factor in enabling children of the upper classes to *maintain* the high position of their parents: children of large families in the upper strata are more likely to be downwardly mobile.[25]

A striking illustration of the relationship between mobility and restricted family size is found in a Swedish study. Using matriculation in secondary schools as an indicator of probable mobility, Moberg found that the educationally successful sons of craftsmen, workers, and minor officials came from smaller families and had fewer children themselves than the matriculated sons of higher-status and better-educated families: it would seem, from his study, that in order to rise, lower-class families must be even smaller than upper-strata families.[26]

It can be argued that "small family" is simply a spurious variable which "intervenes" between the motivation and education of the parents and the motivation and education of the offspring: that it is the better-educated and mobility-motivated parents from the lower strata who tend to restrict the number of their children, and that these are also the parents who motivate their children to advance and would do so whatever the size of their family. Although there is an element of truth in this, research data indicate that the size of family itself has

[19] See J. Nisbet, *Family Environment* (London: Eugenics Society, 1953), for a review of the relevant literature.

[20] Anne Roe, *The Making of a Scientist*, pp. 88–93 and Paul Sheldon, "The Families of Highly Gifted Children," pp. 59–60.

[21] R. E. L. Faris, "Sociological Causes of Genius," *American Sociological Review*, 15 (1950): 689–699.

[22] Anne Anastasi and John P. Foley, Jr., *Differential Psychology*, rev. ed. (New York: Macmillan, 1949), p. 338 f.

[23] J. G. C. Blacker, "Social Ambitions of the Bourgeoisie in 18th Century France and Their Relation to Family Limitation," *Population Studies*, 11 (1957): 46–63. In twentieth century America also, mobile entrants into the upper class have fewer children than the old-family sector of the social elite. See E. Digby Baltzell, "Social Mobility and Fertility Within an Elite Group," *The Milbank Memorial Fund Quarterly*, 31 (1953): 411–420.

[24] Floud, Martin, and Halsey, "Educational Opportunity . . ."; Marcel Bresard, "Mobilité sociale et dimension de la famille," *Population*, 5 (1950): 533–566; Alain Girard, "Mobilité sociale et dimension de la famille," *Population*, 6 (1951): 103–124; Paul Minon, "Choix d'une profession et mobilité sociale"; K. Svalastoga, "An Empirical Analysis of Intrasocietary Mobility Determinants"; Sven Moberg, "Marital Status and Family Size Among Matriculated Persons in Sweden," *Population Studies*, 4 (1950): 115–127; and Alessandro Lehner, "Mobilité sociale par rapport à la dimension de la famille," *Proceedings of the World Population Conference, 1954* (New York: United Nations, 1954), pp. 911–931.

[25] A. Lehner, "Mobilité sociale . . ." In England upper-middle-class parents have been severely limiting their family size in order to afford public school education for their sons. *Royal Commission on Population* (London: His Majesty's Stationery Office), p. 145, cited in E. Digby Baltzell, *Philadelphia Gentlemen* (Glencoe: The Free Press, 1958), p. 318,

[26] S. Moberg, "Marital status . . ."

a number of dynamic consequences which affect social mobility, and should therefore be considered as an "independent variable."

The first consequence is obvious and corresponds to the conscious, manifest intent of parents who restrict fertility. For people of limited income, the fewer the children the better they can be fed, clothed, and educated. Thus one of the French studies found that although size of family had no effect on the ability of wealthy parents to provide higher education for their children, only those in "modest" circumstances who restricted the size of their families could afford secondary education for their children.[27] Two other French studies also show an inverse relationship between size of family and length of education for children of low-status parentage, but indicate that size of family bears no relationship to continuation in school for those with a high-status background.[28] . . .

A second consequence of a small family is perhaps more unintended and latent. Interaction in the smaller family unit, by increasing the involvement of the children with adults, seems to lead to higher intelligence and greater motivation, which, in turn, means greater likelihood of educational and occupational success. In addition to the evidence for this presented earlier, the findings of two national surveys are striking. Although the Scottish Intelligence Survey found the usual associations between (1) high-status occupation and high intelligence-test scores, (2) high-status occupation and small family size, and (3) high intelligence-test scores and small family size, the finding that is significant in the present context is that *within each occupational class, the children from smaller families consistently had higher intelligence test scores.*[29]

Similarly, a French national survey found that performance on intelligence tests varies with rural-urban residence, father's occupation, and size of family. But, except for the children of professionals, there was an inverse relationship between size of family and test performance within each occupational group (residence held constant).[30]

These research findings on the relation of restricted fertility to possibilities for social advancement agree with modern population theory and research, which in recent years has given increasing consideration to the desire for upward mobility as one of the significant factors in the secular trend toward smaller family size.[31]

The recent efforts of sociologists to locate the sources of motivation towards achievement in the cultural values of different groups, and to explain which individuals secure high status by being urged toward education, hard work, proper dress, etc., have been paralleled by the work of psychologists who have sought to find in personality the sources of varying motivations to achieve. The work of David McClelland and his associates has been particularly important in this area. They have developed a number of projective and content analysis techniques that make it possible to analyze the strength of the "need for achievement." The core of this method is a coding of fictional and fantasy materials according to criteria which are measures of the extent to which the described action is interpreted by the respondent as an attempt to "achieve," either relative to some standard or to some other person.[32] Once the strength

[27] A. Girard, "Mobilité sociale . . ."
[28] M. Bresard, "Mobilité sociale . . .," p. 554, and data in table 9.4.
[29] James Maxwell, "Intelligence, Fertility and the Future: A Report on the 1947 Scottish Mental Survey," *Proceedings of the World Population Conference, 1954* (New York: United Nations, 1954), p. 738.

[30] Institut National d'études Démographiques, *Le Niveau intellectuel . . .*, pp. 187–193. Thus while the overall performance of the children of white-collar workers in a given age group is six to eight points higher than that of the children of manual workers, an "only" child from a working-class family tends to have a score equal to or a little higher than that of children from large white-collar families (three or four children).
[31] See Charles F. Westoff, "The Changing Focus of Differential Fertility Research: The Social Mobility Hypothesis," *Milbank Memorial Fund Quarterly*, 31 (1953): 24–38. John F. Kantner and Clyde V. Kiser, "The Interrelation of Fertility, Fertility Planning and Inter-Generational Social Mobility: Social and Psychological Factors Affecting Fertility," *Milbank Memorial Fund Quarterly*, 32 (1954): 76–78; Jerzy Berent, "Fertility and Social Mobility," *Population Studies*, 5 (1952): 244–260. . . .
[32] An exposition of the techniques of this method and some validating materials, along with some preliminary empirical results, are presented in David C. McClelland, *et al.*, *The Achievement Motive* (New York: Appleton-Century-Crofts, 1953).

of the motivation to achieve is measured, it may be related to such other variables as religious affiliation, family structure, child-rearing practices of various cultures, and so on.[33]

There is evidence that this achievement motive is a true personality component that stems in large part from early childhood experiences, much like the propensity to anxiety.[34] Early training for independence is related to high achievement motivation; that is, children who are weaned earlier, who are treated as independent individuals earlier, who are forced to take care of many personal functions at an early age, are much more likely to have an orientation to high achievement than those who are protected in this early period. Early training for independence is, moreover, much more characteristic of middle-class than working-class families. We would therefore expect that middle-class children would possess higher achievement motivation than working-class children and that this fairly common-sense notion could be substantiated by empirical research. This has been done by one of McClelland's associates who found that 83 per cent of New Haven high school boys from the two highest social classes scored high on an achievement scale compared to only 32 per cent of the boys from the three lowest strata.[35]

The few empirical findings which are available not only substantiate the notion that the middle class is more oriented to achievement than the lower class, but also that it is superior to the *upper class* in these traits of drive and ambition. Charles McArthur's study of the personality characteristics of upper- and middle-class men at Harvard shows that the latter are much more likely to be work oriented and to reject both strong family ties in general and in particular their father, whom they desire to surpass in status.[36] . . . Two other studies by Rosen also found that the "need achievement" scores of middle-class respondents are higher than those of the upper class though the differences in each study are very small.[37] According to McArthur these findings on achievement motivation help explain why at elite colleges such as Harvard "public school boys consistently achieve higher grades than do boys with a private school background." A number of investigations agree that "intelligence held constant, college grades showed a constant inverse relation to economic advantage." The scions of the upper class at private schools and Harvard get a "gentleman's C" and are presumably gentlemen first and achievers second in later life, while those from middle-class families are more likely to "make an A," worry about marks, take a pretechnical major, and presumably put

---

[33] M. Winterbottom, "The Sources of Achievement Motivation in Mother's Attitudes Toward Independence Training," *in* McClelland, *et al.*, *The Achievement Motive*, pp. 297–304; D. C. McClelland and G. A. Friedman, "A Cross Cultural Study of the Relationship between Child-training Practices and Achievement Motivation Appearing in Folk Tales," *in* G. Swanson, *et al.*, eds., *Readings in Social Psychology* (New York: Henry Holt, 1952), pp. 243–249; and McClelland, *et al.*, "Religious and Other Sources of Parental Attitudes Toward Independence Training," *in* McClelland, ed., *Studies in Motivation* (New York: Appleton-Century-Crofts, 1955), pp. 389–397.

[34] Havighurst found that upwardly mobile persons do not find relaxation in leisure-time pursuits but "play" in much the same striving, energetic manner in which they approach work and other areas of life. Robert J. Havighurst, "The Leisure Activities of the Middle-Aged," *American Journal of Sociology*, 63 (1957): 158.

[35] Bernard C. Rosen, "The Achievement Syndrome: A Psychocultural Dimension of Social Stratification," *American Sociological Review*, 21 (1956): 206. The most comprehensive summary

of the results of the many psychological studies of socialization during the past twenty-five years concludes: "Though more tolerant of expressed impulses and desires, the middle class parent . . . has higher expectations for the child. The middle class youngster is expected to learn to take care of himself earlier, to accept more responsibilities about the home, and—above all—to progress further in school." Urie Bronfenbrenner, "Socialization and Social Class Through Time and Space," *in* E. E. Maccoby, *et al.*, eds., *Readings in Social Psychology* (New York: Henry Holt, 1958), p. 424.

[36] Charles McArthur, "Personality Differences Between Middle and Upper Classes," *The Journal of Abnormal and Social Psychology*, 50 (1955): 247–258.

[37] B. Rosen, "The Achievement Syndrome . . ." p. 206; and David C. McClelland, "Community Development and the Nature of Human Motivation; Some Implications of Recent Research," (Unpublished manuscript, 1957), table 1.

achievement first after leaving Harvard.[38] Perhaps this superiority in achievement and drive of a rising middle class over established elites is endemic in stratified societies which are economically progressive. In his analysis of the repeated rise of "new men" into the leading positions in the economy from the Middle Ages down to the nineteenth century, Henri Pirenne has pointed to the fact that descendants of the new rich always lose interest in achievement, and ultimately "withdraw from the struggle. . . . In their place arise new men, courageous and enterprising."[39] Thus class differences in personality must be considered a factor in the perennial "circulation of the elites."

Unfortunately, granted the exciting implications for social analysis suggested by the work of these psychologists, they have not yet provided us with actual evidence that high achievement motivation is actually related to occupational success.

There is no evidence that motivation (of the sort measured by the techniques mentioned above) results in higher occupational achievement among those with equal opportunity. We do not know whether those who have achieved the transition from a working-class background into the middle class have stronger motivations than those who only maintain the positions of their families. We also do not know whether motivation for achievement which cannot be fulfilled by a high-status occupation can be easily satisfied, for example, by athletic achievement, or by doing a good job at a lower level.

However there is evidence that achievement *motivation* is related to concrete achievement *behavior* among students. Rosen in his study of New Haven high school boys found that within both upper and lower social strata, boys with high achievement motivation scores received

high grades and boys with low achievement scores received low grades.[40] . . .

The process of social mobility requires, beyond the motivation to achieve, the capacity to leave behind an early environment and to adapt to a new one.[41] This capacity to form social relationships at a higher level and to give up those at a lower level is probably related to personality. Thus, the socially mobile among business leaders show an unusual capacity to break away from those who are liabilities and form relationships with those who can help them.[42] The childhood experiences of lower-status men who later become business leaders often show a pattern of strong mothers and weak fathers, and an emotionally unsatisfying

[38] Charles McArthur, "Personalities of Public and Private School Boys," *Harvard Educational Review*, 24 (1954): 256–261; quote about intelligence is taken by McArthur from A. B. Crawford, *Incentives to Study* (New Haven: Yale University Press, 1929).

[39] Henri Pirenne, "Stages in the Social History of Capitalism," *in* R. Bendix and S. M. Lipset, eds., *Class, Status and Power* (Glencoe: The Free Press, 1953), p. 502. The entire article is pertinent.

[40] Bernard C. Rosen, "The Achievement Syndrome . . .," p. 210. The most recent knowledge available on how achievement motivation is related to differential behavior has been summarized by McClelland: "The 'highs' work harder at laboratory tasks, learn faster, do somewhat better school work in high school even with IQ partialled out, and seem to do their best work when it counts for their record and not when other special incentives are introduced such as pressure from the outside to do well, money prizes, or time off from work. They are more resistant to social pressure, choose experts over friends as work partners, and tend to be more active in college or community activities, like risky occupations, perform better under longer odds, and choose moderate risks over either safe or speculative ones." David C. McClelland, "Community Development . . .," pp. 4–5. This paper contains the references which document each of the above listed findings. See also David C. McClelland, *et al., Talent and Society* (Princeton: Van Nostrand, 1958).

[41] See W. Lloyd Warner and James C. Abegglen, *Big Business Leaders in America* (New York: Harper, 1955), pp. 59–64; W. Foote Whyte, *Street Corner Society*, pp. 94–108; and Peter M. Blau, "Social Mobility and Interpersonal Relations," *American Sociological Review*, 21 (1956): 290–295.

[42] A study which contrasted the socialization patterns in Jewish- and Italian-American families found that certain beliefs, values, and personality traits conducive to high achievement and upward mobility were inculcated in Jewish, but not in Italian families. These included: "a belief that the world is orderly and amenable to rational mastery, and that therefore, a person can and should make plans which will control his destiny; . . . a willingness to leave home to make one's way in life; . . . and a preference for individualistic rather than collective credit for work done." Fred L. Strodtbeck, "Family Interaction, Values, and Achievement," *in* Marshall Sklare, ed., *The Jews: Social Patterns of an American Group* (Glencoe: The Free Press, 1958), pp. 162–163.

family life.[43] If it is assumed that a situation in which the mother has higher social status than the father is likely to result in this pattern of intrafamily relations, then families in which the mother had a higher occupational status than the father before marriage should result in higher social mobility. Two interesting British studies support this hypothesis. The study cited above . . . found that "the mothers of successful [in getting into the highly selective grammar school at the age of 10–11] working class children moreover had frequently followed an occupation 'superior' to that of their husbands."[44] A second study reports that working-class parents are more likely to prefer grammr school education for their children when the mother's occupation, before marriage to a manual worker, was nonmanual rather than manual.[45] A similar pattern has been observed in America by Allison Davis, who writes that "many parents who push children toward social mobility are members of mixed-class marriages. . . . A lower-middle class woman who marries a man from the upper part of the working class usually begins to try and recoup her original social class status either by reforming and elevating her husband's behavior to meet lower-middle class standards or by seeking to train and propel her children toward the status she once had."[46]

The characteristic family experiences in childhood of the upward mobile and his typical personality structure remain still a relatively unexplored area. The contrast among the findings of the studies on these subjects is striking. Douvan and Adelson, who investigated the occupational aspira-

tions of 1,000 high school boys, found that those whose aspirations were upward tended to come from warm, permissive family *milieux* which encouraged the development of achievement and autonomy and of realistic attitudes toward parents and the self. The upward-aspiring boys were more likely to share leisure activities with parents than the boys without higher aspirations.[47] On the other hand, a number of studies of which the one of business leaders by Warner and Abegglen is the most comprehensive, found that the upwardly mobile tended to be escaping from an impoverished home pervaded by a "spiritually bleak and physically depressed family atmosphere," in which quite often the father was an inadequate and unreliable figure. Although these men also show strong traits of independence, they are characterized by an inability to form intimate relations and are consequently often socially isolated men.[48]

Warner and Abegglen's negative picture of family environment and personality structure is supported by a number of more limited studies. . . .

Mental illness rates would seem to provide additional data for the notion that the upwardly mobile tend to be deprived psychodynamically. People who are upward mobile, but *not* those who are downward mobile or geographically mobile, have higher rates of mental disorder than those who are stationary.[49] This suggests that it is not the anomic situation associated with mobility that is responsible for the greater vulnerability, because one would expect downward mobility to be at least as threatening to psychic equilibrium as upward mobility. It is therefore probable that a particular type of ego structure which results from a characteristic family environment is both favorable for upward mobility

[43] Warner and Abegglen, *Big Business Leaders* . . . , pp. 64–107.

[44] Floud, *et al.*, *Social Class* . . .

[45] F. M. Martin, "An Inquiry into Parents' Preferences in Secondary Education," *in* D. V. Glass, ed., *Social Mobility in Britain*, p. 169.

[46] Allison Davis, "Personality and Social Mobility," *The School Review*, 65 (1957): 137. American data which give empirical support to this hypothesis are provided by Cohen, who found that 80 per cent of the boys whose fathers were manual workers, but whose mothers had white-collar family backgrounds were going to college, compared to only 42 per cent of those working-class boys whose mother's background too was working class. E. G. Cohen, *Parental Factors in Educational Mobility*, p. 70.

[47] Elizabeth Douvan and Joseph Adelson, "The Psychodynamics of Social Mobility in Adolescent Boys," *The Journal of Abnormal and Social Psychology*, 56 (1958): 31–44.

[48] Warner and Abegglen, *Big Business Leaders* . . . , pp. 59–83.

[49] A. B. Hollingshead, R. Ellis, and E. Kirby, "Social Mobility and Mental Illness," *American Sociological Review*, 19 (1954): 577–584 and A. B. Hollingshead and F. C. Redlich, "Schizophrenia and Social Structure," *American Journal of Psychiatry*, 110 (1954): 695–701.

and vulnerable to mental illness.[50] The various researches in this area all suggest that the downward mobile have been over-protected and loved as young children, and hence are perhaps better able to cope with stress. They also have much less of a need for achievement and therefore should feel less frustrated by failure.

It seems quite likely that the personality determinants and consequences of upward mobility would differ according to the extent and character of the mobility process. Perhaps it is *extreme mobility*, especially mobility into and within elites such as the professions and the higher positions in business, that attracts personality configurations which are a result of childhood deprivation.

. . . .

These studies suggest that upward mobility selects people who are distinctive in psychodynamic terms. They also indicate that a crucial variable in the motivation for social mobility is the structure of the family, perhaps independently of direct urging toward social mobility.

The relations between motivation for achievement deriving from personality structure and motivation deriving directly from the social structure remain to be investigated, but recent explorations in psychology constitute the most promising line of research yet developed to supplement the sociological analysis of the relation of mobility to structural factors such as class or ethnic background. Such studies may enable us to specify how different positions in the social structure may affect family behavior, and child-rearing practices in particular.

. . . .

On a theoretical level, perhaps the most

interesting effort to bridge the gap between psychological and sociological research may be found in the "reference-group theory," particularly as it has been systematized by Robert K. Merton and Alice S. Rossi.[51] . . . To use a group as a normative reference group, on the other hand, is to take over its norms, to emulate its members. . . . Reference-group theory suggests that the potentially upward mobile usually reveal *anticipatory socialization,* that is, they absorb the norms and behavior traits of higher strata long before they have actually changed their social position. As Merton and Rossi have put it, such people "conform" to the norms of groups of which they are not yet members, thus becoming "nonconformists" within their group of origin.

It should be noted, however, that although conformity to the standards of a group with higher status undoubtedly facilitates upward mobility, such conformity is not always a product of an orientation toward the higher-status group as a reference group, a possibility that is ignored in much of the writing on reference-group theory and mobility. Thus, lower-class individuals who exhibit good work habits, cleanliness, concern for personal appearance, and generally follow the established rules of "middle-class morality" are much more likely to move up in the social structure than those who reject these norms. The motivation to behave in this fashion may, however, have little or nothing to do with having a middle-class reference group, but may, for example, have developed out of the inner dynamics of a religious belief. Thus, ascetic sects which have arisen among the lower classes in various Protestant countries often insist that their members conform strictly to Christian principles, which, from another perspective means conformity to middle-class standards. Similarly, the upward mobility of Japanese-Americans has been explained in terms of a "significant compatibility . . . between the value systems

---

[50] Some of the case-study materials on the adjustment of families to the Depression suggest that those families whose members were motivated to be socially mobile were more rigid in their response than were families less concerned with economic success. See Ruth S. Cavan and Catherine H. Ranck, *The Family and the Depression* (Chicago: University of Chicago Press, 1938), p. 90; Mirra Komarovsky, *The Unemployed Man and His Family* (New York: Dryden Press, 1940), pp. 78–83, 116–122: and Robert Angell, *The Family Meets the Depression* (New York: Scribners, 1936), pp. 17–18, 192–193.

[51] See esp. Robert K. Merton and Alice S. Rossi, "Contributions to the Theory of Reference Group Behavior," in R. K. Merton, *Social Theory and Social Structure,* rev. ed. (Glencoe: The Free Press, 1957), pp. 225–280, and R. K. Merton, "Continuities in the Theory of Reference Groups and Social Structure," *ibid.,* pp. 281–386.

found in the culture of Japan and the value systems found in American middle class culture" rather than in terms of a conscious orientation of lower-status Japanese-Americans to the middle class as a reference group.[52] The study of anticipatory socialization should, therefore, always try to differentiate between that behavior which is manifestly anticipatory and that which is directed towards a different goal, even

[52] W. Caudill and G. DeVos, "Achievement, Culture, and Personality . . .," p. 1107.

though both may serve the same function—that of preparing individuals to succeed in new roles.

Both reference-group theory and the data on role conformity, anticipatory socialization, and reference-group behavior suggest that by merging the sociological and psychological approaches to the study of social mobility we may be able to advance the study of the mechanisms by which individuals and groups reach their positions in the stratification structure.

PART VI
Ethnicity, Race, and Class

Ethnicity and class constitute two major and connected features of a number of contemporary societies. It is therefore important to know the relationship between them. But as yet no over-all sociological theory has been formulated to explain the connection between them in general. What we do have is a series of recent studies about ethnicity and class in given societies. And these show that the relationship is complex and varies sharply from continent to continent and society to society.

We are using the term *ethnic* group in its *broad* meaning of any group of people defined by or singled out because of race, religion, national origin, or a combination of these. Our first reading, however, is primarily concerned with one kind of ethnic differentiation—the racial one—and its relevance to class in Latin America. It will serve as a frame of comparison for the subsequent readings on race and class in the United States.

Despite certain common historical experiences—of European expansion, colonization, and *slavery*—the relationship between race and class in Latin America is fundamentally different from that in the United States, as is made explicit by Julian Pitt-Rivers in his "Race, Color, and Class in Central America and the Andes." It could be said that in Latin America class is a more important determinant of social position than race. Given, for instance, two people with the same racial characteristics, one might be considered white and the other colored, depending on the class to which they belong. In contrast to the United States, with its color bar dividing people into two categories, white and Negro, "color" in Latin America is a matter of degree and class. Class differences are often referred to in Latin America in idioms of race. The reason is the historical association between class and race there. The upper classes were white, the lower Negro or Indian. But the point is that individuals with Negroid or Indian physical features are found in the upper classes. Their standing is secured by other criteria of class, which outweigh the criterion of race. Color in Latin America, in the words of the author, "is an ingredient, not a determinant of class," and can be therefore traded for other ingredients, such as money or power. It is quite common to trade these things in marriage so that an impoverished white person will marry a rich person with Negroid or Indian features.

Pitt-Rivers suggests that the phenotypical association of class (correlation between class and physical appearance) is increasing rather than diminishing in Latin America.[1] He ties this to recent demographic trends. On the one hand, the rural migration to cities means the absorption of people with Indian features into the urban lower classes. On the other, European immigrants are being absorbed into the upper classes. In contrast to the local community where everyone knows everyone's standing and background, color is gaining as a symbolic indicator of status in the big impersonal cities while clothing, speech, and manners are losing ground.

Color in both rural and urban areas of the United States has traditionally been the symbol of caste, not class. Although Negroes belong to different classes, whites react to them more in terms of race than in terms of class membership. But before proceeding to discuss the readings on race and class in the United States, we shall place them in the perspective of the general orientation of sociological studies in this field.

In casually surveying the theoretical discussions and empirical studies that touch on the relationship between class and ethnicity in the United States, one arrives at the conclusion that they center around the following three related questions: (1) What is the relationship between membership in a given ethnic group and the position in the total system of social stratification? (2) What is the class distribution of a given ethnic group and how does it compare with that of the majority population? (3) When the behavior of a given ethnic group differs from that of the majority, to what extent are these differences the result of the differential class distribution of the ethnic group as compared with the majority population?

A concept that connects these questions and may connect our selections is that of *ethclass,* formulated by Milton Gordon.[2] The term refers to the *subsociety* created by the *intersection* of ethnic group and class. By specifying that the ethclass is a subsociety, he gives notice that it is a "... functioning unity which has an integrated impact on the participating individual." Thus, he cites such examples of ethclasses as upper-middle-class white Protestant or lower-middle-class Irish or upper-lower-class Negro. In these ethclasses people tend to concentrate their primary social relationships. As Gordon expresses it, with a person of the same social class but of a different ethnic group "one shares behavioral similarities but not a sense of peoplehood." With those of the same ethnic group but of different social class, one shares the sense of peoplehood but not behavioral similarities. "The only group which meets both of these criteria are people of the same ethnic group *and* same social class."[3] In this last group one feels at home, one interacts with ease. This concrete structure of the ethclass is then the result of the combination of two factors, class and ethnicity, which analytically can be and often are separated, as we shall see in the forthcoming readings.

The consistent note that emerges from studies dealing with race and class in the United States is that the greatest differences in behavior between the races are found in the lower classes. Much discussion, for example, revolves around the

[1] For a systematic exploration and statistical treatment of the association between class and phenotype in the West Indies, see M. G. Smith, *Stratification in Grenada,* Berkeley: University of California Press, 1965, pp. 158–174. On class and ethnicity in Mexico, see: Rodolfo Stavenhagen, "Classes, Colonialism, and Acculturation," in Joseph A. Kahl, ed., *Comparative Perspectives on Stratification,* Boston: Little, Brown and Company, 1968, pp. 31–63.

[2] Milton M. Gordon, *Assimilation in American Life,* New York: Oxford University Press, 1964, pp. 46–54.

[3] *Ibid.,* p. 53.

great instability of the lower-class Negro family. The frequent explanation is the historically based matriarchal tradition that exists in the Negro family.[4] But, as G. Franklin Edwards points out convincingly in the reprinted article "The Negro American—Community and Class Realities: The Ordeal of Change," the instability of the Negro family is only partly explained by the tradition (dating back to slavery) under which the father-child ties of Negroes were not honored. Its continuation is tied to today's socioeconomic conditions, which limit the possibility of the standard American family form replacing the matrifocal one so prominent among Negroes, who are still overwhelmingly lower class. And the same factors are operating here to which Gunnar Myrdal pointed as the causes of social disorganization in the underclass: the unemployment and underemployment of Negro males.[5] Edwards points out the important study by Hylan Lewis that presents evidence of the Negro male's concern about his responsibility to the family. One concludes from this study that, in the words of Edwards, the behavior of these absent fathers "is a practical response to untoward circumstances which undermine the well intentioned, but often unattainable goals" of fulfilling family responsibilities. Similarly, many other differences in the behavior patterns of lower-class Negroes and whites are not only the legacy of slavery but also the fruit of discrimination.

Another consistency in the sociological studies of race and class in the United States are the findings concerning the similarity between the patterns of behavior of the Negro middle class and the white middle class. However, the Negro middle class is proportionally very much smaller than the white middle class. This, Edwards shows, is tied to the fact that social mobility among Negroes until recently was primarily determined by the needs of the Negro community rather than the general conditions in the country. Thus Negro professionals were largely professionals serving Negroes, Negro businessmen largely selling to Negroes, and so on.

Subsequently this type of mobility has been analyzed as a "mobility trap" by Norbert F. Wiley. This concept refers to the structural condition in which the means for moving up within the ethnic group are contrary to those for moving up within the dominant social structure. There are certain opportunities for mobility within the ethnic group (as exemplified by the preceding discussion of Negro businessmen). However, they may constitute mobility traps as far as mobility within the dominant social structure is concerned. The underlying metaphor in this formulation is that of climbing a tree rather than that of climbing a ladder, the metaphor so widely employed in mobility studies. Thus a person who has moved up within a given ethnic group may be visualized as on top of an isolated limb. If he wants to move up in the dominant structure (climb the trunk), he faces the problem of how to get off the limb. And the possibility of accomplishing this varies with ethnic group. As the author puts it, for Negroes it is almost impossible and, one could add, for Mexican Americans it is quite difficult.[6]

[4] For example, Richard Bloom, Martin Whiteman, and Martin Deutsch, "Race and Social Class as Separate Factors Related to Social Environment," *American Journal of Sociology*, January, 1965, p. 472.

[5] For the effects of unemployment on family stability, see the studies of the depression: Bohdan Zawadzki and P. F. Lazarsfeld, "The Psychological Consequences of Unemployment," *Journal of Social Psychology*, Vol. VI, 1935, pp. 225–251, and Marie Lazarsfeld Jahoda and Hans Zeisel, *Die Arbeitslosen von Marienthal*, Leipzig: Verlag von S. Hirzel, 1933. See also E. W. Bakke, *The Unemployed Man*, New York: E. P. Dutton & Co., 1934; and E. W. Bakke, ed., *The Unemployed Worker*, New Haven: Yale University Press, 1940.

[6] Norbert F. Wiley, "The Ethnic Mobility Trap and Stratification Theory," *Social Problems*, Vol. 15, Fall, 1967, pp. 147–159.

One must point out that the smallness of the Negro middle class, contrary to prejudiced views, cannot be explained in terms of lack of ambition. [7] The high educational aspirations of Negroes deserve special attention because, as we recall from the preceding part of our book, education proves to be less profitable for them than for whites. The same amount of education yields considerably less return in the form of occupational status or income to Negroes than to whites. (See pp. 340–352 in this volume).

If indeed the situation is that suggested from the Bloom, Whiteman, and Deutsch study, that mobility aspirations of Negroes do not vary substantially with class, then they are now displaying a characteristic present in those ethnic groups that have advanced fairly rapidly, notably the Jews. The chief obstacle then for Negroes, as far as taking advantage of existing opportunities for advancement is concerned, is not lack of ambition but the problem of inadequate education, as is described by Edwards.

In contrast to the ethnic groups that have advanced rapidly, Celia S. Heller argues, those that have shown small intergenerational advancement display substantial class variation in characteristics conducive to mobility, such as in stress on education, in IQ scores, or in occupational aspirations. The group she concentrates on is America's "forgotten" minority, its third largest: the Mexican Americans. [8] The latest analyzed data show that of all sizable "cultural" minorities (national origin) in the United States, this is the only one that fails to show a substantial intergenerational rise in socioeconomic status. The author explains that the traditional values of this ethnic group, which do not vary with class—honor, respect, family obligation, manliness—are not conducive to early stages of upward mobility. And those qualities that foster upward mobility, such as stress on mental effort and education, differ inversely with social class among the Mexican Americans.

Our last selection by E. Digby Baltzell deals with members of an ethnic group who positionally have succeeded in climbing the trunk to the very top but who, to continue with Wiley's terminology, suffer from reputational inconsistency. It also can be related to the Heller article, for if her essay deals with the problems of ethnic groups in the early stage of advancement (from working-class to middle-class position), the focus of Baltzell's study is on the last stage: members of an ethnic group being allowed to move into the national upper prestige stratum, which is actually nothing but an ethclass—white Protestant—to use Gordon's concept.

The latter problems by and large are those of third-generation and the former of second-generation Americans. But as we gather from the Heller article, third-generation Mexican Americans are showing the manifestations that other ethnic groups displayed in the second generation. Also the Negroes, who are among the oldest American groups, are facing many of the problems that other ethnic groups were confronted with in the second generation.

The key concepts in our reprinted pages from E. Digby Baltzell's "The Protestant

[7] Bloom, Whiteman, and Deutsch, *op. cit.*, pp. 471–476. Also, James S. Coleman, ed., *Equality of Educational Opportunity*, Washington, D.C.: U.S. Government Printing Office, 1966, pp. 278–281. For other evidence showing that the achievement values and educational aspirations of Negroes are high, being comparable to those of Jews, Greeks, and white Protestants, and higher than those of other ethnic groups, such as Italians, see Bernard C. Rosen, "Race, Ethnicity, and the Achievement Syndrome," *American Sociological Review*, Vol. 24, February, 1959, pp. 47–60.

[8] For a brief account of the history and geographic distribution of this minority, see Celia S. Heller, *Mexican American Youth: Forgotten Youth at the Crossroads*, Random House, 1966, pp. 3–21.

Establishment—Aristocracy and Caste in America," as well as in the book as a whole, are the three named in the title plus *elite* and *upper class* (Baltzell does not make use of the term *ethclass*, and in contrast to Gordon, he, like Heller, employs the term *ethnic* in the narrow sense of national origin). He alternately refers to the elite as individuals in top *functional* positions or individuals at the top of the power hierarchy. The upper class in his usage is the group of families at the top of the social-status hierarchy, analogous to Warner's upper-upper. By *establishment* he means the leaders within the elite. Baltzell tells us that during the first decades of our century the *WASP* upper class was in control of the elite. But since then some families from more recent ethnic groups have reached top economic and political positions. In the elite, says Baltzell, class replaces religion, national origin, and even race as the independent variable in social relationships. But here Baltzell seems to use class in a different sense than is usual in his work. Perhaps one could get a better sense of what he means by restating that in the elite *eliteship* replaces *ethnicity* as the important independent variable in primary relationships. The elite reside near one another, marry one another, and so forth, irrespective of national or religious origin. To use Milton Gordon's terminology, the *participational identification* of those people is not the ethclass but the elite. Now, the picture we get from Baltzell's description is that the WASP members of the elite are within the class system, being members of the upper class, but the others are marginal, outside the class system. The latter have either left or never belonged to the ethclass for which they qualify—Jewish upper class, Irish upper class, and so on. But the door is closed to the nationwide upper class that clings to the tradition of being "an Anglo Saxon caste." The author maintains that the WASP establishment has been forced to share its power, but it continues to hoard its social prestige. He sees two opposite tendencies at work in the WASP establishment and WASP upper class: one is toward closure, which he terms *caste*; and the other toward openness to the most prominent and polished families of the nation, regardless of ethnic origin, which he designates as a tendency toward *aristocracy*.

The policies of country club admission committees, Baltzell tells us, are one of the main ways of maintaining the upper class as a caste. And he seems to plead with these clubs to assume "the aristocratic role as leaders of assimilating association" and for the upper class "to regenerate its original ideals of equality of opportunity." Of course, equality of opportunity means something else here than equality of opportunity for the Mexican Americans and Negroes in the initial stage of ethnic mobility. For the latter it means equal opportunity for an education and a job, for the former it is the opportunity to join a WASP country club. Digby Baltzell presents the theme of the American Dilemma in the upper-class key. Although interesting sociologically, it is rather trivial and hardly as moving as the same theme in the lower-class key, except to the top climbers themselves.

RACE, COLOR, AND CLASS IN CENTRAL AMERICA AND THE ANDES

Julian Pitt-Rivers

Among its many *fiestas,* the Hispanic world celebrates one with the name of "El día de la raza" (which is what is called Columbus Day in the United States). Why it should be so called remains something of an enigma. . . .

Quite apart from the mysteries surrounding The Day of the Race, the concept of *race* itself is unclear in Latin America. My concern here is not with what anthropologists mean by *race,* but only with what the people of Latin America think the word means when they encounter it in their daily speech. By minimal definition, it refers to a group of people who are felt to be somehow similar in their essential nature. . . .

The word *race* is, of course, also used to mark differences of ethnic identity within the nation. Sometimes awareness of any implication of heredity is so slight that a man can think of himself as belonging to a race different from that of his parents. The word clearly owes little to physical anthropology but refers, however it may be defined, to the ways in which people are classified in daily life. What are called race relations are, in fact, always questions of social structure.

. . . .

A study that straddles the frontiers of established disciplines requires consideration from . . . varied viewpoints. It must above all achieve a synthesis of the cultural and the social aspects. . . . The preliminary condition of such an enterprise is a clear description of the systems of ethnic classi-

From *Daedalus,* "Race, Color, and Class in Central America and the Andes," by Julian Pitt-Rivers, Spring, 1967. Reprinted by permission of the author, the publisher, and the American Academy of Arts and Sciences.

fication at the local level and a recognition of their social significance. Charles Wagley was making this point when he coined the phrase "social race."[1] He went on to point to the importance of knowing how the terminology varies, for this matter is filled with confusion. Not only do the words used vary from area to area and from class to class, but the conceptions to which they correspond also change, and the criteria on which the system of classification is based vary in relevance. It is difficult to say what is an Indian,[2] but it is scarcely easier to say what is a Negro.

Terminological inconsistencies complicate from the outset discussion of race relations in Latin America. Indeed, there is not even agreement as to whether or not a "problem" of race relations exists in Latin America. The nationals of these countries often deny the existence of racial discrimination. They claim from this fact a virtue that makes them, despite their supposed economic and technological underdevelopment, the moral superiors of their northern neighbor, whose "inhumanity" toward colored people they deplore. Moreover, this opinion is held not only by Latin Americans themselves, but by outside observers, the most eminent of whom is Professor Arnold Toynbee, who speaks of the Latin American's freedom from race prejudice.[3]

This point of view, in many cases a way of expressing criticism of the United States,

---

[1] Charles Wagley, "On the Concept of Social Race in the Americas," *Actas del 33 Congreso Internacional de Americanistas* (San José, 1959). Reprinted in Dwight B. Heath and Richard N. Adams, eds., *Contemporary Cultures and Societies of Latin America* (New York, 1965).

[2] Woodrow Borah, "Race and Class in Mexico," *Pacific Historical Review,* Vol. 23, No. 4 (November, 1954); Julian Pitt-Rivers, "Who Are the Indians," *Encounter* (September, 1965).

[3] "In Latin America happily this racial distinction is not important and this is very much to Latin America's credit." Arnold Toynbee, *The Economy of the Western Hemisphere* (Oxford, 1962), p. 4. "Here is a country [Mexico] whose population is racially diversified yet is socially and culturally united. . . . I can only hope that the Latin American and Islamic freedom from race prejudice is the 'wave of the future.'" Arnold Toynbee, "The Racial Solution," *Encounter* (September, 1965), p. 31.

is also held by many patriotic American citizens, including especially some who are "colored" and whose testimony, if first-hand, might be thought to suffice.[4] Nevertheless, it is not by any means held universally and is sometimes regarded as a myth. Certain critics, both national and foreign, maintain that race is as important in Latin as in North America, once it is admitted that in addition to differences in the form discrimination takes, there is a major difference: The race that is penalized is the Indian rather than the Negro. Neither of these points of view appears correct.[5] Both are confused as to the nature of the question. Yet by examining the observations upon which they are based and how they have come to hold sway, one can understand better the role ethnic distinctiveness plays in ordering the society of Latin America.

"Segregation" as it is found in the United States does not exist in Latin America. "Color" in the North American sense is not the basis of a classification into two statuses to which differential rights attach. Segregated schools, public facilities, transport, or restaurants do not exist in Latin America. The Negro is not formally distinguished at any point. While many institutions are devoted specifically to the Indians, the definition of Indian in this regard is not based on physical criteria. Moreover, neither color nor phenotype has sufficed in the past to debar men from prominence in the national life, as the long list of Negroid or Indian-looking men of eminence in Latin American history shows.[6]

Intermarriage is not regarded with horror. Among the upper classes and in many places among the population generally, it

is, however, considered denigrating to marry someone much darker than oneself. This is so, for example, in Barranquilla, Colombia, where the greater part of the population is more or less Negroid. The idea of physical contact with darker races is nowhere considered shocking, nor is it regarded as polluting by the whites. Dark-skinned people are thought to be more sensual and therefore more desirable sexually. This is not the expression of a neurotic fear of sexual insufficiency but an accepted and openly stated commonplace. Pale-skinned people of both sexes are thought to be more frigid and proud, and less warmhearted. Mistresses tend, consequently, to be more swarthy than wives, whose pale skin indicates social superiority.

The immense majority of the population from Mexico to Bolivia are well aware of their mixed ancestry. "A touch of the tarbrush" can, therefore, never mean total social disqualification. "We are all halfcastes," Mexicans commonly remark, pointing to their forearm to show the color of their skin. Still, they sometimes go on to stress that only a small percentage of their blood is Indian. National unity demands that to be truly Mexican they must have some Indian blood, but social aspirations require that they should not have too much. Color is a matter of degree, not the basis of a division into black and white.

In consequence, physical characteristics cannot be said to be socially insignificant; their significance is only different. Physical traits never account for more than part of the image that individuals present. These images are perceived in terms of what they can be contrasted with; there is no color problem where the population is homogeneous in color, whatever that color may be. Social distinctions must then be made according to other criteria. From one place to another, in greater or lesser degree, physical traits are qualified by cultural and economic indicators in order to produce that total image which accords a social identity. . . .

In Barranquilla, Colombia, color is qualified by other social factors, and the term *Negro* confined to the slum-dwellers of the city. In the modern housing developments where no one is to be seen who would not

[4] For example. Robert S. Browne, *Race Relations in International Affairs* (Washington, 1961), p. 22: "South and Central America have in some places developed veritable interracial societies." The qualification is vital.

[5] Juan Comas reviews some of the more scholarly versions of the two views in "Relaciones inter-raciales en America Latina, 1940–60," *Cuadernos del Instituto de Historia, serie antropologica*, No. 12 (Mexico, 1961).

[6] Paez, Morelos, and Alamán looked Negroid; Porfirio, Díaz, Juarez, and Melgarejo looked Indian. This can be verified from contemporary evidence. In modern popular literature and schoolbooks they are sometimes quite literally "whitewashed."

qualify as a Negro in the United States, one may be told: "Only white people live here." The definition of *Negro* varies from place to place and, of course, from class to class. A man may be defined as Negro in one place, but simply as *moreno, trigueño, canela,* or even white in another. A man who would be considered Negro in the United States might, by traveling to Mexico, become *moreno* or *prieto,* then *canela* or *trigueño* in Panamá, and end up in Barranquilla white. The definition of *Indian* presents a comparable problem once the word no longer refers to a member of an Indian community. Different places and classes use different criteria.

Skin color is merely one of the indices among physical traits that contribute to a person's total image. It is not necessarily more significant than hair type or shape of eye. The relative evaluation of different physical traits varies. . . .

The system of classification makes what it will of the objective reality of the phenotype. The forces of the social structure utilize the raw material of phenotypical distinctions, building out of it the social statuses into which people are classified.

It has sometimes been said that the difference between Anglo and Latin America is that in the former anyone who has a drop of Negro blood is a Negro, whereas in the latter anyone who has white blood is a white.[7] The first statement is approximately true, but the second is emphatically not so. The concept of "blood" is fundamentally different in the two and has, in the past, varied from one century to another.

In Latin America, a person with non-white physical traits may be classed as white socially. A trace of European physique is, however, quite insufficient in itself to class a person as white. Although Indians with pale skin and European traits or gray hair may be found sporadically throughout Latin America, they are considered to be no less Indian on this account. In any market in the Andes one or two can usually be seen, and the *indio gringo* "(fair-skinned" or "blond" Indian) is a recognized type in parts of northern Peru. There is nothing anomalous in this description. "Indian" is

[7] See. for example, Albert Sireau, *Terre d'angoisse et d'espérance* (Paris, 1959), p. 22.

not, in the first place, a physical type but a social status. The Indian is distinguished not by genetic inheritance but by birth in, and therefore membership of, an Indian community and by possession of that community's culture. This is all that is needed for the definition of an Indian, though Indians normally look "Indian." The word *Indian* has, therefore, come to mean "of Indian descent"; it is used of persons who no longer occupy Indian status, but whose physical resemblance to the Indians implies descent from them. Since Indians are the "lowest" or least "civilized" element of the population, the word in this sense means "low class." It can also be used to mean "savage," or "uncivilized," or "bad" in a purely figurative way—equivalent, say, to that of *canaille* in French. *Negro,* on the other hand, denotes a physical type that commonly carries with it the general implication of low class, but culture is usually quite subsidiary to the definition.[8]

Racial status in the United States, defined in terms of "blood" and identified purely by physical appearance, divides the population into two halves within which two parallel systems of class differentiation are recognized. In Latin America, appearance is merely one indicator of social position. It is never sufficient in itself to determine how an individual should be classed. The discrimination imposed on the basis of "color" in the United States has sometimes been called a "caste" system and has been contrasted with class systems. This distinction is impossible in Latin America where color is an ingredient of total social position, not the criterion for distinguishing two racial "castes." A policy of segregation on the basis of color would, therefore, be not merely repugnant to Latin Americans but literally impossible.

Even in Panamá where the bulk of the urban population is Negro and the "oligarchy," as the traditional upper class is called, entirely European, the notion of segregation is repulsive. A member of the Panamanian upper class concluded a bitter

[8] The situation in Panamá, referred to above, is exceptional. It derives from the influx of a large number of persons of different language and culture. Some slight difference in style of speech is attributed to Negroes in certain regions.

criticism of discrimination in the United States with the remark: "After all, it's a matter of luck whether one is born black or white." It remained to be added, of course, that in Panamá it is nevertheless bad luck to be born black and good luck to be born white.

At the time of the race riots in Oxford, Mississippi, Hector Velarde, a distinguished critic, took the occasion to deplore racial discrimination in the United States in an article in a Peruvian newspaper. Why can the North Americans not learn from us the virtue of racial tolerance? he asked. He went on to illustrate his argument with the usage of the word *negrita* as a term of affection. *Negrita de mi alma* was an expression used toward a sweetheart, he said. Indeed he did not exaggerate, for *negrita* and *negra* are both forms of address that imply a certain intimacy or informality (as a diminutive the former carries the implication of a potential sexual interest the latter lacks). Velarde did not mention the Indians (who are very much more numerous in Peru than the Negroes). If he had, it would not have helped his thesis since *Indian* is never used in an equivalent fashion, though *cholo* ("civilized Indian") and *zambo* ("half-caste") are both used as terms of affection among comrades.[9]

The implication of racial equality that he drew from his examples invites precision. Such terms do not find their way into such a context because they are flattering in formal usage, but precisely because they are not. Intimacy is opposed to respect; because these terms are disrespectful, they are used to establish or stress a relationship in which no respect is due. The word *nigger* is used in this way among Negroes in the United States, but only among Negroes. Color has, in fact, the same kind of class connotation in the Negro community as in Latin America. Pale-skinned means upper class. Hence *nigger*, in this context dark-skinned or lower class, implies a relationship that is free of the obligation of mutual respect. Velarde's example, consequently, shows that color is an indicator of class, not a criterion of caste.

[9] The same is true in Ecuador. N. E. Whitten, *Class, Kinship and Power in an Ecuadorian Town* (Stanford, 1965), p. 91.

Those who find no racial discrimination in Latin America take the United States as their model. They point out, correctly, that there is no color bar and that race riots do not occur. (Indian risings are a matter they do not consider.) On the other hand, those who do find racial discrimination in Latin America are concerned with the fact that there exist high degrees of social differentiation that are habitually associated with physical traits and frequently expressed in the idiom of "race." They justify their view by the racial overtones given to social distinctions. In Latin America, these critics are commonly persons of left-wing sympathy who see racial discrimination as a bulwark of class distinction and, evading all nuances, they equate the two. . . . Because there is no color bar but rather a color scale that contributes only partially to the definition of status, they are pushed to an implied definition of race that is worthy of Gobineau. They speak of "racial hypocrisy" to explain why certain people claim a "racial" status to which their phenotype would not entitle them if "race" were really a matter of genes. This "false race-consciousness" is false only by the standards of a theory that would obliterate the historical evolution of the past four hundred years. History may validate these theorists if the Chinese interpretation of Marxist-Leninism acquires authority, and the class struggle, transposed to the international plane, becomes a matter of race.

The contrary opinion is usually held by persons of right-wing views. They regard class distinctions as either unobjectionable, insignificant, or at least inevitable. Once they can cite examples of people of upper-class status who show marked traces of non-European descent, they are satisfied that there is no racial discrimination in their country. (This conviction accords with the liberality of their nature and the official creed of their nation.) They are content that there is no problem if there is no "discrimination" as in the United States.

In the first case, the distinctiveness of class and color must be denied; in the second, the association between the two. The first theory ignores the individual instance; only the statistical aspect counts. The exception is evaded lest it disprove the rule. The second theory takes as significant only the chosen individual instance, overlooking the existence of a statistical norm. Indeed, no one is boycotted on account of his phenotype if his class standing is secured by the other criteria that define high status. In such a case, infrequent as it may be in Panamá, color may properly be said to be a matter of luck in the sense that it is a contingency that carries little of the weight of social definition. Economic power, culture, and community are what count.

The disapproval that Latin American visitors to the United States feel of the segregation they find there is not unconnected with the disrespectful attitude they are likely to inspire as Spanish speakers. They know that as Hispanics they are judged socially inferior in many places. Visitors from the United States, on the other hand, are often highly critical of the treatment the Indians of Latin America receive. This strikes them as much more reprehensible than the treatment of the Negroes in their own country, who have indeed much greater opportunities to improve their economic position and who, as domestic servants, are treated with more courtesy and consideration by their employers than the Indians of Latin America —a fact not unconnected with the shortage of domestic servants in the United States. Moreover, the treatment of Indians appears all the less justifiable to these visitors because Indians are not the object of discrimination throughout the greater part of North America.

Thus, comfortably blinkered by the assumptions of their own culture, each nation sees the mote in the other's eye.

In the United States one does sometimes find strong sentiments of hostility toward Indians in areas surrounding their communities; the same is sometimes true in Latin America of the Negroes (however they happen to be defined there). If Indians are not generally subject to discrimination in the United States nor Negroes in Latin America, it is in the first place due to their numerical weakness. In both countries, they pose local, not national, problems. There is roughly one Indian to fifty Negroes in the United States; in Latin America, the inverse disproportion would be greater even

if one were to include only those recognized as Negro. Such a comparison can be taken no further than this, however, since the nature of social distinctions is different in the two lands.

The Indian's predicament in Latin America can be likened to that of the Negro in the United States in only one way: Both provide a major national problem at the present time. There the resemblance stops. Not only is the nature of race relations fundamentally different in the societies that evolved from the English and Spanish colonies, but Indians and Negroes are different in their physical appearance and cultural origins. They are different above all in their place within the structure of the two societies, and have been so from the very beginning of colonial times. The Indians were the original inhabitants of the land; their incorporation or their refusal to be incorporated into colonial society hinged on the existence of Indian communities with a separate culture and a separate identity. The Negroes came in servile status and were marketed as chattel to the industrialized producers of sugar and metals. Cut off from their fellows, they soon lost their language and their original culture and became an integral part of colonial society.[10]

The Negro's status was within colonial society. The Indian's was not. To the extent that the Indian abandoned his Indian community and changed his culture, he lost his Indian identity. While the status of Negro refers to phenotype and attaches to individuals, Indian status refers to culture and attaches to a collectivity. One might speak of individual versus collective status, with all that these imply in terms of social structure. Consequently, while phenotypical differences are irrelevant to the definition of the Indian—hence the *indio gringo*—they

---

[10] This loss of language and culture does not hold for parts of the West Indies and Brazil. Aguirre Beltran maintains that elements of African culture have survived in Mexico. This is true in the case of certain details of material culture and musical style, though it might be more exact to call these Caribbean rather than African. In any case, they have long since ceased to be recognized as such. See, Aguirre Beltran, *Gonzalo: La Poblacion Negra de Mexico, 1519-1810* (Mexico, 1946), p. 96.

have importance in according an individual status once he becomes "civilized." They establish a presumption as to descent, and this is an ingredient of class status. Paradoxically, the genetic background is important only in social distinctions between persons who are recognized as belonging to the same "non-Indian" race; not in the distinction between them and the Indians. "Race" is a matter of culture and community, not of genes, though class is connected with genes.

The problems of race relations in North America and Latin America are, therefore, fundamentally different. One concerns the assimilation of all ethnic groups into a single society; the other, the status distinction between persons who have been assimilated for hundreds of years but who are still distinguished socially by their appearance. The two are comparable only at the highest level of abstraction. One may wonder, therefore, whether the word *caste,* which is so often used in reference to the status distinction between Indians and *mestizos* (or *ladinos*) in Latin American society is not something of a misnomer. It carries quite different implications in Latin as opposed to North America. It would appear that it comes into the sociological literature about Latin America on the basis of several different and all equally false assumptions which will be dealt with elsewhere.

While the value of color is somewhat similar within the Negro community of the United States and the Hispanic section of Latin America, the Negro community is separated by a *caste* distinction from a socially superior element defined by phenotype; the Hispanic population of Latin America is distinguished by language and customs, beliefs and values and habitat from an element it regards as inferior, which does not participate in the same social system and, for the most part, far from wishing to be integrated into it, desires only to be rid of the *mestizos* physically. For this reason, the aims of Indian rebellions are the opposite of the aims of race riots. The former would like to separate once and for all the two ethnic elements; the latter are inspired by the resentment at the existence of a separation. Indians rebel to drive the intruders out of the countryside; Negroes riot in towns when they are not accorded full civic privileges.

The ethnic statuses of modern Latin America vary in number from the simple division into Indian and *mestizo* found in Mexico north of the Isthmus to the four tiers of highland Peru which include *cholos* and *blancos: (indio, cholo, mestizo, blanco).* These "social races" have much in common with the class distinctions of stratified societies. Woodrow Borah has even maintained that the ethnic distinction in Mexico is no more in essence than a matter of social class. This view raises a further problem in those areas where a regional ethnic consciousness emerges, for example among the Tlascalans, Isthmus Zapotecs, and the wealthy, educated Indians of Quetzaltenango in Guatemala.

Admitting that the class structure of Latin America carries ethnic overtones, how is this structure affected by class differences being thought about largely in the idiom of "race"? Such a view implies that classes are different in their essential nature. If the concept of "social race" teaches us to think about race in terms of social structure, we should also have a concept of "ethnic class" to remind us that class systems no longer function in the same way once class has phenotypical associations. Processes of selection come into operation that cannot exist in a homogeneous population however it is stratified.

This observation leads to a conclusion that does not altogether accord with that of Professor Wagley[11] who states: "At least, theoretically, it is only a question of time until such populations may be entirely classed as mestizo by social race and social differentiation will be entirely in terms of socioeconomic classes."[12]

In terms of his thesis continued racial intermixture produces in Latin America, unlike North America, a blurring of the

---

[11] If I disagree with Professor Wagley ultimately with regard to the prospects of the future (about which wise anthropologists refrain from speculating), I do not wish to obscure my debt to Professor Wagley's thinking on this subject nor to deny homage to his admirable essay. But I would not write about this subject at all if I did not think there remains something more to be said.

[12] Wagley, "On the Concept of Social Race in the Americas," p. 540.

distinctions among different "social races." This would be true enough, if time could be trusted to produce phenotypical homogeneity, but it ceases to be so once one introduces the notion of selection into the theory. The absence of a bar on intermarriage does not necessarily produce homogeneity.

Distinctions of status are not always exhibited in the same ways. The castes of India are held apart by prohibitions on physical contact and commensality, and by endogamy. Feudal Europe accorded no importance to the first two and little to the third. The division of labor implied by any social distinction can bring people into either direct co-operation or segregation, depending upon the range of their ties and the basis of their "complementarity." If their status difference is assured in one way, it may prove indifferent to any other basis of distinction. For this reason the intimacy to which servants were admitted by their masters was greater in an earlier age when social distinctions were more clear-cut.

Physical differences can never be obliterated, but whether they, rather than cultural or social differences, are regarded as significant is a matter each social system decides for itself. It is for this reason that the value accorded to physical appearance varies so greatly from place to place and class to class in Latin America. But the significance of phenotype also varies greatly according to context. Political or commercial alliances are not the same as alliances through marriage. Their products are of a different order. Profits are colorless, children are not. Hence, phenotype may not matter in commercial dealings, but it is never more important than in marriage.

In Latin America today the grandchildren of a rich man who looks Indian or Negroid always appear much more European than he is himself. Color is an ingredient, not a determinant of class. It can, therefore, be traded for the other ingredients. It is not something that can be altered in the individual's life, but it is something that can be put right in the next generation. For this reason, the wives of the well-to-do tend to look more European than their husbands. In the lower classes, paler children are sometimes favored at the expense of their more swarthy siblings; their potential for social mobility is greater.

Individual motivations are ordered to produce conformity with an ideal image of ethnic class. This tends to reinforce the original image. Moreover, demographical factors reinforce this conformity in other ways—through the immigration of Europeans into Latin America and the existence of a pool of unassimilated Indians on the land. Indians are constantly abandoning their Indian identity and becoming integrated into the nation. This process is not unconnected with the current flight to the cities, for you lose Indian status once you settle in the city.[13] The result is a continual influx of persons of mainly Indian physique into the proletariat. At the same time, the immigration of Europeans into these countries has been very considerable in the last two decades, and these Europeans have almost all been absorbed into the upper classes. For demographic reasons, the correlation between class and color is increasing rather than diminishing.

Moreover, the significance of this correlation is also increasing under modern conditions. (It would be rash to say that it will go on increasing in the future, for the structure itself may well change to offset this effect.) The expansion of the open society at the expense of the local community changes the criteria whereby people are defined socially. Where known descent establishes status, color may carry little of the weight of social definition, but the descent must be known. It must be known whose child you are if you are to inherit the status of your father. If you have exchanged your local community for the big city, your descent becomes a matter of conjecture; you can no longer be respected because of your birth despite your Indian features. If you look Indian, it will be concluded that you were born of Indian parents. Thus, in the open society, appearance takes over the function of descent in allocating social status. In a world in flux, the fact that appearance cannot be dissimulated recommends it

---

[13] Only exceptionally, as in the Isthmus of Tehuantepec or Quetzaltenango, can a man become integrated while retaining an Indian (or is it a pseudo-Indian?) identity. Then region replaces community as the defining unit.

above all other indicators. Clothing, speech, and culture are losing force as indicators of status in the context of expanding cities, but color is becoming ever more crucial.

Although these same conditions might create an increase in social mobility that would tend to reduce the phenotypical correlation of class, it appears that the opposite is happening today. If the classification into social races is losing its precision, the ethnic aspect of class is coming to have increased importance. The social structure is changing and with it the criteria of social classification. Under modern industrial conditions, much of Latin America is moving from the systems of social race that flourished in the communities of yesterday to a system of ethnic class adapted to the requirements of the open society of tomorrow.

THE NEGRO AMERICAN— COMMUNITY AND CLASS REALITIES: THE ORDEAL OF CHANGE

G. Franklin Edwards

One of the paradoxes of American life is that though the Negro is an old-line American he is not yet fully American. His presence in this country antedates that of most immigrant groups, but his career and community life are greatly different from those of immigrants from northern and southern Europe. In terms of the basic socialization processes and the community contexts in which they occur, differences between the Negro and these immigrant groups, including the most recent large-scale arrivals, the Puerto Ricans, are apparent.

Immigrant groups from Europe have fol-

Daedalus, "Community and Class Realities: The Ordeal of Change," by G. Franklin Edwards, Winter, 1966. Reprinted by permission of the author, the publisher, and the American Academy of Arts and Sciences.

lowed a somewhat typical process as they moved into the main stream of American life. Most members of these groups entered the work force at the bottom of the economic ladder, as small farmers and as unskilled, semiskilled, and service workers. They lived initially among fellow immigrants in small village communities or in poorer city neighborhoods in which communal institutions helped cushion the cultural shock induced by the differences between life in their countries of origin and life in the United States. Family, church, the foreign language press, and mutual aid organizations helped in the adjustment process. Members of the second and succeeding generations acquired increasing amounts of education and the skills necessary to take advantage of available opportunities; eventually the Americanization process was fairly complete. . . .

In contrast to the pattern of immigrant groups, the Negro has remained socially and morally isolated from the American society. At no time in the almost three and a half centuries of his history in this country has he been "counted in." His caste-like position is owing more to restraints from without than to any centripetal force serving to keep him separated from other groups. He has lived, according to E. Franklin Frazier's characterization, as "a nation within a nation."[1] Robin Williams recently has referred to the general Negro community as "a world in the shadow,"[2] and James Silver, in describing an extreme instance of a local community's exclusion of Negroes, has referred to the "closed society."[3]

One basic difference between the Negro and these immigrant groups is that the former served for nearly two centuries as slaves. Although succeeding generations of Negroes acquired increased amounts of education after the Emancipation, access to opportunities commensurate with formal training often was denied because of color. The failure to learn certain basic skills to

[1] E. Franklin Frazier, *Black Bourgeoisie* (New York, 1957), p. 15.
[2] Robin M. Williams, Jr., *Strangers Next Door* (New York, 1964), p. 252.
[3] James W. Silver, *Mississippi: The Closed Society* (New York, 1963), p. 164.

qualify for jobs in the world of work placed serious limitations upon the horizontal and social mobility experienced by members of the group. As a matter of fact, the social mobility of Negroes up to the present has been determined more by conditions within the Negro community than by those of the broader society. The number and distribution of Negroes within the professions, for example, have been related more directly to the needs of the Negro community for certain types of services than to the demands of the broader society.[4] It is for this reason that clergymen and teachers, functionaries required by the segregated Negro community, have represented at least one-half of all Negro professional persons at any given period.

The segregation of Negroes from the main stream of American life has produced institutional patterns and behavior which have a bearing upon contemporary efforts to eliminate inequalities between the two major racial groups. The behaviors are expressed as deviations of Negroes from many normative patterns of American life and suggest something of the magnitude of the differentials which must be dealt with if reconciliation, rather than further alienation, is to be achieved.

The contrasts in background experiences between the Negro and immigrant groups raise the fundamental question of whether, given the promise of recent changes, the Negro will now be integrated into American society in much the same manner as have these other groups. Any strict analogy between the future course of the Negro's relationship to American society and the processes which occurred in the experiences of immigrant groups, however, is subject to serious limitations and error.

The long history of oppression has profoundly affected the Negro's self-esteem. The fears, suspicions and feelings of inadequacy generated in the Negro by his subordinate status are not duplicated in the experiences of immigrant groups. Moreover, color and other physical traits distinguish the Negro sharply from other groups in the society. In the past these characteristics were taken as physical stigmata which reinforced negative attitudes toward the Negro. Sharp physical differences were not present to complicate the relationships of immigrants to American society, although differences in this regard can be observed between the northern Europeans, on the one hand, and southern Europeans and Orientals, on the other. . . .

It should be observed that significant advancement in the status of the Negro comes at a time when economic conditions are quite different from those faced by immigrant groups. The great influx of immigrants came at a time when there was a market for agricultural labor and unskilled work and mobility through these avenues was still possible. The Negro today has been displaced from the farm and must now compete for work in an urban market which requires a somewhat higher degree of education and technical skill than was the case a half century ago. Given the present educational and occupational inadequacies of a large segment of the Negro population, the task of overcoming these deficiencies is formidable.

While it is clear that further changes in the status of the Negro will occur in the years ahead, moving the Negro nearer to equality with other Americans, the processes by which this will be achieved are certain to be difficult and tortuous. The remainder of this essay is an elaboration of this viewpoint.

Foremost among the indicators of the social isolation of Negroes is the Negro ghetto. It represents at once the restrictions placed upon the living space of the Negro minority and, as Kenneth Clark recently has pointed out, a way of life with a peculiar institutional patterning and psychological consequences.[5] Unlike most immigrant ghettos, which show a tendency to break up, the Negro ghetto, especially in Northern cities, has become more dense. . . .

The growing awareness of the limitations of life in the ghetto, as a result of the influence of mass media, increased physical mobility, and better education, has played a vital part in precipitating the "Negro Revolution." The mass demonstrations for equality of treatment in places of public

[4] G. Franklin Edwards, *The Negro Professional Class* (Chicago, 1959), pp. 23–26.

[5] Kenneth Clark, *Dark Ghetto* (New York, 1965), pp. 63–80.

accommodations, for access to better quality schools, for equal employment opportunities and voting rights are thought of as efforts by Negroes to achieve first-class citizenship. In another sense, they are efforts to overcome the barriers which have isolated Negroes from aspects of American life.

The difficulty of overcoming the problems created by the physical fact of the ghetto is indicated by attempts to improve the quality of education of schools in slum areas. In our large metropolitan cities, because of the segregation in housing and the traditional neighborhood concept of school attendance, a disproportionate number of schools, particularly at the elementary level, becomes predominantly Negro or predominantly white, with the Negro schools being inferior. Opposing theories for dealing with this situation, generally regarded as undesirable, have generated serious community conflicts. There are those who feel that the efforts should be concentrated upon improving the quality of education in these depressed areas by larger allocations for plant improvement, remedial work, new curricula, and better trained teachers. Other students of the problem contend that substantial improvement of slum schools cannot be achieved until such schools lose their predominantly Negro or predominantly white character. It becomes necessary in the thinking of the protagonists of this latter view to develop methods for overcoming racial imbalances in the schools. While a variety of techniques have been proposed, each has generated rather serious opposition. It is patent that this problem, one of the serious concerns of the leaders of the Negro Revolution largely because it is tied to segregation in housing, will not be easily solved.

. . . The ghetto has not only restricted the interaction of Negroes with other members of the society, and hence symbolized the isolation under which Negroes have lived; but it has also been a primary force in the generation and persistence of atypical institutional patterns which are viewed as dysfunctional in any effort at reconciliation. Doubtless the foremost of these institutions is the Negro family which, because of historical circumstances connected with slavery and the isolated conditions under which Negroes have lived in both urban and rural areas, is characterized by rather significant variations from the dominant American family pattern. It is not so much the differences *per se,* or any mere deviation of Negro family characteristics from those of white middle-class families, but the variations in structural and interactional features known to be desirable in family living which become causes of concern.

The most salient feature of Negro family life which captures the attention of those concerned with integration of Negroes into American life is the degree of disorganization represented by structural breakdown. In only three-quarters of all Negro families, as compared with approximately nine-tenths of all white families, were both spouses present. One Negro family in five (21 per cent) was headed by a female and 5 per cent had only the male head present. Thus one Negro family in four, as compared with one white family in ten, was headed by a single parent. This differential in the percentage of families headed by one parent accounts in part for the fact that in 1960 only one-third of Negro children under eighteen years of age, as compared with one in ten white children of comparable age, lived in families in which only one parent was present.

The assumption underlying the desirability of family unity—the presence of both spouses—is that on balance the economic, social, and affectual roles may be best discharged when both mates are present in the home. Divorce, desertion, and separation follow the generation and expression of tensions which, even before rupture occurs, reduce the effectiveness with which the mates can discharge the duties and obligations of family life, as well as deny the satisfactions derived from the intimate sharing of experiences and attainments of goals. In essence, the organized and unified family becomes at once a matrix for the personal satisfaction of the marital partners and for the protection, proper socialization, and well-being of their children. This is not to deny that the basic goals of family life, regarding child-rearing and other functions, may not be achieved by the single-parent family. Given the complexities of modern urban life and the established normative values around which the modern family is organized, however, the discharge of family functions may best be achieved when the family is unified.

In analyzing the statistics on the Negro family one becomes aware that the instability of the Negro family unit is greater than is represented by statistics on the percentages of males and females enumerated as widowed or divorced. In 1960, 15 per cent of all Negro males and 20 per cent of all Negro females, though enumerated by the Census as married, were living apart from their mates. The percentage of Negro males separated from their mates is four times as large as the comparable percentage for white males, and for Negro females four and one-half times as large as for white females.

The instability of Negro family life is explained only in part by the historical conditioning of attitudes toward family life, beginning with slavery, when strong family ties were not encouraged and Negroes, as Elkins has suggested, were made dependent upon whites.[6] The phenomenon arises also from forces of contemporary American life which place limits upon the possibility of successful family organization. These are reflected in the statistics on characteristics of the heads of Negro families.

As reported by the last Census, approximately one-half, 48.5 per cent, of the heads of nonwhite (mainly Negro) families had not finished elementary school. Even in urban areas where access to educational opportunities is somewhat greater and school-attendance laws somewhat better enforced than in rural farm and nonfarm areas, two out of five nonwhite family heads failed to reach the last year of elementary school. Of nonwhite heads living in rural nonfarm and rural farm areas, 70 and 80 per cent, respectively, had failed to attain this level of schooling.[7] The low level of educational achievement for such a large proportion of nonwhite family heads has obvious implications for the cultural life to

which the Negro child is exposed in the home and doubtless for the type of motivation the child receives for achievement in school. It also is related to the labor-force participation and income of nonwhites.

In an economy in which automation is rapidly introducing changes in the demand for certain types of labor, the heads of nonwhite families were disproportionately represented in those occupational categories in which fewer workers are required and monetary returns are small. Only 13 per cent of all nonwhite family heads, as compared with 40 per cent of white heads, were in professional, managerial, and clerical occupations for which labor demands are increasing. One in five white heads, but only one in ten among nonwhite, was a skilled worker. Thus, one in four nonwhite heads, as compared with three in five white, were white-collar and skilled workers.[8] The heavier identification with semiskilled and unskilled work accounts in part for the nonwhite employment rate being twice as large as the comparable rate of whites and for greater underemployment among nonwhites.

The type of job and both underemployment and unemployment influence the relatively low income of nonwhite family heads. The median nonwhite family income of $3,465 in 1963 was only approximately 53 per cent of the white family income of $6,548. More than two-fifths of all nonwhite families (41 per cent) earned less than $3,000 in 1963, which placed them at the poverty level, and only one in twenty earned $10,000 or more in the same year.[9] It is significant to note, in line with our previous discussion regarding the desirability of family closure—both parents in the home— that in 1959 families in which both husband and wife were present in the home had a median income of $3,633 as compared with a median of $1,734 for families having a female head.[10]

[6] Stanley Elkins, *Slavery* (Chicago, 1959), pp. 115–133.

[7] The statistics in this section are taken from G. Franklin Edwards, "Marriage and Family Life Among Negroes," *The Journal of Negro Education*, Vol. 32 (Fall 1963), pp. 451–465.

[8] *Ibid.*, p. 463.

[9] Current Population Reports, "Income of Families and Persons in the United States: 1963," Series P-60, No. 43 (Washington, D.C., 1964), Table 1, p. 21.

[10] *U.S. Census of Population: 1960, U.S. Summary,* Detailed Characteristics, Final Report PC(1)-1D (Washington, D.C., 1963), Tables 224 and 225, pp. 594–603.

The problems of the Negro family, then, in terms of its instability and the associated phenomena of crime, delinquency, school dropouts, high morbidity and mortality are related to a complex of interwoven factors, of which level of educational attainment and income are important components. . . .

A definitive study by Hylan Lewis of child-rearing practices among low-income Negro families in the District of Columbia reveals that there is, indeed, still much to be learned about the operating dynamics and underlying causes of disorganization among such units.[11] What often is accepted as knowledge about these families is in fact mythology. It is noted, in the first instance, that these families are not homogeneous as regards their organization, functioning, and ambitions for their children. In many of them considerable strength is to be noted, but the exigencies of daily living often deny the achievement of the parents' most ambitious plans. Though parents set training and discipline goals for their children, these are often undermined by influences beyond their power, and the actual control over their children may be lost as early as the fifth or sixth year.

Investigation reveals that many of these parents, particularly the mothers, are warm, human, and concerned individuals who, despite deprivation and trouble, are persistent in their desires to have their children become respectable and productive citizens and in their willingness to sacrifice for them. The picture contrasts with the common belief that in an overwhelming majority of low-income families parents reject their children and are hostile to them.

Lewis' study raises questions regarding assigned reasons for alleged male irresponsibility toward family obligations and the degree of family concern with pregnancy out of wedlock and illegitimate births. There does appear to be a greater degree of concern by the male regarding his responsibilities and by family members regarding the sexual behavior of their offspring than is commonly recognized. What in fact

---

[11] Lewis' study, conducted over a period of five years, is now being prepared for publication. The references in this paper were taken from various reports which the investigator made available to the writer.

emerges is that the behavior of these lower-income families is a practical response to untoward circumstances which undermine the well-intentioned, but often unattainable, goals of these units.

The major problems of the Negro family are experienced in urban areas where more than 70 per cent of such families now live. There has been a heavy migration during the past twenty-five years from farms and small towns to large metropolitan areas. The limited extent to which many of these families can cope with the demands of urban life, given the low educational level and obsolescent skills of the adults, raises serious questions for the American society as well as for the families themselves. The War on Poverty, youth opportunity programs, Medicare and other changes in our social security program are certain to exercise some influences in ameliorating existing conditions. But the deep-seated nature of many of those conditions and the personality damage they have produced, as expressed in feelings of powerlessness, hopelessness, and forms of anti-social conduct, give rise to the prediction that no easy solution to problems of the Negro family may be found. This is especially true of those "hard core" or multi-problem families in many of which at least two generations have been dependent on public assistance programs. Present efforts to focus upon the young, as evidenced in Project Head Start and programs for youth, on the assumption that this population is most amenable to change, are based upon sound theory. There remains, however, the complex problem of improving the skills and enhancing the self-esteem of the adult members whose personalities are crystallized and whose levels of expectation have been shaped under an entirely different set of conditions. What is apparent is that the problems of the Negro family are intimately tied to those of the larger community.

The elimination of many of these difficulties depends upon a commitment to invest a great deal more of our resources in improving educational and social services, including more effective family limitation programs.

. . . .

The disabilities of the Negro family discussed in the preceding paragraphs are most characteristic of low-income units. Not all Negro families are affected by inadequate income, education, and employment opportunities, and many of them do not lack strong family traditions. There is a considerable differentiation within the Negro community in terms of status groups and social classes.

E: Franklin Frazier observed that as late as World War I the Negro middle class was composed "principally of teachers, doctors, preachers, trusted persons in personal service, government employees, and a few business men." [12] He stated further that:

This group was distinguished from the rest of the Negro population not so much by economic factors as by social factors. Family affiliation and education to a less degree were as important as income. Moreover, while it exhibited many middle-class features such as its emphasis on morality, it also possessed characteristics of an upper class or aristocracy. [13]

The urbanization of the Negro population, beginning with World War I and continuing to the present, resulted in the formation of large ghettos in Northern and Southern cities and provided the condition for greater occupational differentiation within the Negro community. The differentiation was more pronounced in Northern communities where Negroes had a substantially greater opportunity to enter clerical and technical occupations than was true in Southern cities, and where the large population base provided economic support for a sizable corps of professional functionaries. Education and income became more important than social distinctions in determining class membership.

The Negro middle class today includes a still relatively small, but expanding, number of persons. If occupation is used as a criterion for determining membership and those in professional and technical, clerical, sales, and skilled occupations are included, only approximately 26 per cent of all nonwhite workers belong to the middle class. White workers in these above-mentioned

categories represent 64 per cent of all whites in the labor force. [14] The contrast between the two occupational structures is further indicated by the fact that the percentage of white workers, taken as a proportion of all white workers, is twice as large as the comparable percentage of nonwhite workers in professional and kindred occupations, and in clerical and skilled work; four times as large in managerial occupations; and three times as large in the sales category.

In none of the specific occupational categories associated with the middle class did nonwhite male workers achieve parity with white males in median income. The nearest approximation to parity in 1959 was in clerical and kindred occupations in which the nonwhite male median earnings of $4,072 was approximately 85 per cent of the white male median of $4,785. In none of the other categories did nonwhite male workers receive so much as 70 per cent of the median income of white males in the category. [15]

The expansion of the Negro middle class has been most marked by accretion of persons in professional, technical, clerical, and sales occupations. This expansion by approximately 300,000 persons since 1940 has been influenced in part by government policy which prohibits those business firms holding contracts with the federal government from discriminating against workers on the basis of race, religion, creed, or national origin. In engineering, architecture, and the natural sciences, occupations oriented to the wider world of work rather than to the Negro community, the increases among Negroes, though small in absolute numbers, have been rather dramatic. Between 1950 and 1960, there was a three-fold increase in the number of Negro engineers. The number of Negro architects increased by 72 per cent, and the number of natural scientists by 77 per cent. [16] This expansion

[12] E. Franklin Frazier, "The New Negro," in *The New Negro Thirty Years Afterward* (Washington, D.C., 1955), p. 26.
[13] *Ibid.*

[14] Computed from U.S. Bureau of the Census, *U.S. Census of Population: 1960, U.S. Summary,* Detailed Characteristics, Final Report PC (1)-ID, Table 208.
[15] *Ibid.*
[16] Computed from *U.S. Census of Population: 1940,* Vol. II, *Characteristics of the Population,* Part 1, *U.S. Summary,* Table 128, p. 278; and *U.S. Census of Population: 1960,* Vol. I, *Characteristics of the Population,* Part 1, *U.S. Summary,* Table 205, p. 544.

comes at the end of a half century in which Negroes could hardly expect to earn a living in these fields and thus were not encouraged to prepare for entering them.

The number of Negroes in medicine, dentistry, and law, whose services traditionally have been oriented to the Negro community, has begun to increase rather significantly. During the 1950's, physicians increased by 14 per cent, dentists by 31 per cent, and lawyers by 43 per cent.[17] More substantial fellowship and scholarship aid, ability to pay for professional education, as well as the opening of the segregated professional schools in the Southern states, have contributed to this result.

It is not only the increase in number of these professionals which deserves attention; the improved opportunities for advanced training and learning experiences are also of importance. On the basis of increased opportunities for internships and residency training, the number of Negro physicians who became diplomates of medical specialty boards increased from 92 in 1947 to 377 in 1959.[18] Negro physicians, lawyers, and dentists are admitted today to membership in local societies of national professional organizations in larger numbers and enjoy the privileges these societies provide for continued professional growth.

It should be remembered, however, that these gains, while significant in terms of what has occurred in Negro life heretofore, are relatively small. The ratios of the actual to expected numbers of Negroes in middle-class occupations, as measured by the total labor force distribution, are extremely small.[19]

The differences between Negro and white community life cannot be measured solely by variations in income, occupation, education, and other objective indicators. In assessing the differences, it is important to recognize that the Negro class structure and institutions have emerged in response to segregation and represent adjustments to the isolation under which Negroes have lived. The meaning of relationships within the community and the values placed upon them must be considered.

Frazier has observed, for example, that in the absence of a true upper class based upon old family ties and wealth, the Negro middle class simulates the behavior of the white upper class without possessing the fundamental bases upon which such behavior rests.[20] Moreover, segregation has provided a monopoly for many Negroes in business and the professions and has introduced, in many cases, differential standards of performance. This has important consequences for any consideration of desegregation, for those who enjoy a vested interest in the segregated community are not likely to welcome competition from the broader community. The Negro church represents an extreme instance of vested interest in the Negro community and, at the same time, is the most important institution giving expression to the Negro masses. For this reason no degree of acceptance of Negroes by white churches is likely to bring about the dissolution of Negro churches.[21]

The Negro community doubtless will be the source of social life of Negroes for some time into the future. Sororities, fraternities, clubs, and other organizations will continue to serve a meaningful function. The acceptance by whites of Negroes as fellow workers often bears little relationship to their willingness to share social experiences with them outside the plant or office or to have them as neighbors.

The importance of the Negro community as a source of social life is indicated by the fact that, though the majority of the members of a Negro professional society felt that its members should identify with the local chapter of the national organization representing the profession when the opportunity became available, one-quarter had some reservation about joining and another

[17] Ibid.

[18] From data supplied the writer by W. Montague Cobb, M.D., editor of the *Journal of the National Medical Association.*

[19] Ratios for many of these occupations are supplied in Leonard Broom and Norval Glenn, *Transformation of the Negro American* (New York, 1965), Table 5, pp. 112–113.

[20] This is the thesis of E. Franklin Frazier, *Black Bourgeoisie* (Chicago, 1957). See, especially, pp. 195–212. See, also, Frazier, "Human, All too Human," *Survey Graphic:* twelfth Calling America Number (January 1947), pp. 74–75, 99–100.

[21] E. Franklin Frazier, "Desegregation as a Social Process," in Arnold Rose (ed.), *Human Behavior and Social Processes* (Boston, 1962), p. 619.

5 per cent were opposed to joining. The underlying reasons for reservations to becoming members of the formerly white organization were that, though Negroes may be accepted as professional colleagues, they would not be treated as social equals and that opportunities for leadership roles would be lost if the Negro association were dissolved.[22] What is patently indicated is that most members thought they should have the *right* to membership in the local chapter of the national organization, but they should retain their own association for social and professional reasons.

Despite the effort to conserve the conceived advantages of the Negro community, the larger social forces are introducing changes. Already the small Negro entrepreneurial group is threatened by these forces. Speaking to a group of Negro businessmen in Detroit, the Assistant Secretary of Commerce for Economic Affairs referred to the disappearance of the monopoly Negroes formerly held in certain businesses.[23] The impact of desegregation is being felt, he said, in the Negro market, for, as the income of Negro consumers expands, white businessmen become more conscious of the Negro's purchasing power. To this end they have added a cadre of professional Negro salesmen to their payrolls for the specific purpose of developing the Negro market. The success of this undertaking is indicated by the fact that many of the employed Negroes have risen to top executive posts in these organizations. Moreover, Negroes have begun to buy in increasing amounts from shopping centers serving the Negro community and have begun to patronize places of public accommodations other than those traditionally operated by Negroes. This change in consumer behavior represents a steady and gradual erosion of the position of the Negro businessman. The cruelest blow of all, the Assistant Secretary stated, is that "the large life insurance companies serving the market at large are bidding away Negro life insurance salesmen at an increasing rate."[24] These and other changes are certain to influence the structure of the Negro community.

THE ORDEAL OF CHANGE

From observing current developments in race relations and the operation of the larger social forces in our society, it is evident that several basic conditions operate to influence the pattern and pace at which change is occurring. These provide some insight into what may be expected in the future in regard to the general status of the Negro minority; they document the theory of slow and gradual change for some time to come in most areas and somewhat more rapid change in others.

A first consideration, not prominently mentioned heretofore, is the opposition to change by segments of the white community. Beginning with the school desegregation decision, there has been a mobilization of white community efforts to prevent the attainment of desegregation in many aspects of community life. This opposition has taken a variety of forms: the closing of schools, violence visited upon Negroes, intimidation of Negroes and threats to their job security, the rise of some hate groups—such as Citizens' Councils and Night Riders—and the strengthening of others—such as the Ku Klux Klan—the resurrection of racial ideologies having the purpose of establishing the inferiority of the Negro, and a variety of other techniques designed to slow the desegregation process.[25]

What is important in this connection is that many of the organizations connected with the opposition have had the support, if not the leadership, of prominent persons in the power structure; many governors, mayors, legislators, and prominent businessmen have all given support to the resistance efforts, owing to political and economic expediency, if not to personal sentiment.

---

[22] Martha Coffee, "A Study of a Professional Association and Racial Integration," unpublished Master's Thesis, Department of Sociology, Howard University, Washington, D.C., 1953.

[23] "Desegregation and the Negro Middle Class," remarks of Dr. Andrew F. Brimmer, Assistant Secretary of Commerce for Economic Affairs, Detroit, Michigan, July 16, 1965.

[24] *Ibid.*

[25] A good discussion of these hate groups is given in James W. Vander Zanden, *Race Relations in Transition: The Segregation Crisis in the South* (New York, 1965), pp. 25–54. See, also, Arnold Forster and Benjamin Epstein, *Report on the Ku Klux Klan* (New York, 1965).

Moreover, persons with some claim to scientific respectability in the academic community have contributed to the questioning of whether differentials between Negroes and whites stem from the former's disadvantaged community life or from the Negro's innate biological inferiority.[26] . . .

A second important force affecting change is inherent in the nature of the phenomenon itself, especially the contribution made by the accumulated disabilities of the Negro family, and in individuals in terms of inadequate education, job skills, housing, patterns of dependency, and low self-esteem. The advancement toward a more equalitarian society depends upon how fully these disabilities can be overcome or eliminated. Any analysis must consider the generational problem, for the extent to which the education and job skills of many adult family heads—those over forty-five, for example—can be improved is problematic. A stronger basis of hope rests with the generation which begins school under improved educational conditions and whose levels of aspiration will be shaped by a social context which varies considerably from that of the past half century, and may be expected to vary even more in the future. But even under the most favorable circumstances, the improvement of educational qualifications of Negroes to a position of parity with those of whites, an essential factor for job equality, may not be easily achieved. One prominent sociologist on the basis of statistical calculations concluded:

Whatever the future may hold with respect to the on-coming cohorts of young Negroes, the performance to date, together with the postulate that educational attainment is a "background" characteristic [for employment], enables us to make a most important prediction: the disparity between white and nonwhite levels of education attainment in the general population can hardly disappear in less than three-quarters of a century. Even if Negroes in their teens were to begin immediately to match the educational attainment of white children, with this equalization persisting in-

definitely, we shall have to wait fifty years for the last of the cohorts manifesting race differentials to reach retirement age.[27]

The achievement of educational and occupational equality is far more difficult to attain than equal treatment in public accommodations. Many civil rights leaders recognize this and, now that the public accommodations struggle has been successful, consider that the movement has entered a new and much tougher phase. . . .

The most significant influence in determining the pattern and pace of race relations changes is the federal government. The early court decisions, particularly in the area of public accommodations, orders by the executive, and recent legislation by the Congress have had salutary effects in altering disability-producing conditions. With more rigorous enforcement, they are likely to have an even more important influence in the future. The Civil Rights Act of 1964 provides a wedge for undermining, or at least neutralizing, much of the support for denying the constitutional rights of Negroes. . . . This result, along with the greater political consciousness of Negroes throughout the country, is certain to improve the power position of the group and result in the election of large numbers of Negroes to public office.[28]

The change in the position of the government in respect to the status of Negroes results from the altered position of this country in world affairs since the end of World War II and to a substantial shift in public opinion regarding the position of the Negro during that period. It is important, therefore, to view contemporary changes as a part of broader social movements toward improved welfare for the disadvantaged within the country and in the world. These broad forces tend to override resistances, but they are subject to

[26] See the following: Wesley C. George, *The Biology of the Race Problem* (A report prepared by commission of the Governor of Alabama, 1962); and Dwight J. Ingle, "Racial Differences and the Future," *Science,* Vol. 146 (October 16, 1964), pp. 375–379.

[27] Otis Dudley Duncan, "Population Trends, Mobility and Social Change," a paper prepared for the Seminar on Dimensions of American Society, Committee on Social Studies, American Association of Colleges for Teacher Education, p. 52. (Quoted with the permission of the author.)

[28] For a list of the growing number of Negro office holders, see Harold F. Gosnell and Robert E. Martin, "The Negro as Voter and Office Holder," *Journal of Negro Education,* Vol. 32 (Fall 1963), pp. 415–425.

challenges and counter pressures. If viewed in this broad perspective, it is clear that more significant changes which will bring the Negro greater opportunities for participation in our society lie ahead. When, in fact, basic equalities will be achieved cannot be predicted.

CLASS AS AN EXPLANATION OF ETHNIC DIFFERENCES IN UPWARD MOBILITY

THE CASE OF MEXICAN AMERICANS

Celia Stopnicka Heller

The aim of this paper is to challenge the indiscriminate use of *class* as an explanation of ethnic differences in mobility behavior. The fact that some differences—such as in mobility aspirations—between a given ethnic group and the majority population can be *statistically* accounted for by class is often interpreted to mean that class adequately explains these differences. Our contention is that such an interpretation is both unwarranted and incorrect.

Although the usual procedure involved in the explanation we are questioning is well known, it seems appropriate, for the sake of clarity, to begin by briefly summarizing it. The first step in this procedure is to compare the occupational, educational, material, or other mobility aspirations of a given ethnic group, in which the researcher is interested, with that of the majority population. When substantial differences are discovered, the factor of class is statistically controlled. If the differences disappear

This is a slightly revised version of the article that appeared in the *International Migration Review*, Vol. II, Fall, 1967. Reprinted by permission of the author.

when class is controlled, the relation between ethnicity and aspirations is adjudged to be spurious and class is treated as the explanatory factor. If, on the other hand, the differences do not disappear but shrink, class is considered an important factor and the remaining differences are treated as being the result of the *ethnic* factor (unique characteristics of the group studied).

The procedure initially followed in our study of aspirations and the means of mobility of Mexican American youth was the same in manner. The quantitative data consisted of answers to a questionnaire administered in 1955 by Ralph H. Turner to seniors in ten Los Angeles high schools. These were chosen as a representative sample of the metropolitan area. Of the entire sample of male students, 165, or 12 per cent, turned out to be Mexican American.[1]

In comparing the answers of the Mexican Americans and the white non-Mexican boys, referred to as Anglo Americans, we found substantial differences in their occupational and educational expectations, and also in their IQ scores. (See Tables 1 and 2.) Over twice as many Anglo Americans as Mexican Americans expected to enter a *profession* (36.8 and 15.4 per cent, respectively) and, conversely, the proportion of Mexican Americans who chose *skilled labor* was almost twice that of Anglo Americans (41.3 and 22.4 per cent, respectively). The answers to the question concerning educational expectation were similarly patterned.[2] More than twice as many Mexican Americans did not expect to go beyond high school. At the opposite end of the educational scale, the proportion of Mexican Americans who anticipated graduating from college or better was only one-third that of Anglo-Americans.

As for IQ scores, the differences were still larger. The average score of the Mexican American male high school seniors was 90.5 as compared with 103.3 of the Anglo Americans. Almost half of the Mexican American students were below average in

[1] Celia Stopnicka Heller, "Ambitions of Mexican-American Youth—Goals and Means of Mobility of High School Seniors," unpublished Ph.D. dissertation, Columbia University, 1963.
[2] Table is omitted.

IQ, in contrast to 13 per cent of the Anglo Americans. Only 6 per cent of them, but 30 per cent of the Anglo Americans, fell into the "bright" and "superior" categories. (See Table 2).

Following the commonly used techniques, we controlled statistically the class factor and concluded—in accordance with the prevalent interpretation we are now disputing—that class largely explains the differences in occupational and educational expectations but does not explain IQ differences. In other words, we maintained that the fact of being Mexican American has little explanatory power, but the fact of being lower-class has much explanatory power for the understanding of the lower mobility aspirations of Mexican American youths. This conclusion was based on the findings that when class was statistically held constant, the differences in occupational and educational expectations were small, but the differences in IQ scores remained large. (See Tables 1 and 2.)

However, at this point, it must be admitted that our explanation was faulty. We were not justified in inferring that the relationship between mobility aspiration and Mexican American ethnicity is largely a spurious one. The problem of ethnic differences in mobility is not solved by holding the class factor constant, because the very class structure of the ethnic group is part of the *intrinsic* problem. In other words, *the class distribution of a given ethnic group, whether it differs from or resembles that of the majority population, must be accounted for.*

Because recent immigrants, as a whole, irrespective of country of origin, concentrate at the bottom of the socioeconomic ladder,[3] to make the leap that would enable them to approximate the class distribution of the majority population (let alone improve on it), they must at some point in their history exceed the aspirations of the majority population of the same class. If they simply advanced to the same degree as lower-class individuals in the majority group, the gap between their class distribution and that of the majority population

would continue. And yet we know that there is more than one ethnic group which has not only approximated the class composition of the majority population but exceeded it.[4]

Among many ethnic groups, the process of moving toward the occupational structure of the majority population begins with the second generation; among some it begins later;[5] and among a few, such as Jews and Japanese, it begins in the first generation.[6] Although the occupational aspirations of these last groups undoubtedly varied with class in their countries of origin, transplanted to a relatively mobile society they responded to the promises of that society irrespective of the class they occupied in their country of origin or at the beginning of their stay here. There are indications that among these ethnic groups, in contrast to nonethnic Americans, mobility aspirations do not differ significantly with class.[7]

Similarly, class is not an adequate explanation if one proceeds to an analysis of the educational expectations of Mexican American youth. According to the class explanation, the lower educational expectations of Mexican Americans simply reflect their lower-class background. The general proposition from which it follows is the one

[3] Oscar Handlin, "Historical Perspectives of the American Ethnic Group," *Daedalus*, Spring, 1961, p. 228.

[4] Bernard Rosen, "Race, Ethnicity, and the Achievement Syndrome," *American Sociological Review*, Vol. 24, February, 1959, p. 47.

[5] E. P. Hutchinson, *Immigrants and Their Children, 1850–1950*, New York: John Wiley & Sons, 1956.

[6] Harry J. Crockett, "The Achievement Motive and Differential Occupational Mobility in the United States," *American Sociological Review*, Vol. 27, April, 1962, pp. 191–205.

[7] See Nathan Glazer, "Social Characteristics of American Jews, 1654–1954," in Morris Fine, ed., *American Jewish Year Book*. (Philadelphia: Jewish Publication Society of America, 1955), pp. 32–33.

Perhaps the following finding by McClelland also suggests the above. In comparing the "need" for achievement among four ethnic groups in the United States—French, Canadian, Italian, Greek and Jewish—he concludes that "the Jews are the only group . . . which do not show a drop in average *n* Achievement level for the lower socioeconomic classes." The only reservation is that by McClelland's admission, the "need" for achievement is not necessarily correlated with occupational aspirations. See: David C. McClelland, *The Achieving Society*, New York: D. Van Nostrand Co., 1961, p. 362.

TABLE 1 Occupational Expectations of Male High School Seniors in the Los Angeles Metropolitan Area, 1955 (in percentages)

Occupational Category	ENTIRE SAMPLE			OF WORKING-CLASS BACKGROUND (BREADWINNER'S OCCUPATION: MANUAL)	
	Anglo American	Mexican American	Standardized Anglo American*	Mexican American	Anglo American
1. Unskilled labor	.4	1.8	1.3	1.9	.7
2. Semi-skilled labor	1.3	1.8	3.6	.0	2.3
3. **Skilled labor**	**22.4**	**41.3**	**34.1**	**42.1**	**33.3**
4. Clerical & Sales Clerks	3.1	3.1	2.5	2.8	3.4
5. Small business owners—managers & salesmen	11.7	13.0	12.3	11.2	10.5
6. Semi-professionals	17.9	19.8	16.5	21.5	19.4
7. Business agents & managers	3.1	3.7	2.6	3.7	3.2
8. Large business owners & officials	3.3	.0	1.1	.0	.9
9. **Professionals**	**36.8**	**15.4**	**26.0**	**16.8**	**26.4**
Total	100.0%	99.9%	100.0%	100.0%	100.1%
Total Number	(1057)	(165)		(107)	(443)
No answer & unclassifiable	(10)	(3)		(0)	(4)
Chi square (last two columns)**				$\chi^2 = 3.27$	
				Not significant at .30 level	

* These are calculated Anglo-American rates if the Anglo–Americans had the same occupational background as the Mexican Americans.
**For the chi square test the categories were thus combined: (1, 2, 3), (4, 5, 7, 8).

TABLE 2 I.Q. Scores of Male High School Seniors (in percentages)

IQ Class Interval	Verbal Characterization[a]	TOTAL SAMPLE		OF WORKING-CLASS BACKGROUND[b]	
		Mexican American	Anglo American	Mexican American	Anglo American
1. Below 80	Borderline	19.6	3.6	15.1	4.1
2. 80–90	Dull	28.2	9.7	21.7	12.6
3. 90–99	Average	26.4	22.8	31.1	27.9
4. 100–109	Average	20.2	33.8	26.4	35.0
5. 110–119	Bright	4.3	20.5	4.7	16.5
6. 120–129	Superior	1.2	7.7	.9	3.4
7. 130 and over	Very superior	.0	1.8	.0	.5
Total		99.9%	99.9%	99.9%	100.0%
Total Number		(165)	(1057)	(107)	(443)
No scores available		(2)	(37)	(1)	(6)
Mean IQ		90.45	103.31	92.80	100.43
Standard deviation		12.94	12.68	12.39	11.53
Chi square				$\chi^2 = 65.83$[c]	
				Significant at .001 level	

[a] Used by educators.
[b] Breadwinner's occupation is manual.
[c] Categories 5–7 were combined.

stated by Lipset and Bendix that "the higher the education of the parents, the more likely they would be to instill motivation for upward movement in their children.[8] Its specific reading would be: The parents of Mexican American students, being less educated than the Anglo American parents, are less likely to influence their children to obtain a higher education. And yet the argument is not entirely convincing. The confirmation of the Lipset and Bendix proposition, it could be said, comes from the empirical studies of non-ethnic youth.[9] *Parents' educational achievement and parents' influence on their children's educational motivation is not a necessary, although often found, equation.* The two cases in point are the American Jews and Japanese Americans.

The educational ambition and striving of the children of poor and uneducated Jewish immigrants have become proverbial and well documented. But why is this so? We know that in the traditional Jewish culture, sacred education was stressed as the channel of mobility open to all Jews: poor and rich, of educated and uneducated parents. The immigrants transferred their aspirations for their sons from religious to secular education.[10] They influenced their children to want an education and helped them secure it.

Much less is known about the mainspring of the Japanese Americans' stress on education, although it is easily observed that in terms of educational ambition and achievement they resemble the Jews. The Japanese immigration to the United States was also largely a lower-class immigration, even if in contrast to the Jewish one, it was mostly composed of peasants. These lower-class immigrants put great emphasis on education and influenced their children in that direction.[11] Thus, already in 1940, the educational level of the Nisei was 12.2 median years of school completed, as compared with 10.1 years for American-born white children in the Pacific coast states.[12]

In extreme contrast to the Jewish and Japanese stand the Mexican immigrants, whose cultural heritage—like that of some other immigrant groups, such as the Italian and Polish—did not contain the goal of education for all irrespective of social class. But their relative failure to aspire or influence their children to aspire or achieve higher education must *not* be considered indicative of a low value placed on education, as some writers have argued in studying lower socioeconomic groups of the majority population.[13] Long ago, when studying the immigrants in the United States, Robert E. Park stated that "even the Polish peasant . . . appreciates learning though not for his class."[14] Somehow, the Mexican Americans have long held on to the belief that formal education was useless for *them* and did not get them anywhere.[15] They viewed it as leading their children not toward mobility, but toward frustration and humiliation. To help their children avoid the latter, parents pointed to those Mexican Americans who received an education and yet did not hold a job appropriate to it.[16]

Finally, we should like to examine class as an explanation of ethnic differences in IQ. Although IQ scores are not adequate measures of innate capacity,[17] they do depict the reality of differing socially and culturally structured capacities, that is,

[8] S. M. Lipset and Reinhard Bendix, *Social Mobility in Industrial Society*, Berkeley: University of California Press, 1962, p. 237.

[9] *Ibid.*

[10] Jackson Toby, "Educational Maladjustment As a Predisposing Factor in Criminal Careers: A Comparative Study of Ethnic Groups," unpublished Ph.D. dissertation, Harvard University, 1950, p. 159.

[11] R. A. Schermerhorn, *These Our People*, Boston: D. C. Heath and Company, 1949, p. 214.

[12] William Caudill and George De Vos, "Achievement, Culture and Personality: The Case of Japanese Americans," *American Anthropologist*, Vol. 58, 1956, p. 1124.

[13] Herbert H. Hyman, "The Value System of Different Classes: A Social Psychological Contribution to the Analysis of Stratification," in Reinhold Bendix and S. M. Lipset, eds., *Class, Status and Power*, Glencoe, Illinois: Free Press, 1953, p. 429.

[14] Robert E. Park and Herbert A. Miller, *Old World Traits Transplanted*, New York, 1921, p. 268.

[15] Ruth Tuck, *Not With The Fist*, New York: Harcourt, Brace & Co., 1946, pp. 189–190. Florence R. Kluckhohn and Fred Strodtbeck, *Variations in Value Orientations*, New York: Row, Peterson Co., 1961, p. 248. Celia Stopnicka Heller, "Ambitions of Mexican-American Youth: Goals and Means of Mobility of High School Seniors," unpublished Ph.D. dissertation, Columbia University, 1963, pp. 167–171.

[16] Tuck, *ibid.*, p. 248.

[17] Otto Klineberg, *Social Psychology*, rev. ed., New York: Henry Holt & Co., 1954, pp. 304–312.

capacities for advancement in *our* society. As Anastasi demonstrates, "The criterion employed in validating intelligence tests has nearly always been success in our social system."[18]

Again, class is not an adequate explanation because, first of all, *IQ does not necessarily vary with class.* It is true that it varies with class in many collectivities that have been studied, but some empirical data support the above assertion that such variation is neither universal nor a necessary consequence of social stratification. An interesting study, conducted in London, showed that among the Jews there, IQ did not differ with class. According to this study, the average IQ of non-Jews dropped as the occupational index of parents fell, but the IQ of Jews remained on about the same level.[19]

Even if empirical studies were to prove that some Jewish communities are the only ones among whom the preceding is true, the analysis of this deviant case holds the promise of yielding important clues to further our knowledge about social mobility. It suggests, for example, that in as far as a culture emphasizes intellectual pursuits for all classes as an end in itself, it equips the members of the lower classes with a powerful means for potential mobility. In a relatively nonmobile society such people are more likely to escape through the rigid boundaries of class. Even when bred in a closed system, they are at an advantage when they move to an open society. In contrast to them, lower-class people formed in cultures where intellectual pursuits are expected of the upper class only, are not as well fit to seize the opportunities for advancement when they find themselves in a relatively open society. The Jews seem to represent an extreme case of the first and the Mexican Americans an extreme case of the latter.

In all complex cultures there are certain traits that are considered appropriate for all irrespective of social position and other traits that are class bound. However, the traits that do not vary with class in one culture may be the very ones that differ with class in another. In the case of Mexicans, honor, respect, family obligation, and manliness are some of the elements that are deemed important for all. But these are not the values that are very conducive to mobility; on the contrary, they are obstacles in the initial stages of social advancement, however praiseworthy on other grounds. And, in contrast to the Jews, Mexicans consider those qualities that are especially suited to mobility—intellect and education —to be the domain of the upper classes.

But if some ethnic groups start sooner and proceed faster to catch up with the socioeconomic positions of the population at large and a few even exceed it,[20] all ethnic

---

[18] Anastasi shows that "Scores on the test are correlated with school achievement or perhaps with some more general measure of success in our society. If such correlations are high, it is concluded that the test is a good measure of 'intelligence' ": (See Anne Anastasi, *Differential Psychology*, 3rd ed., New York: The Macmillan Co., 1958, pp. 566–567.)

[19] As reported in Toby, *op. cit.*, p. 204. Parenthetically, the preceding fits rather well the folk beliefs of the Jews in Eastern Europe. They did not tend to think that "smartness" or talent varied with class among Jews, although they recognized that it differed with class among Gentiles. Nowhere in the people's sayings or their behavior do we find an attempt to place intelligence in a certain class of Jews or claim that it is more prevalent there. See Celia Stopnicka Heller, "Social Stratification of the Jewish Community in a Small Polish Town," *American Journal of Sociology*, Vol. 59, July, 1953, p. 10. (Reprinted in this volume, pp. 183–191, C.S.H.)

[20] It is often suggested that the rapid advancement of Jews is largely due to their urban heritage as compared with the rural background of other ethnic groups. (See Lipset and Bendix, *op. cit.*, p. 223.) Another explanation is that Jews more than any other groups were engaged for generations in middle-class occupations. (See Glazer, "Social Characteristics of American Jews," *op. cit.*, p. 30.) Although the factual basis of the latter could be seriously questioned, because the East European immigration to the United States was largely a lower-class immigration, or, if one prefers, an immigration of extremely impoverished sectors of the population, it might suffice to show that neither of the preceding factors are the necessary ingredients of rapid advancement. It should be recalled that the Japanese in the United States were not originally of the urban middle class but of peasant origin, and yet they displayed a similar pattern of mobility to that of Jews. By 1960 the Japanese ranked higher than whites in both occupational and educational status but their income level was lower. (See: Calvin F. Schmid and Charles E. Nobbe, "Socioeconomic Differentials Among Nonwhite Races," *American Sociological Review*, Vol. 30, December, 1965, pp. 909–922; Also, Caudill and De Vos, *op. cit.*, pp. 1102–1126).

groups have eventually responded to the American ideology of advancement. Until now, the only exception appears to be that of the Mexican Americans. On the basis of his careful analysis of 1950 census data, Donald J. Bogue concludes that the Mexican Americans constitute "... *the only ethnic group for which a comparison of the characteristics of the first and second generation fails to show a substantial intergenerational rise in socio-economic status*" (italics supplied).[21]

However, our data seem to suggest that the Mexican Americans are now entering, to borrow Walt W. Rostow's term, the "take off stage" of mobility. We arrive at this new "trend" among Mexican Americans not through holding class statistically constant, but by comparing the sons with the fathers. It can now be said, on the basis of our findings, that there is a portion of Mexican American youth who, if they could fulfill their aspirations and expectations, would substantially exceed their parental generation in occupational, educational, and in self-employment status. Specifically, only 4 per cent of the Mexican American boys expect to be doing unskilled or semi-skilled labor, whereas 42 per cent of them come from such backgrounds. Conversely, 35 per cent of them aspire to semiprofessional or professional occupations, whereas only 2 per cent of their fathers are in these occupations.

As for education, only 5 per cent come from homes where the breadwinner attended college, but 44 per cent of them expect to do so. Eighty-seven per cent of their fathers had no education beyond high school, but only 31 per cent of them foresee not continuing their schooling.

Again, in the comparison of independent-employee status, 41 per cent of them think that they will have their own business or practice, whereas only 13 per cent of them are from homes where the breadwinner works for himself or owns a business. Also distinctive is that, unlike the Anglo Americans, the proportion of Mexican Americans who expect to be employed, is smaller than the proportion of those whose fathers are employees.

If, as Turner argues, the comparable distributions of the Anglo Americans indicate that the movement from an employee to independent status is not regarded by the majority youth as upward movement,[22] then those of the Mexican Americans indicate a contrasting attitude. A shift from employee to independent status seems to mean to them what it has traditionally meant in America: going up in the world. In a sense, the Mexican Americans may only now be taking hold of the pattern that the majority population is already abandoning. Possibly, these third- and fourth-generation Americans of Mexican descent are showing the pattern that some ethnic groups, such as Jews, showed in the first generation. The mobility path of many immigrant Jews was to leave the factory and establish a small business.[23]

In terms of independent-employee status, as well as in terms of occupation and education, we see then that our sample of Mexican American boys does not expect to conform to the Mexican American pattern of no intergenerational difference in socio-economic status. As a matter of fact, if we use the approach of *relative* mobility aspirations, the Mexican American boys seem quite mobility oriented.[24]

The analysis of relative mobility aspirations points to a change in the achievement orientation of Mexican Americans. We could not have detected this new trend by holding class statistically constant because the preceding technique, contrary to the prevalent interpretation of the results it yields, tells us no more than how the pattern of class variation (in the behavior under consideration) of a given ethnic group compares with the majority group *at one specific time* (the time of study). This is insufficient for understanding ethnic differences in mobility aspirations and achievement. For

[21] Donald J. Bogue, *The Population of the United States*, Glencoe: The Free Press, 1959, p. 372.

[22] Ralph H. Turner, *The Social Context of Ambition*, San Francisco: Chandler Publishing Company, 1964, pp. 39, 180, 199.
[23] Fred L. Strodtbeck, "Jewish and Italian Immigration and Subsequent Status Mobility," in McClelland, *op. cit.*, p. 263.
[24] LaMar T. Empey, "Social Class and Occupational Aspiration: A Comparison of Absolute and Relative Measurement," *American Sociological Review*, Vol. 21, December, 1956, pp. 703–709.

that it is necessary to know whether the traits important in upward mobility are class bound in the original culture of the studied ethnic group. Furthermore, one must locate the class variable in the ethnic group's span of time in the United States, not merely at the time of study.

Mexican Americans, similarly to some other ethnic groups—such as Italian Americans, Polish Americans, and so forth—come from a culture where those traits that are especially suited to mobility are restricted to the upper classes. But in addition, the rate of acculturation of Mexican Americans has been slower than that of most of these groups. Mexican Americans have moved rather slowly out of the culture of the immigrants. In the strength of the traditional culture, they resemble more ethnic minorities in Europe than those in the United States. This is in part due to the fact that Mexican American history in this country began with the American conquest of territories in which Mexicans lived. The twentieth-century Mexican immigrants who came to the United States found here an indigenous Spanish-speaking population of long standing. They did not found immigrant colonies so much as move in with relatives.

Also contributing to cultural persistence and limited acculturation is the proximity to Mexico. The Mexican American population is largely concentrated in border states. There is continuous movement back and forth across the border. New immigrants are constantly added to the community; old immigrants, as well as their American born children, grandchildren, and great-grandchildren, "visit with relatives" in Mexico for short or long periods.[25] These then are the special factors that may account for the *apparent* uniqueness of the Mexican American group as compared with other ethnic groups (in the sense of no significant intergenerational advancement).

In conclusion, the analysis of relative mobility aspirations suggests a change in

the Mexican American group showing it not to be the exception to the ethnic pattern in the United States. The process of responding to the American ideology of advancement observed in all other ethnic groups is similarly reenacted here, although it took a few more generations to initiate it. This change could not have been detected through the technique of statistically controlling the class factor.

THE PROTESTANT ESTABLISHMENT— ARISTOCRACY AND CASTE IN AMERICA

E. Digby Baltzell

THE IMMIGRANTS' PROGRESS AND THE THEORY OF THE ESTABLISHMENT

Several years ago an Englishman, visiting America for the first time, remarked to an editor of *Harper's* magazine that nobody had prepared him for his quick discovery that this was not an Anglo-Saxon nation.[1] Although he had long been aware of our multinational, racial and religious origins in the abstract, he simply had not visualized the heterogeneity of our population in general, nor the heterogeneity of the persons of talent and ability in leadership positions. Hollywood, of course, portrays America to people all over the world. Yet the personalities of our screen stars, well-publicized representatives of the American rags-to-riches dream, had done little to dissuade him of our over-all Protestant and Anglo-Saxon ancestry. A brief look at the

---

[25] Carey McWilliams, *North from Mexico— The Spanish-Speaking People of the United States,* Philadelphia: Lippincott, 1949; Celia S. Heller, "Origin and Background," in *Mexican American Youth: Forgotten Youth at the Crossroads,* New York: Random House, 1966 pp. 9–26.

Condensed from *The Protestant Establishment,* by E. Digby Baltzell. © Copyright 1964 by E. Digby Baltzell. Reprinted by permission of Random House, Inc.

[1] *Harper's,* March, 1955, p. 81.

original names of some of our more famous, pseudo-Anglo-Saxon, Hollywood heroes was indeed a revelation. . . . Just as the original names of these famous stars suggest the ethnic diversity of talent in modern America, so their assumed names attest to the Anglo-Saxon ideal which still persists in our culture. For, in spite of the fact that some forty million immigrants of diverse religious and ethnic origins came to America in the course of the nineteenth and early twentieth centuries, we were a predominantly Anglo-Saxon–Protestant people for almost the first two-thirds of our history. Thus our earliest cultural traditions—in language and literature as well as in our legal, political and religious institutions—were modeled on those of seventeenth- and eighteenth-century England. And, above all, our upper class has always been overwhelmingly Anglo-Saxon and Protestant in both origins and values. The "Sixty Families" or the "Four Hundred," the "Rich and the Well-Born," the "Harvard Man," the "Senator," the "Diplomat," the "Socialite," and the "Man of Distinction in the Executive Suite" are all continuing symbols of this Anglo-American ideal which the Hollywood stars, regardless of their own ethnic origins, have tended to perpetuate. The uncomfortable paradox of American society in the twentieth century is that it has tried to combine the democratic ideal of equality of opportunity in an ethnically diverse society with the persistent and conservative traditions of an Anglo-Saxon caste ideal at the top.

. . . As we have seen, the WASP upper class remained more or less in control of the American elite throughout the first three decades of this century.[2] This was perhaps inevitable, and, as it served to maintain a continuity of tradition at the level of leadership, it was a healthy thing for society as a whole. In the meantime, however, new ethnic families were gradually establishing

[2] In the words of the author, "The elite concept has no evaluative connotations such as the 'best' but refers solely to those *individuals* who have succeeded in rising to the top positions in any society. The democratic process means then that the *elite is open* and is based on the American ideal of equality of opportunity." See *The Protestant Establishment*, New York: Random House, 1964, p. 7. (C. S. H.)

themselves on the ladder of economic, political and social mobility. By and large this was a three-generational process.

. . . .

THE ELITE AND THE MARGINAL MAN

Winston Churchill once said that in any hierarchical situation there is all the difference in the world between the number one man and number two, three, four and the rest. Thus, while most Americans, . . . are living and moving up the class hierarchy within each of our larger religious communities, there exists today an important qualitative difference in the nature of social relationships at the very top levels of society. In other words, while there are upper-, middle- and lower-class levels *within the Protestant, Catholic and Jewish communities,* there are Protestants, Catholics and Jews *within the elite.* To put it another way, class tends to replace religion (and even ethnicity and race) as the independent variable in social relationships at the highest levels of our society (see Diagram I).

And this difference as between the elite and the rest of society is more pronounced in the third, as against the first and second generations. Whereas, for instance, Mayor John Francis Fitzgerald was an "FIF" (First Irish Family) within the Boston Catholic community, his son-in-law became a member of the national elite, both as a multimillionaire businessman and Ambassador to the Court of St. James. While the second generation was still emotionally rooted in a *marginal culture,* the third generation was still emotionally rooted in a *marginal man.* This same marginality, as has been shown above, characterized the lives of Baruch, La Guardia and Weinberg, because of their elite positions. While Weinberg, for instance, was very naturally led into such intimate relationships as cruising in Maine with Charles Dickey because of their common elite positions at Goldman-Sachs and J. P. Morgan respectively, the majority of Jewish employees at Goldman-Sachs, even at quite high levels, led their private lives entirely within Jewish communities (and probably had not even met their gentile counterparts at the Morgan

Diagram 1

The Triple Melting Pot and the
Class System, 1900 and 1950

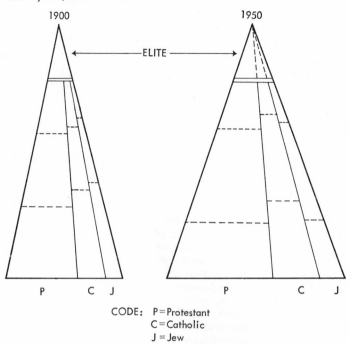

1900   1950

ELITE

P   C   J   P   C   J

CODE: P = Protestant
        C = Catholic
        J = Jew

firm). And similarly, part of the tragedy of La Guardia's life was that, though he had led a rich and convivial social life among his artistic and professional friends of Italian and Jewish extraction while he was a rising young lawyer in Greenwich Village, when he went to Washington, and later when he became Mayor of New York, he was forced by his functional position of leadership either to lead a social life within the elite or to have no social life at all.

The functional necessity that elite members associate with each other regardless of background or religion (or race, as the complications in the lives of such eminent Americans as Ralph Bunche or Marian Anderson attest to) is paralleled in many other areas of life. In residential patterns, for instance, the lower-class Jew will live within an entirely Jewish neighborhood, the middle-class Jew in a predominantly, but not wholly, Jewish suburb, while the elite Jew will more likely be found in an

almost predominantly gentile neighborhood.

This elite pattern also extends to the socialization of children at school and at college. While public schools are largely neighborhood schools, and thus often ethnically homogeneous, the best private schools cater to a class clientele from all parts of the city and its suburbs, and increasingly tend to include a small nucleus of children from elite Jewish families. The boarding school is, of course, even a more powerful class-assimilating atmosphere for the minority of Jewish youths who go there from wealthy and prominent families. Similarly, the sons of the elite will be living in a far more class-bound atmosphere at Harvard than at the College of the City of New York.

Finally, of course, the class-limited way of life at the top is naturally reflected in the frequency of intermarriages and religious conversions. Thus Baruch, La Guardia and Schiff all married gentiles. . . .

· ·

The theory of the triple melting pot, then, must be modified at the elite level in order to take into account the overwhelming factor of class. While in the third generation and at most class levels there is a return to ethnic and religious roots, centered in the suburban synagogue and

church, there is a reversal of this trend today at the top levels of national leadership. And the pinch of prejudice will increasingly be felt as more and more non-Anglo-Saxon Protestants rise to this level of society. At the same time, it should be emphasized that this importance of class makes the theory of the persistence of the Anglo-Saxon Ideal—which many sociologists have seen as an important modifying factor in the melting-pot theory—even

Diagram II

The Establishment and
the Triple Melting Pot

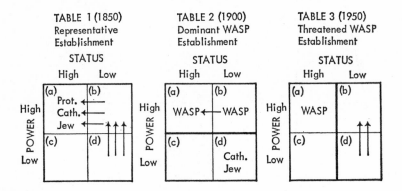

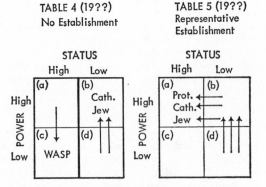

KEY CONCEPTS: Elite: Boxes (a) and (b) (High Functional Power)
Upper Class: Boxes (a) and (c) (High Social Status)
Establishment: Box (a) (Power, Status and Authority)
WASP: White-Anglo-Saxon-Protestant
Caste: Status without Authority (Box (c))
Aristocracy: Status with Authority (Box (a))

more important at the elite level than at other social-class levels. This is of course because the nation's leadership is still dominated by members of the WASP upper class, the primary source and carrier of this ideal.

. . . .

. . . While the social organization of the triple melting pot serves quite effectively in assimilating the descendants of the more recent immigrants into most levels of our pluralistic society, there is, at the same time, constant pressure at the top levels of leadership today, which is increasingly composed of hyphenated-Americans of the third generation, to assimilate *all* talented and powerful men, regardless of their origins or religious convictions, into the main stream of traditional authority by ultimately rewarding them with the dignity, security and family honor implied and nourished by membership in an establishment.

THE TRIPLE MELTING POT AND THE THEORY OF THE ESTABLISHMENT

In order to sharpen and elaborate the theory of the establishment, I have attempted to conceptualize, in a series of logical models shown in Diagram II, the past and possible future relationships between the three main ethnic-religious groupings in American society and the two variables of stratification: *social power* (position and power in the functional hierarchy of politics, business, religion, art, etc.) and *social status* (family position and prestige in the social-class hierarchy). Diagram II, in other words, conceptualizes the logically possible relationships between Protestants (WASPs), Catholics and Jews and the social organization of leadership. The *elite* concept, then, refers to those *individuals* at the top of the social power hierarchy (Diagram II, Box a and b); the *upper-class* concept refers to those *families* at the top of the social-status hierarchy (Box a and c): and the *establishment* refers to those leaders within the elite whose families also belong, or are in the process of belonging, to the upper class (Box a).

All social organizations are, of course, hierarchical. For social action depends on the differential distribution of power as between classes and individuals. The essential problem of social order, in turn, depends not on the *elimination* but the *legitimation* of social power. For power which is not legitimized (Box b) tends to be either coercive or manipulative. Freedom, on the other hand, depends not in doing what one wants but on wanting to do what one ought because of one's faith in long-established authority. An establishment (Box a), then, is composed of families who carry traditional authority deriving from the past, and present, power of their members. Both Franklin Roosevelt and Fiorello La Guardia, for instance, had power because of their personal qualities and functional positions. The Roosevelt family, however, possessed the kind of established authority which was denied the family of La Guardia.

This is not to say that all leaders in a changing society should be members of the establishment (Box a). They definitely should not. For new men (Box b) are always needed in every generation. The trouble comes when whole classes of new men, because of the accidents of ancestry, are denied the opportunity of translating their power and talent into some sort of family authority. But caste[3] not only denies the families of new men access to established authority; caste also weakens established authority itself because it tends to alienate its supposed beneficiaries by emphasizing their *rights* to privilege (Box c) rather than their *duties* to lead (Box a). Both the Roosevelt family's continual assumption of leadership *and* the continuous assimilation of men like La Guardia and Weinberg into the ranks of the upper class tend to strengthen the establishment's authority. On the other

[3] The author explains thus what he means by caste: "When, in any society, there is an upper class which protects its privileges and prestige but *does not continue* (1) to contribute leadership or (2) to assimilate new elite members, primarily because of their *racial or ethnic origins*, I shall refer to the process of *caste*. If an upper class degenerates into a caste, moreover, the traditional authority of an establishment is in grave danger of disintegrating, while society becomes a field for careerists seeking success and affluence. The caste process is the very antithesis of the aristocratic process and inevitably, in the long run if not immediately, leads to the decline of *authority* and a crisis in leadership." See *The Protestant Establishment, ibid.* p. 8. (C. S. H.)

hand, both when the established fail to lead and when leaders fail to become established, authority is in grave danger of degenerating into authoritarianism, and an organic social order becomes an atomized horde of fearful, alienated and manipulated individuals. The most difficult and delicate problem faced by democratic societies is that of balancing the liberal need for the continuous circulation of individual elites (Box b) with the conservative need for maintaining a continuity of family authority (Box a).

It is the theory of the establishment, then, that the processes of history may be conveniently conceptualized in terms of classes of men and their families circulating counterclockwise on the logical model outlined in Diagram II. When the cycle is complete, and is working without the corruptions of caste, the accomplishments and power of individual leaders are translated into family prestige and the continuity of established authority is maintained. From this point of view American leadership has gone through three more or less distinct periods.

In the first period, from the nation's founding and roughly through the first half of the nineteenth century, positions in the establishment were open to all white men, regardless of ethnic origin (Diagram II, Table 1). Thus, although there was a great deal of anti-Catholicism and fear of "Popery," individual Catholics were assimilated into the upper class on the basis of achievement and manners. The famous anti-Catholic riots in Philadelphia during the 1840s were really anti-Irish, and there was little or no antipathy toward middle-class German Catholics and certainly none toward the few distinguished Catholics who belonged to the upper class. At this time many leading families of Irish and Catholic origins became converts and passed on to their descendants solidly established positions in the Eastern Seaboard upper class. This was the case, for example, for such leading members of the Protestant establishment in Philadelphia as the Drexels of banking eminence (originally Austrian Catholics). . . . And this same pattern of accepting men on their merits and manners and assimilating their families into the establishment was followed, as we have

seen, in the case of the Jews. The power of aristocratic assimilation[4] which existed at this time, for example, was implied in a recently published history of the Philadelphia Assemblies—annual balls, attendance at which still marks a family's inclusion within the innermost circles of Philadelphia's upper class and which have been held continuously since George Washington was one's dancing partner. Thus the author of this history was proud to write that "there are on the Subscribers' List of the Assemblies today, families of the following racial strains: English, Welsh, Irish, French, German, Dutch, Swiss, Italian, Spanish, Portuguese, Swedish, and Polish."[5] (What he meant was that the impeccable WASP establishment in the city of Philadelphia was composed of families whose ancestors included Spanish, Portuguese, German and Polish Jews, Irish, French and Italian Catholics, as well as Protestants from all these nations and dominated by those from the British Isles.) In this first historical period, then, the American establishment, though rooted in a mercantile upper class which was exclusive, proud, uniform in manners and certainly less patronizingly democratic in its treatment of the rest of the population than is the case today, was nevertheless still representative of the ethnic and religious composition of the white population.

But all this was to change after the Civil War, when the ethnic composition of

[4] The author explains thus what he means by aristocratic assimilation: "By an aristocracy I mean (1) a *community of upper-class families* whose members are born to positions of high prestige and assured dignity because their ancestors have been leaders (elite members) for one generation or more; (2) that these families are carriers of a set of traditional values which command *authority* because they represent the aspirations of both the elite and the rest of the population; and (3) that this class continues to justify its authority (a) by contributing its share of contemporary leaders and (b) by continuing to assimilate, in each generation, the families of new members of the elite. As with the elite concept, I do not conceive of the aristocracy as the 'best' or the 'fittest' in the sense of the term 'natural aristocracy' as used by Jefferson. The aristocratic process means that the *upper class is open.*" See *The Protestant Esatblishment, ibid.,* pp. 7–8. (C. S. H.)

[5] Joseph P. Sims, *The Philadelphia Assemblies,* 1748–1948, privately printed, p. 8.

American society was radically altered by the new immigration. This second historical period, which reached its peak somewhere between 1900 and the First World War, was marked by an associationally exclusive establishment of White–Anglo-Saxon–Protestants who dominated the leadership of the nation. . . . The WASP establishment during this period was still representative of the elite, even though it was increasingly less representative of the population as a whole (Diagram II, Table 2). For this reason the establishment still possessed authority. In other words, it is not necessary, in the short run at least, that an upper class be representative of the whole people. In fact upper-class families are not recruited from the population at all but only from its leadership. The elite, on the other hand, must in the long run reflect and draw on the pool of national talent which inevitably resides in all classes. This is especially true where the people are literate and where a considerable majority have an opportunity for education. As of 1900, there was an authoritative establishment even though there was a more or less closed caste line drawn at the elite level which excluded those hyphenated-Americans of the Catholic and Jewish communities.

The significant difference in the structure of leadership in America in the third, as against the second, historical period is the fact that the caste line is now drawn in a status rather than a power sense, or, as it were, right down the middle of the elite (Diagram II, Table 3). In other words, our open class system has continued to work quite well and has produced a more or less ethnically representative elite. Our status system, on the other hand, has failed to keep pace. The WASP establishment has been forced to share its power while at the same time continuing to hoard its social privileges. In a very important sense, we now have in America, at the elite level of leadership, a *caste-ridden, open-class* society. And the consequent pressure upon the upper class to open its doors to the most talented and polished descendants of the newer immigrants has increased tremendously. . . .

At this time it is hard to see how the dynamic tension between the pressures of caste exclusion and of aristocratic assimilation which is now characteristic of the nation's leadership will finally be resolved. Today the situation is an ambivalent one. In the long run, there are two logically possible alternatives: either the WASP establishment will eventually develop into a closed caste, protecting its way of life and privileges while gradually abdicating from its position of leadership (Diagram II, Table 4), or a new aristocracy will emerge with the energy and ability to absorb the most prominent and polished families in the nation, regardless of their ethnic origins or religious convictions (Table 5). These strictly logical alternatives are, of course, only polar tendencies, and reality will fall somewhere in between.

CASTE AND THE CLUB

Lacking the communal solidarity which older social structures have inherited from their feudal pasts, American society has always been faced with the dangerous consequences of extreme individualism. Atomized individualism always tends to degenerate into anarchy on the one hand, and more or less extreme forms of centralization on the other. Yet fortunately, up till now, we have avoided both these two extremes through our traditional ability to create a host of mutually excluding, yet interlocking, voluntary associations. "Wherever at the head of some new undertaking," wrote Tocqueville over a hundred years ago, "you see the government in France, or a man of rank in England, in the United States you will be sure to find an association." . . .

At the upper-class level in America, moreover, the club (a private voluntary association) lies at the very core of the social organization of the accesses to power and authority. . . . It is the anachronistic admissions policies of the leading upper-class clubs in America today . . . which lie at the very basis of the decline of upper-class authority, and the resulting confusion in communal and national leadership. The authority structure in this country is indeed in trouble, for instance, when a member of the oldest country club in the nation was able to say, not long before President Kennedy was killed, that he was proud of the fact that his club's admissions policies had not yet descended to the level of accepting any member of the nation's First Family. The absurdity of the statement is more understandable, however, when one takes into account the fact that the vast majority of the distinguished doctors, lawyers and business executives and their families who reside in the Boston suburb where the country club is located (and where John F. Kennedy was born) are categorically unacceptable for membership because of their ethnic origins.

. . . What Henry James found to be one of the uniquely characteristic American institutions was born with the founding of The Country Club, at Brookline, Massachusetts, in 1882. . . .

The boom in suburban clubs since the war has come about for several reasons. Of most importance is the fact that the policies of country-club admissions committees are one of the main ways of perpetuating caste divisions in an age when both the suburbs and elite leadership positions have been greatly democratized. From the time The Country Club, in Brookline, was founded until roughly up to the end of the Second War, the American upper-class suburb was almost entirely the monopoly of Anglo-Saxon Protestants. Country-club membership, then, was largely a reflection of community composition. As the upper classes still lived in large houses with spacious rooms and plenty of servants, moreover, the club was primarily a functional association used for the single purpose of sport (mainly golf, as private tennis courts and swimming pools were the rule).

On the other hand, the country club of today has become a veritable community. Space is at a premium even in the sixty- and seventy-thousand-dollar executive housing developments, while servants are scarce and overdemanding if not unobtainable. Consequently leisure-time and sporting activities have moved to the country club, where restaurants and bars do a thriving business (dues of course can often be written off as a business expense in these days when business and leisure so often interlock). But more than the economic factor is involved. Even the most exclusive suburbs are now no longer the monopoly of Anglo-Saxons, and the club serves to protect one's ethnic purity in increasing heterogeneous neighborhoods. This is especially true as far as elite Jews are concerned, for middle-class Jews are still most likely to settle in predominantly Jewish suburbs. It is the most talented and successful Jewish leaders in the community who of necessity deal on close social terms with gentiles in countless civic and charitable activities, who are also most likely to live in predominantly gentile upper-class neighborhoods. At the same time, as one Jewish civic leader reported: "They'll call on me to lead their Community Chest campaign or help on the Red Cross. But when it comes to the country club, I'm not good enough for them." Catholics are also moving to the suburbs in large numbers. Thus a Democratic political leader who was worried about affluent and suburbanized Catholics deserting to the Republican Party told Theodore H. White during the last Presidential campaign: "These guys whose grandfathers used to want to be captain of the ward now all want to be president of the country club."[6]

In response to the new suburban heterogeneity as well as to the caste values of the old-stock Protestants who got there first, minority country clubs have multiplied since the war and are now preserving the triple melting pot in the elite suburbs.

. . . .

THE CLUB AND THE CORPORATE ELITE: THE TAIL THAT WAGS THE DOG

At noon every day in the week, the men at the top of the executive suites in the city of Pittsburgh gather for lunch in a great brownstone pile which has housed the Duquesne Club since 1889. As one old-timer at the club remarked: "The way to tell if a fellow's getting along in any Pittsburgh company is to see if he's yet a member of the Duquesne. As soon as his name goes up for membership, you know he ought to be watched. He's a comer."[7] . . .

The Duquesne Club lies at the very core of the associational organization of

[6] Theodore White, *The Making of the President, 1960.* New York: Atheneum Press, 1962, p. 240.

[7] Osborn Eliott, *Men at the Top.* New York: Harper & Brothers, 1959, p. 164.

leadership in Pittsburgh. In fact, it has been argued by the club's management in the federal courts that income from dues should not be taxable because it is a business organization.

. . . .

Here indeed is a distinctly American institution where close primary relationships are forged between top management men who have the power of decision over trans-communal corporate activities which affect the lives of men and women all over the world, from the Atlantic to the Pacific, from the Monongahela to the Amazon. It is, too, a kind of associational aristocracy-by-ballot which is ideally suited to a dynamic and democratic society's continual need to assimilate new men of talent and power into the top levels of established leadership.

But at the same time this aristocratic function fails, at clubs like the Duquesne, to reach out beyond the boundaries of nominal-Christian affiliations. In the long run, these caste boundaries will inevitably create embarrassing situations which will be downright dysfunctional to the organization and recruitment of leadership. Even today there is in Pittsburgh an executive at the very top level of leadership in one of the nation's major corporations who has never been taken into the Duquesne because of his Jewish origins (even though he has never been associated in any way with the city's Jewish community).

. . . .

It is not, of course, that the values of the gentile gentlemen who dominate the admissions policies of the Duquesne are out of the ordinary. On the contrary, they mirror the mores of most of the leading metropolitan men's clubs in the nation. In city after city, the admissions policies of the top clubs are increasingly causing our national corporations to bar some of their best-qualified men from top leadership positions. . . .

One wonders how the younger generation of potential executives now coming out of the leading universities and the graduate schools of business will fit into this pattern of caste exclusion at clubs like the Duquesne. Most of them will, of course, go along with the conventional mores. Or they will choose careers elsewhere; which many sons of present business leaders will surely do for this very reason. And they will presumably be the kind of men who prefer a world where convictions count. A world, for example, where men like Angier Biddle Duke are not afraid to resign from organizations whose policies they consider dysfunctional to the nation's leadership. . . . Perhaps the main point at issue here, is the fact that not only are caste policies dysfunctional as far as the associational organization of leadership within the business community itself is concerned; these policies are also dysfunctional in that they will, in the future, alienate more and more young men of talent and principle from seeking careers in the business world. . . .

THE CLUB AND THE RUMBLINGS OF REVOLT

Although policies of caste exclusion still characterize the vast majority of metropolitan men's clubs in America, there are signs of change, even though the bastions of the business establishment still lag behind.

. . . .

. . . Also in accord with our thesis, Amory sees the decline in New York's club life as partly a result of the younger generation's *disenchantment with anti-Semitism*. . . . On the other hand, Amory finds that the most successful social clubs in New York in the 1960s—the Century, the Cosmopolitan, the River, and the Regency, as well as the socio-theatrical and literary clubs like the Lotos, the Players and the Coffee House— all have members who also happen to be of Jewish origins. But above all, the college clubs have been the most successful in the city. Once citadels of snobbery . . . these clubs are now the most useful in the city because, as one member of the Harvard and Century clubs, who recently resigned from the Union after almost a quarter of a century's membership, put it recently: "I want a club where I can take a couple of friends without producing a birth certificate, a marriage license and a blood test."[8] . . . But in spite of the acceptance of change

[8] Cleveland Amory, *Who Killed Society?* New York: Harper & Brothers, 1960, p. 227.

which marks the policies at the Harvard and Century clubs, such eminent clubs as the Union, Knickerbocker and the Links are still dominated by the society and bourgeois ideals of caste exclusion.

The differential response to the social changes of our era are reflected in the club system in New York; indeed they reflect the conflicting social forces which lie at the very heart of our whole social system. Sometimes apparently unrelated sociological facts . . . have a way of hanging together to form a pattern. Thus the nature of American leadership at any given time is partly a reflection of its leaders' attitudes toward clubs. . . . But by far the most important clue to the difference between the Democratic and Republican leadership in America today is to be found by examining the membership and admission policies of the Links and Century clubs in New York City. . . . Although the Knickerbocker and Union clubs have long been strongholds of the Protestant Anglo-Saxon business establishment in America, centered in the family firm and Wall Street investment banking houses, the Links Club, since the war, has become the New York *rendezvous* of the national corporate establishment. It is of symbolic interest that the Links was founded in 1921, not as a purely business club, but rather "to promote and conserve throughout the U.S. the best interests and true spirit of the game of golf." Its out-of-town membership is almost entirely business and includes such eminent members as a Crocker from San Francisco, a Pillsbury from Minneapolis, a Ford from Detroit, a Field from Chicago, a Humphrey from Cleveland, a Mellon from Pittsburgh, a du Pont from Wilmington, a Pew from Philadelphia, and a Cabot from Boston. Of course its membership does not include such eminent and public-spirited business leaders as Sidney Weinberg or Meyer Kestnbaum, even though they may be intimate friends of many members. No Jews, and few if any professors or Democrats, belong to the Links.

The Century Association is far older than the Links and was founded for very different purposes by a group of artists and authors, in 1847. But "authors and artists cannot stand apart from the practical world," wrote the founders. . . . And so they in-

vited into their club "gentlemen of any occupation provided their breadth of interest and moral qualities and imagination make them sympathetic, stimulating and congenial companions to the society of authors and artists." [9] This tone set by the founders has stood the test of time. At the Century today, one meets artists, professors, college presidents and distinguished men of affairs from both business and politics. As artists are not likely to be awed by a man's origins, there are Jews among the membership. . . .

In the middle of the twentieth century, then, the contrasting membership and admissions policies at the Links and Century clubs are arresting examples of the forces of caste, on the one hand, and aristocracy, on the other. On the whole, while the Links represents the authority of the business-Republic establishment, the Century's membership reflects the cultural and political leadership of the nation and is far more receptive to the ideals of the Democratic Party. The club affiliations of the Rockefeller family are of interest here. The family is of course Republican, and Nelson is one of the most eminent members of the party. . . . Nelson lists membership in the aristocratic Century rather than the caste-bound Links. For perhaps Nelson Rockefeller, whose family symbolizes the very essence of established communal authority in this country, may eventually be able to lead his party to a new position of established political authority. But, as the eight Eisenhower years so amply demonstrated, this transformation will not be produced by any single victory or series of victories at the polls; it will not be done through campaign oratory and platforms professing the ideals of civil liberty; it will not be done by putting forth minority candidates for office or by appointing Catholics or Jews to important governmental positions; it will, in the long run, be accomplished only when the established communal leaders who dominate the Republican Party in city after city assimilate within their ranks the most distinguished and talented men in their respective communities, regardless of their ethnic or religious origins. This will not be done until, among other things, the admissions

[9] *Ibid.,* p. 215.

committees of the leading metropolitan men's clubs, in the style of the Century rather than the Links, take seriously their aristocratic role as leaders of assimilating associations in the communal organization of power. Or, as Richard Nixon put it after his recent defeat, until the Republicans "quit being an exclusive social club."

What is needed, then, is a sociological, rather than a political, revolution within the ranks of the establishment. And this revolution, in accord with the Whig tradition in England rather than the radical tradition in France, needs only to regenerate its original ideals of equality of opportunity. . . .

PART VII
Change in Stratification Systems

Social change has for some time been the neglected branch of sociology, a fact generally recognized and deplored in the discipline. As T. H. Marshall assessed it, in no field of study is this neglect more evident than in that of social stratification. Students of stratification not only fail to pay attention to the "dynamic forces" but "often deliberately eliminate these dynamic forces in an endeavor to discover the essence of the present system, viewed in its own right as a system."[1]

Approached from this perspective, all our readings in this section have the distinction of focusing on change. The first is on the "Interaction Between Industrial and Pre-Industrial Stratification Systems," by Bert F. Hoselitz. He distinguishes four different patterns of change that have followed the introduction of Western economic and political elements into relatively stable tradition-oriented societies. His analysis, however, concentrates on only one of these patterns: some form of slow integration of the new elements with the old ones. As examples of societies where it is taking place, he mentions Indonesia, India, and Pakistan. The most important fact here, according to the author, is that industrialization leads to urbanization. The industrially employed labor force is concentrated in cities and at the beginning there is a deep gulf between them and the rest of the population, much larger in number, who continue to be employed in agriculture. However, as economic change proceeds, the rural and urban sectors become increasingly interdependent. The stratification system that evolves first in the urban areas and then spreads to the country at large, tends to resemble that of Western societies. Thus he see this type of stratification—associated with economic growth—compatible with different types of original cultures in the societies prior to industrialization. He predicts that in many countries of Asia and Africa, differing in their cultures, similar systems of stratification will develop in the next few decades.

In a sense, the picture of change in Peru drawn by David Chaplin in our second

[1] T. H. Marshall, "Changes in Social Stratification in the Twentieth Century," in *Class, Citizenship and Social Development*, Garden City, Doubleday, 1964, p. 124.

selection has many points in common with those made by Hoselitz, and yet it does not completely fit into Hoselitz' scheme. The focus is also on urbanization, but Chaplin shows that in Peru urbanization largely precedes rather than follows industrialization. To put it plainly, Peru is more urbanized than industrialized. In that country, marked by a rigid class structure with persisting feudal features and low economic development, some changes have been taking place ahead of industrialization. They are being brought about by urbanization based on foreign trade rather than domestic industrial development. Thus in Peru—as well as in some other countries in Latin America,[2] and perhaps in other parts of the world such as the Near East—we witness effects on the existing stratification system of urbanization ahead of industrialization. One would therefore suppose that Chaplin's analysis of Peru is applicable to some extent to all such countries.

Especially noteworthy is Chaplin's hypothesis that urbanization in Peru, and in Latin America in general, unlike that which occurred in Europe, is having a negative effect on urban lower-class protest, leading to *deradicalization*, that is, the stifling of radicalism in that class. The radicals are the university students of "modest" socioeconomic background who suffer from status deprivation. But once they complete their university training they are easily coopted. One might add that the cooptation of lower-class leaders is a common and perfected procedure in Latin America. It appeared to this writer, while studying stratification in Colombia, South America, from 1953–1956, as if at times the oligarchy were consciously following Pareto's prescription of how a ruling class is to maintain itself in power.[3] That it might not be as successful in the future, nevertheless, is suggested by the case of Cuba. The potential followers of revolutionary leaders in Peru, as in Cuba, according to Chaplin, are the landless peasants. Here he seems in accord with Raymond Aron's generalization that "wherever feudal hierarchies survive and wherever great landowners cultivate, more or less carelessly, the land on which the farmers and agricultural workers labour, propaganda for a classless society will find large numbers of followers."[4] That it has not found them in large numbers among the peasants of Peru is because many of them are Indians who are still nonparticipants in the larger Peruvian society. The Indians in Peru, who comprise about one-third of the total population, fit into one of the four aforementioned patterns outlined by Hoselitz: the pattern of the indigeneous group remaining for a long time a separate entity.

Another possible pattern resulting from the introduction of Western elements into the tradition-oriented societies named by Hoselitz is that of complete reorientation along Western lines. He considers the transformation of Japan in the last hundred years the best example of this pattern.

Perhaps the other case of modernization that could match Japan in its rapidity is that of Isreal. But apart from this, the selection from Eisenstadt's book *Israeli Society* is impressive because it represents the unique case of the study by a sociologist of the inception of a stratification system in a total society. Here is a study

[2] For a general understanding of stratification in Latin America see Ralph L. Beals, "Social Stratification in Latin America," *American Journal of Sociology*, No. 58, 1953, pp. 327–339.

[3] On cooptation of rising leaders by the dominant political party of Mexico, see Claudio Stern and Joseph A. Kahl, "Stratification Since the Revolution," in Joseph A. Kahl, ed., *Comparative Perspectives on Stratification*, Boston: Little, Brown and Company, 1968, p. 27. One lites and development in Latin America, see Seymour Martin Lipset and Aldo Solari, eds., *Elites in Latln America*, New York: Oxford University Press, 1967.

[4] Raymond Aron, "Social Structure and the Ruling Class," *British Journal of Sociology*, Vol. I, March, 1950, p. 86.

of a stratification system emerging in a society whose founders were dedicated to the creation of a classless society. It has then some resemblance to the case of Russia where the founders of the new Soviet regime were committed to the ideology of a classless society. But it differs in other important respects, as will become clear. From a sociological point of view, perhaps the most important difference is that in postrevolutionary Russia the tendency toward equilibrium, as formulated by Pareto, set in: gradually old patterns, or certain aspects of them, returned. But in Israel the stratification system was and is emerging simultaneously with the emerging of a society. Here we find a new society and a new stratification system in the making. Eisenstadt outlines for us the multiple tendencies that are at play, some contradictory to one another and some reinforcing each other. He traces their origin and development through the three periods of the new society: during the *Old Yishuv*, the original pioneer settlement prior to Palestine's becoming an English mandate; during the mandatory period; and in the present period, after the achievement of statehood. To give a simplified characterization of those periods—the specifics of which can be found in the selection—the first was a period of relative social equality; the second of the beginning of the structuring of inequality; and the third of a growing system of social inequality. Although some trends contradictory to the pioneering ideology have become especially strong during statehood—with its unified political framework, increasing economic development, and influx of Jewish immigrants from the Orient—nevertheless the ideology of pioneering, of service to the nation, has put its stamp on the emerging stratification system. One of the contradictory trends, which the author considers especially important and to which he gives considerable attention, is the growing importance of political power as a criterion of evaluation and as an avenue of access to high economic position.

A similarity may be observed here between the situation of the lowest socioeconomic groups in Israel and what Myrdal designated as the underclass in the United States. As Eisenstadt describes them, they are in a sense marginal within the society. There is also a similarity in their composition: in the United States an overrepresentation of Negroes, Mexican Americans and Puerto Ricans, and in Israel of Oriental Jews in the lowest socioeconomic levels.

In the next selection in this part of our book the complex problem of the nature of stratification in industrial society is succinctly discussed by John Goldthorpe. In his essay a poignant critique of the much-accepted view of industrial development as the prime determinant of the pattern of change in the stratification systems of advanced, or what he terms mature, industrial societies is found. This idea is part of a conception of "the standardizing effects upon social structures of the exigencies of modern technology and of an advanced economy."[5] These factors supposedly cancel out the effects of other factors that vary from one society to another—such as the national culture or the political system—and press for an essential similarity in the stratification systems of advanced industrial societies. By the time the reader turns to Goldthorpe's essay he will have already come across this conception in a number of our selections, most recently in the Hoselitz article just discussed. Clearly, Hoselitz adhers to this conception. But one of the first, and perhaps the most explicit sociological expositions of this thesis on stratification in advanced industrial society is found in Theodor Geiger's *Die Klassengeselschaft*

[5] A later rendition of this thesis is found in John Kenneth Galbraith, *The New Industrial State,* Boston: Houghton Mifflin, 1967.

im Schmelztiegel, to which Goldthorpe does not refer. The reader who recalls its main arguments from the selection reprinted in Part II of this book will now have the chance to judge whether it withstands the empirical evidence marshaled by Goldthorpe against later versions of the same thesis.

Goldthorpe breaks down the thesis into three parts and proceeds to show how each is not in accord with empirical data from Western societies. The data he refers to—on distribution of income and wealth, on status inconsistency, and on social mobility—will be familiar to the reader who has studied the earlier selections. What he will find new here is the use Goldthorpe makes of them to test hypotheses concerning changes of stratification systems in advanced industrial societies.

Having shaken the thesis by pointing to the numerous empirical findings at odds with it, he moves on to what he considers more fundamental theoretical criticisms. He arrives at these through examining stratification in the Soviet Union and comparing it with stratification in the West. Although there are similarities between them, Goldthorpe, in contrast to Theodor Geiger, insists that they are of a *phenotypical kind*, that is in appearance only. *Genotypically*, that is in essence, they differ sharply. He makes the point that in the West economic forces constitute the crucial stratifying agency. In the Soviet Union, the system of stratification is subject to political regulation. As he expresses it, the Soviet stratification system is characterized by an important element of deliberateness that sets it apart from the Western system.

It might be appropriate to add here that Goldthorpe's analysis resembles Raymond Aron's formulation. According to the latter "the fundamental difference between a society of the Soviet type and one of the Western type is that the former has a unified *elite* and the latter a divided elite."[6] In the hands of the first are concentrated both political and economic powers, which are absolute and unbounded. They have infinitely more power than the rulers in Western democracies. The main point of Goldthorpe's detailed discussion, as well as of Aron's, is that essentially different systems of stratification exist in Soviet and Western types of societies, although both are in a state of advanced industrialization.

The thesis of essentially different stratification systems in contemporary socialist and capitalist societies is central in our next selection. "Strata and Strata Interests in Socialist Society," a paper delivered at the Sixth World Congress of Sociology by the Polish sociologist Wlodzimierz Wesolowski. However, his argument rests on other grounds than those of Goldthorpe or Aron. Although it deviates from the "official" line on stratification (which is pronounced with boring repetition by Soviet "sociologists" at international meetings) and in this sense is "revisionist," it nevertheless begins with the same assumption. Wesolowski assumes that the classic Marxist criterion of relation to the means of production ceases to play an important part in socialist society because private ownership of the means of production is largely abolished. The author completely disregards the question of who controls the means of production (recall the selections by Theodor Geiger and Djilas). Thus he sees socialism as representing the eventual equalization in relation to the means of production and therefore as a classless society. (But we could add, only as far as formal ownership is concerned; not as far as control over it is concerned.) And his analysis of stratification in socialist society largely ignores

[6] Aron, *op. cit.*, p. 10.

the unequal distribution of power while concentrating on income, education, and prestige inequality. This is especially noteworthy in light of the fact that in an earlier article devoted to the criticism of the functional theory of stratification, he gave much attention on theoretical grounds to inequality in authority and concluded that it is characteristic of all stratified societies. (See pp. 503–511 in this volume.) But when he deals specifically with stratification in socialist society— what he said about Davis and Moore could be said about him—he is "inclined to relegate authority to the background."

Wesolowski analyzes the process of change in the stratification system of socialist society. Even though socialist society succeeds in abolishing the capitalist class, it nevertheless inherits from the capitalist system the *class* of small farmers and the *stratum* of intelligentsia, white-collar workers and professionals. (The first in the "official Marxist" conception is a class because its distinguishing characteristic lies in its relation to the means of production. But this is not the case of the latter and that is why it is termed a stratum whose distinguishing characteristic is nonmanual labor.)

The process of transformation in the class structure inherited from capitalism, according to Wesolowski, varies in speed from one socialist society to another but always proceeds in two directions: (1) equalization of the relation to means of production—small farmers are at first tolerated but eventually eliminated or, as the author expresses it, changed into "employees of the state" and (2) income, prestige, and opportunity cease to be determined by the relation to the means of production.

What is not to be overlooked in Wesolowski's article is the attention he pays to conflicting interests in socialist society. This represents a marked departure from the official Marxist line, which holds that once private ownership of the means of production is abolished, antagonistic interests disappear. But Wesolowski is careful to trace his concept of *contradiction of interests* in socialist society to Marx's writings. (This is a common procedure among scientists in socialist countries who depart from the official line; it takes more exaggerated forms in the Soviet Union than in Poland.) Marx, Wesolowski explains, spoke not only about the opposite interests between classes but also among workers competing for the same jobs. The author argues that socialist society to this very day is marked by a scarcity of generally desired goods or values and "their distribution is by necessity such that any increase of the share of one group is bound to bring cuts in the share of another group." Therein lie the roots of opposite interests in socialist society.

The author does not confine himself to the analysis of the objective side of the contradiction of interests but moves on to an analysis of the subjective perception of these interests as conflicting or not, depending on one's location in the social structure. The wide acceptance of the formula "to each according to his work" as just, he argues, works in the direction of diminishing the awareness of the opposite interests that exist in socialist society. But when there are departures from this formula, even when these are in accordance with other socialist principles, they result in such awareness, especially among the lowest income groups.

As we read Wesolowski's exposition we cannot help but note numerous similarities between stratification in contemporary socialist and capitalist societies. The author himself does not seem to be able to escape them, but he insists in the footnotes that they are only phenotypical similarities. In this sense his position resembles that of Goldthorpe.

Despite the thorough analysis by Goldthorpe and Wesolowski, the question of the similarity and difference between the Soviet type and the Western type of stratification is not yet answered conclusively. Thus our last two selections devoted to change connect rather well with the readings that follow them in the final part of the book, "Unresolved Issues in Stratification Theory."

INTERACTION BETWEEN INDUSTRIAL AND PRE-INDUSTRIAL STRATIFICATION SYSTEMS

Bert F. Hoselitz

A common aspect of economic development, in societies that already have experienced it as well as those engaged in bringing it about, is the increase of the secondary and tertiary sectors in the economy. Although technical and other improvements of agriculture are being considered or carried out in all these societies, the major socioeconomic change with which development is usually associated is the change from technically simple production methods. With this change is associated an increase in the numbers of highly educated people and skilled and specialized workers, and an absolute or proportional decline of the rural, especially the small village population, as towns and urban areas grow.

I offer this crude description of economic advancement here, not in an attempt to describe economic development as a process, but to suggest the very general characteristics of change in economic practices, in residential patterns, and in the nature of economically and socially interacting groups, which are usually associated with economic development. In some countries these changes have been relatively rapid, in others slow, and in others they are just beginning. My purpose is to describe in rather general terms the characteristics of societies in which certain parts are still strongly influenced by the "old-fashioned" conditions of social structure and in which other parts, especially the industrialized urban sectors, have accepted or been forced into new forms of social organization and

From Neil J. Smelser and Seymour Martin Lipset, eds., *Social Structure and Mobility in Economic Development*. Reprinted by permission of the Aldine Publishing Company.

new relations between persons belonging to different and possibly new social classes.

DUALISM AND ECONOMIC DEVELOPMENT

In his doctoral dissertation, presented in 1910, J. H. Boeke set forth a theory of social and economic development founded on the concept of "dualism," and the present analysis is strongly influenced by his work. Boeke's extensive reading and research on Dutch practices and policies in Indonesia brought him to the conclusion that social and economic conditions and life patterns in Indonesia, and possibly in other tropical Asian territories, were so different from those prevailing in Europe that theories concerned with Western social and economic growth and development were an inadequate and unrealistic basis for interpreting socioeconomic relations in the less industrialized, economically non-rationalized societies of tropical Asia.[1] . . .

A very informative statement of the views supporting and objecting to Boeke's ideas was published recently,[2] and some economists have published a series of essays rather critical of dualism, even rebutting Boeke's views, although an anthropologically-inclined sociologist and a few economists concerned with some of the more interesting countries experiencing economic change and growth have adopted certain aspects of dualism.[3] . . .

[1] Julius H. Boeke, *Dualistische Economie* (Leiden: S. C. van Doesburgh, 1930); *Oriental Economics* (New York: Institute of Pacific Relations, 1947).

[2] See the "Introduction" (writer's name not indicated) to *Indonesian Economics: The Concept of Dualism in Theory and Policy*, Vol. 6 of *Selected Studies on Indonesia*, by Dutch Scholars (The Hague: W. van Hoeve, 1961), esp. pp. 30–64.

[3] Among the opposing essays are Benjamin H. Higgins, "The 'Dualistic Theory' of Underdeveloped Areas," *Economic Development and Cultural Change*, 4 (1956), pp. 99–115, and Yoichi Itagaki, "Some Notes on the Controversy Concerning Boeke's 'Dualistic Theory'; Implications for the Theory of Economic Development in Underdeveloped Countries," *Hitotsubashi Journal of Economics*, 1 (October, 1960), pp. 13–28. For a more positive treatment of dualism, see John H. Rex, "The Plural Society in Sociological Theory," *British Journal of Sociology*, 10 (June, 1959), pp. 114–124, and William J. Barber, *The Economy of British Central Africa* (Stanford: Stanford University Press, 1961), *passim*.

. . . Whereas Boeke argued that the imposition of Western social, economic and political elements on non-Western societies would produce a structure permanently bifurcated into Western and non-Western systems, Nash insists that introducing Western social and economic conditions is likely to produce a plural system, subject to change and evolution, and that the more highly developed and the more traditional parts of the society may be interrelated to different degrees in different tropical countries.[4] Since this criticism seems valid, I shall apply it in the following discussion of different patterns of economic growth and political change.

First, I shall outline the general changes that may take place under the impact of various Western economic and political institutions in underdeveloped societies. Let us assume that the societies not yet exposed to foreign technical or economic procedures are relatively well integrated and functionally not highly differentiated, and that they can maintain themselves in their social and economic environment, in which some long-range changes may go on. These societies may appear to many foreign observers to be stable and essentially unchanging. Political activities tend to be hierarchical and probably not democratic in the modern sense. Minor disturbances can be handled without upsetting the social and economic equilibrium and without altering the nature of the society. . . .

The imposition of Western institutions on a relatively stable, strongly tradition-oriented society may destroy the economically simpler society completely, and though its people may survive, they are either integrated with the more advanced population or maintained on a welfare basis. An example of this pattern of change is the destruction, absorption, or socio-economic subjection of the American Indians during the settlement of the United States. Although quite a few Indian communities still exist on United States territory, their independent economic activity has ceased and

their social and political systems have been destroyed. A number of Indians have been assimilated to some extent, but only those who settled in white American areas and completely gave up their associations with other members of the original societies.

A second pattern is the adoption of completely new forms of economic, social, and political organization. Although these non-Western social systems may have been relatively well developed, they become completely reoriented. The transformation of Japan in the last hundred years is perhaps the best example, but the same pattern has also occurred in geographically more limited areas such as Singapore and Hong Kong. There, colonial organization was politically limited by the boundaries between these urban populations and the much more stable populations in surrounding areas. The Japanese case is different, for here a large society adopted new methods of production —and as a result altered its political structure and social organization to produce a new social system. The latter cannot be said to exhibit dualism, for it is an integrated form of socioeconomic organization basically different from the form that existed before the major innovations took place.

In addition to complete destruction of the non-Western society and its complete reorganization, two other possibilities are substantively of greater significance and more closely related to the problem of dualism. One is the situation where an indigenous tribal or related group remains for a long time a self-centered, separate entity. For example, Barber argues that the Barotse tribe of Northern Rhodesia has remained socially and economically isolated and has scarcely interacted in any way with the remainder of the country.[5] Other instances of this type are known, though it is questionable how long these isolated communities can persist. The Indian societies in South America that survived Spanish colonialization belong in this class. Similarly, a number of separate tribal groups in India led a life of their own during all or most of the British colonial rule and did

---

[4] This is a somewhat modified presentation of ideas expressed by Manning Nash in "Southeast Asian Society—Dual or Multiple," *Journal of Asian Studies*, Vol. XXIII, No. 3, pp. 420–422.

[5] See Barber, *op. cit.*, pp. 20 and 44.

not interact with the part of the society that was under Western domination. Similar situations may exist in some Indonesian islands and elsewhere, and in some parts of Africa separate tribal groups have only minimal contact with non-tribal populations.

These situations are probably not permanent, and changes occurring in the surrounding areas will eventually bring about some form of change in the relatively isolated groups. They may become integrated with the surrounding populations; this appears to be an important and powerful development in many parts of the world. Until a few years ago, for example, portions of Tibet formed a self-sustained, economically integrated social and political entity, whose connections with both the Indians and the Chinese were very limited. The Chinese invasion of Tibet altered this situation, and within the next few years the Tibetans will either be exterminated, essentially, or integrated with the Chinese people. Similar developments will probably take place in Africa and Asia, where independent and relatively isolated tribal groups still exist. In the Amazonian areas of Brazil a few very small, extremely isolated tribal communities still exist: they will be exterminated, completely subordinated like North American Indians, or incorporated in the wider Brazilian society. Similar patterns are likely to occur among Canadian and Alaskan Eskimos.

These are, in some ways, the most important and genuine examples of dualism, but modern communication methods, rising political aspirations, and the tendency toward unified political and social communities even among African and other still undeveloped societies, create conditions under which isolated communities can last only a relatively short time. At present, however, a good many such communities do exist, and research on them and their peculiarities during the past may be of some interest.

Finally I come to the fourth case, some form of integration of the more with the less westernized portions of a colonial area. Indonesia, India, Pakistan and many other areas in tropical Asia and Africa represent this situation. . . .

INTERACTION BETWEEN INDUSTRIAL AND PRE-INDUSTRIAL STRATIFICATION SYSTEMS

In countries that have recently become independent and established new sociopolitical systems, the most significant social phenomenon is not dualism, but the fact that industrialization has created an urban, industrially employed labor force, superimposed on or coordinated with a larger number of agricultural workers and producers. In many of these countries, particularly in Africa and Asia, by far the largest proportion of the economically active population—between 60 and 80 per cent or even more—is still in agriculture. Industries, as well as various services, are usually located in urban areas; hence agriculturalists differ substantially from persons in secondary and tertiary occupations, not only in terms of occupational activity but often in terms of the locality where it is carried out.

Where old cultures are well established, however—as, for example, in India—local differentiation between farming and other forms of productive activity is less important than it is in some of the African and Southeast Asian countries where persons in non-agricultural occupations are often foreigners or members of a linguistically or "nationally" distinct group. Examples are the Chinese in various Southeast Asian countries, the Lebanese and Syrians in parts of Africa, and the Indians in various parts of East Africa. Many of these people are in service and trade occupations, but to some extent modern industrial development has brought them into commercial activities as well. Thus, differences between urban and rural populations, between native and originally foreign persons, and between industrially and agriculturally occupied persons have tended to produce different processes of adjustment and change in different areas. Where important and apparently insuperable conflicts arose between two or more sections of the population, dualism or pluralism was discovered. But a more careful analysis of these changes shows that such contrasts and conflicts may not be insuperable and that gradual, if slow, adjustment is possible and even probable.

Manning Nash has written a detailed description of the introduction of industrial production methods in a peasant society: Cantel, in Guatemala.[6] Cantel is a small Indian community, originally based entirely on agriculture, whose relations with other communities and other social groups clearly exhibited traditions prevalent among Central American Indians. Though the different native communities in Guatemala possessed a variety of dialects, costumes, saints, and sacred ceremonies, their interrelations within a village and between villages created a culturally and sociologically stable system, changing little. Then a textile factory was set up in one community. The factory employed Indians from the neighborhood, some of whom had previously not earned money income, few of whom had lived close to the factory, and none of whom had been engaged in an economic activity requiring regular working hours, specific behavior at the work place, or other related forms of behavior.

Nash describes the whole process of change in the article cited and in a book dealing with the same problem; I shall not repeat this here, but I want to stress one point that he discusses, having to do with social relations in Cantel after the factory had been present for about 30 years. Nash discusses differences between the factory workers and those who remained traditional agricultural operators in Cantel and the surrounding area. Changes in industrial workers' houses and their furnishings have been minimal; similarly, foods and cooking arrangements have changed little. Above all, family relations have remained essentially identical. The factory workers share with the remaining peasants the same religious beliefs and practices and enjoy the same festivities. The closeness of personal relations in a number of important social areas is summed up by Nash as follows:

Unquestioning acceptance of folk ideas of reality is part of everyone's life, irrespective of his occupational role. In Cantel this includes acceptance of folk remedies, origin myths, modes of cure, and the belief that foods and persons are "hot" and "cold," that smoke from the candles carried one's prayer to heaven, that the sacrifice of a sheep keeps

[6] This discussion is based on Manning Nash, "Introducing Industry in Peasant Societies," *Science*, 130 (November 27, 1959), pp. 1456–1462.

death from a household, and that an eclipse is a battle between good and evil. What is apparent in this matter of world view is the extent to which spheres of rationality and irrationality coincide among factory and non-factory workers.[7]

Yet, to some extent certain social differences did develop in Cantel, among them the new friendship clubs for factory workers —which previously did not exist at all—a sports club composed of bicycle riders and basketball players (sports introduced from more advanced societies), and labor union activity introduced by organizers from the outside.

In personal relations, in belief systems, in the more intimate behavior patterns, then, change has been negligible or nonexistent. Now, anyone looking at various developing countries in Asia and Africa will also have found that in many regions, personal, familial and other basic life patterns have changed least. Such changes as have occurred have involved new social groupings produced by the new work situation, new political associations arising at least in part from the formation of new states or other new political entities, and new patterns of economic behavior resulting primarily from new and especially industrial methods of production rather than from altered social or cultural conditions.

In general, I think one can argue that the significant differences and patterns of change attributable to the introduction of new productive activities principally reflect changes in economic conditions, together with individual propensities to enter new and previously nonexistent social groups, rather than changes in attitudes or in family structure. It must be emphasized, however, that industrialization took place in Cantel only on a very limited scale. The factory was set up in a rural community, and though the population increased a bit and several new houses were constructed near the factory, and though other changes took place within the community, including the availability, to workers, of new and improved commodities that the peasants were too poor to buy, basic personal and even socio-cultural conditions altered not at all,

[7] *Ibid.*, p. 1460.

or at most only very little. Dualism is absent from Cantel, because the new economic activities were fully integrated into the peasant community.

Now, industrialization often involves productive entities much larger than a small textile firm, and it usually occurs primarily in urban rather than in rural areas. Consequently, persons who enter the industrial enterprises leave their original place of work, move to an urban center, and lose contact with many members of their families and others with whom they have traditionally associated. As observers of Indian or Indonesian cities have often reported, however, members of a given group (whether it is based on a common language, on caste, or on village of origin) try to associate with others from the same group and to maintain close relations with them. Moreover, urban residents in these countries, and in other newly industrializing nations in which urban areas have grown quickly and relatively recently, often return to the villages whence they came, when their urban employment ends. For example, in a survey of migration into and out of major urban centers in India, S. N. Agarwala found that in the older age groups emigration considerably exceeds immigration, an indication that these older people return to the villages or small towns from which they originally came.[8]

This implies that urbanization is an important factor in changes in social structure in the newly developing countries. For, although urban residents from similar social and geographical areas try to establish relations similar to those in the villages, these groups are often small, and in many instances associations of this type are impossible. Workers moving to urban areas in which industrial employment is available often come without their families, and inter-action among temporarily single men differs substantially from interaction among rural families in Asian and African countries.

Hence the increasing settlement of workers in cities, and the urban concentration

of industrial establishments and related services are important factors in breaking up existing social relations and creating new forms of social interaction and social stratification. In short, alteration in stratification systems depends on the growth and increasing urban concentration of the population of developing countries.

Little research has been done on the changing stratification patterns in urban areas of developing Asian and African countries, partly because in many urban areas immigrant workers are still highly mobile. But studies of Indian cities,[9] for example, suggest that stratification in the urban areas of some developing countries generally resembles that of Western countries. Hence, the notion of "dualism" is mainly based on the observation that stratification in agricultural areas has changed little whereas in urban areas it has taken on many Western features. Changes in urban areas have been only partial, however, and without doubt have begun to affect rural areas in some parts of the world, though empirical knowledge on this is still very limited.

An additional problem involves the entry of foreign people, not through colonization, but through the immigration of ordinary people from other Asian or African societies at a similar level of development. The migration of Chinese into parts of South and Southeast Asia, the migration of Indians to parts of Africa and Southeast Asia, and that of various Middle Easterners to many parts of the world are examples. Where these immigrations involved large groups of foreigners, they usually concentrated on certain specialized economic activities, created their own residential centers in urban areas, and in general continued the social relations characteristic of their native countries.

But in a number of areas, as time goes on, changes have been taking place which are likely to increase interaction between the native inhabitants and the immigrants. European colonial powers did not interfere

---

[8] See S. N. Agarwala, "A Method for Estimating Decade Internal Migration in Cities in India from Indian Census Data'" *Indian Economic Review,* 4 (February, 1958), p. 71.

[9] See for example, S. N. Sen, *The City of Calcutta* (Calcutta: Bookland, n.d.—ca. 1960), and C. W. Ranson, *A City in Transition: Studies in the Social Life of Madras* (Madras: The Christian Literature Society of India, 1938).

with or impose special rules on "colored" immigrants from Asian or African countries, but when these developing countries became politically independent, and political power was transferred to the natives, it became important to integrate these foreigners with the domestic social structure. Full integration cannot easily be achieved, and in the process the ethnically and linguistically distinct immigrants must choose whether to return to their home countries or to find a place in the social and economic life of the dominant and politically more powerful native population.

I do not regard the previous situation, which is now being altered everywhere in newly independent countries, as dualism. To be sure, substantial differences in personal associations and in stratification systems have divided immigrants from natives. But with one or two exceptions—Malaya being the principal one—the total number of foreign immigrants was too small to permit economic and political independence from the domestic majority. And with political independence and indigenous political leadership, any apparent elements of dualism in the relations between ethnic minorities and domestic majorities will gradually disappear.

In the United States, the gradual integration and "Americanization" of persons with very different linguistic and national origins, in the pre-World War I and pre-World War II periods, is clearly an instance of this tendency to form a national unity. And although the United States is still "dualistic" with respect to different racial groups, current policies are designed to bring about closer integration and ultimately, perhaps, a complete eradication of various forms of dualism or "segregation."

The process of integrating ethnic groups does tend to produce a system of social stratification in which some difficulties and inconsistencies are inevitable. In many instances the ethnic minorities occupy positions in specialized secondary production, or in commercial activities, and therefore enjoy an income level higher than that of most of the indigenous population. For example, the income of the few thousand Indians who live in Nyasaland was estimated to be, on the average, 15 to 20 times higher than that of the indigenous Nyasas, and though the income differences may be smaller in Thailand between Chinese and Thais, or in Indonesia between Chinese and Indonesians, they still create an obstacle to the social and economic integration of the ethnic minorities. But as these countries achieve political independence, and take moderately successful steps toward modernization, economic growth will improve the social and economic positions of the indigenous people. More than any other factor, this tends to make possible the integration of foreign ethnic minorities into the social structure of newly developing countries. Some phases of the integration of ethnic minorities may be complex and difficult, however, leading to violence or other forms of serious social conflict. But in the long run ethnic "dualism" will disappear, as a structurally more simplified and better integrated society emerges.

CONCLUSION

Among the major issues I have raised, in connection with dualism as a feature of social stratification in societies containing both industrialized and non-industrialized sectors, one of the most important is the problem of social mobility, both between agricultural and industrial sectors and within each of them. As economic change of various kinds takes place in developing economies, the rural and urban, or agricultural and industrial sectors tend to become increasingly interdependent. With the growth of international commerce and the rise of internal markets, assisted by the extension of roads and railways, the old self-sufficiency of the village has been progressively worn down; the rigidity of the old village division of labor has softened; the old social barriers to economic mobility are slowly yielding, and in most villages—at least in most parts of Asia and probably within the next few years also in Africa—cash is replacing barter. At the same time the expansion of towns and the diversification of employment opportunities, the rise of new trades and the somewhat more limited decline of old ones, have been breaking down the formerly rather complete control exercised by the family, though in many developing countries the family is still a strong force. The spread of education, which has been very substantial in many developing countries, is working in the same direction. India, in particular, epitomizes these developments in many ways. There political independence, the formation of indigenous political movements, the formal abolition of large landed estates and the alleged and, in some cases genuine, increase of tenants' rights, have broadened village horizons. The substitution of a new social order for the old one has become concretely associated with more modern patterns of economic and social organization.[10]

In other words, the forms of social stratification characteristic of urban industrial and tertiary occupations have to some extent affected economic and related social patterns in the rural areas of developing countries. In some of the more isolated areas this change has not yet taken place, but with the growth of communication and transport systems the size and importance of these regions will decline. This is especially true in Asia, but it is beginning in Africa and will probably continue on both continents at a rapidly increasing rate.

Thus we may say that dualism either did not exist in the newly developing countries of Asia and Africa, or, where it did exist in some form, it is disappearing. For the changing social and economic conditions in these countries are making individuals in different productive activities more interdependent, and the major bases of social differentiation are increasingly confined to the more intimate spheres, to family relations, religious beliefs, and primary groups whose identity and composition have a long-standing and well-established significance. Changes in social structure are closely based, in my opinion, on changes in the nature and conditions of economic growth, and on the whole the basic processes of economic growth are very similar in all newly developing countries. What varies among these peoples are certain cultural conditions, most of which are inherited from a long past. Though in its intermediate phases the type of stratification associated

with economic growth may appear to be dualistic, it is also compatible with quite different cultural conditions, and in the next few decades systems of stratification in different Asian and African countries should become increasingly similar.

PERUVIAN STRATIFI-CATION AND MOBILITY—REVOLUTIONARY AND DEVELOPMENTAL POTENTIAL

David Chaplin

While Peru's economic development is highly influenced by its resource endowment and the price structure of its exports, the style of industrialization will be determined in large part by the type and amount of social mobility its class structure permits. Although similar ethnically to Guatemala and Bolivia, Peru has so far (1967) managed to forestall a basic social revolution and has developed under one of the most private "free enterprise" regimes in Latin America. It should therefore be interesting to examine the type of class structure and social mobility which underlies this stage of development.

In terms of a model of the process of industrialization, I shall emphasize the distinctive features of the transitional stage. It seems that a folk-urban, traditional-modern dichotomy—or even a transitional type which is merely "half way" between these extremes—is not adequate. There are features of the class structure which are apparently peculiar to the transitional stage, such as the multiple "full-time" occupations of the middle class. This stage is not merely a mixture of "the old and the new." It may turn out on reanalysis that some of these features are not limited to the currently underdeveloped countries into which

[10] On India, and for other related aspects as well, see UNESCO, *Social Change and Economic Development* (Paris: UNESCO, 1963), esp. pp. 90–99, 110–118, and 157–163.

industrialization has been introduced from the outside, but will be found to have existed also in the "Western case" of spontaneous development.

In addition to the above perspectives, the question of downward mobility, which has been neglected in many studies of social mobility,[1] is particularly interesting in Peru. Fox and Miller suggest that the amount of downward mobility in a society is the best measure of its openness.[2] In the case of the United States it could be argued, contrary to its avowed universalism, that its economic development has been such as to allow considerable upward mobility *as well as* considerable upper-class continuity since so much room is being created at the top. . . . Fox and Miller note, for instance, that in comparing the United States, Great Britain, the Netherlands and Japan, "the ability of sons of elite fathers to inherit their father's socio-economic status is greatest in the United States, 24 per cent greater than in Great Britain. . . . The United States has high inheritance [of elite positions] *and* high accessibility."[3]

It may be the case in Peru that, cultural particularism notwithstanding, there is both low internal accessibility *and* relatively low inheritance, the latter arising from high elite fertility, inheritance laws calling for an equal division of property—as well as a small but socially significant foreign immigration moving "in at the top."

PERUVIAN SOCIAL STRUCTURE

Before discussing mobility an attempt will be made to describe Peru's class structure. Its most outstanding feature is its large Indian population. An "Indian" is someone who speaks little or no Spanish, wears Indian garb and sandals or walks barefoot and chews coca (cocaine) leaves. By this cultural definition, they are probably not over a third of the population.

Historically, the Indians were a subordinate "caste" majority, so the process by which they have decreased in relative im-

portance is one of the most significant types of social mobility in Peru. Even after independence the Indians continued to be treated as a separate group with special burdens (tithing for support of the Church until 1854) and few privileges. In fact, most historians agree that their condition worsened markedly after the somewhat restraining hand of the Crown was eliminated in 1821. On the other hand, since a majority of Peruvians today are racially mestizo (Indian and White mixture), a strict caste endogamy has obviously not been maintained.

Paralleling this division between the Indian and non-Indian is the rural-urban difference in class structure. Although some observers feel class to be an urban phenomenon in developing societies, Peru's highland Indians are not an egalitarian subsistence "hunting and gathering" folk culture. Most of them are inside or near large plantations. They have also acquired a strong Western sense of private property, indigenist ideologists notwithstanding.

In cities of the importance of departmental capitals the upper stratum consists of a light-skinned class based on land, profession, governmental office and commerce in rural departments and finance, commerce, land and government in Lima. There is a sharp break between Lima (1,500,000 in 1961), and the rest of Peru's towns (Arequipa, the next largest, is only one-tenth as large).

The major split in Peru's "oligarchy" is found between the inefficient feudal *latifundistas* in the mountains (*gamonales*) and the modern export-oriented cotton and sugar plantation owners along the coast. The former group is still dominant only in local affairs while the national "power elite" is made up largely of coastal plantation owners. This oligarchy, Bourricaud feels, is not a true elite or ruling class but a monopolistic collection of "clans" which is based on the neutralization of the middle classes and "shoving aside" the "forgotten" lower classes.[4] Unfortunately the use of bearer stock (*acciones al portador*) and the secretive nature of Peruvian business

---

[1] Thomas Fox and S. M. Miller, "Occupational Stratification and Mobility: Intra-Country Variations," in *Studies in Comparative International Development*, Vol. I, No. 1, 1965, p. 1.

[2] *Ibid.*, p. 3.

[3] *Ibid.*, p. 8.

[4] See François Bourricaud, "Structure and Function of the Peruvian Oligarchy," *Studies in Comparative International Development*, Vol. II, No. 2, 1966.

TABLE 1   1961 Socio-Economic Status Structure[5]

	Total Peru	Lima	Callao	Ayacucho	Loreto	Pasco
	%	%	%	%	%	%
I. Upper class (administrative)	1.5	3.5	3.2	.3	1.5	1.8
II. Upper middle class (professional, technical)	3.5	6.3	4.4	2.1	3.5	3.0
III. Middle class (office employees)	4.5	11.0	13.9	.8	2.5	3.0
IV. Lower middle class (salesmen, clerks, etc.)	7.6	12.3	10.6	4.9	7.4	5.2
V. Upper lower class (miners, artisans, chauffeurs, factory workers)	19.7	30.6	37.4	8.3	11.5	28.5
VI. Lower lower class (peasants, domestic servants)	63.2	36.3	30.5	83.6	73.6	58.5
	100.0	100.0	100.0	100.0	100.0	100.0

[5] *Censo Nacional de Población, Dirección Nacional de Estadística y Censos,* Vol. I, Tomo IV, Tables 8 and 18, Lima, 1966.

life make a more detailed or reliable evaluation of upper-class economic behavior very difficult. It is fairly clear, however, that Peru's national upper class does have the following characteristics: It is overwhelmingly based in Lima, quite open to infiltration by financially successful European or North American entrepreneurs, and quite disunited by familial, commercial and political competition.

Turning to the 1961 census, there is some "objective" data available on class strata. If we type the eleven explicit occupational categories provided by the census by their median income, the following socio-economic status type strata can be delimited:

For the country as a whole this distribution fits the pattern expected in underdeveloped countries with only 1.5 per cent in the upper class and 15.6 in the middle. The most urban and industrial departments, Lima (86 per cent urban) and Callao (96 per cent urban—Lima's nearby port city), have predictably the largest middle classes. Ayacucho is a prototypical Indian sierra department with a very large lower class and a disproportionately large upper middle class made up predominantly of government officials in the departmental and provincial capitals. The upper and middle classes listed in Loreto (Peru's largest department, consisting of sparsely populated jungle) live largely in one town—the capital at Iquitos. Pasco is the sierra department with the heaviest concentration of modern mining operations. . . .

In terms of the occupational structure (see Table 2), Peru's distinctive features are (1) An excessive tertiary sector composed of both government workers and lawyers as well as surplus "primitive" services such as domestic servants, street vendors, etc. (2) A proliferation of multiple full-time type occupation-holding (not visible in the following Table) most striking in those modern middle-class positions in which such behavior would be judged as diluting professional specialization if not involving actual conflicts of interest. (3) A retarded development of industrial, especially manufacturing jobs. In this category we also find a "premature" exclusion of women owing to their higher cost due to the selective enforcement of labor and welfare laws in this industrial sector.

. . . One of the peculiarities of Peruvian social structure has been that the manual–non-manual gap, already very wide traditionally, was increased in the labor laws passed between 1920 and 1960. In general,

TABLE 2 The Peruvian Labor Force[6] 1940–1961

	The % Male		Total				1940	1961
	1940 %	1961 %	1940 %	1961 %			%	%
1. Agriculture	68.5	86.2	62.4	49.7 }	Primary		64.4	51.8
2. Extractive	97.3	97.3	1.8	2.2 }	sector			
3. Manufacturing	43.5	71.8	15.4	13.1 }	Secondary		17.2	16.6
4. Construction	98.0	99.0	1.9	3.3 }				
5. Commerce	67.8	72.1	4.6	9.1 }				
6. Transportation & communication	95.3	95.1	2.1	3.0 }	Tertiary		16.8	27.2
7. Services	50.9	50.8	10.2	15.2 }				
8. Other	80.1	78.4	1.6	4.4			1.6	4.4
% Male of all economically active	64.6	78.2	100.0	100.0			100.0	100.0

[6] *Censo Nacional de Población y Ocupación,* Vol. I, 1940, *Dirección Nacional de Estadística,* Lima, 1944, pp. 360, 606–607, and 669. *Sexto Censo Nacional de Población—Resultados Finales de Primera Prioridad, 1961, Dirección Nacional de Estadística y Censos,* Lima, March, 1964, p. 230, Table 11.

the benefits of *empleados* (white-collar workers) were twice as good as those of *obreros* (blue-collar workers). In the early 1960s the *obreros'* benefits were pulled up to the level of the *empleados* except for the sharp distinction still maintained in medical facilities. The *obrero* labor and welfare laws are, however, enforced only for a small segment of the labor force, namely the organized workers in the Lima-Callao area and the few provincial centers of industry.

In the white-collar sector there are two major categories in the 1961 census, governmental and private employees. The most striking feature of this white-collar sector is the relative size of government employment. For the country as a whole, the ratio of white-collar workers who worked for the government to those working for private employers was .65. This varied, from a low of .48 in the department of Lima (in which the capital is over 80 per cent of the population) to a high of 3.9 in the jungle department of Amazonas. Thus while both government power and personnel are highly centralized in Lima, commerce and industry are even more concentrated there. Within provincial towns then, government workers are relatively more numerous than in the capital.

The difference between these two types of white-collar occupations is also revealed in this comparison of their income distribution. The private employees span a much wider range of income levels by including more highly paid as well as poorly paid workers than those in government.[7] . . .

The main problem in interpreting this comparison between government and private *empleados* is that the larger the town the more likely government workers are to also have one or more non-governmental jobs. So while the official report (undoubtedly underestimating the income of private employees) presumably avoids double counting, it can not give an accurate picture of the total income of government employees either.[8]

Another way of approaching the question of occupational differentials is to examine the gap between the urban *empleado* and *obrero* income and the per cent urban by

[7] *Censo Nacional de Población,* Vol. I, Tomo IV, Table 115, *Dirección Nacional de Estadística,* Lima, 1966.

[8] An additional problem in Peru is the institution of *acciones al portador* or bearer stock through which the ownership, and hence dividend recipients, of "anonymous societies" remain unknown.

departments. There is a strong negative correlation between the size of this gap and the per cent urban—that is, the more rural an area the greater the distance is between these groups within local towns. In Lima and Callao, therefore, we find a minimal difference in median monthly income of 450 shill between urban *empleados* and *obreros*, whereas in the isolated sierra department of Ayacucho this difference (even at a lower absolute level of income for both) is greatest—at 1150 shill. (Ayacucho also has the fourth highest ratio of government to private *empleados* in the country: 2.7.)

Turning to the Peruvian middle class, we find a dearth of empirical studies. The most distinctive feature of this stratum has already been described—namely multiple occupation-holding. The "ideal" combination of occupations would be a university professorship for prestige, a government position for power and prestige, and various private jobs related to the governmental post for income. It is partly through the latter activities that a European type of bourgeois consciousness is diluted. As Bourricaud observed, "the middle class has not evolved an original value system . . . vis-a-vis the oligarchs. . . . The characteristic trait of [the] Peruvian middle class—whether . . . old or new . . . is that it is a *dependent* group." This dependence arises from the fact that "this country has no bureaucracy in the Weberian sense" nor has it produced a nineteenth-century type of entrepreneur. The few successful men of this type were generally foreigners who "were bought out by the oligarchy, enjoying a rapid absorption into the traditional ruling class."[9]

This blurring of occupational identity could be interpreted as illustrating the point that in this transitional phase of industrial development, in the middle and upper classes, occupations are perhaps least relevant to a man's over-all status. I am assuming, perhaps incorrectly, that there was a somewhat greater tendency for the very small (but certainly existent) colonial and nineteenth-century middle class to have one major occupation as is still more the case in small towns. Today, the expansion of the "infrastructure" beyond the supply of qualified personnel, and the depressing effect of inflation—cause middle-class professionals to take on as many sources of income as possible even if they are all full-time type occupations whose various commitments they could not properly meet. . . . Multiple occupations are linked with a leisure-oriented basis for social status. It is the middle-class man's style of consumption rather than production which determines his prestige.[10] Such an ephemeral basis for status naturally leads to a high degree of social instability and anxiety. One aspect of this behavior is the abuse of the title Doctor, or Engineer, for almost anyone with a university level education.

Peru's middle classes are different from Western also in being made up largely of employees of the government or large foreign firms. The independent businessman is relatively rare and usually foreign in origin (even if Peruvian in nationality as in the case of the Chinese).

A central factor in the situation of such a salaried class is inflation. MacLean y Estenos places the first proletarianization of the lower middle class during the inflation of World War I.[11] It would be extremely difficult to pinpoint when the better paid factory workers surpassed the income of the lower white-collar workers, but this "modern" phenomenon had occurred at least by 1958.[12] This latter shift was not primarily a matter of a relative decline in white-collar wages, but rather the substantial gains in welfare benefits as well as wages enjoyed by

---

[9] Bourricaud, *op. cit.*, p. 27. MacLean y Estenos suggests that the absence of independent guilds (the Indians were used for artisan work, or such goods were imported) is one factor accounting for the non-bourgeois character of Peru's middle class. Robert MacLean y Estenos, *Sociología Peruana*, Lima, 1942, p. 118. We could add the absence of a "free city" tradition. Lima has always been dominant over Peru but until recently subservient to a landowning plutocracy.

[10] François Bourricaud, "Algunas características originales de la cultura mestiza en el Peru contemporaneo," *Revista del Museo Nacional*, Tomo XXIII, 1954, p. 165.

[11] MacLean y Estenos, *op. cit.*, p. 118.

[12] David Chaplin, "Industrialization and the Distribution of Wealth in Peru," *Studies in Comparative International Development*, Vol. III, No. 3, 1967–1968, p. 58.

the privileged sector of Lima's organized factory workers.

The urban lower class has been studied primarily in Lima. Its most outstanding characteristic is its failure to radicalize. The urban proletariat has looked (successfully) more to paternalistic military dictators than middle-class revolutionary leaders. In Peru's case the famous Aprista party (one of the earliest significant non-Communist radical parties after the Mexican revolution) must also share the credit or blame for this situation since it has used its lower-class base largely to benefit its middle-class leadership. It is closely linked to the textile federation, the earliest major urban industrial union, but even so, most of the considerable benefits enjoyed by these workers were enacted by the military dictators, Benavides (1933–1939) and Odría (1948–1956), rather than by more democratic regimes.

It seems that urbanization in Latin America, unlike the case of the West, dilutes lower-class protest so effectively that a de-radicalization (or stifling of radicalization) could be said to be occurring.[13] An explanation for this "deviant" transitional phenomenon could be that: (1) As in other Latin American countries, the small group of highly organized urban factory workers (the only group which could effectively protest) are relatively well taken care of by the selective enforcement of very advanced labor and welfare benefits. This can be done because factory owners are not yet a major sector of the national elite. They are also largely foreign in Peru. In addition, Peru's factories are more capital intensive and protected than were England's at a comparable level of economic development, hence they can afford to pay higher wages. (2) This industrial sector is still very small and, thanks to its relative capital inten-

sity, it is not likely to ever be as large a per cent of the national labor force as was the case in Western development. The great lead of the tertiary sector is not likely to be reversed. (3) Although 70 per cent of Peru's industrial establishments are located in the Lima-Callao area, they are overshadowed by the size and complexity of this metropolis.[14] Moreover, the median size of employment per manufacturing establishment is under 300. The few mining towns in Peru, however, do reveal the same pattern of polarized intense labor-management conflict that Kerr and Seigel noted for Western countries.[15] (4) The mass of Lima's lower class has its political and economic leverage diluted by the enormous influx of increasingly "Indian" migrants. Most slum dwellers try to handle their problems in an individualistic manner since they seem to be unable to develop effective voluntary associations. (Many are created but few accomplish anything.)

NINETEENTH-CENTURY SOCIAL MOBILITY

Contrary to the stereotyped view, the nineteenth century was not a period of "feudalistic" stability but one of turbulent change even in rural areas. Factors increasing the level of elite change in Peru during this period are (1) The abolition of primogeniture and entail. Landed estates were divided up equally among all children—of both sexes, legitimate and illegitimate. One must also remember that fertility in Peru at this time undoubtedly varied directly rather than inversely with wealth. Most of the poor died before adolescence and so could barely reproduce themselves. Thus there existed a demographic pressure for downward mobility for some of the descendants of wealthy families. (2) With a custom of dowries together with the chance sex ratio among children—the wrong mixture of children and marriages could ruin a family. In fact, one could say that only

---

[13] Ratinoff, in his survey of middle-class ideology in Latin America, sees several stages to this deradicalization. At first, the rising middle class is in favor of limits on individual freedoms—especially property rights since they are interested in undercutting the power of the plutocratic elite. Later when their position is more established they favor a return to individual property rights. Luis Ratinoff, *La clase media en América Latina, Revista Paraguaya de Sociología,* Año 2, No. 4, Set.–Dic. 1965, pp. 16–18.

[14] *Censo de Manufactura—1963, Dirección Nacional de Estadística y Censos,* Lima, 1965, p. v.
[15] Clark Kerr and Abraham Siegel, "The Interindustry Propensity to Strike—An International Comparison," chap. 14 in Arthur Kornhauser, *et al., Industrial Conflict,* New York: McGraw-Hill, 1954.

an extraordinarily adroit and lucky family could preserve their status in rural Peru generation after generation.[16]

It should also be noted that Peru's nineteenth-century plutocratic families did not maintain any sense of "racial" or ethnic purity with respect to the few European or North American migrants who came to Peru during this period. Like the sixteenth–seventeenth-century British landed aristocracy they were only too happy to effect ties to an entrepreneurial group.[17] From a period of extreme provincial isolation when even the elite in Lima could cherish a sense of being the center of a universe, the devaluation of Peru's culture has grown to a national disease. As a result, Peru's elite is denationalized by various foreign cultures of orientation—often not shared even within the same family. The committed nationalists are then only a segment of the middle class—and, of course, the politicians, since the largely disenfranchised Indians are not yet part of Peru's "civic culture."

TWENTIETH-CENTURY SOCIAL MOBILITY

The major change in social stratification in Peru's provincial towns has been the exodus of the original creole landed "aristocracy."[18] There has always been a pattern of absenteeism, but before the turn of the twentieth century it usually took the form of having a town house in the provincial or departmental capital so that frequent and prolonged visits to the plantation could be made. Thereafter a redefinition of an acceptable level of physical comfort and style, together with the eroding effect of Indian unrest, caused these provincial elites to abandon their landholdings to managers while they fled to Lima. Such a move usually

meant a downgrading to upper middle clas at best since the Lima pyramid towers above that of all other cities. In a similar manner, movement out of Lima makes relative upward mobility possible although acceptance by provincial society would be slower. Subsequently even an upper-middle-class status in Lima may be difficult to maintain since absentee-managed highland plantations are likely to yield declining revenues—especially today in the face of Indian invasions and the threat of land reform. As a result, unless such ex-provincial elite families can rise to the challenge of developing a new urban economic base they are likely to slip still further.

The most striking effect of the heavy waves of rural migration to Lima has been the ruralization of sections of the city. At the same time Peru's upper class, located overwhelmingly in Lima, becomes more cosmopolitan in its outlook—thus there is less of a shared culture in Lima today than 50 years ago due not only to the increase in the absolute size of the population but more crucially to these divergent influences.

Another current of migration also of growing significance since 1940 has been the increasing number of middle-class Peruvians educated abroad. Education in general is the most important means of upward mobility (a good professional education can, of course, also cushion the fall of the son of an ex-provincial "aristocrat"). As the national universities are increasingly democratized the prestige value of their degrees declines and hence a foreign education becomes even more desirable aside from its usually much greater functional utility. Before World War II the majority of Peruvians studying abroad were upper class. With the closing off of Europe during the Second World War and the growing importance of the United States in the Peruvian economy, the predominant locale of the foreign educated changed. The surplus demand in North American universities meant that no longer could scions of the best families count on getting into the elite foreign universities. Their places were increasingly likely to be taken by more talented and ambitious middle-class Peruvians.

The initial expectation of the North

[16] Lenski has also noted a high level of agrarian elite turnover in studies on medieval Europe. See Gerhard E. Lenski, *Power and Privilege*, New York: McGraw-Hill, 1966, p. 239.

[17] Lawrence Stone. "Marriage Among the English Nobility in the Sixteenth and Seventeenth Centuries," *Comparative Studies in Society and History*, Vol. III, No. 2, January, 1961, pp. 182–206.

[18] Gabriel Escobar M., *La estructura política rural del departamento de Puno*, Published doctoral thesis in Anthropology, Universidad Nacional de San Antonio Abad del Cuzco, Cuzco, December, 1961.

American foundations paying for the education of this new group was that they would "of course" return to their countries where the need for their talents was so great. The actual outcome is now described as the problem of the Brain Drain (inadequately compensated for by the importation of short-term foreign "experts"). The problem for the foreign schools is that if they selected Peruvian students only on the basis of ability they could be turning out some graduates of such modest social background that the gap between the position they were trained for and the one they could hope to obtain would be unbearable—and so they would return to "their" foreign country or become revolutionaries. Even where "excessive" social mobility is not involved, a prolonged period of training in the "West" tends to have the following disadvantages: (1) The student may unlearn the *criollo* (creole, or in this context, "operator") approach to career success and instead come to expect to win a position on merit alone. He thus is psychologically unprepared to play the game—as it still must be played in Peru.[19] (2) He may also simply lose touch with his clique or patron.

A related matter for those not working primarily for the government is whether they seek employment with a national or foreign-owned firm. Each has obstacles to advancement. The national firm is normally a family enterprise in which the best positions will go to relatives. The foreign firm for its part often reserves the top positions for its own countrymen. However, in the latter case there are two countervailing factors. The average total size and relative proportion of higher level positions are larger in foreign firms. They are also, at least, true corporations and not family enterprises. Moreover, they can be pressured by the government into "nationalizing" their personnel up to the highest local

level. Some of those top positions, however, are also particularistic in a "functional" way. Each foreign firm needs a protective wall of local influentials whose only talent need be personal ties to the ruling oligarchy. These positions are therefore not open to talented "upstarts."

LOWER-CLASS MOBILITY

Lower-class rural mobility occurs mainly through migration to cities precipitated by available education and transportation routes. Culturally, it is described as the process of *cholificación*—of Indians becoming *cholos*.[20] *Cholos* are viewed as the next higher stratum to Indians (followed by mestizos and then creoles). However, they are also in a different situs since Indian communities have their own internal stratification system based on wealth, age and political office. Their distinguishing traits are bilingualism and an aggressive self-reliant relationship to the dominant mestizo and creole classes. They have sloughed off the deference and inferiority complex of the Indians without compromising their aggressions through the adoption of middle-class aspirations. As a marginal category, they lack stable reference groups and so live a disorganized existence. They are, however, the most dynamic element in the sierra even if this involves taking advantage of the Indian.

In the 1920s a series of Indian revolts against further encroachment on their lands by plantation owners in the southern sierra brought about an "Indigenous Community" reform law. It was designed to protect the surviving *ayllus* (traditional Indian communities created by the colonial *reducciones*) from further expropriation. In principle, this seemed to promise a United States-type reservation system which could slow down the acculturation of the Indian, thus keeping him out of national life. In fact, the results were quite different. (The traditional subsistence plantation with its "attached" Indians is actually the most effective isolating institution.) Since taking advantage of this law required the employment of a lawyer

[19] See Anthony Leeds, "Brazilian Careers and Social Structure: an Evolutionary Model and Case History," *American Anthropologist*, Vol. 66, No. 6, Part 1, December, 1964, for an excellent description of the operation of this same prebendary *patronazgo* (patronage) system in Brazil. Ratinoff generalizes Leeds' findings to all of Latin America (Luis Ratinoff, *La clase media en América Latina, Revista Paraguaya de Sociología*, Año 2, No. 4, *Set.–Dic.* 1965).

[20] Gabriel Escobar M., *El mestizaje en la región andina: el caso del Perú, Revista de Indias*, Nos. 95 and 96, *Enero–Junio*, Madrid, 1964, pp. 197–220.

and a direct relationship with the Ministry of Labor and Indian Affairs in Lima, the registered communities were actually projected into greater participation in national life. A related factor accelerating acculturation is that although some Peruvian intellectuals and folklorists idealize the Indian (primarily the defunct Incaic civilization) the contemporary Indian is generally despised for his "dirty uncultivated" habits.

Mobility within Indian communities occurs largely through the lavish patronizing of fiestas and election to local political office. But even this internal mobility requires participation in the national economy to raise the necessary money.

DISTRIBUTION OF INCOME AND WEALTH

For the middle third of the twentieth century some data is available on changes in the distribution of wealth and income.[21] All of the available sources suggest that while a small proportion of the organized urban industrial labor force is gaining both relatively and absolutely, the over-all distribution of wealth and income has become increasingly unequal both by class and region. The reasons for this are

1. Movement into the market economy of the relatively larger, elite-owned resources previously possessed but not evaluated in commercial market terms. The extension of commercialism also means that real estate is exchanged for money rather than primarily as familial inheritance or bridal dowries. Hence the possibility for a more rational concentration of holdings.

2. Since only the upper class can save significantly, commercialization increases the economic opportunities of those already on top.

3. There is an increasing gap between the urban and rural world resulting from the concentration of industrialization in the largest cities—in Peru's case almost exclusively in Lima—since increases in per capita productivity come more rapidly in the urban industrial sector.

4. Excessive population growth decreases the level of living of the mass of landless

[21] See Chaplin, *op. cit.*

peons thus widening the gap even if the wealth of the elite remains stable.

5. The usual inflation which undercuts the position of the majority group of employees in favor of the owners of land and other flexible price assets.

AGRARIAN REFORM

In this connection the question of the aims and the probable consequences of land reform should be raised. They are (1) Social justice through a redistribution of wealth; and (2) increased food production for Peru's booming population. A not so explicit goal is the creation of a conservative petit bourgeois peasantry to offset the danger of a revolutionary landless proletariat. (I am speaking of the type of "bourgeois-reformist" land reform as it is generally defined in Latin America—not of Soviet-type collectives or state farms.) Of course there are still some obtuse die-hards who view this program as itself revolutionary because it will require the expropriation of the notoriously inefficient (but also economically unpromising) mountain *latifundia*. Actually land reform is sophisticated conservatism in the same sense as is birth control for the masses. Communists do, or should from their own perspective, see it as a bourgeois trick to repeat the unintended effect of the early Soviet (which created the ultra-conservative Kulaks) or the Napoleonic land reforms.[22] Nevertheless, they must pay it lip service since land reform has become an article of faith with most Latin American progressives.

As to its practical consequences for changing the social structure, we can perhaps turn to Bolivia. There the old class of landlords was indeed destroyed in the 1952 revolution and a new rural political base developed with which the government could offset the persistently rebellious mine union and its militia. (A comparable goal was achieved in Venezuela.) The same type of minimal immediate improvement in economic condition could be accomplished in

[22] Karl Marx, *The Eighteenth Brumaire of Louis Bonaparte,* George Allen and Unwin, London, 1943, pp. 135–137. Marx also observed that the benefits to the peasantry of such a division of land had to be transitory—enough to buy support and time for one regime but subsequently equally great poverty would result.

Peru in spite of the extremely conservative and laggard nature of their law and program. (In Peru no redistribution of wealth is contemplated since the landlords would be well compensated by government bonds with extraordinary financial support.) On the other hand, it seems unlikely that the ultimate development of land redistribution in Peru will be·much structured by this law since most of the division of land so far has been a legalization of the many land invasions outside the law. Moreover, it seems very unlikely that, were the Indians to default on their mortgage payments, the government would forcibly eject them en masse.

In the long run, even an immediately successful land reform program can not avoid the inevitable reconcentration of land which seems to occur in any industrialized society, Communist or capitalist—only a system of uneconomic subsidies (such as those of the United States, which Peru could not afford) could maintain an agricultural sector of independent farm families. This reconcentration will be hastened by the desperate need for more food for the production of which there is not enough time or personnel to painfully retrain the mass of Peruvian Indians. Moreover, it seems likely that one of the consequences of land reform would be an increase in peasant fertility thus wiping out, in a generation, the gain in food production and increase in land holdings to lots of minimal scale efficiency which land reform provides initially. In traditional communities, an Indian does not establish his own family until he can acquire land. A land shortage thus results in postponed marriages and/or emigration. The sudden provision of more land for all would lower the age at marriage and probably increase the per cent married, thereby increasing the size of completed families in such a "non-contracepting" population.

Land reform, then, can be viewed as a short-term stop-gap and a politically unavoidable effort to buy time (against a Communist revolution—and/or regression to chaos) which can only work if parallel efforts are made in the urban industrial sector in which most of the subsequent generations will be living.

EDUCATION

The primary avenue to social mobility in Peru is formal education. In this respect Peru is not following the pattern of Western industrialization but is rather "prematurely" up to date. Unlike the United States in the nineteenth century (and this source has been much exaggerated) there are very few Peruvians who have risen primarily through business activities. As mentioned above, entrepreneurs in Peru have been overwhelmingly of foreign extraction.

Education thus has to bear an especially heavy burden of ambition which it creates or aggravates only to then frustrate due to either its nonfunctional or poor quality or to the many obstacles to merit mentioned above. It is for this reason that the primary source of revolutionary ferment is in the universities rather than the factories. Rebel leaders are those who suffer the widest gap between their aspirations and achievements, rather than those at the most deprived level of existence or in "classic" proletarian situations.

This radicalizing effect of higher education may, in part, account for the decision of the Peruvian government to reopen or establish universities in provincial towns rather than merely adding more in Lima. The expectation may have been that either such unsophisticated locales would restrain radicalization—or that it could be more easily contained—and the accessibility of the national government to intimidation by student unrest reduced. Only the latter goal could be said to have been partially accomplished. From the start, in the late 1950s, the program of establishing additional provincial universities has been plagued with staffing problems. Most educated Peruvians want to move to or stay in Lima. Only those lacking either influential connections, talent or those imbued with considerable idealism (often revolutionary) would have to or care to teach outside of Lima. As a consequence, students at provincial universities tend to be exposed to more radical faculty influence than in Lima.

This radicalization of the university educated tends, however, to be a transitory phenomenon for the individual even if it increases for the country as a whole due to the larger proportion in school. The radicalization of the university student is a feature of the middle years of his studies and tends to disappear, except perhaps in private conversation, as he comes to terms with careerist pressures. There is, as Theisenhusen notes, "an unseemly willingness of the liberal-minded university-trained in Latin America to be co-opted by the establishment."[23]

Primary and secondary education in Peru remain highly class stratified and hence reinforce the current class structure, except at the bottom. . . . The government-run schools (with a few exceptions in Lima) are for the lower class. Middle- and upper-class children attend private schools. All primary and secondary students wear official uniforms which differ by school and hence bear explicit class stigma.

THE MILITARY AND THE CHURCH

There are two other major institutions which also offer increasing opportunities for lower-class mobility—the armed forces and the Church. The former has its internal stratification system with the navy being the most elite, followed closely by the air force and then the army. The Guardia Civil apparently suffers a much lower status, drawing its officer corps from the *cholo* class, while the army officers are largely *mestizo* and the navy and air force largely white and upper middle class. One could interpret these differences both as a matter of the differential pressure for practical performance (the navy is largely decorative while the Guardia Civil—as a sort of "state police" in the United States sense—is constantly employed), or attempt to explain them in terms of different foreign cultures of orientation since the air force and navy are largely United States-trained, while the army, until 1939, was French trained. In any case, the army and Guardia Civil do offer the possibility for career mobility to thousands of lower-class males—much more so than the civilian government services.

Such "social democracy" has no necessary tie to a preference for parliamentary democracy. In fact, the military ethos of

[23] William C. Theisenhusen, "How Big Is the Brain Drain?" Land Tenure Center Paper No. 29, University of Wisconsin, Madison, January, 1967, pp. 20–22.

discipline and disdain for "politicians" leads, at best, to a technocratic professionalism at the higher levels while at the lower ranks it serves to so alienate the Indian recruit from his people that he will willingly kill them if necessary. The army's system of training and assignments effectively turns Indians into *cholos* who tend to despise "their people."

The Catholic clergy also offers an increasing opportunity for lower-class mobility due to the decline in the attractiveness of this profession for the middle and upper class. Today, although the highest positions in the Peruvian hierarchy are still held largely by upper-class priests (with Peruvian congressional and presidential approval), this group has few successors among the coming generation. The clergy, in general, has shrunk due to the decline in recruits and also "darkened" as it declined—that is, a larger proportion of the declining numbers of entrants are lower class in origin.

CONCLUSION AND FURTHER SPECULATION

In concluding this discussion it should be reiterated that more solid evidence is needed for most of the foregoing assertions. While all are based on field observations, few are buttressed by systematic empirical investigations. There is, however, some concrete evidence that the distribution of wealth and of income is becoming even more unequal than it was some 50 years ago. The crucial exception to this is a small elite segment of urban manufacturing workers whose income has risen relatively as well as absolutely since 1940.

In terms of economic development, the small but strategic flow of foreign migrants to Peru could be said to have the following alternative consequences: (1) a replacement for Peruvians lost through the brain drain; (2) an obstacle to upward mobility within Peru; (3) dynamic entrepreneurship in the form of creating their own—as well as other —positions for Peruvians, rather than blocking internal mobility. (Peruvian writers tend to view foreigners at least as an obstacle if not as outright exploiters of national resources and manpower.) The major obstacle to the entrepreneurship role is the high degree of acceptance of "elite strangers" by Peru's established elite. Such absorption tends to dilute the dynamic function of at least the next generation.

Over all, it seems probable that, in spite of Peru's low level of economic development and supposedly rigid social structure, there may be a rather high level of social mobility down as well as up. The significant size of the educational system, the military and the Church provide various channels of upward mobility while inheritance practices, inflation, high upper-class fertility and other factors foster a high rate of downward mobility.

It is hoped that this discussion also contributes toward a model, or at least models, of the transitional stage as not merely derivable from a traditional and modern era. At the present level of abstraction, we would have to include such factors as: (1) whether a country had ever been a colony —and if so, whether freed before or after the first Industrial Revolution; (2) its economic structure; (3) whether a revolutionary, traditionalist or "reform-mongering" regime was in power.

Some of the general features of the current transitional stage seem to be (1) the "advantage" of a late start—which, depending on one's evaluation, might include a relatively wide franchise and very ample (but selectively enforced) labor and welfare legislation; (2) urbanization and population growth ahead of local industrialization; and (3) multiple occupation-holding.

In terms of revolutionary potential, Peru's most subjectively deprived category is its nationally educated university students. They are the major exception to the peculiarly deradicalizing effect urbanization has had on Peru's class conflict. This phenomenon illustrates the central point that Peru is far more urbanized than industrialized, since its level of urbanization is based on foreign trade rather than domestic industrial development or an adequate internal hinterland.

At present the most "promising" mass base for the student middle-class revolutionary leadership is the landless peasantry. The acceptance by this leadership of the petit bourgeois type of land reform program popular in Latin America as a necessary intervening stage threatens to deprive them

of the continued support of the small number of peasants they have been able to attract.

At this over-urbanized stage, the potential protest of the industrial proletariat has been "bought off" or deflected. However, the relatively high wages and fringe benefits required for this situation have already raised the prices of Peru's manufactured goods so far above the level of comparable imports that a productivity showdown has only been postponed. Some future government will have to reorganize Peru's industrial system. The resultant labor reaction could be exploited by either a rightist or a leftist party.

THE EMERGING PATTERN OF ISRAELI STRATIFICATION

S. N. Eisenstadt

1
SOCIAL ORGANIZATION AND STRATIFICATION IN THE YISHUV[1]
Introduction—The Problem and the Setting.
. . . We have seen that one of the major aims of Zionist ideology was to create a new type of modern society—one in which some of the pitfalls of other societies would be avoided. As it developed, however, more and more problems similar to those of other modern societies became apparent and varied social groups and organizations, with different styles of life, values, and traditions emerged. The activities which crystallized from them had to be evaluated —in terms of the major social rewards— money, power, and prestige. Israeli society —as any other—was therefore faced with

From *Israeli Society*, by S. N. Eisenstadt, Basic Books, Inc., Publishers, New York.

[1] This refers to the Jewish community in Israel, formerly Palestine, from its beginnings in the late 1880s. (C. S. H.)

the problems of organizing different social positions, and the allocations of people into these positions. . . .

In one important aspect the development of the Yishuv differed from normal, peasant or traditional societies, and even from most colonizing societies: in the initial stages of development ecological units and basic ascriptive solidarities such as kinship groups, territorial or class divisions, etc., did not constitute the most important or binding factor from which the more specific groups developed and crystallized.

Initially, the basic groups within the Yishuv were the various pioneering groups and sects. Some ecological ·groups of the older Yishuv existed throughout the initial period, and most new ones—whether agricultural settlements or new urban quarters —were, at first, offshoots of these sects and did not develop any strong traditions or symbols of identification of their own.

Moreover, the special nature of the migratory movement to Palestine implied that no strong ascriptive solidarities such as kinship or ethnic groups or social strata developed initially. It was only much later that such different collectivities—sometimes of a rather special type—developed, and ecological settings as well as ascriptive solidarities acquired some autonomy and tradition of their own. But even these were greatly influenced by the characteristics of the sects from which they stemmed and the most important of which was perhaps that these sects and groups were orientated towards complex social, economic, political, and cultural activities which soon outstripped their concrete needs. . . .

From these beginnings, the social structure of the Yishuv developed in two "idealtype" directions which, though greatly differing, had some common characteristics.

One can be seen in the rural and urban settlements of the first aliya,[2] and in what came to be called the "private" sector of the Yishuv. The second trend developed from within the more sectarian groups which comprised the "workers'" camp. In

between these two several meeting points existed in various cultural, educational, and even professional activities.

· ·

The Structure of the Major Roles. . . . Initial Zionist ideology, common to a large extent to the different branches of the Zionist movement, envisaged the full development of all occupational, economic, social, cultural, and political functions, as being permeated by a spirit of national identification and social justice and equality.

In this image the only real role was that of the pioneer with its basic dedication to national goals and pioneering movements.

More autonomous demands of such functions—their claim for prestige, for technical competence, or for intrinsic achievement and performance were very often looked down on as infringing on the purity of the pioneering role. In more ideological formulations this lack of emphasis on any concrete task was seen as a manifestation of the lack of "human self-alienation," characteristic of so many modern, and especially capitalist, societies. In the more realistic-political terms which developed during the third aliya, such demands for the autonomy of different functions were considered as weakening political ardour and identification with the various sects and parties of the workers' sector.

Ideological orientations against such tendencies were also greatly reinforced by the fear of "premature normalization"—as in the case of the first aliya.

This fear of premature normalization coupled with strong ideological orientations was seen most clearly in one of the most vital roles of the period—that of the agriculturist which crystallized as early as the first aliya, matured in the period of the second aliya[3] and fully developed in the mandatory period.

The most important characteristic of this "peasant" role was the de-emphasizing of occupational and "traditional" aspects of peasant life, at the expense of the more élitist conception of agricultural work as the main symbolic expression of pioneering.

[2] The first wave of immigration to Palestine, 1882–1903. It consisted of 20–30,000 immigrants. See S. N. Eisenstadt, *Israeli Society,* New York: Basic Books, 1967, pp. 23–24.(C. S. H.)

[3] Second wave of immigration, 1904–1914. It consisted of 35–40,000 immigrants. *Ibid.* (C.S.H.)

Later, during the third aliya,[4] these élitist orientations were consolidated in the various kibbutz movements,[5] which placed greater importance on ideological orthodoxy than on agricultural activities or a rural way of life.

Although the moshavim[6] established during the third aliya placed greater emphasis on agricultural activities and family life, these tendencies were yet part of a socio-political movement and ideology.

A similar, though perhaps less intensive, tendency developed within the cultural and educational sectors, in which the role of the teacher was defined and developed so as to include the cultural ingredient in the general image of the pioneer.

Evaluation of Roles. Closely related to the definition of different roles was their evaluation and the status levels that developed in the various sectors of the Yishuv.

The criteria of evaluation in the private sector were in many ways the "usual" criteria of economic and professional competence with somewhat stronger emphasis being placed on family status by economic standing and family lineage. But even within this sector strong emphasis was placed on national goals and service, although several of the basic assumptions of the pioneer group were rejected.

The situation was necessarily different in the pioneer groups and in the workers' sector. There, the basic criterion of status evaluation was devotion to pioneering-collective tasks with prestige in the eyes of the community the main reward. It was assumed that material rewards—and especially *differential economic* (and even prestige and power) rewards—were not only unimportant but even dangerous and poten-

tially disruptive to the solidarity of the pioneering group.

These evaluations of activities in the workers' groups and in the first settlements were, in their pure form, much more adapted to the small avant-garde élite groups than to wider and functionally differentiated settings. Hence it is no accident that the fullest manifestation of these criteria of evaluation was to be found in the collective settlements. Because of this, the maintenance of these criteria by the élite groups was greatly dependent on the minimizing of the occupational and status aspects of their peasant orientations and on the stress of the élitist orientations to the settlement and the movement. Within these groups such criteria and rewards could be upheld in all their purity...

The Image of Society. These variations in social stratification were closely related to the image of a society developed by these groups and derived from their basic ideology. . . .

The views as expressed there are mainly concerned with a "classless" society, composed of different groups and movements, and bound by common aspirations and activities, in which there is but little division of labor and small difference in wealth. However, these images were purely ideological and utopian, and bore few connexions to existing society.

It is significant that neither in the basic ideologies nor in this embryonic image of society was there any reference to the problems of distribution of power, or of power as a basis for social status. This omission was due to the limited scope of the settlements and groups, to the strong utopian elements of their ideology and to the fact that the main resources of most groups came from outside the Yishuv. This fact had many important repercussions on the developing social organization and stratification.

Interrelations Between the Scale of Collectivities, Role Structure and Criteria of Status. The three major aspects of social organization—the nature of collectivities, the definition of roles, and the criterion of status, tended to complement each other in controlling incipient social differences.

This was due to various factors: One was the relatively small degree of differentiation

---

[4] Third wave of immigration, 1919–1923. It consisted of 35,000 immigrants. *Ibid.* (C.S.H.)

[5] *Kibbutz:* an agricultural collective founded on the principle "from each according to his ability to each according to his need." (C.S.H.)

[6] Plural form of *moshav:* an agricultural co-operative, the land of which is divided into equal farmsteads, each of which is worked by a family. For a comparative analysis of the kibbutz and moshav and the bearing that these organizations have on stratification theory, see Richard D. Schwartz, "Functional Alternatives to Inequality," *American Sociological Review*, Vol. 20, August, 1955, pp. 424–430. (C.S.H.)

in the Yishuv's social structure, a tendency which was reinforced by the fact that the Yishuv was at that time composed of many small "parallel" settlements and organizations, allowing little occupational or economic differentiation to develop. Little specialization took place among the many similarly composed yet different groups, and even the activities of the professional and cultural bodies were not geared to any specific needs but rather to those of a "future" society. Only gradually a more concrete interrelationship between the various groups developed and with it a growing change in tasks.

The second major reason for the limited differences was rooted in the ideology of the pioneering group.

Historically, these two conditions were closely connected. However, each was more strongly operative in one sector than in another and hence their development varied between the sectors and probably influenced later developments in the Yishuv's social structure.

These initial tendencies left their imprint in several crucial areas. The first important characteristic, common to the Yishuv as well as to many other colonizing countries, was the absence of an aristocracy. This was due not only to lack of special family tradition but also to the fact that much of the land, and the available capital, was vested in public hands, often abroad. The second characteristic was the concentration of wealth in various public bodies and organizations. Thirdly, the strong egalitarian emphasis in the social structure of the Yishuv became apparent even at this stage, and fourthly, side by side with the strong egalitarianism, there was also the emphasis on the élite inherent in the image of the pioneer. This combination had many interesting repercussions on the social structure and organization of the Yishuv.

Growing Differentiation in the Mandatory Period—Competition Between the Sectors. Patterns of Voluntary Associations. With the mandatory period the relatively homogeneous social structure became more complex and diversified, and distinct from older types of homogeneous sects and small, "under-developed" ecological communities.

With the growing expansion of the Yishuv's economy, many new occupational activities—industrial, professional, and clerical—developed. These were connected with the growth of more diversified ecological settings, with the many new types of organizations and groups, and with the growing interdependence of the different sectors of the Yishuv. The growth of autonomous functions and specialized groups as well as the growing importance of monetary and economic rewards also influenced this development.

These developments created new tendencies in the distribution of wealth and power, giving rise to growing differences between economic groups and between the incipient occupational groups.

Concomitantly, ascriptive solidarities began to develop in the private sector, based on kinship, and ecological and occupational traditions, with more widespread emphasis on criteria of economic status, occupational achievements, and differential remuneration.

Within the workers' sector these developments constituted a challenge to the basic ideological pioneering premises. . . .

Patterns of Institutionalization of Ideology. The challenges of growing social differences were taken up by the leaders of the working sector in several ways . . . ideology became institutionalized partly through the selection of élites, and partly through affiliation by the élites with the pioneering groups as well as by allocating symbolic élite status to the settlements. . . .

. . . .

Ideologically, many attempts were made to define the industrial workers as individual or group pioneers whose duties and image did not differ greatly from those of the older pioneer type. . . .

The worker's function was defined more and more in collective terms of social and political identification and, even less than in the case of the agricultural pioneer, in terms of occupational or technical contribution.

Criteria of Allocation and Organizations in the Workers' Sectors. Attempts to institutionalize the pioneering ideology brought to light some of the structural implications and potential contradictions inherent in this ideology.

Access to different functions and resulting rewards became important at that time.

Although official formulation of the pioneering ideology emphasized the importance of free access by all to the pioneering tasks, strong selectivism was in fact practised within it. This was stressed by the importance placed on membership in the various collective organizations and was inherent in the nature of élitist orientation. With the growing problem of adapting the ideology to the developing social structure, this became even more general, applying to the allocation of rewards, the organizational patterns within the movements, and the different ways of life in the workers' sectors. Such ways were based on membership of different élitist groups and movements centred in the communal settlements, the youth movements, and the workers' quarters in the cities, but showed few autonomous class or strata orientations.

Leaders of the workers' sector aimed at maintaining the older homogeneity of status criteria. Membership in these associations became an important means of access to different positions, and resources.

The Social Structure at the End of the Mandate—Social Differentiation and Ideology. By the end of the mandatory period, social organization and stratification in the Yishuv was already much more complicated than in the incipient stages of its development. A greater variety of collective bodies existed, as did ecological groups, functional organizations, voluntary associations, broad movement organizations, and fraternities, as well as various types of latent ascriptive solidarities—and the differences between urban and rural settings continuously increased.

However, gradually a greater number of more specific occupational, political, and cultural functions and functional groups emerged which, although as yet embedded in the collective and ideological definitions of the pioneering image, acquired growing autonomy and began to cut across their initial collective sectors. As a result of these developments the differences in standards and ways of life between groups grew.

Most of these differences were still small compared to those in other modern countries, but nevertheless "lower-class" areas or even slums developed as, for instance, in the Hatigvah quarter of Tel Aviv. These were mostly composed of groups from a lower class and educational background with little pioneering orientation.

Adherence to the sects of the official pioneering ideology as the major framework to all social developments, and the continuous expansion of the social structure, prevented these inequalities and incipient social problems from being fully perceived; one by-product was the slow, and initially inadequate, development and recognition of social work. . . .

. . . .

Moreover, the attempts made by leaders of the workers' groups to institutionalize the ideology gave rise to new tensions and problems, as well as to many paradoxical and unintended consequences.

Among these was the growing and yet not fully-recognized importance of power and power positions in the system of social organization and stratification.

Few clear norms therefore emerged to deal with the distribution or regulation of power. Most economic and organizational frameworks constituted important power positions, and the gradual transition of the Yishuv from a series of groups connected mostly by "mechanical" solidarity and ideological orientation, to a more differentiated social structure, necessarily enhanced the power positions and value of all these groups and enterprises. The growing importance of power positions was only partly offset by the "federative" nature of the expanded social structure, and by continuous preoccupation with the implementation of collective goals. This naturally changed with the establishment of the State.

2
SOCIAL ORGANIZATION AND STRATIFICATION IN THE STATE OF ISRAEL—EMERGING TRENDS

The Establishment of the State — Major Changes in Social Organization. With the establishment of the State of Israel, the trends, tensions, and problems of social organization and stratification described in the preceding section were thrown into greater relief. In many ways national independence proved to be a turning point in development and crystallization, highlighting several factors of crucial importance:

1. The first was the growing unification of different sectors with their often separate "systems" of stratification and social organization. This was accompanied by a weakening of relative autarchy and the dissolution of the "federative" nature of relations between the sectors.

   This unification was caused by the establishment of a central political framework and by the growing importance of political considerations and criteria in the allocation of "material" and prestige rewards.[7]

2. The second major development which influenced social organization was the great influx of new manpower in the form of new immigrants, with their special social, cultural, and educational backgrounds and with their specific motivations for immigration. . . . This influx created great problems in terms of pressures on various resources, the extent of mobility open to these groups, and in tendencies to maintain or develop their own styles of life and traditions.

3. This process of absorption was closely connected with continuous economic development and social and economic differentiation. The very establishment of the state with its administrative and political frameworks created new occupational and prestige positions, which were enhanced by the expansion in the economic structure, giving rise to new occupational roles, organizations, and patterns of mobility. Equally, new problems of differential mobility with regard to both old and new immigrants emerged.

4. The fourth major development was the growing importance of political power

as a social reward, a criterion of social status and position, and as a means of access to major occupational and economic positions.

5. This development also brought out important changes in value-orientations among the different sectors, the most important of these being a weakening in the "forward-looking" outlook and, instead, a growing emphasis on the present as an important dimension of social action. Growing emphasis was therefore placed on a wider spectrum of rewards and on the struggle and competition for these rewards. . . .

6. All these trends necessarily sharpened the conflict between the official pioneering ideology and the developing social reality. The establishment of the state brought the bearers of the pioneering-socialist ideology to power but, at the same time, a new reality resulted from their own policies and their change into a ruling élite.

Growing Differentiation of Roles and Organization. . . . The most general trend in this period was a growing change from the predominant pattern (whereby various functions of society were performed by the same people in a given group) through a process of gradual emphasis on separate tasks which crystallized into distinctive roles and organizations.

Many new industrial enterprises developed, bringing with them a growing managerial and professional class and increased differentiation between technical, skilled, and semi-skilled jobs. In addition, the army and the civil service provide conspicuous examples of entirely new or previously underdeveloped functions.

Similar developments took place in other spheres. In the field of public services banking was greatly expanded and new sectors, such as a growing hotel trade, evolved. Continuous expansion also took place in the older professions, such as law, medicine, and teaching, while engineering and architecture which had not developed much in the previous period, grew very rapidly. Relatively "underdeveloped" professions such as social work also gained in importance. Moreover, there was a continuous inclination towards professionalization in

---

[7] The growth in importance of overall political considerations in the allocations of material rewards was most clearly shown in the fact that major problems of wage policy and differences as well as labor conditions were decided by the central political authorities on a more or less country-wide basis, thus becoming a focal point in the central political struggle.

many new occupations. This showed itself in a growing emphasis on formal educational standards for the attainment of occupational grades in the civil service, in the army, and in business, as well as in the growing tendency of such groups to organize themselves in relatively autonomous professional organizations.

Closely connected with this was the development of new forms of large, bureaucratic administrative and economic organizations—a tendency which could also be found in agriculture. . . .

. . . .

However, the most important structural result of this growing occupational differentiation was perhaps that it created a situation of irreversibility of occupational roles. Unlike the original pioneer-ideology which assumed that a person can easily shift his occupational role according to collective demands, the economic development after the establishment of the State caused commitment to an occupational role to become more set.

People could and did retrain, but the time spent and the specialized demands of most jobs were such that the possibilities of continuous shifts in occupation by adults became more difficult.

This growing occupational specialization constituted the most important breakthrough to economic modernization in Israel.

However, all these changes and trends to differentiation did take place within the framework of a relatively small-scale society. Although the population of this society has, since the establishment of the state, been almost quadrupled—yet its absolute numbers were yet relatively small in terms of comparison with other modern facilities.

This fact had . . . many repercussions on the very direction of these processes of differentiation, on their structural repercussion and on the relations between the élite and the broader groups of the population. . . .

. . . .

Trends in Crystallization of Status. The continued impact of the various social, economic, and occupational differences and the policies evolved by the élite, produced some lasting, if unexpected, tendencies in the Israeli social organization.

The most obvious change was in the manifestations of different styles of life and in the ways in which accessibility to basic resources became organized. . . .

Perhaps the most important general development here was the weakening of the "movement" style of life. The growing emphasis on common standards of consumption diminished the differences between private and collective sectors, but accentuated the differences between occupational, economic, and ethnic groups and strata.

This gave rise to a blurring of differences between the major formal or semi-formal sectors in the Yishuv, and affected all sections of the population.

At the same time relations between the different sectors accentuated the stress on power and greatly increased in importance as a basic element in the system of stratification. This was part of the wider process of proliferation of the various centres of power in Israeli society, rooted in the establishment of the State, in the diversification of administrative-bureaucratic agencies, and in the growing importance of political positions within the social organization. . . .

This weakening of the élitist and movement orientations, intensified the problems of access to various positions and resources—partly because this development went against the egalitarian assumptions of the élites and partly because the process of differentiation itself was apt to weaken the control by the élite over access to major positions and resources.

The most important transformation in stratification developed around economic differentiation and the diverse styles of living. . . .

While the growing importance of consumption as a criterion of status strengthened the class or stratum in the social stratification at the expense of the older élite movement ideologies, yet within it new trends, specific to the Israeli scene, developed.

Trends in Class Crystallization. An analysis of the trend of occupational, positional, and income differentials may well be the best approach to these developments.

In order to analyse the specific characteristics of Israeli society, it is not enough to indicate general trends—rather it is essential to analyse the constellations and coalescence between criteria of status, education, occupation and income—as they developed.

Some peculiar characteristics emerged, closely related to some of the aspects of social mobility analysed above.

The data in Table 35 give a preliminary view of this problem.[8]

Analysis shows a high discrepancy between the different scales, and the lower grades, especially people at the lowest educational level, emerge with a fair chance of achieving a relatively high-level income.

Thus, whereas 51.1 per cent of all Israelis belong to the lowest educational grade, only 33.2 per cent belong to the lowest income level. Unlike the United States of America where we find a high correspondence between occupational prestige and income in the *upper grades* of the two scales, in Israel the trend seems to be the opposite.

[8] Bar-Yosef, R. and Padan, D.: "The Oriental Communities in the Class Structure of Israel," *Molad*, Vol. XXII, Nov. 1964, pp. 195–6.

The upper grades show a marked discrepancy between occupational prestige and income: 10.5 per cent of Israelis are in the higher occupational prestige grade but only 3.9 per cent are counted in the highest income level.

This means that when distributing the population on an income scale, the slant is toward the lower grades, whereas in the *occupational scale* this distribution points toward the *upper* ones.

As most of the statistical data are more reliable with regard to wage-earners than to self-employed, these findings and implications have, to be corrected accordingly, even though exact data for a full correlation are not yet available. . . . It is possible that this indicates a discrepancy between income and occupational prestige in the higher levels which may be somewhat smaller than assumed, especially with regard to non-professional occupations in the private or semi-public sectors.

However, whatever the extent of these cleavages, the class system in Israel tends towards a strong emphasis on the lower middle and middle class, a fact which is also borne out by the preliminary data on mobility. . . .

An interesting paradox of this is the fact

TABLE 35   Status Crystallization (Percentage of Population) in Isreal

	Income	*Occupation*	*Education*
High	3.9	10.5	12.2
Upper middle	19.5	34.0	35.1
Lower middle	43.4	24.7	—
Low	33.2	25.5	51.1*

* The following criteria were used to characterize the class scale:—
Education: Low   = no schooling—elementary education
             Middle = high school
             High   = University or its equivalent of after high school education
Occupation: Low   = unskilled manual work services
      Lower Middle = skilled workers, semi-skilled workers, minor clerical positions and minor business and sales groups
      Higher Middle = white collar employees in middle range positions
             High   = business men, self-employed and employed professionals, highest managerial grade
Income: the grade frontiers are based mostly on the socially accepted evaluation of low, middle, and high income:
             Low   = 1,000–1,999 IL
      Lower Middle = 2,000–3,999 IL
             High   = 7,500–10,000 + IL

Source: R. Bar-Yosef and D. Padan, *op. cit.*

that the economic situation of the lower groups is very low indeed and that they form a marginal group within the society.

Even more important, the relative percentage of these lower groups has not decreased, despite the heavy emphasis of official social policies on minimizing inequality. Some of these policies, such as the lack of full-scale health insurance, as well as the importance of political pressures in their implementation, may well tend to reinforce and perpetuate this situation.

On the other end of the scale, the various middle classes greatly stressed differential symbolic consumption, and encouraged the continuous growth of a small, but continuously expanding, "upper" class of millionaires or very affluent groups of industrialists, bankers, foreign investors, and some professionals.

It was also partially legitimized by the general emphasis on conspicuous consumption and by the participation of many public figures and officials in such consumption. . . . This, in its turn, greatly influenced the direction of the processes of mobility in Israeli society.

This overall trend towards middle-class crystallization becomes even more evident in the self-evaluation of Israelis in terms of status and class criteria. One preliminary research[9] has shown that, in spite of the fact that Israel is known for strong ideological and political orientation towards labor movements, and although the USA is regarded as the stronghold of capitalism the data on class identification in the two countries show a reverse picture. Interestingly enough even a third of the members of socialist collective settlements (kibbutzim) considered themselves as belonging to the middle class.

Another research[10] which used a somewhat different questionnaire indicates what at first glance may seem to be different results, but are basically rather similar ones. This research used the following status

categories, derived to some extent from the "pioneering" ideology: (1) Middle class; (2) Working intelligentsia; (3) Labour class; (4) Working class.

It was found that self-identification with one of these class-categories is closely connected with objective occupational status and educational attainment. Fifty per cent of the non-matriculated wage-earners who were investigated identified with "working class" and less than 20 per cent with "middle class." Fifty-one per cent of the non-matriculated and 62 per cent of the matriculated self-employed identified with "middle-class"; while 50 per cent of the matriculated wage-earners categorized themselves as "working-intelligentsia," an additional 22 per cent as middle-class and only 10 per cent as "working-class."

Thus here also there seems to be a strong emphasis on the "middle" strata—even if defined by somewhat different categories—than on the "truly" proletarian or "low" ones.

All these data indicate an interesting trend of development of the Israeli status system. They do indeed indicate that occupation has become an important, even if not a single, determinant of socio-economic status in Israel. During the pre-state period the objective process of downward intergenerational mobility was recognized and idealized ("proletarization," "normalization of the occupational pyramid"). Formal education was devalued and the stereotype of the "cultured worker" fostered by the "halutzic sector" enhanced the self-image of the "class-conscious worker" (at least so we are told). Remnants of this idealization are probably still operating today. Yet no doubt there exists today a greater variety of significant status components than in the past competing with "class," occupation, and ideology as potential foci of identification and solidarity. . . .

The plurality of status components and the relative absence of congruity between the various criteria prevents the emergence of a status-consciousness based upon the primacy of a single deprecatory factor even of the most basic kind. Through increasing the salience of status-enhancing factors low-status individuals are enabled to form a

[9] A. Antonovsky: "Social and Political Attitudes in Israel," *Allot,* June–July, 1963.
[10] Adapted from fieldwork for: A. Zloczower: *Mobility Patterns and Status Conceptions in an Urban Israeli Setting.* Ph.D. Thesis, The Hebrew University of Jerusalem, 1966.

relatively favourably status-image for themselves. . . .

NEW STATUS CRYSTALLIZATION: OCCUPATIONAL, ETHNIC, POLITICAL, AND RELIGIOUS AFFILIATIONS

These crystallizations of "middle class" orientations indicate the growing importance of occupational criteria in evaluation of status. But in spite of this, there also developed growing differences in hierarchies of prestige according to various non-professional criteria, among the most important of which were religion and ethnic background. . . .

THE ETHNIC ELEMENT IN THE TRANSFORMATION OF TRADITIONAL STRUCTURES

Due to the basic characteristics of the various immigrant groups and because of the initial conditions of absorption . . . some of the major "ethnic" groups tended to concentrate, at least temporarily, in special clusters.

Although these groups maintained some of their traditions and ways of life, they were naturally strongly affected by the impact of the absorbing society—the educational system, the army, and economic and occupational pressures.

These clusters were indicative of the common "fate" of the different immigrant groups in the process of absorption.

In this context the extent of coalescence between economic "class" and "ethnic" criterion, achieved a special importance. . . .

Ethnic background and identity were most strongly articulated among the oriental, but, to a smaller degree, also among some European groups—and became an important new factor in the pattern of social organization. Effects were also felt in the re-crystallization of the avenues of access to different occupational and political positions and to economic and political resources.

The development by the oriental immigrants of specific subcultures within the Israeli system of stratification is indicated by several different reinforcing trends and is closely related to the continuous coalescence—especially within oriental groups—of low occupational, educational, and economic status.

Among oriental groups the less differentiated images of society seem to be more prevalent. Similarly, they evince patterns of mobility aspiration, which emphasize larger incomes rather than the attainment of advance education. This is related to findings that, at the same level of income, the oriental group tends to invest less in education and more in direct consumption. The continuous educational backwardness of many of these groups . . . is, of course, closely related to this.

The crystallization of the specific ethnic element as distinct and divisive, also becomes apparent in the data on intermarriage between groups of different origin. These show that in 86 per cent of all marriages performed in 1959, partners were of similar ethnic origin, whereas in only 14 per cent were their origins "mixed." . . .

We see thus that the ethnic and especially the oriental element could crystallize as a specific new ascriptive element in the Israeli social structure, a development which constitutes one of the most important within Israeli society and a challenge to it. In addition, the ethnic factor also caused new cleavages and tensions in the social and political fields.

Closely connected with these developments were the many attempts made to change the negative relationship between ethnic background and access to occupational and educational positions. One attempt was a demand for more help in acquiring the resources (especially education) necessary for the achievement of various positions and occupations.

The other attempt made was to increase demands for more direct access to such positions by virtue of belonging to a given ethnic group.

These directions combined through the political organizations of various ethnic groups and reinforced several broader tendencies of crystallization of status in Israeli society.

POLITICS AND POWER IN THE CRYSTALLIZATION OF STRATA AND STATUS

A similar picture emerges with regard to the second new criterion of status—the political-administrative one.

Of the many organizations which, increasingly, affected the life of the Israeli citizen, the most important, encompassing almost every sphere of life, was the Histadrut. This organization controlled areas of work (and until lately also access to work through the various labour exchanges), health services (through *Kupat Cholim*), and a large part of the access to housing and other basic necessities.

The various government departments and agencies constituted another important conglomeration of organizations dominating the access to basic areas and facilities. For many of the new immigrants the Jewish Agency and the different parties constituted the all-important sources of allocation of resources and goods. These various organizations often competed among themselves and had to take recourse to the central political and administrative organs of the State to develop some *modus vivendi*. This greatly increased the importance of power in the context of social organization—as a criterion of status, as a resource, and as a focus of conflict within the social structure.

Many of the élite policies tried to enhance the value of power and the prestige of political position and their control over access to resources. The growth of large-scale economic organizations in both private and public sectors, encouraged by the Government's economic and tax policies, reinforced the importance of political and organizational criteria in the state system.

Seen from the political and administrative criteria of stratification, the Israeli population divides according to differences in access to the various facilities, and according to the channels through which such access is organized.

Since the various political groups largely control access to major facilities, membership in one of them may be virtually essential. While it is relatively easy to evaluate different groups according to relative standard of living, wealth, and education, the picture becomes more complicated with additional criteria. In many cases the lack of affiliation to any collective, party, or bureaucratic organization, is a sign of the lowest possible status group. Among many groups of new immigrants, however, while access to collective agencies certainly mitigates low status, a too exclusive dependence on only one organization, may freeze different groups of the population at a relatively low occupational level.

There is no doubt for example that a very large percentage of those who are not members of any Sick Fund belong to the lowest strata of the population for whom the attainment of full rights in the *Kupat Cholim* of the Histadrut would mean a very great advance.

As in many other welfare societies, social services in Israel tend to discriminate in favour of the more powerful or rich, so that the lower rungs who have neither additional income nor the pull of membership in other organizations, receive only minimal attention which may well minimize their possibilities of advancement. Therefore the access to a number of more active organizations may be of crucial importance for the achievement of higher mobility.

On the other hand, especially among the higher occupational groups, constant recourse to such organizations becomes a constricting factor which may impede the possibility of further social mobility and participation.

Among these groups, especially among the professional ones, more autonomous hierarchies of prestige emerged, and with them important tensions and cleavages in reaction to restrictions imposed by political and administrative bodies. . . .

The first cleavage appeared between the salaried and self-employed sectors, and was particularly pronounced among the upper and middle groups. The second cleavage seems to be developing within the salaried professionals, between those employed in sectors (like government service) where official wage policy is more or less maintained, and those private sectors and government companies where this is not the case. These cleavages explain the growing conflicts and tensions between professionals and non-professionals in the public service.

These tensions produced two broad tendencies of structural crystallizations of great importance for the merging patterns of stratification in Israel. The first such tendency found expression in growing occupational and social differentiations, in multiplication of avenues of mobility, and in heterogeneous points of prestige and status.

The second tendency developed in the direction of growing concentration on and restriction of access to resources, positions, and prestige, affecting members of various, either new political, or ethnic (or religious) organizations.

Thus, within the professional groups, attempts were made to break the monopoly of the Histadrut, while at the same time new ascriptive groups were organized which could become a second Histadrut, assuring members of various benefits.

....

ECOLOGICAL PATTERNS OF STRATIFICATION

It may be worthwhile to describe briefly some of the major social organizations that crystallized in different ecological settings.

As a result of factors analysed above, different social patterns and groupings are in constant development. The strong movement patterns as seen in the kibbutz and the moshav are at one extreme, with new immigrant settlements—especially the moshavim—constituting a special sub-category within this framework. These patterns are mostly characterized by a more positive attitude to agriculture, by growing interests in urban patterns of life, and by more organized leisure activities, interwoven within different patterns and traditions. In the non-movement rural sectors and in the older moshavot, a wealthy suburban peasant type developed with close family tradition, connected with economic and occupational orientations, around which the new semi-urban immigrant groups tended to settle.

However the most varied development took place in the various urban centres of Jerusalem, Tel Aviv, and Haifa.

It is here that the different occupational, professional, and economic groups changed and crystallized most dramatically. Here also many of the religious groups are concentrated, and the most conspicuous "ethnic" problem areas developed.

....

An entirely new pattern of social organization in which some of the "new trends"

have crystallized can be found in the various development towns and areas, such as Beersheba, and the much less urbanized development areas, such as Kiryat Shmona and Kiryat Gat.

Within these frameworks the criterion of occupation and origin—as well as the length of stay in the country is gaining increasing importance, and different groups and strata tend to crystallize according to occupation, education, ethnic origin, etc.

While many variations exist in the development areas, the following survey[11] of one of these medium-sized towns may give an indication of some of the emerging trends in the development areas.

The town under study was established as the result of a twofold policy: development of arid areas and settlement of the numerous immigrants who entered Israel in the 'fifties. The construction of the town was part of a plan which included the establishment of agricultural settlements. An industry based on agriculture was to be set up, and the town was also intended to serve as an administrative, commercial, and cultural centre.

The first settlers were new immigrants from North Africa who came to the town directly from the port. Within a few years more North African immigrants followed, mainly from Morocco, as well as some immigrants from Egypt, Eastern Europe (mainly from Poland and Romania), and a small group from English-speaking countries.

From the beginning these groups were joined by veteran citizens who came from all parts of the country, and at the time the study was undertaken, the population of the town was about 10,000.

The main criteria of social differentiation in the town are length of stay in the country and ethnic origin. Ethnic origin also determines affiliation to different communities with their own cultural and religious traditions: the Ashkenazi community which includes mainly European Jews, and the Sephardic community which includes Jews of Spanish descent and oriental Jews. The

[11] This is based on: E. Cohen, L. Shamgar and Y. Levy. Research Report: *Absorption of Immigrants in a Development Town*. The Hebrew University, Department of Sociology, 1962.

differentiation among these various groups embraces all spheres of life, including politics.

At first the old settlers filled all the central roles in the occupational sphere. They were sent to the town in order to function as an administrative and cultural élite, to teach, to instruct, and to build up the municipal and public institutions. Their occupational concentration, relatively high standard of living, and common culture and way of life, made them into a rather closed social stratum in which members enjoy high social status.

This strata contains the senior officials in the municipal institutions and in government service, such as social welfare and health, as well as the first political party officials sent there as the population grew. In this way the veterans were at the head of the political organization from the very beginning.

In contrast to the veterans, the new immigrants generally lack economic resources and means of obtaining employment, and are dependent on various governmental and municipal agencies for such basic needs as housing and work.

After the first difficult period of adaptation, differences among the several groups of new immigrants became apparent, mainly in their economic situation and way of life.

Highest average incomes and occupational positions are held by the immigrants from English-speaking countries, who form a small group. They live in the best part of the town, together with many veterans and some prosperous immigrants from Eastern Europe. They are active mainly in the economic field, whereas in public-political life their impact is hardly felt. In general, the situation of the East European immigrants is less good, particularly as regards the many elderly persons who have difficulties in getting re-established. . . .

Due to their higher level of education and professional training, and because of their cultural closeness to the Old Yishuv, as well as their personal ties with the old settlers, the European and Anglo-Saxon immigrants have access to many avenues of individual social mobility.

The situation of the oriental immigrants who lack the above mentioned character-istics is much harder. Among the Egyptian immigrants there is a small nucleus of persons whose educational and professional formation is European. They occupy relatively good positions and form an élite at the centre of their group.

The North African immigrants who constitute half the town's population are the most backward of all newcomers and form the greater part of unemployed and relief workers. The average income of a Moroccan family is often inadequate even for minimum food requirements. Their level of formal education is usually very low. Most Moroccan families are large and a considerable number of them are under the care of governmental social welfare. Many of these immigrants live in the oldest housing quarters which are now near-slum areas. The older Moroccan immigrants are traditionalists and the synagogue to them is a social institution of prime importance. However, they lack central traditional—or other—leadership, and they are socially divided into a number of rival groups.

The study has shown that the various ethnic groups, and the veteran residents, form distinct social units with major social ties. Nevertheless these groups are not homogeneous from the point of view of stratification, and within each group economic and educational differences exist. Indications show that different ethnic groups, of a relatively high economic or educational level, tend to tie up in "status-groups" which cut across ethnic barriers and create new social units whose bases are economic and cultural. However, they do not, normally, cut across the boundaries between the two community formations: the Ashkenazim and the orientals.

Thus economic and cultural criteria gradually assumed increased importance in the more developed groups of the population, which, in turn, led to greater emphasis on divisions among the communal groups.

Naturally, the organizational settings of the various development towns differ in many details, especially in those towns where the original political or administrative élite was composed of "oriental" settlers who received the newcomers, among them also European groups. But nonetheless, the crystallization of status and ethnic groups with concomitant ethnic tensions was of equal importance.

The Importance of Ascriptive and Power Elements. It is interesting to see to what extent the new patterns of "strata" crystallization and the growing importance of power and ascriptive criteria, influenced the perception of the social structure.

Several recent research projects arrived at the conclusion that, in modern industrial societies, most stratification images can be classified into one or two types, or into a combination of the two. These two types are: (a) The hierarchic image, in which society is seen as a composition of usually three groups forming an "open-class" system. These groups differ in their functions and in their way of life, but together they are conceived as constituting a relatively harmonious social entity with few overall conflicts. . . . (b) The power image, in which society is seen as a dichotomy of two sharply distinguished classes.

Some studies undertaken in Israel[12] substantiated these findings and have shown that here, as in most other societies, the more hierarchic image is characteristic of the higher social groups, while the second is typical of the lower. But some specific characteristics seem to emerge.

The survey mentioned above showed that the most common images of social structure among the dwellers of our development town were found to be the following: (1) A non-hierarchical, multi-group image, in which the groups differ in the ethnic origin of their members (18.1 per cent of the total answers). According to this conception, the community is made up of a number of ethnic groups of equal status and without conflict. No possibility of mobility between them exists since the distinguishing criterion is ascriptive and one simply "belongs" to the group. As these groups have equal status, this image was named "the egalitarian image." (2) A hierarchical, multi-class image, in which classes differentiate according to economic criteria (12.8 per cent of the total answers). According to this conception, the community is a hierarchy of economic groups, mostly occupational, income-bracket groups. The distinction be-

tween them is not as clear-cut as in the previous image, for, together, they constitute an organic entity without contrasts or appreciable discrepancies. Since the distinguishing criterion is one of economic achievement and the groups form a hierarchy, mobility from one group to another is possible. (3) A hierarchical, two-class image in which distinction is made along the lines of economic criteria (17 per cent of the total answers). According to this conception the community is made up of two groups whose economic situations differ sharply. The existence of social conflict is inherent in this image. Thus, free movement between the two classes is more limited than in the previous image, although the distinguishing criterion is one of economic achievement. Here the differential *economic power* status of the groups is emphasized. (4) A hierarchical, two-group image, in which the groups are differentiated by the criterion of origin (26.9 per cent of the total answers). With this approach, the community is also made up of two groups, but these are distinguished either by length of stay in the country or by ethnic origin and communal affiliation (veteran-new immigrant; Ashkenazi-oriental). The groups constitute a dichotomy, and there is a conflict of interests between them. As the distinguishing criterion is ascriptive, there is no possibility of mobility between the groups; and this image may be labelled as the "caste image."

The project concludes that the egalitarian image which is non-hierarchic, is characteristic of those of higher status. The extent of hierarchization increases as status decreases, and, among those of lowest status, we find the "caste" image, which is extremely hierarchical by nature. The usual two images—"the hierarchic image" and "the power image," are therefore placed between the two new images which were encountered in our research; they are characteristic of the groups which occupy the highest and the lowest positions in the social structure of the town. It is also interesting to note that both groups have ascriptive bases of valuation, while the common base of the two intermediary groups is achievement.

These findings are based mostly on

---

[12] E. Cohen, L. Shamgar, Y. Levy, *op. cit.*, 1962.

material gleaned from development areas and necessarily reflect some of the specific problems of these areas. Tentative comparison between the stratification images of the town and of the whole country shows that, on the national level, both the "conflicting" images (the "power" and the "caste" images) and the ascriptive images (equality and caste) were stressed to a smaller, but not insignificant, degree.

The picture of Israeli society as perceived by some groups, differs greatly from the more official ideological view of a "classless" working society—the ideological image of the élite.

Our picture indicates not only the emergence of growing differences between various groups but also the growing importance of several new elements of power and ascription, both in the actual processes of crystallization of social stratification and in the perception of the social structure.

SOCIAL STRATIFICATION IN INDUSTRIAL SOCIETY

John H. Goldthorpe

For a decade or so now, a growing interest has been apparent, chiefly among American sociologists, in the pattern of long-term social change within relatively mature industrial societies. This interest appears to derive from two main sources.

In the first place, it can be seen as resulting from broadly based studies of the sociology of industrialization, concentrating originally on the underdeveloped or developing countries of the world. For example, work conducted as part of the Inter-University Study of Labour Problems in Economic Development led up to the theoretical statement on the "logic" of industrialism

From *The Development of Industrial Society*, Paul Halmos, ed., the *Sociological Review*, Monograph No. 8, 1964. Reprinted by permission of the *Sociological Review* and the Sociological Review Monographs.

attempted by Clark Kerr and his associates in their book, *Industrialism and Industrial Man*.[1] Secondly, this interest has undoubtedly been stimulated by the revival in comparative studies of social structure and social processes in economically advanced countries. Important here, for example, has been the work of Professor Lipset and a number of other members of the Berkeley campus of the University of California; and even more so, perhaps, studies which have chiefly involved comparisons between Western and Communist societies, such as those produced in connection with the Harvard Project on the Soviet Social System by Professor Inkeles and his colleagues.[2]

However, it is notable that in spite of possibly different origins, current American interpretations of the development of industrial societies often reveal marked similarities. Basically, it may be said, they tend to be alike in stressing the standardizing effects upon social structures of the exigencies of modern technology and of an advanced economy. These factors which make for uniformity in industrial societies are seen as largely overriding other factors which may make for possible diversity, such as different national cultures or different political systems. Thus, the overall pattern of development which is suggested is one in which, once countries enter into the advanced stages of industrialization, they tend to become increasingly comparable in their major institutional arrangements and in their social systems generally. In brief, a *convergent* pattern of development is hypothesized.

Kerr and his associates have been the most explicit in this connection—and also in the matter of specifying the type of society on which the process of convergence is focussed. In their conception, "the road ahead" for all advanced societies leads in the direction of what they call "pluralistic" industrialism. By this they mean a form of industrial society in which the distribution

[1] Clark Kerr, J. T. Dunlop, F. H. Harbison and C. A. Myers, *Industrialism and Industrial Man*, 1960.

[2] See, e.g., Raymond A. Bauer, Alex Inkeles and Clyde Kluckhohn, *How the Soviet System Works*, 1956; Inkeles and Bauer, *The Soviet Citizen*, 1959.

of power is neither "atomistic" nor "monistic", nor yet radically disputed by warring classes; but rather a social order in which an "omnipresent State" regulates competition and conflict between a multiplicity of interest groups on the basis of an accepted "web of rules," and at the same time provides the means through which a degree of democratic control can be exercised over the working of the economy and over other key social processes such as the provision of welfare and public services, education and so on.[3] Other theorists have usually been a good deal more guarded than this in their formulations; but it would nonetheless be fair to say that, in the main, they have adopted views which have been broadly consistent with the Kerr thesis. In general, the "logic" of industrialism has been regarded as powerfully encouraging, even if not compelling, the emergence of a new type of society from out of former "class" and "mass" societies alike.

Clearly, then, a central theme in the interpretations in question concerns the development in advanced societies of systems of social stratification. And it is perhaps indicative of the importance of this theme that it has on several occasions been singled out for special discussion. In this paper[4] my main purpose will be to consider this particular aspect of current theories of industrialism and, further, to raise certain doubts and objections which seem to me to be of a serious kind and to have negative implications for these theories *in toto*. But at the outset I should say that I in no way intend to criticize the *kind* of sociological endeavour which is here represented. On the contrary, we are, I believe, much indebted to the authors of these theories for showing us a way to escape from the cramped quarters of trivialized empiricism without falling victim to highly speculative building with "empty boxes."

The arguments concerning the development of social stratification which form a core element in American interpretations

of industrialism can be usefully stated under three main heads: differentiation, consistency and mobility.[5] To begin with, I would like to consider these three sets of arguments in turn.

DIFFERENTIATION

In regard to differentiation, the major proposition that is put forward is that, in course of industrial advance, there is a decrease in the degree of differentiation in all stratification subsystems or orders. In other words, to follow Inkeles' formulation: "a process of relative homogenization takes place, reducing the gap or range separating the top and bottom of the scale"—in income and wealth, in status formal and informal, and in political power.[6] As a result of this process, a marked increase occurs within each stratification order in the proportion of the total population falling into the middle ranges of the distribution. The "shape" of the stratification hierarchy thus ceases to be pyramidal and approximates, rather, to that of a pentagon or even of a diamond.

This trend is related to the "logic" of industrialism in several different ways. But, primarily, the connection is seen as being through the changing division of labour. An advancing technology and economy continually repattern the occupational structure, and in ways which progressively increase the number of higher level occupational rôles; that is to say, rôles requiring relatively high standards of education and training and at the same time commanding relatively high economic rewards

---

[3] Kerr, *et al., op cit.*, Chs. 1, 2 and 10 especially.

[4] I am indebted to my friend M. Alfred Willener for his criticisms of an earlier draft of this paper and also to colleagues in the Faculty of Economics and Politics of the University of Cambridge who have discussed many specific points with me.

[5] The following exposition is derived from Kerr, *et al., op. cit.*; Inkeles, "Social Stratification in the Modernization of Russia" in Cyril E. Black (ed.), *The Transformation of Russian Society*, 1960; and W. E. Moore (ed.), *Industrialisation and Society*, 1963, pp. 318–322, 353–359 especially. It is, however, important to note the very marked differences in tone and style between these contributions. Kerr and his colleagues are most dogmatic and "prophetic", but also the most diffuse in their arguments; Inkeles, on the other hand, is the most explicit yet is clearly writing, as he says, "not to settle a point but to open a discussion"; while Moore, aiming at the summing-up of a body of research data, puts forward by far the most cautious and qualified statements.

[6] *Loc. cit.*, p. 341. Cf. Kerr *et al., op. cit.*, pp. 286–294. . . .

and social status. Thus, the middle of the stratification hierarchy becomes considerably expanded.

So far as Western societies are concerned, a further factor in this homogenizing process is also recognized in the growing intervention of the state in economic affairs; particularly in governmental policies which lead to the redistribution and control of economic power. For example, it is observed that policies of progressive taxation and of social welfare in various ways modify for the benefit of the less privileged the division of income and balance of social advantage which would have resulted from the free operation of market mechanisms. However, in this case great stress is placed on the close relationship that exists between this expansion in the regulatory functions of government and the direct requirements of the industrialization process. The state, it is argued, *must* be the key regulatory organization in any advanced society: the complexity of its technology and economy demand this. At minimum, the state must be responsible for the general rate of economic progress, and thus ultimately, for the overall allocation of resources between uses and individuals, for the quality of the national labour force, for the economic and social security of individuals and so on.[7]

In other words, even where greater social equality results directly from the purposive action of governments, the tendency is to see behind this action not a particular complex of socio-political beliefs, values or interests but rather the inherent compulsions of "industrialism" itself.[8]

. . . Furthermore, one should note, a similar viewpoint is taken in arguing that greater equality in political power—in the form of a pluralistic system—will tend to emerge in societies which now have totalitarian (or autocratic) regimes. In the first place, it is held, the production technology of an industrial society is such that any regime must become increasingly interested in the consent of the mass of the labour force; for the efficient use of this technology requires responsible initiative and freely given co-operation on the part of those who operate it. Secondly, the growing complexity of technical problems arising in the process of government itself necessitates the greater involvement in decision-making of experts and professionals, and in this way the latter come to acquire some independent authority. Thus, a monolithic structure gives way to one in which there are a number of "strategic" elites and of different foci of power. In brief, industrialism is regarded as being ultimately inimical to any form of monistic political order.[9]

CONSISTENCY

In this respect, the central argument is that as societies become increasingly industrial, there is a growing tendency within the stratification system towards what Inkeles terms "equilibration"; that is, a tendency for the relative position of an individual or group in any one stratification order to be the same as, or similar to, their position in other orders.[10] In traditional societies, it is observed, inconsistencies in the stratification system may have been contrary to the prevailing ideology but were nonetheless frequent because of the rigidity of the levels

[7] Cf. Kerr, *et al., op. cit.,* pp. 31, 40–41, 273–274, 290–292; Moore, *op. cit.,* pp. 357–359.

[8] For a discussion of the strengths and weaknesses of attempts to apply this approach to the explanation of the development of social policy in 19th century England, see John H. Goldthorpe, "Le développement de la politique sociale en Angleterre de 1800 à 1914", *Sociologie du Travail,* No. 2, 1963. (English version . . . in *Transactions of the Vth World Congress of Sociology,* Vol. IV, 1964).

[9] Cf. Kerr *et al., op. cit.,* pp. 274–276, 288–290; Inkeles, p. 346. As earlier noted, Moore diverges here. He notes (p. 359) the empirical probability of increased political participation as societies become industrial, but argues that so far there is no evidence of a *necessary* incompatibility between industrialism and totalitarianism.

[10] Inkeles' "equilibration" (following E. Benoit-Smullyan, "Status Types and Status Interrelations", *Am. Soc. Rev.,* Vol. 9, 1944) thus largely corresponds to what Lenski and Landecker have referred to as "crystallization" and Adams and Homans as "congruence". See Gerhard E. Lenski, "Status Crystallization: a Non-Vertical Dimension of Social Status", *Am. Soc. Rev.,* Vol. 19, 1954; Werner S. Landecker, "Class Crystallization and Class Consciousness", *Am. Soc. Rev.,* Vol. 28, 1963; Stuart Adams, "Social Climate and Productivity in Small Military Groups", *Am. Soc. Rev.,* Vol. 19, 1954; G. C. Homans, "Status Congruence" in *Sentiments and Activities,* 1962. Moore refers simply to "consistency" or "coalescence".

within the different subsystems and the relatively low degree of interaction between them. For example, a merchant might become extremely wealthy yet be debarred from "noble" status; in fact, legally, he could be of peasant status and might be treated as such in certain circumstances in spite of his wealth. In industrial societies, by contrast, there are far fewer difficulties in the way of "adjustments" which serve to bring the position of individuals and groups more or less into line from one stratification order to another. Moreover, there is also a shift away from the relative diversity of the bases of stratification which is characteristic of traditional society. With industrialism, the occupational structure takes on overwhelming primacy in this respect. The occupational rôle of the individual is in general in close correlation with most other of his attributes which are relevant to his position in the stratification hierarchy as a whole: his economic situation, his educational level, his prestige in the local community and so on.[11]

In the same way as the trend towards greater equality, the trend towards greater consistency in stratification systems is also treated as an integral part of the industrialization process and as being directly linked to technological and economic advance. In industrial society, it is argued, the distribution of both economic rewards and prestige must come into a close relationship with occupational performance since this type of society in fact presupposes an overriding emphasis upon achievement, as opposed to ascription, as the basis of social position—and specifically upon achievement in the sphere of production. At the same time, though, as a result of technological progress, occupational achievement becomes increasingly dependent upon education, and in this way closer ties are formed between economic standing on the one hand and life-styles and subculture on the other. The ignorant and vulgar tycoon and the poor scholar are seen alike as figures of declining importance. In other words, the argument is that inevitably in modern societies, the various determinants of an individual's

placing in the overall stratification hierarchy come to form a tight nexus; and that in this nexus occupation can be regarded as the central element—providing as it does the main link between the "objective" and "subjective" aspects of social inequality.

Implicit, then, in this interpretation is the view that in industrial societies stratification systems tend to become relatively highly integrated, in the sense that specifically class differences (i.e. those stemming from inequalities in the economic order) are generally paralleled by status differences (i.e. those based on inequalities in social evaluation); and, thus, that changes in the pattern of the former will automatically result in changes in the pattern of the latter. For example, Kerr and his associates see the growth of "middle incomes" as making for a "middle class society"; that is, a society in which middle class values are widely accepted, both among manual workers and elite groups, and in which the bulk of the population share in "middle class" status.[12]

MOBILITY

In regard to mobility, the central proposition that is made is one which complements the previous arguments concerning differentiation and consistency. It is that once societies have reached a certain level of industrialization, their overall rates of social mobility tend to become relatively high—higher that is, than is typical in preindustrial or traditional societies. The increasing number of intermediate positions in the stratification hierarchy widens the opportunity for movement upward from the lower levels, while the emphasis upon occupational achievement rather than on the ascription of social positions means that intergenerationally the talented will tend to rise at the expense of those whose talent is unequal to their birth. In this respect, the educational system is seen as the crucial allocative mechanism, sieving ability and matching capacity to the demands and responsibilities of occupational rôles.[13]

In other words, then, industrial society

---

[11] Cf. Kerr *et al.*, *op. cit.*, pp. 272–273, 284, 292–293; Inkeles, *op. cit.*, pp. 341–342; Moore, *op. cit.*, pp. 356–357.

[12] Kerr, *et al.*, *op. cit.*, pp. 272–273, 286.
[13] Cf. *ibid.*, pp. 35–37; Moore, *op. cit.*, pp. 319–321, 343–344.

is regarded as being essentially "open" and "meritocratic". And once more, one should note, the interpretation derives from a conception of the structural and functional imperatives of this type of social order. . . .

In this approach, thus, there is little room for consideration of institutional variations or of value differences between industrial societies which might be associated with *differing* patterns of mobility. It is taken that the overall similarities in this respect are, or at any rate are certainly becoming, the feature of major significance.

. . . I would now like to turn to what I have to say by way of criticism of these arguments and, to begin with, I would like to comment on each of the three themes on which I based the foregoing exposition. My main purpose here will be to indicate that the views which I have outlined are not always in entire accord with empirical data, and in this connection I shall refer primarily to the industrial societies of the West. . . .

On the question of reduced differentiation—or greater equality—in stratification systems, my remarks at this stage will be largely confined to the economic order. This is because it is chiefly in this regard that we have data which will permit, at least in principle, some test of the arguments involved; that is, data on the distributions of income and wealth.[14]

At the outset it may be said that, although the evidence is often very patchy, a broad trend towards greater economic equality *does* seem to be discernible in the case of all those societies which have so far progressed from a traditional to an industrial form. Myths of "golden ages" of economic equality in pre-industrial times are now little heeded, and, as a rough generalization, it would, I think, be widely accepted that the poorer the society, the greater the "skew" one may expect in its distributions

of income and wealth alike.[15] With this view I would not wish to quarrel—provided that it is taken merely as a formula summing up historical experience, and as one which is subject to exceptions. But there are no grounds at all, in my view, for regarding the regularity in question as manifesting the operation of some process inherent in industrialism—of some general economic law—which will necessarily persist in the future and ensure a continuing egalitarian trend. Rather, the possibility must be left quite open that where such a trend exists, it may at some point be checked—and at a point, moreover, at which considerable economic *in*equality remains. In fact, in my assessment, the relevant data suggest that such a check may already be occurring in some of the more advanced societies of the West; or, at any rate, I would say that on present evidence *this* conclusion is indicated as much as any other.

For the distributions of income and wealth alike, it is true that figures exist to show a movement towards greater equality in most western industrial societies over the years for which adequate time-series are available; that is, from the late inter-war or early post-war period onwards.[16] However, it is now becoming increasingly clear that these figures, which are largely based on tax returns, are not always to be taken at their face value. And, in general, their defects appear to be such that they tend on balance to underestimate the income and wealth which accrue to the economically more favoured groups and in this and other ways to give a somewhat exaggerated idea of the degree of "levelling" that has taken place. In fact, for some western societies at least, there are now grounds for believing

---

[14] It should be acknowledged, however, that for the West, at least, there is clear evidence on one other important point; that is, on the reduction, indeed virtual elimination, of *formal* inequalities of status. This has been the concomitant of the growth of "citizenship" through which all members of national communities have been granted equal civil, political and social rights. Cf. T. H. Marshall, "Citizenship and Social Class" in *Sociology at the Crossroads*, 1963.

[15] Cf. United Nations, *Preliminary Report on the World Social Situation*, 1952, pp. 132–134; and *Report on the World Social Situation*, 1961, pp. 58–61.

[16] See, e.g., United Nations, *Economic Survey of Europe in 1956*, 1957, Ch. VII; R. M. Solow, "Income Inequality since the War" in Ralph E. Freeman (ed.), *Postwar Economic Trends in the United States*, 1960. Recent studies relating specifically to Great Britain are H. F. Lydall, "The Long-term Trend in the Size Distribution of Income", *Journ. Royal Stat. Soc.*, Vol. 122, Part I, 1959, and H. F. Lydall and D. C. Tipping, "The Distribution of Personal Wealth in Britain", *Oxford Inst. Stat. Bull.*, Vol. 23, 1961.

that during the last twenty years or so, overall economic inequality has in reality declined only very little, if at all. And particularly so far as wealth is concerned, it is likely that such changes as have occurred have been virtually negligible in their implications for social stratification.[17] Such conclusions have been suggested for the United Kingdom, for example, in Professor Titmuss' recent study, *Income Distribution and Social Change*.[18] . . .

A similar point of view is maintained, with reference to the United States, in Gabriel Kolko's somewhat neglected book, *Wealth and Power in America*. . . . Kolko supplements material from official sources with generally more reliable survey data, and on this basis suggests that over as long a period as 1910 to 1959 there has been no significant *general* trend in the United States towards greater income equality.[19]

Kolko's study prompts one to note the often overlooked point that simply because there may be some levelling of incomes going on in *certain ranges* of the total income distribution, this does not necessarily mean that *overall* equality is increasing; for in other ranges inegalitarian trends may simultaneously be operating. For example, there may be a tendency towards greater equality in that the number of middle-range incomes

is growing; but at the same time the position of the lower income groups, relative to the upper and middle groups alike, may be worsening.

In fact, it seems more than possible that a pattern of change of this kind is now going on in the United States. This is indicated by a good deal of recent investigation, apart from that of Kolko, and particularly by the growing volume of work on the extent of poverty. Gunnar Myrdal, for example, has argued in his book, *Challenge to Affluence*, that while many Americans in the intermediate social strata may well be benefiting from a levelling upwards of living standards, at the base of the stratification hierarchy there is increasing inequality, manifested in the emergence of an "underclass" of unemployed and unemployable persons and families. In other words, the middle ranks of the income distribution may be swelling, but the gap between the bottom and the higher levels is, if anything, tending to widen.[20]

Moreover, what is also significant in Myrdal's study for present purposes is the way in which he brings out the *political* aspects of the problem. Myrdal observes that structural unemployment, resulting from technological innovation in industry, is a basic, and increasingly serious, cause of poverty in America, whereas in a country like Sweden, in which technological advance is also proceeding rapidly, full employment has been steadily maintained. Again, he notes the relative failure of the United States, compared with most western European countries, to stabilize aggregate demand in its economy on a high and rising level.[21] The explanation of these differences, Myrdal then argues, while not of course entirely political, must nonetheless be regarded as

[17] Chiefly, this is because much levelling which appears to have gone on at the top of the distribution has in fact taken place simply *within* families—particularly between parents and children and generally as a means of avoiding taxation. E.g., Lydall and Tipping (*op. cit.*) note the "growing tendency for owners of large properties to distribute their assets amongst the members of their families well in advance of death" (p. 85). However, it is, of course, the family, not the individual, that must be regarded as the basic unit of stratification.

[18] See, e.g., the critical review of Titmuss' book by A. R. Prest, and Titmuss' reply, in *British Tax Review*, March–April, 1963. *Income Distribution and Social Change*, 1962, p. 198. In this connection it should also be remembered that certain major developments which have made for greater equality in incomes in the recent past are of a non-repeatable kind—notably, the ending of large scale unemployment and the considerable expansion in the number of working class wives in gainful employment.

[19] *Wealth and Power in America*, 1962, Ch. 1. The data in question refer to pre-tax incomes, but Kolko is prepared to argue (Ch. 2) that "Taxation has not mitigated the fundamentally unequal distribution of income. . . ."

[20] *Challenge to Affluence*, 1963, Ch. 3. The data assembled by the Conference on Economic Progress, *Poverty and Deprivation in the United States*, 1962, suggest that there was real improvement in the income position of low-income groups during World War II but that since then the economy has not greatly enhanced the living standards of the low-income population. In regard to the distribution of wealth, Robert J. Lampman, *The Share of Top Wealth-Holders in National Wealth*, 1962, has produced data to show that the share of personal sector wealth held by the wealthiest 1% of adults in the USA has steadily increased from 1949 to 1956.

[21] Myrdal, *ibid.*, pp. 13–15, 27–30.

being significantly so. In particular, he stresses the inadequate achievement of government in America in long-range economic planning, in redistributional reforms, and in the provision of public services and advanced social welfare schemes. And the sources of this governmental inadequacy he traces back to certain basic American socio-political dispositions and also to a relative lack of "democratic balance" in the institutional infrastructure of the American policy. On the one hand, Myrdal claims, there is among the powerful business community and within government itself a reluctance to take the long view and to envisage more central direction and control of the economy; also "a serious and irrational bias against public investment and consumption." On the other hand, among the lower strata of American society there is an unusual degree of political apathy and passivity which is most clearly seen in the general failure of the poorer sections of the population to organize themselves effectively and to press for the fundamental social reforms that would be in their interest. In this way an imbalance in organized power is brought about within the "plural society" which makes the need for initiative on the part of government all the more pressing—at the same time as it seems to paralyse this.[22]

If, then, Myrdal's analysis has any general validity—and it has yet, I think, to be seriously disputed—it follows that we should look somewhat doubtfully on arguments about a new equality which "has nothing to do with ideology" but which is the direct outcome of technological and economic advance. Such new equality there may be for some. But for those at the base of stratification hierarchies at least—how "equal" they are likely to become seems to have a good deal to do with ideology, or at any rate with purposive social action, or lack of this, stemming from specific social values

[22] *Ibid.*, chs. 4, 6 and 7. A basically similar view is presented in Michael Harrington, *The Other America*, 1962. On the organizational, and thus political, weakness of the poor, see pp. 13–17; on the past failure and present responsibility of the Federal Government, pp. 163–170. Cf. also Stephen W. Rousseas and James Farganis, "American Politics and the End of Ideology", *Brit. Journ. Soc.*, Vol. XIV, No. 4, 1963.

and political creeds as well as from interests.[23] And differences between some industrial societies in these respects may well be giving rise to divergent, rather than convergent, patterns of change in their stratification systems.

On the second set of arguments—those concerning growing consistency between different stratification orders—I shall have relatively little to say for the good reason that there is little empirical data which directly bears on the crucial issue here; that is, the issue of whether there really is a *continuing* increase in the degree of integration of the stratification systems of *advanced* societies. About the long-term historical trend, one would not wish to argue; but again it is a question of whether such a trend is a reliable guide to the present and the future.

My main comment is that such evidence as does appear relevant to this issue indicates that in some industrial societies, at least, on-going economic progress is resulting in stratification systems becoming, if anything, somewhat *less* well integrated in certain respects. This evidence refers to what has become known as the "new working class." It suggests that the appreciable gains in income and in general living standards recently achieved by certain sections of the manual labour force have not for the most part been accompanied by changes in their life-styles of such a kind that their *status* position has been enhanced commensurately with their *economic* position. In other words, there is evidence of cultural and, in particular, of "social" barriers still widely existing between "working class" and "middle class" even in cases where immediate material differences have now disappeared.[24] Thus it seems that,

[23] Cf. Harrington's emphasis on the fact that "If there is to be a way out (of poverty) it will come from human action, from political change, not from automatic processes" (p. 162). . . .

[24] See, e.g., for Great Britain, John H. Goldthorpe and David Lockwood, "Affluence and the British Class Structure," *Soc. Rev.*, Vol. II, No. 2, 1963; for the USA, Bennet Berger, *Working Class Suburb: a Study of Auto Workers in Suburbia*, 1960; for France, A. Andrieux and J. Lignon, *L'Ouvrier D'Aujourd'hui*, 1960. In all these contributions a common emphasis is that on the growing *disparity* between the situation of the manual worker as *producer* and *consumer*.

contrary to the expectations of Kerr and his associates, "middle incomes" have not resulted, as yet at least, in the generalization of "middle class" ways of life or of "middle class" status.

Moreover, there are grounds for believing that notable discrepancies in stratification will persist in industrial societies. As Kerr himself recognizes, there will still exist in the foreseeable future in such societies a division between "managers" and "managed"—between those who are in some way associated with the exercise of authority in productive and administrative organizations and those who are not. And this division, one would suggest, will remain associated with differences in prestige as well as in power, while at the same time managers and managed overlap to some extent in terms of living standards. One would agree that in an economically advanced society a broad stratum of workers, performing skilled or, one would add, particularly arduous or irksome jobs, are likely to earn middle-range incomes. But there are no grounds for automatically assuming that they will thereby become socially accepted and assimilated into even the lower levels of what Renner has usefully termed the "service class".[25] After all, it must be recognized that groups which have some serious basis for claiming superior status generally take advantage of this. And further, it should be borne in mind that, increasingly, the members of this "service class" will be selected through their educational attainments rather than being recruited from the rank and file. Thus, if anything, they are likely to become more set apart from the latter in terms of culture and life-styles than they are at present.

In sum, one might suggest that the "increasing consistency" argument is flawed because it fails to take into account first, that occupational rôles with similar economic rewards may in some instances be quite differently related to the exercise of authority; and secondly, that relatively high income may serve as recompense for work of otherwise high "disutility" to the opera-

tive as well as for work involving expertise and responsibility.

Lastly, then, we come to the matter of social mobility. In this case, the first question which arises is that of whether it is in fact valid to regard industrial societies as having regularly higher rates of mobility than pre-industrial societies. Several writers, one should note, have recently argued that this view should not be too readily taken and have produced evidence to suggest that certain pre-industrial societies were far less rigidly stratified than seems generally to have been supposed.[26] Nevertheless, I would not wish to argue here against the more orthodox view, except to make the point that an increased rate of *inter*generational mobility in advanced societies is likely to be associated with some limitation of *intra*generational or "career" mobility. To the extent that education becomes a key determinant of occupational achievement, the chances of "getting ahead" for those who start in a lowly position are inevitably diminished. This fact is most clearly demonstrated in recent studies of the recruitment of industrial managers. These show that as the educational standards of managers have risen, the likelihood of shop floor workers being promoted above supervisory level has been reduced.[27] Furthermore, in an advanced society, increasingly dominated by large scale organizations, the possibilities for the "little man" of starting up a successful business of his own also tend to be more limited than they were at an earlier phase in the industrialization process. Thus, for that large proportion of the population at least, with rank-and-file jobs and "ordinary" educational qualifications, industrial society appears to be growing significantly *less* "open" than it once was.

However, other, and perhaps more basic,

---

[25] Karl Renner, *Wandlungen der modernen Gesellschaft; zwei Abhandlungen über die Probleme der Nachkriegzeit,* 1953.

[26] See, e.g., for China, Robert M. Marsh, *The Mandarins: the Circulation of Elites in China, 1600–1900,* 1961, and "Values, Demand and Social Mobility," *Am. Soc. Rev.,* Vol. 28, 1963, also, Ping-ti Ho, *The Ladder of Success in Imperial China: Aspects of Social Mobility, 1368–1911,* 1963.

[27] For Great Britain, see Acton Society Trust, *Management Succession,* 1965, and R. V. Clements, *Managers: a study of their careers in industry,* 1958. For the USA, see W. Lloyd Warner and James C. Abegglen, *Occupational Mobility in American Business and Industry,* 1955.

issues arise from the arguments concerning mobility which I earlier outlined; in particular issues relating to the determinants of mobility patterns and rates. What are the grounds, one might ask, for believing that in advanced societies the crucial factor here is the occupational distribution, and thus that from one such society to another social mobility will tend to be much the same? Support for this view can be found in the well-known Lipset and Zetterberg study which led, in fact, to the conclusion that Western industrial societies have broadly similar rates of intergenerational mobility, and which produced no evidence to suggest that factors other than the "standardizing" one of the occupational structure were of major significance.[28] Their data, the authors claim, give no backing for the idea that differences in social ideologies, religious beliefs or other aspects of national cultures exercise a decisive influence on mobility. But it has to be noted that, as Lipset and Zetterberg themselves make quite clear, their findings in this respect refer only to "mass" mobility; that is, simply to movements across the manual–nonmanual line. And indeed they point out that the investigation of some aspects of "élite" mobility —for example, the recruitment of higher civil servants—has indicated some important national variations.[29]

Moreover, we have more recently the outstanding study of comparative social mobility made by Professor S. M. Miller.[30] This covers a still greater amount of data than Lipset and Zetterberg's work and demonstrates fairly conclusively that when *range* as well as frequency of mobility is taken into consideration, industrial societies do reveal quite sizeable differences in their mobility patterns. Such differences tend to be most evident in the case of long-range mobility. This is generally low—another reason for querying just how "open" and "meritocratic" industrial societies have so

far become—but certain countries, the USA and USSR, for example, appear to have attained quite significantly higher rates of "élite" mobility than do others, such as many in western Europe. Further, though, Miller shows that countries with low long-range mobility may still have relatively high short-range mobility—as, for instance, does Great Britain: there is no correlation between rates of mobility of differing distance. Thus, industrial societies have quite various "mobility profiles"; the overall similarity indicated by the study of "mass" mobility turns out to be somewhat spurious.

On this basis, then, Miller is able to argue very strongly that patterns of social mobility in advanced societies cannot be understood *simply* in terms of occupational structure[31] —or, one would add, in terms of any "inherent" features of industrialism. Their diversity precludes this. It appears necessary rather, to consider also the effects on mobility of other, and more variable, aspects of social structure—educational institutions, for example, and their articulation with the stratification hierarchy itself—and further, possibly, *pace* Lipset and Zetterberg, the part played by cultural values.[32] As Miller points out, what is perhaps most surprising about his data is the *lack* of convergence in mobility patterns that is indicated between societies at broadly comparable levels of economic development. The "logic" of industrialism, it appears, is often confused by "extraneous" factors.

These, then, are some of the objections that may be made on empirical grounds to the hypotheses concerning changes in stratification systems which I previously outlined. . . . In conclusion of this paper, I would like to make a more basic objection which relates to the theoretical position underlying these arguments. Specifically, I would like to question the idea that the stratification systems of all industrial societies are *ipso facto* of the same generic type, and thus that they may in principle be

---

[28] See S. M. Lipset and Hans L. Zetterberg, "A Theory of Social Mobility," *Transactions of the Third World Congress of Sociology,* 1956, Vol. III, pp. 155–177, and Ch. II, "Social Mobility in Industrial Society" in S. M. Lipset and R. Bendix, *Social Mobility in Industrial Society,* 1959.

[29] *Ibid.,* pp. 38–42.

[30] S. M. Miller, "Comparative Social Mobility," *Current Sociology,* Vol. IX, No. 1, 1960.

[31] *Ibid.,* pp. 22–23, 57–58.

[32] As an example of the kind of study which would seem particularly relevant and valuable, see Ralph H. Turner, "Modes of Social Ascent through Education: Sponsored and Contest Mobility" . . . [reprinted in this book].

expected to follow convergent or parallel lines of development. Against this view, I would like to suggest that social stratification in the advanced societies of the Communist world—or at any rate in the USSR and its closer satellites—is *not* of the same generic type as in the West and that, because of this, the hypotheses earlier discussed cannot in this case really apply.

Soviet society is, of course, stratified; and, furthermore, it is true that in spite of the absence of private property in production, it appears to be stratified on an often similar pattern to the capitalist or post-capitalist societies of the West. For example, to a large degree there is apparent similarity in the connections between occupational rôle, economic rewards and social prestige, in the part played by education in determining occupational level, in the operation of an informal status system, and so on. But, I would argue, this similarity is only of a phenotypical kind: genotypically, stratification in Soviet society is significantly different from stratification in the West.

Primarily, it may be said, this difference derives from the simple fact that in Soviet society 'the economy operates within a "monistic", or totalitarian, political order and is, in principle at least, totally planned, whereas in advanced Western societies political power is significantly less concentrated and the economy is planned in a far less centralized and detailed way. From this it results that in the West economic, and specifically market, forces act as the crucial stratifying agency within society. They are, one could say, the major source of social inequality. And consequently, the *class* situation of individuals and groups, understood in terms of their economic power and resources, tends to be the most important single determinant of their general life-chances. This is why we can usefully speak of Western industrial society as being "class" stratified. However, in the case of Soviet society, market forces cannot be held to play a comparable rôle in the stratification process. These forces operate, of course, and differences in economic power and resources between individuals and groups have, as in the West, far-reaching social and human consequences. But, one would argue,

to a significantly greater extent than in the West, stratification in Soviet society is subjected to *political* regulation; market forces are not permitted to have the primacy or the degree of autonomy in this respect that they have even in a "managed" capitalist society. Undoubtedly, the functional requirements of the economy exert pressures upon the system of stratification, and these pressures may in some cases prove to be imperative. But the nature of the political order means that far more than with Western democracy, the pattern of social inequality can be shaped through the purposive action of the ruling party, and still more so, of course, the "life-fates" of particular persons.[33]

For example, during the years of Stalin's rule, economic inequality in the USSR generally increased.[34] . . . By the end of the war decade, these developments had led to a degree of inequality in Soviet society which, in the view of many commentators, was greater than that which was generally to be found in the industrial societies of the West.[35] However, in more recent years it has become clear that contrary to most expectations, this inegalitarian trend in the USSR has been checked and, moreover, that in certain respects at least it has even been reversed. Minimum wages in industry have been increased several times since the late 1950s and the incomes of the *kolkhozy* have for the most part risen quite considerably. This latter development has had the effect of closing somewhat the income gap between industrial and agricultural workers and has also been associated with a reduction in differentials in the earnings of the *kolkhoz* peasants themselves. At the same time, there is evidence of limitations being placed on the more excessive salaries of higher officials and of more stringent measures being taken against the abuse of

[33] Also relevant here, of course, is a further distinctive feature of a totalitarian political system —the absence of the "rule of law".

[34] Probably the best analysis in this respect is that provided by Barrington Moore, Jr., *Soviet Politics—the Dilemma of Power*, 1950.

[35] See, e.g., Alex Inkeles, "Social Stratification and Mobility in the Soviet Union: 1940–1950," *Am. Soc. Rev.*, Vol. 15, 1950. This paper contains an excellent factual account of the ways through which both economic and status inequality were increased during the Stalin era.

privileges. Finally, tax changes in the past few years have tended to favour the poorer against the richer groups, and various kinds of welfare provision have been substantially improved. In these ways, then, economic differences between the manual and non-manual categories overall have almost certainly been reduced to some extent, as well as differences within these categories.[36]

Now these changes can, of course, be rightly regarded as being in some degree economically conditioned. Clearly, for instance, the increased differentiation in wages and salaries in the Stalin era must in part be understood in terms of the exigencies and consequences of rapid industrialization. But, I would argue, there can be little question that at the same time these changes were the outcome of political decisions—of choices made between realistic alternatives—and, furthermore, that frequently they were brought about with political as well as with specifically economic ends in view. Stalin, it is true, wanted rapid industrialization: but he had the further political objective that this process should be carried through under his own absolute control. Thus, this entailed not only depriving a large section of the population of material returns from their labour in order to achieve maximum expansion of industrial capacity, but also the building-up of a group of exceptionally favoured administrators and managers who would be highly motivated to retain their enviable positions through loyalty to Stalin and through high level performance. To this latter end, in fact, appropriate status as well as economic inequalities were also developed. For example, during and after the war years, formal titles, uniforms and insignia of rank were introduced into various branches of industry and the governmental bureaucracy. Moreover, the wide social distance which was in this way created between the top and bottom of the stratification hierarchy had the manifest function of insulating the "élite" from the masses and from their

needs and wishes. And thus, as Professor Feldmesser has pointed out, those in high positions were helped to learn "that success was to be had by winning the favour not of those below them but of those above them, which was exactly what Stalin wanted them to learn."[37]

Similarly, the more recent moves towards reducing inequalities have again fairly evident political aims, even though, in some cases, they may also have been economically required.[38] On the one hand, it seems clear that the present Soviet leadership is working toward a future Communist society which will be characterized by a high level of social welfare, and indeed eventually by private affluence, while still remaining under the undisputed dominance of the Party. In other words, the creation of the "good life" for all appears destined to become one of the régime's most important sources of legitimacy. In fact, as Professor Shapiro has noted, the 1961 Programme of the CPSU makes this more or less explicit. The Programme, he writes,

enunciates squarely the concrete fact that party rule has come to stay. It calls upon the Soviet citizen to recognize and accept this fact, and to abandon the illusion that in this respect, things are going to change. In return, it promises him great material benefits and prosperity.[39]

On the other hand, the security of the régime also requires that the bureaucratic and managerial "élite" does not become so well established as to gain some measure

---

[36] For a general discussion of these changes, see Robert A. Feldmesser, "Towards the Classless Society?". Also Alec Nove, "Is the Soviet Union a Welfare State?", both in Alex Inkeles and Kent Geiger (eds.), *Soviet Society*, 1961.

[37] *Ibid.,* p. 579. This political subordination of members of the "élite", concomitant with their economic and status elevation, is the reason for using inverted commas [quotes]. As Feldmesser notes, the "élite" created by Stalin is surely distinctive by virtue of its general lack of autonomy.

[38] As, e.g., in the case of the increase in peasant incomes which was essential if genuine incentives to improve production were to be offered in agriculture. Cf. Seweryn Bialer, "But Some Are More Equal than Others," *Problems of Communism,* Vol. IX, No. 2, 1960.

[39] Leonard Shapiro, "From Utopia towards Realism" in Shapiro (ed.), *The USSR and the Future: an Analysis of the New Program of the CPSU,* 1963. See also in this volume Erik Boettcher, "Soviet Social Policy in Theory and Practice". The text of the Programme itself is printed as an Appendix; note, in particular, Part Two, Sections II, III, V and VII.

of independence from the Party chiefs. Thus, Krushchev has been concerned to show the members of this group that they remain the creatures of the Party and that their privileges are not permanent but still rest upon their obedience and service to the Party. Those whom Djilas has referred to as the "new class" in Communist society[40] cannot in fact be allowed by the Party leadership to become a class—in the sense of a collectivity which is capable of maintaining its position in society (and that of its children) through its own social power, and which possesses some degree of group consciousness and cohesion. For the emergence of such a class would constitute a serious threat to the Party's totalitarian rule, different only in degree from the threat that would be posed by the emergence of an independent trade union, professional body or political organization. It is awareness of this danger, one would suggest, which chiefly lies behind the recent attacks —verbal as well as material—which have been made upon higher officialdom and the top industrial personnel. For apart from the curtailment of economic rewards in some cases, it is interesting to note that the quasi-military status distinctions of the war decade have now been largely abolished and that the Party has actually encouraged rank-and-file employees in industry and agriculture to expose inadequacy and inefficiency on the part of their superiors.[41] Furthermore, there has been some weeding out of superfluous posts, and demotions appear to have become much more common.[42] Finally, though, it is probably Krushchev's educational reforms which have been of greatest significance. These were carried through at a time when pressure on the institutions of secondary and higher education was reaching a peak; yet they were designed to make access to these institutions less dependent than previously upon economic resources and the new rules for competitive entry which were introduced seem, if anything, to shift the balance of "social" advantage away from the children of the "élite" and towards candidates from

worker or peasant families. As Feldmesser notes, if a "new class"—a "state bourgeoisie"—were in fact in existence in the USSR, then exactly the reverse of this might have been expected; that is, a move to make access to these scarce facilities *more*, rather than less, dependent upon the ability to pay.[43]

It is then not too much to say that in Soviet society hierarchical differentiation is an instrument of the régime. To a significant degree stratification is *organized* in order to suit the political needs of the régime; and, as these needs change, so too may the particular structure of inequality. In other words, the Soviet system of stratification is characterized by an important element of "deliberateness", and it is this which basically distinguishes it from the Western system, in spite of the many apparent similarities. In the industrial societies of the West, one could say, the action of the state sets limits to the extent of social inequalities which derive basically from the operation of a market economy: in Soviet society the pattern of inequality also results in part from "market" forces, but in this case these are subordinated to political control up to the limits set by the requirements of the industrial system.[44] For this reason, one may conclude, Soviet society is not, in the same way as Western society, *class* stratified. As Raymond Aron has observed, class stratification and a monistic political system are to be regarded as incompatibles.[45]

If, then, the foregoing analysis is accepted, it follows that the arguments I earlier outlined on the development of stratification systems can have no general validity. Their underlying rationale, in terms of the exigencies of an advanced industrial technology and economy, is destroyed. The experience of Soviet society can be taken as

[40] Milovan Djilas, *The New Class,* New York: Frederick A. Praeger, 1957.
[41] Feldmesser, *op. cit.,* pp. 573–575.
[42] Bialer, *op. cit.,* pp. 576–578.

[43] Feldmesser, *op. cit.,* pp. 576–578.
[44] This assessment is consistent with the more general interpretations of the Soviet social system advanced by writers such as Brzezinski and Daniel Bell, in some opposition to the interpretation of Inkeles and his associates. . . . Zbigniew K. Brzezinski, *Ideology and Power in Soviet Politics,* 1962, p. 31. Daniel Bell, "Ten Theories in Search of Reality: the Prediction of Soviet Behaviour" in *The End of Ideology,* New York: Collier Books, 1961, pp. 340–341.
[45] See his "Social Structure and the Ruling Class," *Brit. Journ. Soc.,* Vol. I, 1950.

indicating that the structural and functional imperatives of an industrial order are not so stringent as to prevent quite wide variations in patterns of social stratification, nor to prohibit the systematic manipulation of social inequalities by a régime commanding modern administrative resources and under no contraints from an organized opposition or the rule of law.

The crucial point, in fact, at which the rationale breaks down is in the supposition that industrialism and totalitarianism cannot "in the long run" co-exist; that is, in the idea that with industrial advance a progressive diffusion of political power must of necessity occur. Were this idea valid, then it would become difficult to maintain the claim that differences between the stratification systems of the Western and Communist worlds are of a generic kind. However, it may be said that no serious grounds exist for believing that within Soviet society any such diffusion of power is taking place, or, at least, not so far as the key decision-making processes are concerned.[46] The régime may be compelled to give more consideration to the effect of its decisions on popular morale and to rely increasingly on the expertise of scientists, technicians and professionals of various kinds; it may also find it desirable to decentralize administration and to encourage a high degree of participation in the conduct of public affairs at a local level. But the important point is that all these things can be done, and in recent years *have* been done, without the Party leadership in any way yielding up its position of ultimate authority and control. Indeed, it is far more arguable that since the end of the period of "collective" rule, the power of the Party leadership has become still more absolute and unrivalled. This situation, one would suggest, has been brought about as a result of Krushchev's success in reducing the power and independence, relative to the Party machine, of the other major bureaucratic structures within Soviet society—those of

the political police, of the military and of government and industry. In some cases, it might be noted, the changes involved here can be seen as aspects of "destalinization"—for example, the mitigation of the terror or the dissolution of a large part of the central state apparatus. Yet at the same time these changes have had the effect of accentuating still further the totalitarian nature of Party rule. As Bialer points out:

The party bureaucracy is at present the only remaining apparatus which is centralized in its organization, which operates at all levels of the society, and which "specializes" in every sphere of societal activity. In its functions of communicating, controlling and to an ever greater degree directly organizing the tasks set forth by the leadership, it influences the operation of the other bureaucratic apparatuses, but is not in turn subject to any outside interference. It is subordinate only to the top leadership and to its own hierarchical line of authority.[47]

. . . What one would wish to stress, then, is that if such views as these are sound (as I believe they are), it becomes difficult to see how one can formulate *any* general and comprehensive propositions concerning stratification change as part of a "logic" of industrial development. For the essential assumption involved in such propositions —that of some necessary "primacy" of the economic system over the political—is no longer a reliable one. It has to be recognized, rather, that stratification systems are not to be understood as mere "reflections" of a certain level of technology and industrial organization but are shaped by a range of other factors, important among which may be that of purposive political action; and further, that the importance of this latter factor in societies in which political power is highly concentrated is such as to create a distinctive type of stratification which is

---

[46] For recent discussion of the issue of the compatibility of industrialism and totalitarianism from both empirical and theoretical points of view, see Brzezinski, *op. cit.*, Chs. I and III, and R. Aron (ed.), *World Technology and Human Destiny*, 1963.

[47] Bialer, *op. cit.*, pp. 48–49. In addition to Bialer's paper, see also on the strengthening of Party rule under Krushchev, Brzezinski, *op. cit.*, Ch. III, and Edward Crankshaw, *Krushchev's Russia*, 1957, pp. 69, 76–79. Crankshaw shows how this process is in no way inconsistent with the widening of opportunities for popular participation in administrative work at a local level via the "public organizations". See pp. 94–98.

difficult even to discuss in terms of concepts developed in a Western, capitalist context.[48]

STRATA AND STRATA INTEREST IN SOCIALIST SOCIETY

TOWARD A NEW THEORETICAL APPROACH

Wlodzimierz Wesolowski

INTRODUCTION

The question of the class structure of socialist society is the subject of lively discussion among Polish sociologists and economists. Apart from the findings of empirical research on particular classes and

Paper delivered at Sixth World Congress of Sociology, Evian, France, September 1966. Printed by permission of the author.

[48] As Feldmesser has indicated, the argument that Soviet society is not "class" stratified in the manner of Western industrial societies can also be supported from the "subjective" point of view. See his paper, "Social Classes and the Political Structure" in Black (ed.), *op. cit.*, pp. 235–252. The available evidence suggests that Soviet citizens exhibit a relatively low level of class consciousness in the sense that their class situation is not of fundamental importance in patterning their dominant modes of thought and action. Members of different social strata in Soviet society seem more alike in their social ideologies and attitudes than their counterparts in the West, while the feature of the social structure which is most strongly reflected in their social consciousness at all levels is that of the division between "Party people" and "non-Party people". On this latter point see Inkeles and Bauer, *op. cit.*, Ch. XIII.

[1] Cf. Bronislaw Mino, *Klasy i warstwy w spole-czeństwie socjalistycznym,* "Classes and Strata in Socialist Society," *Polityka,* Nos. 39, 42, 46, 1961; J. Wiatr, *Uwarstwienie spoleczne a tendencje egalitarne,* "Social Stratification and Egalitarian Tendencies," *Kultura i Spoleczeństwo,* No. 2, 1962; B. Gałęski, *Niektóre problemy struktury spolecznej w świetle badań wiejskich,* "Some Problems of Social Structure in the Light of Investigations of the Rural Communities," *Studia Socjologiczne,* No. 1, 1963; Bronislaw Mino, *O rozwarstwieniu spoleczeństwa socjalistycznego,* "Social Stratification in Socialist Society," *Kultura i Spoleczeństwo,*

strata conceived in the traditional fashion as the working class, the stratum of intelligentsia, and the class of small peasants, several articles recently appeared with new theoretical propositions regarding the class structure of socialist society.[1] In their interest in these problems Polish scientists are by no means alone. A similar trend can be noted in other socialist countries.[2]

The present paper is intended as a contribution to the current discussion. This discussion is steadily widening in scope and hence it seems worthwhile to present some of its problems to the wider circles of experts working in the field of social stratification. The ideas outlined below constitute a preliminary inquiry rather than a definite solution.

In the current discussion in Poland the economist Bronislaw Minc has advanced the most original and at the same time controversial conception. Lack of space prevents a full exposition of that conception. It is nevertheless necessary to mention it at least briefly since I advance a clearly varying proposition. Both our conceptions are based on general Marxist sociological principles. But they propose different concrete theoretical solutions.

Minc proposes[3] to distinguish in socialist society, where socialist construction has been completed, where there are no longer any private factories, nor the private ownership of the means of production, two social classes: a class of workers of the State sector and a class of workers of the cooperative sector. His point of departure is the assumption that a socialist society retains the "relation to the means of production" as

No. 3, 1963; W. Wesolowski, *Proces zanikania roźnic klasowych,* "Process of Disappearing of Class Differences," *Studia Socjologiczne,* No. 2, 1964; S. Widerszpil, *Interpretacja przemian struktury spolecznej w Polsce Ludowej,* "An Interpretation of Changes of Social Structure in People's Poland," *Nowe Drogi,* No. 1, 1963.

[2] Cf. P. N. Fiedosijew, ed., *Ot socjalizma k komunizmu,* "From Socialism to Communism," Moscow 1962; *Socjologija w SSSR,* "Sociology in the Soviet Union," Vol. I, Moscow 1965; *Socjologija* Nos. 1–2, 1966, Beograd, special issue of the Yugoslav sociological journal devoted to the problems of "Socialism and the Changes in Class Structure."

[3] Cf. Minc, *Klasy i warstwy w spoleczeństwie socjalistycznym, op. cit.*

the criterion of class differentiation, since two different economic sectors continue to exist. One is the State sector in which the means of production are the general property of the nation; the second is the cooperative sector in which the means of production are owned by a smaller group, members of a given cooperative.

According to Mino, two manual workers, turners, for example, will be considered to belong to two different classes only on the basis that one works for the government and the other in a cooperative enterprise. Analogically, the class affiliation of two engineers or two directors would be determined by the fact that they are employed in two different economic sectors. . . .

Sociologists cannot accept these propositions since they are too formalistic. The crucial argument against them is that under the socialist economic system the social consequences of being employed in the State or in the cooperative sector are not important enough to be regarded as a basis for social differentiation. Sectors do not determine in any significant extent the distribution of crucial stratificational variables or, in other words, the distribution of the important social status characteristics such as income, life chances, power, prestige, and so on.

Through the theory of the two classes, based on the two sectors of economy, Mino wants to stress the lasting role of the "relation to the means of production" in the socialist society and in this way to retain the classical Marxist criterion of classes as valid for that type of society. This author believes, on the contrary, that the new social situation resulting from the "socialized" economic system demands a new theoretical approach. It is unwarranted to stress so heavily the classical criterion, while its role is gradually diminishing and some other factors enter in its place.

THE MARXIAN CLASS THEORY AND SOCIALIST SOCIETY

The Marxian theory of class structure stipulates first of all the existence of two mutually antagonistic groups involved in the process of production. These are so-called basic classes. They differ from each other by their relations to the means of production. One of these classes owns them; the other is deprived of them although it operates them. This relation determines the character of the first as an exploiting, and of the second as an exploited class.

The objective conflict of interests is rooted in the antagonistic positions of the two classes, and a different consciousness arises on the foundation of these antithetic social positions. The emergence of the class struggle demonstrates the existence of such classes.

This brief summary leads to what has become a commonplace, that proletarian revolution abolishes the thus conceived class structure. Socialization of the capitalist owned means of production means the liquidation of one of the elements of the antagonistic capital-labor relations. And with this disappears the fundamental class relation typical for capitalist society. Without their opposite pole the workers cease being a class in the old sense of the term. For there has ceased to exist the basic characteristic constituting them as a class in capitalist society: exploitation by the owners of the means of production. In the Marxist sense, they are no longer an *actual class,* but rather a *former class.*

The above statement is deliberately simplified to underscore the fundamental difference. When the workers free themselves from their "Siamese Twin" they lose the principal characteristic of their social position but they are not thereby automatically deprived of other characteristics. These other traits make it advisable to continue to call them the workers, although not the class in Marx's sense of that term. Perhaps it would be convenient to call them stratum of workers. The workers continue to be linked with a certain type of production, industrial production, and a specific type of labor, manual labor. They are characterized by certain social and cultural traits. In other words, the workers occupy a given place in the social division of labor; they have a definite type of income, education, way of life, political attitude, and a number of other important social characteristics or attributes.

Involved here is one of the important, though not always clearly perceived, characteristic traits of the Marxian theory of classes. In that theory one characteristic and one social relation connected with it—the monopoly of the means of production on one side and deprivation of them on the other—are regarded as the bases of the complex structure of class characteristics.

The class characteristics create a sort of specific hierarchy and causal chain of interrelations. There is a constellation of characteristics on the side of the capitalists and a different one on the workers' side. Ownership of the means of production puts the capitalist in control of the production process and gives a privileged position in the division of income derived from production. The worker carries out orders in the course of the production process and suffers discrimination in the division of income derived from production. From the combination of these elements flow further characteristics of the social position of capitalists and workers. These may be defined as unequal opportunities to attain and benefit from various values, such as education, health, enjoyment of cultural assets. On the basis of all these characteristics of the social position there take shape different ways of life, a different consciousness and dissimilar political attitudes.

It is true that some of these attributes were heavily stressed by Marx, while others were merely mentioned. In writings of many later Marxists some of these attributes were overlooked. But they were present in Marx's deliberations.

It should be noted in addition that the causal relations are not like a uniform linear chain. For instance, the relation to the means of production shapes class consciousness by determining the income level and status in the social organization of the labor process. The magnitude of income reacts on class consciousness by the opportunities it offers and by social prestige. There is furthermore an interaction between some characteristics.[4]

... The following facts are important for our treatment of the question of transformation in the class structure of socialist society: (1) the abolition of the capitalist production relations eliminates the fundamental connections and basic characteristics distinguishing the workers in capitalist society, setting in motion the means of production belonging to another class, but (2) all the other characteristics of their social position do not automatically disappear as a result. While free or cut out from the previously determining characteristic, namely relation to the means of production, these other attributes of workers are retained. They continue to fulfill their differentiating role, no longer in relation to the capitalists, but to other groups or strata.[5]

Capitalist society is composed not only of basic classes: capitalists and workers but also of some other classes and strata. These strata are "inherited" by socialist society. Usually they are conceived by Marxists as the *stratum of intelligentsia*, understood as the broad group of white-collar workers, and the small commodity agricultural producers, farmers.

Those other strata also have definite characteristics of social position, similar to those included in our schemes. The characteristics of intelligentsia are peculiar in that they do not comprise any "relation to

---

[4] The above enumeration of class characteristics of social position reveals that the difference between Marxists and non-Marxist students of social stratification is not so much in their choice of the set of characteristics as in their perspectives in approaching that set of characteristics. The Marxist approach could be called deterministic, the non-Marxist approach, operational. Marxists look at the whole structure of status characteristics

from the bottom up. Most of the non-Marxists divide all inhabitants of a given community into *prestige classes,* being less interested in the underlying structure of other characteristics. Of course, there are other differences between the two approaches, but it is worthwhile to see also similarities. This point was further elaborated in the present author's introduction to the Polish edition of C. W. Mills' *White Collar, cf. Białe kołnierzyki: Amerykańskie klasy średnie,* Warsaw, 1965.

[5] The current tendency in capitalist countries is for the government to exert its influence on some of the status characteristics of the working class by introducing social legislation, giving grants, fixing minimum wages, and so on. As a result, the direct dependence of some of the status characteristics on the relation of the given social group to the means of production is weakened, though the two basic classes, capitalists and workers, continue to differ sharply in their status characteristics which in the last analysis depend on the relation to the means of production.

the means of production" which would put this stratum in antagonism to any other class. Marxists therefore insist on calling the intelligentsia a stratum, rather than a class. What distinguishes the white-collar workers as a stratum are: type of occupation (nonmanual labor), income (usually defined as medium, that is somewhere between the income of capitalists and that of the laborers), opportunities, way of life, prestige, and so on.

The peculiar characteristics of the farmers as small-scale agricultural producers consist in the specific nature of their means of production and their relations to those means of production. In capitalist society, the farmers, similar to the white-collar workers, have no direct polar relationship to any other class, unlike the laborers and capitalists. The farmers are owners of their means of production but they employ their own labor to use them. As in the case of the laborers or capitalists, the above characteristic of the farmers determines a number of other characteristics of their social position. . . .

Thus the small-commodity agricultural producer—like the worker and the representative of the intelligentsia—is characterized by a certain syndrome of traits. With respect to individual characteristics, his position may be compared to that of the worker or white-collar in the proportion of manual and mental labor, size of income, and so on.

The transformation of the class of small-commodity producers under socialism takes the direction of turning its members into employees of the socialized sector. The aim of the socioeconomic policy of the State is to make their relation to the means of production conform to that of laborers and white-collar workers. This means a desire to eliminate their relation to the means of production as a characteristic distinguishing this group from others. This is accompanied by the desire to deprive this characteristic of its role of decisive determinant of the social position and psychological attributes specific to that group.

This process may be of shorter or longer duration and it may also take different forms. We shall leave that question aside. It may be said, however, that the trans-

formations in the class structure inherited from capitalism evolve towards: (a) equalization of the relation to the means of production of the former small-commodity producers, the workers and intelligentsia, (b) complete deprivation of the relation to the means of production of its decisive role in determining other status characteristics, income, prestige, opportunity, and so on. *From here on the relation to the means of production is uniform for all citizens. And if there appear differences in income, character of labor, prestige, opportunity, political attitude, it is not this relation which determines them.*

PROCESS OF DISINTEGRATION OF CLASS CHARACTERISTICS

The following conclusion is suggested by the above: the evolution of the class structure in socialist society consists of the gradual evening out of the relation of different groups of the population to the means of production. Parallel with that occurs a gradual diminution of the role of that relation as a determinant of other status characteristics and of the content of social consciousness.

Hence the role of differentiating characteristics of society is assumed to an ever-growing degree by such status characteristics as: the nature of labor, income, education, prestige, and so forth.[6] These characteristics, removed from the determining influence of the relation to the means of production, retain an autonomous existence under socialism. Thus, although classes, in Marx's sense of that term, disappear in a developed socialist society, there remain social differentiations which may be called social stratification.

This stratification may be conceived in a dual manner. The first conception refers to income, occupational or prestige stratifications along its various dimensions. This is a fairly simple theoretical concept which

[6] Until now we used the terms *class characteristics* or *class attributes*. From here on we will use rather the term *status characteristics* or *status attributes* since the *relation to the means of production* ceases to play any important role in our deliberations. The characteristics of social position from the upper layers of our schemes are usually associated with the term *status* or *social status*.

lends itself easily to research. It would involve the application of a simplified concept of multidimensional stratification to an investigation of socialist society. Each characteristic would then constitute a separate research subject and its intensity would be a criterion for distinguishing the individual stratification levels.

The second concept is more complex, but it therefore enables a better grasp of social processes and structures. It is the multidimensional approach proper.

It should be recalled here that for Marx classes differ in respect to a number of related characteristics. The bourgeoisie enjoys a high income, high education level and high prestige. The workers have low incomes, a low educational level and low prestige. The petty bourgeoisie have a medium income, enjoy medium prestige and their educational level is above that of the workers and below that of the bourgeoisie. This class concept appeared not only in Marx but in a number of non-Marxist theoreticians.

There hence arises the exceptionally important question: To what extent is there a congruence of certain characteristics among the strata of a socialist country? Is there a correspondence, for instance, between income on the one hand and education and prestige on the other? Is it the problem of status crystallization, in Lenski's terms?[7]

The processes of revolutionary transformation effect a certain disintegration or *decomposition* of status characteristics. The given character of labor, size of income, level of education, and degree of prestige tends to disintegrate. There are groups with low education and high incomes, or with high incomes and low prestige, and so on. This is brought about by the changes in the economic system and in ideology. Many evidences of these disintegration processes are to be found in Poland. The theoretical significance of them is overlooked by sociologists and economists.

[7] G. Lenski, "Status Crystallization: A Non-Vertical Dimension of Social Status," *The American Sociological Review*, No. 4, 1954. See also, L. Broom, "Social Differentiation and Stratification," in R. K. Merton, L. Broom, L. S. Cottrell, Jr., eds., *Sociology Today*, New York, 1959.

The processes of disintegration of status characteristics intermingle with the processes of evening out some differences. Some decompositions may be considered as the processes leading to equalization. If for instance an unskilled laborer earns as much as a doctor, this may be considered an equalization of their social position in respect to one area of difference, income, while the difference in another area, education, is retained. The same applies to the equalization of the earnings of a turner and an engineer, for example. But other processes are also taking place when a turner earns more than an engineer, or a miner enjoys a greater prestige than a lawyer; the disintegration of status characteristics exceeds the bounds of the equalization of levels and leads to a deeper or more distant dislocation. Certain groups begin to differ one from another as being in a reverse relation with respect to certain attributes than was the case in the previous socio-economic system.

The disintegration of social-status characteristics may hence assume two forms. One is the equalization of the levels of some characteristics pertaining to some particular former classes or strata. The second is the case of one class leaping ahead of another in relation to some of these characteristics.

By way of example we present below some empirical material on the disintegration of three status characteristics in contemporary Poland. These are the nature of labor, size of income, and degree of prestige.

In interwar Poland virtually every white-collar worker earned more than manual workers. The average wage of a white-collar worker was more than double that of a manual worker. Table 1 presents the comparative income structure of the two groups today.[8]

True, the table shows a higher percentage of manual workers among the lowest paid and a higher percentage of white-collar workers among the highest paid. Nevertheless, two other phenomena indicated in the table are no less important. Thus a high percentage of manual and nonmanual workers earns the same amount, from 1200 to 2000 zlotys a month. This speaks for income

[8] *Poland in Figures 1944–1964*, Warsaw, 1965, p. 104.

TABLE 1 Gross Monthly Earnings of Employees by Income Groups in 1963

Income Group	Manual Workers, Per cent	Nonmanual Workers, Per cent
701–800	10.7	1.3
801–1000	7.2	5.4
1001–1200	8.7	9.1
1201–1500	15.6	17.1
1501–2000	24.7	26.3
2001–2500	15.9	16.3
2501–3000	8.5	10.4
Over 3000	8.7	14.1
	100.0	100.0

equalization. Then there is a large number of workers who earn more than white-collar workers. Of manual workers 33.1 per cent earn more than 2000 zlotys, while 59.2 per cent of nonmanual workers earn less. Here we enter the trail of the disintegration of two characteristics: nature of labor and size of income.

An investigation of occupational prestige in Poland today suggests the disintegration of another pair of characteristics: the nature of labor and social prestige. It indicates that some manual occupations enjoy greater prestige than some nonmanual vocations. Thus skilled workers occupy a higher place in the prestige hierarchy than do clerks and similar categories of white-collar employees. In contrast a sociologist wrote about the corresponding prewar situation: "Perhaps nowhere is the social gulf so glaring as in Poland between nonmanual work— even of the most subordinate kind—and manual work, no matter how constructive." [9]

Also evident is a partial separation of income and prestige. For instance, earnings in the teaching and nursing professions are relatively low today. A school teacher earns from 1500 to 2000 zlotys monthly and a nurse about 1500. But they occupy a higher place on the prestige ladder than does the turner with three to four thousand zlotys

or the private merchant whose income is still higher.

Members of the society are of course aware of this disintegration process. In the above cited investigations the respondents were asked to evaluate the same two occupations according to the criteria of material benefit and prestige. The hierarchies of the two did not correspond. Each occupation occupied one place on the income scale and another on the prestige scale. In contracted form this is shown in Table 2.

It should also be noted here that a certain decomposition of status characteristics of some categories of manual and nonmanual workers is also to be noted in some contemporary capitalist societies. But its range is much smaller than in the socialist societies.

CONTRADICTION OF INTERESTS IN SOCIALIST SOCIETY

The problem of interests, and especially of contradictions of interests plays an important role in Marx's theory of social structure. Discussing the changes in class structure in the socialist society we shall focus on the sphere of social interests. The problems involved here are of extreme complexity. Until now they were rarely and rather incidentally studied by Marxist scholars. . . .

At the very beginning some distinctive features of the capitalist versus the socialist society should be pointed out. This might help to understand some peculiarities of the socialist society.

According to Marx, the capitalist mode of production is characterized by the presence of two social classes of which one appropriates the results of the labor of the other. The capitalist class seizes the *surplus value* produced by the workers. This kind of class relation is connected with the distribution of goods according to "the ownership principle of distribution." When this principle is in operation a person need not be working to take part in the distribution of economic goods, or even to enjoy privileges in this distribution.

The ownership principle of distribution ceases to operate with the abolition of the capitalist ownership of the means of

[9] W. Wesołowski and A. Sarapata, *Hierarchia zawodów i stanowisk*, "Hierarchies of Occupations and Positions," *Studia Socjologiczne*, No. 2, 1961, p. 101.

TABLE 2   Evaluation of Occupational Groups According to Material Rewards
and Social Prestige[10]

Occupational Group	MATERIAL REWARD		PRESTIGE	
	Rank	Score	Score	Rank
Private entrepreneurs	1	1.81	2.81	3
Professionals	2	2.35	1.74	1
Skilled workers	3	2.40	2.33	2
White-collar	4	3.30	3.17	4
Unskilled workers	5	4.12	4.06	5

[10] *Ibid.*, p. 104. In this table all nonmanual workers, called in the present paper intelligentsia and white collar, are divided into two groups: professionals and white collar. The reason for this division is that university professors, physicians, engineers, lawyers are evidently on different layers of the hierarchy than nurses, bookkeepers, office department directors, etc. (See Table 1.)

production. This also means an end to the contradiction of class interests characteristic of capitalist society, that is between the class of capitalists and the working class.

In socialist society, the place of the ownership principle is taken by the principle of distribution according to work. Thus an individual's share in the social product is determined by the quality and quantity of work done by that individual. This principle is not entirely new. In capitalist society it applies to people without capital, that is to say, to people who live from their own labor. With the abolition of the interest rate on capital in socialism the principle of distribution according to work acquires universal validity. In socialist society there is only one criterion of an individual's share in the social product: the amount and quality of the work done by him.[11]

Let us examine some questions connected with the application of the formula "to each according to his work." The problems of social stratification are related to that part of the formula which postulates wages as a function of the quality of labor, that is a function of the level of skill and education

[11] In this paper the question of the unity of interests in a socialist society is omitted. This important problem has been discussed in the present author's *Klasy, Warstwy i Wladza,* "Classes, Strata and Power," Warsaw, 1966, chap. 4. The need for relativism in the treatment of "interests" is discussed in W. Wesolowski, "Ruling Class and Power Elite," *The Polish Sociological Bulletin,* No. 1, 1965.

required for the performance of a given job. There is a marked difference in that level between, for example, the unskilled laborer and the university professor.

It is necessary to clarify what situation we have in mind as creating the "contradiction of interest." It should be recalled that Marx had a very broad concept of the contradiction of interests. He wrote about contradictions of interests between classes as well as between two workers competing for the same job. Following his approach, this author is inclined to look for a contradiction of interests wherever there is a scarcity of generally desired goods, or broader values, and their distribution is by necessity such that any increase of the share of one group is bound to bring cuts in the share of another group.

TWO TYPES OF CONTRADICTION RESULTING FROM THE UNEVEN DISTRIBUTION OF GOODS

If we consider the formula "to each according to his work" and the proposed definition of the contradiction of interests we come to the conclusion that the uneven distribution of goods among the socio-occupational groups, or strata, may take two forms. The first occurs when the uneven distribution of goods is conditioned by the operation of the principle "to each according to his work." The second, when the uneven distribution is due to other factors than the operation of this principle, or to inadequacies in the application of this principle. In either case we face an objective contradiction of interests. And yet there is a significant difference between these two situations.

The principle "to each according to his work" is regarded as the basic principle of distribution in socialist society, but it is not always strictly implemented. In the first place because economists have failed so far to develop precise measures of labor quality that would account for the level of skills involved and some other factors which should be taken into account, for example, the degree of responsibility and risk, existing measures are largely intuitive. As long as precise measures are not available, it is extremely difficult to tell to what extent the wage of, for instance, a loader and a nurse, or a public servant and a factory manager, or a turner and a university professor, and in general, the whole system of wages, conforms to the principle "to each according to his work."

Two problems have to be considered here. One is connected with the extent to which the objective contradiction of interests is compatible with the socialist system. It could be said that a departure from the socialist principle of distribution may result in the "overpayment" of one and "underpayment" of others due to their particular work. As a result, the socialist contradictions of interests could grow into something like antagonistic contradictions, for the overpayment or underpayment may be viewed as a peculiar form of the exploitations of some people by other people (in conditions of the social ownership of means of production).

On the other hand, there is the psychological aspect of interest contradictions in socialism. The employees in Poland, for instance, are sensitive not so much to inequalities in wages as to the relative level of wages paid to people in different occupations. There is a general feeling that a just and equitable pay is the one which conforms to the principle "to each according to his work." People are on their watch lest somebody else gets their "sawbuck." These findings suggest that overpayment-underpayment practices may result not only in a quasiexploitation but also in augmentation of discontent. It seems that the objective contradiction of interests involved in the uneven distribution of goods in conformity with the principle "to each according to his work" itself does not evoke such strong conflict-generating tendencies.

The term *contradiction of interests* is used here to denote an objective state of affairs. The term *conflict of interests* is conceived as reflecting the subjective interpretation of a state of affairs as being the subject's interests. These being two different phenomena, the need was felt for two different terms.

Limitations on the Principle "To Each According to His Work." We shall now turn to some additional factors influencing the system of wages. The principle "to each according to his work" fails to be applied with consistency not only because of the lack of precise measurements. There are some other formulas that are considered part of the socialist credo and hence translated into practical policies.

Thus, we may have overpayments and underpayments compatible with the principles of socialism in spite of the discordance with the cardinal formula of remuneration.

One such departure from the formula is the overpayment of less skilled laborers and underpayment of highly skilled workers. Both minimum wages and limitations on extra-high wages are in all likelihood departures from the principle "to each according to his work." And both these phenomena seem to exist in socialist society.[12]

The second departure consists in giving advantages to workers employed at big investment projects located far from the existing urban and industrial centers. . . . The comparatively higher wages for workers employed in those conditions should be seen as a kind of compensation for the unfavorable working and living conditions he had agreed to accept. Such a wage may be viewed as a normal wage multiplied by a factor that accounts for the additional social and psychological costs incurred by the worker. In contrast with the purely *economic* wage, this kind of payment has

---

[12] Z. Morecka, *Placa w gospodarce socjalistycznej*, "Wage in a Socialist Economy," in O. Lange, ed., *Zagadnienia ekonomii politycznej socjalizmu*, 1960.

been termed *socioeconomic wage*.[13] In addition to labor as such, this wage accounts for a number of deprivations suffered by the worker.

We have defined some of the departures from the principle "to each according to his work" which are due to the operation of other principles which are also consistent with the ideas of socialism. But the mechanics of social life being today a highly complex affair, there is no room in everyday life for the man in the street to follow it in all details. There is a tendency for people to assume standards of judgment based on plain facts and simplified formulas that catch their imagination and suit their sense of morality. And for that reason it seems that any departure from the formula "to each according to his work," whether fully justifiable on social and economic grounds, or caused by unwarranted and inequitable privileges, or else generated by lack of objective measures of quality of labor—all these appear to lead to one and the same result: a deepening of the awareness of conflicts of interests in socialist society. Of course it is a matter for future empirical studies to decide to what extent awareness of conflict is generated by the very objective contradiction of interests involved in the operation of the socialist distribution principle "to each according to his work," on the one hand, and by departures from this principle, on the other. Difficult as they are, such studies would prove very revealing.

Certain other hypotheses deserve to be tested empirically. For instance, there are probably two factors that either generate, or simply aggravate, the awareness of conflict. One could be defined as the burden of the past and the other as anticipation of the future.

The burden of the past is felt among members of those groups that received higher wages in the past, in the capitalist system. These people keep asking, "Why does a laborer get so much, and why does a physician get so little?" Conversely, members of the previously handicapped groups tend to anticipate the future, that is, the principle "to each according to his

[13] Z. Morecka, *Płaca ekonomiczna czy socjo-ekonomiczna,* "Economic or Socio-Economic Wage?" *Życie Gospodarcze,* Nos. 8, 9, 1958.

needs," postulated for communism, by asking, "Why does the charwoman get so little and the manager so much?"

Moreover, there seems to be a natural tendency toward conflict awareness among members of extreme income groups. Consequently, even in the socialist system some people, especially those earning little, tend to speak of the rich and the poor, of the privileged and the plain folks. This is understandable if we consider the relativism of human judgment with respect to one's own economic position.

Interest Contradiction and the State.   In the socialist society the uneven distribution of goods in high demand is mediated by the mechanism of government decisions. The general system of wages is determined by the government, as is the income of the individual citizen. Contradictions of interest may occur here on two planes: one is the plane of contradictions between groups with different incomes, the other is the plane existing between these groups and the *general regulator* represented by the government, in a wide sense of the word.

Objective contradictions between the interests of groups who share in different degrees in the national product exist irrespective of the mechanism of distribution. When this mechanism is the market, the government also acts as regulating factor by maintaining market relations, or by direct intervention in market relations, for example, by fixing a wage minimum, or interfering with collective agreements. Such is the situation in present-day capitalism.

In the socialist system, the government acquires the role of direct regulator. This accounts for a peculiar psychological situation. People with discrepant incomes tend to blame the government, as the regulator of their income, rather than the better-off groups. This tendency is much less common and much less explicit in the capitalist system. There, interest contradictions are chiefly conceived as contradictions between different social groups. This difference between the two systems is of tremendous importance for any discussion of conflicts of interests.

Equipped with the concepts of overpayment and underpayment, as well as the distinction between objective interest contradictions and subjectively felt conflicts, we can now attempt to delve deeper into the theoretical complexities of the situation created by the direct regulatory function of the State. Let us consider a number of possibilities.

In determining the system of wages, the government may be acting in one of the following ways: (1) respecting fully the principle "to each according to his work," (2) applying this principle with certain departures in favor of the highly skilled, (3) applying this principle with departures in favor of unskilled strata. Considering the marked discrepancies in the systems of wages of the various socialist countries, those three alternatives are likely to exist in reality.

In the first example, the government acts as a just and impartial regulator of wages. The better skilled workers are assigned higher wages, in line with the socialist principle of remuneration. But the contradiction of interest arising in this case between different social and occupational groups, or strata, is a direct result of government policies. This alone may give rise to an awareness of conflict on the part of the lower-paid people, and their feelings will be directed against the state (government). There is an objective contradiction between the interests of different social and occupational groups, but at the same time there is also the awareness of conflict on the part of the lower-paid people directed against the government. We are facing here a *transfer* of conflict awareness against the *general regulator*. Evidently, this type of intergroup contradiction of interests is unavoidable in socialism.

The situations described under (2) and (3) are of a different nature. Here the government overpays some and underpays other social and occupational groups, or entire strata. This may well enhance the satisfaction of some but will also aggravate the awareness of conflict among some others. The conflict-generating tendencies are born from the "partiality" of the government; the resultant contradictions transgress the framework of the socialist system of remuneration. The awareness of conflict among the people is heightened in

view of such bias, the more so when the underpayment concerns the unskilled, and hence, less well-off people. The reverse occurs perhaps more frequently in practice. In Poland, for example, if any group is overpaid. it is the less-skilled group. For society as a whole this appears to result in a reduction of the awareness of the conflict.

Finally, one more possibility is given in the situation in which the group responsible for fixing the wage system, meaning the political leaders of the country at large, is overpaid. Whereas in the previous examples the leaders as a group did not stand in a nonsocialist contradiction of interests to the, or some, other groups, the latter example provides for precisely such a contradiction. This is a fertile ground for a sharp rise in awareness of conflict.

The situations listed above are purely theoretical. They derive from a specific, broadly conceived interpretation of interest contradictions and from the conception of overpayment and underpayment. In order to employ those conceptions in empirical research we must first determine objective measures of the social value of different types of labor. These measures will have to account for not only the purely economic value of labor but also for some other factors of a socioeconomic nature. Though it might not be easy to determine such measures, one cannot think of any other way of effectively studying the objective interest contradictions existing in socialism. . . .

Contradictions of Interests Concerning Noneconomic Goods. Besides an uneven distribution of income, we also find in socialist society an uneven distribution of various other values. The distribution of income involves the distribution of some other goods, owing to the partial convertibility of those values. In a situation where a wide range of noneconomic values, for example, cultural, can be obtained for money in the market, the acquisition of other goods is determined by the distribution of income. We may therefore feel justified to focus our attention on the distribution of income. Being fully characteristic of capitalist society, the above conditions apply to a marked degree to socialist society also. But a peculiar feature of the latter is the weakened interrelation between size of income and participation in other values. In effect, the noneconomic goods distributed through separate channels are subject to extremely important contradictions of interests. Among those values are education, some goods in the sphere of so-called cultural consumption, for example, holidays at reduced rates, health benefits, and many others.

Take for example education. . . . In any industrial society, the individual level of education is a major component of professional qualifications, and the latter form the foundation of the individual's general status. In capitalist society, however, this interdependence does scarcely apply to members of the capitalist class. Their status and opportunities are chiefly determined by the amount of capital at their disposal, rather than by their education. Education represents here only an additional bonus enabling the capitalist to take up some occupation.

In socialist society, the situation of any individual is largely determined by his occupational status, and the latter depends very much on his education and the skills ensuing from that education. . . . And since there is a direct link between occupation and both income and social prestige, education amounts to an important instrument for obtaining various other values.

We have just referred to the intragenerational instrumental role of education, but there is also an intergenerational one. . . . Education is the chief instrument serving to define the future occupational position of a young man on his entering adult social life.

It should be borne in mind that in those societies where school education is not free, the level of education acquired by a young person depends largely on the income of his parents; his future income is in turn determined by his education. As a result of that mechanism, the status is subject to a *hereditary* tendency. In the above general model, no consideration is given to modifications resulting from the system of scholarships and grants for gifted children from poor homes.

In socialist society, where education at all levels is free, the interrelation between the parents' income and the educational opportunities of their children is greatly reduced, although the education acquired by an individual is a major determinant of his future income and social status. This reflects the reduced intergenerational instrumental role of income and the increased intergenerational instrumental role of education in socialist society.

But there is as yet no abundance of secondary and higher schools in the socialist countries. Consequently there is ground for interest contradictions between social strata as regards the criteria of admission to educational institutions at secondary and higher levels. This contradiction applies to the operation of channels through which education, an instrumental and "autonomous" factor with regard to income, is distributed.

The peculiar social conditions underlying that contradiction are connected with the discrepancies in the general intellectual development of children from workers and peasant homes on one hand and the children of the intelligentsia. This is highlighted during entrance examinations at universities and colleges, but also during similar examinations at secondary schools.

The differentiated cultural conditions in individual homes account for differentials in the initial achievements of children from different social strata. In view of this, the workers and farmers favor the preferential system of school admission, under which their children are granted additional counts for social background. This system works toward reducing the chances of admission of the children of the intelligentsia. Hence the educated people are in favor of a system of selection based on the outcomes of purely competitive examinations. The latter system tends to reduce the chances of admission of children from workers' and farmers' homes, of course.

In conditions of free education, the lack of equilibrium between the supply of educational facilities and the demand for education is the source of contradictions of interests concerning the principles of selection.

The Cumulative and Noncumulative Distribution of Values. The distribution of values in capitalist society is largely cumulative:

high income, great political influence, high education, and high prestige are vested in some persons, while other persons suffer from inadequacies in those respects. Thus there is a high congruence of status characteristics in capitalist society, especially when we consider the two basic classes in the Marxist sense.

In socialist society we observe a decomposition of characteristics of social status as resulting from the noncumulative distribution of generally desired values. Income, education, political influence, and prestige are distributed more or less independently from one another. The effect of this phenomenon on the sphere of interests is enormous.

Two general hypotheses may be advanced in this connection: (1) the cumulative distribution of values and, as its result, the congruence of status characteristics both favor the development of fairly well-defined social strata or classes. (2) The same phenomena result in an aggravation of objective interest contradictions between the groups (strata), by creating parallel and correlated spheres of social inequalities.

Those two hypotheses lead us to another general proposition: Both the objective contradictions of interests and the subjective awareness of conflicts of interests tend to decrease in socialist society when compared with capitalist society.

TWO TENDENCIES

We have stressed the decomposition of status characteristics in socialist society because of the relative novelty of this phenomenon, often neglected or overlooked by sociologists. It would be wrong, however, to forget the existing congruences of characteristics. The latter may be either a heritage of the past, or may result from the socialist mechanisms of distribution. In fact, there is good reason to search for the sources of congruence in status characteristics.

The principle "to each according to his work" operates toward synchronizing at least some of the status characteristics.

It may be assumed that certain severe decompositions observed in Poland were caused, among other things, by disregard for this principle under the pressure of an egalitarian ideology and of economic necessities, for example, manpower shortages in certain occupations.

The principle "to each according to his work" contributes to the synchronization of status characteristics because it regulates income according to the *quality* of work and hence according to education and the ensuing professional skills. Formal, that is, school, education is of decisive influence on professional qualifications in highly developed industrial societies. Adherence to the principle "to each according to his work" tends to increase the congruence between education and income. There is a similar tendency toward congruence between position, in power or management structures, and income. The same synchronizing tendency is reinforced by the dependence of prestige on education.

At the same time an opposite tendency is at work. Certain decomposition tendencies are aroused by those deliberate departures from the principle "to each according to his work" that are aimed at raising the income of the least-skilled people. The result is a discrepancy between skills, for example, low, and income, for example, medium. Similar effects are produced by departures from the principle such as wage limitations for highly skilled people.

Generally speaking, the scale of skills seems to be greater than the scale of income. Thus, a leveling out of income to a middle position results in certain decompositions of status characteristics. These are decompositions in the form of leveling out rather than in the form of leaping ahead. A rise occurs in one status characteristic of a social and occupational group or a whole stratum, while all other characteristics remain unchanged. Such decompositions are probably the most common.

It is easier to observe such a partial decomposition of status characteristics against the background of a wide range of status characteristics. Take prestige, for example.

There are groups of highly skilled people in Poland who enjoy great prestige but get only medium pay, for example, physicians, or junior research workers. There are occupations that require medium qualifications, ensure low income, and enjoy medium prestige, for example, nurses. In the first case the skill and prestige are uniformly high, while income is lowered toward the middle of the scale. In the latter case, qualifications and prestige are the same (medium), and again income lags behind. Both cases exemplify a partial decomposition of status characteristics, and both demonstrate a higher congruence of prestige and qualifications than prestige and income. There is also some indication in both cases for an autonomization of prestige in relation to other status characteristics.[14]

Thus in socialist society we find two opposite tendencies in the realm of the distribution of values representing important status characteristics—education, income, and social prestige. Either tendency is connected with different socialist principles. One tendency, the congruence of status characteristics, is connected with the principle "to each according to his work." The other tendency is associated with egalitarian ideals and leads to a decomposition, at least partial, of status characteristics. . . .

[14] The nature of social prestige seems to be changing gradually in socialist society over what it was in a capitalist society. Hence it is subject to greater autonomization in relation to certain objective status characteristics, income, power, and so on. The present paper leaves no room for any wider discussion of that problem.

PART VIII
Unresolved
Issues in
Stratification
Theory

The great unanswered questions, the unsettled issues in stratification theory are in many ways the most intriguing ones. In studying them, what we know and what we do not know about structured social inequality come to a most intellectually exciting confluence. Our readings concern two types of unresolved issues. The first four center around the problem of the nature of stratification in general. Here these questions loom large: Why is stratification universal—or more accurately—nearly universal? Is stratification necessary for society? Is it the usual consequence of or a necessary condition for society's existence? The last three readings here deal with a different kind of issue. They struggle to grasp the outline of the new system of structured inequality that is now shaping in advanced industrial society.

We know that two opposed theoretical models for interpreting social phenomena are used in contemporary sociology: the structural-functional and the conflict models. The field of stratification is no exception. Here also these two antithetical theories have vied with each other for years as explanations of stratification. The most recent manifestation is the recognition that each of them contains a measure of validity. And it takes two forms: (1) the assertion that each theory is suited to a different set of empirical phenomena and problems and (2) the assertion that a theory representing a synthesis of the functional and conflict theories is needed, is possible, and, sometimes, has already been at least partially achieved.

The controversy between functional and conflict interpretations has been fought on two fronts. To simplify it, one is the intellectual battle over the problem of what stratification is, and the other concerns the reason why stratification exists. In the first, the functionalists were led so to speak by Parsons; in the second by Davis and Moore. To begin with the first, the functionalists take the position that stratification is integrative because it results from common values; the conflict theorists maintain that conflict is endemic to it because it results from coercion. The exponents of or adherents to the *integrative* theory emphasize the common values that bind the different strata; those of the *conflict* theory emphasize the divergent interests that divide them. Whereas the former see consensus as the basis of social unity, the latter see unity achieved by coercion.

We have already encountered in our previous readings the emphasis on the integrative function of stratification, especially in Warner. But, as expressed by Dahrendorf in our first selection, the most eminent sociological theorist of integration is Talcott Parsons. And Dahrendorf gives us a rendition of Parsons' theory. [1] Dahrendorf's writing preceded and therefore made no mention of M. G. Smith's test of Parsons' assumption that a common value system is the indispensable basis of all society. In reading Dahrendorf's discussion of Parsons' theory, we should bear in mind the results of Smith's study of Grenada in the British Caribbean. Smith was guided by J. S. Furnivall's theory of plural society, which explicitly denied that such overarching systems of common values are found in plural societies. Smith's analysis revealed a substantial divergence of values among the Grenadian society. In his words,

At one extreme, among the highest-ranking Westernized Creole "whites," we find an undiluted ascriptive orientation with solidary particularistic stress; at the other, in the dark, low-ranking elite levels above the folk, the prevailing set of values is individualistic and achievement-oriented. These two value sets challenge and clash with each other. *Their coexistence at different levels of the elite hierarchy represents dissensus rather than the prevalence of common system of values* [2] (italics supplied).

Thus, the empirical facts, as studied by Smith, seem at odds with Parsons' theory, which postulates that a common value system is "a *condition* of the stability of social systems" (italics supplied). [3]

Dahrendorf's essay may also be read as a compact presentation of conflict theory or what he calls coercion theory. This is an important contribution in itself, for, as has been stated by the Danish sociologist Kaare Svalastoga, "... the conflict centered theories have nowhere received a level of elaboration comparable to functional theory." [4] Dahrendorf reduces the conflict theory to its basic tenets. One of these is that "every society is based on the coercion of some of its members by others." The differential distribution of authority is the determining factor of systematic social conflicts. He proceeds to develop this idea further by pointing to social organizations as the *locus* of conflict: "they generate conflict of interests and become the birthplace of conflict groups."

According to Dahrendorf each theory—integration and conflict—is suitable for only one "face" of society but society is Janus-headed and has two faces. Thus he views these theories as complementary rather than mutually exclusive. He does raise the issue of a *unified* theory, which would explain both the integration and conflict inherent in society. But, as far as he is concerned, there is no such theory today and, moreover, its feasibility in the future is questionable.

[1] For the first statement of this theory, see "An Analytical Approach to the Theory of Social Stratification," in *Essays in Sociological Theory*, Glencoe, Ill.: Free Press, 1954, pp. 69–88. Parsons presented later a revised version of his stratification theory. See Talcott Parsons, "A Revised Analytical Approach to the Theory of Social Stratification," in Reinhold Bendix and Seymour Martin Lipset, eds., *Class, Status and Power*, Glencoe, Ill.: Free Press, 1953, pp. 92–128.
[2] M. G. Smith, *Stratification in Grenada*, Berkeley: University of California Press, 1965, p. 253.
[3] Parsons, "A Revised Analytical Approach to the Theory of Social Stratification," *op. cit.*, p. 93.
[4] Kaare Svalastoga, *Social Differentiation*, New York: David McKay Company, 1965, p. 4.

Others seem more optimistic about theoretical synthesis. In his book, *Power and Privilege,* Gerhard Lenski makes the claim that his theory represents such a synthesis. (But some critics say that he failed to achieve this goal.)[5] Lenski asserts that the reason why theorists of the two opposing schools have gotten into so many impasses is that "both parties have asked the same wrong question or utilized the same faulty concepts."[6] And he sees himself lifting stratification theory from the impasses and moving it toward a synthesis by a process of reformulating problems and concepts. Lockwood, on the other hand, ascribes the achievement of synthesis to Marxian theory.[7] He charges that the contemporary conflict theorist cannot answer why some conflict results in change, and other conflict, equally endemic and intense in a social system, does not lead to change. But the answer is implicit in Marx's thought, for there we find a distinction between *the propensity* to class antagonism and the *dynamics* of class antagonism. According to Lockwood, Marx saw the *tendency* toward conflict as resulting from the character of production relationships. (This Lockwood designates as the *social integration aspect.*) But Marx saw dynamics of change as related to the growing contradictions in the economic system. (Lockwood labels this aspect *system integration.*) Thus structural contradictions are central to Marx's theory of change.

And it is most important that Marx's idea of a contradiction between the material conditions of production and the productive institutions of the economic system should not be ignored by sociologists. Lockwood assures the sociologists that if they were to use Marx's idea of a *functional incompatibility* between the dominant institutional order and the material base of a social system, they would *not* necessarily have to adopt Marx's conclusion that this inevitably leads to the breakdown of a system and its replacement by another.

The reading that follows the Dahrendorf selection is the much discussed article "Some Principles of Stratification," by Kingsley Davis and Wilbert E. Moore. The controversy generated by it is one of the most enduring disputes in current sociology. The authors present a functional theory of why stratification exists. They contend that social stratification—which they equate with the unequal distribution of rewards—is functionally necessary and that is why it is a universal and permanent feature of society. The main functional necessity, they say, which explains the universality of stratification "is precisely the requirement faced by any society of placing and motivating individuals in the social structure." Throughout the reprinted article they develop the theme that stratification is an "unconsciously evolved device by which societies insure that the most important positions are conscientiously filled by the most qualified persons" (p. 497).

Future historians and sociologists of knowledge might see this functional theory as a rationalization of social inequality existing in advanced industrial society. This suggests itself as plausible when we read R. H. Tawney's interpretation of the ideological significance of the functional theory that prevailed in the Middle ages.

The facts of class status and inequality were rationalized in the Middle Ages by a functional theory, as the facts of competition were rationalized in the eighteenth by

[5] For example, Seymour M. Lipset's criticism at the "Author Meets the Critic" session at the annual meeting of the Eastern Sociological Society, New York, N.Y., on April 16, 1967.

[6] Gerhard Lenski, *Power and Privilege,* New York: McGraw-Hill Book Co., 1966. The quote is from p. 20.

[7] David Lockwood, "Social Integration and System Integration," in *Explorations in Social Change,* George K. Zollschan and Walter Hirsch, eds., New York: Houghton Mifflin, 1964, pp. 244–257.

the theory of economic harmonies. . . . Society, like the human body, is an organism composed of different members. Each member has its own function; prayer, or defence, or merchandise, or tilling the soil. Each must receive the means suited to the station, and must claim no more. . . . Between classes there must be inequality; for otherwise a class cannot perform its function . . . .[8]

For more than twenty years since its appearance, the Davis-Moore theory has been extensively criticized, sometimes on grounds of ideological bias but more often on grounds of lacks in the validity of its concepts and propositions. For example, Foote and Hatt questioned whether stratification would continue in "massified" societies such as the one in the United States.[9] Buckley found fault with Davis' and Moore's neglect of the family as a determinant of status, contending that ". . . positions are determined on the whole by social inheritance, and only secondarily by . . . performance." He also criticized their use of the term *social stratification*, charging that they confused it with social differentiation.[10] In reply to Buckley, Davis reiterated that he and Moore applied the term *social stratification* ". . . to the system of unequal rewards attached to different positions in society. It is the existence of such unequal reward systems that the theory tries to explain."[11]

On the other hand, Dennis Wrong in an article that appeared about fifteen years after the Davis and Moore essay, surveying the criticisms directed at it, concluded that the critics succeeded only in showing that there are many things about stratification that are not explained by the Davis and Moore theory but that "they have not succeeded in seriously denting the central argument that unequal rewards are necessary in any societies with a division of labor extending much beyond difference in age and sex."[12] He explains that Davis and Moore are only committed to the view that there must be unequal rewards. How unequal these rewards need to be— the subject of some of the critics of their theory—is another question and a question to which Davis and Moore did not address themselves. Their theory, says Wrong, does not deny that the distribution of rewards in a given society may be way in excess of the "minimum inequalities necessary to maintain a complex division of labor."[13]

Of the many discussions of the Davis and Moore theory, the one by Wesolowski reprinted here is among the latest and seems to me to have succeeded where Dennis Wrong claims the earlier ones have failed, that is, in denting the central argument. This is not to say that this is the only one that has succeeded. Quite germane, for example, is a note by Huaco. We are referring to his criticism *on logical grounds* of the Davis-Moore theory and especially of its proposition that those positions convey the best rewards which have the greatest functional importance for society. Huaco argues that in the present state of social science we have no scientifically adequate empirical evidence as to which roles make the greater contribution to the

[8] R. H. Tawney, *Religion and the Rise of Capitalism*, Harmondsworth, England: Pelican Books, 1938, p. 37, as quoted in Barber, *op. cit.*, p. 201.

[9] Nelson N. Foote and Paul K. Hatt, "Social Mobility and Economic Advancement," *American Economic Review*, Vol. XLIII, May, 1953, pp. 387–394.

[10] Walter Buckley, "Social Stratification and Social Differentiation," *American Sociological Review*, Vol. 23, August, 1958, pp. 369–375.

[11] Kingsley Davis, "The Abominable Heresy: A Reply to Dr. Buckley," *American Sociological Review*, Vol. 24, 1959, p. 82.

[12] Dennis Wrong, "The Functional Theory of Stratification: Some Neglected Considerations," *American Sociological Review*, Vol. 24, December, 1959, p. 773.

[13] *Ibid.*, pp. 774–776.

survival of a given society. Thus the concept of unequal functional importance "is a complete unknown; and as it stands, it cannot serve as a legitimate explanation for 'unequal rewards,'" for it is a rule of logic that you cannot explain one unknown by another unknown.[14] In the same issue of the *American Sociological Review* in which this note appeared, another important contribution is found by Arthur Stinchcombe. He points out that the Davis-Moore theory, despite all the attention it has received, has "stimulated remarkably few studies." He therefore sets before himself the task of outlining some empirical implications of the theory, convinced that, like other scientific theories, it contains implications which can be demonstrated to be either true or false. "Deciding whether they are true or false," he says, "is not a theoretical or ideological matter, but an empirical one." And this decision therefore awaits empirical testing.[15]

The article by Wlodzimierz Wesolowski deserves attention not only because of its exceptional clarity and logical rigor, but also because it represents a reaction to the functional theory by a sociologist from Poland, a "socialist" society. He reduces the theory to three main propositions, each of which he examines critically. Contrary to Davis and Moore's claim that theirs is a theory of stratification in general, Wesolowski convincingly demonstrates that it is only a theory of the stratification of systems that rely principally on achievement rather than on ascription in filling positions. But even if limited to such systems, he charges, the theory contains erroneous assumptions about human nature, patterns of society, and structure of values. Concerning the last, Davis and Moore see as the main goals material advantages and prestige. But it is possible, argues Wesolowski, to have a society where other goals, such as education and authority, are ultimate. In such a society positions calling for education and training, as well as positions of authority, would be filled not because of their material advantages but because of their intrinsic attributes—skill, knowledge and power—which could be sufficiently attractive. Those latter values, which in the Davis-Moore theory are treated as intermediate values, may appear as terminal values. (Although Wesolowski's point is well taken, one may wonder whether a stratification system that recruited into positions of power solely people who enjoy power would not prove more oppressive and rigid than the systems where material rewards attract people into such positions. But, of course, this does not damage his thesis.)

Wesolowski further criticizes the Davis-Moore theory for concentrating on material advantages and prestige and neglecting authority, the more important element of stratification from a functional point of view. Moreover, he attempts to demonstrate that if there is any functional necessity for stratification, it is the necessity of unequal authority rather than of unequal material goods or prestige. Hierarchies of authority are inevitable in large social structures. There is a great similarity between this conclusion and Dahrendorf's thoughts on inequality. Dahrendorf maintains that inequality in power and authority inevitably accompanies social organization. There are those who have the right to control the action of others and issue commands and others who are controlled and have to obey. What makes Wesolowski's conclusion especially noteworthy is that its implications are not in line with the Soviet conception of nonantagonistic classes in Soviet-type

---

[14] George A. Huaco, "A Logical Analysis of the Davis-Moore Theory of Stratification," *American Sociological Review*, Vol. 28, October, 1963, pp. 801–803.

[15] Arthur L. Stinchcombe, "Some Empirical Consequences of the Davis-Moore Theory," *American Sociological Review*, 28, October 1963, pp. 805–808.

societies. If there is inequality in authority in such societies, there is also potential conflict.[16]

Missing in Wesolowski's criticism of the Davis-Moore theory is a challenge to their assertion that stratification is universal. And yet for some time anthropologists have been saying that this is not the case, that stratification is a feature of some but not all societies. Gunnar Landtman, for instance, in the book he published in 1938, proclaimed as a fact "that a condition of almost complete equality reigns among peoples in the lowest degrees of culture.[17] One of the latest anthropological essays on this subject cites various concrete examples of unstratified societies in East Africa and Australia. Its author, M. G. Smith, also addresses himself to the fascinating question of why so many sociologists proceed on the assumption that stratification is universal when social anthropologists are denying it. He suggests that sociologists see in inequality the proof that stratification exists. Anthropologists, on the other hand, first ask what form inequality takes and what its degree and scale are before they decide that stratification is present in a given society. In the view of the latter, Smith says "the principles by which observable inequalities are institutionalized are the critical data." Thus, according to Smith, inequality in a given society does not per se mean that it is stratified, but institutionalized inequality in the access to favored positions is "decisive for societal classification as stratified."[18]

If sociologists tended in the past to equate inequality with stratification, then it is no longer true of some, as is reflected in the two readings by Moore and Wrong that follow Wesolowski's. The reprinted selection by Wilbert Moore represents the last step in the last round of the Tumin-Moore debate, which appeared at the end of the second decade of the theoretical controversy generated by the Davis and Moore essay. It is worthwhile to recall that Tumin was one of the first to challenge the Davis-Moore theory. In his initial criticism of that theory he objected, among other things, to its assumption of a scarcity of trained and talented personnel. He asserted that, contrary to what the theory postulates, stratification interferes with rather than facilitates the selection of talented people.[19] He thus directed himself to some of the dysfunctions of stratification. In addition, he challenged the Davis-Moore assumptions concerning human motivation:

A generalized theory of social stratification must recognize that the prevailing system of inducements and rewards is only one of many variants in the whole range of possible systems of motivation which, at least theoretically, are capable of working in human society.[20]

[16] Various empirical studies conducted in these countries show that social conflict did not cease with state ownership of the means of production. However, the term social conflict is used only by some Polish sociologists. Sociologists in other socialist countries use such guarded terms as *problem of technological and social progress* or *functional differentiation of socialist society* when discussing problems of conflict in their own societies. See Gabor Kiss, *Gibt es eine Marxistische Soziologie,* Köln: Westdeutscher Verlag, 1960, pp. 43–60. As we saw in the other article by Wesolowski in a preceding part of this book (which the author presented subsequently to the one we are now discussing), he did address himself to conflict in interests in socialist countries but, significantly, left out of it the dimension of power. See pp. 465–477 in this volume.

[17] Gunnar Landtman, *The Origin of the Inequality of the Social Classes,* London: Kegan Paul, Trench Trubner and Co., 1938, p. 3.

[18] Michael G. Smith, "Pre-Industrial Stratification Systems," in Neil J. Smelser and S. M. Lipset, eds., *Social Structure and Mobility in Economic Development,* Chicago: Aldine Press, 1966, pp. 141–176. Direct quotes from p. 149.

[19] Melvin Tumin, "Some Principles of Stratification: A Critical Analysis," *American Sociological Review,* Vol. 18, August, 1953, pp. 387–394.

[20] *Ibid.,* p. 388.

The last round of the debate appeared in the February, 1963 issue of the *American Sociological Review*. In it is found the article by Wilbert Moore, "But Some Are More Equal than Others," in which he summarized the criticisms raised by sociologists, with special attention to those of Tumin, accepting some and rejecting others. He conceded to the critics that the functional theory of stratification neglected dysfunctions of stratification. Also, he made it clear that he considered his and Davis' equating of social stratification with unequal rewards unfortunate, thus expressing some sympathy for Buckley's criticism on this point. But he did not find the critics persuasive on the possibility of eliminating inequality. He therefore reiterates the original contention that functional differentiations of positions "will inevitably entail unequal rewards" and adds to it that "differences in performance must be expected to be and will be differentially valued."[21] Moore maintains then that social inequality is "an essential feature of social systems."[22] The implication of Moore's argument seems to be, although he does not express it thus, that stratification may not be necessary but that inequality is. (As noted here, he no longer considers stratification synonymous with unequal rewards.)

The article by Moore was followed in the same issue of the *Review* by Melvin Tumin's "On Social Inequality." In it Tumin expressed the conviction that the difficulty in the past exchanges with Moore arose partially from the ambiguity of the term social inequality. He proceeds therefore to specify five forms of inequality, no known society being without some or all of these: (1) role differentiation; (2) ranking in accordance with the intrinsic attributes of a role; (3) ranking in terms of approximation to social values and norms; (4) ranking according to functional contribution; and (5) diffusion and transfer of "differentials in property, power, and prestige."[23] His contention is that any of these can become subject to stratification, and some are more likely to than others, but *none must become stratified in order that society survive*. According to him, little can be learned about existing stratification, or about existing society in general, by focusing on what is necessary for minimum social survival. He insists that most existing stratification ". . . enjoys little or no consensus, has little to do with social integration, and is probably seriously dysfunctional for social productivity."[24]

Tumin finishes on a moral note in behalf of equality, the logic of which is easily dented, and this is accomplished by Moore in the reprinted rejoinder, which we have titled "The Tumin–Moore Polemics—Remaining Points of Disagreement." Still, Moore gives recognition to the main accomplishment of the Tumin article: It has reduced substantially the previous area of disagreement between them by addressing itself to the general issues of inequality. Moore specifies the points on which there is no longer disagreement and moves on to the ones on which they are still divided. He takes special issue with Tumin's contention that most social differentiation does not involve invidious valuation, asserting that "it is not at all established that functional differentiation and unequal valuation are independently variable."

Moore ends his rejoinder by pointing out that the exchange between him and Tumin has not touched on some important issues relevant to stratification. Foremost among them is whether class continues to be a useful explanatory concept.

[21] Wilbert E. Moore, "But Some Are More Equal than Others," *American Sociological Review*, Vol. 28, February, 1963, pp. 13–18.

[22] *Ibid.*, p. 14.

[23] Melvin Tumin, "On Social Inequality," *American Sociological Review*, Vol. 28, February, 1963, pp. 19–26.

[24] *Ibid.*, p. 25.

This is precisely the central question in the last three essays in this section, and the authors take opposite positions on it. Dennis Wrong in his "Social Inequality Without Social Stratification" allies himself with the view—which he tells us is rejected by the majority of American sociologists—that the concept of social class is becoming irrelevant to the understanding of advanced industrial society because social classes have disappeared or are disappearing therefrom. In a sense, Suzanne Keller's argument—in the selection that follows Wrong's—that elites may exist independently of a ruling class is related to Wrong's argument that inequality may exist apart from a class system. To the contrary, Bottomore, in the excerpt from his *Classes in Modern Society,* puts forth the view that the concept of class, and specifically ruling class and working class, has not lost all its meaning, but that the manifestations of class in advanced industrial society are different from what they were in the earlier stages of industrial society.

In the essay prepared especially for this volume, which she based on her book *Beyond the Ruling Class,* Keller maintains that the concept of ruling class does not fit the realities of today's emerging stratification system. Modern society is characterized by a proliferation of elite groups. [25] The ones she concentrates her attention on are what she labels *strategic elites.* They are distinguished from the rest of the elites in that their "judgments, decisions and actions have determinable consequences for all or most members of society." She argues that they are not ruling classes but the *structural alternatives* to them. In addition to the difference in internal organization, they are marked by greater functional specialization than the ruling classes that preceded them. Another distinguishing feature is that they are recruited on the basis of proven capacity to perform. In this respect Keller's strategic elites bear some resemblance to Michael Young's meritocracy, which is discussed by Dennis Wrong in the essay preceding Keller's.

Dennis Wrong is convinced that the now-emerging social structure can be best understood by abandoning the concept of social class and by concentrating on the sociology of equality and inequality. He makes it clear that although he does contend that contemporary industrial society is classless he is not implying that it represents a trend toward general equality. The keen observation by Bernard Barber might fit here: In *styles of life* the trend has been and is toward the pattern of *gross equality* and *subtle inequality.*[26] But Wrong points to the "considerable institutionalized social inequalities" and asserts that the absence of social classes may hide them more effectively than does a class society. He also outlines other major differences between class societies and what he considers the modern classless societies. In the process, he reviews and rejects the arguments of those theorists, notably Dahrendorf, who hold that the concept of class should be retained. He labels Dahrendorf's conception of class "the most quixotic effort" in recent sociological writings to hold on to the concept of class. Subsequent to Wrong's article, another major effort has been made, this time by Lenski, to uphold the continuing usefulness of the concept of class, and one cannot help but wonder whether Wrong would apply the same label to it. As did Dahrendorf, Lenski contends that a single individual may simultaneously be a member of several

---

[25] For an analysis of the conflict between the underlying egalitarian assumptions of the modern welfare state and the use of an elite of trained personnel, see Piet Thoenes, *The Élite in the Welfare State,* New York: Free Press, 1966.

[26] Bernard Barber, "Social Stratification Structure and Trends of Social Mobility in Western Society," in Talcott Parsons, ed., *American Society,* New York: Basic Books, 1968, p. 192.

different classes. But the reasons are different. According to Dahrendorf there are as many class systems in a modern society as there are functional hierarchies of power in it. To Lenski there are a number of class systems in a society, a class system being a hierarchy of classes ranked in terms of a single criterion, such as occupation, property, ethnicity, education, *sex and age*. Thus he refers to a "sexual class system" and "age class system" as well as to occupational, educational, and power class systems.[27]

In light of these curious attempts at redefinitions of class, Bottomore's use of class represents continuity in the meaning of the concept. It is reflected, for example, in his analysis of the working class in modern industrial society as exercising an independent force in political life, despite the fact that it has in many respects not followed the course that Marx and the early Marxists expected it to follow. Very thought provoking is Bottomore's warning against accepting the view of relative peace in industrial society. He thinks it not only possible but likely that there will be new discontent as the disadvantaged become aware that there is no general trend toward greater economic equality and that "there are very powerful movements which tend to produce a more unequal distribution of income and wealth whenever the industrial and political pressure of the working class is relaxed." More important yet than this in generating discontent, according to Bottomore, is the growing discrepancy between conditions of work and conditions of leisure for the working class. There is an increasing freedom of choice and independence of action outside the workplace, but work is still characterized by "constraint, strict subordination, lack of responsibility, absence of means of self-expression."[28] Note, these formulations by Bottomore were made in 1965. Subsequent events— such as the 1968 General Strike in France and the Poor People's Campaign in the United States—dramatically bore out his thesis and gave a note of obsolescence to the opposite thesis of the affluent society and *embourgeoisement* of the working class.

In a way similar to Dennis Wrong's, but on different grounds, Bottomore finishes with a criticism of recent sociological studies. Wrong criticizes them for holding to the concept of class, which he considers obsolete. Bottomore critizes them for the lack of a "historical sense" in their treatment of contemporary social classes. He considers the historical analysis of the changing class structure "one of the most important unfulfilled tasks of sociology today."

Implicit in the last two articles is the general problem of a lack of a basic, standardized vocabulary in the field of stratification studies. Although it is characteristic of sociology in general the malady is especially pronounced here. It is superfluous to spell it out at this time, for the reader is by now well acquainted with it—having been subjected in the readings to the various explicit or implicit meanings of such terms as class, status, stratification, class consciousness, and so on. Perhaps what should be stated is that much energy in the sociological controversies is spent in argument over words. And yet there is no immediate solution in sight for this Tower of Babel. It seems that the best one can do at this stage of our science is to make explicit what he means by a given term when employing it in a manner consequential to the exposition of a thesis, but one must admit that this is a cumbersome procedure, easier to preach than to practice.

[27] Lenski, *op. cit.,* p. 80.

[28] We might add to Bottomore's list of present sources of discontent, the lack of a "humane and informed administration of social service." See: Richard M. Titmuss, "Goals of Today's Welfare State," in Joseph A. Kahl, ed., *Comparative Perspective on Stratification*, Boston: Little, Brown and Company, 1968, p. 90.

SOCIAL STRUCTURE, GROUP INTERESTS, AND CONFLICT GROUPS

Ralf Dahrendorf

INTEGRATION AND VALUES VERSUS COERCION AND INTERESTS: THE TWO FACES OF SOCIETY

Throughout the history of Western political thought, two views of society have stood in conflict. Both these views are intended to explain what has been, and will probably continue to be, the most puzzling problem of social philosophy: how is it that human societies cohere? There is one large and distinguished school of thought according to which social order results from a general agreement of values, a *consensus omnium* or *volonté générale* which outweighs all possible or actual differences of opinion and interest. There is another equally distinguished school of thought which holds that coherence and order in society are founded on force and constraint, on the domination of some and the subjection of others. To be sure, these views are not at all points mutually exclusive. The Utopian (as we shall call those who insist on coherence by consensus) does not deny the existence of differences of interest; nor does the Rationalist (who believes in coherence by constraint and domination) ignore such agreements of value as are required for the very establishment of force. But Utopian and Rationalist alike advance claims of primacy for their respective standpoints. . . .

Conflicting philosophical positions must inevitably, it seems to me, reappear constantly in theories of science. Even if this should not generally be the case, I would claim that the philosophical alternative of a Utopian or a Rational solution of the pro-blem of order pervades modern sociological thinking even in its remotest manifestations. Here, as elsewhere, philosophical positions do not enter into scientific theories unchanged. Here, as elsewhere, they pass through the filter of logical supposition before they become relevant for testable explanations of problems of experience. The sociological Utopian does not claim that order *is based on* a general consensus of values, but that it *can be conceived of in terms of* such consensus, and that, if it is conceived of in these terms, certain propositions follow which are subject to the test of specific observations. Analogously, for the sociological Rationalist the assumption of the coercive nature of social order is a heuristic principle rather than a judgment of fact. But this obvious reservation does not prevent the Utopians and the Rationalists of sociology from engaging in disputes which are hardly less intense (if often rather less imaginative and ingenious) than those of their philsophical antecedents. The subject matter of our concern in this study demands that we take a stand with respect to this dispute. . . . Generally speaking, it seems to me that two (meta-)theories can and must be distinguished in contemporary sociology. One of these, the *integration theory of society,* conceives of social structure in terms of a functionally integrated system held in equilibrium by certain patterned and recurrent processes. The other one, the *coercion theory of society,* views social structure as a form of organization held together by force and constraint and reaching continuously beyond itself in the sense of producing within itself the forces that maintain it in an unending process of change. Like their philosophical counterparts, these theories are mutually exclusive. . . .

In recent years, the integration theory of society has clearly dominated sociological thinking. In my opinion, this prevalence of one partial view has had many unfortunate consequences. However, it has also had at least one agreeable consequence, in that the very onesidedness of this theory gave rise to critical objections which enable us today to put this theory in its proper place. Such objections have been stimulated with increasing frequency by the works of the most

Reprinted from *Class and Class Conflict in Industrial Society* by Ralf Dahrendorf with permission of the publishers, Stanford University Press. © 1959 by the Board of Trustees of Leland Stanford Junior University.

eminent sociological theorist of integration, Talcott Parsons. It is not necessary here to attempt a comprehensive exposition of Parsons' position; nor do we have to survey the sizable literature concerned with a critical appraisal of this position. . . . There is one objection to Parsons' position, however, which we have to examine if we are to make a systematic presentation of a theory of group conflict. In a remarkable essay, D. Lockwood claims "that Parsons' array of concepts is heavily weighted by assumptions and categories which relate to the role of *normative* elements in social action, and especially to the processes whereby motives are structured normatively to ensure social stability. On the other hand, what may be called the *substratum* of social action, especially as it conditions interests which are productive of social conflict and instability, tends to be ignored as a general determinant of the dynamics of social systems."[1] . . . Lockwood's claim touches on the core of our problem of the two faces of society. . . .

It is certainly true that the work of Parsons displays a conspicuous bias in favor of analysis in terms of values and norms. It is equally true that many of those who have been concerned with problems of conflict rather than of stability have tended to emphasize not the normative but the institutional aspects of social structure. The work of Marx is a case in point. Probably, this difference in emphasis is no accident. It is nevertheless as such irrelevant to an understanding of or adoption of the alternative images of society which pervade political thought and sociological theory. The alternative between "normative elements in social action" and a factual "substratum of social action," which Lockwood takes over from the work of Renner, in fact indicates two levels of the analysis of social structure which are in no way contradictory. There is no theoretical reason why Talcott Parsons should not have supplemented (as indeed he occasionally does) his analysis of normative integration by an analysis of the integration of social systems in terms of their institutional sub-

stratum. However we look at social structure, it always presents itself as composed of a moral and a factual, a normative and an institutional, level or, in the doubtful terms of Marx, a superstructure and a substratum. The investigator is free to choose which of these levels he wants to emphasize more strongly—although he may be well-advised, in the interest of clarity as well as of comprehensiveness of his analysis, not to stress one of these levels to the exclusion of the other.

At the same time, there is an important element of genuine critique in Lockwood's objection to Parsons. When Lockwood contrasts stability and instability, integration and conflict, equilibrium and disequilibrium, values and interests, he puts his finger on a real alternative of thought, and one of which Parsons has apparently not been sufficiently aware. For of two equivalent models of society, Parsons has throughout his work recognized only one, the Utopian or integration theory of society. His "array of concepts" is therefore incapable of coping with those problems with which Lockwood is concerned in his critical essay, and which constitute the subject matter of the present study.

For purposes of exposition it seems useful to reduce each of the two faces of society to a small number of basic tenets, even if this involves some degree of oversimplification as well as overstatement. The integration theory of society, as displayed by the work of Parsons and other structural-functionalists, is founded on a number of assumptions of the following type:

1. Every society is a relatively persistent, stable structure of elements.
2. Every society is a well-integrated structure of elements.
3. Every element in a society has a function, i.e., renders a contribution to its maintenance as a system.
4. Every functioning social structure is based on a consensus of values among its members.

. . . However, it is abundantly clear that the integration approach to social analysis does not enable us to comprehend all problems of social reality. . . . On the 17th

[1] David Lockwood, "Some Remarks on 'The Social System,' " *British Journal of Sociology*, Vol. VII, No. 2, 1956, p. 136.

of June, 1953, the building workers of East Berlin put down their tools and went on a strike that soon led to a generalized revolt against the Communist regime of East Germany. Why? . . . Evidently, the uprising of the 17th of June is neither due to nor productive of integration in East German society. It documents and produces not stability, but instability. It contributes to the disruption, not the maintenance, of the existing system. It testifies to dissensus rather than consensus. The integration model tells us little more than that there are certain "strains" in the "system." In fact, in order to cope with problems of this kind we have to replace the integration theory of society by a different and, in many ways, contradictory model.

What I have called the coercion theory of society can also be reduced to a small number of basic tenets, although here again these assumptions oversimplify and overstate the case:

1. Every society is at every point subject to processes of change; social change is ubiquitous.
2. Every society displays at every point dissensus and conflict; social conflict is ubiquitous.
3. Every element in a society renders a contribution to its disintegration and change.
4. Every society is based on the coercion of some of its members by others.

If we return to the problem of the German workers' strike, it will become clear that this latter model enables us to deal rather more satisfactorily with its causes and consequences. The revolt of the building workers and their fellows in other industries can be explained in terms of coercion.[2] The revolting groups are engaged in a conflict which "functions" as an agent of change by disintegration. A ubiquitous phenomenon is expressed, in this case, in an exceptionally intense and violent way, and further explanation will have to account for this violence on the basis of the acceptance of conflict and change as universal features of

social life. I need hardly add that, like the integration model, the coercion theory of society constitutes but a set of assumptions for purposes of scientific analysis and implies no claim for philosophical validity—although, like its counterpart, this model also provides a coherent image of social organization.

Now, I would claim that, in a sociological context, neither of these models can be conceived as exclusively valid or applicable. They constitute complementary, rather than alternative, aspects of the structure of total societies as well as of every element of this structure. We have to choose between them only for the explanation of specific problems; but in the conceptual arsenal of sociological analysis they exist side by side. Whatever criticism one may have of the advocates of one or the other of these models can therefore be directed only against claims for the exclusive validity of either.[3] Strictly speaking, both models are "valid" or, rather, useful and necessary for sociological analysis. We cannot conceive of society unless we realize the dialectics of stability and change, integration and conflict, function and motive force, consensus and coercion. In the context of this study, I regard this point as demonstrated by the analysis of the exemplary problems sketched above.

It is perhaps worth emphasizing that the thesis of the two faces of social structure does not require a complete, or even partial, revision of the conceptual apparatus that by now has become more or less generally accepted by sociologists in all countries. Categories like role, institution, norm, structure, even function are as useful in terms of the coercion model as they are for the analysis of social integration. In fact, the dichotomy of aspects can be carried through all levels of sociological analysis; that is, it can be shown that, like social

---

[2] For purposes of clarity, I have deliberately chosen an example from a totalitarian state. But coercion is meant here in a very general sense, and the coercion model is applicable to all societies, independent of their specific political structure.

[3] This, it seems to me, is the only—if fundamental—legitimate criticism that can be raised against Parsons' work on this general level. In *The Social System,* Parsons repeatedly advances, for the integration theory of society, a claim that it is the nucleus of "the general" sociological theory—a claim which I regard as utterly unjustified. It is Lockwood's main concern also, in the essay quoted above, to reject this claim to universal validity.

structure itself, the notions of role and institution, integration and function, norm and substratum have two faces which may be expressed by two terms, but which may also in many cases be indicated by an extension of concepts already in use. . . . The notions of interest and value indeed seem to describe very well the two faces of the normative superstructure of society: what appears as a consensus of values on the basis of the integration theory can be regarded as a conflict of interests in terms of the coercion theory. Similarly, what appears on the level of the factual substratum as integration from the point of view of the former model presents itself as coercion or constraint from the point of view of the latter. . . .

While logically feasible,[4] the solution of the dilemma of political thought which we have offered here for the more restricted field of sociological analysis nevertheless raises a number of serious problems. It is evidently virtually impossible to think of society in terms of either model without positing its opposite number at the same time. There can be no conflict, unless this conflict occurs within a context of meaning, i.e., some kind of coherent "system." No conflict is conceivable between French housewives and Chilean chess players, because these groups are not united by, or perhaps "integrated into," a common frame of reference. Analogously, the notion of integration makes little sense unless it presupposes the existence of different elements that are integrated. . . .

Inevitably, the question will be raised, also, whether a unified theory of society that includes the tenets of both the integration and the coercion models of society is not at least conceivable—for as to its desirability there can be little doubt. Is there, or can there be, a general point of view that synthesizes the unsolved dialectics of integration and coercion? So far as I can see, there is no such general model; as to its

---

[4] As is demonstrated most clearly by the fact that a similar situation can be encountered in physics with respect to the theory of light. Here, too, there are two seemingly incompatible theories which nevertheless exist side by side, and each of which has its proper realm of empirical phenomena: the wave theory and the quantum theory of light.

possibility, I have to reserve judgment. It seems at least conceivable that unification of theory is not feasible at a point which has puzzled thinkers ever since the beginning of Western philosophy.

For the explanation of the formation of conflict groups out of conditions of social structure, we shall employ a model that emphasizes the ugly face of society. In the following sections of this chapter I shall try to show how, on the assumption of the coercive nature of social structure, relations of authority become productive of clashes of role interest which under certain conditions lead to the formation of organized antagonistic groups within limited social organizations as well as within total societies. . . .

POWER AND AUTHORITY

From the point of view of the integration theory of social structure, units of social analysis ("social systems") are essentially voluntary associations of people who share certain values and set up institutions in order to ensure the smooth functioning of cooperation. From the point of view of coercion theory, however, the units of social analysis present an altogether different picture. Here, it is not voluntary cooperation or general consensus but enforced constraint that makes social organizations cohere. In institutional terms, this means that in every social organization some positions are entrusted with a right to exercise control over other positions in order to ensure effective coercion; it means, in other words, that there is a differential distribution of power and authority. One of the central theses of this study consists in the assumption that this differential distribution of authority invariably becomes the determining factor of systematic social conflicts of a type that is germane to class conflicts in the traditional (Marxian) sense of this term. The structural origin of such group conflicts must be sought in the arrangement of social roles endowed with expectations of domination or subjection. Wherever there are such roles, group conflicts of the type in question are to be expected. Differentiation of groups engaged in such conflicts follows the lines of differentiation of roles that are relevant from the point of view of the exercise of authority. Identification of variously equipped authority roles is the first task of conflict analysis;[5] conceptually and empirically all further steps of analysis follow from the investigation of distributions of power and authority.

. . . So far as the terms "power" and "authority" and their distinction are concerned, I shall follow in this study the useful and well-considered definitions of Max Weber. . . . We say—as does Max Weber—that while power is merely a factual relation, authority is a legitimate relation of domination and subjection. In this sense, authority can be described as legitimate power.

In the present study we are concerned exclusively with relations of authority, for these alone are part of social structure and therefore permit the systematic derivation of group conflicts from the organization of total societies and associations within them. The significance of such group conflicts rests with the fact that they are not the product of structurally fortuitous relations of power but come forth wherever authority is exercised—and that means in all societies under all historical conditions. (1) Authority relations are always relations of super- and subordination. (2) Where there are authority relations, the superordinate element is socially expected to control, by orders and commands, warnings and prohibitions, the behavior of the subordinate element. (3) Such expectations attach to relatively permanent social positions rather than to the character of individuals; they are in this sense legitimate. (4) By virtue of this fact, they always involve specification of the persons subject to control and of the spheres within which control is permissible.[6]

Authority, as distinct from power, is never a relation of generalized control over others. (5) Authority being a legitimate relation, noncompliance with authoritative commands can be sanctioned; it is indeed one of the functions of the legal system (and of course of quasi-legal customs and norms) to support the effective exercise of legitimate authority.

Alongside the term "authority," we shall employ (and have employed) in this study the terms "domination" and "subjection." . . .

It seems desirable for purposes of conflict analysis to specify the relevant unit of social organization in analogy to the concept of social system in the analysis of integration. To speak of specification here is perhaps misleading. "Social system" is a very general concept applicable to all types of organization; and we shall want to employ an equally general concept which differs from that of social system by emphasizing a different aspect of the same organizations. It seems to me that Max Weber's category "imperatively coordinated association" (*Herrschaftsverband*) serves this purpose despite its clumsiness.[7] . . . In looking at social organizations not in terms of their integration and coherence but from the point of view of their structure of coercion and constraint, we regard them as (imperatively coordinated) associations rather than as social systems. Because social organizations are also associations, they generate conflicts of interest and become the birthplace of conflict groups.

I have assumed in the preceding remarks that authority is a characteristic of social organizations as general as society itself.

---

[5] To facilitate communication, I shall employ in this study a number of abbreviations. These must not however be misunderstood. Thus, "conflict analysis" in this context stands for "analysis of group conflicts of the class type, class being understood in the traditional sense." At no point do I want to imply a claim for a generalized theory of social conflict.

[6] This element of the definition of authority is crucial. It implies that the manager who tries to control people outside his firm, or the private lives of people inside his firm, trespasses the borderline between authority and power. Although he has authority over people in his firm, his control assumes the form of power as soon as it goes

beyond the specified persons and spheres of legitimate control. This type of trespassing is of course frequent in every authority relation; and an empirical phenomenon well worth investigating is to what extent the fusion of authority and power tends to intensify group conflicts.

[7] Parsons, in his translation of Weber's *Wirtschaft und Gesellschaft*, suggests "imperatively coordinated group." Any translation of Weber's term is bound to be somewhat awkward, but it seems to me that the word "group" in Parsons' translation is false. Weber uses *Verband*, e.g., to describe the state, or a church—units of organization which can hardly be called "groups." "Association" is probably as precise an English equivalent of *Verband* as is likely to be found.

Despite the assertion of Renner—and other modern sociologists—that in some contemporary societies the exercise of authority has been eliminated and replaced by the more anonymous "rule of the law" or other nonauthoritative relations, I should indeed maintain that authority is a universal element of social structure. It is in this sense more general than, for example, property, or even status. . . . Authority relations exist wherever there are people whose actions are subject to legitimate and sanctioned prescriptions that originate outside them but within social structure. This formulation, by leaving open who exercises what kind of authority, leaves little doubt as to the omnipresence of some kind of authority somehow exercised. For it is evident that there are many forms and types of authority in historical societies. There are differences of a considerable order of magnitude between the relations of the citizen of classical Athens and his slaves, the feudal landlord and his villeins and serfs, the nineteenth-century capitalist and his workers, the secretary of a totalitarian state party and its members, the appointed manager of a modern enterprise and its employees, or the elected prime minister of a democratic country and the electorate. No attempt will be made in this study to develop a typology of authority. But it is assumed throughout that the existence of domination and subjection is a common feature of all possible types of authority and, indeed, of all possible types of association and organization. . . .

It is certainly true that for many purposes of analysis, power or—as I should prefer to say—authority, both realizes and symbolizes the functional integration of social systems. To use a pertinent illustration: in many contexts, the elected president or prime minister of democratic countries represents his country as a whole; his position expresses therefore the unity and integration of a nation. In other contexts, however, the chief of government is but the representative of the majority party, and therefore exponent of sectional interests. I suggest that as in the position of the prime minister neither of these elements is primary or secondary, thus neither the integrative nor the disruptive aspect of authority in social analysis is primary or secondary.

Like all other elements of social structure, authority has two faces—those, so to speak, of Mills and of Parsons—and on the highest level of abstraction it is illegitimate to emphasize either of these to the exclusion of the other. Authority is certainly not *only* productive of conflict; but neither is it *only* (or even primarily) "a facility for the performance of function in and on behalf of the society as a sytem." If we are concentrating in this study on what Parsons would call the "negative functions" of authority, we do so because this aspect is more appropriate and useful for the analysis of structurally generated systematic social conflicts.

In referring to the ugly face of authority as a "zero-sum" concept, Parsons brings out one further aspect of this category which is essential for our considerations. By zero-sum, Parsons evidently means that from the point of view of the disruptive "functions" of authority there are two groups or aggregates of persons, of which one possesses authority to the extent to which the other one is deprived of it. This implies—for us, if not for Parsons—that in terms of the coercion theory of society we can always observe a dichotomy of positions in imperatively coordinated associations with respect to the distribution of authority. Parsons, in his critique of Mills, compares the distribution of authority to the distribution of wealth. It seems to me that this comparison is misleading. However unequally wealth may be distributed, there always is a continuum of possession ranging from the lowest to the highest rank. Wealth is not and cannot be conceived as a zero-sum concept. With respect to authority, however, a clear line can at least in theory be drawn between those who participate in its exercise in given associations and those who are subject to the authoritative commands of others. Our analysis of modern societies in later chapters will show that empirically it is not always easy to identify the border line between domination and subjection. Authority has not remained unaffected by the modern process of division of labor. But even here, groups or aggregates can be identified which do not participate in the exercise of authority other than by complying with given commands or prohibitions. Contrary to all criteria of social stratification, authority does not permit the construction of a scale. So-called hierarchies of authority (as displayed, for example, in organization charts) are in fact hierarchies of the "plus-side" of authority, i.e., of the differentiation of domination; but there is, in every association, also a "minus-side" consisting of those who are subjected to authority rather than participate in its exercise.

In two respects this analysis has to be specified, if not supplemented. First, for the individual incumbent of roles, domination in one association does not necessarily involve domination in all others to which he belongs, and subjection, conversely, in one association does not mean subjection in all. The dichotomy of positions of authority holds for specific associations only. In a democratic state, there are both mere voters and incumbents of positions of authority such as cabinet ministers, representatives, and higher civil servants. But this does not mean that the "mere voter" cannot be incumbent of a position of authority in a different context, say, in an industrial enterprise; conversely, a cabinet minister may be, in his church, a mere member, i.e., subject to the authority of others. Although empirically a certain correlation of the authority positions of individuals in different associations seems likely, it is by no means general and is in any case a matter of specific empirical conditions. It is at least possible, if not probable, that if individuals in a given society are ranked according to the sum total of their authority positions in all associations, the resulting pattern will not be a dichotomy but rather like scales of stratification according to income or prestige. For this reason it is necessary to emphasize that in the sociological analysis of group conflict the unit of analysis is always a specific association and the dichotomy of positions within it.

As with respect to the set of roles associated with an individual, total societies, also, do not usually present an unambiguously dichotomic authority structure. There are a large number of imperatively coordinated associations in any given society. Within every one of them we can distinguish the aggregates of those who dominate and those who are subjected. But since domination in industry does not necessarily involve domination in the state, or a church, or other associations, total societies can present the picture of a plurality of competing dominant (and, conversely, subjected) aggregates. This, again, is a problem for the analysis of specific historical societies and must not be confounded with the clearer lines of differentiation within any one association. Within the latter, the distribution of authority always sums up to zero, i.e, there always is a division involving domination and subjection.

I need hardly emphasize that from the point of view of "settling" the concepts of power and authority, the preceding discussion has raised more problems than it has solved. I believe, however, that for the purposes of this study, and of a sociological theory of conflict, little needs to be added to what has been stated here. In order somewhat to substantiate this perhaps rather bold assertion, it seems useful to recapitulate briefly the heuristic purpose and logical status of the considerations of this section.

I have introduced, as a structural determinant of conflict groups, the category of authority as exercised in imperatively coordinated associations. While agreeing with Marx that source and level of income—even socioeconomic status—cannot usefully be conceived as determinants of conflict groups, I have added to this list of erroneous approaches Marx's own in terms of property in the means of production. Authority is both a more general and a more significant social relation. The former has been shown in our critique of Marx; the latter will have to be demonstrated by subsequent considerations and analyses. The concept of authority is used, in this context, in a specific sense. It is differentiated from power by what may roughly be referred to as the element of legitimacy; and it has to be understood throughout in the restricted sense of authority as distributed and exercised in imperatively coordinated associations. While its "disruptive" or conflict-generating consequences are not the only aspect of authority, they are the one relevant in terms of the coercion model of society. Within the frame of reference of this model, (1) the distribution of authority in associations is the ultimate "cause" of the formation of conflict groups, and (2), being dichotomous, it is, in any given association, the cause of the formation of two, and only two, conflict groups.

The first of these statements is logically an assumption, since it underlies scientific theories. It cannot as such be tested by observation; its validity is proven, rather, by its usefulness for purposes of explanation. We shall derive from this assumption certain more specific hypotheses which, if refuted, would take the assumption with them into the waster-paper basket of scientific theories. We assume in this sense that if we manage to identify the incumbents of positions of domination and subjection in any given association, we have identified the contenders of one significant type of conflicts— conflicts which occur in this association at all times.

As to the second statement, the one concerned with the dichotomy of authority positions in imperatively coordinated associations, it is not, I suggest, either an assumption or an empirical hypothesis, but an analytical statement. It follows from and is implicit in the very concept of authority that within specified contexts some have authority and others not. If either nobody or everybody had authority, the concept would lose its meaning. Authority implies both domination and subjection, and it therefore implies the existence of two distinct sets of positions or persons. This is not to say, of course, that there is no difference between those who have a great deal and those who have merely a little authority. Among the positions of domination there may be, and often is, considerable differentiation. But such differentiation, while important for empirical analysis, leaves unaffected the existence of a border line somewhere between those who have whatever little authority and the "outs." Strictly speaking, an analytical statement which states that there is a dichotomy of authority positions is tautological; but as this example shows, there are tautologies which are worth stating. . . .

LATENT AND MANIFEST INTERESTS

The analytical process of conflict group formation can be described in terms of a model. Throughout, the categories employed in this model will be used in terms of the coercion theory of social structure. With this restriction in mind, the thesis that conflict groups are based on the dichotomous distribution of authority in imperatively coordinated associations can be conceived of as the basic assumption of the model. To this assumption we now add the proposition that differentially equipped authority positions in associations involve, for their incumbents, conflicting interests. The occupants of positions of domination and the occupants of positions of subjection hold, by virtue of these positions, certain interests which are contradictory in substance and direction.

. . . .

For purposes of the sociological analysis of conflict groups and group conflicts, it is necessary to assume certain structurally generated orientations of the actions of incumbents of defined positions. By analogy to conscious ("subjective") orientations of action, it appears justifiable to describe these as "interests." It has to be emphasized, however, that by so doing no assumption is implied about the substance of these interests or the consciousness and articulate orientation of the occupants of the positions in question.[8] The assumption of "objective" interests associated with social positions has no psychological implications or ramifications; it belongs to the level of sociological analysis proper.

CLASSES OR CONFLICT GROUPS?

. . . In my opinion, the problem of the applicability of the concept of class is a purely terminological problem. In positive terms, this means that it is in part a matter of arbitrary decision, and in part a matter of convenience. Logically, there is no reason why we should not call quasi-groups and interest groups classes or anything else. Pragmatically, of course, the usage and history of words has to be considered; it is unwise to provoke misunderstandings by choosing words which carry associations that are not intended.

. . . .

[8] This statement will be qualified below by the distinction of "latent" and "manifest interests." Strictly speaking, it holds for latent interests only.

It is hard to weigh the "pros and cons" ... entirely rationally; an element of personal preference will probably enter into any decision. Without trying to argue for this decision at any length, I will therefore state immediately that in my opinion the case in favor of retaining the concept of class is still sufficiently strong to warrant its application to even the most advanced industrial societies. This decision does involve, of course, a polemical stand against all those who "falsify" the term "class" by applying it to what should properly be called social strata. It also involves considerable extensions of the concept as it was used by Marx as well as by all Marxists and Marxians. But it emphasizes that in class analysis we are concerned (*a*) with systematic social conflicts and their structural origin, and (*b*) with but one specific type of such conflicts.

In terms of our model, the term "class" signifies conflict groups that are generated by the differential distribution of authority in imperatively coordinated associations. This definition implies no assumption as to the looseness or rigidity of their coherence, the presence or absence of a common culture or ideology (beyond specific interests) among their members, and the intensity or lack of intensity of their engagement in social conflicts. . . .

SOME PRINCIPLES OF STRATIFICATION

Kingsley Davis and Wilbert E. Moore

In a previous paper some concepts for handling the phenomena of social inequality

American Sociological Review, "Some Principles of Stratification," by Kingsley Davis and Wilbert E. Moore, Vol. 10, April, 1945. Reprinted by permission.

were presented.[1] In the present paper a further step in stratification theory is undertaken—an attempt to show the relationship between stratification and the rest of the social order.[2] Starting from the proposition that no society is "classless," or unstratified, an effort is made to explain, in functional terms, the universal necessity which calls forth stratification in any social system. Next, an attempt is made to explain the roughly uniform distribution of prestige as between the major types of positions in every society. Since, however, there occur between one society and another great differences in the degree and kind of stratification, some attention is also given to the varieties of social inequality and the variable factors that give rise to them.

Clearly, the present task requires two different lines of analysis—one to understand the universal, the other to understand the variable features of stratification. Naturally each line of inquiry aids the other and is indispensable, and in the treatment that follows the two will be interwoven, although, because of space limitations, the emphasis will be on the universals.

Throughout, it will be necessary to keep in mind one thing—namely, that the discussion relates to the system of positions, not to the individuals occupying those positions. It is one thing to ask why different positions carry different degrees of prestige, and quite another to ask how certain individuals get into those positions. Although, as the argument will try to show, both questions are related, it is essential to keep them separate in our thinking. Most of the literature on stratification has tried to answer the second question (particularly with regard to the ease or difficulty of mobility between strata) without tackling the first. The first question, however, is logically prior and, in the case of any particular individual or group, factually prior.

[1] Kingsley Davis, "A Conceptual Analysis of Stratification," *American Sociological Review.* 7: 309–321, June, 1942.

[2] The writers regret (and beg indulgence) that the present essay, a condensation of a longer study, covers so much in such short space that adequate evidence and qualification cannot be given and that as a result what is actually very tentative is presented in an unfortunately dogmatic manner.

THE FUNCTIONAL NECESSITY OF STRATIFICATION

Curiously, however, the main functional necessity explaining the universal presence of stratification is precisely the requirement faced by any society of placing and motivating individuals in the social structure. As a functioning mechanism a society must somehow distribute its members in social positions and induce them to perform the duties of these positions. It must thus concern itself with motivation at two different levels: to instill in the proper individuals the desire to fill certain positions, and, once in these positions, the desire to perform the duties attached to them. Even though the social order may be relatively static in form, there is a continuous process of metabolism as new individuals are born into it, shift with age, and die off. Their absorption into the positional system must somehow be arranged and motivated. This is true whether the system is competitive or non-competitive. A competitive system gives greater importance to the motivation to achieve positions, whereas a non-competitive system gives perhaps greater importance to the motivation to perform the duties of the positions; but in any system both types of motivation are required.

If the duties associated with the various positions were all equally pleasant to the human organism, all equally important to societal survival, and all equally in need of the same ability or talent, it would make no difference who got into which positions, and the problem of social placement would be greatly reduced. But actually it does make a great deal of difference who gets into which positions, not only because some positions are inherently more agreeable than others, but also because some require special talents or training and some are functionally more important than others. Also, it is essential that the duties of the positions be performed with the diligence that their importance requires. Inevitably, then, a society must have, first, some kind of rewards that it can use as inducements, and, second, some way of distributing these rewards differentially according to positions. The rewards and their distribution become a part of the social order, and thus give rise to stratification.

One may ask what kind of rewards a society has at its disposal in distributing its personnel and securing essential services. It has, first of all, the things that contribute to sustenance and comfort. It has, second, the things that contribute to humor and diversion. And it has, finally, the things that contribute to self respect and ego expansion. The last, because of the peculiarly social character of the self, is largely a function of the opinion of others, but it nonetheless ranks in importance with the first two. In any social system all three kinds of rewards must be dispensed differentially according to positions.

In a sense the rewards are "built into" the position. They consist in the "rights" associated with the position, plus what may be called its accompaniments or perquisites. Often the rights, and sometimes the accompaniments, are functionally related to the duties of the position. (Rights as viewed by the incumbent are usually duties as viewed by other members of the community.) However, there may be a host of subsidiary rights and perquisites that are not essential to the function of the position and have only an indirect and symbolic connection with its duties, but which still may be of considerable importance in inducing people to seek the positions and fulfill the essential duties.

If the rights and perquisites of different positions in a society must be unequal, then the society must be stratified, because that is precisely what stratification means. Social inequality is thus an unconsciously evolved device by which societies insure that the most important positions are conscientiously filled by the most qualified persons. Hence every society, no matter how simple or complex, must differentiate persons in terms of both prestige and esteem, and must therefore possess a certain amount of institutionalized inequality.

It does not follow that the amount or type of inequality need be the same in all societies. This is largely a function of factors that will be discussed presently.

THE TWO DETERMINANTS OF POSITIONAL RANK

Granting the general function that inequality subserves, one can specify the two factors that determine the relative rank of different positions. In general those positions convey the best reward, and hence have the highest rank, which (a) have the greatest importance for the society and (b) require the greatest training or talent. The first factor concerns function and is a matter of relative significance; the second concerns means and is a matter of scarcity.

Differential Functional Importance. Actually a society does not need to reward positions in proportion to their functional importance. It merely needs to give sufficient reward to them to insure that they will be filled competently. In other words, it must see that less essential positions do not compete successfully with more essential ones. If a position is easily filled, it need not be heavily rewarded, even though important. On the other hand, if it is important but hard to fill, the reward must be high enough to get it filled anyway. Functional importance is therefore a necessary but not a sufficient cause of high rank being assigned to a position.[3]

Differential Scarcity of Personnel. Practically all positions, no matter how acquired, require some form of skill or capacity for performance. This is implicit in the very notion of position, which implies that the incumbent must, by virtue of his incumbency, accomplish certain things.

[3] Unfortunately, functional importance is difficult to establish. To use the position's prestige to establish it, as is often unconsciously done, constitutes circular reasoning from our point of view. There are, however, two independent clues: (a) the degree to which a position is functionally unique, there being no other positions that can perform the same function satisfactorily; (b) the degree to which other positions are dependent on the one in question. Both clues are best exemplified in organized systems of positions built around one major function. Thus, in most complex societies the religious, political, economic, and educational functions are handled by distinct structures not easily interchangeable. In addition, each structure possesses many different positions, some clearly dependent on, if not subordinate to, others. In sum, when an institutional nucleus becomes differentiated around one main function, and at the same time organizes a large portion of the population into its relationships, the *key* positions in it are of the highest functional importance. The absence of such specialization does not prove functional unimportance, for the whole society may be relatively unspecialized; but it is safe to assume that the more important functions receive the first and clearest structural differentiation.

There are, ultimately, only two ways in which a person's qualifications come about: through inherent capacity or through training. Obviously, in concrete activities both are always necessary, but from a practical standpoint the scarcity may lie primarily in one or the other, as well as in both. Some positions require innate talents of such high degree that the persons who fill them are bound to be rare. In many cases, however, talent is fairly abundant in the population but the training process is so long, costly, and elaborate that relatively few can qualify. Modern medicine, for example, is within the mental capacity of most individuals, but a medical education is so burdensome and expensive that virtually none would undertake it if the position of the M.D. did not carry a reward commensurate with the sacrifice.

If the talents required for a position are abundant and the training easy, the method of acquiring the position may have little to do with its duties. There may be, in fact, a virtually accidental relationship. But if the skills required are scarce by reason of the rarity of talent or the costliness of training, the position, if functionally important, must have an attractive power that will draw the necessary skills in competition with other positions. This means, in effect, that the position must be high in the social scale—must command great prestige, high salary, ample leisure, and the like.

How Variations Are to Be Understood. In so far as there is a difference between one system of stratification and another, it is attributable to whatever factors affect the two determinants of differential reward—namely, functional importance and scarcity of personnel. Positions important in one society may not be important in another, because the conditions faced by the societies, or their degree of internal development, may be different. The same conditions, in turn, may affect the question of scarcity; for in some societies the stage of development, or the external situation, may wholly obviate the necessity of certain kinds of skill or talent. Any particular system of stratification, then, can be understood as a product of the special conditions affecting the two aforementioned grounds of differential reward.

MAJOR SOCIETAL FUNCTIONS AND STRATIFICATION

Religion. The reason why religion is necessary is apparently to be found in the fact that human society achieves its unity primarily through the possession by its members of certain ultimate values and ends in common. Although these values and ends are subjective, they influence behavior, and their integration enables the society to operate as a system. Derived neither from inherited nor from external nature, they have evolved as a part of culture by communication and moral pressure. They must, however, appear to the members of the society to have some reality, and it is the role of religious belief and ritual to supply and reinforce this appearance of reality. Through belief and ritual the common ends and values are connected with an imaginary world symbolized by concrete sacred objects, which world in turn is related in a meaningful way to the facts and trials of the individual's life. Through the worship of the sacred objects and the beings they symbolize, and the acceptance of supernatural prescriptions that are at the same time codes of behavior, a powerful control over human conduct is exercised, guiding it along lines sustaining the institutional structure and conforming to the ultimate ends and values.

If this conception of the role of religion is true, one can understand why in every known society the religious activities tend to be under the charge of particular persons, who tend thereby to enjoy greater rewards than the ordinary societal member. Certain of the rewards and special privileges may attach to only the highest religious functionaries, but others usually apply, if such exists, to the entire sacerdotal class.

Moreover, there is a peculiar relation between the duties of the religious official and the special privileges he enjoys. If the supernatural world governs the destinies of men more ultimately than does the real world, its earthly representative, the person through whom one may communicate with the supernatural, must be a powerful individual. He is a keeper of sacred tradition, a skilled performer of the ritual, and an interpreter of lore and myth. He is in such close contact with the gods that he is viewed as possessing some of their characteristics. He is, in short,

a bit sacred, and hence free from some of the more vulgar necessities and controls.

It is no accident, therefore, that religious functionaries have been associated with the very highest positions of power, as in theocratic regimes. Indeed, looking at it from this point of view, one may wonder why it is that they do not get *entire* control over their societies. The factors that prevent this are worthy of note.

In the first place, the amount of technical competence necessary for the performance of religious duties is small. Scientific or artistic capacity is not required. Anyone can set himself up as enjoying an intimate relation with deities, and nobody can successfully dispute him. Therefore, the factor of scarcity of personnnel does not operate in the technical sense.

One may assert, on the other hand, that religious ritual is often elaborate and religious lore abstruse, and that priestly ministrations require tact, if not intelligence. This is true, but the technical requirements of the profession are for the most part adventitious, not related to the end in the same way that science is related to air travel. The priest can never be free from competition, since the criteria of whether or not one has genuine contact with the supernatural are never strictly clear. It is this competition that debases the priestly position below what might be expected at first glance. That is why priestly prestige is highest in those societies where membership in the profession is rigidly controlled by the priestly guild itself. That is why, in part at least, elaborate devices are utilized to stress the identification of the person with his office—spectacular costume, abnormal conduct, special diet, segregated residence, celibacy, conspicuous leisure, and the like. In fact, the priest is always in danger of becoming somewhat discredited—as happens in a secularized society—because in a world of stubborn fact, ritual and sacred knowledge alone will not grow crops or build houses. Furthermore, unless he is protected by a professional guild, the priest's identification with the supernatural tends to preclude his acquisition of abundant wordly goods.

As between one society and another it seems that the highest general position awarded the priest occurs in the medieval type of social order. Here there is enough economic production to afford a surplus, which can be used to support a numerous and highly organized priesthood; and yet the populace is unlettered and therefore credulous to a high degree. Perhaps the most extreme example is to be found in the Buddhism of Tibet, but others are encountered in the Catholicism of feudal Europe, the Inca regime of Peru, the Brahminism of India, and the Mayan priesthood of Yucatan. On the other hand, if the society is so crude as to have no surplus and little differentiation, so that every priest must be also a cultivator or hunter, the separation of the priestly status from the others has hardly gone far enough for priestly prestige to mean much. When the priest actually has high prestige under these circumstances, it is because he also performs other important functions (usually political and medical).

In an extremely advanced society built on scientific technology, the priesthood tends to lose status, because sacred tradition and supernaturalism drop into the background. The ultimate values and common ends of the society tend to be expressed in less anthropomorphic ways, by officials who occupy fundamentally political, economic, or educational rather than religious positions. Nevertheless, it is easily possible for intellectuals to exaggerate the degree to which priesthood in a presumably secular milieu has lost prestige. When the matter is closely examined the urban proletariat, as well as the rural citizenry, proves to be surprisingly god-fearing and priest-ridden. No society has become so completely secularized as to liquidate entirely the belief in transcendental ends and supernatural entities. Even in a secularized society some system must exist for the integration of ultimate values, for their ritualistic expression, and for the emotional adjustments required by disappointment, death, and disaster.

Government. Like religion, government plays a unique and indispensable part in society, But in contrast to religion, which provides integration in terms of sentiments, belief, and rituals, it organizes the society in terms of law and authority. Furthermore, it orients the society to the actual rather than the unseen world.

The main functions of government are, internally, the ultimate enforcement of norms, the final arbitration of conflicting interests, and the overall planning and direction of society; and externally, the handling of war and diplomacy. To carry out these functions it acts as the agent of the entire people, enjoys a monopoly of force, and controls all individuals within its territory.

Political action, by definition, implies authority. An official can command because he has authority, and the citizen must obey because he is subject to that authority. For this reason stratification is inherent in the nature of political relationships.

So clear is the power embodied in political position that political inequality is sometimes thought to comprise all inequality. But it can be shown that there are other bases of stratification, that the following controls operate in practice to keep political power from becoming complete: (a) The fact that the actual holders of political office, and especially those determining top policy must necessarily be few in number compared to the total population. (b) The fact that the rulers represent the interest of the group rather than of themselves, and are therefore restricted in their behavior by rules and mores designed to enforce this limitation of interest. (c) The fact that the holder of political office has his authority by virtue of his office and nothing else, and therefore any special knowledge, talent, or capacity he may claim is purely incidental, so that he often has to depend upon others for technical assistance.

In view of these limiting factors, it is not strange that the rulers often have less power and prestige than a literal enumeration of their formal rights would lead one to expect.

Wealth, Property, and Labor. Every position that secures for its incumbent a livelihood is, by definition, economically rewarded. For this reason there is an economic aspect to those positions (e.g., political and religious) the main function of which is not economic. It therefore becomes convenient for the society to use unequal economic returns as a principal means of controlling the entrance of persons into positions and stimulating the performance of their duties. The amount of the economic return therefore becomes one of the main indices of social status.

It should be stressed, however, that a position does not bring power and prestige *because* it draws a high income. Rather, it draws a high income because it is functionally important and the available personnel is for one reason or another scarce. It is therefore superficial and erroneous to regard high income as the cause of a man's power and prestige, just as it is erroneous to think that a man's fever is the cause of his disease.[4]

The economic source of power and prestige is not income primarily, but the ownership of capital goods (including patents, good will, and professional reputation). Such ownership should be distinguished from the possession of consumers' goods, which is an index rather than a cause of social standing. In other words, the ownership of producers' goods is, properly speaking, a source of income like other positions, the income itself remaining an index. Even in situations where social values are widely commercialized and earnings are the readiest method of judging social position, income does not confer prestige on a position so much as it induces people to compete for the position. It is true that a man who has a high income as a result of one position may find this money helpful in climbing into another position as well, but this again reflects the effect of his initial, economically advantageous status, which exercises its influence through the medium of money.

In a system of private property in productive enterprise, an income above what an individual spends can give rise to possession of capital wealth. Presumably such possession is a reward for the proper management of one's finances originally and of the productive enterprise later. But as social differentiation becomes highly advanced and yet the institution of inheritance persists, the phenomenon of pure ownership, and reward for pure ownership, emerges. In such a case it is difficult to prove that the position

is functionally important or that the scarcity involved is anything other than extrinsic and accidental. It is for this reason, doubtless, that the institution of private property in productive goods becomes more subject to criticism as social development proceeds toward industrialization. It is only this pure, that is, strictly legal and functionless ownership, however, that is open to attack; for some form of active ownership, whether private or public, is indispensable.

One kind of ownership of production goods consists in rights over the labor of others. The most extremely concentrated and exclusive of such rights are found in slavery, but the essential principle remains in serfdom, peonage, encomienda, and indenture. Naturally this kind of ownership has the greatest significance for stratification, because it necessarily entails an unequal relationship.

But property in capital goods inevitably introduces a compulsive element even into the nominally free contractual relationship. Indeed, in some respects the authority of the contractual employer is greater than that of the feudal landlord, inasmuch as the latter is more limited by traditional reciprocities. Even the classical economics recognized that competitors would fare unequally, but it did not pursue this fact to its necessary conclusion that, however it might be acquired, unequal control of goods and services must give unequal advantage to the parties to a contract.

Technical Knowledge. The function of finding means to single goals, without any concern with the choice between goals, is the exclusively technical sphere. The explanation of why positions requiring great technical skill receive fairly high rewards is easy to see, for it is the simplest case of the rewards being so distributed as to draw talent and motivate training. Why they seldom if ever receive the highest rewards is also clear: the importance of technical knowledge from a societal point of view is never so great as the integration of goals, which takes place on the religious, political, and economic levels. Since the technological level is concerned solely with means, a purely technical position must ultimately be subordinate to other positions that are religious, political, or economic in character.

---

[4] The symbolic rather than intrinsic role of income in social stratification has been succinctly summarized by Talcott Parsons, "An Analytical Approach to the Theory of Social Stratification," *American Journal of Sociology.* 45:841–862, May, 1940.

Nevertheless, the distinction between expert and layman in any social order is fundamental, and cannot be entirely reduced to other terms. Methods of recruitment, as well as of reward, sometimes lead to the erroneous interpretation that technical positions are economically determined. Actually, however, the acquisition of knowledge and skill cannot be accomplished by purchase, although the opportunity to learn may be. The control of the avenues of training may inhere as a sort of property right in certain families or classes, giving them power and prestige in consequence. Such a situation adds an artificial scarcity to the natural scarcity of skills and talents. On the other hand, it is possible for an opposite situation to arise. The rewards of technical position may be so great that a condition of excess supply is created, leading to at least temporary devaluation of the rewards. Thus "unemployment in the learned professions" may result in a debasement of the prestige of those positions. Such adjustments and readjustments are constantly occurring in changing societies; and it is always well to bear in mind that the efficiency of a stratified structure may be affected by the modes of recruitment for positions. The social order itself, however, sets limits to the inflation or deflation of the prestige of experts: an over-supply tends to debase the rewards and discourage recruitment or produce revolution, whereas an under-supply tends to increase the rewards or weaken the society in competition with other societies.

Particular systems of stratification show a wide range with respect to the exact position of technically competent persons. This range is perhaps most evident in the degree of specialization. Extreme division of labor tends to create many specialists without high prestige since the training is short and the required native capacity relatively small. On the other hand it also tends to accentuate the high position of the true experts— scientists, engineers, and administrators— by increasing their authority relative to other functionally important positions. But the idea of a technocratic social order or a government or priesthood of engineers or social scientists neglects the limitations of knowledge and skills as a basic for performing special functions. To the extent that the social structure is truly specialized the prestige of the technical person must also be circumscribed.

VARIATION IN STRATIFIED SYSTEMS

The generalized principles of stratification here suggested form a necessary preliminary to a consideration of types of stratified systems, because it is in terms of these principles that the types must be described. This can be seen by trying to delineate types according to certain modes of variation. For instance, some of the most important modes (together with the polar types in terms of them) seem to be as follows:

(*a*) *The Degree of Specialization.* The degree of specialization affects the fineness and multiplicity of the gradations in power and prestige. It also influences the extent to which particular functions may be emphasized in the invidious system, since a given function cannot receive much emphasis in the hierarchy until it has achieved structural separation from the other functions. Finally, the amount of specialization influences the bases of selection. Polar types: *Specialized, Unspecialized.*

(*b*) *The Nature of the Functional Emphasis.* In general when emphasis is put on sacred matters, a rigidity is introduced that tends to limit specialization and hence the development of technology. In addition, a brake is placed on social mobility, and on the development of bureaucracy. When the preoccupation with the sacred is withdrawn, leaving greater scope for purely secular preoccupations, a great development, and rise in status, of economic and technological positions seemingly takes place. Curiously, a concomitant rise in political position is not likely, because it has usually been allied with the religious and stands to gain little by the decline of the latter. It is also possible for a society to emphasize family functions—as in relatively undifferentiated societies where high mortality requires high fertility and kinship forms the main basis of social organization. Main types: *Familistic, Authoritarian* (*Theocratic* or sacred, and *Totalitarian* or secular), *Capitalistic.*

(*c*) *The Magnitude of Invidious Differences.* What may be called the amount of social distance between positions, taking into account the entire scale, is something that should lend itself to quantitative measurement. Considerable differences apparently exist between different societies in this regard, and also between parts of the same society. Polar types: *Equalitarian, Inequalitarian*.

(*d*) *The Degree of Opportunity.* The familiar question of the amount of mobility is different from the question of the comparative equality or inequality of rewards posed above, because the two criteria may vary independently up to a point. For instance, the tremendous divergences in monetary income in the United States are far greater than those found in primitive societies, yet the equality of opportunity to move from one rung to the other in the social scale may also be greater in the United States than in a hereditary tribal kingdom. Polar types: *Mobile* (open), *Immobile*, (closed).

(*e*) *The Degree of Stratum Solidarity.* Again, the degree of "class solidarity" (or the presence of specific organizations to promote class interests) may vary to some extent independently of the other criteria, and hence is an important principle in classifying systems of stratification. Polar types: *Class organized, Class unorganized*.

EXTERNAL CONDITIONS

What state any particular system of stratification is in with reference to each of these modes of variation depends on two things: (1) its state with reference to the other ranges of variation, and (2) the conditions outside the system of stratification which nevertheless influence that system. Among the latter are the following:

(*a*) *The Stage of Cultural Development.* As the cultural heritage grows, increased specialization becomes necessary, which in turn contributes to the enhancement of mobility, a decline of stratum solidarity, and a change of functional emphasis.

(*b*) *Situation with Respect to Other Societies.* The presence or absence of open conflict with other societies, of free trade relations or cultural diffusion, all influence the class structure to some extent. A chronic state of warfare tends to place emphasis upon the military functions, especially when the opponents are more or less equal. Free

trade, on the other hand, strengthens the hand of the trader at the expense of the warrior and priest. Free movement of ideas generally has an equalitarian effect. Migration and conquest create special circumstances.

(*c*) *Size of the Society.* A small society limits the degree to which functional specialization can go, the degree of segregation of different strata, and the magnitude of inequality.

COMPOSITE TYPES

Much of the literature on stratification has attempted to classify concrete systems into a certain number of types. This task is deceptively simple, however, and should come at the end of an analysis of elements and principles, rather than at the beginning. If the preceding discussion has any validity it indicates that there are a number of modes of variation between different systems, and that any one system is a composite of the society's status with reference to all these modes of variation. The danger of trying to classify whole societies under such rubrics as *caste, feudal,* or *open class* is that one or two criteria are selected and others ignored, the result being an unsatisfactory solution to the problem posed. The present discussion has been offered as a possible approach to the more systematic classification of composite types.

SOME NOTES ON THE FUNCTIONAL THEORY OF STRATIFICATION

Wlodzimierz Wesolowski

One might be tempted to find many reasons for the length and pertinacity of discussion aroused by the articles of K. Davis and W. Moore. No doubt one reason would be the

Reprinted from *The Polish Sociological Bulletin*, No. 3–4 (5–6), (1962), pp. 28–38, by permission of the author and the publisher.

abbreviated and abstract form in which the theory is presented, making it subject to various interpretations, as well as the "ideological overtone" attached to it. In my view, however, the most important reason for the length of discussion is the importance of the problem itself.

In the form in which it was presented in the *American Sociological Review*,[1] the theory would seem to contain three main assertions:

1. Social stratification (uneven distribution of material rewards and of prestige) is functionally necessary and is therefore a universal and permanent feature of society;
2. Stratification is functionally necessary because every society needs a mechanism inducing people to occupy positions which are socially important and require training; material rewards and prestige act as stimuli towards the occupation of such positions;
3. The existence of the above mechanism ensures that "the most important positions are conscientiously filled by the most qualified persons" ("the most qualified" here means: the ablest and best trained).

During the discussion following the articles,[2] and even earlier (in K. Davis'

[1] K. Davis, "A Conceptual Analysis of Stratification," *American Sociological Review*, Vol. 7, 1942, No. 3; K. Davis and W. Moore, "Some Principles of Stratification," *American Sociological Review*, Vol. 10, 1945, No. 2.

[2] M. M. Tumin, "Some Principles of Stratification: A Critical Analysis," *American Sociological Review*, Vol. 18, 1953, No. 4; K. Davis and W. Moore, "Reply and Comment," *American Sociological Review*, Vol. 18, 1953, No. 4; M. M. Tumin, "Reply to K. Davis," *American Sociological Review*, Vol. 18, 1953, No. 6. Among the large number of contributions to the discussion, the following should be especially noted: W. Buckley, "Social Stratification and the Functional Theory of Social Differentiation," *American Sociological Review*, Vol. 23, 1958, No. 3; D. H. Wrong, "The Functional Theory of Stratification: Some Neglected Considerations," *American Sociological Review*, Vol. 24, 1959, No. 6. The theory is also discussed in the following books: J. F. Cuber and W. F. Kenkel, *Social Stratification in the United States*, New York, 1954; J. A. Kahl, *The American Class Structure*, New York, 1957; M. M. Gordon, *Social Class in American Society*, North Carolina 1958; L. Reissman, *Class in American Society*, Glencoe 1959.

book, *Human Society*), the third assertion, suggesting the "perfection" of this social mechanism of selection, was withdrawn by the authors owing to its blatant inconsistency with many sociological facts. Attention was drawn to the fact that the occurrence of cases where (1) status is ascribed, (2) status is "prepared" by the position and efforts of the parents, and (3) the status and career of the individual are influenced by various group and clique determinants, means that (a) not all those who have equal ability have equal opportunity to acquire training, (b) not all those who are equal in training have equal opportunity to occupy positions bringing high prestige and income. For these reasons I shall not deal with the third assertion.[3] I should like, however, to make some comment on the first two assertions, which seem to me the core of the theory.

These assertions are concerned not so much with the system of selection, as with the system of motivation. When the third assertion is rejected, the theory asserts only that if positions which are important and require training are to be filled, then they must provide greater prestige and higher income; otherwise no-one would bother to train himself to fill them. Nevertheless, the theory does not say that everyone occupies a position suitable to his talents and, his training. There are some people who, although capable, had no chance to acquire a training. There are others, who, although trained, had no opportunity to gain high positions. But the very fact that there is differentiation of prestige and differentiation of income nevertheless acts as a stimulus encouraging people to make the effort to win a higher position.

The central point of the theory, then, is the hypothesis concerning motivation. According to this hypothesis, the striving for high income and high prestige is an indispensable and principal motive which drives people to make the effort to occupy positions which are important and require training. It is this assertion which will be the subject of our comment. Before we come to

[3] The present author discusses this at greater length in an article: "Davis' and Moore's Functional Theory of Stratification," *Studia Socjologiczne*, 1962, No. 4.

this, however, a certain concept which is used in the theory calls for explanation. This is the concept of "importance" of position.

" Importance " of position. According to this theory, greater prestige and greater material rewards give positions which have greater importance for society and require greater training or talent. It is more or less clear what the authors mean by "training or talent." In this article I will take training into account and by it I will mean education (general and specific) which in modern industrial society is the chief means of attaining basic knowledge and skill required for most highly valued jobs (e.g., doctor, lawyer, engineer).[4] It is less clear, however, what should be regarded as making importance of position. Here we are left to our own suppositions and interpretation.

The authors write: "Unfortunately, functional importance is difficult to establish. To use the position's prestige to establish it, as is often unconsciously done, constitutes circular reasoning from our point of view. There are, however, two independent clues: (a) the degree to which a position is functionally unique, there being no other positions that can perform the same function satisfactorily; (b) the degree to which other positions are dependent on the one in question. Both clues are best exemplified in organized systems of positions built round one major function. Thus, in most complex societies the religious, political, economic, and educational functions are handled by distinct structures not easily interchangeable. In addition, each structure possesses many different positions, some clearly dependent on, if not subordinate to, others. In sum, when an in-

stitutional nucleus becomes differentiated around one main function, and at the same time organizes a large portion of the population into its relationships, the key positions in it are of the highest functional importance."[5]

Let us examine these assertions.

As "functionally unique" (see point *a* above) one can regard those positions that call for specific training. The "specific" character of this training and talent may consist in its "quality" or "quantity." The training of a doctor and of an engineer are qualitatively different and yet quantitatively similar (high educational level). Likewise, the training of a fitter in a factory and that of a nurse are qualitatively different, yet quantitatively similar.

The engineer cannot be replaced in his duties by the doctor; neither can the fitter be replaced by the nurse. Owing to their different "qualitative" training, both the doctor and engineer are equally "irreplaceable." Likewise with the fitter and the nurse. On the "horizontal" plane, therefore, it would be difficult to find differences in extent of "irreplaceability" between the various occupations. Such differences can only be found in the "vertical" plane. The doctor is more irreplaceable than the nurse because he can carry out the nurse's duties (although less efficiently), but the nurse cannot carry out the doctor's duties. Similarly, it would be easier for the engineer to carry out the duties of the fitter, than for the fitter to carry out the duties of the engineer; and easier for the manager to carry out the clerk's duties than the clerk to carry out the duties of the manager. Thus those occupational positions which call for higher specialized training (in industrial societies it means chiefly higher education) are more "irreplaceable." Thus the first clue indicating the "functional importance" of a position does not seem to contribute any new element to the theory, since the role of training is mentioned as the first determinant of the height of position (besides "functional importance" as the second determinant).

But the second clue indicating "functional

---

[4] Attention given here to the training and not to the talent seems to me in accordance with the main features of the theory under discussion since it is dealing with the mechanism of motivation to attain the positions that require training. This attention is also justified by the author's assertions that: (*a*) gaining the doctor's training is in capacity of anyone with average talent (the same is probably true about lawyer, engineer and many other occupations); (*b*) in cases of many occupations talents are fairly abundant in the population, but only training is long and costly. One can add also that even the artistic occupations in which inborn talents play a greater role, demand today not only talents but training.

[5] K. Davis and W. Moore, "Some Principles of Stratification," *American Sociological Review*, Vol. 10, 1945, No. 2, p. 243, footnote 3.

importance" (mentioned in point *b*) does seem to introduce a new element. Explanations given by Davis and Moore suggest that the second factor determining the functional importance of position is authority. For—according to them—those positions are important, which other positions are subordinate to, or which they depend on; formulated differently, they are "key positions." Examples given by the authors point to the highest positions in hierarchic structures of social institutions.[6]

The above analysis leads us to the conclusion that, according to this theory, unequal distribution of material advantages and prestige is needed to make people train for positions requiring higher occupational skills and, perhaps, positions of high occupational skill and of authority. A good example of the first position is the position of a medical doctor; examples of the second would be the position of a business executive or of a general.

The Mechanism of Motivation. The authors regard their theory as being universally applicable to all known societies throughout history. But this is a view which is easy to disprove. It is very doubtful, for example, if ever differences of prestige and differences of income were "functionally necessary" for the filling of positions in stabilized societies where statuses were ascribed. And it should be remembered that societies of this type have been predominant throughout by far the greater part of history.

But the theory does seem to grasp the essential connections which occur in societies where statuses are achieved. This would appear to be the reason for the great liveliness of discussion on the articles by Davis

[6] Authority is a kind of power—"institutionalized" power. Authority belongs to a person who as a result of his position in some institutional structure has the right to issue orders to other people who also occupy a position in that structure. These orders are carried out because of the customs or laws concerning the functioning of the structure as a whole. In any modern organization (industrial or political), the hierarchy of positions is the simplest example of the hierarchical system of positions in which authority, as here understood, is to be found. See R. Bierstedt, "An Analysis of Social Power," *American Sociological Review*, Vol. 15, 1950, No. 6.

and Moore. For modern industrial societies —both capitalist and socialist—are societies with achieved statuses. And in these societies are to be found many facts confirming the existence of the motivational mechanism described by the authors of this theory. The question arises, therefore, whether the theory holds good for all industrial societies where there is far-reaching division of labour and where statuses are attainable.

In Davis' and Moore's theory, it is this problem which is of the greatest interest. It seems possible, however, that a number of weighty theoretical arguments, as well as certain factual data, can be brought up against the theory.

SOME GENERAL ARGUMENTS

The main theoretical argument against Davis' and Moore's conception is that their theory contains three erroneous assumptions. These are concerned with (*a*) the human nature, (*b*) the pattern of society, (*c*) the structure of values.

It has already been pointed out that in many respects Davis' and Moore's theory recalls the classical theory of political economy, for example its implicitly assumed conception of unchanging "human nature." According to Davis and Moore, human nature is characterized, on the one hand by a drive towards personal advantages, and on the other by laziness. In a society where human nature is such, then stratification (the unequal distribution of material rewards and prestige) is an unavoidable necessity if important positions requiring training are to be filled properly. It must be said, however, that whereas such a concept of human nature has not yet completely disappeared from the economic text-books, it does not occur at all in modern text-books of sociology, psychology, or cultural anthropology. In fact is may be said that the psychological content of Davis' and Moore's theory is inconsistent with modern theory of social psychology.

Here is what T. Newcomb says on this very subject: "Many motives which we, as members of our own society, think of as being part of human nature, are by no means dependable the world over. Motives of wanting prestige, wanting to be free from the dominance of authority of others, jealousy in love relationships as well as motives of acquiring property, seem utterly natural to us. They are, in fact, fairly dependable in large sections of American society. Their dependability rests, however, upon the dependability of the cultural conditions under which they are acquired. They may, perhaps, be said to represent 'contemporary middle-class American nature,' but they do not correspond to anything dependable in human nature" (dependable = universal).[7]

The statement that the motives of people's behaviour depend on the type of culture in which they were brought up in and in which they live is today universally accepted by sociologists, social anthropologists, and social psychologists. The same is true of the thesis that motives of behaviour are affected by two essential elements in any culture— the system of values and the objective living conditions.[8]

It can be said that each culture has its own specific values. But it is possible to hold a less extreme view, that certain cultures have similar, or even identical, sets of accepted values, but that these cultures differ from each other in the importance they attach to the various values. In other words, they differ as to the position of the various values in the structure of values as a whole. Both in the first and in the second case it is at least theoretically possible to have a culture in which the motive of personal material advantage and prestige is not one of the fundamental motives of human behaviour, not one of the fundamental motives underlying choice of occupation and job training (or, as a result, choice of social position).

I should like to put forward the hypothesis that in industrial societies which differ in their social organization (e.g., capitalist societies and socialist societies), it is possible that at least the inner structure of their system of values differs. The difference in this structure may consist not only of the different "weight" given to the diverse

values in their whole system, but perhaps in the different "character" of the separate values.

Some values may be recognized as desirable because they themselves represent something desired; others may be recognized because they are a good means of attaining some other values. According to Davis and Moore, in the motivation of individuals education (knowledge, skill) and authority occur as values which are means of attaining the other values, material reward and prestige. In my opinion, the relationship between the values education and authority, and material reward and prestige, may be different. I also think that the striving for education or the striving for authority may be the chief motives of human behavior. Generally speaking, there is not any fixed constellation of values in their division between values-means and values-ends: there is not any universally pursued end-value either.

In Davis' and Moore's theory not only is it assumed that the motivation of the human individual is unchanging. It also assumes a certain unchanging "pattern" of society, or at least it assumes that some of the characteristics of that society are universal and permanent (this pattern again reminds us of classical political economy). If the authors assert that unequal distribution of material goods and of prestige must exist because otherwise people would not take the trouble to prepare for positions requiring training, then they assume that the acquisition of training is a matter of individual choice and effort, and that the acquisition of training also demands a certain amount of sacrifice. They also assume an insufficiency of products, the unequal distribution of these products according to position, and an insufficiency of trained personnel.

But other patterns of industrial societies are also possible. This may be illustrated by certain trends in the socialist countries or the *kibbutz* in Israel, although certain tendencies towards change can also be observed in contemporary capitalist societies. Trends towards the planned training and employment of qualified cadres, or towards the award of scholarships which relieve parents of the cost of educating their

---

[7] T. M. Newcomb, *Social Psychology,* New York, 1950, p. 137.

[8] Cf. J. W. Atkinson (Ed.), *Motives in Fantasy, Action and Society. A Method of Assessment and Study.* Part V. "Motivation and Society."

children, are becoming more and more marked in the modern world, especially in the socialist countries, but in the capitalist countries as well.

MATERIAL ADVANTAGES

The values which drive people to acquire a training are material advantage and prestige. Both occur together in Davis' and Moore's theory. But they are separate values. They should therefore be examined separately. Let us first deal with material advantages.

Let us assume the existence of a society with the following attributes: (*a*) income differences are small, and the basic needs of most families are met; (*b*) education is assured without any sacrifice either on the part of the parent or of the child; the level of education of the community as a whole is relatively high; (*c*) the dominant ideas in the system of values are equality, social service, education and full development of personality.

In such a society, even where certain differences of income exist according to qualifications, it is possible that material advantages are not the main stimulus to education and training. Although the differences in material advantages exist, they may not result in significant differences in the standard of living. The system of values may not attach much importance to these differences, whereas the desire for full development of personality, and awakened interest in learning may make the desire to acquire education suiting the person's talents the principal motive for acquiring training. Education (knowledge, skill) which in Davis' and Moore's theory are values that are a means to an end, may in themselves become ends.

Certain elements in the situation described above are to be found in some contemporary societies. For example, in Poland (and similarly in Norway) there has been a distinct curtailment of the range of income. In Poland free education is open to all. At the same time, in propaganda more and more emphasis is being placed on education. Education, as some researches show, is very high on the scale of values accepted by the people for our country. Egalitarianism also has wide support—

both in the sphere of postulates and in everyday behaviour.[9]

Like education, "authority" may appear as a value in itself and not as a means to an end. We assumed that, in Davis' and Moore's theory, material advantage and prestige are regarded as rewards for those who occupy positions of authority. But authority itself may be such a reward. Max Weber and Harold Lasswell wrote of this convincingly. In this connection it is worth noting that in industrial societies planning, and the general organizing of society, is becoming more common. In such a situation positions of authority provide an immense opportunity for the individual to express his own personality, his talents and ideas, quite apart from the opportunity such an individual has of satisfying his thirst for power, his desire to direct others.

Examples may be given illustrating the high value placed on authority by many people, even if it is not accompanied by material advantage or prestige. In present day conditions in Poland the factory foreman would seem to provide a good example. Neither in earnings nor in prestige is he superior to those under his authority. But the very fact that a foreman does have people under him is one of the assets of such a position, even although in other respects it does not stand very high.

Thus it seems quite possible to have an industrial society in which the differentiation of material advantages is not a "functional necessity." Positions calling for education and training, as well as positions of authority, may be filled not because they offer material advantages, but because their

[9] Cf. W. Wesołowski and A. Sarapata, "Hierarchia zawodów i stanowisk" ["Hierarchy of Jobs and Occupations"], *Studia Socjologiczne* 1961, No. 2. In recent research carried out in Łódź by Dr. A. Sarapata, 50% of the respondents replied "No" when asked if some occupations were more important than others—which should be regarded as a sign of an egalitarian attitude. In a new survey carried out by the present author on a sample of the rural population throughout Poland, the respondents were asked what should be the difference between incomes. About 65% declared that differences of income should be small. When asked who should earn more than the others, the majority of the respondents said "people whose work is the hardest."

principal attributes—skill, knowledge and power—prove to be sufficiently attractive. Those values, which in Davis' and Moore's theory are treated as intermediate values, may appear as end-values.

PRESTIGE

As in the case when we analysed income differentiation, likewise in the case of prestige differentiation must we distinguish between: (*a*) the very existence of such differentiation, and (*b*) the role it fulfils as a stimulus for the occupation of "important positions requiring training." From the empirical point of view, such a differentiation may turn out to be extremely difficult; from the point of view of analysis, however, it is extremely important.

If differences of prestige were to be eliminated entirely, then we would have to have such a system of values in which "equality" would be a value completely outweighing all the other values (probably this would also necessitate the complete disappearance of differences in income, education, power and other social attributes). Even if we take it that egalitarian values are growing in favour and that more practical steps are being taken towards ensuring objective equality between people one can hardly imagine that a world without differences of prestige is imminent.

Yet the very fact that differences of prestige exist does not mean that Davis and Moore are right. For their theory states that prestige must occur as one of the main motives leading people to prepare for and fill social positions. Thus their theory would not hold true where education and authority were end-values, sufficiently strong to induce people to occupy certain positions in society. Differences in prestige connected with these positions would then cease to be "functionally necessary."

It is true that then there would be certain difficulties of interpretation.

If we accept the view that a desire for education (knowledge, skill) and a desire for authority act as motives for the occupation of important positions requiring training, then we must accept that education and authority are important values. And it would be difficult to imagine differences of education and differences of authority dis-

appearing completely. In this situation, on the basis of differences of education and authority, there may arise different estimates as to the prestige of positions which have varying elements of skill and power.

The question therefore arises: should prestige differentiation then be treated as an epiphenomenon incapable of acting as principal stimulus, or should it be treated as an important stimulus giving rise to the desire to occupy positions which despite everything have greater prestige?

It is impossible at present to give an answer to this question. The whole situation is hypothetical. If ever such a situation were to exist, this question could be settled by means of research on the strength of various motives on the choice of social positions.[10]

THE FUNCTIONAL ASPECT OF POWER AND STRATIFICATION

Material advantage and prestige are the two elements of stratification on which Davis and Moore concentrate their attention. They are inclined to relegate authority to the background. But from the functional point of view authority may be regarded as an important stratificatory element—perhaps even more fundamental than material advantage or prestige.

The "functionalism" of Davis' and Moore's theory consists mainly in the fact that it places stratification in the group of phenomena which in "functional analysis" are called "functional requirements," or "functional prerequisites" of every society.

There is no divergence of views that biological reproduction, the production of consumer goods, the socialization of the younger generation (together with indoctrination in some system of values), and social organization are functional prerequisites. The functionalists, however, tend to add to the number of these prerequisites.

[10] In our discussion we have avoided the question of divergence of motives of human behaviour, since this is a separate and extensive subject. It may only be mentioned that the values accepted in present-day societies are very varied and rather "autonomous" and in consequence there is a great variety of motive in choice of education and career. When a sufficiently high standard of living would be assured, this variety might be much more marked.

Because of the tendency to expand the "functional requirements" of any social system and in this way to attribute universality and permanence to the various elements of social life, the idea of these "functional requirements" has been fairly severely criticized. There has been a suggestion that "functional alternatives" should be sought and studied, that is, phenomena which may occur as the equivalents of other phenomena.[11]* Davis and Moore may be criticized because they declare stratification is universal by including it among the "functional prerequisites" of social life, and do not take into account the possibility that other phenomena may occur in its place, in the form of functional alternatives (e.g., such a system of values as would cause people to train and to fill positions of skill or authority without reckoning on future material advantages or prestige).

It is worth noting, however, that among the functional prerequisites of social life it would be difficult not to take social organization into account. Social life is group life. And group life involves the inner structuralization of the group. This structuralization consists among other things in the emergence of positions of command and subordination (as well as of "intermediate" positions at further stages of development). In such a structure, authority is unevenly distributed. For as soon as the positions of authority are filled, those who occupy the positions have the right (and duty) to give orders, while the others have the duty to obey them.

The inevitable occurrence of power relations of this kind in every complex social structure was long ago pointed out by social thinkers of very divergent theoretical orientations (quite independently of how they differed as to how positions of authority are, or should be, filled, or in whose interest authority is wielded, or what connection exists between the distribution of

authority and the distribution of other values which occur as factors stratifying society, etc.). Engels, for example, who said that in a communist system the State as a weapon of class domination would wither away nevertheless declared that it would be impossible to think of any great modern industrial enterprise or of the organization of the future communist society without authority—or superiority-subordination relationships.[12] Mosca wrote, "There can be no human organization without rankings and subordination. Any sort of hierarchy necessarily requires that some should command and others obey."[13] M. Weber gave a number of reasons for the necessity of a functional division of authority in large administrative and political structures.[14] W. L. Warner is a contemporary author who explains in a brief form but explicitly the functional inevitability of stratification, pointing out that positions of authority are bound to occur.[15]

Davis and Moore seem to perceive the functional inevitability and stratifying role of authority relationships. Remarks on that are to be found in their considerations on "major societal functions" and the institutions fulfilling these functions. For example when they discuss "government" they say that "stratification is inherent in the nature of political relationships."[16] Yet they make no use of such a kind of observations in the construction of their theory. Neither do they explain how such statements are to be connected with the main propositions of their theory. Meanwhile it seems that these observations may lead us to quite a different explanation of the "functional inevitability" of stratification. This explanation may be as follows: The existence of great social structures creates social hierarchies built on authority. Thus if we are to take stratification to mean the

[11] Cf. R. K. Merton, "A Paradigm for Functional Analysis in Sociology," in *Social Theory and Social Structure*, Glencoe 1949.
* For an empirical study on this subject, see Richard D. Schwartz, "Functional Alternatives to Inequality," *American Sociological Review*, Vol. 20, August, 1955, pp. 424–430. (C. S. H.)

[12] F. Engels, "O zasadzie autorytetu" ["On the Principle of Authority"] in: K. Marx and F. Engels, *Dziela Wybrane* [*Selected Works*], Vol. I, Warszawa 1949.
[13] G. Mosca, *The Ruling Class*, New York 1939, p. 397.
[14] Cf. H. H. Gerth and C. W. Mills, *From Max Weber: Essays in Sociology*, New York 1958.
[15] W. L. Warner, M. Meeker and K. Eels, *Social Classes in America*, Chicago 1949, p. 8.
[16] Davis and Moore, *op. cit.*, p. 245.

occurrence of social positions among which there is an unequal distribution of some value, then it can be said that in the given structures there are positions among which the value which we call authority is unevenly distributed; in such cases, then, there is stratification along the dimension of authority.

In consequence it may be said that if there is any functional necessity for stratification, it is the necessity of stratification according to the criterium of authority and not according to the criterion of material advantage or prestige. Nor does the necessity of stratification derive from the need to induce people for the acquirement of qualifications, but from the very fact that humans live collectively.

THE TUMIN–MOORE POLEMICS–REMAINING POINTS OF DISAGREEMENT [1]

Wilbert E. Moore

The opportunity for this further exchange has served both to reduce radically the previous area of disagreement and—because Tumin has addressed himself to the general issues of inequality creatively and not just defensively—to open up some new issues worthy of theoretical and empirical attention. Let me note some of the major points of agreement. (These represent a substantial modification of "original" positions on both sides of the controversy.)

It is agreed that performances will be differentially evaluated in terms of approximations to social values and normatively defined standards of conduct.

From the *American Sociological Review,* Vol. 28, February, 1963. Reprinted by permission.

[1] Title supplied. Appeared originally as "Rejoinder."

It is agreed that some social differentiation entails "intrinsic" inequality of position.

It is agreed that the relationship between such ubiquitous "inequalities" on the one hand and "stratification" as generalized and ranked social categories on the other is subject to investigation but by no means definitionally the same. Thus, one may theoretically imagine and, here and there, empirically encounter social differentiation with unequal rewards without this becoming a component of a "generalized" social status. Put the other way around, what Tumin calls the "diffusion" of inequality and its self-reinforcement have no intrinsic and necessary relationship to differential valuation of performance or differential valuation of functional positions.

It seems also to be agreed that the "utilization of human potential" is sub-optimal in all known social systems, and that in all known social systems the institutionalization of existing differentials is incomplete and subject to dynamic tensions. The implications of these dysfunctions and dynamic properties of unequal valuations seem still in dispute. I see no reason to suppose that the predictive inference to be drawn from them is a tendency to greater equality of position and reward.

Now what remains in useful contention? The first debatable issue, I suggest, revolves around Tumin's "minimal" estimate of the relevance of inequality. Let me start with his assertion of "the fact that in all societies the largest number of socially differentiated roles and social types do not involve differential evaluation and reward." Now if this allegation refers to evaluation of *performance* it is not only contradictory to the clearly stated concession on this point, but, more to the scientific point, it is overwhelmingly contravened by the evidence. If *positional* differentiation is the basis of the allegation, the matter is in principle subject to mensuration but none is in fact at hand. In the present state of knowledge, I suggest that the formulation is a non-fact. And although I shall note below that I dislike Tumin's extreme relativism concerning societies and cultures, I suggest here that any measurement of positions differentially evaluated or not would be highly relative to the degree of coalescence and consistency in status categories in one or another system of social "stratification." Thus the allegation appears patently false in a traditional "caste" system and probably in a totalitarian system of bureaucratic positions, as, say, in the Soviet Union.

I have spent some precious space on this point because Tumin reiterates twice more the assertion that most differentiation does not involve invidious valuation, but in the modified context of "stratification," narrowly speaking. I think it *is* agreed that functionally specific inequalities *may* not be generalized into a singular status or aggregates of such statuses into a stratum, but it is not at all established that functional differentiation and unequal valuation are independently variable.

The general position Tumin has espoused in his latest statement is debatable in several respects that warrant specification. He has adopted an extremely relativistic view of cultural values and social institutions that seems to me empirically unwarranted and theoretically doubtful. Without using the Sumnerian phrase, "the mores can make anything right," that is the position he has taken. As I read the evidence, the evaluation of functionally differentiated positions is by no means as randomly variable as his discussion asserts or implies. I suggest that behavior relevant to the maintenance of order, the provision of economic support, the protection of the society, and the exemplifications of religious and esthetic values *always* involves differential positional as well as merely personal valuation. Tumin's cultural relativism and his notion that anything is possible through socialization represent a kind of denial of orderly and reliable generalizations about human societies. I do not think this denial is immoral; it is just wrong.

Although Tumin asserts that scarce personnel can be motivated to take up functionally critical tasks without differential rewards, "or at least with much less and much less enduring forms of such invidious distinctions," there is surely no evidence for the bald assertion, without the modification, which he reiterates in subsequent paragraphs. I spoke of improbable "martyrdom" in the performance of exceptional tasks without unequal recognition

and I still have no reason to retreat from my critical positions.

Tumin links an extreme cultural relativism and extensive randomness of cultural components with an extreme bio-social determinism within a *given* system. His final moral argument in behalf of rather extensive equality is to the effect that there is little social justice in rewarding differential talent (and performance?) which derives either from hereditary accident or the character of socialization that is imposed by the very system that allocates rewards. But here he uses a tell-tale, saving phrase, "assuming equal conscientiousness." Surely by now our understanding of the complex interplay between the individual and the social order does not permit so deterministic a view of human motivation or so easy a dismissal of the importance of purpose in human behavior. Though it is extremely unlikely that any social system will be able to overlook the consequences of the accident of birth in either the biological or sociological sense, since differential placement will likely take such consequences into account, there surely remains some interstitial area of human effort, or purpose, or conscientiousness that cannot be readily reduced to the influence of human heredity or the social environment. Though it is clearly the business of the sociologist to seek out the social sources and correlates of patterned human behavior, I do not think the evidence warrants the comfortable and individual guilt-absolving or excellence-degrading view that society is all and the complexities of individual motivation a purely dependent variable. Perhaps this difference of view only confirms the notion that assumptions regarding human nature underlie most if not all structural propositions of substantial generality.

Tumin and I have both been guilty, in these short statements, of anthropomorphizing "society." Such ellipsis is normally harmless, but I do want to dissent on one point. When Tumin stipulates as a condition for the "functional theory" of social inequality that the society be "rational," I suggest two modifications. The first is the evolutionary, "survival" test which Tumin has earlier doubted but not destroyed. The second point is that the denial of rationalism in a social decision-making is untenable, since it conspicuously exists as a norm in all contemporary societies, and, now and then, as a practice.

The protagonists in the current renewal of an enduring controversy are scarcely the designated spokesmen for recognizable clienteles. And lest it be thought that the issues relevant to stratification are all resolved or clarified, it should be noted that the whole concept of "class" as an explanatory variable has been barely touched in this exchange. Tumin in his suggested desiderata for the next steps in analysis of social inequality happily does not use the term "class"—which unfortunately our neighboring social scientists think is one of our most useful analytic tools—and his way of putting the questions does not presuppose that conceptual category. Can we get anyone to join the joyful march to sensible investigation?

SOCIAL INEQUALITY WITHOUT SOCIAL STRATIFICATION

Dennis H. Wrong

Recently, several sociologists have, notwithstanding the increased preoccupation of their colleagues with the subject of class, argued that the concept of social class is becoming more and more irrelevant to understanding advanced industrial societies.[1] They have largely confined their

This is a revised version of a paper presented to the annual meeting of the American Sociological Association in Los Angeles, August, 1963, and published in the *Canadian Review of Sociology and Anthropology*, Vol. 1. Reprinted by permission.

[1] Arnold M. Rose, "The Concept of Class and American Sociology," *Social Research,* XXV, Spring, 1958, 53–69; Robert A. Nisbet, "The Decline and Fall of Social Class," *Pacific Sociological Review, II,* Spring, 1959, 11–17; Wilbert E. Moore, "But Some Are More Equal Than Others," *American Sociological Review,* XXVIII, February, 1963, 14–15.

remarks to the United States. Several European writers, however, have made similar suggestions with respect to the major countries of Western Europe, though rather more tentatively since much that has already become a reality in America remains a trend on the other side of the Atlantic.[2] On the whole, the claim that social classes have disappeared or are disappearing has been rejected by the majority of American sociologists. For the most part their rejection has been based on little more than a preference for different definitions of class and has been offered good-humoredly as if the matter were merely a trivial issue of terminology. Yet, as so often in sociology, definitions defended on pragmatic or operational grounds turn out on closer examination to obscure full recognition of the contrast between past and present and of the new possibilities latent in contemporary social reality.

Sociologists who argue that social class is no longer a useful concept take what has been called a "realist" position regarding the existence of classes. They are committed, that is, to the view that, in the words of one of them, social classes "are groups possessed both of real and vital common economic interests and of a group-consciousness of their general position in the social scale."[3] Their contention that social classes are disappearing in industrial societies rests on the failure to locate such groups. The opposing "nominalist" point of view regards classes as a useful classificatory concept for grouping together for purposes of analysis individuals who possess certain attributes in common, whether or not they feel any unity or are even aware of having something in common with their fellow class members. The sociologist, in effect, creates the "class structures" he describes, which are no more than a means of organizing his data on variations in human behavior. He may find several different class systems or pyramids of

[2] T. H. Marshall, "General Survey of Changes in Social Stratification in the Twentieth Century," *Transactions of the Third World Congress of Sociology,* International Sociological Association, 1956, III, 1–17; George Lichtheim, *The New Europe: Today and Tomorrow* (New York, 1963), 198–215.

[3] Marshall, *ibid.,* 15.

stratification within a society, none of which are perceived or experienced as collective realities, as real social groups, by their members.

A denial of the existence of social classes as defined by the "realist" perspective, however, in no way implies a trend towards general equality or social uniformity. Inequalities in the distribution of income, the invidious ranking of occupations with respect to prestige or status, and functional hierarchies of power and authority may remain solidly established in the absence of social classes. Individuals or social roles may be ranked with respect to varying income, status or power, as is commonly done by sociological researchers, but the categories or percentiles into which individuals or roles are grouped are not social classes in the realist sense unless there is independent evidence that their members are internally cohesive and see themselves as a distinct collectivity with *common* rather than merely *like* goals, interests and values.

The so-called "realist versus nominalist" dispute over the kind of objective reality that should be ascribed to social classes has long been a standard theoretical and methodological issue in discussions of social stratification. Yet it has not always been acknowledged that all of the major nineteenth- and twentieth-century theorists of class were unmistakably "realists," regardless of whether they thought classes were based on economic interests, shared values, or common access to social power.

To Marx, a class was not fully formed until it had ceased to be merely a potential membership-group (*Klasse an sich*) and had achieved a solidarity based on awareness of the common interests of its members in opposition to those of another class (*Klasse für sich*).

Joseph Schumpeter wrote: "Class is something more than an aggregation of class members. . . . A class is aware of its identity as a whole, sublimates itself as such, has its own peculiar life and characteristic 'spirit.'"[4]

Max Weber is frequently cited by American sociologists in support of the contention that stratification in modern

[4] Joseph A. Schumpeter, *Imperialism and Social Classes* (New York, 1955), 107.

societies involves at least three partially independent hierarchies, one of wealth, one of prestige, and one of power. He is also often invoked to justify the treatment of status rankings of occupations as synonymous with "class structure." Weber is the source of the "wealth–status–power" triad so favored by contemporary sociologists, but he was clearly concerned with identifying relatively cohesive groups differentiated with respect to these three bases of stratification and did not consider each as forming a continuous scale on which individuals or positions could be located. Thus, defining "class," like Marx, in strictly economic terms, he saw classes as "possible, and frequent, bases for communal action," although he was less certain than Marx that aggregates of people sharing like interests would become aware of their common interests and resort to "communal action" to advance them. Commonly regarded as the first modern social theorist to stress the importance of status, Weber was chiefly concerned to describe "status groups" or *Stände*—a term that clearly designates self-conscious collectivities. With reference to power, he used the less fortunate term "party," which nevertheless is unambiguous in connoting a collective entity rather than an attribute with respect to which individuals or roles vary continuously.

Finally, W. Lloyd Warner has always insisted that the six social classes he discovered in Newburyport, Massachusetts, were ultimately derived from "the way in which people in American communities actually classify themselves," although his critics have repeatedly challenged the validity of this claim after re-analyzing Warner's own data.

I doubt that any of these men would have devoted so much time and effort to the study of class had they thought it a matter of indifference whether classes "really" existed in the experience of their members or were no more than artifacts constructed by the sociologist as a means of ordering and summarizing his observations. The grouping together by the sociologist of individuals sharing a common position with respect to several distinct variables is a thoroughly legitimate and useful procedure in certain kinds of empirical research. But to call the resultant groupings "social classes" is to risk confusion with the quite different meaning of class in the writings of the leading theorists of stratification. Researchers who use such terms as "socioeconomic group" or "level" at least implicitly recognize the distinction. But there are others who persist in referring to combined measures of occupation, income, or education as "indexes" of social class, although the entity these measures allegedly indicate appears to have no independent reality and "class" becomes no more than a shorthand expression for the ensemble of the very variables that have been combined to form the index.[5]

Critics of the realist conception of social classes have attributed to it the necessary implication that members of a society must be fully aware of the class system and that its nature can therefore be determined by a simple opinion poll.[6] Surely, this is a specious argument. To assert that social controls and expectancies are present in the minds and sentiments of the people whose conduct they influence is not to maintain that these people can readily put them into words. Consider social norms in primary groups, which are clearly operative influences on behavior; those who conform to them are not always able to provide a coherent account of the codes that guide and restrain them in their day-to-day interactions with others.[7] The kind of awareness-in-behavior that frequently characterizes social class relations may involve still less self-consciousness since classes (except in small isolated local communities) are not even potential primary groups; hence the frequent use of the term "quasi-group" to describe them.

The existence of classes, however, is a matter of degree depending upon the extent to which their members are conscious of their unity and of the boundaries separating them from other classes.[8] But recognition of this does not invalidate the realist position. All the theorists previously mentioned, with the exception of the ahistorical Warner, dealt at length with what Schumpeter called *class formation* and saw it as a process frequently falling short of the eventual emergence of fully developed classes. All of them attempted to specify the conditions under which aggregates of similarly situated individuals acquire cohesion and begin to behave as if they constitute at least a fictive membership-group. Nor does the existence of individuals or families whose position is marginal within the class structure pose special theoretical difficulties, for this is an inevitable result of inter-class mobility, which is also a temporal process of uncertain outcome.

Finally, if the existence of a class system implies *some* stratification, it is also possible for particular classes—most frequently new and rising classes—to exist which do not fit into an orderly hierarchical system.[9] Thus if we regard social stratification as a stratification of groups, classes may be formed in partial independence of stratification. But,

[5] Marshal, *op. cit.,* 5–6; Rose, *op. cit.,* 65–69.

[6] See, for example, Bernard Barber, *Social Stratification* (New York, 1957), 76–7; Nelson N. Foote, Walter Goldschmidt, Richard Morris, Melvin Seeman and Joseph Shister, "Alternative Assumptions in Stratification Research," *Transactions of the Second World Congress of Sociology,* International Sociological Association, 1953, II, 386–7.

[7] William F. Whyte reports that his main informant, Doc, remarked to him: "Now when I do something, I have to think what Bill Whyte would want to know about it and how I can explain it. . . . Before I used to do these things by instinct." *Street Corner Society* (Chicago, 1943), 10.

Many of the simplifications to which sociologists are prone in discussing the question of the degree to which people are aware of the determinants of their own behavior result from a failure to take into account Ryle's distinction between "knowing how" and "knowing that." See Gilbert Ryle, *The Concept of Mind* (New York, 1949), 25–61.

[8] As Andreas Miller has written: "A social class is a real group, set aside from its social environment by natural boundaries. . . . In a classless society one can speak of differences in social status. It would, however, be of no value to look for a class-system in a society without differences in social status. . . . An adequate conception of the class-system can only be reached by answering the question whether the community investigated is divided into strata by clear boundaries, what is their number, location, and strength." "The Problem of Class Boundaries and Its Significance for Research into Class Structure," *Transactions of the Second World Congress of Sociology,* 1953, II, 343, 348–9.

[9] Stanislaw Ossowski, "Old Notions and New Problems: Interpretations of Social Structure in Modern Society," *Transactions of the Third World Congress of Sociology,* 1956, III, 18–25.

more important, inequalities in the distribution of income, prestige, and power may exist in complete independence of it.

So far, my emphasis has been primarily definitional and I have done no more than insist on a number of distinctions that are widely recognized in principle, although often ignored in research practice. Applied to contemporary industrial societies, however, these distinctions are acquiring new relevance, for modern societies are unmistakably moving in the direction of maintaining considerable institutionalized inequality in the absence of a class system, a condition that the Polish sociologist, Stanislaw Ossowski, has characterized as "non-egalitarian classlessness." [10] This condition has not yet been fully achieved even in the United States, much less in Western Europe. But the steady approach toward it increasingly transforms social classes into "ghost" communities preserving a fitful and wavering identity rooted in historical memories, similar to that ascribed by Nathan Glazer to the " ghost nations " of third-generation American immigrants which continue to play a minor role in American politics. [11]

Since so many American sociologists have failed to see any significance in the disappearance of social classes in view of the survival of pronounced status inequalities, I shall briefly suggest several differences between societies where classes to some degree are present and societies where social inequality is relatively detached from stratification.

1. Income, educational and status mobility are experienced differently in the two societies. The person who moves upward (or downward) in a classless society does not encounter a class boundary in addition to the career obstacles he has to overcome in order to rise. Surely, it is the relative absence of classes in American society, whatever the historical causes for this absence, that accounts for the general belief that mobility is greater in the United States

than in Europe, a belief that Lipset and Bendix have shown to be unfounded. [12] Quite minor improvements in status or income are more readily perceived as mobility where no class boundary has to be crossed or confronted. There have been no real counterparts in the United States to the British "angry young men": persons of provincial and working-class origin who rise through educational or occupational attainment but become embittered on experiencing real or imagined exclusion when they try to cross a class line. The closest American equivalent is the experience of upwardly mobile Negroes and members of ethnic or religious minorities. The fact that occupational status rankings are similar in America and Britain, and indeed in all advanced industrial societies, [13] merely underlines the difference between these rankings and a social class system.

2. More important, a distinction between stratification and social inequality aids us in understanding the political sociology of modern industrial societies. The distinction holds, it should be noted, regardless of whether economic interest or style-of-life is considered the essential basis of class. The latter—the " Marx vs. Warner " issue— is a separate definitional problem. However, last-ditch defenders of the relevance of the class concept, such as Rudolph Heberle in a recent paper, [14] fall back on the Marxist view of classes as interest-groups divided by ownership or non-ownership of the means of production. They plausibly argue that, although classes separated by sharp status and associational boundaries have been largely supplanted by a continuous hierarchy of status, conflicts of interest have by no means disappeared and the major opposing groups continue to think and act in concert politically, at the very least in their voting behavior. The prediction of American Marxists in the 1930s that national cleavages of economic interest would increasingly

[10] Stanislaw Ossowski, *Class Structure in the Social Consciousness* (New York, 1963), 100–18.

[11] Nathan Glazer, "Ethnic Groups in America: From National Culture to Ideology," in Morroe Berger, Charles H. Page and Theodore Abel, editors, *Freedom and Control in Modern Society* (New York, 1954), 172–3.

[12] Seymour Martin Lipset and Reinhard Bendix, *Social Mobility in Industrial Society* (Berkley, 1959), 11–75.

[13] Alex Inkeles and Peter H. Rossi, "National Comparisons of Occupational Prestige," *American Journal of Sociology*, LXI, January, 1956, 329–39.

[14] Rudolph Heberle, "Recovery of Class Theory," *Pacific Sociological Review*, II, Spring, 1959, 18–28.

supersede regional and ethnic divisions as the main basis of political alignment has on the whole been borne out.

But a second part of the prediction was that more tightly drawn class lines would result in an intensification of the political class struggle between Left and Right. The opposite has occurred: "class" has become a more important determinant of voting at the same time that the bitterness of class struggle has unmistakably abated.[15] While it may, therefore, be formally correct to insist that the term "class" in the Marxist sense is still applicable where society-wide conflicts of interest find political expression, it is surely more relevant to the understanding of modern politics to recognize that today economic interest-groups and the political associations based on them do not, in T. H. Marshall's words, "permeate the whole lives of their members, as social classes do, nor are they always in action, and at times the constituent sub-groups may be more important than the largest aggregates."[16]

Ralf Dahrendorf attributes the obsolescence of the Marxist two-class sytem to what he aptly calls the "institutional isolation of industry" in modern society. But he tries to preserve the emphasis on conflict and change in Marxist class theory by redefining classes as the result of tension between power-holders and their subordinates, arguing that the division between owners and non-owners of property, and even conflicts of economic interest in general are merely special cases of this more fundamental phenomenon.[17] Dahrendorf does not hesitate to conclude that there are as many class systems in a modern society as there are functional hierarchies of power and that a single individual may therefore simultaneously be a member of several different classes if he belongs to several associations each with its own structure of authority. In effect, Dahrendorf makes three main contentions: that social conflict is generated by differences in power; that

classes are conflict-groups; and that all conflict-groups are classes. He may be right on the first two points (I am inclined to think that he is), but the third assertion surely represents the most quixotic effort to uphold the continuing usefulness of the concept of class in recent sociological writing.[18] Moreover, it would seem to be of no use at all in understanding the major political divisions in modern societies, although this has been precisely the most valuable feature of class theories which take their point of departure from Marx. Yet notwithstanding the inadequacies of his own class theory, Dahrendorf shows a far more acute grasp of the many differences between stratified and non-egalitarian classless societies than most American sociologists.

3. The absence of classes also helps account for the invisibility of poverty in the United States, to which several writers have recently called attention. The poor are composed of a number of categories of persons with particular demographic characteristics whose economic plight is no longer clearly linked to what Marx or Weber would consider a "class situation."[19] Both in status and in economic terms, only the American Negroes come close to constituting a definable and cohesive deprived group, with the possible exception of tenant farmers and

---

[15] Seymour Martin Lipset, *Political Man* (New York, 1960), especially chapters IX and XIII.

[16] Marshall, *op. cit.,* 13.

[17] Ralf Dahrendorf, *Class and Class Conflict in Industrial Society* (Stanford, Calif., 1959), especially Part Two.

[18] Both Kurt B. Mayer and Lewis A. Coser have similarly criticized Dahrendorf's thesis in reviews of his book. See Mayer's review of the German edition, *American Sociological Review,* XXIII, October, 1958, 592–3, and of the English edition, *ibid.,* XXV, April, 1960, 288; and Coser, *American Journal of Sociology,* LXV, March, 1960, 520–1.

[19] An exhaustive study of poverty in the United States by Oscar Ornati indicates that the following were "poverty-linked characteristics" in 1960: Non-white, Female head of household, Age 65 and over, Age 14–24 head of household, Rural Farm, Residence in South, Non-wage earner, Part-time wage earner, More than Six Children under 18, Education less than 8 years. None of the groups defined by these characteristics, with the possible exception of Rural Farm, represents a socioeconomic class. Ornati, *Poverty in an Affluent Society,* Preliminary Draft, New York: The New School for Social Research and The Twentieth Century Fund (Mimeographed), chapter 5. For a discussion of the non-class nature of contemporary American poverty see Henry M. Pachter, "The Income Revolution," *Dissent,* IV, Summer, 1957, 315–18.

laborers in certain sectors of the agri-cultural economy. There is indeed some justification for calling Negroes *the* Ameri-can lower class.[20]

The emerging social structure of post-bourgeois industrial society can best be understood if, except for secondary pur-poses and for historical analysis, we abandon the concept of social class and re-define much of the work done under this label as a contribution to the sociology of equality and inequality. But American sociologists have been unwilling to make this necessary redefinition, in part for ideo-logical reasons.

Celebrations of the United States have traditionally affirmed its "classlessness" and extolled at the same time the equality of opportunity to attain unequal rewards it allegedly provides. In challenging the reality of the latter, sociologists have been unwilling to concede any truth to the claim of classlessness lest they should appear to be denying the facts of inequality and barriers to opportunity. A spirit of liberal muckrak-ing still pervades much American sociolog-ical writing on stratification whether the writer's intent is to deplore or, like W. Lloyd Warner to counsel adjustment to the "brute facts" of inequality that are concealed or minimized by the official egalitarian ideolo-gy. The result has been that sociologists have perpetuated the very confusion of classless-ness with equality that the official ideology makes.

American sociologists have failed to see that the absence of classes may both in ideology and in social fact *more* effectively conceal existing inequalities than a social structure clearly divided into recognizable classes. The invisibility of poverty in the United States, already referred to, suggests such a conclusion, as does the fact that income distribution has become more unequal in the past decade,[21] the very decade of the "affluent society," which has witnessed so much individual and collective mobility, the mass diffusion of formerly restricted status symbols, and

the breakdown of long-standing ethnic, religious, and even racial barriers to oppor-tunity.

In distinguishing conceptually between stratification and inequality and noting some of the consequences of their increasing factual separation in contemporary society, I have avoided direct discussion of mobility and equality of opportunity. Many writers who have insisted as I have that stratification involves a hierarchy of groups rather than of positions or of individuals possessing unequal amounts of income, prestige, and power, have gone on to argue that stratified groups, or social classes, must necessarily be hereditary.[22] By transmitting the unequal privileges of one generation to the next through the family, classes thus inevitably prevent the full institutionalization of equality of opportunity.

The class systems of the past have un-deniably been hereditary, though permitting sufficient mobility to justify distinguishing them from *caste* systems. But need this be so in the future? Historically, biological continuity has been the major means of preserving the internal solidarity and the distinctive ethos of classes from generation to generation, but is it necessarily the only possible means? George Orwell wrote: "The essence of oligarchical rule is not father-to-son inheritance, but the per-sistence of a certain world-view and a certain way of life imposed by the dead upon the living. A ruling group is a ruling group so long as it can nominate its successors. Who wields power is not important, provided that the hierarchical structure remains always the same."[23] Orwell was writing of political elites, but his point that permanence of structure need not de-pend on biological continuity may well have a broader relevance. Hereditary social classes may not be succeeded by non-egalitarian classlessness but by new classes whose members are not recruited by

---

[20] Rose, *op. cit.,* 64.

[21] I am indebted to Oscar Ornati for having shown me the data from a later section of his study, *Poverty in an Affluent Society,* indicating this to be unmistakably the case.

[22] See especially Walter Buckley, "Social Strati-fication and the Functional Theory of Social Differentiation," *American Sociological Review,* XXIII, August, 1958, 369–75; and Kurt B. Mayer, "The Changing Shape of the American Class Structure," *Social Research,* XXX, Winter, 1963, 458–68.

[23] *Nineteen Eighty-Four* (New York, 1949), 370–1.

the intergenerational transmission of privileges through the family and whose cohesion does not depend on familial socialization.

Equality of opportunity could literally be achieved in full only by a method of allocating individuals to social positions that was strictly random, such as drawing lots. In contrasting equal opportunity with the inheritance of social position, however, sociologists obviously mean by the former the allocation of individuals to positions according to the single criterion of demonstrated ability to carry out the position's requirements. They have usually assumed that equality of opportunity thus defined is not only morally superior to any hereditary principle but would also prove to be more humanly tolerable, eliminating the social gulf that has existed between hereditary social classes and removing the envy and sense of injustice of low-status individuals who feel deprived of social rewards only by the accident of birth.

There is some evidence that the absence of clear-cut class lines in the United States and the prevailing "democracy of manners" make it easier for low-status individuals to tolerate hereditary inequalities provided they continue to believe that at least *some* opportunity to rise is available to them and their children.[24] But the most devastating attack on the belief that an inegalitarian order combined with full equal opportunity would reduce social conflict has been made by the English sociologist, Michael Young, in his brilliant sociological satire *The Rise of the Meritocracy: 1870–2033*.[25] . . .

Young's book is cast in the form of an historical interpretation written by a sociologist in the year 2033. His meritocratic social order is located in England, rather than "nowhere," and its evolution under the pressure of social forces powerfully at work in today's world is fully described. . . . The meritocracy is the result of three forces: the attack by socialists on all hereditary privileges, the pace of international economic competition requiring Britain to maintain high rates of economic growth,[26] and improvements in intelligence testing which have made it possible to reorganize the school system so that students can be segregated by intelligence at progressively earlier ages and trained for their eventual positions in the social order. The testing centers and the school system thus have become the vehicles for selecting the ruling elite of meritocrats. Possessing a monopoly of ability, the meritocracy easily prevails in conflicts of interest with the lower strata, who are completely bereft of leadership since all their potential leaders have been elevated into the meritocracy, and who must live with the knowledge that they have been scientifically proven to be inferior in ability to their rulers. The family, however, has survived in its present form and, echoing the functional theory of inequality, Young sees this as the Achilles heel of the regime. The meritocratic parents of inferior children and women, whose occupational skills suffer as a result of their withdrawal to bear and raise children, become infected with a discontent that eventually leads to revolution.

In Young's account the meritocracy clearly constitutes a unified ruling group, sharing common interests and a similar style of life, even though it is not recruited by heredity. And the same is true to a lesser degree of the "technicians"—the regime's euphemism for the industrial working class. Rather than defining class and stratification by the hereditary principle and calling the meritocracy a "classless" or unstratified society, it is surely more reasonable to see it as a new form of class society.

Yet one must raise some doubts about the general relevance of Young's meritocracy to contemporary trends in advanced industrial societies. One might question, to begin with, his assumption that the family will remain cohesive and unchanged when so much else has been transformed. More important, the very plausibility of Young's account

---

[24] Robert E. Lane, *Political Ideology: Why the American Common Man Believes What He Does* (New York, 1962), 57–81.

[25] London, 1958, *passim*.

[26] Several writers have recently argued that the maintenance of high rates of economic growth sets severe limits to the achievement of greater equality of condition as distinct from equality of opportunity. See George Lichtheim, *The New Europe,* New York: Frederick A. Praeger, 1963, 188–9; also C. A. R. Crosland, *The Conservative Enemy* (New York, Schocken Books, 1962), 29–34.

depends heavily on the roots of the meritocracy in English history with its characteristic "inevitability of gradualness." Thus
Young sees the sharpness of class lines and
the steepness of the status hierarchy that
have existed in English society from feudalism to the present day as surviving even
when birth has been entirely supplanted by
merit as the basis of status. While the independence of stratification in general from
the particular form of stratification by
hereditary social classes is thus brilliantly
suggested, one is forced to wonder whether
a meritocracy would have the same consequences in an industrial society that
lacked the pervasive continuities of English
history—in, say, the United States.

I know of only one even sketchy account
of a possible American meritocracy. It is
provided, not by a sociologist, but by a
lawyer and unsuccessful politician, Stimson
Bullitt, in his perceptive little book *To Be a
Politician*.[27] Bullitt envisages an American
meritocratic order as being far more stable
and less riven by class conflict than Young's
Britain. He writes:

> The free flow up and down and the narrow
> range of variations in revealed ability among
> members of the great majority will make class
> differences less sharp. Also, the classes will be
> equally well fed and in most ways equally free;
> people on different levels of talent will be closer
> in many ways than were the social classes of
> the past. All people will have greater under-
> standing, and therefore sympathy, for persons
> on other levels of talent than used to be the
> case between classes whose members lived like
> different species. (177–8.)

While Bullitt attributes the absence of
class tensions in a meritocratic United
States in part to general prosperity and a
high degree of material equality, conditions which are absent in Young's less
economically self-sufficient England—the
traditional classlessness of American society
clearly leads him to anticipate an American
meritocracy that would resemble a continuous hierarchy of unequal positions
rather than Young's more stratified order.

Will the decline of hereditary social
classes and the trend toward meritocracy
eventuate in non-egalitarian classlessness or

[27] (New York, Doubleday Anchor Books,
1961), 162–93.

in a new class society allocating individuals
by specialized abilities rather than by birth?
What will be the peculiar discontents of
each order? What form will the ancient
dream of an egalitarian society, equally
frustrated by both, take under these con-
ditons? These are likely to be the questions,
only dimly adumbrated in our present imperfectly affluent society, with which future
sociologists of inequality will concern themselves. We are not likely to make much
progress in answering them if we cling to a
conceptual apparatus that does not distinguish between stratification and inequality or between stratification in general
and the particular form it has taken in the
hereditary class societies of the past.

BEYOND THE RULING CLASS—STRATEGIC ELITES

Suzanne Keller

Influential minorities exist in all organized
societies. Whether a community is small or
large, rich or poor, simple or complex, it
always sets some of its members apart as
very important, very powerful, or very
prominent. The notion of a stratum elevated
above the mass of men may prompt approval, indifference, or despair, but regardless of how men feel about it, the fact remains that their lives, fortunes, and fate are
and have long been dependent on what a
small number of men in high places think
and do.

The reasons for the ubiquity and persistence of such leading minorities are not
easy to fathom, being rooted in complex
needs for social leadership in simple and
more advanced societies. Wherever we
find large-scale multipurpose organizations

This selection was especially prepared for this
volume. Part of it is drawn by the author from
her book, *Beyond the Ruling Class*, 1963. Reprinted by permission from Random House, Inc.

called societies, sustained by such leadership groups, we may anticipate the presence of such leadership groups. And just as individual leaders of small primary groups have been shown to embody the salient characteristics and aims of their followers, so the leadership of a society will likewise exhibit that society's characteristic traits, ideals, and purposes, and will vary in structure, style, and stance as these do.

Modern industrial societies may thus be expected to possess leadership groups appropriate to their structure and purposes. Mass democracy, social mobility, and technological diversity notwithstanding, socially significant elites are no less essential in these societies than in feudal, classical, or primitive ones. In fact, in certain respects, their significance is actually growing as one of the striking trends of our time is not, as many would have supposed, toward a decline of elite groups, but toward their proliferation, greater variety, and more extensive, though highly specialized, powers. The very fact of social, technical, and economic differentiation makes imperative the emergence of unifying and coordinating elements which these elites, as guardians and creators of common purpose and as managers of collective aims and ambitions, exemplify.

Elites are therefore fundamental to social continuity and social order in any differentiated aggregate, from delinquent gangs, to socialist political parties, to pluralist societies. And everywhere, their rule is rather similar even if their specific characteristics, tactics, and tastes vary with time, place, and circumstances. Essentially, they are expected to keep their establishments in working order, confronting and surpassing the minor and major crises that occur by giving a sense of purpose and direction to the totality. How they do so and how successful they are affect for good or ill the destinies of men and of nations.

This brings us to the question of which elites to study, and this depends on how they are defined. In noting that all elites are important in some social and psychological context, we must not fall into the error of attributing equal social importance to all. Those elites having major and sweeping social significance must somehow be distinguished from the rest. There is in effect a hierarchy among elites with some—beauty queens, criminal masterminds, champion bridge players, and master chefs—holding top rank in specific pyramids of talent or power but lacking a sustained general social impact. Other elites—leading generals, scientists, and statesmen—do have such an impact, as their judgments, decisions, and actions have determinable consequences for all or most members of society. These we designate as the *strategic* elites thereby distinguishing them from segmental elites. Strategic elites, in our view, comprise not only political, economic, and military leaders, but also normal, cultural, and recreational ones. Whether or not an elite is counted as strategic depends not so much on its particular activities than on its scope, impact, and society-wide influence.

The social significance of an elite cannot be discerned by examining either the intrinsic nature of activities, or the intrinsic motives and desires of its actual and potential members. It is thus misleading to make the subjective desires of individuals for wealth, fame, or power account for the existence of elite positions that provide such rewards. For this confuses the role of an elite in the life of society with individual reasons and justifications for wanting to participate in that role. The objective responsibilities of elites and the subjective rewards of their members are distinct dimensions that cannot be inferred from one another. For example, an individual may understandably aspire to a leading position in the world of big business in order to amass a personal fortune, but from this one can hardly conclude that the major social task of the business elite is the private accumulation of wealth. Even if this were the principal preoccupation of an individual member, it would not describe their collective responsibilities of directing the economic affairs of society in accord with prevailing standards and values. In any case, objective function and subjective reward must be considered apart if they are to aid our understanding of the system of values underlying the preeminence of given elites.

Elites as a Special Form of Societal Leadership. Strategic elites have both novel and familiar aspects, reflecting their kinship with older social forms from which they sprang as well as the new forces at work in a complex and changing world. The ruins of many extinct civilizations and the pasts of living ones are replete with a family of institutions with whom these elites are frequently confused—ruling castes, aristocracies, high estates, and ruling classes. Close scrutiny suggests that strategic elites are a crystallization, an outgrowth, a further development of these precursors, and may be viewed as structural alternatives to them, representing a more specialized form of social leadership. In this sense, of course, strategic elites are as old as the first organized human societies, with their leading minorities of priests, elders, warrior kings, or legendary sages and heroes—agents for and symbols of the common life. The new features stem from changed patterns of selection and reward as well as the changed demands made on them.

STRATEGIC ELITES AND RULING CLASSES

To help clarify this point let us contrast two of the five principal types of social leadership groups—that of a ruling caste and that of a ruling class. A ruling caste comprises a homogeneous stratum expected to perform the most important social tasks and recruit its personnel through biological reproduction. Ranking highest in prestige, it is set apart from the rest of society by religion, kinship, language, residence, economic standing, and occupational activities. Social control is enforced by religious ritual rather than by a centralized body of law, and the state is either nonexistent or plays a minor role in the life of society. Individuals enter the ruling caste through birth and leave it through death. The chief characteristics of caste systems—their rigidity and permanence—can be traced to how the ruling caste is recruited and maintained.

Social leadership concentrated in a ruling class also exhibits the presence of a single stratum in charge of various key social functions. However, it is recruited in a variety of ways and although heredity continues to provide access to this class it no longer constitutes the chief justification for such access. Lineage makes way for

property and wealth, whether ascribed or achieved. The members of a ruling class share not only their functional positions but also more general habits and culture.

Social leadership exercised by strategic elites differs from each of these. For one thing, several social strata may supply personnel to the leading social positions. Merit, regardless of other attributes—sex, race, class, religion, or even age—is the predominant justification for attaining elite positions, thus destroying the notion of all-round excellence or over-all superiority.

Selection on the basis of individual competence implies dismissal for incompetence, and this principle links these modern elites to the primitive institution of chiefship, where the chief—be he priest, king, or warrior—may be killed if he fails to bring about the desired end: peace, the harvest, or health. Thus strategic elites are marked by functional specialization and recruitment on the basis of proven capacity to perform their specialized roles. Along with the specialization, diversity, and impermanence of elites, new problems arise—those of cohesion and unity, morale, balance, and a new type of interdependence at the top, now requiring the cooperation of several interdependent strategic elites. No single elite can outrank all others because no one elite knows enough about the specialized work of all others. In sum, strategic elites differ from ruling classes and castes in their manner of recruitment, internal organization, and degree of specialization. Strategic elites, in some form, exist in every organized human society; ruling classes do not and need not. And although strategic elites have emerged from ruling classes and castes, they cannot be equated with them. As modern equivalents of these earlier historic forms, they also have their unique aspects, which must be assessed and appraised in their own right.

STRATEGIC ELITES AND SOCIAL CLASSES

Elites have often been discussed as if they were interchangeable with social classes. But although the two are related they are by no means identical. The origin of strategic elites (as of all top leadership groups) lies in the heterogeneity of the community—as regards age, sex, ethnicity, skills, strength, and the like. The origin of social classes lies in the social division of labor and the hierarchy of values associated with it.

Both phenomena increase as social differentiation increases. Even without attributing to primitive societies a perfect harmony and homogeneity, it is evident that their relatively small degree of differentiation separates them sharply from the occupationally and technologically more advanced communities. And it is this internal differentiation that permits the rise of strategic elites—where it is slight, elites are few in number and comprehensive in scope; where it is extensive, elites are many and specialized. The tremendous variety of cultures and social structures should not obscure a fundamental similarity in the patterns with which societies have responded to the facts of growth and diversity. At one point in time, we find neither social classes nor an extensive social differentiation, but we do find strategic elites in the form of single chiefs, groups of elders, or high priests performing their functions sporadically and on a temporary basis. At some later time, perhaps a hundred years, or a thousand, or only a few decades, the population increased, a variety of occupations emerged, social classes arose, and the minorities in charge of social leadership became more numerous, more extensive, and more enduring. The organized boundaries of society no longer coincided with its numerical boundaries and in that sense, society became separate from the total membership, as well as longer-lived. Once a certain degree of social differentiation was reached, the emergence of a societal center, a core, a fulcrum, existing apart from and above the community, sacred and exalted, was mandatory. This core symbolized at once the most precarious and the most exalted aspects of organized collective life.

Strategic elites and social classes must therefore be considered as twin-born but not identical. Their development, although related in complicated ways, is not interchangeable. Just as there is a close association between social classes and the existence of a state, but each is a separate consequence of a series of social developments, so elites and classes are independent social occurrences. The subdivision of a population into occupations, castes, guilds, or classes is paralleled by its unification around a symbolic center. The shape of this center is determined by the complexity and variety of the whole—the more varied and complex the one, the more varied and complex the other.

There is one way, however, in which strategic elites have been historically dependent on particular aspects of the social class structures of their societies—via their recruitment and selection. As long as these elites were principally recruited from a small exclusive circle tied by economic position and kinship—that is, from an upper class— it was difficult, if not impossible, to distinguish between the strategic elites and the class that supplied most of their membership. This was even truer if class background rather than social functions was used to justify the holding of strategic elite positions in society. This confusion between the characteristics of functioning leadership groups and the characteristics of the reservoir from which they were drawn arose from the historic fusion of function, attributes, and rewards. An aristocrat, for example, was a leading politician, born of an ancient and noble family, who became merged with his mode of recruitment (kinship and lineage) and his manner of reward (wealth and an elegant style of life). If most politicians were indeed to the manor born, it might readily be assumed that noble birth was indispensable for the exercise of political leadership. As long as these elements were fused, in fact, they were not analytically distinguished. Thus, in the past, strategic elites had two sources of social superiority. One derived from their crucial role in preserving and furthering key social values and goals, the other from their traditional modes of recruitment. In the popular mind, social class and elite rankings were readily confused as the high status of the one reflected on that of the other.

In this age of specialization, demands for specialized excellence have altered the class-linked recruitment patterns of the past and with them some of our traditional assumptions about their indispensability. This is not to say that social class has ceased to play a significant role in recruitment, selection, and opportunity for access to elite positions in society, but only that its role has become attenuated. High social-class position is no longer a formal prerequisite for the attainment of elite positions or for the performance of elite functions. The study of strategic elites must therefore endeavor to keep three factors separate and distinct. The first refers to the duties, responsibilities, and tasks of these elites, the second to their manner of recruitment. If they reproduce themselves, then society is managed by one or more ruling castes; if they are drawn only from the rich and propertied, then the society has a ruling class; if incumbents must demonstrate proven abilities, in specialized spheres, then we have strategic elites in modern dress. The third factor refers to the manner of rewarding these elites for adequate performance. In some instances they get more of the desirable things of life, in others less.

In sum, although the emergence of social classes divides a society, the development of its symbolic center, manned by strategic elites, integrates and reunifies it once more. In this way a society can act in concert even though its various parts are not identical or coequal. With this two-fold development, new and perplexing questions arise: Who is to participate in this center? How large should this group be? How long should given individuals participate? How should they be rewarded? The fate of many societies, including our own, has hung on the ways in which these questions have been answered.

CLASSES IN MODERN SOCIETY

T. B. Bottomore

The egalitarian movement which came to life in socialist clubs, trade unions, cooperative ventures and utopian com-

Condensed from *Classes in Modern Society*, by T. B. Bottomore. © Copyright 1965 by George Allen and Unwin Ltd. Reprinted by permission of Pantheon Books, a Division of Random House, Inc.

munities grew stronger throughout the nineteenth century as capitalism developed. In the course of time this movement has taken many different forms—struggles for women's rights and against racial discrimination, and most recently the efforts to close the gap between rich and poor nations—but its driving force has remained the opposition to the hierarchy of social classes. The class system of the capitalist societies is seen as the very fount of inequality, from which arise the chief impediments to individual achievement and enjoyment, the major conflicts within and between nations, and the political dominance of privileged minorities.

In this movement Marx's analysis of capitalist society acquired—directly or indirectly—a large influence. . . .

The appeal of Marx's theory is twofold: it provides a clear and inspiring formulation of the aspirations of the working class, and at the same time it offers an explanation of the development of forms of society and government, and especially of the rise of the modern labour movement itself. There are not lacking, in the present age, governments which are quite plainly the instruments of rule by an upper class, as in those economically backward countries where the landowners dominate an uneducated, unorganized and dispirited peasantry. When Marx undertook his studies the class character of governments was just as apparent in the European countries which had embarked upon industrialization. During much of the nineteenth century only property-owners in these societies enjoyed full political rights; and it was scarcely an exaggeration to conceive the government as "a committee for managing the common affairs of the *bourgeoisie* as a whole." In many European countries it was only during the first two decades of the twentieth century that universal suffrage was finally established. . . .

The existence of large working-class parties has become a normal feature of the democratic capitalist countries, and this is one of the principal circumstances (another being the political system in the Soviet societies) which raise new problems concerning the relationship between class and politics. In a political system of this kind can the owners of property be regarded any longer as a permanent ruling class? Is the working class still a radical, revolutionary force which seeks to bring about an egalitarian society? Are the relations between classes in the political sphere still the same as they were in the nineteenth-century societies with their restricted franchise? Have new political divisions emerged alongside, or in the place of, those between classes; or have political conflicts lost some of the urgency and importance which they acquired in the period which saw the rise and growth of the labour movement? These questions lie at the heart of present controversies about the changing class structure of industrial societies.

It has become common, for example, to remark upon the great complexity of government in modern societies, and upon the influence which is exerted by the diverse interest groups which are consulted in the course of policy-making; and then to argue that where power is divided among many different groups, whose interests do not always coincide, the notion of a "ruling class" has lost all meaning. But if power is really so widely dispersed, how are we to account for the fact that the owners of property—the upper class in Marx's sense— still predominate so remarkably in government and administration, and in other elite positions; or that there has been so little redistribution of wealth and income, in spite of the strenuous and sustained effort of the labour movement to bring it about? Is it not reasonable to conclude, from the evidence provided in the last chapter, that notwithstanding political democracy, and despite the limited conflicts of interest which occur between elite groups in different spheres, the upper class in the capitalist societies is still a distinctive and largely self-perpetuating social group, and still occupies the vital positions of power? Its power may be less commanding, and it is certainly less arrogantly exercised, than in an earlier period, because it encounters an organized opposition and the test of elections, and because other classes have gained a limited access to the elites; but the power which it has retained enables it to defend successfully its most important economic interests.

There are other difficulties with the concept of a "ruling class," but I have examined them at length elsewhere[1] and I shall not consider them further in the present context. It is in any case the changes in the condition of the working class, and especially in its political role, which have most impressed students of class structure in the postwar period. The "new working class," it is claimed, is economically prosperous and aspires to middle-class standards of living:[2] and in consequence it has become less class conscious and less radical in politics. How far are these political inferences warranted? Class consciousness, in a broad sense, may be regarded as one form of the "consciousness of kind" which develops in all enduring social groups; for example, the consciousness of belonging to a particular nation. In this sense, the emergence of class consciousness, the increasing use of the term "class" to describe an individual's position in society, is itself a sign that new social groups have come into existence.[3] But in Marx's usage, which has had a profound influence both upon sociological theories and upon political doctrines, "class consciousness" involves something more than this; namely, the gradual formation of distinctive ideologies and political organizations which have as their object the promotion of particular class interests in a general conflict between classes.

The growing class consciousness of the working class was represented by Marx as showing these characteristics in an exceptional degree; for it was expressed in ideologies and political movements which strongly emphasized the conflict of economic interest between capitalists and workers, and which proposed radical social changes in order to end the system of society based upon classes. The working class was, therefore, a revolutionary element in society; more revolutionary indeed than any earlier oppressed classes, since it aimed consciously at abolishing the whole class system. . . .

[1] See my *Elites and Society* (New York, 1965), Chapter 2. (Reprinted in this volume, pp. 160–168, C. S. H.)

[2] See *ibid.*, pp. 28–31.

[3] There is a good account by Asa Briggs, "The Language of 'Class' in Early Nineteenth Century England" in Asa Briggs and John Saville (eds.), *Essays in Labour History* (New York, 1960).

This conception of the working class, as the animator of a revolutionary movement which is to establish a classless society, appears to many sociologists to be highly questionable in the light of recent investigations. It is not that the prevalence of class consciousness in a broad sense, or the association between class membership and political affiliation, is generally denied. Social surveys have shown plainly that most people are familiar with the class structure of their society, and are aware of their own position within it. Equally, it has been shown that class membership is still the strongest single influence upon a person's social and political attitudes; and that the major political parties in most countries represent pre-eminently class interests. What is brought into question by recent studies is the view that the working class, in the advanced industrial countries, is striving to bring about a revolutionary transformation of society, rather than piecemeal reforms within the existing social structure; or that there is a total incompatibility and opposition between the doctrines and objectives of political parties which draw their main support from different classes. In Marx's theory the working class was revolutionary in two senses: first, that it aimed, or would aim, to produce the most comprehensive and fundamental change in social institutions that had ever been accomplished in the history of mankind, and secondly, that it would do so in the course of a sustained conflict with the *bourgeoisie* which was likely to culminate in a violent struggle for power. The nascent working class of the mid-nineteenth century fitted reasonably well into this scheme, which was constructed largely out of the experiences of the French Revolution. The "new working class" of the mid-twentieth century, it is argued, fits badly.

Studies of industrial workers during the past decade agree broadly in finding that there has been a decline in their attachment to collective ends, and so also in their enthusiasm for action as a class in order to establish a new social order. F. Zweig, in his study of workers in four modern enterprises, observes that "when speaking about classes a man would seem to be thinking primarily about himself, about the individual aspect

of the problem, and not about the social situation or the social structure,"[4] and he goes on to say that although two-thirds of the workers he interviewed placed themselves in the working class, this recognition of their *class identity* was not accompanied by any strong feelings of *class allegiance*. A study of French workers[5] arrives at very similar conclusions. The authors distinguish three types of reaction among factory workers to their situation in the economy and in society: (1) evasion (the attempt to escape from industrial work either by rising to a higher position within the firm or by setting up in business on one's own account); (2) resignation (a dull and resentful acceptance of industrial work as an inescapable fate); and (3) revolt (opposition and resistance to the capitalist organization of industry). Of these three types, the second is by far the most common, while the third is the least so; and even the 9 per cent of workers in this category, who believe that they can improve their situation by collective action, no longer believe that any future society will be able to alter fundamentally the subordinate position of the worker in the factory. The authors summarize their results by saying that although the workers they studied still have a group consciousness (i.e., they regard themselves as "workers," clearly distinguished from other groups in the population), they no longer have any collective aims. The present-day workers is "a man who is cut off from working-class traditions and who possesses no general principles, no world-view, which might give a direction to his life."[6] This conclusion, they observe, agrees entirely with those reached in a number of studies in Germany, by Popitz, Bednarik and others. Popitz and his collaborators, in their study of workers in the Ruhr steel industry,[7] show that there is a strong working-class consciousness, which is built around the distinction between manual workers and those who plan, direct and command work;

[4] F. Zweig, *The Worker in an Affluent Society* (New York, 1961), p. 134.
[5] A. Andrieux and J. Lignon, *L'Ouvrier d'aujourd'hui* (Paris, 1960).
[6] *Ibid.*, p. 189.
[7] H. Popitz, H. P. Bahrdt, E. A. Jüres, H. Kesting, *Das Gesellschaftsbild des Arbeiters* (Tübingen, 1957).

but those who still think in Marxist terms of the victory of the working class and the attainment of a classless society are a small minority. Similarly, Bednarik concludes his essay on the young worker of today by saying that "society has ceased to be an ideal for the working class," and that the worker "tends more and more to withdraw into private life."[8]

Several of these ideas are brought together by Goldthorpe and Lockwood, in their analysis of the notion of *embourgeoisement*,[9],[*] where it is suggested that there has been, in the Western industrial countries, a convergence between the "new middle class" and the "new working class," leading to a distinctive view of society which diverges both from the radical individualism of the old middle classes and from the comprehensive collectivism of the old working class. In this new social perspective collectivism is widely accepted as a means (and this accounts for the spread of trade unionism among white-collar workers), but no longer as an end (which accounts for the weakening of class allegiance among workers). Goldthorpe and Lockwood use the terms "instrumental collectivism" and "family centredness" to describe the complex of beliefs and attitudes in this conception of society. The second term refers to the phenomenon which other writers have described as a withdrawal into private life, and which is revealed by the individual worker's predominant concern with his family's standard of living, his own prospects of advancement, the education of his children and their opportunities to enter superior occupations.

The second feature of the working class as a revolutionary force, namely its involvement in violent class struggles, can be discussed more briefly. In all the advanced industrial countries the violence of class conflict has greatly diminished over the past few decades, and the working-class parties which still regard their aims as likely to be achieved by the use of force are few in number and insignificant. The change from the conditions at the end of the nineteenth century has been produced by several factors, among which we may single out the development of political democracy, the more effective power of modern governments, aided by the great advances in military technology, in administration and in communication, and the changes in the nature of working-class aims as well as in the relations between classes. . . .

Changes in the relations between classes in the capitalist societies have accompanied the changes in the character of the major social classes, influencing and being influenced by the latter. In so far as social mobility has increased, and the middle class has grown in numbers, the image of society as divided between two great contending classes has become blurred by the superimposition of another image, in which society appears as an indefinite and changing hierarchy of status positions, which merge into each other, and between which individuals and families are able to move with much greater facility than in the past. In addition, the everyday economic struggle between workers and employers has been regulated more and more by the state, through the creation of new social institutions for negotiation, arbitration and joint consultation. It is this situation which leads Ralf Dahrendorf, in his *Class and Class Conflict in Industrial Society,* to write of "post-capitalist societies" in which industrial conflicts have been institutionalized and thereby insulated from the sphere of politics; and although this is an exaggeration, inasmuch as political conflicts are still very largely about class interests, and are widely recognized as such, it contains an element of truth in so far as it points to the emergence of political issues which are in some measure detached from questions of class interest. There is unquestionably some common ground between the main political parties in the Western industrial countries; and the development of science and technology, economic growth and rising levels of living, urban congestion and crime, are among the issues which

---

[8] K. Bednarik, *Der junge Arbeiter von heute— ein neuer Typ* (1953), pp. 138–9, 141.

[9] John H. Goldthorpe and David Lockwood, "Affluence and the British Class Structure," *Sociological Review,* XI (2), July, 1963.

[*] For a subsequent specification of this notion, see Garvin MacKenzie, "The Economic Dimensions of Embourgeoisement," *The British Journal of Sociology,* Vol. XVIII, March, 1967, pp. 29–45. C. S. H.)

have to be dealt with politically along much the same lines in *all* the industrial countries.

The social changes which have produced the "new working class," as well as a political climate in which violent confrontations between the classes are rare, have been interpreted by some sociologists as a crucial phase in a process which is leading to the complete assimilation of the working class into existing society, as a beginning of the "end of ideology" in the precise sense of the decline of socialist doctrines which offer a radical criticism of present-day society and the hope of an alternative form of society. But this interpretation goes beyond the facts which have been discovered by sociological research. It relies, for instance, upon a tacit comparison between the present state of working-class consciousness and its state in some vaguely located and imperfectly known past age, which is seen as a time of heroic resolution and militancy. Against this it should be observed that in the past few decades, in the very period in which the working class is supposed to have become more middle class in its outlook, the support for socialist parties in Europe has been maintained or has substantially increased. It may be objected that this support has been gained by the progressive elimination of distinctively socialist ideas from the programmes of such parties. But this too is doubtful. The language of socialism has changed over the past century, in ways which it would be rewarding to study more closely, but the ends of the labour movement—collectivism and social equality—have not been abandoned or even seriously questioned.

The picture of working-class apathy and lack of enthusiasm for collective ends which is given by the studies mentioned earlier has to be seen, therefore, as a portrait taken at one moment of time and not as the final episode of a serial film. Even as a momentary picture it may not do justice to all the features of the situation. Serge Mallet, in his study of the "new working class" suggests that because the worker as a producer is still dominated and constrained, while as a consumer he experiences a new freedom and independence, it is in relation to the working environment that class consciousness is most vigorously expressed;[10] and this is apparent, he thinks, in the changing nature of trade-union demands in the modern sectors of industry, which are concerned increasingly with shorter hours of work, longer holidays, and greater control over the policies of management. These demands reflect the desire of the "new working class" to alter radically its position in the system of production, in a sense which is close to the ideas of classical socialist thought. The same aspirations, it may be added, find expression in the widening discussion of various forms of producers' co-operation, which has been inspired very largely by the progress of workers' self-management in Yugoslavia.

There are several other influences at work in the Western industrial societies which sustain the ideological controversies over the future form of society, and which lend support, in particular, to the socialist doctrines of the working class. One of the most important is the extension, and the more general acceptance, of public ownership of industry, public management of the economy, and public provision of a wide range of social and cultural services. The contrast between "private opulence" and "public squalor," to which J. K. Galbraith has pointed, has awakened many people to the fact that in modern societies many of the most valuable private amenities can only be got or preserved through public action. Individuals may be prosperous enough to provide adequately for their personal needs in food, housing, transport, and some kinds of entertainment, but they cannot individually assure what is needed for full enjoyment in the way of roads, facilities for sport and recreation, good working conditions, or a congenial and attractive urban environment. The unrestricted pursuit of

[10] This appears very clearly in the comments of workers reported in the study by Andrieux and Lignon (op. cit.). They mention frequently and bitterly the different in the treatment which they receive from other people according to whether they are recognized as workers (in the factory, travelling to work) or as citizens (in leisure time). One worker summed it up by saying that as a worker he was pushed around, but ". . . when I am out in my car and stop to ask for directions the policeman comes up touching his cap because he thinks he is dealing with a gentleman" (pp. 31–32).

private wealth and private enjoyment leads, indeed, to the impoverishment of these vital public services.

In the economic sphere the growth in the size of firms in major branches of industry, and the approach to monopolistic control in some sectors, has reduced the difference between the operations of publicly owned and privately owned enterprises; and if there is, at the present time, no great public excitement over the issue of "nationalization" of industry, this is in part because it is taken for granted that a change of ownership would not affect the economic performance of the industry. In part, also, it is due to recognition of the fact that the economy as a whole, in a modern society, must anyway be increasingly regulated and directed by the political authorities if a consistently high rate of growth is to be achieved, through the systematic application of science to production. Today the entrepreneur has become much less important; while the trained manager (who can perfectly well be a public servant) and the scientist have become much more important.

The increasing provision of social services by the state, which in recent times has been largely brought about by the pressure of the labour movement, has also fortified the socialist conception of a more equal, more collectivist society. Social legislation in the Welfare State may not be preponderantly egalitarian, either in intention or in effect,[11] but as it is extended and comes eventually to include an "incomes policy" so it approaches the conditions in which, as a German social scientist has observed, the task of social policy is to determine the order of priority of claims against the national product.[12] And these are conditions which would accord most fully with the institutions of a classless society.

This discussion of classes and ideologies in the Western societies, if it suggests that the working class may still be considered an independent force in political life, and one which still aims to bring about radical changes in the social structure, also indicates that the development of the working class has diverged in many respects from the course which Marx and the early Marxists expected it to follow. Marx's theory dealt, necessarily, with the first stages in the formation of the working class, and it proposed broad hypotheses rather than settled conclusions based upon intensive research. The Marxist sociologists—in any case few in number—have not greatly advanced the empirical study of social classes. Often they have seemed to be writing about an imaginary society, in which a pure class struggle continues inexorably, unsullied by such events of practical life as the advent of political democracy, the extension of welfare services, the growth of national income, or the increasing governmental regulation of the economy. . . .

Neither Marx not his followers examined sufficiently the strengths and weaknesses of the major social classes in capitalist society, many of which, indeed, have only become apparent through the experiences of the past fifty or sixty years. Marx insisted that the ruling ideas in any society are the ideas of the ruling class. But he did not seriously consider how important the ideas themselves might be in sustaining that rule, or how difficult it would be for the working class to oppose them with its own ideas.[13] Doubtless he thought that his own social theory would have a great effect (as it has), and he also counted upon the economic failure of capitalism—the ever-worsening crises—to discredit bourgeois ideas. In fact, bourgeois ideas have only been discredited, for brief periods, in those societies which have suffered defeat in war, and it is in such circumstances that the major revolutions of the twentieth century have occurred. Otherwise it is true to say that the working class in all countries has continued to be profoundly influenced by the dominant ideas of capitalist society; for example, by nationalism and imperialism, by the competitive,

---

[11] For a discussion of this point see T. H. Marshall, *Social Policy* (New York, 1965), Chapter 13, "Retrospect and Prospect."

[12] Quoted by T. H. Marshall, *Social Policy*, p. 183.

[13] Among later Marxists, Gramsci was the only one who gave much serious attention to these questions, and I should think that he was influenced in this direction by the work of his compatriot Mosca, who had introduced the term "political formula" to describe the body of doctrine which every ruling class, in his view, has to develop and to get accepted by the rest of society if it is to retain power.

acquisitive and possessive conceptions of human nature and social relations, and in recent times by a view of the overriding purpose of society as being the creation of ever greater material wealth. The attempts to combat these ideas reveal the immense difficulties involved in doing so. The ideal of working-class internationalism, in opposition to national rivalries and war between nations, has never been realized in more than a fragmentary form, in the face of differences of language and culture, and the manifold problems of establishing international associations at any level. On the other side, the idea of competition and of activity as mainly acquisitive easily becomes acceptable when it is associated with equality of opportunity—real or supposed —for which the working class itself has striven; while the idea of uninterrupted economic growth must clearly appeal, with reason, to those who are struggling to escape from cramping poverty.

Yet in spite of these difficulties, egalitarian and collectivist ideas have spread widely during this century. . . . The question now is whether these ideas have lost their vigour and have begun to recede, or whether they are still active and effective. A number of sociologists, as we have seen, observe a decline in the enthusiasm of the working class for collective ends, a loss of interest in any social mission, and the gradual erosion of a distinctive working-class culture. A few, among them S. M. Lipset, regard the combination of political democracy and high levels of living as the final achievement of the "good society," and thus as the terminal point of the labour movement: "democracy is not only or even primarily a means through which different groups can attain their ends or seek the good society; it is the good society itself in operation."[14] Lipset concedes that there is still a class struggle of sorts in the capitalist countries, but he sees it as being concerned only with the distribution of income, not with any profound changes in the social structure or culture; and he assumes that there is a constant trend towards greater equality of income which is turning the struggle into a process of limited bargaining between in-

terest groups, while denuding it of all ideological or political significance.

There are several reasons to be cautious about accepting this view that the relative peace on the ideological front, and the apparent decline in the vigour of working-class social ideals, have become permanent features of the capitalist societies; that the final form of industrial society has been reached. First, it is likely that there will be growing discontent as it becomes evident that there is no general trend towards greater economic equality, and that, on the contrary, there are very powerful movements which tend to produce a more unequal distribution of income and wealth whenever the industrial and political pressure of the working class is relaxed. . . .

A second consideration, which seems to me still more important, is that there is a growing discrepancy between the condition of the working class at work and in leisure time. Security of employment and rising levels of living have brought greater freedom of choice and independence of action for industrial workers outside the workplace, and younger workers in particular have taken advantage of their new opportunities. But one result of this is that the contrast between work and leisure has become more intense: at work there is still constraint, strict subordination, lack of responsibility, absence of means for self-expression. All the studies of the modern working class which I reviewed earlier bring out clearly that workers are profoundly aware of this division in their lives, and that they have a deep hatred of the present system of industrial work. They would undoubtedly recognize their condition in Marx's observation that a worker " does not fulfil himself in his work but denies himself, has a feeling of misery rather than well-being, does not develop freely his mental and physical powers but is physically exhausted and mentally debased," that "his work is not voluntary but imposed, *forced labour*," and that he "feels himself at home only in his leisure time."[15]

It is hard to believe that such a division can continue unchanged, but it may be overcome or mitigated in several different ways.

[14] S. M. Lipset, *Political Man* (New York, 1960), p. 403.

[15] Karl Marx, *Economic and Philosophical Manuscripts* (1844).

Sustained economic growth may result in such a reduction of working hours and expansion of leisure time that the hierarchical and authoritarian structure of industry comes to play a negligible part in the individual's personal and social life, and is no longer a matter for concern. Or, on the other hand, there may be renewed efforts to introduce into the sphere of economic production some of the freedom and independence which exist in leisure time, and these efforts may be helped by changes in the character of production itself, as it becomes increasingly a scientific activity—using both the natural and the social sciences—which needs the services of highly educated and responsible individuals to carry it on. Most probably, there will be some combination of these two movements; but in so far as the second one takes place at all it will be through the action of working-class organizations seeking to control the labor process, which still appears, as it did to Marx, as the fundamental activity in every social system.

The rise of the working class in modern societies has been a more protracted affair than Marx supposed, and it has only rarely approached that state of decisive struggle with the *bourgeoisie* which he expected. In the future a similar gradual development appears most likely, but the end may still be Marx's ideal society, a classless society. Indeed, it is only now, when the tremendous development of the sciences has created the possibility of truly wealthy societies—but for the uncertainties of population growth and nuclear warfare—that the economic foundations of a classless society can be regarded as assured. What kinds of inequality would remain in the absence of social classes, and in conditions where individuals had independence and responsibility both at work and in leisure, can only be conjectured. There would doubtless be some differences in the prestige of occupations, in incomes, and in the social position of individuals, but there is no reason to suppose that these would be very large, or that they would be incompatible with an awareness of basic human equality and community.

The principal fault in many recent studies of social classes has been that they lack an historical sense. Like the economists of whom Marx said that they believed there had been history, because feudalism had disappeared, but there was no longer any history, because capitalism was a natural and eternal social order, some sociologists have accepted that there was an historical development of classes and of class conflicts in the early period of industrial capitalism, but that this has ceased in the fully evolved industrial societies in which the working class has escaped from poverty and has attained industrial and political citizenship. But this assumption is made without any real study of the evolution of social classes in recent times, or of the social movements at the present time which reveal the possibilities of future social change. An historical analysis of the changing class structure in modern societies, such as I have merely outlined here, remains one of the most important unfulfilled tasks of sociology today.

NAME INDEX

Abegglen, James C., 370, 371, *459*
Adams, Stuart, 454
Adelson, Joseph, 371
Alford, R. R., 217
Allen, Philip J., 366
Amory, Cleveland, 411
Anastasi, Ann, 316, 367, 401*n.*
Anderson, Arnold, 313
Anderson, C. A., 353
Andreski, Stanislav, 109
Andrieux, A., 458, 526, 528
Angell, Robert, 205, 372
Annaklychev, Shikhberdy, 292
Ansell, C., 257
Antonovsky, Aaron, 249, 257–70, 446
Appel, C., 86
Aptekman, D. M., 290
Archer, William, 210
Aristotle, 2, 9, 65
Aron, Raymond, 59*n.,* 416, 418, 463, **464**
Arutiunian, V., 286
Atkinson, E. T., 80
Atkinson, J. W., 507
Awad, Mohamed, 51

Bahrdt, H. P., 526
Bailey, A. H., 258
Bailey, F. C., 75, 76, 79
Bakke, E. W., 377
Baltzell, Digby, 251, 367, 378–79, 403–13
Banks, O., 359
Barber, Bernard, 1, 58, 126, 256, 486, 515
Barber, William J., 421, 422
Barghoorn Frederic C., 314
Baron, G., 359
Barrow, R. H., 66
Bar-Yosef, R., 445
Bastide, Roger, 73
Bauer, Raymond, 130, 452, 465
Beals, Ralph L., 416*n.*
Becker, Howard, 355
Bednarik, K., 526, 527
Belknap, George, 172
Bell, Daniel, 172
Bell, Gerald D., 315
Bello, Francis, 366

Beltran, Aguiree, 384
Bendix, Reinhard, 1, 2, 7, 58, 124, 199, 315–16, 339, 353 362–73, 400, 401*n.,* 516
Benoit, F., 89
Benoit-Smullyan, E., 454
Bensman, Joseph, 117–18, 168, 169, 170
Berelson, B., 217
Berent, Jerzy, 368
Bergel, Egon E., 51
Berger, Bennet, 458
Bergson, Abram, 145, 146, 149, 150
Berreman, Gerald D., 56–57, 74–81
Beshers, James, 299
Bialer, Seweryn, 462, 463, 464
Bierstedt, Robert, 506
Black, Cyril E., 453
Blacker, J. G. C., 367
Blau, Peter M., 313, 341–52, 370
Bloch, Marc, 57–59, 81–91, 160
Blood, Robert O., 281
Bloom, Richard, 377, 378
Boeke, Julius H., 421
Boettcher, Erik, 462
Bogue, Donald J., 402
Borah, Woodrow, 380
Bose, N. K., 76
Bottomore, T. B., 12, 51, 59, 108, 113–14, 160–68, 487, 524–31
Bouglé, C., 317
Bourricaud, François, 429, 431
Box, Steven, 253
Breslow, Lester, 263, 265
Briggs, Asa, 525
Brimmer, Andrew F., 394
Britten, Rollo H., 260, 267
Brockington, Fraser C., 266
Brogan, Dennis, 361
Bronfenbrenner, Urie, 253, 302, 369*n.*
Broom, Leonard, 393, 469
Brown, R. G., 259
Bruno, Frank J., 260
Brzezinski, Zbigniew K., 463, 464
Buckland, W. W., 66, 67
Buckley, Walter, 482, 504, 518
Buechley, Robert, 265
Buell, Philip, 263

533

SUBJECT INDEX

Achievement, 52, 61
   motivation, 314–15, 360–73, 396–403
    and home socialization, 369, 369n.
    and occupational success, 370
   need for, 368–69
   occupational, and family size, 349–52
    and sibling position, 349–52, 350t.
Achievement aspiration, class variation in, 230–31, 255, 294, 294t., 305–306, 315, 363
   Negro, 378
Africa, social change in, 420–27
Agrarian reform, 435–36
American Dream, The, 175
Anomie, theory of, 255, 256
   test of, 296–307
Anticipatory socialization, 315, 372–73
Aristocracy, 36–39, 41–44
   in U.S., 177, 181, 379, 403–13
   see also Nobility
Ascription, 52, 56–57, 61
Asia, social change in, 420–27
Aspiration, and achievement, discrepancy between, 293–94, 296, 305t.
   egoistic *vs.* fraternalistic, 228–30
Austria, class and mortality, 265
Automation, unemployment and, 137–38

Blue-collar marriage, 253–54, 276–84
Bolivia, social change in, 435
Bourgeoisie, 8, 14n., 14–20, 160–61
Bureaucracy, in capitalist society, 101–102, 156
   in socialist society, 100–101, 156–57
   in Soviet Union, 154–56, 462–64

Capitalist society, industrial society and, 59
   stratification in, 8–9, 14–16, 97–101, 467–68, 527–28
Caste, 29–31, 56–57, 74–81
   club and, 379, 409–13
   defined, 56, 74
   ethnicity and, 29–31, 404–409
   in India, 56, 74–78, 310, 317, 319
   India and U.S. compared, 56, 74–81

Latin America and U.S. compared, 384
   race and, 55–56, 67–68, 80–81, 181–82
   sexual gain in, 77
   social mobility and, 37, 310, 319
   in U.S., 55, 56, 181, 211, 404–409
Change, in income distribution, in U.S., 136–38
   in Soviet Union, 143–54
   in occupational structure of U.S., 192–93
   in stratification, 14–18, 235, 235n., 320, 415–77, 513–31
    patterns of developing nations, 415, 422–27
    perception of, 130–31, 243–44
    role of landless peasants, 416, 434–35
China, *literati* in, 166
Circulation of elites, 11–12, 34–39, 354–56
Class
   dichotomous conceptions, 8–9
   ethnicity and, 375–413, 447, 449–51
    mobility trap, 377–78
   as explanation of ethnic differences, 378, 396–403
   function and rank of, 49–50
   Marx's concepts, 8–10, 14–24, 125
   modern concepts, 486–87, 495–96, 514–15
   in modern society, 91–103, 486–87, 513–20, 522–31
   objective, 9, 105–23, 125, 133–206
   as rank, 115
   strategic elites and, 522–24
   as stratum, 8, 12
   subjective, 9, 123–32, 206–47
   Weber's concept, 10, 25–27
   see also Stratification
Class action, *see* Class consciousness
Class conflict, 14–24, 26–28, 38–39, 59, 75, 78–79, 93–96, 491–95, 517, 527
   avoidance of, 356–57
   institutionalization of, 60, 96, 527–28
   perception of, 244–46, 451–52
   in socialist society, 160, 212–13, 215–16, 244–46, 295–96
Class consciousness, 9, 19, 26, 91–92, 140, 158, 514–15
   in Britain, 128–29, 228–29, 234–35